CRIMINAL VIOLENCE

PATTERNS, EXPLANATIONS, AND INTERVENTIONS

FOURTH EDITION

Marc Riedel, Ph.D.

SOUTHEASTERN LOUISIANA UNIVERSITY,
LOUISIANA

Wayne N. Welsh, Ph.D.

TEMPLE UNIVERSITY,
PHILADELPHIA

NEW YORK OXFORD
OXFORD UNIVERSITY PRESS

Oxford University Press is a department of the University of Oxford.
It furthers the University's objective of excellence in research,
scholarship, and education by publishing worldwide.

Oxford New York
Auckland Cape Town Dar es Salaam Hong Kong Karachi
Kuala Lumpur Madrid Melbourne Mexico City Nairobi
New Delhi Shanghai Taipei Toronto

With offices in
Argentina Austria Brazil Chile Czech Republic France Greece
Guatemala Hungary Italy Japan Poland Portugal Singapore
South Korea Switzerland Thailand Turkey Ukraine Vietnam

For titles covered by Section 112 of the US Higher Education Opportunity Act, please visit www.oup.com/us/he for the latest information about pricing and alternate formats.

Published by Oxford University Press
198 Madison Avenue, New York, New York 10016
http://www.oup.com

Library of Congress Cataloging-in-Publication Data
Riedel, Marc.
Criminal violence : patterns, explanations, and interventions / Marc Riedel, Wayne Welsh. --
Fourth Edition.
pages cm
Includes bibliographical references and indexes.
ISBN 978-0-19-938613-0 (alk. paper)
1. Violence--United States. 2. Violent crimes--United States. I. Welsh, Wayne N., 1957- II. Title.
HN90.V5R54 2015
364.150973--dc23
2014044734

Printing number: 9 8 7 6 5 4 3 2 1

Printed in the United States of America
on acid-free paper

DEDICATION

To *Laurine* and the memory of *Paul G. Kreipe*, who have provided support and helpful advice over these many years.

To my friend and companion, *Patricia Vickers Moore*, for her love and support.

—*MR*

To *Dea Silbertrust and Ilana Welsh*
It is only with their continued patience, love and support that I am able to keep my balance and occasionally strike out on large projects such as this.

—*WW*

CONTENTS

FOREWORD *xiv*
PREFACE *xvi*
ABOUT THE AUTHORS *xxiii*

SECTION I INTRODUCTION

CHAPTER 1 Violence and Criminal Violence *3*

Defining Violence *3*
Turning Violence into Criminal Violence *5*
Perspectives on Criminal Violence *7*
  A Criminological Perspective *7*
  A Criminal Justice Perspective *8*
  Public Health Perspectives *8*
How Is Criminal Violence Studied? *11*
  Theoretical Perspectives *11*
  Research Methods *12*
  Challenges of Violence Research *13*
What Lies Ahead? *15*
  A Tripartite Approach to Understanding Violence *15*
Conclusions *17*
Discussion Questions *18*
Suggested Readings *18*
References *18*

SECTION II TOOLS

CHAPTER 2 **Measures of Violence** *23*

The Application of Measures of Violence *23*

Overview *24*

Crime Rates *24*

Uniform Crime Reports *27*

Collecting Violent Crime Data *27*

National Incident-Based Reporting System *30*

Comparing the Uniform Crime Report and the National Incident-Based Reporting System *30*

National Crime Victimization Survey *33*

The Redesign of the National Crime Victimization Survey *33*

The National Crime Victimization Survey Today *35*

Strengths and Limitations of the National Crime Victimization Survey *36*

Limitations of the National Crime Victimization Survey *37*

Discussion Questions *39*

Suggested Readings *39*

References *39*

CHAPTER 3 **Violence in Other Times and Places** *43*

Violence in the Early United States *43*

White and Native American Warfare *45*

The Trail of Tears *45*

Slavery, African Americans, and Violence *46*

Lynching *48*

Social Banditry *49*

Prohibition *51*

The Role of Organized Crime *52*

Contemporary Trends in Violence *54*

Impersonalization of Homicide *55*

Violence in Other Places *55*

Conclusions *59*

Discussion Questions *59*

Suggested Readings *60*

Note *60*

References *60*

SECTION III TYPES OF CRIMINAL VIOLENCE

CHAPTER 4 **Homicides and Assaults** *65*

Homicides and Assaults in the United States *65*
Age, Gender, and Race *66*
Other Characteristics *68*
Arrest Clearances *69*
Multiple Murders *72*
Trends *78*
Trends in Arrest Clearances *79*
Trends in Serial Homicide *79*
Explanations *80*
Symbolic Interaction *80*
Subcultural Theories *81*
Explaining the Characteristics of Arrest Clearances *81*
Explaining Serial Homicides *82*
Interventions *83*
Increasing Clearance Rates *84*
Apprehending Serial Killers *87*
Conclusions *88*
Discussion Questions *89*
Suggested Readings *89*
References *89*

CHAPTER 5 **Robbery** *92*

Patterns and Trends *92*
Explanations *95*
Strain Theory and Differential Opportunity Theory *96*
Control Theory *97*
Differential Association Theory *98*
Symbolic Interaction Theory *98*
Feminist Theory *99*
Routine Activities Theory *101*
Interventions *102*
Criminal Justice Approaches *102*
Opportunity Reduction Strategies *103*
Conclusions *105*
Discussion Questions *105*

Suggested Readings *106*
Note *106*
References *106*

CHAPTER 6 **Rapes and Sexual Assaults** *109*
Definitions *110*
Patterns and Trends *111*
Characteristics of Victims, Offenders, and Offenses *111*
Explanations *115*
Psychiatric Perspectives *115*
Feminist Theories *116*
Social Cognitive Theories *117*
Multifactor Theories *118*
Interventions *119*
Rape Law Reform *119*
Incarceration *121*
Sex Offender Notification and Registration Laws *121*
Victim Resistance *122*
Victim Services *123*
Sexual Violence Education *124*
Sex Offender Treatment Programs *126*
Conclusions *129*
Discussion Questions *129*
Suggested Readings *130*
Notes *130*
References *130*

CHAPTER 7 **Hate Crimes** *135*
Definitions *136*
Patterns and Trends *137*
Explanations *141*
Group Conflict Theories *141*
Strain Theory *142*
Social Learning Theory *143*
Interventions *144*
Law Enforcement Responses *144*
Hate Crime Legislation *145*
Civil Lawsuits *147*
Educational Strategies *148*

Conclusions 149
Discussion Questions 150
Suggested Readings 150
Notes 150
References 150

SECTION IV VIOLENCE IN SPECIFIC SETTINGS AND CONTEXTS

CHAPTER 8 Intimate Violence 155

"People Hit Family Members Because They Can" 155
Patterns and Risks 155
Intimate Partner Violence 155
Violence Toward Family Members 161
Trends 167
Intimate Partners 167
Child Killings 169
Explanations 169
Intimate Partner Violence 169
Violence Toward Children 172
Interventions 173
Reducing Intimate Partner Violence 173
Reducing Family Violence 174
Conclusion: Is It Time for Another Look? 175
Discussion Questions 175
Suggested Readings 176
References 176

CHAPTER 9 Workplace Violence 179

Introduction 179
Multiplier Effects 180
Patterns and Trends 181
Types of Workplace Violence 181
Nonfatal Workplace Violence 184
Workplace Homicides 186
"Going Postal" 188
Explanations 189
Routine Activities 189
Rational Choice and Aggression in the Workplace 192

Interventions *193*
Prevention Policies and Strategies *194*
Empirical Evidence *197*
Discussion Questions *199*
Suggested Readings *199*
References *199*

CHAPTER 10 **School Violence** *201*
Patterns and Trends *202*
Fear and Avoidance *202*
School Security Responses *203*
School Incidents and Disciplinary Actions *203*
Student Victimization *204*
Teacher Victimization *206*
Self-Reported School Violence *206*
Explanations of School Disorder *206*
Individual Explanations *206*
School-Level Theories *207*
Community and Multilevel Explanations of School Disorder *208*
Interventions *211*
School-Based Violence Prevention: What Works? *211*
The National Study of Delinquency Prevention in Schools *213*
Examples of School-Based Prevention Programs *215*
Conclusions *217*
Discussion Questions *218*
Suggested Readings *218*
References *218*

CHAPTER 11 **Gangs and Gang Violence** *223*
Patterns and Trends *223*
Growth and Change in Gangs *225*
Gang Organization and Violence *226*
Explanations *228*
Strain Theories *228*
Cultural Deviance *230*
Social Control *231*
Interactional Theory *232*

Interventions *233*
Reducing Gang Violence in Boston *233*
Pulling Levers in Other Jurisdictions *237*
Conclusions *237*
Discussion Questions *238*
Suggested Readings *238*
References *238*

CHAPTER 12 **The Role of Firearms in Violence** *241*
Patterns and Trends *242*
Crimes Involving Firearms *242*
Victims *242*
Characteristics of Offenders *244*
Firearm Acquisition, Ownership, and Use *245*
Explanations *246*
Symbolic Interaction Theory *246*
Routine Activities and Illegal Markets *247*
Cultural Theories and Firearm Availability *248*
Media Violence *249*
Interventions *251*
Disrupting Illegal Gun Markets *251*
Gun Control Legislation *255*
Right-to-Carry Laws *260*
Firearm Injury Prevention Programs *261*
Conclusions *261*
Discussion Questions *261*
Suggested Readings *262*
Note *262*
References *262*

CHAPTER 13 **The Role of Drugs and Alcohol in Violence** *266*
Patterns *267*
Explanations *270*
Biological and Psychological Effects *270*
Routine Activities *273*
Cultural Explanations *273*
Structural Explanations *274*
Situational Explanations *275*

Interventions *276*
Criminal Justice Approaches *276*
Public Health Approaches *280*
Conclusions *281*
Discussion Questions *282*
Suggested Readings *282*
Notes *282*
References *283*

CHAPTER 14 **Terrorism** *287*
Definitions *288*
Patterns and Trends *289*
A Brief History of Terrorism *289*
State-Sponsored Terrorism *291*
Terrorist Tactics *292*
Types of Terrorists *292*
Terrorist Incidents *294*
Explanations *298*
Strain Theory *298*
Social Learning Theory *305*
Conflict Theory *307*
Interventions *308*
The 9/11 Report *308*
The Patriot Act *309*
Military Action *311*
Diplomacy and International Cooperation *312*
Conclusions *315*
Discussion Questions *316*
Suggested Readings *316*
Notes *316*
References *316*

SECTION V CONCLUSION

CHAPTER 15 **Prevention and Punishment: A Delicate Balance** *323*
Criminal Justice Approaches *323*
Criminal Justice Goals *323*
The Death Penalty *327*

Three-Strikes Laws 330
The Limits of Punishment 331
Public Health Approaches to Punishment and Prevention 333
The Multilevel Risk Approach 333
Evidence-Based Practices and Programs 334
Office of Juvenile Justice and Delinquency Prevention's Comprehensive Strategy for Serious, Violent, and Chronic Juvenile Offenders 336
Community-Based Approaches 342
Blueprints for Healthy Youth Development 345
When Violent Crime Goes Down, Do We Know Why? 348
Conclusions 349
Discussion Questions 350
Suggested Readings 350
References 351

AUTHOR INDEX 357
SUBJECT INDEX 365

FOREWORD

In the foreword to the third edition of Marc Riedel and Wayne Welsh's *Criminal Violence*, I wrote that violent crime rates in the United States were flat or declining during the most serious economic downturn since the Great Depression. The recession has ended and crime rates are up in some cities and continuing to fall in others.

What accounts for the recent changes in criminal violence? Why are the declines occurring in some cities but not in others? Why are violent crime rates declining during an economic crisis? We do not know. Despite the impressive accumulation of research findings on the sources and patterns of criminal violence documented in this important text, knowledge of the factors underlying variations in violent crime over time and across places remains spotty, inconclusive, and plainly inadequate for guiding or evaluating policy responses.

Exhibit A in the case for improving our knowledge of violent crime is the crime decline of the 1990s. Early in the decade, criminologists were sounding public alarms about a coming tidal wave of violent crime in the United States, a "blood bath," as one called it, led by growing numbers of remorseless young "super predators," as another labeled inner-city teenagers who committed violent crime at high rates. No sooner had the ink dried on the editorials than violent crime rates began to plummet, and the largest reductions occurred among young black men. For example, whereas the overall homicide rate decreased by 40% between 1993 and 2004, the rate for black males aged 15 to 24 dropped by 53%.[1]

This was not American criminology's finest hour. No one had correctly predicted the longest crime drop on record, and the alarmists' mayhem scenario, widely circulated in the press, was absurdly off base. The problem was not that a few criminologists went out on a limb with inaccurate crime predictions—social scientists make incorrect predictions all the time. The problem was that no established theory or research base existed that other criminologists, reporters, and commentators might have consulted to evaluate the plausibility of the predictions, produce alternative forecasts, or address more recent crime changes. For example, the homicide rate of young black men has continued to fall since 2005. We do not know why.

The nation requires a policy-evaluation infrastructure to support the continuous and timely collection and dissemination of crime information, an active research program on the factors associated with changes in crime rates over time, and rigorous assessments of the crime-reduction effects of criminal justice policies and programs. In the absence of an ongoing program of information, research, and evaluation, we will continue to stumble blindly into and out of crime reductions and increases, with little sense of where we are, how we got here, or where we are headed. A broadly informed public, we must hope, would demand better from criminologists and policymakers alike.

Riedel and Welsh's accessible and informative text covers the patterns, explanations, and interventions related to a broad range of violent crimes across diverse social settings, from homicide, robbery, and rape to violence in the home, school, and workplace. Relevant research and data have been updated throughout. The book not only fills an academic void, it also can help stimulate public demand for improved information, research, and policy on criminal violence.

Richard Rosenfeld
University of Missouri-St. Louis
April 2015

NOTE

1. Computed from mortality data compiled by the National Center for Injury Prevention and Control, available at http://www.cdc.gov/injury/wisqars/fatal_injury_reports.html (accessed April 13, 2015).

PREFACE

We have both taught undergraduate and graduate courses in criminal violence for many years. During that time, we searched for a text on violence that could satisfy several important criteria. For example, could a single text provide comprehensive coverage of major topics and theories of violence, provide a coherent analytical framework, and yet remain interesting and easy to understand? We were dissatisfied with what we found.

Instead, like many instructors, we used a constantly evolving series of paperbacks, journal articles, and book chapters, in addition to drawing on our own research, expertise, and experience. One of the shortcomings of that approach is that students do not easily acquire an overview of the area from a perspective that provides continuity across different topics. Assigning a book on serial murder, for example, may generate great student interest, but it tends to give students a rather narrow view of criminal violence. It appeared to us that there was a need for a text that would provide a coherent approach to the study of criminal violence without oversimplifying, on the one hand, and without losing students in specialized terminology and disparate perspectives, on the other.

The result, we hope, is a text that provides broad coverage of major topics and controversies in criminal violence, based on the most current knowledge available. We attempt to provide the "big picture" without oversimplifying. Our approach provides the student with a consistent and coherent framework for analyzing different types of violence, taps the most up-to-date research and knowledge available, employs diverse theoretical perspectives, and examines state-of-the-art prevention and intervention methods. We attempt to communicate to students in a lively, straightforward manner that stimulates critical thinking and interest.

One of the most original features of the book is the use of a consistent and engaging approach to discuss each type of violence. This framework should help students to understand the important relationship between research, theory, and application. Using a tripartite framework, each type of violence is discussed in terms of major patterns, explanations, and interventions:

- *Patterns* include characteristics of victims, offenders, and offenses; situational correlates (e.g., places where violence occurs frequently); and trends over time. The search for relevant explanations must be informed by knowledge of major patterns.
- *Explanations* examine major theories that have been used to understand each type of violence. The search for effective interventions must be preceded by the identification of relevant causes.
- *Interventions* represent proposed solution to each type of violence, including diverse legal and social strategies, both proactive (e.g., prevention) and reactive (e.g., punishment).

The first chapter examines meanings of violence. Definitions, assumptions about causes, and choices of interventions are seen not as simple facts but as the products of social and political processes. We suggest at the outset that violence is not a rare or exotic phenomenon in society but is expressed in a wide variety of activities, such as sports and accidents. The first chapter shows how violence is regulated, with criminal law being an important mode of social control. This chapter also discusses the similarities and differences between legal and criminological approaches to violence.

The next two chapters are necessary tools to understanding the wide variety of violence that is discussed in the next 13 chapters. The second chapter examines the challenge of getting reliable and valid information about violence. Three sources of information are examined in detail: Uniform Crime Reports, the National Incident-Based Reporting System, and the National Crime Victimization Survey.

The third chapter provides a historical and comparative perspective on violence in the United States, addressing stereotypes about the current nature and amount of violence in the United States and comparing it with other countries. For example, levels of violence in the United States were much higher in the past century than they are at present.

Using the tools and skills developed in the first three chapters, Chapters 4 through 7 examine specific types of violence, using the tripartite perspective. Chapter 4 discusses criminal homicides and aggravated assaults. Not only are patterns, explanations, and interventions discussed with respect to homicides and assaults generally, but we also discuss the decline in arrest clearances and serial homicides. The section on the decline in arrest clearances discusses why only about 62% of murders in the United States result in an arrest. In this edition, the section on multiple murders has been expanded to discuss the similarities and differences between mass and serial homicides.

Chapter 5 discusses robbery, one of the most feared crimes in cities, including its frequency, environmental influences, and the psychological and physical consequences for the victims. While persistent robbers are attracted to robbery as a means of getting quick cash, they are also motivated by participation in street culture and a desire to demonstrate physical toughness and even ruthlessness to others. Interventions discussed include targeted law enforcement, mandatory sentencing, and Crime Prevention Through Environmental Design.

Chapter 6 examines definitions, patterns, and trends in rape and sexual assault offenses, as well as characteristics of offenders and victims. Examples illustrate the diversity of rape and sexual assault incidents. We examine causal theories (e.g., psychological theories, feminist theories) and major interventions, including rape law reform, victim counseling and assistance, and sex offender treatment.

In Chapter 7 we define the category of hate crimes and the laws behind it and examine the characteristics of incidents, offenders, and victims. We provide examples of how racial tensions can escalate to interpersonal violence. Explanations include group conflict, strain, and social learning theories. We examine promising intervention strategies, including specialized police bias units, hate crime legislation, and educational approaches.

In Chapters 8 to 15 we describe violence in specific settings and contexts. Chapter 8 examines the types of violence occurring between intimate partners and violence by and toward other family members. The many significant changes aimed at reducing violence between intimate partners are discussed in this chapter. Not only do we have a better understanding of the phenomenon, but we also have developed a wide variety of interventions for dealing with "people who hit people because they can." The section on violence toward other family members discusses lethal and nonlethal violence by parents against children.

The chapter on workplace violence, Chapter 9, describes the various types of workplace violence, including the attacks in post offices, that have drawn enormous media attention. We examine a report on post office attacks that concludes that much of the attention on that type of workplace violence has been exaggerated. This chapter not only includes patterns, trends, and interventions but also discusses the most dangerous jobs, those that are most likely to result in violent victimization.

Chapter 10, on school violence, looks at the total amount of violence in schools, including attacks on teachers as well as students. While serious school violence is rare, it generates fear and avoidance for all concerned. This chapter also discusses prevention activities in schools.

Chapter 11, "Gangs and Gang Violence," discusses various definitions and focuses on street gangs largely because that is the focus of most research. Although their image is one of violence, involvement with violent crimes is a surprisingly small part of their daily activities.

Chapter 12 examines the role of firearms in violence. This chapter illustrates the need to examine situational correlates of violence, including the roles firearms play, the types of crimes involving firearms, what injuries are sustained as a result of firearm use, and various theories explaining the use of firearms (e.g., symbolic interaction, routine activities, and cultural theories). Intervention strategies examined include gun control legislation and targeted law enforcement (e.g., disrupting illegal gun markets).

Chapter 13 examines the evidence linking alcohol and drug use to violence. There are different types of drug-related violence, and the apparent connections between drug use and violence are considerably more complex than commonly acknowledged. Explanations include biological, psychological, routine activities, cultural, structural, and situational theories. Intervention strategies examined include criminal justice approaches (e.g., Weed and Seed), and public health approaches (e.g., prison-based drug treatment programs).

In Chapter 14, we turn to an examination of terrorism. It is critical to examine the use of power and propaganda in such conflicts. Across different places and time periods, violence has been used by the powerful to preserve existing power relations, but violence has also been used by marginalized groups to challenge the status quo. Explanations include conflict, strain, and social learning theories; interventions include political, legal, military, and diplomatic approaches—many of them controversial (e.g., unauthorized wiretaps).

The final chapter discusses more general approaches to reduce violence that do not fit easily or neatly into any one specific subtopic. We examine criminal justice approaches (e.g., capital punishment, three-strikes laws) as well as public health approaches (e.g., risk-based prevention, community-based approaches). We develop two arguments: (1) an effective strategy to reduce violence must balance both preventive and punishment approaches and (2) public policy must be better informed by valid information regarding violence patterns, explanations, and interventions.

Criminal violence is a broad, multidimensional topic that has often defied easy categorization or analysis. There are simply a multitude of topics, theories, and interventions that cut across many different disciplines and perspectives. No one text can address everything; certainly, as authors we had to set some limits for ourselves. For example, some of our reviewers suggested more coverage of international and cross-cultural perspectives on violence. Others wanted more in-depth historical analysis of conditions in the United States. Some wanted more detailed examination of violence measures and statistics, others less. Some wanted more focus on theories of violence; some wanted more attention to public policies and interventions. We suspect that no single text on violence could ever fully satisfy the needs of everyone. We firmly believe, however, that the major topics, theories, and interventions associated with criminal violence can be usefully and coherently interwoven into a single text that introduces students to one of the most challenging and interesting problems of our time. We hope that we have been moderately successful in our aspirations so far, and we invite our students and colleagues to continue to give us their valuable (and valued) feedback.

NEW TO THIS EDITION

All of the chapters were updated. The following chapters were updated more extensively.

CHAPTER 5

- Updated statistics on patterns (e.g., characteristics of victims, offenders, and places) and trends in robbery over time
- Added material on gendered violence (feminist theories) and female robbers

CHAPTER 6

- Updated statistics on patterns (e.g., characteristics of victims, offenders, and places) and trends in rape and sexual assault
- Added material on date rape and campus sexual assaults
- Discussed revised (2013) definitions of rape and sexual assault in UCR
- Added material on multifactor theories. Single-factor theories (e.g., feminist or social cognitive theories) usually attempt to explain a single underlying cause of sexual aggression. In contrast, multifactor theories attempt to explain how different relationships among underlying causes can interactively shape sexual offending.

- Added material on interventions, including recent meta-analyses of studies evaluating effects of Sex Offender Registration and Notification Act (SORNA)
- Expanded and added material on sexual violence education (e.g., Sex & Ethics Violence Prevention Program).

CHAPTER 7

- Updated statistics on patterns (e.g., characteristics of victims, offenders, and places) and trends in hate crimes
- Added discussion and comparisons of NCVS and UCR statistics on hate crimes
- Updated discussion of the Matthew Shepard and James Byrd, Jr. Hate Crime Prevention Act (revised 2009)

CHAPTER 10

- Updated statistics on patterns (e.g., characteristics of victims, offenders, and places) and trends in school violence
- Updated discussion of studies testing multilevel theories of school violence
- Updated discussion of school-based prevention programs and evaluations

CHAPTER 12

- Updated statistics on patterns (e.g., characteristics of victims, offenders, and places) and trends in firearm violence
- Added recent examples, including mass shootings in Colorado and Connecticut
- Added discussion on effects of media violence, including theories and studies (e.g., the "weapons effect": simply seeing a weapon can increase aggression)
- Added extensive material on "stop and frisk" strategies (also known as "stop, question, and frisk" [SQF]), including examination of controversies and new empirical evidence examining the effects of these laws
- Updated material on gun control legislation, including legal challenges to gun ownership laws (e.g., Washington DC handgun ban), gun buybacks, banning assault weapons

CHAPTER 13

- Updated statistics on patterns (e.g., characteristics of victims, offenders, and places) and trends in drug-related violence
- Added material on the Mexican drug cartels ("A Case Study of Systemic Violence")

CHAPTER 14

- Updated statistics on patterns (e.g., characteristics of victims, offenders, and places) and trends in domestic and international terrorism
- Updated discussion of federal legislation and new definitions related to domestic and international terrorism

- Added discussion of similarities and differences between collective violence and terrorism
- Expanded discussion of state-sponsored terrorism
- Updated and expanded discussion of major sources of data on international terrorism (including the National Consortium for the Study of Terrorism and Responses to Terrorism [START]), highlighting some of the issues involved with reliability and validity
- Updated discussion of interventions, especially diplomacy and international cooperation

CHAPTER 15

- Updated discussion and statistics on the death penalty
- Updated discussion and evaluations of three-strikes laws
- Updated discussion of evidence-based practices and programs (EBPP)
- Added discussion of the Standardized Program Evaluation Protocol (SPEP), which translates guidelines for effective juvenile justice programs into practical form
- Added case study and discussion of Ceasefire: A Public Health Approach to Reduce Shootings and Killings
- Updated discussion of Blueprints for Healthy Youth Development initiative.

SUPPLEMENTS

- The instructor's manual features (for each chapter) lecture notes, review questions, case studies, suggested readings, teaching suggestions and exercises, web links, PowerPoint slides, and a test bank.

ACKNOWLEDGMENTS

We would like to thank Shannon Forbes Rushing, a research assistant in Southeastern Louisiana University's graduate program in applied sociology, for reading and correcting errors in many of the chapters. We would also like to thank Karon M. Donahue, who read and corrected errors in many of the chapters in the first edition, corrections that proved invaluable in this edition. Thanks also to Scott Decker, Arizona State University, for taking the time to read the chapter on gang violence and offer a large number of valuable suggestions.

Thank you to the reviewers of this edition: David Bugg (SUNY Potsdam), Amy Cook (Virginia State University), James Densley (Metropolitan State University), Abu K. Mboka (California State University Stanislaus), Carol Higgins O'Brien (University of Massachusetts Lowell), Christopher J. Schreck (Rochester Institute of Technology), Ginger D. Stevens (Louisiana State University), and Margaret A. Zahn (North Carolina State University). Thanks also to the reviewers of the prior editions Jeffrey S. Adler (University of Florida), Alex Alvarez (Northern Arizona University), Thomas J. Bernard (1945–2009) (The Pennsylvania State University), Derral Cheatwood (University of Texas at San Antonio), Scott Decker (Arizona State University), Edna Erez (Kent State University), Anne Goetting (Northern Kentucky University), Gary Jensen (Vanderbilt University), Steven P. Lab (Bowling Green State University),

Alex Piquero (University of Texas, Dallas), Wendy C. Regoeczi (Cleveland State University), Dean G. Rojek (University of Georgia), Frank Scarpitti (University of Delaware), Nanci Koser Wilson (Indiana University of Pennsylvania), Richard A. Wright (Chicago State University), and Margaret A. Zahn (North Carolina State University), Geriann M. Brandt (University of St. Louis, Maryville), Robert Cadigan (Metropolitan College, Boston University), George Capowich (Loyola University), Michelle Emerson (Kennesaw State University), Tom Petee (Auburn University), Margaret A. Zahn (North Carolina State University), John G. Boulahanis (Southeastern Louisiana University), Kenneth Colburn (Butler University), Stan Crowder (Kennesaw State University), Alex Obi Ekwuaju (Kennesaw State University), Michelle Emerson-Lewis (Kennesaw State University), Matthew R. Lee (Louisiana State University), Kristine Miller (Southern Illinois University, Carbondale), Wendy Regoeczi Cleveland State University), and V. Lynn Tankersley (Mercer University).

It is somewhat misleading to label authors in a large undertaking of this type as first and second author or senior and junior authors. Both of us have contributed equally to this work, and we wish to see it regarded as a product of both of us.

We would also like to thank our many students and colleagues who provided constructive feedback on earlier versions of chapters. We, however, are responsible for any errors in this book and for any instances of not taking the sound advice that was given by others.

ABOUT THE AUTHORS

Marc Riedel is Professor in the Department of Sociology and Criminal Justice at Southeastern Louisiana University. He is also Emeritus Professor of Sociology and Administration of Justice at Southern Illinois University. He does research on prescribed and prohibited forms of violence. His articles on the death penalty and homicide have appeared in the *Annals of the American Academy of Political and Social Science, Journal of Criminal Law and Criminology*, and *Temple Law Quarterly*. He is the author or editor of 10 books on different aspects of violence. Riedel has served on the Executive Council and as Vice President of the American Society of Criminology. In 1985, Riedel received the Herbert A. Bloch award from the American Society of Criminology for outstanding service to the society and the profession.

Wayne N. Welsh is a Professor of Criminal Justice at Temple University. He received his Ph.D. in Social Ecology from the University of California, Irvine, in 1990 and his M.A. in Applied Social Psychology from the University of Saskatchewan (Canada) in 1986. Welsh has conducted research in three broad areas: (1) applications of organizational theory to criminal justice and examinations of organizational change; (2) theories of violent behavior and intervention/prevention programs; and (3) substance abuse treatment in criminal justice settings. He is the author of *Counties in Court: Jail Overcrowding and Court-Ordered Reform* (Temple University Press, 1995) and *Criminal Justice Policy and Planning* with Philip Harris (Elsevier/Anderson, 2013, 3rd ed.). Recent articles have appeared in *Administration and Policy in Mental Health, Drug and Alcohol Dependence, Criminal Justice and Behavior,* and *Journal of Experimental Criminology*. Welsh served as Deputy Editor of *The Prison Journal* from 1993 to 2000.

SECTION I

INTRODUCTION

CHAPTER 1

VIOLENCE AND CRIMINAL VIOLENCE

DEFINING VIOLENCE

If we pay attention to newspapers, television, and other types of media, violence appears to be a pervasive part of life. Even if we ignore fictional accounts, newspapers, magazines, television, and the World Wide Web provide a plethora of violence both in types and amount. But what is violence? Is there a difference between violence and criminal violence?

Violence is difficult to define because there are so many different kinds. There is violence associated with the forces of nature. Tornados, hurricanes, earthquakes, rainstorms, floods, and forest fires are frequently described as violence that results in loss of life and property.

Violence may be the outcome of extreme emotional states such as rage, anger, or hate. While rage, anger, or hate may be directed toward people, these emotions may also be directed toward animals or even objects. Kicking the dog after a frustrating day at the office is the most commonly given example, although there are far more serious instances of animals being excessively beaten, starved, or otherwise abused (Newman, 1979). The definition of violence used in this book is taken from the National Academy of Sciences Panel on the Understanding and Control of Violent Behavior: "behavior by persons against person that intentionally threatens, attempts, or actually inflicts physical harm" (Reiss & Roth, 1993, p. 35).

Violence may be the inevitable accompaniment of socially approved activities. An enormous amount of *sports violence* is not only legal but also acceptable because of the circumstances in which it occurs. Atyeo (1979, p. 11) wrote:

> The thing about sport is that it legitimizes violence, thereby laundering it acceptably clean. Incidents routinely occur in the name of sport which, if they were perpetrated under any other banner short of open warfare, would be roundly condemned as crimes against humanity. The mugger in the parking lot is a villain; the mugger on the playing field is a hero. The pain inflicted in sport is somehow not really pain at all; it is Tom and Jerry pain, cartoon agony which doesn't hurt.

Because violence is legitimated on the playing field, there is a tendency for athletes to be involved in more violence off the field than nonathletes. According to a study of Judicial Affairs offices for 10 Division I universities, male student-athletes made up 3.3% of the population but accounted for 19% of cases of sexual assault and domestic violence (Crossett, Benedict, & McDonald, 1995; Crossett, Ptacek, McDonald, & Benedict, 1996).

What is the source of a far greater number of deaths and injuries than workers assaulting one another in the workplace? *Corporate violence.* Corporate violence is behavior that produces an unreasonable risk of physical harm to employees, the general public, and consumers resulting from deliberate decisions by corporate managers or executives (Brownstein, 2000; Kramer, 1983).

The Deepwater Horizon was a floating oil drilling unit, managed by British Petroleum (BP), that was anchored in the Gulf of Mexico and was completely destroyed in April 2010. The destruction led to the death of 11 workers and many injuries. What follows is a brief description of what the *New York Times* described as the one of the worst environmental catastrophes in United States history.

> With government inquiries under way and billions of dollars in environmental fines at stake, most of the attention has focused on what caused the blowout. Investigators have dissected BP's well design and Halliburton's cementing work, uncovering problem after problem.
>
> But this was a disaster with two distinct parts—first a blowout, then the destruction of the Horizon. The second part, which killed 11 people and injured dozens, has escaped intense scrutiny, as if it were an inevitable casualty of the blowout.
>
> It was not.
>
> Nearly 400 feet long, the Horizon had formidable and redundant defenses against even the worst blowout. It was equipped to divert surging oil and gas safely away from the rig. It had devices to quickly seal off a well blowout or to break free from it. It had systems to prevent gas from exploding and sophisticated alarms that would quickly warn the crew at the slightest trace of gas. The crew itself routinely practiced responding to alarms, fires and blowouts, and it was blessed with experienced leaders who clearly cared about safety.
>
> On paper, experts and investigators agree, the Deepwater Horizon should have weathered this blowout . . . What emerges is a stark and singular fact: crew members died and suffered terrible injuries because every one of the Horizon's defenses failed on April 20. Some were deployed but did not work. Some were activated too late, after they had almost certainly been damaged by fire or explosions. Some were never deployed at all. (Urbina, 2010, p. A1)

In January 2013, BP agreed to plead guilty to 14 criminal offenses, including manslaughter, as well as pay a record fine in connection with the 2010 oil spill in the Gulf of Mexico.

Occupationally related deaths also have occurred because the employer did not provide adequate safeguards to prevent contact with toxic substances. For example, people have died from cancer at disproportionate rates because of exposure to high levels of asbestos or vinyl chloride (Swartz, 1975).

In addition to attempts or actual use of physical force, there is *psychological violence*, which can consist of persistent negative attributions to others, particularly those emotionally close to the speaker. For example, it can be emotionally damaging to one intimate partner if the other steadily threatens, denigrates, or verbally abuses him or her. Other examples include controlling another in a way that provides an opportunity to criticize and denigrate (i.e., a husband may allocate too little money to the household food budget, then constantly criticize the wife for the type and quality of food served).

What is notable about the preceding examples is that the violence may or may not be criminal. Does psychological abuse carry a criminal penalty? Although there are numerous instances of sports and corporate violence, few of those responsible for the acts are criminally prosecuted. What is the difference between violence and criminal violence?

TURNING VIOLENCE INTO CRIMINAL VIOLENCE

What turns the threat, attempt, or use of physical force by one or more persons toward others into criminal violence is *law*. Without law, the violence may be outrageous, immoral, depressing, hurtful, demoralizing, and lamentable, but it is not a crime. Certain acts of violence cannot be tolerated in an ordered society, so representatives of a government create rules prohibiting some forms of violent behavior outright and circumscribing their expression in other instances. Sanctions, such as incarceration, are imposed for violations of these laws.

One view of how such laws are created is the *consensus* model, which assumes that members of society by and large agree on what is right and wrong and the law codifies these agreed-upon social values (Adler, Mueller, & Laufer, 1998). The nearest approximation to this view are laws prohibiting homicide, which are among the oldest criminal laws.

The laws regarding homicide used in the United States developed out of English common law. When the Pilgrims landed at Plymouth Rock, they brought English common law with them. One of the first murders reported in the U.S. colonies occurred in 1630, when John Billington, one of the original band of 102 Pilgrims to land at Plymouth Rock, fired his blunderbuss at a neighbor from behind a rock and killed him. Billington was charged with murder, tried, convicted, and hanged (Nash, 1973).

A second view is a *conflict* model, in which power is the key to lawmaking. According to the conflict model, people with political and economic power make laws that protect their interests while keeping the poor at a disadvantage. The conflict model is used to explain why laws governing white-collar and environmental crimes are infrequently and lightly enforced. Those responsible for exposing humans to toxic wastes that shorten lives or those who make unsafe automobiles are rarely prosecuted as violent criminals because of their high social status (Hills, 1987).

Related to the conflict perspective is the view that social reality in general, including criminal laws, is *socially constructed* (Berger & Luckmann, 1967; Spector & Kitsuse, 1987). Brownstein (2000, p. 4) provides a succinct statement of this perspective:

> From the social constructionist perspective, social reality is a product of social interaction in the form of individual decisions, interpretations, and actions. In that individuals act

> and interact, make decisions, and interpret their experience in the context of their unique social positions and interests, social reality, and hence all social phenomena, are necessarily constructed in an ideological and political context. That is, the social world in which we live is designed by us in the context of our own values and interests, or, more precisely, by those among us who have the power to design that world in the context of their own values and interests.

Brownstein is suggesting that social problems such as violence comprise images and ideas that appear as subjective perceptions to us. These perceptions, however, are socially constructed; that is, they become social problems as the result of interaction with others, particularly interaction with groups or organizations that have the capacity to socially define a condition as problematic, in a literal sense. These groups and organizations also provide solutions in the form of laws or prevention programs. Among the most powerful of these claims makers are the media, who present constructions of violence that come to be accepted as objectively real even though, in many circumstances, what is uncovered by research shows the constructed reality to be grossly exaggerated or nonexistent. For example:

> In the mid-eighties, the public was led to believe by media and government officials that we were in the midst of a crack cocaine epidemic that was leading to high levels of violence. At the same time, Henry Brownstein, Paul Goldstein, and Pat Ryan were studying whether crack caused violence. They found a relationship between crack and violence, but 85 percent of crack-related homicides involved disputes over crack-market dealing. Only five of the 414 New York homicides studied were the result of using crack, and two of these involved other drugs as well. Clearly, the "drug-crazed killer" was the product of media claims making. (Brownstein, 2000, p. 29)

Another example of social construction in the seventies was the discovery of a new deviant—the Halloween sadist, who gives dangerous and adulterated food to children. For example, the apples given by the nice lady down the street may have razor blades inside. Media warnings to parents went out, and California and New Jersey legislatures passed laws against Halloween sadism. Best and Horiuchi (1985) searched four major newspapers for all instances of Halloween sadism between 1959 and 1984. Of the 76 instances uncovered, only 2 resulted in the death of children. In one case, the child ate heroin that was hidden in his uncle's home, not in Halloween candy. In the second case, the child died of cyanide in candy that had been placed there by his father, not some anonymous sadist. The remaining cases had minor injuries.

The eighties saw the emergence of a moral panic about serial killings, which represented, according to widespread accounts, up to 20% of all homicides. Upon investigation, however, Jenkins (1994) concluded that serial murders represented fewer than 1% of all murders. The exaggerated count of serial murders emerged from dubious statistics presented in congressional hearings by Federal Bureau of Investigation (FBI) representatives that were treated as objective fact by media. Media claims were reinforced and extended by groups such as homosexuals, African Americans, feminists, and various cults who claimed victimization by serial killers.

The focus of the media on drug-crazed killers, Halloween sadists, and serial killers occurs partly because they are unusual forms of violence. In the United States, murders, sexual assaults, domestic batteries, aggravated assaults, and robberies occur so frequently that they are barely newsworthy. We are suggesting, then, that there must be something unusual about criminal violence to warrant special media attention. The issue is captured by the old saying, "It's not news when dog bites man. It's news when man bites dog."

The fact that the media rarely present a representative view of violence in the United States has an important policy implication. The views carried by the media have an impact on legislators, policymakers, and the public; criminal laws can and do result from exaggerated and distorted views of the problem. Perhaps the best example is the fact that severe sanctions are imposed for the possession and use of marijuana although the drug has been shown repeatedly to have little or no relationship to violence (Reiss & Roth, 1993).

A large number of laws govern the expression of criminal violence. We know them under laws prohibiting homicide, assault and battery, robberies, sexual assaults, and collective and political violence, such as terrorism, labor violence, and hate crimes. We will describe these laws in the chapters dealing with the latter forms of violence.

PERSPECTIVES ON CRIMINAL VIOLENCE

The three perspectives of criminology, criminal justice, and public health provide different ways of viewing criminal violence. We will discuss the similarities and differences between the two most closely related disciplines, criminology and criminal justice, in the following section. Although criminological issues overlap with those of criminal justice and public health, we will focus on distinctions between criminal justice and the public health perspective in the second section. All three approaches contribute to policy and practice.

A CRIMINOLOGICAL PERSPECTIVE

Criminology in the United States got an important impetus and legitimization from the work of sociologists at the University of Chicago who studied crime and social disorganization in the 1920s and 1930s. Criminology is defined as "the scientific study of the making of laws, the breaking of law, and society's reaction to the breaking of laws" (Adler, Mueller, & Laufer, 1998).

We have discussed the making of laws in a previous section, in which we described how criminal law is made through consensus and conflict. For the latter, we discussed the contributions of social constructionists.

The second part of our definition, the breaking of laws, is what is typically thought of as the main concern of criminology. What is important to recognize is the difference between a legal and a criminological approach to crime. Practitioners in the criminal justice system (e.g., law enforcement, prosecutors, judges, probation officers, and correctional personnel) are primarily interested in processing offenders according to criminal law. They are, of course, very interested in any measures that would reduce the appearance or, more likely, the reappearance of offenders, but their job is to work within the limits of law. Criminologists, on the other hand, have the task of explaining why the behavior occurred.

The final component, society's reaction to the breaking of laws, indicates that criminologists are interested in the effect that lawbreaking has on general society. Do people feel that some sanctions are more effective than others? Does the punishment handed out by courts fit the crime in the view of the public?

A CRIMINAL JUSTICE PERSPECTIVE

Criminal justice achieved its current prominence as a result of legislation funding criminal justice education during the administration of President Lyndon Johnson in the 1960s and 1970s. Although criminology has been heavily influenced by sociology, criminal justice is multidisciplinary, assimilating the insights of a variety of social sciences (e.g., psychology, economics, history, geography, and political science).

While criminology focuses on why criminal behavior occurred, the focus of criminal justice is the criminal justice system: law enforcement, the criminal courts, and corrections. Gottfredson (1999) describes four themes that are central to understanding the criminal justice system:

- The conflict between personal liberty and community safety, which is reflected in daily criminal justice decisions. While we value liberty, we also recognize that the behavior of some people must be controlled for the safety of others.
- Law enforcement agencies, criminal courts, and correctional agencies are part of an interacting system. What happens in one part affects all the other parts.
- An emphasis in the study of criminal justice is on the quality of decision making by those who work in the system. Decisions should be made in a framework that is legal and ethical.
- The main resource for making decisions and understanding the criminal justice system should be scientifically gathered and evaluated information.

The different emphases of criminology and criminal justice are complementary. Criminology focuses on the "front end" of the criminal justice system, criminal justice on the remainder of the system itself. Criminology considers not only the causes of individual crime, but also the components of a criminogenic society. Criminal justice examines organizations and how decisions have an impact on the offender and on other parts of the system.

Both criminology and criminal justice rely on scientific theory and the use of the scientific method to understand and evaluate criminality. Because the public health perspective also relies on the scientific method, we will postpone discussion of how criminal violence is studied until we have described the public health perspective.

PUBLIC HEALTH PERSPECTIVES

The public health approach views violence as emerging from a complex causal system that includes, but is not limited to, offender intentions, motivations, and characteristics (Moore, 1995). The public health approach focuses on reducing the probability (risk) of harm. It emphasizes prevention rather than reaction, and reducing risk factors rather than simply incapacitating violent offenders (Prothrow-Stith, 1991). Moore (1995) outlines three key distinctions between public health and criminal justice approaches to violence. Each provides different ideas about the problem, its causes, and effective interventions.

First, each sees the *problem* of violence differently. Criminal justice personnel view interpersonal attacks as crimes; public health specialists view them as *intentional injuries.* Intentional injuries are viewed as part of a larger category of health problems that include both disease and injuries; injuries include intentional injuries as well as unintentional injuries (e.g., auto accidents, falls, and fires).

Criminal law and the public both place greater weight on violent incidents resulting in serious injury or the threat of injury (Moore, 1995). Public health professionals, in contrast, traditionally have focused more on diseases and unintentional injuries. If data show that the death rate due to homicide for young black males is more than 10 times the rate for young white males, however, then one must seek to find ways to reduce the level of harm to this population (Mercy & O'Carroll, 1988).

Differences in problem definition also result in different views regarding offenders and victims. In general, the criminal justice system attempts to prevent violent crime through deterrence, incapacitation, or rehabilitation. *Deterrence* refers to the inhibiting effect that punishment has on potential offenders in the public (general deterrence). This may involve increasing the probability of arrest, conviction, or incarceration, or increasing sentence severity. Specific deterrence, in contrast, would seek to prevent future criminal acts only by the individual punished. *Incapacitation* refers to the fact that an offender is restrained from committing any further crimes against the public, at least during the period he or she is confined. *Rehabilitation* refers to any postconviction treatment aimed at reducing an offender's future likelihood of committing crimes. We review some evidence for the effectiveness of each in Chapter 15. In reality, though, many criminal justice programs and policies today address multiple goals simultaneously, and traditional distinctions among these goals are less pronounced than they once were (Welsh, 1993).

To public health specialists, the essential task is to repair the damage caused by the attack and reduce future attacks rather than assign blame. Similarly, the public health community traditionally has been more sensitive to violence occurring among intimates, because much violence unreported to police is likely to turn up in emergency rooms, schools, and other noncriminal justice settings.

Criminal justice also tackles *causes* differently. Criminal justice specialists tend to focus on individual offender intentions, motivations, and backgrounds. Indeed, violence would be treated as accidental rather than criminal were there not some level of intent on the part of the offender. The criminal justice system's emphases on deterrence, incapacitation, and rehabilitation flow naturally from its focus on the intentions and motivations of individual offenders (Moore, 1995).

Public health tends to see violence as emerging from complex causes, including, but not limited to, the individual offender. *Risk factors* can be defined as statistical or conditional probabilities that elevate the likelihood of violent victimization. Protection is indicated when certain factors, such as being raised in a two-parent rather than a single-parent family, lower the statistical likelihood of violent victimization.

A four-step "risk-based" approach guides prevention and intervention efforts (Mercy & O'Carroll, 1988): (1) surveillance (collect, analyze, interpret, and report health data), (2) risk group identification (identify persons at greatest risk of disease or injury, and the places, times, and circumstances associated with increased risk), (3) risk factor exploration (analyze to explore potentially causative factors), and (4) program implementation and evaluation (design, implement, and evaluate preventive interventions based on understanding of risk factors and the population at risk). This approach is thus highly empirical and pragmatic rather than theoretical. Public health specialists are informed by theoretical research, although they are more directly concerned with identifying risk factors that are malleable or changeable through ethical and humane methods. Part of the test for a useful theory or a useful risk factor is whether interventions based on its logic will work or not (Moore, 1995).

Public health perspectives focus on at least three broad classes of risk factors: (1) structural and cultural, (2) criminogenic commodities, and (3) situational (Moore, 1995). Poverty, for example, is a structural risk factor. Poverty exposes children to higher rates of trauma, victimization, and poor health, with the result that the likelihood of future success is lowered and the likelihood of future victimization and/or offending is increased. Criminogenic commodities are items that increase both the likelihood of violence and the seriousness of injury: guns, alcohol, and drugs (see Chapters 12 and 13). Situational risk factors are specific types of interactions and settings in which the risk of violence is elevated. The notion of *dangerous offenders,* central to criminal justice, is conspicuously missing from the public health perspective (Moore, 1995).

As Moore suggests, the public health perspective complements, not replaces, criminal justice. It widens strategies for prevention and intervention. It identifies important opportunities for preventing and controlling violence that go beyond deterrence, incapacitation, and rehabilitation. It also challenges our moral values about who should be blamed for violent incidents. At least some interpersonal violence may be seen as heavily influenced by structural, cultural, and situational factors rather than the moral depravity of offenders. If the causes of violence go beyond the individual, then so must solutions.

Indeed, the different focuses of intervention for criminal justice and public health advocates is the third key distinction between the two approaches (Moore, 1995). Traditionally, criminal justice is more *reactive,* while public health is more *proactive,* attempting to intervene before violence occurs. As a result, three types of prevention are distinguished by public health:

Primary prevention attempts to prevent the occurrence of disease, injury, or death by targeting and altering one or more critical risk factors. One might seek to prevent, for example, the initial occurrence of child physical or sexual abuse. Public health strategies typically emphasize the importance of primary prevention.

Secondary prevention attempts to identify and change key stages in the development of disease, death, or injury that, if left unaltered, are likely to lead to more serious physical or mental health consequences. Secondary prevention programs often target individuals who have already begun to experience some negative health consequences as a result of their exposure to certain risk factors but have not yet progressed to serious illness or injury.

Tertiary prevention attempts to intervene after an illness has been contracted or an injury inflicted. It seeks to minimize the long-term consequences of the disease or injury and reduce the likelihood of its reoccurrence. Tertiary prevention programs tend to focus on targets who have already suffered serious, negative consequences (e.g., serious injury, physical or mental disability, and/or criminal justice involvement) as a result of their exposure to certain risk factors.

Preferred interventions are at the level of primary prevention, the prevention of harm before it occurs. The public health perspective complements criminal justice efforts, which mostly take place at secondary and tertiary levels, when the risk of violence has been identified and when violence has already occurred. The public health approach brings a different set of strategies for observation and intervention, additional resources for developing and using data, and a broader constituency. The public health approach is not limited to reducing victimization; it extends to reducing violent offending. To reduce harm, public health specialists are equally interested in interrupting the processes that produce violent offenders (Moore, 1995). For example, a primary prevention approach attempting to reduce drug abuse by adolescents would seek to reduce the likelihood of initial experimentation. Secondary prevention programs target users who have tried drugs but have not yet experienced serious physical or mental health consequences. Tertiary prevention programs target users who have already experienced serious, negative health or behavioral effects (Greenwood, 1992).

The extension to violent offending is clear. Public health specialists prefer primary prevention, wherever possible, and thus emphasize the desirability of trying to prevent *first offenses*, or initial occurrences of violent behavior (Moore, 1995). Public health specialists, in contrast to criminal justice professionals, also tend to target structural, cultural, environmental, and situational risk factors much more than individual characteristics. When behavioral approaches are considered (e.g., altering adolescents' attitudes and behavior regarding drug use), educational approaches rather than legal interventions (e.g., massive mobilization of police resources to combat drug sales in high-crime neighborhoods) are emphasized.

HOW IS CRIMINAL VIOLENCE STUDIED?

THEORETICAL PERSPECTIVES

The study of criminal violence is anchored in criminal law; without criminal law, as we said at the beginning of the chapter, the behavior may be violent, but it is not criminally violent. Criminology, criminal justice, and public health perspectives are not compelled to view criminal violence through the lens of criminal law, however. The essential characteristic of a discipline is that it contributes its unique view to an understanding of a phenomenon. The three perspectives discussed in the preceding pages may each view the same phenomena differently from the way they are viewed by criminal lawyers and other practitioners.

To use an example from criminology, the major legal difference between aggravated assault and criminal homicide is the existence of a dead body. Thus, if an offender robs and beats a victim, leaving him or her in a coma, the offender can be charged with aggravated assault and robbery. If the victim dies, however, the charge is changed to criminal homicide.

Viewing criminal homicide and aggravated assault as separate categories of violence may not be the most useful way of looking at them from the viewpoint of developing a scientific theory to understand this type of violence. The two crimes are legally distinct and are processed differently because the homicide ends in death and the assault does not. An analysis of police records, however, indicates that the two types of crimes have very similar characteristics (Block, 1977; Pittman & Handy, 1964; Pokorny, 1965). In a more recent comparison of assaults and homicides in Dallas, Harries (1989) found results similar to earlier studies. Homicides are similar to assaults with respect to socioeconomic status, temporal patterns, and racial, age, and gender distributions. Homicides differ from assaults primarily in the more frequent use of firearms.

From the viewpoint of understanding the causes of criminal homicides and assaults, does it make sense to have a theory of homicides and a theory of assaults because they represent different legal categories? A more useful approach is to assume that because they share many characteristics, criminal homicides and assaults may be subsets of one general theoretical category of violence. From this perspective, the causes of both crimes are similar. The differences between the two are the result of factors related to the situation (i.e., differential availability of firearms) or the process of the violent event. In other words, a scientific explanation of criminal violence may call on criminologists to conceptualize violent behavior in ways that are substantially different from the goals of criminal law and criminal justice processing.

RESEARCH METHODS

The preceding discussion on theoretical perspectives illustrates how researchers can view violence using their particular perspectives. In many instances, research is carried out to answer policy or practice questions using legal categories. For example, homicide rates have been declining in the United States since the mid-nineties. Using the criminal law definition of homicide, researchers continue to explore the reasons for the decline (Blumstein & Rosenfeld, 1998).

What binds the three perspectives together is that they use scientific methods to acquire information about criminal violence. For example, Sherman, Shaw, and Rogan (1995) did an *experiment* in which police intensified their efforts to enforce existing gun laws on an experimental patrol beat in Kansas City. The results of their efforts were compared to those in another patrol beat (control beat) in which no increased effort was made to enforce gun laws. The results show that gun-related crimes in the target beat decreased from 37 per 1,000 persons to 18.9, while gun crimes in the control beat showed little change. Other positive findings included a decline in homicides and less public fear in the experimental area as compared to the control area.

The National Crime Victimization Survey (NCVS), discussed in detail in the next chapter, is an example of how a *survey* is used to study violence (Rennison & Rand, 2007).

In addition to questions on violence, the NCVS asks a nationally representative sample a series of questions about how often they have been victimized and the nature of their victimizations.

Researchers use *interviews* as a method of learning about violence. Giordano and colleagues (1999) interviewed a representative sample of 12- to 19-year-old young men and women in Toledo in 1982 and again in 1992. The authors wanted to know whether prior delinquency involvement and self-concept played a role in relationship violence, particularly among females. The results of their analysis supported the view that prior delinquency involvement did, indeed, increase relationship violence among females.

Participant observation is one of a number of qualitative research techniques used to study violence. For example, Jankowski (1991) conducted studies of 37 gangs in Boston, New York, and Los Angeles. The gangs were of African American, Jamaican, Puerto Rican, Dominican, Chicano, Central American, Irish, and mixed ethnic membership. Jankowksi studied these gangs by participating in their daily activities, even to the extent of fighting with them when it became impossible to do otherwise. He became accepted by the gangs and took notes and made tape recordings of their activities.

Secondary data and *content analysis* are frequently used because violent phenomena are statistically rare (Riedel, 2000). Somewhat less frequently used is content analysis to determine the kinds of information that are available—and, presumably, read—by selected audiences. Social constructionists who study the impact of media interpretations of public opinion and legislation use content analysis of television, magazines, the World Wide Web, and newspapers. Best and Horiuchi's (1985) study of Halloween sadism is an example of how content analysis of newspapers is used to study violence.

CHALLENGES OF VIOLENCE RESEARCH

The challenge in doing research on violence has little to do with method and everything to do with content, because it is criminal violence, rather than violence, that is being studied. Because it is *criminal* violence, the research has to be anchored, in some fashion, in a legal concept of crime. This fact alone shapes and limits the kind of information that is available for research purposes. For example, there are relatively few studies of violent offenders who are not incarcerated. Studies of incarcerated offenders indicate awareness that they are committing a violent crime. Although such research is enormously useful, it is clear that offenders interviewed may or may not be a representative sample of, for example, robbery offenders.

Much research on violent crime draws on secondary data—that is, information gathered for another purpose. Most of this research draws on official records, such as police department records or official statistics, such as the *Uniform Crime Reports*, an annual summary of crime in the United States published by the FBI. We will discuss the law enforcement record and other sources of data in the next chapter.

The following considers some characteristics of crime that make access to reliable and valid data on violent crime difficult.

The first obstacle to obtaining valid and reliable data is the rarity of the event. As a rule, the more serious the crime, the less frequently it occurs and the less likely it can be observed directly. For example, in 2011, there were only 1,794 murders and nonnegligent manslaughters in a California population of 35,578,616, which is 0.000050% of the population (State of California, 2012). Given its rarity and generally unannounced occurrence, information about criminal homicides is obtained as a byproduct of police investigation and apprehension of offenders.

Readers may be puzzled because the opening pages of this chapter give numerous examples of violence and criminal violence, yet in the preceding paragraph we say that violent crime is statistically rare. In one sense, both statements are true, depending upon what is being compared. When we consider 1,794 murders and nonnegligent manslaughters in a population of more than 35 million people, they are, indeed, rare events. When we consider violent crime in comparison to other technologically advanced nations, however, rates of criminal violence are extremely high in the United States. We consider these issues in Chapter 3.

Second, there are violent crimes more prevalent than criminal homicides, but they cannot be observed easily for other reasons. For example, Harries (1989) found that aggravated assaults ($n = 32{,}096$) occurred 27 times more frequently than criminal homicide ($n = 1{,}228$) in Dallas from 1981 through 1985. Aggravated assaults, however, occur in settings that are not routinely subject to surveillance. Thus, robberies and rapes, as well as crimes like burglaries, occur in locations and in ways that reduce the possibility of the offender being identified and apprehended.

Violent assaults also occur in settings that are legally protected from outsiders. Thus, the study of domestic violence must be limited to voluntary reporting by the victims or offenders because of the protected privacy of the settings (Gelles & Straus, 1988).

Third, a major premise of the criminal justice system is that victims or bystanders will report crimes. In many instances, victims have a clear interest in reporting crimes because they seek justice, retribution, and/or restitution for an injury suffered. Crimes go unreported, however, because victims may be legally implicated in offenses like prostitution, gambling, and possession of controlled substances. Aside from legal accountability, victims may not report crime because they fear humiliation, embarrassment, or reprisal from the offenders. For this reason, spousal and child abuse, sexual assaults, and rapes are underreported.

Generally, violence involving family members and relatives is less frequently reported than violence involving strangers, for several reasons. There is a tendency to "normalize" violent attacks by people known to the victim, which does not occur for attacks by strangers. A violent attack is "normalized" by a victim's effort to attribute a socially acceptable and benign meaning to it. The older literature on violence between spouses is replete with examples of normalizing. The wife believes that a beating by her husband has to be forgiven and understood in the context of his fears and insecurities over losing his job, for example.

In addition, the criminal justice system is less willing to deal with violent offenses involving people known to one another compared to offenses involving strangers, although recent legislation has compelled more attention by law enforcement to domestic violence. Gottfredson and Gottfredson (1988, p. 259) summarize the impact of strangers on discretionary decisions:

> The major pattern may be stated succinctly: It is preferred that the criminal justice process not deal with criminal acts between nonstrangers. Nearly every decision maker in the process seeks alternatives for criminal acts between relatives, friends, and acquaintances. The gravest dispositions are reserved continuously for events between strangers. Victims report nonstranger events less frequently, police arrest less frequently, prosecutors charge less frequently, and so on through the system.

Fourth, victims may respond differently, depending on what is considered "normal" in their particular environments. For example, victimization surveys find that victimization by assault is positively correlated with education, despite the fact that police files indicate that most victims of assault are less educated. It may be that better-educated persons are better respondents and give more information. It is also likely, however, that less-educated persons may see certain types of violence as a normal part of life, whereas the better-educated have had very little contact with physically assaultive behavior and see such acts as criminal violence (Skogan, 1982).

Fifth, because crime is stigmatizing and carries with it penal sanctions, large portions of the record may be missing even though the crime is reported. Obviously, offenders have the greatest interest in concealing events. Except for observations supplied by the victim, information about the offender depends on "clearing" an offense by the arrest of one or more offenders. Clearance percentages are very low, however; the clearance percentage for the most serious crime, homicide, was 64.8% in 2011 (FBI, 2012). If the offender is not known and the victim is dead, police records are missing information about an important participant in the crime in 35.2% of these cases.

WHAT LIES AHEAD?

The first three chapters of this book provide a background for understanding subsequent chapters on specific forms of violence. Chapter 2 reviews and discusses the strengths and limitations of different measures of violence. These include data available from police and medical professionals at the local and national levels and the NCVS.

Chapter 3 focuses on historical and comparative perspectives. Was the United States always a violent society, or is it more violent now than in previous historical periods? How does the rate of criminal violence in the United States compare to those in other technologically advanced, and Third World, countries?

A TRIPARTITE APPROACH TO UNDERSTANDING VIOLENCE

Following Welsh and Harris (2004) we suggest a *tripartite approach* to violence in Chapters 4 through 15. For any specific type of violence, we first examine *patterns* of violence (who is involved, where, how much, how often, how long, and so on). Second, we attempt to understand or *explain* violence based on those observed patterns. Third, we need to explore *solutions* (interventions) to specific types of violence that are consistent with *both* observed patterns and explanations. Failure to do so increases the likelihood of failed interventions. Using the tripartite approach, Chapters 4 through 7 discuss specific types of violent crimes (homicide, robbery, rape, hate crimes). Also using the tripartite approach, Chapters 8 through 14 discuss criminal violence in specific settings and contexts. Thus, there are separate chapters on family, workplace, school, and gang violence as well as on gun and drug violence. Chapter 14 discusses terrorism and Chapter 15 examines the relationship between punishment and prevention.

Patterns

We begin analysis of any specific type of violent behavior by examining information about it. We are interested in questions like: How do we define a specific behavior (e.g., homicide, robbery)? How prevalent is it? Where is it most frequently found? Who are the offenders, and who are the victims? How long has the problem existed? How has it changed over time? We need to be careful, because problems are socially constructed by the media, politicians, or even criminal justice officials. In other words, certain problems are perceived, and decisions are made to focus attention and resources on a particular problem (Welsh & Harris, 2004). Perceptions of a problem and reactions to it, however, may be quite different from the actual size or distribution of a problem (Spector & Kitsuse, 1987; Walker, 1998). We need methods to document, describe, and analyze patterns for any specific type of violence.

We also need to look at some kind of data to estimate the degree and seriousness of a problem. Wherever time and resources allow, it is always desirable to use as many techniques as possible to analyze a specific issue. Social indicators, such as police and NCVS data, are perhaps the most accessible and widely used information for analyzing criminal justice problems. Other types of data include interview and participant observation.

Examining Potential Explanations of the Problem

What causes any specific type of violence? How can we explain why people commit particular acts of violence? This is a critical stage of analysis, because different causes imply different solutions. If we choose a solution (e.g., changing existing laws) before examining causes, it is likely that the solution will be ineffective. Any intervention should be aimed at a specific cause or causes. Causes may be identified at different levels of analysis ranging from individual to social structural:

Individual: Presumed causes lie within individuals (e.g., personality traits, such as "aggressiveness").

Group: Presumed causes lie within the dynamics of particular groups to which a person belongs (e.g., patterns of roles and relationships within a family or a gang).

Organizational: Presumed causes lie within the particular culture and procedures of a specific organization, such as the police, courts, or prisons (e.g., how police officers are recruited, selected, or trained; how criminal justice officials use their discretion in case processing).

Community: Presumed causes lie within the behavioral patterns and dynamics existing within a specific community (e.g., community "cohesiveness" or the degree of involvement in community organizations, such as churches and community associations; attitudes toward deviance; supervision of juveniles).

Social Structure or Cultural: Presumed causes lie within the underlying social structure of society (e.g., the unequal distribution of wealth and power engendered by the economic system of capitalism) or its cultural attitudes regarding behaviors, such as drug use, sexuality, education, crime, and so on.

We explicitly examine our causal assumptions about a specific type of violence and examine empirical evidence for any cause or theory. One should look at journal articles, books, and government and agency reports (e.g., numerous branches of the U.S. Department of Justice, including the National Institute of Justice).

Interventions

We usually need to discover what types of previous interventions have been attempted to reduce a specific type of violence. We attempt to find out what major interventions have addressed specific types of violence and identify which specific causes the intervention was attempting to modify. Excellent sources of information about interventions are officials working in justice-related positions, criminal justice journals and books, and government reports. Numerous databases can be searched by key words and terms. Criminal justice literature searches can be conducted online, via computer software, and in printed index format (e.g., the National Criminal Justice Reference Service Abstracts sponsored by the U.S. Department of Justice).

CONCLUSIONS

This chapter has introduced the topic of violence and criminal violence. Violence may be legally neutral. We gave examples of violence in nature and instances of sports violence. Violence in sports is looked on as part of the sport, regrettable as that may be.

What turns violence into criminal violence is law. Laws are constructed by consensus or conflict. We discussed how laws are socially constructed and the powerful effect media claims have on shaping our image of violence and shaping the laws that define criminal violence.

In the third part of the chapter, we discussed criminology, criminal justice, and public health perspectives that will inform the discussion of criminal violence in this book. The final pages of that section described the difficulties of doing research on criminal violence because of the limitations of the data. We hope we have left the reader with curiosity to read the next chapter, in which we describe sources of data about criminal violence and how some of the shortcomings are addressed.

The final section discussed how the remainder of the book is organized. In the first three chapters, we provide a background, describing data sources, and historical and comparative perspectives. Chapters 4 through 7 approach specific forms of violence, while Chapters 8 through 14 discuss violence in specific settings through the tripartite approach of patterns, explanations, and interventions.

Although our responses to violence have become more punitive over the past few years, new and promising prevention strategies are being developed and tested. *Arguably, the best responses to violence can, must, and will include a balance of both punishment and prevention.* Chapter 15 will examine promising prevention and intervention strategies in more detail.

DISCUSSION QUESTIONS

1. Discuss the three different ways that criminal law is made.
2. Discuss how the public health perspective differs from the criminological perspective.
3. Explain the importance of the research on the "razor blade in the apple."
4. Describe the similarities and differences between criminology and criminal justice.
5. What is meant by "clearing" an offense and how does that affect research on offenders?

SUGGESTED READINGS

Best, J. (1999). *Random violence: How we talk about new crimes and new victims.* Berkeley: University of California Press.

Messner, S. F., & Rosenfeld, R. (2001). *Crime and the American dream* (3rd ed.). Belmont, CA: Wadsworth.

Zahn, M. A., Brownstein, H. H., & Jackson, S. L. (Eds.). (2004). *Violence: From theory to research.* Cincinnati: Anderson/Lexis Nexis.

REFERENCES

Adler, F., Mueller, G. O. W., & Laufer, W. S. (1998). *Criminology* (3rd ed.). Boston: McGraw-Hill.

Atyeo, D. (1979). *Blood & guts: Violence in sports.* New York: Paddington Press.

Berger, P. L., & Luckmann, T. (1967). *The social construction of reality: A treatise in the sociology of knowledge.* Garden City, NY: Doubleday.

Best, J., & Horiuchi, G. T. (1985). The razor blade in the apple: The social construction of urban legends. *Social Problems, 32,* 188–499.

Block, R. (1977). *Violent crime: Environment, interaction and death.* Lexington, MA: Lexington Books.

Blumstein, A., & Rosenfeld, R. (1998). Explaining recent trends in U.S. homicide rates. *Journal of Criminal Law and Criminology, 88,* 1175–1216.

Brownstein, H. H. (2000). *The social reality of violence and violent crime.* Boston: Allyn and Bacon.

Crosset, T. W., Benedict, J. R., & McDonald, M. A. (1995). Male student-athletes reported for sexual assault: A survey of campus police departments and judicial affairs offices. *Journal of Sport and Social Issues, 19,* 126–140.

Crosset, T. W., Ptacek, J., McDonald, M. A., & Benedict, J. R. (1996). Male student-athletes and violence against women: A survey of campus judicial affairs offices. *Violence Against Women, 2,* 163–179.

Federal Bureau of Investigation (FBI). (2012). *Crime in the United States 2011.* http://www.fbi.gov/ucr/cius2007/index.html. (accessed December 8, 2009).

Gelles, R. J., & Straus, M. A. (1988). *Intimate violence.* New York: Simon and Schuster.

Giordano, P. C., Millhollin, T. J., Cernkovich, S. A., Pugh, M. D., & Rudolph, J. L. (1999). Delinquency, identity, and women's involvement in relationship violence. *Criminology, 37,* 17–40.

Gottfredson, D. M. (1999). *Exploring criminal justice: An introduction.* Los Angeles: Roxbury.

Gottfredson, M. R., & Gottfredson, D. M. (1988). *Decision making in criminal justice: Toward the rational exercise of discretion.* New York: Plenum Press.

Greenwood, P. W. (1992). Substance abuse problems among high-risk youth and potential interventions. *Crime and Delinquency, 38,* 444–458.

Harries, K. D. (1989). Homicide and assault: A comparative analysis of attributes in Dallas neighborhoods, 1981–1985. *The Professional Geographer, 41,* 29–38.

Hills, S. L. (Ed.). (1987). *Corporate violence: Injury and death for profit.* Totowa, NJ: Rowman & Littlefield.

Jankowski, M. S. (1991). *Islands in the streets.* Berkeley: University of California Press.

Jenkins, P. (1994). *Using murder: The social construction of serial homicide.* New York: Aldine de Gruyter.

Kramer, R. C. (1983). A prolegomena to the study of corporate violence. *Humanity and Society, 7,* 149–178.

Mercy, J. A., & O'Carroll, P. W. (1988). New directions in violence prevention: The public health arena. *Violence and Victims, 3,* 285–301.

Moore, M. (1995). Public health and criminal justice approaches to prevention. In M. Tonry & D. F. Farington (Eds.), *Building a safer society: Strategic approaches to crime prevention* (Vol. 19, pp. 237–262). Chicago: University of Chicago Press.

Nash, J. R. (1973). *Bloodletters and badmen: A narrative encyclopedia of American criminals from the pilgrims to the present.* Philadelphia: Lippincott.

Newman, G. (1979). *Understanding violence.* New York: Lippincott.

Pittman, D., & Handy, W. (1964). Patterns in criminal aggravated assault. *Journal of Criminal Law, Criminology, and Police Science, 55,* 462–470.

Pokorny, A. D. (1965). A comparison of homicide in two cities. *Journal of Criminal Law, Criminology, arid Police Science, 56,* 479–487.

Prothrow-Stith, D. (1991). *Deadly consequences.* New York: Harper Collins.

Reiss, A. J., & Roth, J. A. (Eds.). (1993). *Understanding and preventing violence* (Vol. 1). Washington, DC: National Academy Press.

Rennison, C. M., & Rand, M. R. (2007). Introduction to the national crime victimization survey. In J. P. Lynch & L. A. Addington (Eds.), *Understanding crime statistics: Revisiting the divergence of the NCVS and UCR* (pp. 17–54). New York: Cambridge University Press.

Riedel, M. (2000). *Research strategies for secondary data: A perspective for criminology and criminal justice.* Thousand Oaks, CA: Sage.

Sherman, L. W., Shaw, J. W., & Rogan, D. P. (1995). *The Kansas City gun experiment* (Research in Brief). Washington, DC: National Institute of Justice.

Skogan, W. G. (1982). *Issues in the measurement of victimization* (NCJ-74682). Washington, DC: Government Printing Office.

Spector, M., & Kitsuse, J. I. (1987). *Constructing social problems.* New York: Aldine de Gruyter.

State of California. (2012). E-4 population estimates for cities, counties and the state, 2001–2009, with 2000 benchmark. Retrieved from http://www.dof.ca.gov/ research/demographic/reports/ estimates/e-4/2001–09/.

Swartz, J. (1975, Spring-Summer). Silent killers at work. *Crime and Social Justice,* 15–20.

Urbina, I. (Dec. 25, 2010). "Deepwater Horizon's Final Hours." *New York Times.*

Walker, S. (1998). *Sense and nonsense about crime.* Belmont, CA: Wadsworth.

Welsh, W. N. (1993). Ideologies and incarceration: Legislator attitudes toward jail overcrowding. *Prison Journal, 73,* 46–71.

Welsh, W. N., & Harris, P. W. (2004). *Criminal justice policy and planning* (2nd ed.). Cincinnati: Anderson/Lexis Nexis.

SECTION II

TOOLS

CHAPTER 2

MEASURES OF VIOLENCE

THE APPLICATION OF MEASURES OF VIOLENCE

Measures of violence are important to a society for several reasons. They are social indicators, which enable us to assess where we stand and where we are going with respect to our values and goals, and to evaluate specific programs and determine their impact (Bauer, 1967, cited in MacCrae, 1985, p. 5). Statistics on a wide variety of criminal violence provide information as to the severity of the problem and form a foundation for prevention programs and policies.

For example, data from the Uniform Crime Reporting Program of the Federal Bureau of Investigation (FBI) are being used to allocate federal funds. Maltz (1999) reports that in reauthorizing the Omnibus Crime Control and Safe Streets Act of 1968, the U.S. Congress provided additional funding under a block grant program. The amount of money available was to be based on the amount of violent crimes experienced in the jurisdiction in the three most recent years. The source of data for determining the amount of violent crime was to be the Uniform Crime Reports or what is also known as *Crime in the United States.*

When communities and governments believe they have a problem of violence, there are a wide variety of statistics available to document their problems and form a foundation for prevention programs. There are statistics on such diverse topics as domestic violence; homicide, robbery, rape and sexual assault, aggravated and simple assault; hate crimes; assaults on the elderly and children; and drug-related violence. Beyond descriptions of the event, there are a wide variety of data on arrests, prosecutions, convictions, and final dispositions for violent crimes; final dispositions include probation, parole, prison, release from prison, and reentry into the community. The large amount of information available can be illustrated by reviewing a publication like *The Sourcebook of Criminal Justice Statistics* online (http://www.albany.edu/sourcebook/).

Violence statistics are important for a second reason. Detailed information on the amount of violence collected by the major data sources is readily available on the Internet. Data from the UCR, the National Crime Victimization Survey (NCVS), and the National

Incident-Based Reporting System (NIBRS), to name the major data sources, are available for downloading from the National Archive of Criminal Justice Data (Inter-University Consortium of Political and Social Research, 2014, http://www.icpsr.umich.edu/icpsrweb/landing.jsp). Because the data can be analyzed in many different ways and for many different purposes, it is important that the user learn the characteristics of the data source, as well as its strengths and limitations, to be able to reach valid and reliable conclusions (Riedel, 2000).

OVERVIEW

Before discussing the three major measures of violence, the following section discusses crime rates. Rates are used so frequently that many people fail to recognize important differences between rates and amounts; the next section distinguishes the two and discusses their strengths and limitations.

Three measures of violence are discussed and compared in this chapter. The first official statistics source is the UCR program administered by the FBI. *Crime in the United States*, more commonly known as the *Uniform Crime Reports* or simply the *UCR*, is an annual publication that summarizes and synthesizes information on crimes reported by the police.

The second source of official statistics is the NIBRS. After more than 60 years of use, the criminological and law enforcement community called for a reevaluation and expansion of the UCR to meet the challenges of the 21st century. The result in 1985 was a final report, *Blueprint for the Future of the Uniform Crime Reporting Program*, which provided new guidelines (Poggio et al., 1985). Now, for each crime incident that comes to the attention of police, NIBRS collects a wide variety of data: nature and types of specific incidents, characteristics of victims and offenders, detailed information on the nature and value of property stolen as well as recovered, and characteristics of arrestees.

The third source of information is the NCVS, administered by the Bureau of Justice Statistics and the U.S. Census Bureau. The NCVS is based on a national survey and provides detailed information about a variety of criminal and violent victimizations. The Bureau of Justice Statistics issues regular reports on criminal victimization in the United States as well as reports on specialized topics.

CRIME RATES

In 2012, according to FBI reports, New York City had 419 murders and Chicago had 500. It appears that both cities had about the same number of murders (http://www.fbi.gov/about-us/cjis/ucr/crime-in-the-u.s/2012/crime-in-the-u.s.-2012/tables/8tabledatadecpdf/table_8_offenses_known_to_law_enforcement_by_state_by_city_2012.xls/view). If we look at the number of murders and ask which city posed the greatest risk of murder victimization, however, we come up with a very different answer. To answer that question, we need to consider the size of the city population at risk, and that is the purpose of rates.

It is important to distinguish between rates and what are variously called raw numbers, volume, incidence, prevalence, and amount. The latter (we use the term *amount*) is how much violent behavior there is of whatever type defined by location and time span. Thus, in terms of amount, there were 500 murders in Chicago and 419 murders in New York in 2012.

Rates are a measure of the amount of change in relation to some basis of calculation, such as a population at risk. Crime rates have five components: (1) amount of the crime in question, (2) population at risk for that crime, (3) a constant multiplier, such as 100,000, (4) location, and (5) time span. The components for a given jurisdiction and time are as follows:

Crime Rate = (Amount/Population at Risk) * 100,000

If we plug in the numbers for New York and Chicago, we have the following 2012 murder victim rates:

(New York) 5.05 = (419/8,289,415) * 100,000
(Chicago) 18.46 = (500/2,708,382) * 100,000

Because Chicago has the higher rate of 18.46 murders per 100,000, persons living in that city have a risk of being murdered that is almost three times as high as the risk for people living in New York, where the murder rate is 5.05 per 100,000. Thus, although the amount of murders for the two cities is similar, the risk of being victimized is dramatically different; relying only on the amount of murders without taking into account population differences can be very misleading.

Let us take an example where the populations are somewhat similar, but the amount of murder in 2012 is very different: Baltimore, Maryland, and Austin, Texas.

(Austin) 3.72 = (31/832,901) * 100,000
(Baltimore) 34.85 = (218/625,471) * 100,000

Although Austin has a larger population by about 200,000 in comparison to Baltimore, the risk of being a murder victim is more than nine times higher in Baltimore in comparison to Austin. Beyond policies and procedures, such comparisons become useful to people anticipating moving to a specific city.

In addition to specifying risk for defined populations, crime rates are useful for comparing the same population groups at different times or different population groups at the same time. Thus, we can compare how the murder victim rate has changed in Chicago over a period of years, or we can compare Chicago rates to those of other cities with smaller or larger populations.

To get an idea of how crime rates can vary, the murder victimization rate for the United States in 2012 was 4.7 per 100,000 (FBI, 2012). Although this is lower than New York's rate, it is important to keep in mind that crime rates are generally lower in rural areas and small towns than in large cities; hence, the murder rate is going to be lower for the entire country than for specific large cities. At the other extreme is San Salvador, El Salvador, which had a homicide rate in 2009 of 94.6 per 100,000 (United Nations Office on Drugs & Crime, 2011).

Two other features of crime rates deserve mention. First, the constant multiplier of 100,000 is a number conventionally used to convert a decimal to a whole number. In some measures, such as the NCVS, the constant multiplier is 1,000. Beyond making certain that all comparisons of rates use the same multiplier, the number has no significance. Second, although there is generally a question about the extent to which a violent offense is reported accurately, the greatest problem resides in specifying the denominator, the population at risk. For a crime rate to be useful, there must be a match between the characteristics of the entities in the numerator and in the denominator. Thus, we can argue that all residents of Chicago and New York are at risk of being homicide victims, although the level of risk obviously varies.

But what about offender rates? How many newborn babies can manage to fire a handgun with felonious intent? How about hospitalized people in a coma? Strictly speaking, a murder offender rate would have to exclude the latter from the population at risk.

If rates are being computed for approximate comparisons between two cities, for example, offender rates might use the total population, even though it is not completely accurate. In using the total populations, the person computing the rates has to assume the two populations are similar along dimensions that would affect the rate. In other words, if it can be assumed that the two populations have about the same proportion of people unable to offend for one reason or another, the crude rate can lead to meaningful comparisons.

But that is frequently not a valid assumption. For example, African American and white homicide victimization rates for Los Angeles cannot be usefully compared to the same two groups in Chicago even if the proportion of African Americans is the same in both cities. The reason is that there are many more Latinos in Los Angeles than in Chicago; they are an ethnic, not a racial, group, but they are frequently classified as white. Hence, Latino homicide rates and patterns are distinct from both racial groups (Riedel, 2003). What is required is that the amount or number of homicides for each racial or ethnic group be divided by the appropriate racial or ethnic population before multiplying by 100,000. This gives us a race/ethnic-specific homicide victimization rate.

Obviously, crime rates can be refined even further by age and gender groups. Thus, we can have race/ethnic-age-gender-specific rates or any combination of the four categories, depending on the purpose of the comparisons. Specific rates are used to help explain differences in the rates that we have described in preceding paragraphs. Thus, the differences in rates between Chicago and New York, as well as Austin and Baltimore, might be accounted for by race/ethnic-age-gender-specific rates or some simpler combination of demographic groups. The major constraint that limits the extent to which rates can be refined is determined by the availability of data that can be used to construct a population at risk. Although population data are generally available for age, race, ethnicity, and gender, there are no population data available, for example, on the number of strangers in a population.

Crime rates have been criticized because city population data are not sufficiently accurate to support the kinds of rates needed. Block (1987), in her study of Chicago homicides, avoided the use of rates because the city population base is not appropriate when substantial numbers of homicide victims are nonresidents. In addition, the use of interpolation for population numbers between census years may not correspond to actual changes in the population. Finally, young black and Latino men are undercounted in the census, yet they represent a large number of homicide victims and offenders. For many of her comparisons, Block (1987) relied on percentages in which the denominator was the total number of homicides.

UNIFORM CRIME REPORTS

The UCR began in the late 1920s, when the FBI, with the support of the International Association of Chiefs of Police, began a program to collect national crime data. In 1930, the U.S. House of Representatives passed a bill authorizing the FBI to be the official national clearinghouse for information on crime obtained from the nation's police departments.

Initially, the UCR program cooperated with police departments on a voluntary, individual basis. As the number of law enforcement agencies grew, however, the UCR program supported the development of state-level mandatory reporting systems. A state-level system, created by legislation, designates an official crime-reporting agency in that state and mandates reporting by all law enforcement agencies within that state.

In 2012, law enforcement agencies active in the UCR Program represented more than 308 million of the United States population (98.1 percent). This amount of total coverage amounted to 98.9 percent of Metropolitan Statistical Areas, 93.3 percent of the population in cities outside metropolitan areas, and 94.2 percent of the population in nonmetropolitan counties (FBI, 2012).

COLLECTING VIOLENT CRIME DATA

The process of collecting information about violent crime begins most often with a complaint to law enforcement officials, who investigate and determine whether a criminal offense has occurred. The process of compiling records, what records are compiled, and how they are transmitted to the UCR program is illustrated in Figure 2.1.

As Figure 2.1 indicates, states with mandatory reporting programs collect information consistent with UCR requirements. They may collect additional information from local law enforcement agencies, but at a minimum they collect information needed by the UCR. The state UCR agency issues its own report; for example, the UCR agency in Illinois is the Department of State Police, and it publishes an annual report, *Crime in Illinois*. States without a mandatory reporting system and some large cities, such as Chicago, report directly to the UCR program.

The UCR program collects information on the following four violent crimes: murder and nonnegligent manslaughter, forcible rape, robbery, and aggravated assault. Violent crimes are defined in the UCR Program as those offenses which involve force or threat of force.

Information is also collected on the following property crimes: offenses of burglary, larceny-theft, motor vehicle theft, and arson. The object of the theft-type offenses is the taking of money or property, but there is no force or threat of force against the victims.

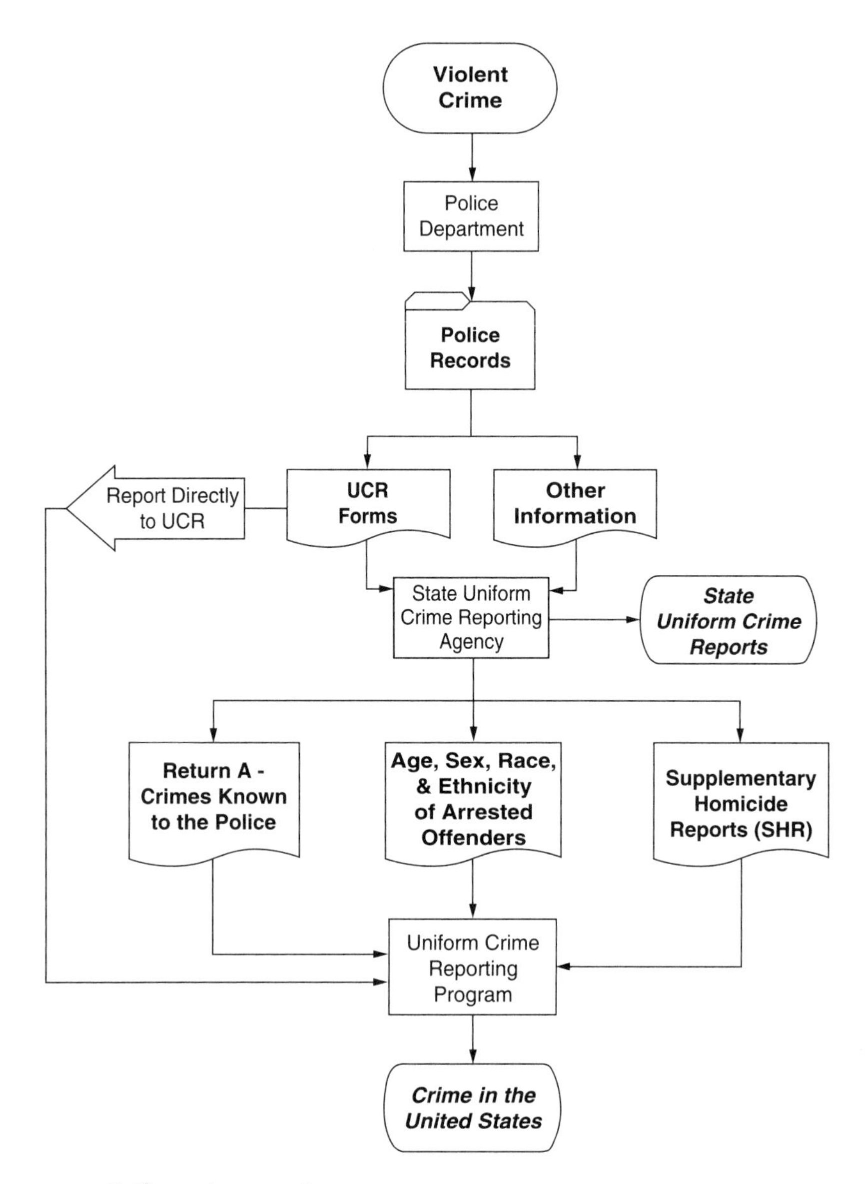

FIGURE 2.1 Uniform crime reporting program.

In addition, the UCR collects information on whether someone has been arrested for the offense. Expanded offense data is also collected such as location of robberies, time of day, and type of larcenies. Expanded homicide data include such variable as age, race, and sex of victim and offender, type of weapon, and victim/offender relationship. (FBI, 2012)

Although the UCR program requires a number of forms, three have the most relevance to violent crime: Return A, Crimes Known to the Police; Age, Sex, Race, and Ethnic Origin of Arrested Offenders; and the Supplementary Homicide Report (SHR). Information from these three forms is the primary source for the annual UCR report.

Return A: Crimes Known to the Police

As the name implies, this form contains the following information:

- Offenses reported or known
- Founded or unfounded complaints
- Number of actual offenses (founded complaints)
- Total number cleared by arrest or exceptionally cleared (described below)
- Number of clearances for persons under 18.

A number of features of this form need to be noted. First, because not all jurisdictions report, the numbers of crimes given in annual editions of UCR are estimates based on Return A reports.

Second, there is no information on specific cases. The published numbers are aggregated and reported monthly. In other words, the annual number of forcible rapes reported in the UCR is a 12-month summary of Return A reports.

Third, the number of *arrest clearances* refers to the number of offenses for which an arrest was made, not the number of offenders arrested. One arrest can clear many crimes; conversely, the arrest of many people may clear only one crime. *Exceptional clearances* refers to the administrative closing of cases for a variety of circumstances beyond the control of police departments. When cases have been adequately investigated, some of the reasons for not effecting an arrest include offenders who committed suicide or died from accidents or natural causes before being arrested; who made deathbed confessions; or who were killed by police or citizens. Other reasons include confessions by offenders prosecuted for other crimes in other jurisdictions; extradition to the jurisdiction where the crime occurred is denied, or the refusal of the district attorney to prosecute.

Age, Sex, Race, and Ethnic Origin of Persons Arrested

There is one paper form of this type for adults and another for persons under age 18. The two forms are the same except that the juvenile form requests information about curfew violations and runaways. Unlike the clearance measure for offenses, this form asks for the number of arrested offenders.

Offenders are classified into four racial groups: white, black, American Indian, and Asian or Pacific Islander. Ethnicity is coded as Hispanic or not Hispanic. Hispanic refers to Mexicans, Puerto Ricans, Cubans, Central or South Americans, or any persons of "Spanish culture or origin, regardless of race" (FBI, 1984, p. 58). In practice, ethnicity of offenders is determined by investigating officers, who may use a variety of definitions.

Supplementary Homicide Reports

While Return A and Age, Sex, Race, and Ethnic Origin of Persons Arrested forms represent aggregated monthly and annual information, the SHR provides information on each recorded case of murder and nonnegligent manslaughter. From 1962 to 1975, the SHR was primarily a record of the age, race, and gender of victims, weapon used, and circumstances of the offense. Readers interested in the history of the SHR as well as research on the current version are referred to Riedel (1990, 1999).

Revision of the SHR was completed with information received in 1976. The revision substantially improved its usefulness as a data source. The current version of the SHR contains the following information:

- A situation code indicating combinations of single or multiple victims and single, multiple, or unknown offenders
- Age, sex, race, and ethnicity of all victims and offenders involved in the event
- Weapons used
- Victim/offender relationships
- Circumstances, including type of involvement in other felony crimes associated with the homicide.

NATIONAL INCIDENT-BASED REPORTING SYSTEM

The UCR was subject to severe criticism for its shortcomings from the 1950s onward (Beattie, 1962; Robison, 1966; Sellin, 1951; Wolfgang, 1963). Two events have reduced the amount of criticism directed toward the UCR program. First, the appearance of the NCVS in the late 1960s and early 1970s provided information about violent crime that was not available from the UCR. In addition, because of their experience with victimization surveys, criminologists began to appreciate some of the difficulties involved in collecting valid and reliable data about violence (Gove et al., 1985).

Second, although there were some modifications and improvements of the UCR in 1976, a major evaluation and redesign began in 1982 as the result of an FBI/Bureau of Justice Statistics task force (Akiyama & Rosenthal, 1990; Poggio et al., 1985). The resulting system, the NIBRS, was based on reporting major characteristics of serious crimes rather than aggregate or summary counts of incidents and arrests. In short, the kind of detail that was requested for the SHR in the traditional UCR system was also being requested for a large number of serious offenses in the NIBRS.

The NIBRS is designed to gather detailed information on 46 Group A offenses in 22 categories, such as robbery, types of homicides, assaults, sex offenses, fraud, and stolen property offenses. Group A offenses were selected, in part, because of their seriousness, frequency, prevalence, and visibility to law enforcement. Group B offenses consist of 11 less serious offense categories, including bad check offenses, curfew violations, disorderly conduct, and drunkenness. For Group A crimes, a detailed incident report is filed, whereas only an arrest report is filed for Group B crimes (FBI, 1992).

COMPARING THE UNIFORM CRIME REPORT AND THE NATIONAL INCIDENT-BASED REPORTING SYSTEM

While both data sources provide information on violent crime, the NIBRS provides much more data, and in greater detail. Rantala and Edwards (2000) describe the differences between the UCR and NIBRS in Table 2.1.

To better understand Table 2.1, we need to define what the NIBRS means by an "incident." "With regard to the NIBRS, the FBI UCR Program defines an incident as one or more

Table 2.1 Differences Between Summary UCR and NIBRS

Summary UCR	NIBRS
• Consists of monthly aggregate crime counts for 8 index offenses	• Consists of individual incident records for 8 index crimes and 38 other offenses
• Records 1 offense per incident as determined by hierarchy rule	• Records each offense occurring in incident
• Does not distinguish between attempted and completed crimes	• Distinguishes between attempted and complete crimes
• Applies hotel rule to burglary	• Expands burglary hotel rule to include rental storage facilities
• Records rapes of females only	• Records rape of males and females
• Collects weapon information for murder, robbery, and aggravated assault	• Collects weapon information for all violent offenses
• Provides counts on arrest for the 8 index crimes and 21 other offenses	• Provides detail on arrests for the 8 index crimes and 49 other offenses

Source: Table adapted from Rantala and Edwards (2000, p. 1).

offenses committed by the same offender, or group of offenders acting in concert, at the same time and place." (FBI, 2014, p. 9). A single incident may have as many as 10 offense types, 999 victims, and 99 offenders (Biderman & Lynch, 1991; Maxfield, 1999).

The UCR is described as "summary data" because the UCR provides little or no detailed information on serious offenses other than homicide. The NIBRS, in contrast, collects information for Group A offenses on type of victim, victim characteristics, victim–offender relationship, use of force or weapon, type and nature of injury, time, type of location, and residence status of victim.

The NIBRS abandoned the hierarchy rule, which was one of the most controversial features of the UCR. The hierarchy rule required that in an incident in which several crimes were committed, only the most serious crime was counted; the remaining offenses were ignored. Thus, if a female victim were robbed, beaten, raped, and murdered, the traditional UCR system counts that as one murder or, to use UCR terminology, a murder and nonnegligent manslaughter. The hierarchy rule applies to all index offenses except arson, which, if committed concomitantly with another offense, is counted in addition to the other offense. In contrast, the NIBRS records each offense as an incident, as Table 2.1 indicates.

The next element to note in Table 2.1 is what the hotel rule means.

> Burglaries of hotels, motels, lodging houses, and other places where lodging of transients is the main purpose are scored under provisions of the hotel rule. This principle of scoring dictates that if a number of dwelling units under a single manager are burglarized, and the offenses are most likely to be reported to the police by the manager rather than the individual tenants, the burglary must be scored as one offense (FBI, 2004). In the NIBRS, the hotel rule is expanded to include self-storage, "mini-storage," and temporary rental storage facilities. (Rantala & Edwards, 2000)

Advantages and Disadvantages

First, one of the major problems with the traditional UCR system is that, except for homicide, it is impossible to link together victims and offenders for a given incident. In other words, there is no way of connecting a robbery reported on Return A with an arrest reported on the Age, Sex, Race, and Ethnic Origin of Arrested Offenders. In the NIBRS, however, all segments of an incident are linked together with originating agency numbers, incident numbers, and sequence numbers when multiple victims and offenders are involved (Akiyama & Nolan, 1999; Jarvis, 1992).

Second, in the UCR, Return A reports whether the offense is cleared (i.e., whether an offender or offenders are arrested on the charge). Beyond that, there is no information that can be linked directly to the offender. In the NIBRS, information is available on many more items, such as whether offenses are cleared or exceptionally cleared; data about the age, race, ethnicity, and gender of arrestees; dates of arrests; codes to distinguish arrests for each offense; whether arrestees were armed; what weapon was used; and disposition of arrestees under age 18.

Finally, in contrast to the UCR, the NIBRS provides information on offenses attempted and completed, drug and/or alcohol use, bias crime involvement, type of premise entry, and property crime characteristics.

One criticism directed toward the NIBRS was that with enhanced recording, the number of crimes would increase. For example, with the abandonment of the Hierarchy Rule, would the number of offenses increase? With careful comparisons, Rantala and Edwards (2000) found that the NIBRS rates differ only slightly from the UCR:

- Murder rates are the same.
- Rape, robbery, and aggravated assault rates in the NIBRS are about 1% higher, on average, than in Summary UCR.
- NIBRS burglary rates are lower by an average of 0.5%.
- NIBRS larceny rates are higher by an average of 3.4%.
- NIBRS motor vehicle theft rates are higher by an average of 4.5%.

The NIBRS is an enormously flexible data system that opens the door to areas of analysis that have remain closed because of the absence of reliable data. For example, Finkelhor and Ormrod (2001a, 2001b, 2004) have used NIBRS data to examine crime by babysitters, child abuse by parents and other caretakers, and child pornography.

On a more negative note, the NIBRS is plagued by missing data just as the UCR is. In comparison with SHR, Addington (2004) found more missing data for weapons and circumstances, less for offender information and victim/offender relationships, and an underutilization of the updating capability. Addington (2008) also compared the response rate of police agencies to the traditional UCR. She found the highest response rates for cities that had a population of less than 10,000 and rural and suburban counties. The lowest response rates were for agencies with populations over 250,000.

Maxfield (1999) notes that the NIBRS is an extremely complex dataset that presents challenges to not only experienced researchers but also the police officers who have to provide the initial data. The NIBRS has a multiple record structure and the ability to link together files at incident, victim, and offender levels, and it offers a wide variety of analysis opportunities, but it is also difficult to manage due to its complexity.

Full implementation of the NIBRS will take decades. The Justice Research and Statistics Association (http://www.jrsa.org/) reports that as of 2012, 32 states were certified to report the NIBRS to the FBI. Approximately 29% of the population was covered by NIBRS reporting, representing 27% of the nation's reported crime. Another 13 states or agencies were in the testing phase. NIBRS was still in the developmental stage in seven states or territories. According to the FBI, only six states had no formalized plan to report incident-based data. The largest agency reporting as of September 2012 was Fairfax County, Virginia, with a population of 1,055,204. http://www.jrsa.org/librrc/background/nibrs_states.shtml.

NATIONAL CRIME VICTIMIZATION SURVEY

The other major source of information about violent crime is the NCVS. Crime surveys, unlike information collected from police or medical examiners, rely on interviews with victims. One purpose of crime surveys is to get an idea of how much crime occurs that is not reported to or by the police. The first crime surveys of victims were conducted in the mid-1960s and were sponsored by the President's Commission on Law Enforcement and Administration of Justice. In addition to a national survey, surveys were conducted in Washington DC, Boston, and Chicago. One of the most surprising findings of these studies was that the crime rates reported by the UCR were only one half to one third of those based on victim reports (O'Brien, 1985).

After a few years of preliminary research to determine questions of reliability and validity, the National Crime Survey was started in 1972. Questions of reliability included such issues as how likely respondents were to answer questions, how far back victims' memories were reliable in reporting victimization, and how questions should be worded. Victimization surveys of large cities were done from 1972 to 1975 and then dropped. What remained is the nationwide survey and, since 1991, the National Crime Survey has been known as the NCVS.

THE REDESIGN OF THE NATIONAL CRIME VICTIMIZATION SURVEY

The NCVS underwent a major redesign in 1992 involving several needed changes. A screening questionnaire (to determine whether the respondent has been the victim of any crime within the scope of the survey) uses extensive, detailed cues to help respondents recall and report incidents. These new questions and cues jog respondents' memories and let them know that the survey is interested in a broad spectrum of incidents, not just those involving weapons, severe violence, or strangers. Because of these changes, victims are more likely to tell the interviewers about simple assaults (assault without a weapon, resulting in minor injury) and sexual crimes.

Because of the limited capacity of the original National Crime Surveys, the redesign included more and better questions about domestic violence and sexual assaults. For example, multiple questions and cues on crimes committed by family members, intimates, and acquaintances have been added. The survey also encourages respondents to report incidents even if they are not sure whether a crime has been committed. The survey staff review these reported incidents using standardized definitions of crimes.

One of the reasons for the redesign and the addition of more questions about sexual violence is that public attitudes about sexual violence have changed since the inception of the National Crime Survey in the 1970s. At that time, it was deemed inappropriate for a government-sponsored survey to ask respondents directly about rape. Reports of rape and attempted rape were obtained only if the respondent volunteered this information in response to questions about assault and attacks. The new survey asks directly about rape and attempted rape. It also distinguishes among sex crimes by asking directly about sexual attacks, coerced and unwanted sexual activity (with and without force), and verbal threats of rape or sexual attack.

These new categories, broadened coverage, and more extensive questions on sexual victimizations have elicited information on about three to four times as many sexual crime victimizations as in the past. The redesign changes made were done in such a way as to maintain continuity between the older and newer versions of the NCVS; results from the redesign began to be available in October 1994 (Bureau of Justice Statistics, 1994b, 1995).

What Is Collected?

There are two steps in interviewing victims. In the first stage, screening questions are asked to determine whether the respondent has been the victim of a crime in the past 4 months. If the respondent indicates that someone in the household has been a victim, then an individual victimization report is completed for each incident mentioned in response to the screening questions.

Perhaps the most important change in the redesign of the NCVS was the total revision of screening questions. Taylor & Rand (1995) has suggested that the most effective approach was to pepper respondents with a number of short cues to help recall the context in which the victimization occurred. This would include location of the attack, people present, and types of property that might have been stolen, and types of weapons that might have been used in an attack.

To test the difference in screening questions, half of the 1992 sample was given the old victimization survey and half was given the survey with new screening questions. In comparing the redesign with the original, estimated rate was 49% higher for crimes of violence (Kinderman, Lynch, & Cantor, 1997).

The new screening questions increased the number of completed and attempted acts and showed a greater increase of nonstranger victimizations compared to stranger victimizations (Kinderman, Lynch, & Cantor, 1997). Nonstranger victimizations (attacks by family and people known to the victim) tend to be forgotten over time or not thought of as crimes. Thus, without the prompting provided by the new screening questions, nonstranger victimizations are underreported (Riedel, 1993).

With respect to rape and sexual assault, rather than the general attack and threat screening question, the following wording was used:

> Incidents involving forced or unwanted sexual acts are often difficult to talk about. Have you been forced or coerced to engage in unwanted sexual activity by

(a) Someone you didn't know before
(b) A casual acquaintance
OR
(c) Someone you know well? (Bureau of Justice Statistics, 1994b, p. 4)

In addition, new response codes were added that allow recording of nonrape sexual assault and unwanted sexual contact. Key elements in the definition of rape were physical and/or psychological coercion as well as penetration (Taylor & Rand, 1995). The results of the redesign indicated that rapes had increased by 157% and assaults by 57% (Kinderman, Lynch, & Cantor, 1997).

The survey categorizes crimes as personal or property. In addition to rape and assaults, personal victimizations include robbery, simple and aggravated assault, and purse snatching or pocket picking. Property victimizations include burglary, theft, and motor vehicle theft. Unlike the UCR, the NCVS does not collect information about homicide or arson.

In addition to estimating the number of victimizations, the NCVS gathers details on each incident. These include:

- Characteristics of the victim (age, sex, race, ethnicity, marital status, income, and educational level)
- Characteristics of the offender (sex, race, and approximate age)
- The relationship between victim and offender
- The month, time, and location of the crime
- Self-protective actions taken by the victim during an incident
- Results of those actions
- Consequences of the victimization, including any injury or property loss
- Whether the crime was reported to police and reasons for reporting or not reporting
- Offender use of weapons, drugs, and alcohol.

How Are Incidents Collected?

The NCVS collects victimization data from a nationally representative sample of about 100,000 individuals age 12 or older living in about 50,000 U.S. households. Basic demographic information (e.g., age, race, sex, and income) is collected to enable analysis of victimizations of various subpopulations. Interviews are translated for non–English-speaking respondents. The NCVS does not cover individuals living in institutions.

Each month the U.S. Bureau of the Census selects respondents for the NCVS using a panel design. Panel designs mean that the same household is randomly selected and interviewed every 6 months for a total of seven interviews over a 3-year period. At the conclusion of this 3-year period, a new household is selected. Once in the sample, all age-eligible individuals in the household become part of the panel. The first and fifth interviews are face to face; the remainder are done by telephone.

THE NATIONAL CRIME VICTIMIZATION SURVEY TODAY

The NCVS has undergone several major changes since 1972. With the redesign in 1992, screening questions were improved to capture more information from the respondent.

With some subsequent changes, the 2005 NCVS measures not only sexual assault and vandalism but also crimes against the disabled and identity theft, which were not measured in 1972. The NCVS also has moved from using exclusively in-person interviews to an increasing proportion of interviews done with CATI. The sample size has decreased markedly over time. In 1972, a sample of 72,000 housing units was selected; by 2005, it had decreased to 42,000 households.

However, several characteristics remain the same. The NCVS uses the same sampling design as was used in the National Crime Survey versions. Households remain in the sample for 3 years and are interviewed seven times at 6-month intervals. Interviews are conducted with every household member aged 12 or over, and the interview is conducted in two parts: the screening interview and the interview to collect information about each victimization (Rennison & Rand, 2007).

STRENGTHS AND LIMITATIONS OF THE NATIONAL CRIME VICTIMIZATION SURVEY

It is difficult to show the advantages or disadvantages of the NCVS in comparison to the UCR and the NIBRS because the NCVS is not in competition with police-based statistics; it is not a matter of the NCVS *versus* the UCR or the NIBRS. Rather, the reporting systems complement each other; that is, the strengths of one system compensate for the weaknesses of the other systems, and vice versa, to provide a well-rounded picture of violence in the United States. Some of the ways that the three systems complement one another are as follows:

- The data sources measure the same subset of serious crimes, defined similarly: rape, robbery, aggravated assault, burglary theft, and motor vehicle theft. The UCR includes rape against women, whereas the NCVS and the NIBRS include rape against both genders. There is also a small variation in the definition of burglary between the NCVS and the other two sources.
- The NCVS measures both reported and unreported crime. The UCR and the NIBRS focus only on crimes reported to the police. Hence, the NCVS is not affected by the extent to which people report crime to the police or improvements in police record-keeping technology.
- The NCVS provides information on a national sample. The UCR and the NIBRS provide police department data from cities, towns, counties, and states.
- The NCVS does not interview children under 12, whereas the UCR and the NIBRS measure crime affecting young children. Survey experts cannot agree whether children under 12 can be reliably interviewed.
- The NCVS does not collect information on homicide, commercial crimes, or arson, whereas the UCR and the NIBRS do collect that information.
- The UCR collects only summary information about violent offenses other than homicide. The NCVS collects detailed information about each offense. The NIBRS collects detailed information on each offense, but, unlike the NCVS, it does not rely on a sample.

Except for homicides, the UCR provides only aggregated and summary information about offenders and arrests. The NCVS collects detailed information on victims' perceptions of offenders and relates it to victimizations. The NIBRS collects detailed information on arrests and offenders from police statistics (U.S. Department of Justice, 1995).

LIMITATIONS OF THE NATIONAL CRIME VICTIMIZATION SURVEY

Cost of Large Samples

Probability samples are used to achieve representativeness and to avoid the unacceptable costs of interviewing a population. Done within the rules of scientific sampling, we can obtain information on a population of millions by correctly sampling a few thousand. If that is the case, why does the Bureau of the Census sample 50,000 households when doing the NCVS?

Although everyone agrees there is too much crime, from a sampling and statistical point of view it is a rare event, particularly violent crime. Therefore, to capture a substantial number, a large sample must be taken. For example, suppose we knew that 10% of the population were victims of crime, and the victims were distributed more or less randomly throughout the population. Therefore, if we took a representative sample of 100, we would, on average, get only 10 victims. On the other hand, if we took a sample that is ten times larger, 1,000, we would get 100 victims, which would provide better statistical validity and reliability. Thus, to get a reliable number of victimizations, a very large number of people must be sampled. Because of the enormous cost of sampling, only organizations that have access to the economic resources of a nation can afford to carry out national victimization surveys (Glaser, 1978; Hagan, 1997).

There are two major reasons homicide is not part of the NCVS. Of course, a homicide victim cannot be interviewed, but the survey unit in the NCVS is a household, not an individual. It seems likely to us that if a homicide occurred in a household in recent months, someone in that household would be inclined to remember and report it to an NCVS interviewer.

But there are two more definitive reasons for excluding homicide from the NCVS. First, among the violent crimes of homicide, robbery, rape, and aggravated assault, homicide is by far the rarest. For example, in 2012, in a population of more than 312 million people, there were 84,376 forcible rapes, 354,520 robberies, and 760,739 aggravated assaults reported in the UCR, but only 17,827 reported homicides (FBI, 2012). To draw and interview a national sample large enough to obtain reports on, for example, 100 homicides would be prohibitively expensive and time-consuming.

Second, there are two national systems already in existence that provide detailed information on homicide, the UCR and the National Center for Health Statistics (NCHS). It makes greater economic sense to take the additional funds needed to include homicide in the NCVS and give them to the UCR program and the NCHS, which collect data on homicide as part of their national mortality records.

Poor Memory and Telescoping

As a rule, the longer the time between the actual victimization and the interview, the greater the likelihood of memory failure. To minimize recall decay, the NCVS requests that respondents recall victimization that occurred within the previous 6 months.

The difficulty with that approach is what is called "telescoping"; that is, a victimization that occurred a year ago is recalled as occurring within the last 6 months. The NCVS controls for this problem by using the first interview as a "bounding" interview. In other words, the actual number of victimizations reported in the first interview is not published because of uncertainty over when they occurred. By comparing later interviews with the first, however, the NCVS interviewers and analysts can determine whether telescoping has occurred.

Errors in Reporting

There are several types of errors in reporting. Mistaken reporting occurs when the respondent believes he or she was the victim of a crime and was not. It may be that a person who reports that his lawnmower was stolen neglected to check with his unreliable brother-in-law who borrowed it without informing him. Persons may report that others were trying to break into their homes when no such incident took place. Most of these kinds of events would be treated as unfounded crimes by police, but they may end up being published in victimization surveys.

People may report crimes to NCVS interviewers that they regarded as too trivial or unimportant to report to the police. One reason the NCVS reports a greater volume of crime than the UCR is that it reports many more minor property crimes that would have been labeled unfounded by the police (Gove, Hughes, & Geerken, 1985).

Sampling Bias. NCVS surveys fall victim to the same problems that affect census surveys of the population: the undercounting of young people, males, and members of minority groups. This poses a problem not only for crime rates, noted earlier, but also for a lack of responses in the NCVS (Hagan, 1997).

Violence Statistics, Policy, and Practice

There is no doubt that violence statistics have improved immeasurably since the revision of the SHR in 1976, but there remain some substantial challenges in the use of violence data for policy and practice.

A major problem in the use of violence statistics is missing data. Although there is a need to better understand the circumstances that lead citizens to report or not report a crime, the problem is even more evident when it is known a crime occurred but there is no information about the offenders. The reason there is no information about the offenders is that they have not been arrested or, if arrested, no information was recorded. While research is beginning to explore reasons for the low clearance, it is clear that not only are violence statistics suffering from omission, but, quite literally, offenders are getting away with murder. A second major problem is the failure of data sources to provide any linkage between and among them. One of the few examples comes from research that explores the linkage between SHRs and death certificates on homicide filed by coroners/medical examiners as part of the mortality statistics published by the NCHS. Since the definitions of homicide used by the two data sources are similar, we might expect a high level of agreement. Wiersema, Loftin, and McDowall (2000) examined the amount of agreement between SHR and death certificate records for 3,111 counties or county equivalents in the United States from 1980 to 1988. The authors found that the two agreed exactly in only 670 (22%) counties. For more than two thirds of the counties (2,120) the difference was four homicides or less. The full distribution of differences, however, extended from 474, indicating more homicides reported to the SHR than the medical examiner, to 3,121, indicating more homicides reported in death certificates.

At least for homicide records, linkage is possible and useful. Beginning in 2003, a major step forward was accomplished by the Centers for Disease Control and Prevention (CDC) through the establishment of the National Violent Death Reporting System (NVDRS), which collects data on both homicides and suicides. Data on both victims and perpetrators are integrated in a single homicide event. For each event NVDRS integrates data from a number of sources that include death certificates, medical/coroner records, police reports, SHR, hospital records, Alcohol, Tobacco, and Firearms records, crime laboratory data, and information from Child Fatality Review Teams. Currently, NVDRS contains more than 700 data elements and include data on homicide for 32 states (CDC, 2008; Karch et al., 2008).

The implementation of the NIBRS system promises much more detailed information on violent crime than was available with the UCR. There is a major problem that cannot be addressed by more elaborate data collection systems, however: The forms used by the UCR and the NIBRS depend on the quality of the persons entering the data. Until some system of quality control is implemented for police decisions and records, information on crime and violence will continue to suffer from limitations that will inevitably hamper policy, practice, and research.

DISCUSSION QUESTIONS

1. What are the similarities and differences between the Uniform Crime Reports (UCR) and the National Incident-Based Reporting System (NIBRS)?
2. Explain some of the limitations and strengths of the National Crime Victimization Survey (NCVS)
3. What are "exceptional clearances"?
4. What is the difference between crude and specific rates?
5. Why are numbers, such as the number of murders, not as important as population when discussing murder rates in similarly sized cities?

SUGGESTED READINGS

Lynch, J. P., & Addington, L. A. (Eds.). (2007). *Understanding crime statistics: Revisiting the divergence of the NCVS and UCR*. New York: Cambridge University Press.

Maltz, M. D. (1999). *Bridging gaps in police crime data* (No. NCJ 176365). Washington: Bureau of Justice Statistics.

Poggio, E. C., Kennedy, S. D., Chaiken, J. M., & Carlson, K. E. (1985). *Blueprint for the future of the Uniform Crime Reporting Program: Final report of the UCR study*. Boston: Abt Associates.

REFERENCES

Addington, L. A. (2004). The effect of NIBRS reporting on item missing data in murder cases. *Homicide Studies, 8*, 193–213.

Addington, L. A. (2008). Assessing the extent of nonresponse bias on NIBRS estimates of violent crime. *Journal of Contemporary Criminal Justice, 24*, 32–48.

Akiyama, Y., & Nolan, J. (1999). Methods for understanding and analyzing NIBRS data. *Journal of Quantitative Criminology, 15,* 225–238.

Akiyama, Y., & Rosenthal, H. M. (1990). The future of the Uniform Crime Reporting Program: Its scope and promise. In D. L. MacKenzie, P. J. Baunach, & R. R. Roberg (Eds.), *Measuring crime: Large-scale, long-range efforts* (pp. 49–74). Albany: SUNY Press.

Bauer, R. A. (1967). *Social indicators.* Cambridge: The MIT Press.

Beattie, R. (1962). Problems of criminal statistics in the United States. In M. E. Wolfgang, L. Savitz, & N. Johnston (Eds.), *The sociology of crime and delinquency* (pp. 37–43). New York: John Wiley.

Biderman, A. D., & Lynch, J. P. (1991). *Understanding crime incidence statistics: Why the UCR diverges from the NCS.* New York: Springer-Verlag.

Block, C. R. (1987). *Homicide in Chicago: Aggregate and time series perspectives on victim, offender, and circumstances (1965–1981).* Chicago: Loyola University of Chicago.

Bureau of Justice Statistics (BJS). (1994a). *Questions and answers about the redesign* (NCJ-151171). Washington DC: Government Printing Office.

Bureau of Justice Statistics (BJS). (1994b). *Technical background on the redesigned National Crime Victimization Survey.* Bureau of Justice Statistics. Washington DC: Government Printing Office.

Bureau of Justice Statistics (BJS). (1995). *National Crime Victimization Survey redesign.* Washington DC: U.S. Government Printing Office.

Centers for Disease Control and Prevention. (2008). *National Violent Death Reporting System (NVDRS) coding manual revised* [Online]. Retrieved September 2008 from http://www.cdc.gov/injury.

Federal Bureau of Investigation (FBI). (1984). *Uniform Crime Reporting handbook.* Washington DC: U.S. Government Printing Office.

Federal Bureau of Investigation (FBI). (1992). *Uniform Crime Reporting handbook* (National Incident-Based Reporting System Edition). Washington DC: U.S. Government Printing Office.

Federal Bureau of Investigation (FBI). (1998). *National Incident-Based Reporting System, Vol. 1. Data Collection Guidelines.* Washington DC: U.S. Department of Justice.

Federal Bureau of Investigation (FBI). (2004). *Uniform Crime reporting Handbook.* Washington DC: U.S. Government Printing Office.

Federal Bureau of Investigation (FBI). (2012). *Crime in the United States 2012.* Washington DC: U.S. Government Printing Office.

Federal Bureau of Investigation (FBI). (2013). *National Incident-Based Reporting System (NIBRS) User Manual.* Washington DC: U.S. Government Printing Office.

Finkelhor, D., & Ormrod, R. (2001a). *Child abuse reported to the police.* Washington DC: Office of Juvenile Justice and Prevention.

Finkelhor, D., & Ormrod, R. (2001b). *Crimes against children by babysitters.* Washington DC: Office of Juvenile Justice and Prevention.

Finkelhor, D., & Ormrod, R. (2004). *Child pornography: Patterns from NIBRS.* Washington DC: Office of Juvenile Justice and Prevention.

Glaser, D. (1978). *Crime in our changing society.* New York: Holt.

Gove, W. R., Hughes, M., & Geerken, M. (1985). Are Uniform Crime Reports a valid indicator of index crimes? An affirmative answer with some minor qualifications. *Criminology, 23,* 451–501.

Hagan, F. E. (1997). *Research methods in criminal justice and criminology.* Boston, MA: Allyn and Bacon.

Inter-University Consortium of Political and Social Research. (2014). *Data access and analysis.* Retrieved January 25, 2014, from http://www.icpsr.umich.edu/icpsrweb/landing.jsp.

Jarvis, J. P. (1992). The National Incident-Based Reporting System and its application to homicide research. In C. R. Block & R. Block (Eds.), *Questions and answers in lethal and non-lethal violence* (pp. 81–85). Washington DC: U.S. Government Printing Office.

Justice Research and Statistics Association. (2012). *Incident-Based Reporting Center.* Retrieved December 2012 from http://www.jrsa.org/ibrrc/index.html.

Kinderman, C., Lynch, J. P., & Cantor, D. (1997). *Effects of the redesign on victimization estimates* (No. NCJ-164381). Washington DC: Bureau of Justice Statistics.

Karch, D. L., Lubell, K. M., Friday, J., Patel, N., & Williams, D. D. (2008). Surveillance for violent deaths—National Violent Death Reporting System, 16 State, 2005. *MMWR, 57(SS03)*, 1–43, 45.

MacCrae, D. J. (1985). *Policy indicators: Links between social science and public debate.* Chapel Hill: University of North Carolina Press.

Maltz, M. D. (1999). *Bridging gaps in police crime data* (No. NCJ 176365). Washington DC: Government Printing Office, Bureau of Justice Statistics.

Maxfield, M. G. (1999). The National Incident-Based Reporting System: Research and policy applications. *Journal of Quantitative Criminology, 15,* 119–149.

National Archive of Criminal Justice Data. (2005). *Access data.* Retrieved June 12, 2005, from http://www.icpsr.umich.edu/NACJD/.

National Violent Death Reporting System. (2012). *The National Death Reporting System.* Retrieved December 27, 2012. http://www.cdc.gov/violenceprevention/pdf/nvdrs_overview-a.pdf.

O'Brien, R. M. (1985). *Crime and victimization data.* Beverly Hills, CA: Sage.

Poggio, E. C., Kennedy, S. D., Chaiken, J. M., & Carlson, K. E. (1985). *Blueprint for the future of the Uniform Crime Reporting Program: Final report of the UCR study.* Boston: Abt Associates.

Rantala, R., & Edwards, T. J. (2000). *Effects of NIBRS on crime statistics* (NCJ 178890, pp. 1–15). Washington DC: U.S. Government Printing Office (Revised 2001).

Rennison, C. M., & Rand, M. R. (2007). Introduction to the National Crime Victimization Survey. In J. P. Lynch & L. A. Addington (Eds.), *Understanding crime statistics: Revisiting the divergence of the NCVS and UCR* (pp. 17–54). New York: Cambridge University Press.

Riedel, M. (1990). Nationwide homicide datasets: An evaluation of UCR and NCHS data. In D. L. MacKenzie, P. J. Baunach, & R. R. Roberg (Eds.), *Measuring crime: Large-scale, long-range efforts* (pp. 175–205). Albany: SUNY Press.

Riedel, M. (1993). *Stranger violence: A theoretical inquiry.* New York: Garland.

Riedel, M. (1999). Sources of homicide data: A review and comparison. In M. D. Smith & M. A. Zahn (Eds.), *Homicide: A sourcebook of social research* (pp. 75–95). Thousand Oaks, CA: Sage.

Riedel, M. (2000). *Research strategies for secondary data: A perspective for criminology and criminal justice.* Thousand Oaks, CA: Sage.

Riedel, M. (2003). Homicide in Los Angeles County: A study of racial and ethnic victimization. In D. Hawkins (Eds.), *Violent crime: Assessing race and ethnic differences* (pp. 44–66). New York: Cambridge University Press.

Robison, S. M. (1966). A critical review of the Uniform Crime Reports. *University of Michigan Law Review, 64,* 1031–1054.

Schneider, V. W., & Wiersema, B. (1990). Limits and use of the Uniform Crime Reports. In D. L. MacKenzie, P. J. Baunach, & R. R. Roberg (Eds.), *Measuring crime: Large-scale, long-range efforts* (pp. 21–48). Albany: SUNY Press.

Sellin, T. (1951). The significance of records of crime. *Law Quarterly Review, 67,* 489–504.

Sourcebook of criminal justice statistics. (2003). Retrieved March 25, 2003, from http://www.albany.edu/sourcebook.

Taylor, B. M., & Rand, M. R. (1995). *The National Crime Victimization Survey redesign: New understandings of victimization dynamics and measurement.* Paper presented at the American Statistical Association, Orlando, Florida.

United Nations Office on Drugs and Crime. (2011). *2011 Global Study on Homicide: Trends, Contexts, Data*. Vienna: United Nations Office on Drugs and Crime.

U.S. Department of Justice. (1995). *The nation's two crime measures* (No. NCJ-122795). Washington DC: U.S. Government Printing Office.

Wiersema, B., Loftin, C., & McDowall, D. (2000). A comparison of supplementary homicide reports and national vital statistics system homicides estimates for U.S. counties. *Homicide Studies, 4,* 317–340.

Wolfgang, M. E. (1963). Uniform Crime Reports: A critical appraisal. *University of Pennsylvania Law Review, III,* 708–738.

CHAPTER 3

VIOLENCE IN OTHER TIMES AND PLACES

VIOLENCE IN THE EARLY UNITED STATES

To understand our present beliefs, attitudes, and behavior, it is important to understand our history of violence, both in the United States and in the United States compared with other countries. In his historical review of violence, Richard Maxwell Brown stated that "historically, American life has been characterized by continuous and often intensive violence" (1979, p. 40). Criminal activity, political assassination, and racial conflict are part of this picture of profound violence.

Noncriminal violence has also been prevalent, Brown suggests. Violence has formed a "seamless web" (Brown, 1979, p. 40), incorporating some of the most positive accomplishments of U.S. history: independence from Britain, freedom for slaves in the Civil War, stabilization of the frontier through vigilante initiative, and social elevation of farmers and laborers through agrarian and labor conflict.

Brown (1989, pp. 50–51) points out that:

> Historical patterns of violence survive and are deeply embedded in our heritage and habits. Violence is strongly rejected for inclusion in the American creed, but so great has been our involvement with it over the long sweep of American history that violence has become a compelling, although unacknowledged, element in our values and in our culture.

As Brown has suggested, violence is the instrument not merely of the disorderly criminal, but of the most upright and honorable. Prior to the American Revolution, mob protest and violence against British rule were common, usually involving young males loosely organized in gangs. Lane (1997, p. 70) gives an instance:

> On the cold winter night of March 5, 1770, following several days of tense encounters, a big crowd, mostly young men and boys, pinned eight redcoats and their Irish captain, Thomas Preston, against the wall of the Customs House, center and symbol of imperial rule. Yelling insults and waving sticks, throwing stones and snowballs, they dared the

> Brits to shoot. One threw a club; it hit a soldier. A single shot rang out immediately; then, after a pause of about six seconds, a whole round of shots—without Preston's order. A number of townsmen were hit in this Boston Massacre, five of them mortally including the escaped slave Crispus Attucks, traditionally counted as the first victim of the American Revolution. The crowd fell silent; Preston screamed at his panicked troops, lined them up, and marched them off, without pursuit or retaliation. The royal governor quieted the city with the promise that the troopers would stand trial for murder.

John Adams, revolutionary radical and later U.S. president, orchestrated the trial carefully, eliminating jurors with strong anti-British feelings to demonstrate the importance of lawful proceedings. Adams argued that the soldiers were endangered and fired in self-defense. Some were provoked into firing, which was, at worst, manslaughter. None of the soldiers was sentenced to death; Preston and six soldiers were acquitted, and two were found guilty of manslaughter and branded on their thumbs.

Feuds and dueling were other forms of early American killing. Dueling was used to settle insults to a person's honor, with probably the most famous duel being the one between Alexander Hamilton and Aaron Burr. Less well known were two pre-presidential duels by Andrew Jackson and a duel by Senator Thomas Hart Benton, a famous antebellum leader, who killed a man early in his career. Dueling as a practice faded after the Civil War.

In the decades after the Civil War and before World War I, feuds became a popular and violent way of settling matters. In addition to the famous Hatfield–McCoy feud of the Kentucky–West Virginia border, there were the Martin–Tolliver and Hargis–Cockrell feuds of eastern Kentucky and the Allen family feud in the Virginia Blue Ridge country of West Virginia.

The feuds of Texas and the Southwest were as bloody as any found in Appalachia, however. The most deadly was the "Pleasant Valley War" in Arizona between the Graham family (cattle ranchers) and the Tewksbury family (sheep ranchers), which finally ended with only one survivor (a Tewksbury) (Brown, 1989).

Before proceeding further, it is worth noting that the study of violence is plagued by myths and outright fabrications that characterize historical events in general and violence in particular. Perhaps the cruelest blow to mythology was struck by Lane (1997, p. 171), a leading historian of crime, who said:

> . . . it is a historian's unpleasant duty to inform readers steeped in Hollywood legend that nowhere in the Wild West, nor ever, did any two cowboys or anyone else stand in the middle of a street, revolvers strapped to their sides, and challenge each other to a fatal "quick-draw" contest.

It is also important to understand that information about interpersonal violence in the United States prior to the 20th century is fragmentary and unreliable. The little information that exists from that time is based on coroners' reports, indictments, and convictions rather than on arrests or incidents. By relying on information from later stages of the criminal justice process, cases that dropped out at earlier stages, such as arrests, are not available for historical analysis. Further, no accurate crime information was kept in the unsettled areas of the Midwest and the West. Finally, given popular prejudice, few records were kept if the victim of violence was a Native American or an African American.

The next two sections of this chapter will focus on violence involving Native Americans and African Americans. Conflicts between these nonwhite groups and whites have had a long-term impact on our history and society. A third section deals with a group of offenders sometimes characterized as "social bandits," such as Jesse James, Billy the Kid, Bonnie and Clyde, and Al Capone. The final section of the chapter examines current trends in homicide and compares them to trends in other countries.

WHITE AND NATIVE AMERICAN WARFARE

The earliest contacts between European settlers and Native Americans were generally peaceful. What is regarded as the first Thanksgiving in the United States occurred in 1621, after the completion of the harvest. Governor William Bradford proclaimed a day of thanksgiving and prayer for the Plymouth colonists and neighboring Native Americans.

In a similar but rare moment of cooperation between whites and Native Americans, William Penn, a Quaker, obtained from the British king, in 1681, a grant of territory in North America in payment for a debt owed to his father. In 1682, Penn sailed for the United States, where he planned and named the city of Philadelphia, established peaceful relations with the local Native American tribes, and ruled the colony for two years.

The usual history of the relationship between whites and Native Americans is as follows: Treaties are made, treaties are broken, and warfare ensues, with Native Americans losing and being pushed westward off their land. For example, encounters between whites and Cherokee Indians ended in the Trail of Tears, a typical episode and one of the saddest in the history of conflicts between whites and Native Americans.

THE TRAIL OF TEARS

Although the Cherokee initially sided with the British during the American Revolution, they negotiated a peace treaty with the United States in 1785. Because Cherokee resistance had continued for a decade, a new treaty was signed in 1791, giving the Cherokees land in parts of Georgia, Tennessee, and North Carolina. By 1820, the tribe had established a governmental system similar to that of the United States, with a principal chief, a senate, and a house of representatives. In 1827, it drafted a constitution and incorporated as a Cherokee nation.

Problems started when valuable gold deposits were discovered on tribal lands. In 1819, Georgia appealed to the U.S. government to remove the Cherokee from Georgia lands. This failed, so attempts were made to purchase the territory. The Cherokee nation retaliated by enacting a law prohibiting any sale of lands under penalty of death. In 1828, the Georgia legislature outlawed the Cherokee government and confiscated the tribe's land.

The Cherokee nation appealed for federal protection and the request was rejected by President Andrew Jackson, who used the Indian Removal Act of 1830 to force the Cherokees from their land. In 1832, the U.S. Supreme Court ruled the Georgia legislation was unconstitutional, but federal authorities, following Jackson's policies, ignored the decision.

In 1835, 500 Cherokees agreed to cede territory in return for $5,700,000 and land in Oklahoma, which was then called Indian Territory. This action was repudiated by 90% of the tribe, however, and several dissenters among the Cherokee were assassinated by tribal members. Federal troops began to forcibly evict the Cherokee. About 1,000 of the tribe escaped to the North Carolina mountains and purchased land there. The remaining 18,000 to 20,000 people were forcibly marched about 800 miles to Indian Territory. Because about 4,000 perished in the march from hunger, disease, and exposure to the elements, this exodus became known as the Trail of Tears (Microsoft, 1998a).

In the process of removal, the U.S. Army divided the large number of people into 13 detachments. The Army commanded some of the detachments, while others were directed by contractors who were paid $65 for each person in their care—money that did not always go for its intended purpose. Two of the detachments traveled by river and the others traveled over land. Of those traveling by water, 311 people drowned when an overloaded flatboat capsized. Among those traveling by land, cholera broke out and, of 800 in the detachment, only 489 survived (Mulligan, 1970).

Other tribes were similarly offered treaties that were also broken as European settlers wanted more of their land and, like the Cherokee, other tribes were herded into reservations. By the 1850s, only scattered groups of Native Americans remained in the eastern half of the United States.

Much the same fate awaited Plains and western Native Americans, even though history acknowledges the combat expertise of the First Peoples. For example, on a one-on-one basis, Native American warriors were better fighters than U.S. cavalrymen. Moreover, without Native American scouts from enemy tribes, the army was helpless. Given better tactics, artillery, and no women or children to slow them down, however, the army eventually could not lose. George Armstrong Custer's famous 1876 loss at the Little Big Horn was more an exception than the rule.

What really defeated Native Americans was loss of habitat, and attrition. By the early 1880s, white hunters with repeating rifles had reduced the buffalo herds, central to Native American lifestyle and survival, to a few hundred. Hemmed in by miners and farmers, decimated by European diseases, exhausted by cold and hunger, the last of Native Americans were pushed onto reservations by the 1890s (Lane, 1997).

SLAVERY, AFRICAN AMERICANS, AND VIOLENCE

Slavery got its start with the rise of farming tobacco, the first commercially viable crop that was grown in the early settlement of Jamestown, Virginia. Tobacco is a very labor-intensive business, however. Initially, Native Americans were used as a labor source, but they either ran away or had to be coerced to the point of death.

Another approach to the labor shortage was the use of indentured servants. Under England's new Poor Laws, young men could sell themselves and their labor for a period of four to seven years. They received no pay, the master provided for their keep, and they were given 50 acres of land when their indenture ended. Often, however, the "free land" consisted of swampy ground that would not allow them to sustain a livelihood.

There were two problems with indentured servitude. First, the death rate among these young men was appalling. Around 1620, for instance, the annual death rate among indentured servants was 80%, the result of malaria, typhoid, overwork, malnutrition, and general ill treatment. Although the men could be replaced free of charge, communities faced yet a bigger challenge: Once free of their masters' control, a class of discontented young men—who typically had guns—often played a role in local power struggles (Lane, 1997).

The first Africans were purchased as early as 1619 in Jamestown. Initially, Africans were treated as indentured servants, but they spoke no English, knew no law, and frequently had no idea when their term of indenture was up. Thus, they could be kept in bondage for long years, even for life. Lane (1997, p. 43) stated it well:

> Over the years practice became custom, and custom law. In 1664 the legislature of Maryland took the final step, decreeing not only that all "negroes" were to be slaves for life but that the children of all female slaves were also to be slaves, ensuring that those with known African ancestry were doomed to serve forever.

Meanwhile, due to improved conditions in England, the number of people available for indenture declined toward the end of the 17th century. To meet the increasing demand for labor in the colonies, larger and larger numbers of slaves were imported. In Virginia, for example, slaves represented about 7% of the population in 1680 and more than 40% by the middle of the 18th century (Microsoft, 1998b). Slavery was a system to meet the labor demands of the South, with respect to growing tobacco at first and subsequently cotton. Neither indentured servants nor slaves played a large role in Northern states, for two reasons: (1) the religious origins of such states as Massachusetts and (2) there was no need in the North for unskilled labor to grow labor-intensive crops like tobacco (Lane, 1997). Hence, by the middle of the 18th century, 90% of slaves lived in Southern states (Microsoft, 1998b).

Slavery was an unstable system, however. First, the rhetoric of equality was part of the ideology that supported the American Revolution, so it was difficult to justify the obvious inequality represented by slavery. There was a persistent fear and sense of unease among Southerners that their slaves would one day rise up and kill them. Second, plantation owners had daily evidence that their slaves were not happy with their lot. Third, slaves had low productivity, making slavery a very inefficient system. There was a constant problem with foot-dragging or deliberate slowdowns by slaves who pretended to be sick, feigned difficulty understanding instructions, and "accidentally" misused tools and animals.

There were constant plots, real and imagined, but the best known is the Nat Turner Rebellion. Nat Turner was born a slave in Southampton County, Virginia, in 1800. Turner was a popular religious leader among his fellow slaves. In 1831, he believed that he had received a sign from God, by means of the color of the sun, indicating that he should lead his people to freedom.

In August of that year, Turner and five other slaves killed their master and his family. Over the next 40 hours, they were joined by about 60 other slaves from neighboring plantations. They then moved about the county, slaughtering about 50 whites. Consequently, an unknown number of blacks were lynched in reprisal by white mobs. The revolt lasted until August 24, when it was put down by federal and state troops and associated volunteers, but Turner was not found for another six weeks. After his capture, Turner and 15 of his companions were tried, convicted, and hanged.

As a result of the Nat Turner Rebellion, the movement to abolish slavery, which had enjoyed some support in the South, became a Northern phenomenon. In contrast, Southern legislatures used the enormous level of white fear generated by the revolt to impose even greater restrictions on slaves (Lane, 1997).

LYNCHING

There is good reason to agree with Lane that, in comparison to previous centuries, the 19th was the most violent. As the conflicts over slavery became more intense, they ended not only more often in violent death, but also in the Civil War. Of the 2,500,000 who served during this war, in either the Southern or Northern armies, 620,000 young men, or one in four, died.

The amount of race hatred expressed on both sides led to unbelievable atrocities—gross exceptions to the rules of combat. After Lincoln's Emancipation Proclamation in 1863, black soldiers began to serve in Union units. In April 1864, after Confederate troops overran Fort Pillow, Mississippi, General Nathan Bedford Forrest refused to accept the surrender of the many black soldiers in the Union garrison. With their hands up, they were methodically bayoneted to death. Forrest later stated the river ran red for nearly 200 yards downstream (Lane, 1997).

The most murderous outbursts of the Civil War accompanied the New York City Draft Riots of 1863. During the early stages, the government had relied on voluntary enlistment to obtain recruits for the Union armies. Because of pressing need, however, Congress passed the Enrollment Act in 1863, which imposed liability for military duty on every able-bodied male between the ages of 20 and 45. There were draft riots in several cities, but none as large as in New York, with its heavy concentration of Irish immigrants. Irish immigrants did not believe the Civil War was their war, and they were further angered by the Emancipation Proclamation, which increased their antagonism toward African Americans. In addition, critics of President Lincoln's administration objected to policies exempting potential draftees who could supply a substitute or $300.

The Monday after the law became effective, a crowd gathered, set ablaze the draft headquarters, and prevented the efforts of firefighters. As a result, the flames spread and destroyed a city block. Rioters roamed freely throughout the city attacking, murdering, and lynching many black men, whom they blamed for the war. The mob attacked and burned the Colored Orphan Asylum, and only the courageous intervention of one Paddy McCaffrey and several firemen kept the children from being killed as well. The riot lasted from July 13 to July 16, when troops returning from the Battle of Gettysburg dispersed the rioters. Fatalities from the four days of havoc were estimated at more than 1,000.

Violence toward African Americans in the form of lynching became especially pronounced after the Civil War. Although the South technically lost the war, between 1865 and 1877, it informally won back much of what it had lost by using murder as an instrument of social policy (Lane, 1997). Lynching, hanging, or other forms of execution carried out by self-appointed commissions or mobs without due process of law have occurred, at some time, in every state—for instance, these were used for punishing Tories during the American Revolution—but more than 3,700 lynchings occurred between 1889 and 1930, and well over 80% occurred in the South.

What has fascinated and occupied scholars over the decades is the sheer barbarity of such incidents:

> The results included the most barbaric episodes in the history of American homicide: special excursion trains took passengers to Paris, Texas, in 1893, to watch a retarded black man die, over the course of an hour, of red-hot irons thrust into his body and down his throat; in 1911 an accused rapist was tied to a stake on the opera house stage in Livermore, Kentucky, and tickets bought the privilege of shooting at him from the seats. (Lane, 1997, p. 151)

Lynching finally declined because white fears had been put to rest by U.S. Supreme Court decisions that all but excluded African Americans from the political process by poll taxes and literacy requirements. When these barriers were coupled with practices of legal segregation, African Americans found themselves economically dependent and politically powerless. Nothing more was needed to hold them down, so the practice of lynching declined because it simply was no longer needed.

SOCIAL BANDITRY

The period after the Civil War was one of enormous industrial growth in the United States, particularly in the North. It was also a period of unrestrained capitalism. While the Rockefellers, Carnegies, and Morgans grew wealthy, sharecroppers, farmers, ranchers, and small merchants were caught by economic cycles that left them in poverty. Further, in the South and Civil War border states, many men who had been sympathetic to the Confederacy were left to find their own way after the war, which meant an increase in gangs organized for robbery and murder. Rather than being appalled by the violence of people like Wild Bill Hickok, Jesse James, Billy the Kid, the Daltons, the Younger brothers, and a host of others, however, we turned them into romantic figures who form the basis of contemporary notions of "real men," heroes who, it was said, "fight and die for the things that make America great."

There are several reasons that this particular group of "Wild West" killers became romantic figures. First, in addition to weak law enforcement in border and Western regions, a great many Confederate sympathizers admired outlaws who were former Confederate soldiers. Nash (1973, p. 275) related the story of Cole Younger, a member of the James–Younger gang. In the course of a stagecoach robbery, a passenger with a Southern accent turned over a gold watch. Younger asked him if he had served in the Confederate Army and, if so, to name his rank, regiment, and commanding officer. After the man did so, Younger gave back the watch to the startled passenger and said, "We are all Confederate soldiers. We don't rob Southerners, especially Confederate soldiers."

Second, in the latter half of the 19th century, many small landowners and merchants suffered economically and blamed their troubles on Eastern banks and the growth of railroads. Thus, a kind of vicarious revenge grew in these people, who rejoiced to hear of outlaws who had come from the same humble backgrounds and inflicted damage on banks and railroads by robbery and murder of their agents (Brown, 1969).

Finally, it is difficult to underestimate the impact of favorable publicity from Eastern newspapers, pamphlets, and dime novels.1 New York detective magazines churned out dozens of pamphlet-sized stories that portrayed the outlaws of the time as simple farmers driven to violence by unscrupulous and vindictive lawmen serving the interests of greedy railroad owners and bankers.

Nowhere was the image of outlaw as social bandit cultivated more carefully than with Jesse Woodson James, his brother Frank, and the Younger brothers, Cole, James, John, and Robert. Frank was born in 1843 and Jesse in 1847 to Robert James, a minister, and his wife, Zerelda. The Younger brothers were cousins of the James boys and lived a few miles from the James homestead in Clay County, Missouri.

Although the James and Younger boys were neighborhood troublemakers, the pivotal event in their lives was the Civil War. Frank James and Cole Younger rode with the Southern guerrilla leader William Clarke Quantrill, and Jesse, when he got old enough, joined with "Bloody Bill" Anderson's gang. Both the Quantrill and Anderson gangs were exceptionally violent and brutal toward Union soldiers and sympathizers. Quantrill's Raiders burned the town of Lawrence, Kansas, and killed all its male inhabitants in 1863; Anderson and his gang massacred 75 unarmed Union soldiers in Centralia, Missouri, in 1864. The Civil War provided an education in violence, and after the war the James and Young boys turned to robbing trains and banks. If they managed to escape to their home territory on the Missouri–Kansas border, they were safe, because of strong sympathies for the Southern cause and because local people thought the James and Younger brothers were being victimized by the same railroads and banks that were also victimizing them.

The Robin Hood image of robbing from the rich and giving to the poor was cultivated assiduously by the James gang. Whenever they visited friends and neighbors in the western wilds of Missouri while on the run from lawmen, they paid handsomely for their board and room. One story, more myth than fact, illustrates the heroic legend of Jesse James. Jesse and his gang reportedly stop at the cabin of a lonely widow. Although impoverished, she feeds the gang. On seeing tears in the woman's eyes, Jesse inquires about the problem. She tells him that a banker is coming that very day to foreclose on her small farm unless she can produce $3,000 to cover the mortgage. Jesse gives her the money before riding away with his gang.

According to one version of the story,

> A few hours later the banker arrives and is astounded when he receives the amount due him. The widow woman demands her note and mortgage (remembering Jesse's warning to do exactly that) and these are handed over to her by the startled banker. Fondling his money, the greedy banker leaves in his buckboard. Three miles from the cabin, Jesse James emerges from the brush, pistol in hand and leveled at the banker, he recoups his $3,000, plus the banker's watch for his trouble, and rides away chuckling. (Nash, 1973, p. 268)

The James–Younger gang continued to rob banks and trains and kill uncooperative employees. Even though they could be identified by living victims and pursued by posses, they always managed to escape back to their home territories, where they were protected by local people who would not cooperate with law enforcement. Victims who did identify one of the gang would, within a short period of time, become unwilling to testify because of threats from supporters of the gang.

Things changed when the gang attempted to rob the First National Bank of Northfield, Minnesota. One of the Northfield residents was alerted to the robbery, and the local residents, rather than running and hiding, grabbed guns and started shooting. Cole and Jim Younger were both shot, but not fatally. They survived and were sentenced to life imprisonment at the Minnesota state penitentiary.

Jesse and Frank James escaped the Northfield debacle, moved to Tennessee, and went into hiding as farmers for three years. Then, in 1879, they organized a new gang and robbed a bank in Riverton, Iowa, as well as, five days later, a train, in which robbery a passenger and the engineer were killed. Responding to the public outcry over the murders, the governor of Missouri offered a reward of $10,000 for the capture and conviction of the James brothers.

The promise of the reward was sufficient incentive for Robert Ford to kill Jesse James. Ford had never been a full-fledged member of the gang, but he had moved about the periphery along with others who helped the outlaws escape after a robbery. While Ford was visiting Jesse and talking about the dissolution of the gang, Jesse got up, unbuckled his gun belt, picked up a chair, and went over to adjust a picture on the wall. Seeing Jesse's unprotected back, Ford drew his pistol and fired several shots, killing Jesse. He then proceeded to collect the reward.

Subsequently, Frank James turned himself in to the governor for a promise of protection and a fair trial. The unscrupulous shooting of Jesse James aroused and upset the nation, especially Missouri, which improved Frank's chances of acquittal. After a series of trials, Frank James was freed and returned to his farm to die a natural death in 1915.

PROHIBITION

The Eighteenth Amendment to the Constitution prohibited the sale, manufacture, distribution, and importing of intoxicating liquors in the United States. The Prohibition amendment became effective in 1920 and was repealed in 1933. Most people have been taught that this 13-year period resulted in wholesale violation of Prohibition laws in the form of illicit drinking, violence in the face of legal efforts to enforce the laws, and the appearance of organized crime. This is somewhat of an oversimplification. Prohibition produced a switch from low-potency drinks, such as beer, to distilled spirits, a high-potency source of alcohol. This occurred for two reasons. First, distilled spirits are much easier and cheaper to transport, while beer is bulky and expensive. Second, prior to refrigeration, beer would spoil, whereas distilled spirits would not. Thus, one unanticipated result of Prohibition was that people began consuming a higher volume of a more dangerous beverage.

Another impact of Prohibition was that more people, desperate to get their hands on an alcoholic drink, ended up consuming toxic forms of alcohol, such as methyl alcohol, which caused blindness, paralysis, and death. Of course, organized crime came to assume the organizational shape we know today because illicit alcohol was a major source of revenue for high-level gangsters.

But it is not correct to believe that Prohibition increased the amount of alcohol consumption. Based on the available evidence, consumption declined with Prohibition and increased only after the Eighteenth Amendment was repealed.

Although there are no hard data on alcohol consumption because it officially no longer existed, other indicators were used. One such indicator was the rate of death from cirrhosis of the liver, which is closely correlated with alcohol consumption in the population. Between 1900 and 1919, the death rate was between 12 and 17 per 100,000 individuals; during Prohibition, the rate dropped to between seven and nine per 100,000. By the mid-1930s, however, the rate of death from cirrhosis of the liver began to increase again (Goode, 1999).

The message to be drawn from the preceding is that "there is no free lunch." True, alcohol consumption declined, but at what cost to other important social values? Prohibition encouraged disrespect for the law, increased consumption of distilled spirits, increased the general risk of consuming toxic substances, corrupted law enforcement, and increased organized crime. We leave it to our readers to determine whether similar arguments might be used with respect to contemporary laws against the use of marijuana.

THE ROLE OF ORGANIZED CRIME

It is important to recognize that the production, distribution, and sale of alcohol are like the production, distribution, and sale of a loaf of bread: Both require a complex organization to move from raw material to a finished product. When the product is legal, a large variety of laws govern relationships between employers, employees, and the public. Labor unions, for example, are monuments to the types of relationships that prevail between workers and managers.

The situation becomes dramatically different when the product carries criminal penalties. Assuming there is a market for the illegal product, the objective tasks of production, distribution, and sale remain the same with respect to needing a complex bureaucracy to accomplish the task. These interrelated series of tasks must be accomplished without alerting law enforcement, however, and discipline must be maintained in the ranks of illegal workers.

Moreover, there are several consequences accompanying the production of illegal alcohol. Costs will increase because of the need for concealment. These costs include paying workers more because they are taking greater risks, costs of using more circuitous routes and means of transportation and distribution, and costs associated with bribing police, lawyers, and court officials. Such costs can, of course, be passed on to consumers, because they are willing to pay more for the forbidden substance.

Above all, there is the need to maintain discipline within the ranks. Large amounts of money will be changing hands at various levels, and the managers of an organized bootlegging operation must make certain that they are not cheated. The difficulty is that they have no recourse to law if their employees are dishonest; they must be able to enforce their own rules, which means injury or death to anyone who betrays them.

Finally, it is a simple fact that organizations become larger and more profitable if they have no competition. In the violent world of Prohibition, there was a constant violent struggle to eliminate the competition.

No one illustrates these characteristics better than "Scarface" Al Capone. Capone was originally from New York and spent his formative years as a member of the Five Points gang in Brooklyn. He beat up union leaders unwilling to kick money back to the gang, and acted as a bouncer and bartender in a brothel-saloon, the Harvard Inn, owned by "Big Jim" Colosimo. Capone moved to Chicago to work for Colosimo's immense brothel empire, but he kept in touch with Johnny Torrio, the leader of the Five Points gang.

When Prohibition became law in 1920, Torrio and Capone saw a chance to make a fortune in bootlegging. Colosimo didn't agree and wanted nothing to do with it, so Capone killed him. The next day, Torrio took over Big Jim's empire with Capone as his right-hand man.

Competition was fierce in the bootlegging business in Chicago. The main rivalry was between Dion O'Bannion's North Side gang and Torrio and Capone's gang on the South Side. So long as each gang stayed on agreed-on territory, there was peace.

Of course, gang members occasionally needed discipline. A hood named Joe Howard spent some time bragging about how easy it was for him to hijack beer trucks, particularly those belonging to Torrio. He made his big mistake when he slapped around and insulted Capone's financial wizard, Jake "Greasy Thumb" Guzik. Guzik complained to Capone who, minutes after the event, went into the bar where Howard was, stuck a gun to his temple, and emptied all six bullets. Loyalty was important to Capone, and those who were loyal to him could expect to be repaid.

On another occasion, Capone heard that three of his associates—John Scalise, Albert Anselmi, and Joseph Giunta—were planning to kill him. The three had been loyal Capone gunsels and had killed numerous rival gangsters and uncooperative politicians over the years. Capone invited them to an elaborate dinner, along with his usual collection of associates. At the conclusion of the meal, he praised the work of the three men, grabbed a baseball bat concealed under the banquet table, and beat each one to death.

The peace between the rival O'Bannion and Capone–Torrio gangs did not last. Capone and Torrio gunned down O'Bannion. Hymie Weiss, an infuriated O'Bannion supporter, almost killed Torrio and made an attempt on Capone's life. Torrio had had enough. After he recovered from his wounds, he turned everything over to Capone. Capone was now the number-one man in Chicago's gangland, with an annual income of $5,000,000, but he had a war on his hands. Capone managed to kill Weiss and most of the remainder of the O'Bannion gang, with the exception of George "Bugs" Moran.

Capone, now living in Miami, arranged for the St. Valentine's Day Massacre by phone. Capone's men, dressed as police, raided the garage that was Moran's bootleg headquarters. They lined up seven of the mobsters and machine-gunned all of them on February 14, 1929. At last, Capone completely controlled bootlegging in Chicago, but he forgot one thing—to pay his taxes! Capone was finally brought to his knees by the federal government on a charge of income tax evasion. He served eight years at Leavenworth and Alcatraz and was paroled in 1939.

By this time, his lifestyle had turned his life to shambles. He had contracted syphilis years before from a prostitute in Colosimo's brothels. Left untreated, the spirochete that causes syphilis travels up the spinal cord and destroys the brain. The bug, in other words, ate Capone alive, and he died at his Palm Island mansion near Miami in 1947.

What can be concluded from this brief survey of violence? We are forced to agree with Brown that violence is a persistent feature of our historical landscape: "We have resorted so often to violence that we have long since become a 'trigger-happy' people" (Brown, 1979, p. 41).

Americans express a curious ambivalence about violence. Although we oppose it, there is a tradition of admiration for figures like Frank and Jesse James and John Dillinger, whose robberies of banks and the railroad made them popular among poor people. Billy the Kid retained the respect and admiration of Mexicans and poor people in villages of the Southwest. "Pretty Boy" Floyd was admired by sharecroppers from whose stock he came.

Ambivalence toward violence is also expressed in television programs and movies. Silberman, in his 1978 book (p. 33), pointed out that

> Hollywood has made no fewer than twenty-one movies about Billy the Kid: in one version, the hero was played by Paul Newman, and in another, by Kris Kristofferson, although in real life Billy was described as a "slight, short, buck-toothed, narrow-shouldered youth" who "looks like a cretin."

CONTEMPORARY TRENDS IN VIOLENCE

Lane (1997) points out that historians of criminal violence are frequently asked how current rates compare to violent crimes in the past. By and large, any answer to that question would involve focusing on homicides, because those are records that come closest to meeting minimum standards of validity and reliability. Even then, comparing rates involves a large amount of guesswork.

Before the 1900s, there were no national data of any kind. Lane's (1979) Philadelphia research from 1839 to 1901 could only suggest that the murder rate, based on indictments, was down from the period before the Civil War. Lane also suggested that murder rates in rural areas were higher than in cities.

What makes the count of homicides impossible to ascertain with any degree of accuracy, however, is the number of infanticides (the killing of newborns). Lane reported that in the middle of the 19th century in Philadelphia, dead infants were often found in gutters and privies several times a week. What further complicates any accurate estimate of homicide is the absence of a system for counting the number of black-on-black or white-on-black killings, which must have been substantial, particularly in the South. Finally, at least until the 1880s, when the last of Native Americans were herded onto reservations, the killing of Native Americans was rarely subject to counting or legal action by either tribal or white authorities (Lane, 1997). Taking these kinds of homicides into account may mean that the homicide rate was higher than it is today, but it is really impossible to tell. History is useful in providing a perspective, and, in that context, it is worth considering some of Lane's suggestions about how contemporary homicide has changed or might change in comparison to the past.

IMPERSONALIZATION OF HOMICIDE

The overriding image that Lane conveys is the growing impersonal nature of homicide. Frightening forms of homicide have emerged in recent decades, such as serial murder and domestic terrorism. We would like to point to the close links between terrorism and serial murder. The Unabomber, Theodore Kaczynski, represents an instance of this new and frightening combination.

Both serial killing and terrorism undermine the legitimacy of the existing legal, political, and cultural order by generating an enormous amount of fear and suspicion within a community. Second, serial offenders and terrorists operate in very small groups, either one or two individuals. Third, both types of killers select their victims carefully to maximize media attention and are successful at eluding law enforcement. Finally, on the surface, the acts of serial killers and terrorists appear to be incomprehensible and irrational, the acts of a maniac. Although serial killers seem to retain this characteristic, terrorists are believed to be committed to a rational ideology in irrevocable conflict with the existing order. Distinctions about rational behavior are highly relative, however; after all, one group's "terrorist" is another group's "freedom fighter" (Riedel, 1998).

A different side of the impersonal nature of homicide is given by Lane (1997, p. 326) in explaining contemporary homicide: "The bad news that more Americans are being killed by strangers, criminals, and teenagers has been balanced by good news, in that lower percentages are being killed by family, friends, and acquaintances."

Within recent history, there is little doubt that family killings, particularly spousal homicides, have declined. This issue is explored in Chapter 8. The question of an increase in stranger homicides is more difficult to evaluate. The difficulty is one that was discussed in the first chapter: There had been a precipitous decline in arrests for homicide, from over 93% in 1960 to about 63% in 2008. Therefore, it has been suggested that many of the homicides for which no offender has been arrested involved offenders who are strangers.

It is likely that in the future there will be a greater number of stranger homicides because, if for no other reason, there will be more strangers. Urban areas are the domain of strangers, and it appears that the United States will continue to be more urbanized.

VIOLENCE IN OTHER PLACES

It is also important to know how violence in the United States compares to violence in comparable countries. Archer and Gartner (1984, p. 4) indicate that without an understanding of violence in other societies, our knowledge "remains provincial at best and at worst, simply wrong." If knowledge of violence is based on a single society, the United States, we have no way of generalizing about the size of the problem.

For example, are homicide rates higher in the United States than in comparable countries? Transnational comparisons allow researchers not only to determine the relative amount of violence, but also to explore the generalizability of causes. Such research allows us to understand whether a specified cause is peculiar to the social structure and culture of one society or is more generally important. Likewise, cross-cultural research helps us explore and understand a variety of treatment and prevention programs. If a specific program is successful in another country, policymakers may be willing to consider its application in the United States (Archer & Gartner, 1984).

Even though it is difficult to determine whether the United States is more violent today than in previous centuries, it is clear that in this century, the United States is more violent than in comparable technologically developed countries. Unfortunately, international data sources did not begin until the 1950s, are still limited to reports of homicide, and involve only a limited number of countries. International sources of crime data can be divided into datasets collected by private researchers and those collected on a regular basis by the United Nations (UN) and mortality data collected by the World Health Organization (WHO).

International Data on Violence

The best-known privately collected data source is the 110-nation Comparative Crime Data File, compiled by Dane Archer and Rosemary Gartner (1984). The Comparative Crime Data File reports annual frequencies on crime for 110 nations and 44 cities from 1900 to 1970. A second privately collected source is the Human Relations Area Files, which contain data on homicides from a sample of small, nonindustrial societies that are representative of major world cultural regions (LaFree, 1999).

The UN has collected information from member nations since 1946. Starting then, the UN began conducting a series of surveys covering crime trends and operations of the criminal justice system. The first survey had 49 member member states responding (Newman & DiCristina, n.d.). The most recent, the tenth, covers the years 2005 and 2006 and includes reports from 86 nations (UN, 2009). The tenth survey includes counts for homicide, assault, rape, robbery, theft, burglary, fraud, embezzlement, drug trafficking, drug possession, bribery, and corruption. There are also counts of suspects, persons prosecuted, persons convicted, and prison admissions by crime, gender, and adult or juvenile status. Other variables include the population of the country and largest city; budgets and salaries for police, courts, and prisons; and types of sanctions, including imprisonment, corporal punishment, deprivation of liberty, control of freedom, and warnings (UN, 2009).

In 2011 the UN Office on Drugs and Crime published the Global Study on Homicide, which that provides homicide data from 177 countries from 1995 to 2010. In addition to using UN data, the report uses estimates of homicide from national police, WHO, national statistical officers, and others.

Generally believed to be the best data source, WHO has collected mortality statistics, categorized by cause of death, from national health organizations since 1900. The definition of homicide used by WHO (death due to injuries purposely inflicted by others) has varied; at times, it included deaths due to legal intervention and war. Raw data and rates are provided only on victims of homicide. Classifications are given for age and gender (Beuscher, 2003).

Information on homicide for more than 60 countries is classified using the International Classification of Diseases (ICD), published by WHO. The participating nations, including the United States, meet approximately once every 10 years to review and update the classification system. In the United States, homicide data are collected and sent to international archives by the National Center for Health Statistics, which is part of the Centers for Disease Prevention and Control and the U.S. Department of Health and Human Services. The 11th revision of the ICD is the current one.

Generally, cross-national data on homicide are more reliable than data on other crimes, such as rape, robbery, and assault. There are limitations on cross-national homicide research designs, however. For example, time-series studies of homicide are more reliable than cross-sectional comparisons of national rates. Ultimately, however, researchers who rely on official statistics from national agencies must use what is available; there are few opportunities to adjust data for over- or underreporting or misclassification of events.

Cross-national homicide statistics provide few variables and limited detail: The data consist of total homicides, classified by age and gender. Data on whether the homicide involved robbery, originated in domestic conflict, or involved weapons are absent, as is information on race and ethnicity. Although such information would provide valuable insights, variations in cultural definitions make it difficult to collect this kind of cross-national data.

Finally, available cross-national data are biased toward more developed countries that have sufficient resources and political stability to develop an adequate reporting system. Some countries are involved in devastating civil wars and civil unrest, which provides little opportunity for governments to function and control crime or count it. Afghanistan, Croatia, and Somalia fall into this category. Other countries, such as Zaire (Democratic Republic of Congo), Iraq, Afghanistan, and Albania, have had, or are undergoing, profound political changes in which the government's capacity to report crime is nonexistent.

Transnational Comparisons

Although we may question whether homicide rates were higher in previous centuries, there is little doubt that homicide rates in the United States are substantially higher than those in comparably developed countries.

To show this, the homicide rates for eight other economically and socially developed democracies were selected for the period 1995 to 2011 (UN Office on Drugs and Crime, 2011). Mean rates were obtained for all countries, including the United States, for which data were relatively complete from 1995 to 2011. Excluding the United States, the highest mean rate was in Finland; the lowest was for Switzerland. The mean rates of the remaining seven countries (Austria, Denmark, France, Italy, the Netherlands, Norway, and Sweden) generally fell somewhere between those of Finland and Switzerland.

To show comparisons, Figure 3.1 plots the homicide rates for the United States, Finland, and Switzerland. The homicide rate for the United States was 2.82 times the rate of Finland in 1995. The U.S. homicide rate declined (we will discuss this in Chapter 4) but remained just over twice the rate in Finland. Compared to Switzerland, the U.S. homicide rate was between four times (in 2002) and eight times higher (in 2008).

Of course, the homicide rates just described are not the highest and lowest in the world. According to the UN Office on Drugs and Crime (2011), the highest rate in their dataset was Honduras, with a rate of 82.1 per 100,000 in 2010. The lowest homicide rates were in Japan (0.5) in 2008 and Iceland (0.3) in 2009 (UN Office on Drugs and Crime, 2011).

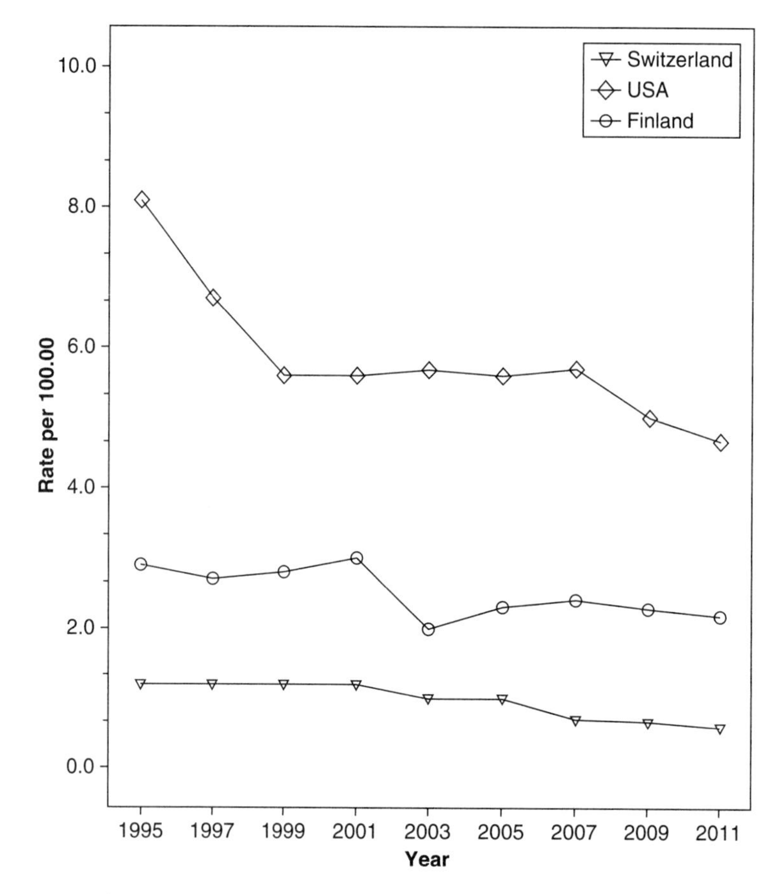

FIGURE 3.1 Homicide Rates in U.S., Finland, and Switzerland 1995–2011. *Source:* United Nations Office on Drugs and Crime. (2013). Global Study on Homicide: Trends, Contexts, Data. UNODC Homicide Statistics (2013).

Why the United States Has Higher Homicide Rates than Finland

Conclusions about differences in homicide rates among countries based exclusively on statistics assume they are, in fact, comparable. The context in which homicides occur not only serves to explain large differences, but also suggests methods of reducing homicides.

Savolainen, Messner, and Kivivuori (2000) constructed 1988 and 1996 datasets for Finland and the United States to examine the contexts in which homicides occur: criminal activity, intimate/romantic relationships, nonintimate disputes/grievances, gang/group homicides, other, and undetermined circumstances. The percentage of homicides involving nonintimate disputes and grievances was about 37% in Finland and about 26% in the United States. The percentage of homicides involving intimate/romantic relationships was about 20% in Finland and about 7% in the United States. The number of homicides involving criminal activity such as robberies, rapes, and burglaries was much larger in the United States in comparison to Finland: 22% of homicides occurred as part of criminal activity in the United States but only about 6% in Finland. The difference between criminal activity in the two countries is almost a mirror image of what was found for intimate/romantic relationships.

To determine why the U.S. homicide rate was much higher than the rate for Finland, Savolainen and colleagues removed all of the homicides involving criminal activity from the data. In this analysis, U.S. homicides decreased by 22% while the Finland numbers showed almost no change. This reduced the difference between the two countries by 35%.

The authors also compared the two countries in terms of weapons used: handguns, rifles/shotguns, unspecified firearms, sharp instruments, blunt instruments, personal force, and other/unknown. Handguns were involved in 55.5% of U.S. homicides but only 9.5% in Finland. The researchers then compared non-handgun homicides committed with and without criminal activity. With criminal activity, U.S. homicides were still 20% higher than in Finland. Without criminal activity, however, Finland's rate was 95% that of the United States.

What this research shows is the importance of taking into account the context of homicides when comparing homicide rates among countries. At least with regard to Finland, the primary reason, accounting for 81% of the difference, why the homicide rate is much higher in the United States is criminal activity associated with the homicides. What further reduces the difference in rates between the two countries is the use of handguns. Thus, the difference in rates is not simply attributable to the greater prevalence of handguns in the United States.

CONCLUSIONS

The first part of this chapter provided a brief review of the history of violence in the United States. We have shown that violence is not only a persistent feature of our past, but it has also served both positive and negative goals. Violence was a prominent part of our historical development from the Revolutionary period to Prohibition and the appearance of organized crime.

The second part of the chapter examined current trends in violence. We focused on homicide because that is the crime for which we have the most reliable information—yet even this is of limited value before the 20th century. We can draw three major conclusions. First, violence will become more anonymous as Americans become more urbanized and come to rely more heavily on technological forms of protection. Second, although violence rates have declined since the mid-1990s, homicide rates in the United States are much higher than in comparable technologically developed countries. Third, comparing different countries based exclusively on homicide rates without understanding the context of homicide can be misleading. For example, the United States has much higher homicide rates than Finland even though Finland has some of the highest homicide rates among European counties. Examining the context of homicides indicates that the United States have many more homicides involving criminal activities, especially those involving handguns.

DISCUSSION QUESTIONS

1. Why did Prohibition begin a wave of organized crime in the United States?
2. Why was slavery instituted in the United States? Where was slavery most prevalent?
3. What was the significance of the Trail of Tears?
4. What is meant by the impersonalization of homicide?
5. Explain why social banditry became so popular.

SUGGESTED READINGS

Menjivar, C. (2002). Immigrant women and domestic violence *Gender and Society, 16*, 898–920.

Nash, J. R. (1973). *Bloodletters and badmen: A narrative encyclopedia of American criminals from the pilgrims to the present*. Philadelphia: Lippencott.

Lane, R. (1997). *Murder in America: A history*. Columbus: Ohio State University Press.

LaFree, G. (1999). A summary and review of cross-national comparative studies of homicide. In M. D. Smith & M. A. Zahn (Eds.), *Homicide: A sourcebook of social research* (pp. 125–145). Thousand Oaks, CA: Sage Publications.

Gartner, R. (1990). The victims of Homicide: A temporal and cross-national comparison. *American Sociological Review, 55*, 92–106.

NOTE

1. Dime novels were called that because of their cost—one dime. The University of Minnesota has a collection of more than 3,000 titles published from 1840 to the early 1900s. These popular books reveal the ideals of the time and, to some extent, our own. The colorful characters—frequently outlaws—display American virtues of patriotism, rugged individualism, frontier virtues, and faith in hard work as the road to success (University of Minnesota Research Collections, 2000).

REFERENCES

Archer, D., & Gartner, R. (1984). *Violence and crime in cross-national perspective*. New Haven, CT: Yale University Press.

Beuscher, P. A. (2003). *The International Classification of Diseases (ICD)*. Raleigh, NC: State Center for Health Statistics.

Brown, R. M. (1969). Historical patterns of violence. In H. D. Graham & T. R. Gurr (Eds.), *Violence in America: Historical and comparative perspectives* (vol. 1, pp. 35–64). Washington, DC: U.S. Government Printing Office.

Brown, R. M. (1979). Historical patterns of violence. In H. D. Graham & T. R. Gurr (Eds.), *Violence in American: Historical & comparative perspectives* (pp. 19–48). Beverly Hills, CA: Sage.

Brown, R. M. (1989). Historical patterns of violence. In T. R. Gurr (Ed.), *Violence in America: Protest, rebellion, reform* (vol. 2, pp. 23–61). Newbury Park, CA: Sage Publications.

Goode, E. (1999). *Drugs in American society* (5th ed.). New York: McGraw-Hill.

LaFree, G. (1999). A summary and review of cross-national comparative studies of homicide. In M. D. Smith & M. A. Zahn (Eds.), *Homicide: A sourcebook of social research* (pp. 125–145). Thousand Oaks, CA: Sage.

Lane, R. (1979). *Violent death in the city: Suicide, accident, and murder in 19th-century Philadelphia*. Cambridge, MA: Harvard University Press.

Lane, R. (1997). *Murder in America: A history*. Columbus: Ohio State University Press.

Microsoft. (1998a). *Cherokee, Encarta encyclopedia*. Redman, WA: Microsoft.

Microsoft. (1998b). *Slavery, Encarta encyclopedia*. Redman, WA: Microsoft.

Mulligan, E. (1970). Accounts of the "Cherokee Trail of Tears" with reference to "Princess Otahki." *St. Louis Post Dispatch*. Retrieved May 16, 2000, from http://www.yvwiiusdinvnohii.net/articles/princes.html.

Nash, J. R. (1973). *Bloodletters and badmen: A narrative encyclopedia of American criminals from the pilgrims to the present*. Philadelphia: Lippincott.

Newman, G., & DiCristina, B. (n.d.). Data set of the 1st and 2nd United Nations world crime surveys. Retrieved Dec. 6, 2009, from http://www.uncjin.org /stats/wcsascii/readme.txt.

Riedel, M. (1998). Serial murder, communities, and evil: A review essay. *Criminal Justice Review, 23,* 220–232.

Savolainen, J., Messner, S. F., & Kivivuori, J. (2000). Crime is part of the problem: Contexts of lethal violence in Finland and the USA. *Journal of Scandinavian Studies in Criminology and Crime Prevention, 1,* 41–55.

Silberman, C. E. (1978). *Criminal violence, criminal justice.* New York: Random House.

United Nations. (2009). *The tenth United Nations Survey of Crime Trends and Operations of Criminal Justice Systems.* Retrieved November 23, 2009, from http://www.unodc.org/unodc/en/data-and-analysis/Tenth-United-Nations-Survey-on-Crime-Trends-and-the-Operations-of-Criminal-Justice-Systems.html.

United Nations Office on Drugs and Crime. (2011). *2011 Global Study on Homicide: Trends, Contexts, Data.* Vienna: Author.

World Health Organization Regional Office for Europe. (2006). *Mortality indicators by 67 causes of death, age and sex (hfa-mdb).* Retrieved June 2006 from http://www.euro.who.int/Information-Sources/Data/20011017_1.

SECTION III

TYPES OF CRIMINAL VIOLENCE

CHAPTER 4

HOMICIDES AND ASSAULTS

This chapter provides an overview of homicides and assaults in the United States. Because aggravated assaults are closely related to, and sometimes precede, homicides, we discuss the two offenses together. As we pointed out in Chapter 1, the two offenses share behavioral similarities. We have, however, drawn on two different data sources to describe patterns, trends, explanations, and interventions. For homicides, the most reliable sources of information are police reports and their representation in *Crime in the United States* or the Uniform Crime Reports (UCR) of the Federal Bureau of Investigation (FBI). While the latter does present aggregate information of aggravated assaults, we believe that data from the National Crime Victimization Survey (NCVS) provides a more adequate picture of the offense. Hence, we used that data source in describing aggravated assaults.

In this chapter, we also discuss multiple murders (mass and serial homicides), a topic that has captured public imagination. We discuss how much of the taken-for-granted knowledge about multiple murder offenders and victims is not supported by research, and how we came to that position. We also discuss trends in multiple homicide, what passes for explanations, and efforts made to apprehend serial offenders.

It has become clear in recent years that a significantly larger proportion of violent offenses have not resulted in the arrests of offenders. Following a discussion of homicides and aggravated assaults, we review the available knowledge on homicides that have not been cleared by arrest. This includes a discussion of patterns, the remarkable decline in clearance percentages, explanations for this decline, and interventions in the form of cold case squads.

HOMICIDES AND ASSAULTS IN THE UNITED STATES

The UCR divides criminal homicides into murder, nonnegligent manslaughter, and manslaughter by negligence. Murder and nonnegligent manslaughter are defined as "the willful (nonnegligent) killing of one human being by another" (FBI, 2012).

According to nationwide FBI statistics for 2012, there were 14,827 murders and nonnegligent manslaughters in the United States, a rate of 4.7 per 100,000 inhabitants. The rate for 2012 is the same as for 2011, which departs from the pattern of a continuing decline in violence in the United States (FBI, 2012). We will return to this issue in a later section.

The NCVS defines aggravated assault as an

> Attack or attempted attack with a weapon, regardless of whether or not an injury occurred and attack without a weapon when serious injury results. *With injury*—An attack without a weapon when serious injury results or an attack with a weapon involving any injury. Serious injury includes broken bones, lost teeth, internal injuries, loss of consciousness, and any unspecified injury requiring two or more days of hospitalization. *Threatened with a weapon*—Threat or attempted attack by an offender armed with a gun, knife, or other object used as a weapon, not resulting in victim injury. (http://www.ojp.usdoj.gov/bjs/abstract/cvus/definitions.htm.)

For 2012, the NCVS reported 996,110 aggravated assaults, a rate of 3.8 per 1,000 persons age 12 or older. Among all aggravated assaults, the rate of 3.8 represents a slight decrease from 4.1 per 1,000 in 2011 (Truman, Langton, & Planty, 2013). Aggravated assaults are much more common than murders. Using estimates from *Crime in the United States* (14,827) and the estimate just described (996,110), aggravated assaults occur more than 60 times more often than homicides. Harries (1989) found that in Dallas, Texas, aggravated assaults reported to the police (32,096) were 27 times more frequent than homicides (1,228).

AGE, GENDER, AND RACE

Perhaps the most persistent finding reflected in Table 4.1 is the predominance of males as both murder victims and offenders. Men represented 77.7% of murder victims and 64.6% of offenders. Females were more frequently victims (22.2%) than offenders (7.5%), a fact reflected in their higher level of victimization in intimate partner murders. There was no information on gender for 27.8% of the offenders.

Generally, most murder victims and offenders are found in the over-18 age group; 90.5% of the victims and 62.4% of the offenders are over 18.

Table 4.1 Percentage of Murder Victims and Offenders by Age, Gender, and Race (2012)

		Victims	Offenders
Age	Under 18	9.7	4.2
	18 and over	90.5	62.4
	Unknown	00.9	33.4
Gender	Males	77.7	64.6
	Females	22.2	7.5
	Unknown	00.1	27.8
Race	White	45.9	31.4
	Black	50.6	37.9
	Other	2.6	1.6
	Unknown	1.0	29.0

Source: FBI. (2012). *Crime in the United States 2012.* Retrieved March 2014 from http://www.fbi.gov/about-us/cjis/ucr/crime-in-the-u.s/2012/crime-in-the-u.s.-2012/violent-crime/murder.

The percentages dealing with race given in Table 4.1 do not take into account differences in the size of the black and white populations. Table 4.1 would lead the reader to believe a slightly larger proportion of murder victims (50.6%) and a slightly smaller proportion of offenders (37.9%) are black. However, using rates rather than percentages reveals extraordinarily high rates of homicide victimization for blacks in comparison to whites, because blacks make up only 13.6% of the population. For example, in 2005, the murder victimization rate for blacks was 20.6 per 100,000, which is more than six times higher than the rate for whites (3.3) (Bureau of Justice Statistics, 2009; *World Almanac and Book of Facts*, 2006).

The UCR asks police departments to supply information about whether murder victims and offenders are of Latino origin which was not reported in the 2012 statistics.

Table 4.1 also indicates a large number of "unknowns" with respect to the age, gender, and race of offenders. The unknowns range from 27.8% for gender to 31.0% for age. The unknowns reflect the fact that only 62.5% of murders were cleared by arrest, which means that someone was taken into custody by law enforcement. Obviously, if the offender is not arrested, there is no information on age, race, and gender. In practical terms, this means that more than one third of murder offenders are free and walking the streets. We will return to this issue in a later section.

Age, gender, and race comparisons of aggravated assault and murder must be made with caution. The NCVS uses rates rather than percentages; uses a rate base of 1,000 rather than 100,000; gives a different classification of ages; and only reports on victimization of persons age 12 or older.

Table 4.2 provides details on aggravated assaults and confirms the predominance of males in violent crime that we saw in Table 4.1. Males represent most of the murder victims

Table 4.2 Rates of Aggravated Assault Victimization by Gender, Age, Race, and Ethnicity (2009)

	Victim Characteristic	Aggravated Assault Rates per 1,000
Gender	Male	4.3
	Female	2.3
Age	12–15	6.9
	16–19	5.3
	20–24	7.5
	25–34	4.5
	35–49	2.6
	50–64	1.9
	65 plus	0.30
Race	White	2.7
	Black	6.8
	Other	1.9
Hispanic Origin	Hispanic	3.2
	Non-Hispanic	3.3

Source: From Truman, J. L., & Rand, M. (2009). *Criminal victimization, 2009* (NCJ 231327). Bureau of Justice Statistics. Washington, DC: U.S. Department of Justice.

and offenders; they are also much more likely than women (3.9 vs. 2.8 per 1,000 for females) to be victims of aggravated assaults. Similarly, young people are more involved in serious assaults, just as they are more involved in murders. Table 4.2 shows that the age ranges of 12 to 15 and 20 to 24 have the highest rates of serious assault victimization. For the 12- to 15-year-old group, the victimization rate per 1,000 is 6.1, while for the 20- to 24-year-old group, it is 8.7.

Tables 4.1 and 4.2 also show the large amount of minority involvement in violent crime. Black murder victim and offender rates are very high; black aggravated assault victimization rates are also higher than those of whites, but Latino serious assault rates are lower than for whites. We can summarize research on the demographic characteristics of victims and offenders thusly: Murders and aggravated assaults predominantly involve young black males.

OTHER CHARACTERISTICS

While there were 14,827 murders in 2012, there was information on other characteristics for only 12,765 of them. With respect to victim–offender relationships, intimate partner murders represented 10.16% of the 12,765 murders in 2012. "Other family" relationships were somewhat less common (7.8%), other murders involving friends and acquaintances made up the largest proportion (24.9%), and strangers were the offenders in 12.2% of murders. There was no information on the victim–offender relationship in 45.1% of the 12,765 murders.

Half of the murders in 2012 were committed with handguns. If we include the 11.7% attributed to other types of firearms, almost 62% of murders involved the use of firearms. Knives and blunt objects made up 16.5% and 14.1% involved other types of weapons.

The information contained under the heading of "circumstances" is sometimes referred to as "motives." These crimes are events that occur in the course of a murder; for example, felony murders like robbery or rape. The most frequent circumstances were brawls and arguments (25.3%), juvenile gang killings (5.6%), robberies (5.1%), and narcotic law violations (2.8%). Felony or nonfelony involvement of 35.9% of the cases was unknown.

Many homicides occur as a result of confrontations among friends, acquaintances, and strangers. Indeed, homicides involving friends, acquaintances, and strangers made up about 24% of reported murders in 2012. This type of homicide is characterized by conflict that proceeds from verbal disagreements, to the display of weapons, to death, sometimes with great rapidity. The following case from the first author's files is an example.

> Dan Smith, a female friend, and her 3-year-old son were in a truck leaving an apartment complex when another car attempting to enter the parking lot could not pass. The vehicles apparently stopped facing each other, with the driver of the other car jumping out and saying to Smith, "You motherfucker, you need to learn how to drive." Smith reached for a pool cue behind him in the gun rack in the window, while the man approached the truck on Smith's side. Smith said, "You're the one who needs to learn how to drive." The other driver then pulled a pistol out of his front pocket and fired three times at Smith, hitting him in the neck, chest, and abdomen. The murderer was apprehended within moments of the incident.

These confrontational homicides involve victims and offenders of the same race/ethnicity more often than is the case with robbery homicides. Victims and offenders are of similar age, and the homicides tend to occur in bars or other recreational settings. Victims and offenders, mostly male, participate in a lethal event that is more frequently witnessed than felony homicides (Riedel, 1993; Zahn & Sagi, 1987).

The total rate for aggravated assaults in 2009 was 3.2 per 1,000 persons; the rate for simple assault was 11.3 for victims age 12 or older. Male NCVS respondents who acknowledge being victims of aggravated assaults are attacked more often by strangers (52%) than by nonstrangers (47%), with 1% unknown. Female victims are also more often attacked by nonstrangers (65%) than by strangers (36%), with no unknowns.

Among the nonstrangers who victimize females, 40% are friends and acquaintances, 18% are intimates, and 7% are other relatives. For males, 41% of such victimizations are by friends and acquaintances, which is not very different from the percentage for females. Males are victimized much less frequently by intimates (6%) and other relatives (0%) than females (Truman & Rand, 2009).

ARREST CLEARANCES

It is obvious that in the event of any crime, particularly homicide or aggravated assault, the offender should be arrested. In recent decades, however, it has become clear that this is not happening in a large number of cases. As noted earlier, only 62.5% of murders in 2012 led to an arrest. For the same year, only 55.8% of aggravated assaults were cleared by arrest (FBI, 2012).

On occasion, police will refer to a crime as "solved," rather than describing an arrest. "Solvability" will sometimes refer to someone whom the police believe committed the crime but who has not been arrested. Because there are clear legal requirements for an arrest that do not apply to solvability, the status of the designated offender is unclear, and we have avoided use of the term when possible.

In the FBI's UCR program, offenses can be cleared by arrest or exceptionally cleared. The UCR states that a law enforcement agency clears an offense by arrest when "at least one person is arrested, charged with the commission of an offense, and turned over to the court for prosecution" (FBI, 2012). The number of arrest clearances refers to the number of offenses for which an arrest is made, not the number of offenders arrested; the arrest of one individual may clear a large number of crimes and, conversely, the arrest of many persons may clear only one offense.

Exceptional clearances occur where law enforcement cannot arrest or charge offenders. The offender must be identified, enough evidence is available to support an arrest, and the location of the offender is known. However, because of circumstances beyond the control of law enforcement, such as death of the offender, the agency cannot make an arrest (FBI, 2012).

One of the few studies comparing clearance by arrest to exceptional clearances was done by Jarvis and Regoeczi (2009). Using NIBRS data from 1996 to 2002, they found that homicides involving females are more likely to result in exceptional clearances in comparison to clearance by arrest, especially if the woman is murdered by an intimate partner, who then commits suicide. Exceptionally cleared offenses are more likely to involve older offenders, which may reflect a pact to end their lives together. Family-related homicides, homicides by acquaintances, and homicides involving an unknown victim–offender relationship are more likely to be cleared by arrest than exceptionally. "Mercy killings" that involve suicide pacts and gang-related homicides that lead to the death of the offender may be exceptionally cleared.

Arrest clearances are extremely important to individual officers, law enforcement agencies, policymakers, and the public for several reasons:

- Regardless of the goals of criminal justice, the process begins with the arrest of offenders. Without arrests, there is neither further processing of offenders nor reduction of crime.
- If offenders are not arrested, they are free to offend again, which increases the risk of victimization.
- Failure to arrest further traumatizes the victim's families and contributes to an increase in the fear of violent victimization.
- Because clearances are a performance measure, failure to arrest undermines the morale of law enforcement personnel and agencies.

When there are no arrests, there is no information on offenders, which obviously hampers criminologists doing research on the characteristics of offenders (Riedel & Jarvis, 1998). But because of recent interest in arrest clearances, there is a small body of research on the kinds of offenses that are cleared and uncleared.

With the increased implementation of the National Incident-Based Reporting System (NIBRS), an additional measure of arrest clearance has become available. Rather than a simple dichotomy of arrest versus no arrest, NIBRS data make it possible to examine the time between the incident and the arrest. Time to clearance is a more useful measure because it recognizes that different kinds of homicide require different amounts of investigator time. The following sections draw on a review of the research literature by Riedel (2008).

Gender, Race/Ethnicity, and Age

Homicides with female victims have a higher probability of being cleared by arrest than homicides with male victims. This is true whether dichotomous or time-to-clearance measures are used. The greater likelihood of female clearances probably occurs because there are more female homicides that result from intimate partner relationships.

It is not clear that there is a racial factor in arrest clearances. Studies generally indicate that either homicides involving white victims are cleared more quickly, or there are no racial differences. Research by Roberts and Lyons (2011) shows that homicides with Latino victims had a lower risk of clearance compared to those involving non-Hispanic white or black victims.

There seems to be general agreement with respect to age: Homicides involving younger victims are cleared more frequently and more quickly than those involving older victims. One possible reason is that police are more sympathetic and work harder to clear cases involving very young homicide victims. Another is that, in contrast to older victims, children are more frequently in the company of others who can provide information to the police (Cardarelli & Cavanagh, 1992).

Weapons and Felonies

Nine of the 11 studies reviewed by Riedel (2008) indicated that homicides with weapons other than firearms were cleared more frequently and more quickly. Firearms, especially widely available handguns, kill at a distance and are less likely to leave forensic evidence. Evidence is more likely to be present for crimes involving other weapons, including personal weapons, such as hands and feet. Concomitant felonies are rape or robbery homicide, and they are generally more difficult to clear. Roberts (2007), however, found concomitant felonies to be more easily cleared. Using time-to-clearance models, Regoeczi, Jarvis, and Riedel (2007) found that homicides involving concomitant felonies are not influenced by whether the case involved a rape or robbery homicide; some concomitant felonies may be cleared swiftly, while others take more time. Concomitant felonies are difficult to clear because they occur in locations where there are unlikely to be witnesses, involve hit-and-run attacks, and are frequently perpetrated by strangers.

Drug-related homicides were found to be more difficult to clear for two of three studies that included them in the research. Roberts (2007) found that drug-related homicides were more easily cleared. Wellford and Cronin (1999), however, disagreed and found that one of the major factors increasing the probability of clearance was the absence of a drug-related homicide.

Victim–Offender Relationship

Combining private residence, family member, and domestic homicides, eight of the 11 studies reported higher clearances for that combined category. It is generally believed that homicides involving strangers are less frequently cleared because they involve felonies or drugs (Ousey & Lee, 2010).

Using event history analysis, Roberts and Lyons (2011) examined the impact of victim–offender dyads using NIBRS data. Homicides with nonwhite offenders were more likely to be cleared by arrest, regardless of the victim's race.

Consider two types of homicide clearances. The first is when a wife kills a physically abusive husband, calls the police, awaits their arrival, and freely confesses. When this does not occur, family members may be witnesses, and arguments and gunshots may be heard by neighbors. Clearing this type of case with an arrest occurs easily and quickly.

On the other hand, for felony-related homicides, police may be called to the scene of a late-night convenience store robbery homicide, sometimes hours after it occurs. Because of the time and location of the offense, there may be no witnesses, little or no third-party cooperation, and little evidence. Facing such odds, even in the face of extensive investigation, it is likely that no offender will be arrested (Riedel & Jarvis, 1998).

To test the hypothesis that strangers disproportionately account for uncleared homicides, Decker (1993) recoded 777 homicide cases using all available paper records from the St. Louis Police Department until only 4% of the victim–offender relationships remained unknown. When he compared the results to the national distribution available from the FBI, he concluded that stranger homicides do not account for the majority of homicides classified as unknown relationships; indeed, they may be distributed among uncleared cases in the same proportions as they are among cleared homicide cases.

Using statistical methods to impute missing data, Regoeczi and Riedel (2003) found results for Los Angeles that were consistent with Decker's findings for St. Louis. In Chicago, however, the same imputation method found a 10% increase in stranger homicides.

Organizational and Investigation Variables

In most cases, arrest clearances are regarded as performance measures, both within and external to a police department. The research by Waegel (1982) shows how police officers manage their workload to maintain a level of clearance that is satisfactory to their superiors.

While no arrest quotas were used in the department studied by Waegel, the informal understanding was that an officer should produce at least two arrests per week to remain in the detective division. These constraints lead to "skimming"—that is, selecting for vigorous investigative effort cases from the assigned workload that are most likely to result in an arrest.

In determining law enforcement factors related to clearances, Greenwood (1970) and Greenwood and associates (Greenwood & Petersilia, 1975; Greenwood et al., 1977) placed primary responsibility for clearing cases on patrol officers, who determine whether the necessary leads are present and the conditions are favorable for an arrest. By contrast, research done by Eck and the Police Executive Research Forum (1983) concluded that both patrol officers and detectives make substantial contributions.

Wellford and Cronin (1999) found 51 characteristics of homicide events and investigative practices associated with arrest clearance. Of these, 37 were associated with police practices, which suggests that law enforcement policies and practices can make a difference in clearing cases. Some of these included a computer check on decedents, witnesses, suspects, guns, use of the local Criminal Justice Information System, and using three or more detectives. Regoeczi and colleagues (2007) did not find a relationship between the time of the police shift and clearances. In other words, homicides occurring late at night and early in the morning were not cleared any quicker than homicides occurring in other shifts.

Keel, Jarvis, and Muirhead (2009) used surveys from 55 police agencies with an average of 25 or more homicides between 2000 and 2004 who also reported to the FBI to determine what management, investigative, and analytical practices were related to homicide clearances. Two major findings were that formal training of homicide detectives greatly improves homicide clearance rates. Second, the use of analytical tools such as blood spatter, criminal investigative analysis, and voice stress analysis were found to increase clearance rates.

MULTIPLE MURDERS

Multiple murders are one of the most frightening events of modern society. An early event was the 1986 killing of 14 postal workers by Patrick Sherrill. This mass murder occurred in a post office in Edmond, Oklahoma, and helped generate the term "going postal" (Fox & Levin, 2015). We will examine the research on mass and serial murders that disputes many of the popular beliefs. We begin with definitions.

The FBI defined mass killings as homicides involving the murder of four or more victims in a single episode. The definition used by Fox and Levin (2015, p. 162) is similar: "Mass murder consist of the slaughter of four or more victims by one or few assailants within a single event, lasting anywhere from a few minutes to as long as several hours."

There is less agreement about serial murders. The FBI adopted the following definition: "Serial murder is the unlawful killing of two or more victims by the same offender(s) in separate events" (FBI, 2013, p. 12). Fox and Levin (2015, p. 43) argue that two homicides should not be considered a series and use the following definition: "serial murder involves a string of four or more homicides committed by one or a few perpetrators that spans a period of days, weeks, months, or even years."

Mass Murders

A number of characteristics distinguish mass from serial homicides or murders. First, mass murders, unlike serial murders, do not possess much of a challenge to law enforcement. Serial killers are frequently hard to identify while mass killers are found at the scene, having committed suicide, having been shot by the police, or waiting to be arrested.

Second, unlike serial killings, which can go on for weeks, months, and years, mass killings are a one-time event. Serial killings energize a community, and each new event increases the state of alarm. Initially, a mass killing may generate horror, but since it is done and over, little anxiety is generated.

Third, because mass killers are generally dead, there is little primary information about them. For example, in the Sandy Hook school killings of 20 first-graders and six adults and the suicide of the offender, the Connecticut state investigators reported they did not know why Adam Lanza committed the crimes (Sedensky, 2012).

Finally, mass murders do not generate the same excitement as serial murders. However, if the murders involve sex and sadism, they attract much attention from the public, press, and researchers (Fox & Levin, 2015).

Public interest in mass murders increased sharply in the mid-1960s, but mass murders have been around in large numbers since at least 1900. Duwe (2007) cites Fox and Levin (1988) as well as others who suggest that the history of mass murder in the United States did not fully emerge until the 1960s (Chester, 1993; Lane, 1997; Petee et al., 1997). However, Duwe's research shows that mass murder has a much longer history than that: "Although the 1960s marked the beginning of a mass murder wave, it was not unprecedented. Indeed, mass murder was nearly as common during the 1920s and 1930s as it has been since the 1960s" (Duwe, 2007, p. 214).

GENDER, RACE, AND AGE. One of the most consistent characteristics of mass killers is that they are male. As Table 4.3 shows, over 90% are male. In their data file that extends from 1976 through 2012, Fox and Levin (2015) also found that 94.1% of mass killers were males compared to 88.4% of homicide offenders, according to FBI data.

From 1976–2011, males are more common among homicide victims (76.7%) while females are more frequent among mass murder victims (43.4%).

Table 4.3 indicates that 68.5% of mass murder victims were white while 50.5% were homicide victims. Blacks clearly predominate among homicide victims compared to mass murder victims. For the 76–11 period 47.7% were homicide victims while 27.1% were mass murder victims (Fox & Levin, 2015).

Mass murder victims tend to be young; Fox and Levin found that 17.6% of mass murder victims were younger than 10 while only 4.1% of homicide victims were in that age range.

Table 4.3 Comparison of Mass Murders and Homicide Victims and Offenders Sex and Race 1999–2012

Characteristic	Mass Murder	Homicide
Offender Count	1,176	648,244
Race (%)		
White	59.3	46.6
Black	36.5	51.4
Other	4.2	2.0
Sex (%)		
Male	94.1	88.4
Female	5.9	11.6
Victim Count (%)	4,212	689,319
Race (%)		
White	68.5	50.5
Black	27.1	47.3
Other	4.2	2.0
Sex (%)		
Male	56.6	76.7
Female	5.9	11.6
Age (%)		
Under 10	17.6	4.1
10–19	17.0	12.1
20–29	23.1	33.7
30–39	16.4	22.3
40–49	12.5	13.1
50+	13.4	14.7

Source: Fox and Levin (2015) pp. 166–168.

For the age interval of 10-19 in Table 4.3 the percent of mass murder victims (17.6%) were also higher than for homicide victims (12.1%).

For the two age categories of 20–29 and 30–39 there were more homicides than mass murders. According to Fox and Levin (2015), the younger age of victims are a consequence of a large proportion of mass murders in which the offender kills his family. After the age of 40, the percent of mass murders and homicides remain very similar.

VICTIM/OFFENDER RELATIONSHIPS. Prior to the increase in the mid-1960s of public attention and interest in mass murders, a large proportion involved families. For the 1900-to-1975 period, Table 4.3 shows that 38.2% of the mass murders involved families. It fell to 40% in the subsequent period.

The percentage of mass murders and homicides involving strangers were similar; 1976 to 2011; 23.5% of mass murders and 21.5% of the homicides involved strangers. The family classification of acquaintances, was the only category in which homicides were higher (49.3%) than mass murders (38.3%).

WEAPONS. The weapons of choice in mass murders are firearms. Guns were used in 77.5% of the mass murders and 67.4% of the homicides. Other types of weapons were used in less than 12% of the mass murders and less than 18% of homicides.

CIRCUMSTANCES. Felony-related mass murders accounted for 30.1% of the mass murders and 23.6% of the homicides Arguments account for 24.5% of mass murders and 50.6% of the homicides (Fox & Levin 2015). In other words, homicide predominate in relation to homicides while felonies are more important in mass murders.

ROLE OF THE NEWS MEDIA. Fox and Levin provide a disturbing picture of the relationship between multiple murderers and the media. This relationship has become so intertwined that it has been described as "symbiotic" (Haggerty, 2009). The media seek the attention of their captivated audience by exploiting its interest in scintillating themes. For their part, the murderers look to the media to help them construct their serial killer identities. In fact, reading their own press clippings helps them to complete an identity transformation in the same way that reading the press does for athletes and entertainers (Fox & Levin, 2015).

MASS MURDER AT A MOVIE. While there are a number of recent mass murders that would illustrate these characteristics, this section describes the July 20, 2012, shooting in Aurora, Colorado, in which 12 people were killed and 58 injured.

The killing began in a packed movie theater that was showing a midnight premiere of "The Dark Knight Rises," the latest Batman sequel. As the theater darkened, the gunman entered the theater through a parking lot exit door wearing a throat protector and leggings, a gas mask, and a long black coat. He threw two tear gas grenades, walked to the front of the theater, and opened fire.

"It was just chaos. You started hearing screaming. You looked up and people were falling. It was like a dream," said Jamie Rohrs, 25, who was there with his fiancée, cradling his 4-month-old son, Ethan, in his arms as the movie began.

The police found the shooter, James Holmes, standing beside his car in the parking lot. Inside his car they found an AR-15 assault rifle, a Remington 12-gauge shotgun, and two .40-caliber Glock handguns that were used in the shootings. Police learned that prior to the shooting, Holmes had purchased 6,000 rounds of ammunition.

> In a subsequent investigation, Holmes indicated that the explosives in his apartment were set to detonate with a trip wire when the apartment was entered. The explosives removed included more than 30 homemade grenades and 10 gallons of gasoline. Five buildings, including Holmes apartment building, were evacuated prior to search and entry. (Frosech & Johnson, 2012, A1)

Serial Homicides

When people think of violence, they are more likely to think of being victimized in public places than in their homes. In 2013, about 85% of the U.S. population lived in urban areas, which means that we interact on a daily basis with a large number of people about whom we know almost nothing (*World Almanac*, 2014).

Nothing better illustrates the vulnerability of being an urban dweller among strangers than the case of the Washington DC–area serial snipers, John Allen Muhammad and Lee Harvey Malvo. Between October 2 and October 24, 2002, 10 people were randomly selected and killed or critically injured. The violence occurred while people were going about their everyday lives: mowing the lawn, pumping gas, shopping, or reading a book.

A massive investigation ensued, led by the Montgomery County (MD) Police Department with the assistance of the FBI, the Maryland State Police, and the Montgomery County SWAT team. Finally, on October 24, Muhammad and Malvo were arrested at a rest stop parking lot off I-70.

What evidence experts from the FBI and other police forces found there was both revealing and shocking. The 1990 Chevy Caprice had a hole cut in the trunk near the license plate so that shots could be fired from within the vehicle. It was, in effect, a rolling sniper's nest (FBI, 2007).

Both Muhammad and Malvo were convicted. Muhammad was executed by lethal injection and Malvo was given a life sentence without parole (FBI, 2007, http://www.fbi.gov/page2/oct07/snipers102207.html).

Citizens must feel free to move about in public in comparative safety if a society is to continue to exist. The major task of a government is to maintain public order; when that fails, or appears to be failing, as in terrorism or where a serial murderer is believed to be present, chaos may follow. This is one reason governments place a premium of responding quickly to this type of violence.

In addition, serial homicides represent unpredictable attacks on citizens as they go about their routine activities. Because, as we will see, serial killers are not readily distinguishable from the multitude of strangers we see every day, their activity undermines the tenuous trust we have as we interact with strangers. Fisher (1997) explores how, in this situation, members of an entire community come to regard one another with doubt, mistrust, and suspicion until the serial murderer is arrested.

Serial homicides are extremely rare; Jenkins (1994) suggests that they represent fewer than 1% of all homicides. Using this estimate, there were no more than 141 serial homicide victims of the 14,121 murder and nonnegligent manslaughter victims reported to the FBI in 2004 in a population of more than 290 million. If we assume that each serial offender kills two victims, we are left with 70 offenders. On the other hand, Fisher (1997) estimates that there are 10 serial killers operating in the United States every year, an even smaller number of offenders. Although serial homicide is a frightening phenomenon, the small number of offenders makes the study of serial homicides very difficult.

Prior to the 1980s, most experts believed that serial homicides made up 1% or 2% of total homicides. During the 1980s, however, the most widely quoted claims were that serial homicides represented 20% to 25% of all homicides. How did this enormous, and false, statistic gain credence among otherwise rational and thoughtful people?

The use of statistics to distort social issues has three characteristics (1) it is an issue of public concern that can be shaped into a major social problem with the help of the media, (2) there is a lack of valid and reliable statistics, or pertinent statistics are ignored, and (3) constituencies are organized to use statistics to promote specific agendas.

Best (1988, p. 26) described the importance of statistics in discussing child abductions: "Three principles seem clear: big numbers are better than small numbers; official numbers are better than unofficial numbers; and big, official numbers are best of all." With respect to serial homicides, it was the Behavioral Sciences Unit (BSU) of the FBI that was prepared to provide "big, official numbers."

Although there were a number of events propelling the publicity given to serial homicide in the 1980s, the belief that serial homicides made up a fifth of all homicides received an enormous amount of credence during congressional hearings in which William Webster, the FBI director, described large numbers of murders by one person in large numbers with no apparent pattern (U.S. Senate, 1984).

The way this conclusion was supported was to factor in cases from the "unknown" category. "Unknown" was interpreted to mean "with no apparent motive," which meant it was "motiveless" and therefore belonged to the serial homicide category. In fact, "unknown" in homicide data simply means that the police did not know the circumstances: It is a confession of ignorance rather than an affirmation of serial homicides (Jenkins, 1994). The reason that police do not know the circumstances is usually because the offender has not been arrested. Adding the "unknowns," which represented a large number in the 1980s, to the tiny number of known serial killers led to the claim that serial homicides represented 20% to 25% of all homicides.

In addition to their rarity, the traditional image of serial killers has been shaped by the media and by case studies done by forensic psychiatrists of offenders held by the court. In more recent decades, criminologists using a social science perspective have examined social and cultural forces underlying serial killings. In addition, law enforcement operatives have shown greater sophistication in using research-based techniques to track and apprehend serial killers (Fox & Levin, 2015).

One of the myths discussed by Fox and Levin (2015) is that serial killers are unusual in appearance and lifestyle. Virtually all researchers on the subject agree that serial killers are "extraordinarily ordinary" (Egger, 1998; Fisher, 1997; Hickey, 2002; Holmes & Holmes, 1998; Jenkins, 1994). Indeed, one reason serial killers are difficult to identify and apprehend is that they do an excellent job of blending in with the crowd and not drawing attention to themselves. They frequently hold full-time jobs, are involved in stable relationships, and are members of various community groups.

The most popular social and demographic myth is the image of the serial killer as a lone white male, a mad slasher, or a ripper. In fact, from 10% to 20% of serial killings can be attributed to two or more individuals working together (Jenkins, 1994).

Not all serial killers are males. Hickey (2002) studied 337 male and 67 female serial killers who were responsible for at least 2,526 homicides between 1800 and 1995. The female killers, who represented 16% of the total pool of serial killers, represent *known* cases. Both Jenkins (1994) and Hickey (2002) point out that the number of female offenders may be underrepresented, because they are more likely to use asphyxiation or poisoning, which were less likely to be noticed until the emergence of modern forensic medicine.

Not all serial killers are white. Until the arrest of Wayne Williams, claims were made that no serial killers were African Americans. Hickey (2002), however, found that African Americans constituted 20% of the offenders in his study.

Finally, serial killers do not generally move about the country. The claim in the 1980s that the typical killer moved about in 10 to 20 states was made to justify increased federal involvement. Although there are a minority of serial offenders who do move about, the majority tend to operate in one city or even in one neighborhood (Jenkins, 1994).

TRENDS

One of the more surprising recent events in the study of violence has been the recent decline of violence in the United States, especially murders, as Figure 4.1 indicates. Beginning in 1991, there was a downturn in the murder rates that continued through 2010. In 1991, the murder rate was 9.8 per 100,000; by 2005, it was 5.6; in 2012, it was 4.7. Aggravated assaults have likewise declined, according to the NVCS. In 2003, the aggravated assault rate was 5.7 per 1,000; by 2012, it had decreased to 3.8 (Truman et al., 2013).

FIGURE 4.1 Homicide Rates in the United States, 1960–2012. *Source:* Annual editions of the UCR (1960–2012).

TRENDS IN ARREST CLEARANCES

Arrest clearances are measured by the number of offenses cleared by arrest divided by the number of offenses for a year, with the resulting proportion multiplied by 100. These annual percentages are also referred to as clearance rates. Clearance percentages are used by departments to measure individual performance, and departments are compared on annual clearance percentages. Figure 4.2 gives the clearance percentages for murders from 1960 to 2008.

It seems unlikely that the decline in homicides shown in Figure 4.1 can be accounted for by the increase in arrest clearances. The percentage of homicides cleared declined from 92.3% in 1960 to 62.5% in 2012. Another way of looking at the picture is that in 2012, of 13,092 homicides, no one was arrested for 37.5%, or 4,909 events.

TRENDS IN SERIAL HOMICIDE

Serial murder offenders have increased in number. Hickey (2002, p. 132) summarizes the growth of male serial offenders:

> Of the 337 male offenders in this study, approximately 94% began their killing since the year 1900. . . . Between 1900 and 1924, 5% of offenders appeared; 8% between 1925 and 1949; 35% between 1950 and 1974; and 45% between 1975 and 1995. More offenders were identified in the 20-year time frame between 1975 and 1995 than during any previous 25-year span.

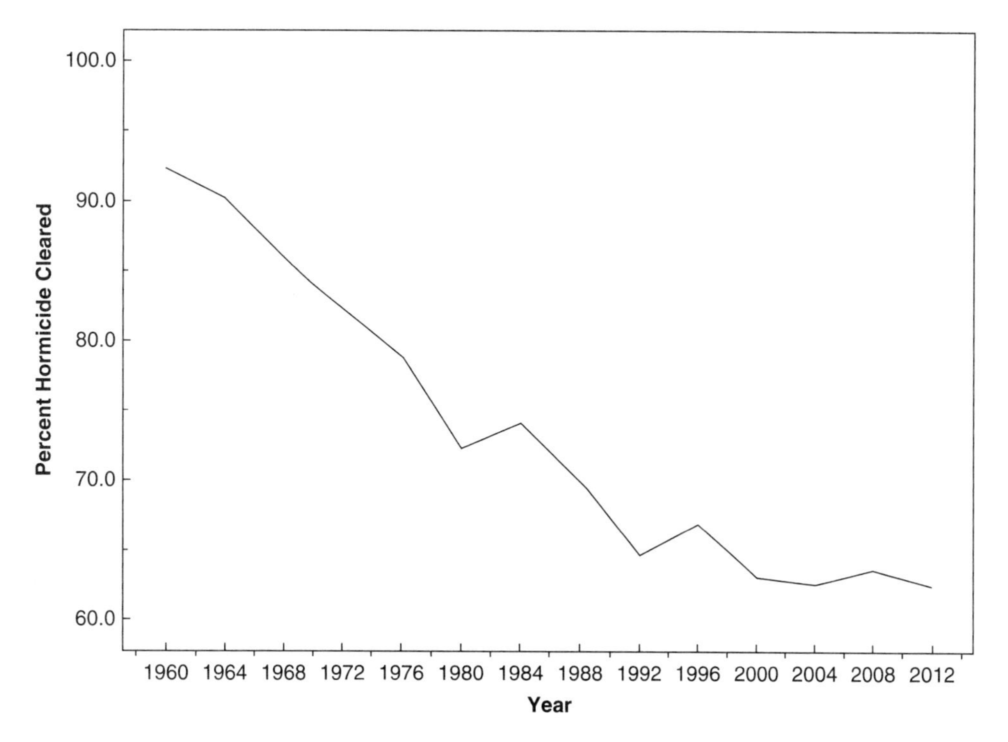

FIGURE 4.2 Homicide Clearances by Year, 1960–2012. *Source:* Annual editions of the UCR (1960–2012).

There were relatively few known cases during the first half of the 20th century, but the pattern emerging during the past few decades is radically different. The number of serial killers and teams grew rapidly from the 1960s into the 1980s. Following the 1980s peak, the number of cases slipped somewhat in the 1990s and then declined even more during the first decade of the 21st century.

The central question, however, is whether the increase is the result of better reporting or a genuine increase in the number of serial killers (Fox & Levin, 1999).

Two problems have an impact on the recording of serial homicides. First, there is no publicly available source of homicide data that records serial homicides. Neither the UCR nor the National Center for Health Statistics (see Chapter 2) maintains a separate category for serial homicides. The estimates given are drawn from stranger homicide records and newspaper accounts; these are useful but of unknown validity and reliability.

Second, until recently it has been possible for a serial offender to move among jurisdictions, killing one or two victims in each place, without ever alerting law enforcement that a serial offender was active. Serial offenders could be mobile and kill with impunity because the absence of sharing or coordinating of investigative information and the absence of networking by law enforcement agencies.

EXPLANATIONS

SYMBOLIC INTERACTION

Although there are a large number of theories that might be used to explain homicides and aggravated assaults, one characteristic makes interactional theories particularly appropriate: Except for multiple murders, few murders or assaults are planned. Murders planned to the last intricate detail and unraveled by a master sleuth happen in fiction, but almost never in reality. Murders and assaults typically evolve in social situations and begin with a conflict.

One of the more amazing characteristics of assaults and homicides is the wide range of motives that compel people to injure or kill others. There are some conflicts that we understand, and even sympathize with, such as the battered wife who finally kills her tormentor after years of abuse. Others defy understanding, such as the case in which one person killed another because he allegedly stole the offender's beer and refused to buy him another (Athens, 1980).

Trying to understand homicide and aggravated assault by determining the "reality" or "importance" of causes is a futile endeavor. Instead, Felson takes the view that violence is goal-oriented or instrumental behavior that results from aggressive attempts to achieve what people value. "Aggressive actions seek to compel and deter others, to achieve a favorable social identity, and to obtain justice, as defined by the actor" (Felson, 1993, p 104). In other words, the validity of motives for the killing has to be examined from the perspective of what the offender hoped to achieve. The battered wife has decided that she will not be beaten again; the offender may perceive the stolen beer as an insult to his ego that he will not tolerate.

As the conflict comes to be defined as an effort to frustrate or "put the other down," the interaction escalates with insults and counter-insults. At some point, either one of the participants withdraws or violence occurs. The violence may take the form of pushing, shoving, or hitting, or it may result in one or the other's death from injuries.

Not all ego insults result in escalation and violence. It takes two to play the escalation game, which raises the question of what happens to potential conflicts when one party simply gets up at the first sign of trouble and leaves the setting.

SUBCULTURAL THEORIES

Wolfgang and Ferracuti (1967) would agree that violence occurs as the result of what participants perceive as insults to their self-image. They carried the analysis one step further, however, by positing a subculture of violence: norms, values, and behavioral expectations that violence represents problem-solving behavior. Values and beliefs that sanction violence as problem-solving behavior are differentially distributed. Lower-class youths are more likely to express these beliefs than middle-class youths. When other males with the same beliefs are present, a violent response is reinforced, as the following case illustrates:

> The offender and his friend were sitting in a booth at a tavern drinking beer. The offender's friend told him that the offender's girlfriend was "playing" with another man (victim) at the other end of the bar. The offender looked at them and asked his friend if he thought something was going on. The friend responded, "I wouldn't let that guy fool around with [her] if she was mine." The offender agreed, and suggested to his friend that his girlfriend and the victim be shot for their actions. His friend said that only the victim should be shot, not the girlfriend. (Luckenbill, 1977, p. 181)

But since there are more flirtations than assaults and homicides, we can only conclude than many encounters of the type described above end without violence. It is consistent with the subculture of violence theory that if one of the parties does not regard the behavior of the other as a threat to his or her self-image, there will be no violence. The insulted party may respond by simply leaving the setting.

EXPLAINING THE CHARACTERISTICS OF ARREST CLEARANCES

There are no theories that explain the decline in arrest clearances, although there is one theory that has been explicitly applied to an understanding of clearance rates. A series of hypotheses is drawn from Black's (1976) *The Behavior of Law*. While Borg and Parker (2001) used Black's theory to investigate homicides, we will use the formulation given by Litwin (2004).

Litwin argues that Black's theory is about discretionary factors in law enforcement, whereas perspectives by Wolfgang (1958), Gottfredson and Hindelang (1979), and Klinger (1997) argue that homicide is the most serious crime, and police will diligently work to resolve the cases, regardless of the characteristics of the victim or location. Therefore, nondiscretionary factors beyond the control of police officers such as body location, weapons, homicide circumstance, and area population should be more important.

Hypotheses drawn from Black's theory by Litwin (2004) are as follows:

- *Stratification*: Homicide cases with victims who are female, nonwhite, or younger are less likely to be cleared than cases with victims who are male, white, or older, because the former have less social wealth.

- *Socioeconomic areas*: For the same reasons (less wealth), homicide cases occurring in lower socioeconomic areas are less likely to be cleared by arrest than cases occurring in higher socioeconomic areas.
- *Social control*: Because some people may have deviant lifestyles, they are less respectable and susceptible to more law. Therefore, homicide cases with victims who have a prior arrest record are less likely to be cleared by arrest than cases with victims who have no prior arrest records.
- *Morphology, or the horizontal distribution of individuals*: Homicide cases occurring in areas with higher unemployment are less likely to be cleared by arrest than cases occurring in areas with lower unemployment.
- *Culture*: Homicide cases occurring in areas where people have less education are less likely to be cleared by arrest than cases occurring in areas where people are better educated.
- *Organization, or collective action*: Homicide cases occurring in areas with a smaller percentage of owner-occupied dwelling units are less likely to be cleared by arrest than cases occurring in areas with a greater percentage of owner-occupied dwelling units.

Using homicide data from Chicago from 1989 to 1991, Litwin (2004) found very limited support for the police discretionary hypotheses drawn from Black's theory. There were no statistically significant differences between cleared and uncleared homicides for females, African Americans, other racial/ethnic groups, prior arrest record, income, unemployment, or level of education. Homicides with Latino victims and older victims were less frequently cleared; homicides occurring in areas of higher home ownership were more frequently cleared.

There is greater support for the nondiscretionary factors in Litwin's research. Homicides were less frequently cleared if a firearm was used, if the homicide occurred with a concomitant felony, or if it was drug- or gang-related; homicides were more frequently cleared if they occurred in homes and in areas with higher home ownership.

Homicides where the body was found in a tavern were less likely to be cleared than if the body was found in a public location. Litwin speculates that these homicides occurred in neighborhood bars where witnesses were known to each other and were less likely to inform police.

While nondiscretionary factors appear to be more important than discretionary factors in this study, Litwin raises an interesting question with regard to the decrease in Latino clearances. Along with homicides involving high home-ownership rates, occurring in taverns, and involving drug- or gang-related events, the ability to clear offenses may be related to the willingness of witnesses to provide information. As Reiss (1971, p. 105) noted several decades ago: "There is no feasible way to solve most crimes except by securing the cooperation of citizens to link a person to the crime." If so, establishing and maintaining a good working relationship with the community will increase witness cooperation and lead to higher clearances (Litwin, 2004).

EXPLAINING SERIAL HOMICIDES

The difficulty with explaining serial homicides is not a shortage of explanations, but an abundance of them. Among the biological factors that are implicated in serial homicide are the XYY chromosome, blood levels of neurotransmitters, and types and levels of hormones. Psychological factors include psychoses, dissociative disorders, psychoanalytical factors, personality disorders, and psychopathies. Among the more sociologically inclined theories are those relating to urbanization, aggression, child abuse, neutralization, labeling, and social control.

Explanations after the fact and an excess of false positives are two major problems with explanations of serial murderers. False positives occur when a person is predicted to have a condition but does not, although he or she shares characteristics used to predict the condition with those who actually turn out to have it. False positives are illustrated with Egger's (1998) discussion of the diagnosis of Kenneth Bianchi, the Hillside Strangler, as having an "antisocial personality disorder 301.70," according to the American Psychiatric Association's *Diagnostic and Statistical Manual of Mental Disorders*. Yet Egger points out that many of his students demonstrated, at some point in their lives, an inability to maintain consistent work behavior and a failure to accept social norms with respect to lawful behavior; these are two of the four characteristics required to make the diagnosis of antisocial personality disorder.

Explaining after the fact occurs once the offender is identified; hindsight makes possible a description of some negative trait or flaw that is supposed to cause the killing. "Postdicting," in contrast to predicting, is a theoretical analogue to Monday-morning quarterbacking.

Finally, as noted at the outset, serial homicide is a rare event, and the theories used have little applicability to rare events. When physical theories attempt to explain a rare event, such as a large asteroid hitting the Earth, they make use of general laws. Sociological and psychological theories, however, have ill-defined boundaries, are imprecise, and are largely untested. They provide few insights and no predictions when applied to serial killers, who are extremely rare and remarkably diverse.

INTERVENTIONS

Because crime rates follow a fluctuating pattern, it is not always clear whether a decline (or increase) signals a trend or is merely an annual fluctuation. Unlike politicians who attribute any positive fluctuation, however minor, to the effect of their pet programs, criminologists recognize that understanding trends, much less forecasting them, is a challenging enterprise.

Homicides have been declining because of social changes and criminal justice interventions. With respect to social changes, Blumstein and Rosenfeld (1998) have found support for the following causes of the nationwide decline in homicide:

- The growth of homicide during the 1980s was largely due to the 15- to 24-year-old age group. The decline beginning in about 1992 was partly accounted for by a decline in this age group.
- Beginning about 1993, there was a decline in handgun homicide among both whites and Latinos, but the decline was greatest among black youth.
- Authors hypothesize that drug markets have matured and stabilized, and other dispute resolution mechanisms have emerged.

- In the late 1990s and the early 21st century, economic expansion has increased the number of legitimate job opportunities and increased the amount of opportunities legal and illegal activities to earn money.

With respect to interventions, the increased use of incarceration may have contributed to a decline in violence. Spelman (2000) found that since the 1970s, the prison population has expanded fourfold. While it might be suspected that increased incarceration had an effect, especially for repeat offenders, we must remember that violence increased substantially during the 1980s, when incarceration was also increasing.

Spelman draws on a wide variety of studies to derive statistical estimates of the impact of incarceration. He suggests that about 25% of the drop in crime is attributable to incarceration. The question that both Spelman (2000) and Rosenfeld (2000) ask in their essays, however, is whether this decrease justifies the massive social and financial cost of prisons. The nation's corrections budget is more than $40 billion annually, money that could conceivably be spent on other crime reduction endeavors such as welfare, education, and health.

It is also possible that programs to control the use of guns have played a role in reducing homicides. Wintemute (2000) presents evidence on the role of guns from studies of changing police practices of stopping and frisking gang members, increasing criminal justice sanctions, tracing guns used in crime, limiting the number of dealers, and placing restrictions on buyers. With respect to the latter, the Brady Bill has prevented more than 400,000 handgun purchases. However, Sheley and Wright (1995) suggest that handguns are carried by young males for self-protection in high-crime areas and dispute the effectiveness of gun legislation (see Chapter 12).

As we will see in Chapter 8, another successful intervention has involved legislation and social policies that have led to a decline in intimate partner homicides. In 1976, there were more than 2,000 intimate partner murders, but by 1996, this number had declined to 987. These laws, programs, and policies have had the effect of reducing the number of male intimate partners killed by females, but not the reverse.

Eck and McGuire (2000) assessed the effect of different types of policing on violence and found only weak effects. They examined the effects of increasing the number of police, community policing, firearms enforcement, and problem-oriented policing programs and found that they had little or no effect on violence rates. Directed patrols in "hot spots"—that is, increasing police patrols in small areas with very high rates of violence—had reasonably strong support and may have contributed to the reduction in homicide rates.

INCREASING CLEARANCE RATES

While various programs in community policing include reducing crime by increasing arrests, police departments in the United States have begun using cold-case squads (Lab, 2000). Cold-case squads continue the investigation of a homicide after the usual amount of time devoted to clearing the case has been exceeded. Two reasons that cold-case squads are particularly useful in clearing homicides is that murders have no statute of limitations, and conventional wisdom holds that homicides that have not developed significant leads or witness participation within 72 hours after the event are unlikely to be cleared (Turner & Kosa, 2003).

The statute of limitations refers to the time period following the crime during which an offender can be prosecuted. Unless there is some special legal procedure to obviate the statute of limitations, most crimes cannot be prosecuted after a certain time period has elapsed. Murders have no statute of limitations.

Cold-case squads address many of the consequences of declining clearance rates that we mentioned earlier. They remove offenders responsible for the homicide from society and prevent them from committing new homicides. An arrest can produce positive feedback from a family that has been frustrated by the inability of law enforcement to clear by arrest the homicide of a loved one. Finally, an arrest in a previously unsolved murder presents the image to the community of a law enforcement agency that never stops caring about unsolved cases. These types of actions also improve the morale of police agencies that are overworked, understaffed, and subject to criticism because of low clearances (Turner & Kosa, 2003).

Cold-case squads vary enormously in structure, size, permanence, and interrelationships with other agencies. Some are part time, focusing on one or two cases; others have full-time personnel. Some squads consist of one or two investigators and one supervisor, while others have 10 or 12 investigators and a supervisor. Some squads work out of police departments, while others are housed in prosecutors' offices.

Not all cold-case squads reside in police departments or prosecutors' offices, however. The Naval Criminal Investigative Service (NCIS) and the Air Force Office of Special Investigations investigate cold-case homicides that involve military personnel or occur on military bases. The extent to which they may get involved with local law enforcement activity is limited by the scope of their jurisdictions, but they work together where jurisdictions permit.

As an example of cooperation between cold-case squads, on May 22, 2002, *The Washington Times* reported about a case in which NCIS and the Fairfax County (VA) Cold Case Squad had been investigating two murders believed to have been committed by Paul Stanley Sorenson, who had served 20 years in the Navy. The first murder occurred in a convenience store before Sorenson joined the Navy. Sorenson turned himself in to authorities on May 21, 2002, for a murder committed 27 years before, on January 19, 1975. Sorenson was charged with first-degree murder and his bail was set at $100,000.

The U.S. Marshals Service has several joint agency fugitive task forces around the nation. Local law enforcement agencies may send an officer to work with these task forces, giving the officer wider experience as well as giving assistance to a cold-case squad. The FBI provides assistance to local agencies through its National Center for the Analysis of Violent Crime. It offers assistance in homicides that involve gangs or drugs.

Reviewing Cases

The process by which cases are selected and reviewed varies among cold-case squads. Generally, the cases are at least a year old and are referred because of time constraints, workload, or lack of viable leads. Cases may be referred by police supervisors as well as prosecutors.

In some instances, a witness who was previously uncooperative or unknown will come forward and cause the case to be reopened.

Cases are reviewed and assigned priorities. According to Turner and Kosa (2003, p. 4):

> The highest priority cases are those in which the murder victim, or even a second surviving victim, has been identified; the death was ruled a homicide; suspects were previously named or identified through forensic methods; an arrest warrant was previously issued; significant physical evidence (such as fingerprints, DNA, or shell casings) can be reprocessed for further clues; newly documented leads have arisen within the last 6 months; and critical witnesses are accessible and willing to cooperate.

Following this list of priorities are cases in which witnesses can identify suspects or evidence can identify possible suspects, or cases in which the initial investigation identified a witness who could not be located, or when there is a need to reinterview the original person.

Cases of midlevel priority are those in which preserved evidence can be processed with modern technology, such as automated fingerprint identification, DNA analysis, or a computerized program that can track signatures on spent shell casings (DRUGFIRE). Cases with the lowest priority are those in which there is no known physical evidence or witnesses to help the investigative process (Turner & Kosa, 2003).

Cold-case investigators begin by reviewing all possible documentation relating to the case, locating gaps in information, such as people mentioned in the original investigation who were not interviewed, and reinterviewing significant witnesses. After working all visible leads, the detective writes a summary of the follow-up investigation that recommends further investigation or inactivation.

The case is closed either by the arrest of a suspect or by administrative decision. The case may be closed administratively because the original offender has died or because he or she is in prison for another crime and is behind bars for life.

Resources

There is no doubt that cold-case squads have access to technology, investigative methods, and resources that were not available one or two decades earlier. The two most frequently mentioned technologies are DNA analysis and advances in fingerprint technology. Advances in fingerprint technology include systems that make it possible to lift prints from leather and cloth as well as systems that use lasers to lift fingerprints.

Although law enforcement sometimes has had an uneasy relationship with media outlets, publicizing a cold-case arrest through the media has sometimes led to people contacting police with information on other cold cases. Newspapers and television stimulate public interest in old cases by articles, pictures, and reenactments that have a wide reach and may cause community members to come forward.

While technology and the media play an important role in clearing cold cases, "The resolution of cold cases is primarily rooted in a squad's ability to identify, locate, and secure the testimony and cooperation of witnesses and informants" (Turner & Kosa, 2003, p. 5). Locating previously unknown or uncooperative witnesses can be a time-consuming and formidable task. Witnesses may not testify or make themselves available in any form to the police because they fear retaliation. With the passage of time, witnesses may no longer feel intimidated by threats or they may become aware of information previously unknown to them through boasting by the offender. The offender may have been killed by rivals or the potential witness may find that coming forward is necessary to his or her changed personal, professional, or legal circumstances. In some instances, the witness himself or herself may need help from law enforcement.

APPREHENDING SERIAL KILLERS

One of the greatest investigative challenges for law enforcement is apprehending a serial killer. As we have discussed, serial killers are nondescript, lead conventional lifestyles, and are exceptionally skilled in their self-presentation so that they appear beyond suspicion. These are major reasons they are difficult to apprehend.

Egger (1998, 2002) discusses the wide variety of police strategies used in investigating serial murders and how some of them can be used to increase cooperation among agencies. He discusses in detail interagency conferences, information clearinghouses, task forces, central coordination efforts, profiling, investigative consultants, forensic consultants, major incident room procedures, solicitation from the public, computer analysis systems, offender rewards, psychics, rapid response teams, and centralized investigative networks.

The approach that receives the most public attention is investigative profiling. Three types of investigative profiling have emerged in the past 20 years. The first investigative profiling approach was done by the Behavioral Sciences Unit of the FBI. The model developed by the FBI depends heavily on the intuition and experience of the profiler. The experienced profiler studies the crime scene carefully and attempts to construct a psychological profile of the offender. This kind of profiling is usually productive in crimes in which there is evidence of psychopathology, such as sadistic torture, lust and mutilation murders, and evisceration. This type of profiling has been evaluated and the results have been inconclusive (Godwin, 1978; Levin & Fox, 1985).

A more useful approach is that of David Canter, at the University of Liverpool, who is building an empirical base in which he considers victim information and relies on statistical analysis and the generation of probabilities from continuously updated information (Egger, 1998).

The third approach is geographic profiling, which is based on the criminal geography research by Brantingham and Brantingham (1978). Research by Rossmo (1999) has led to the use of spatial data to generate a three-dimensional probability map that indicates areas (home, work site, travel routes) most likely to be associated with the offender.

There seems to be relatively little variation on what will be done with serial offenders once they are apprehended. Clearly, they will be sentenced to long prison terms with essentially no chance of release. In many instances, these offenders are sentenced to death and executed. Although the latter may feed the public's need for vengeance and retribution, it may be more useful to keep them incarcerated, not only to protect the community, but also for purposes of research. Given the phenomenal advances that are occurring in research on the human genome, for example, serial killers would offer an opportunity to resolve some longstanding questions about biology and crime.

CONCLUSIONS

This chapter focused on national patterns of homicide and aggravated assaults, arrest clearances, and serial homicide. For each topic, we followed the same order of risks and patterns, trends, explanations, and interventions in describing the phenomenon.

For murders and aggravated assaults, the general pattern seems to be young black males as offenders and victims, victims known to the offenders, and violence as the outcome of brawls or arguments. What has been happening since the mid-1990s has been a decline in homicides and aggravated assaults. The section on interventions explores some of the reasons for the decline and what can be done to further increase the decline.

Many homicides and aggravated assaults are situationally determined—that is, someone insults someone else and the conflict escalates until blows are exchanged or a weapon is drawn. What also has to be considered, however, is that not everyone responds to situational cues that lead to violence. Not everyone sees an insult to his girlfriend or mother as an occasion to respond violently; some will simply get up and leave.

A comparatively new topic in the study of violence is the decline in arrest clearances—that is, the percentage of offenses cleared by the arrest of one or more offenders. As of 2008, the clearance rate stood at 63.6% for murders; other violent crimes have lower clearance rates.

What are some of the risks and patterns of offenders and victims arrested in comparison to those not arrested? Although there is some disagreement, many of the studies find little or no differences between cleared and uncleared offenses in terms of gender. The results are mixed for race/ethnicity, although it appears that crimes involving Latino victims are less likely to be cleared. Cases involving younger victims are more likely to be cleared than those with older victims. Murders involving nonstrangers, such as intimate partners, friends, and family members, are cleared more frequently than those involving strangers. Finally, murders involving firearms are less likely to be cleared than those involving other types of weapons, because the use of firearms is less likely to leave any evidence.

There are two major kinds of multiple murder: mass and serial killings. Mass killers kill four or more victims on one occasion, while serial killers continue killing for a period of time. Mass killers are generally killed or apprehended at the scene, while serial killers are difficult to identify. Mass killers generate a great deal of public excitement at the time of the offense or shortly thereafter, while serial offenders continue to terrorize the community.

Serial killers are the most puzzling of violent offenders. They are extremely rare, and the cruelty and brutality of their murders exceed anything found in other arenas of violence. What is most amazing about these people is their ability to conceal themselves and to commit offenses for a long time. Modern law enforcement makes it more difficult to continue offending without discovery, but serial killers remain the most difficult type of violent offender to apprehend, describe, and explain.

The arrest of serial homicide offenders depends as much on luck as skill. As Egger (1998) has indicated, law enforcement agencies need to practice an enhanced degree of cooperation; they need to avoid "linkage blindness."

DISCUSSION QUESTIONS

1. Describe two myths and two facts about serial homicides.
2. What does Donald Black mean that law is "quantitative"? How does that apply to arrest clearances?
3. Discuss the relationship between weapons and clearances.

SUGGESTED READINGS

Jenkins, P. (1994). *Using murder: The social construction of serial homicide.* New York: Aldine de Gruyter.

Riedel, M. (1998). Serial murder, communities, and evil: A review essay. *Criminal Justice Review, 23,* 220–232.

Rosenfeld, R. (2000). Patterns in adult homicide: 1980–1995. In A. Blumstein & J. Wallman (Eds.), *The crime drop in America* (pp. 130–163). Cambridge: Cambridge University Press.

Sheley, J. F., & Wright, J. D. (1995). *In the line of fire: Youth, guns, and violence in urban America.* New York: Aldine de Gruyter.

REFERENCES

Athens, L. H. (1980). *Violent criminal acts and actors.* Boston: Routledge & Kegan Paul.

Best, J. (1988). Missing children: Misleading statistics. *The Public Interest, 92,* 84–92.

Black, D. (1976). *The behavior of law.* New York: Academic Press.

Blumstein, A., & Rosenfeld, R. (1998). Explaining recent trends in U.S. homicide rates. *Journal of Criminal Law and Criminology, 88,* 1175–1216.

Borg, M. J., & Parker, K. F. (2001). Mobilizing law in urban areas: The social structure of homicide clearance rates. *Law & Society Review, 100*(1), 435–466.

Brantingham, P. J., & Brantingham, P. L. (1978). A theoretical model of crime site selection. In M. Krohn & R. Akers (Eds.), *Theoretical perspectives* (pp. 105–118). Thousand Oaks, CA: Sage.

Bureau of Justice Statistics. (2009). Trends by race. *Homicide Trends in the United States.* Retrieved December 9, 2009, from http://bjs.ojp.usdoj.gov/content/ homicide/race.cfm.

Cardarelli, A. P., & Cavanagh, D. (1992). Uncleared homicides in the United States: An exploratory study of trends and patterns. Paper presented at the American Society of Criminology, New Orleans, LA.

Chester, G. (1993). *Berserk! Motiveless random massacres.* New York: St. Martin's Press.

Decker, S. H. (1993). Exploring victim-offender relationships in homicide: The role of individual and event characteristics. *Justice Quarterly, 10,* 585–612.

Duwe, G. (2004). The patterns and prevalence of mass murder in twentieth-century America. *Justice Quarterly, 21,* 729–761.

Duwe, G. (2007). *Mass murders in the United States: A history.* Jefferson, NC: McFarland & Co.

Eck, J. E. (1983). *Solving crimes: The investigation of burglary and robbery.* Washington, DC: Police Executive Research Forum.

Eck, J., & McGuire, E. (2000). Have changes in policing reduced violent crime? In A. Blumstein & J. Wallman (Eds.), *The crime drop in America* (pp. 207–165). Cambridge: Cambridge University Press.

Egger, S. A. (1998). *The killers among us.* Upper Saddle River, NJ: Prentice-Hall.

Egger, S. A. (2002). *The killers among us* (2nd ed.). Upper Saddle River, NJ: Prentice-Hall.

Federal Bureau of Investigation (FBI). (2006). *Crime in the United States 2004.* Retrieved June 2006 from http://www.fbi.gov/ucr/cius_04/c100.

Federal Bureau of Investigation (FBI). (2007). A byte out of history: The beltway snipers, Part 1. Retrieved December 2009 from http://www.fbi.gov/page2/oct07/snipers102207.html.

Federal Bureau of Investigation (FBI). (2012). *Crime in the United States*. Retrieved March 2014 fromhttp://www.fbi.gov/about-us/cjis/ucr/crime-in-the-u.s/2012/crime-in-the-u.s.-2012/violent-crime/violent-crime.

Federal Bureau of Investigation (FBI). (2013). *Serial Killers, Part 1: The FBI's Role Takes Shape*. Washington, DC. Retrieved from http://www.fbi.gov/news/stories/2013/september/serial-killers-part-1-the-fbis-role-takes-shape.

Felson, R. B. (1993). Predatory and dispute-related violence: A social interactionist approach. In R. V. Clarke & M. Felson (Eds.), *Routine activity and rational choice* (Vol. 5, pp. 103–125). New Brunswick, NJ: Transaction Publishers.

Fisher, J. C. (1997). *Killer among us: Public reactions to serial murder*. Westport, CT: Praeger.

Fox, J. A., & Levin, J. (1999). Serial murder. In M. D. Smith & M. A. Zahn (Eds.), *Homicide: A sourcebook of social research* (pp. 165–175). Thousand Oaks, CA: Sage.

Fox, J. A., & Levin, J. (2015). *Extreme killing: Understanding serial and mass murder*. Thousand Oaks, CA: Sage Publications.

Frosech, D., & Johnson, K. (2012). Gunman kills 12 at Colorado theatre; scores are wounded, reviving debate. *New York Times*, July 20, 2012.

Godwin, J. (1978). *Murder USA: The ways we kill each other*. New York: Ballantine Books.

Gottfredson, M. R., & Hindelang, M. J. (1979). A study of the behavior of law. *American Sociological Review, 44*, 3–18.

Greenwood, P. (1970). *An analysis of the apprehension activities of the New York City police department*. New York: Rand Institute.

Greenwood, P., Chaiken, J., & Petersilia, J. (1977). *The criminal investigation process*. Lexington, MA: Lexington Books.

Greenwood, P. W., & Petersilia, J. (1975). *The criminal investigation process: Vol. 1. Summary and policy implications* (No. R-1776-DOJ). Santa Monica, CA: Rand Corporation.

Haggerty, K. D. (2009). Modern serial killers. *Crime Media Culture, 5*, 168–187.

Harries, K. D. (1989). Homicide and assault: A comparative analysis of attributes in Dallas neighborhoods, 1981–1985. *The Professional Geographer, 41*, 29–38.

Hickey, E. W. (2002). *Serial murderers and their victims* (3rd ed.). Belmont, CA: Wadsworth.

Holmes, R. M., & Holmes, S. T. (1998). *Serial murder*. Thousand Oaks, CA: Sage.

Holmes, R. M., & Holmes, S. T. (2009). *Serial murder* (3rd ed.). Thousand Oaks, CA: Sage Publications.

Jarvis, J. P., & Regoeczi, W. C. (2009). Homicides clearances: An analysis of arrest versus exceptional outcomes. *Homicide Studies, 13*, 174–188.

Jenkins, P. (1994). *Using murder: The social construction of serial homicide*. New York: Aldine de Gruyter.

Keel, T. G., Jarvis, J. P., & Muirhead, Y. E. (2009). An exploratory analysis of factors affecting homicide investigations: Examining the dynamics of murder clearance rates. *Homicide Studies, 13*, 50–68.

Klinger, D. A. (1997). Negotiating order in patrol work: An ecological theory of police response to deviance. *Criminology, 35*, 277–306.

Lab, S. P. (2000). *Crime prevention: Approaches, practices, and evaluations* (5th ed.). Cincinnati, OH: Anderson Publishing Co.

Lane, R. (1997). *Murder in America: A history*. Columbus: Ohio State University Press.

Levin, J., & Fox, J. A. (1985). *Mass murder*. New York: Plenum.

Litwin, K. J. (2004). A multivariate analysis of factors affecting homicide clearances. *Journal of Research in Crime and Delinquency, 41*, 327–351.

Luckenbill, D. F. (1977). Criminal homicide as a situated transaction. *Social Problems, 25*, 176–186.

Newman, K. S., Fox, C., Harding, D. J., Mehta, J., & Roth, W. (2004). *Rampage: The Social Roots of School Shootings*. New York: Basic Books.

Ousey, G. C., & Lee, M. R. (2010). To know the unknown: the decline in homicide clearance rates, 1980–2000. *Criminal Justice Review, 35,* 141–158.

Petee, T. A., Padgett, K. G., & York, T. S. (1997). Debunking the stereotype: An examination of mass murder in public places. *Homicide Studies, 1,* 317–337.

Regoeczi, W. C., Jarvis, J. P., & Riedel, M. (2007). Clearing murders: Is it about time? *Journal of Research in Crime and Delinquency, 45,* 142–162.

Regoeczi, W. C., & Riedel, M. (2003). The application of missing data estimation models to the problem of unknown victim/offender relationships in homicide cases. *Journal of Quantitative Criminology, 19,* 155–183.

Reiss, A. J. (1971). *The police and the public*. New Haven, CT: Yale University Press.

Riedel, M. (1993). *Strange violence: A theoretical inquiry.* New York: Garland.

Riedel, M. (2008). Homicide arrest clearances: A review of the literature. *Sociology Compass, 2,* 1145–1164.

Riedel, M., & Jarvis, J. (1998). The decline of arrest clearances for criminal homicide: Causes, correlates, and third parties. *Criminal Justice Policy Review, 9,* 279–305.

Roberts, A. (2007). Predictors of homicide clearances by arrest: An event history analysis of NIBRS incidents. *Homicide Studies, 11,* 82–93.

Roberts, A., & Lyons, C. J. (2011). Hispanic victims and homicide clearance by arrest. *Homicide Studies, 15*(1), 48–73.

Rosenfeld, R. (2000). Patterns in adult homicide: 1980–1995. In A. Blumstein & J. Wallman (Eds.), *The crime drop in America* (pp. 130–163). Cambridge: Cambridge University Press.

Rossmo, D. K. (1999). *Geographic profiling.* Boca Raton, FL: CRC Press.

Sedensky, S. J. (2012). *Report of the State's Attorney for the Judicial District of Danbury on the Shootings at Sandy Hook Elementary School and 36 Yogananda Street*. State of Connecticut, Division of Criminal Justice.

Sheley, J. F., & Wright, J. D. (1995). *In the line of fire: Youth, guns, and violence in urban America.* New York: Aldine de Gruyter.

Spelman, W. (2000). The limited importance of prison expansion. In A. Blumstein & J. Wallman (Eds.), *The crime drop in America* (pp. 97–130). Cambridge: Cambridge University Press.

Truman, J., Langton, L., & Planty, M. (2013). *Criminal victimization, 2012.* NCJ 243389.

Truman, J. L., & Rand, M. (2010). *Criminal victimization, 2009.* NCJ 231327.

Turner, R., & Kosa, R. (2003). *Cold case squads: Leaving no stone unturned* (NCJ 199781). Washington DC: Bureau of Justice Assistance.

Waegel, W. B. (1982). Patterns of police investigation of urban crimes. *Journal of Police Science and Administration, 10,* 452–465.

Wellford, C., & Cronin, J. (1999). *An analysis of variables affecting the clearance of homicides: A multistate study.* Washington, DC: Justice Research and Statistics Association.

Wintemute, G. (2000). Guns and gun violence. In A. Blumstein & J. Wallman (Eds.), *The crime drop in America* (pp. 45–96). Cambridge: Cambridge University Press.

Wolfgang, M. E. (1958). *Patterns in criminal homicide.* Philadelphia: University of Pennsylvania Press.

Wolfgang, M. E., & Ferracuti, F. (1967). *The subculture of violence: Towards an integrated theory in criminology.* London: Tavistock Publications.

World Almanac. (2014). *The world almanac and book of facts 2014.* New York: World Almanac Books.

Zahn, M. A., & Sagi, P. C. (1987). Stranger homicides in nine American cities. *Journal of Criminal Law and Criminology, 78,* 377–397.

CHAPTER 5

ROBBERY

Robbery is the theft or attempted theft, in a direct confrontation with the victim, by force or threat of force. Robbery is one of the most feared crimes in cities, not only because of its relative frequency but also because of its psychological and physical consequences for victims.

Below are three newspaper accounts of robbery incidents (Marder, 1992). What patterns do these incidents suggest about robbery offenses, victims and offenders, settings where robberies occur, and motivations of offenders? How typical do you think these incidents are of most robberies?

1. Two men stopped at an ATM after a Saturday evening of dinner and drinks in a fashionable area of the city. Although the hour was late, there was a line. A 17-year-old clutching a .22-caliber handgun approached one man and announced, "This is a stickup." The man hesitated and was shot in the back of the head. Thus ended the life of Richard L. Barbour, Jr., 27, an assistant county prosecutor in New Jersey. Yerodeen Williams, the 17-year-old convicted murderer, later said: "He brung this on himself." Williams said Barbour had failed to follow a basic rule of robbery: When you are approached by a thief, do what he says. "Give it up," Williams said. "If he'd have done that, that man would still be here. If you hesitate, somebody gonna give it to you. Shoot you."
2. Andre Johnson, 16, and two friends were walking through Clark Park in West Philadelphia when they encountered Seung Ki Leung, 25, a University of Pennsylvania graduate student coming home from a touch football game. Johnson picked up a tree limb and smashed Leung's skull. As the student lay dying, Johnson and his friends went through the student's pockets and took $11.61. He was obliged to kill, Johnson later said from prison, because Leung had looked him directly in the eye. "You walk past somebody, you don't look them right in the eye . . . You keep walking; you mind your business. If our eyes meet, the dude's looking for trouble."
3. Ruth Wahl, a 22-year-old drugstore cashier in Detroit, was driving with three friends in her shiny white Suzuki Sidekick, her first car. About midnight, she drove into the parking lot of the Vernor Elementary School and parked. She and her friends were just opening a beer when three young men in a brown station wagon drove into the lot and approached. One of the women warned Ruth that nobody comes there, and that they had better go. Ruth drove away with the station wagon in pursuit but lost a race down deserted streets when the wagon finally trapped the Suzuki against a curb. A man with a gun jumped out, shouting, "Gimme your truck, bitch." He opened fire, killing Ruth Wahl.

PATTERNS AND TRENDS

Using official statistics such as the National Crime Victimization Survey (NCVS) and Uniform Crime Reports (UCR) (see Chapter 2), we can examine important patterns and trends in robbery over time. As with other types of crimes, the NCVS shows higher rates of

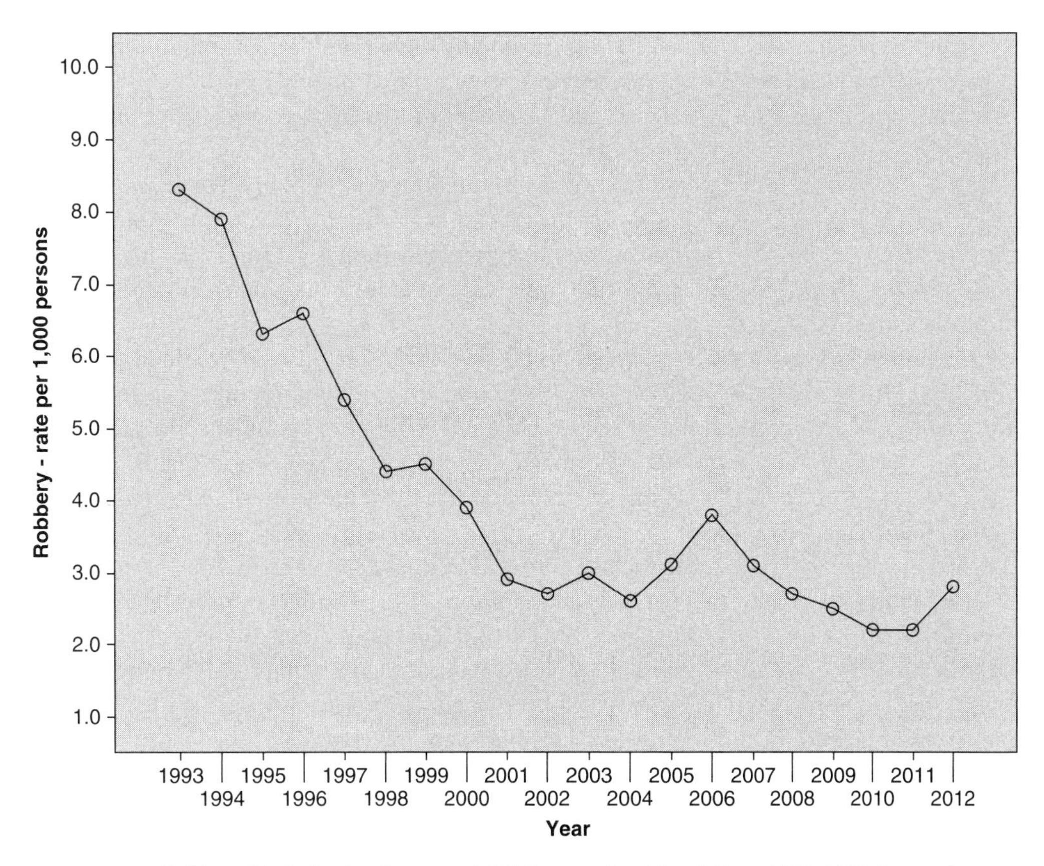

FIGURE 5.1 Robbery Victimization Rates per 1,000 Persons Age 12 and Over, 1993–2012. *Source*: Bureau of Justice Statistics, National Crime Victimization Survey, 1993–2012. Retrieved April 22, 2014, from the BJS website at: http://www.bjs.gov/index.cfm?ty=pbdetail&iid=4781.

robberies than the UCR, even though the NCVS excludes commercial robberies and victims aged younger than 12. We focus mainly on victimization figures here, because they reflect a greater proportion of actual crime that has occurred.

Robbery rates recorded by the NCVS since 1993 have generally declined over time (Fig. 5.1). From 1993 to 2012, robbery rates decreased 66% (from 8.3/1,000 to 2.8/1,000). The bad news is that robberies still occur far too frequently. An estimated 741,760 robberies occurred in 2012, accounting for 11% of all violent crime victimizations (Truman et al., 2013).

Over a longer period of time (since World War II), however, robberies of banks and convenience stores have increased. The number of robberies of small branch banks has increased tremendously, possibly because these are often located in vulnerable areas, such as small malls in residential areas. Numbers of convenience stores have also increased dramatically, offering potentially attractive targets to offenders. Suitable targets include businesses that are open 24 hours a day and have rapid cash flow, poor visibility from the outside of the store, or poor security features (Cohen & Felson, 1979). We will return to this point later in this chapter.

Needless to say, robbery figures are unacceptably high, even though recent trends have been encouraging. Next, we attempt to find some general patterns in robbery offenses, offenders, and victims, and perhaps question some popular myths or exaggerations about robbery.

First of all, we examine possible patterns in the offense of robbery. For example, how often does *injury* occur during a robbery? Injuries are common, but serious injuries are rare. About 38.2% of robbery victims in 2012 suffered *some* physical injury during the robbery, but only 16.9% were injured seriously enough to require medical treatment (Bureau of Justice Statistics [BJS], 2013a).

How many robberies result in the *death* of the victim? The answer, obtained from the UCR (FBI, 2013), may surprise you: The likelihood that any one robbery victim will be killed is quite low—only 1.8 out of 1,000. The total number of robberies counted by the UCR in 2012 (354,520), rather than homicides, is the appropriate denominator to use in answering this question. The appropriate numerator is the number of robbery victims who were killed in 2012 (652).

Next, what do we know about the likelihood of an offender using a *weapon*, or the effects of weapon usage? In 51% of all personal robberies in 2012, offenders were armed, but only about 29% of robberies involved a gun (BJS, 2013b). For commercial robberies (businesses such as banks or convenience stores), the likelihood of a gun being used is much higher (about half) (Cook, 1987). In general, the use of a gun seems to increase the likelihood of robbery success and the amount stolen but minimizes the chances of the victim being attacked (Cook, 1983). Usually, the "take" in personal robberies is relatively small (BJS, 2006). The value of items stolen was less than $50 in 23% of cases; the value exceeded $250 in only 24% of cases (36% of cases for commercial robbery). The median loss was $140.

Wright, Rossi, and Daly's (1983) data showed that offenders' most common self-reported motivations for use of weapons during a crime were, in order of importance, "to intimidate the victim," "to protect myself," and "to get away." Numerous studies have reported high correlations between victim resistance and violence by robbery offenders (Block, 1977; Conklin, 1972; Luckenbill, 1981), but Cook (1986) points out that the actual causal direction of violence is difficult to determine from police records. For example, do victims "resist" before they are attacked by the robber, thinking it is prudent to do so, or do they "resist" after being attacked, perceiving that the offender is so bent on vicious conduct that the victim has nothing to lose by resisting?

Where do robberies occur, and why might the *location* be important? Most robberies (43.5%) happened on streets or highways (FBI, 2013). Much smaller percentages occurred at residences (16.9%), banks (1.9%), gas stations (2.4%), convenience stores (5.1%), or other miscellaneous locations (16.9%). Most robbers reside in impoverished areas and strike close to home; those who do travel tend to seek more lucrative targets in commercial areas of the city (Rhodes & Conly, 1991).

Next, we examine *offender and victim demographics* and detect striking similarities. Robberies tend to be committed by young (60% younger than age 25) males (87%); about 55% of all offenders arrested for robbery in 2012 were black (FBI, 2013). Victims largely (though not exclusively) match the same categories (BJS, 2013c, 2013d, 2013e). Victimization rates in 2012 were highest for those aged 21 to 24 (5.9 per 1,000) but also were high for ages 18 to 20 (4.2 per 1,000). Those aged 65 or older experienced the lowest robbery victimization rates (0.7 per 1,000). Males were more than twice as likely as females (3.9 vs. 1.8 per 1,000) to be robbery victims. Blacks were victimized (5.2 per 1,000) at more than twice the rate for whites (2.5 per 1,000).

The likelihood of robbery victimization corresponds inversely with *income*: the lower the income, the higher the robbery victimization rate. For example, those earning less than $7,500 (household income) were nearly eight times more likely to be robbery victims (14.3 per 1,000) as those earning above $75,000 (1.9 per 1,000) (BJS, 2013f).

What do we know about the *relationship between robbery victims and offenders*? Unlike other violent crimes, the likelihood that robbery offenders and victims are strangers is much higher. In 2012, for example, 74% of female victims of rape and sexual assault knew their attackers, in contrast to 53% of female robbery victims and only 18% of male robbery victims (BJS, 2013g). The likelihood of a victim reporting a robbery to police (56%) was also much greater than for rape or sexual assault (28%) (BJS, 2013h).

Finally, we want to know if robbers *specialize* in robbery, or if, instead, robbery is part of a more general pattern or career of criminal behavior. Evidence suggests that a small number of robbery offenders are indeed very active (Wish & Johnson, 1986), but most offenders commit robbery only opportunistically and occasionally (one or two a year). Robbers are likely to be involved in many other types of crime as well.

EXPLANATIONS

Now that we have examined some of the most significant patterns and trends associated with robbery, we are better equipped to ask two questions: (1) How can we *explain* such behavior (i.e., what are the causes?) and (2) What can we *do* about it (i.e., what are strategies for intervention and prevention?). Again, we caution that any useful theory must be capable of addressing known patterns and trends. Any theory that is incapable of explaining observable patterns cannot possibly yield useful information. In addition, any useful theory about what causes robbery or motivates offenders should provide useful suggestions for prevention and intervention.

Earlier in this chapter we examined three specific robbery incidents to search for similarities. We will return to these incidents to explore offender motivations for committing such terrible crimes. Although their explanations varied, these and many other offenders focused on the negative influence of family, friends, or the brutal environment they had to contend with. As you read the following sections, ask yourself five questions: What are some of the different explanations that offenders offer for committing robbery? To what degree does the evidence suggest individual responsibility on the part of the offender? How much responsibility is due to the victim's behavior? Do external factors, such as the offender's income and environment, help us understand robbery? Do different causes or explanations call for different solutions?

STRAIN THEORY AND DIFFERENTIAL OPPORTUNITY THEORY

Violence, heavily concentrated in the poorest of neighborhoods, decimates young men of color (Prothrow-Stith, 1991; Prothrow-Stith & Spivak, 2004). Disputes that were once resolved by fistfights now end in gun battles, and young men, frequently young black men, willingly use violence for economic gain. Homicides committed by teenagers often occur during robberies or after minor arguments. One convicted offender was quoted as saying that mainstream America has created the formula for violence (Marder, 1992):

> White America is placing drugs into the neighborhood. No black 15-year-old is bringing drugs into the neighborhood. . . . My mind was thinking as a monster. The white community created that.

While the blame-diverting nature of such justifications is obvious, some support exists for such views. Prothrow-Stith (1991) argues that white teenagers will never feel the hopelessness or alienation of black teenagers. Such disenfranchisement reduces hope and investment in the future and instead encourages short-term, impulsive (sometimes violent) behavior. These arguments fit Agnew's General Strain Theory (2007). In particular, the *presentation of negative stimuli* such as child abuse/neglect, excessive physical punishment, negative relations with peers, and negative school experiences can facilitate aggression and delinquency.

Some offenders said that their behavior was a logical adaptation to an environment in which there are only two readily available means, each illegal, to earn a living. "The drug dealers are the only ones who can give you a job: lookout person, holder, pusher," one convicted offender said (Marder, 1992). "You either become a drug dealer or a stickup person." Such statements evoke differential opportunity theory. Cloward and Ohlin (1960) argued that legitimate opportunities may be blocked, but illegitimate ones must be available before the individual can choose one or the other. The deprivation of legitimate means produces a strain toward delinquency, but behavioral adaptations can take many different forms, depending on exactly what illegitimate opportunities are available in the environment. If delinquency emerges because of unequal opportunity and the widespread availability of illegitimate opportunities, then the clear policy implications of this theory are that alternatives to delinquent subcultures and illegitimate opportunities must be provided. Cloward and Ohlin's differential opportunity theory heavily influenced social interventions under the Johnson presidency, known as the "War on Poverty" and the "Great Society" (e.g., education, job training, skill training, community resource centers).

While there are good theoretical reasons to expect the economy to affect crime rates, many theorists disagree about what constitutes "objective" economic indicators. Rosenfeld and Fornango (2007) argue that collective *perceptions* of the economy are more likely to influence many types of social behavior, including criminal behavior. The Index of Consumer Expectations, taken from monthly consumer surveys, is part of the Leading Indicator Composite Index published by the Bureau of Economic Analysis of the U.S. Department of Commerce. The Index of Consumer Sentiment (ICS) comprises five items from the monthly consumer surveys that measure respondents' perceptions of change in their financial situation during the previous year and expected change over the next 12 months; outlook for the economy over the near and long term; and appraisal of buying conditions for household durables. Rosenfeld and Fornango (2007) found that collective perceptions of the economy, as measured by the ICS, had significant effects on robbery and property crime rates between 1970 and 2003, even when controlling for the effects of unemployment and economic growth.

CONTROL THEORY

Social Bonding Theory

As Hirschi (1969) and others have suggested, weak social bonds to parents, schools, and other institutions of socialization lead to weakened transmission of values and ineffective social and cultural constraints against delinquency. Social bonding, in contrast, is the mechanism by which effective controls and constraints are learned. Most young offenders did not grow up in two-parent families: One parent, grandparents, or foster parents typically raised these children. Most do not recount happy family lives. "Mom's using drugs, Pop's not around, so they bring up their own selves," according to Kerry Marshall, a young offender serving a life sentence for a robbery-murder (Marder, 1992, p. A01). He said that even mothers like his, who are hardworking and are not on drugs, are preoccupied. Another offender said he sold drugs and gave some of the proceeds to his mother: "I'd tell her somebody gave it to me . . . Eventually she knew, but she couldn't do nothing. Mom'd say: 'As long as you don't get caught.'" Andre Johnson, who robbed and killed the student in the incident described earlier in this chapter, never lived with his father and last saw him two years before committing murder: "I barely knew him," he said. "I seen him a few times. He's not my father except medically. I give him respect and stuff 'cause he's the dude that brought me into the world. But as far as giving me advice—forget it.'"

In such an environment, school is not taken seriously: "I wasn't much interested in learning," one offender said. "School wasn't happening. I'd go to advisory, check in and leave." Nor was the risk of life imprisonment much of a deterrent to committing violent crime: "My brothers used to tell me, don't ever go to jail . . . But I saw that they went to jail and they were all right. They survived."

Techniques of Neutralization

In the first two robbery incidents described in this chapter, the assailants were both young males who expressed justifications for their actions by blaming their victims. Interviews with defendants, lawyers, and family members in 57 cases showed a disturbing pattern: With few exceptions, the teenagers felt little remorse (Marder, 1992). Such expressions are reminiscent of the techniques of neutralization described by Sykes and Matza (1957). These are essentially inappropriate extensions of common excuses for rule violations found in the larger culture. According to Sykes and Matza, delinquents are part of the larger culture and subscribe to many of its values, but they episodically "drift" into delinquency by using techniques of neutralization that reduce constraints on their behavior and rationalize deviations from conventional values.

DIFFERENTIAL ASSOCIATION THEORY

Many robberies, about 40%, are committed by young males acting in groups of two or more (FBI, 2013), often in response to peer influence. Among the basic propositions of differential association theory is that criminal behavior is learned in interaction with other persons through a process of communication, primarily within intimate personal groups (Akers & Sellers, 2012). Learning involves techniques for committing the crime as well as motives, drives, attitudes, and rationalizations.

According to results from the Habitual Offenders Survey (Petersilia et al., 1977), many offenders' careers progressed from auto theft and burglary to an increasing proportion of robberies. Rightly or wrongly, offenders perceived that robberies would require little preparation and few tools, were easy, usually did not require hurting anyone, and provided unlimited targets. *Juvenile* offenders tended to report expressive needs for committing such crimes (thrills, peer influence). They were less likely to plan their crimes than adults and more likely to use partners. *Adults* tended more often to report motivations of financial need and the desire for high living (e.g., drugs, alcohol, and women) (for similar findings, see recent research by Jacobs & Wright, 1999). Adults were more likely to plan their offenses and were much less likely to use partners as they got older.

SYMBOLIC INTERACTION THEORY

Symbolic interaction theory focuses on the *meaning* of events as perceived by participants in specific interactions with one another. Those meanings, as we shall soon see, have significant implications for understanding the motives of robbers.

Not all robbers commit their offenses with equal frequency. The term *persistent offenders* refers to a small group of criminals who commit an unusually large share of robberies and assaults (Chaiken & Chaiken, 1982). Persistent robbers continue their criminal careers despite lengthy periods of incarceration in their youthful years. Violence itself may be part of the attraction of robbery for these offenders (Katz, 1991).

Purely materialistic explanations for robbery are of limited usefulness, according to Katz (1991). Although legitimate opportunities are lacking in the communities where robbery typically occurs and offenders typically live, the rewards of street robbery are minimal (Katz, 1991). In fact, nonviolent forms of criminality, such as burglary, are often more rewarding and present fewer risks. Further, why should robbery be so overwhelmingly (90%) a male endeavor, if poverty is the primary motivating factor? Instead, Katz suggests, we should focus less on looking for common background factors of persistent robbers and focus more on how persistent robbers, a small and unique group accounting for the largest proportion of robberies, construct and sustain the attractions of robbery, in fact overcoming numerous discouragements, such as the low gain, high risk, and lengthy periods of incarceration that accompany persistent robbery. Methodologically, this perspective requires less emphasis on statistical data and more emphasis on life histories and narratives told from the perspectives of offenders (Katz, 1988).

Katz argues that persistent robbers recall adolescent years during which they attempt to perfect "bad-ass" identities, demonstrating their willingness to use violence beyond any calculation of legal, material, and physical costs to themselves. Even in their younger years, persistent offenders report using violence to silence insults of peers, to avoid being made a fool of, and to dominate a threatening environment. Evidence suggests that violent predators maintain a constant readiness for violence, expecting that others will similarly launch unprovoked attacks (Wright & Rossi, 1994). In robberies, unprovoked violence may also allow the offender to gauge the victim's compliance, and perhaps fulfill other monetary desires (e.g., kidnapping the victim and escorting him or her to his or her home or an ATM to increase the take) or nonmonetary desires (e.g., sexual assault, demonstrating to one's peers that one is indeed a "bad-ass"). Despite such anticipations, "persistent robbers know intimately that the crime is shot through with uncertainties and uncontrollable risk" (Katz, 1991). Indeed, it is acting in the face of such wild uncertainty that allows the robber to present himself as a "bad-ass." Persistent robbers, heavily involved in deviant lifestyles, engage frequently in other types of crime, drinking, drug use, gambling, partying, sexual promiscuity, and so on, scoffing at conventional lifestyles and presenting themselves as more brave, more adventurous, and more "alive" than others. The pursuit of physical pleasure and awareness, reinforced by constructing and strengthening a "bad-ass" identity, provides strong motivation for persistent robbers.

Similarly, interviews conducted with 86 active armed robbers found that robbery stems most directly from a perceived need for quick cash, but this decision is activated, mediated, and shaped by participation in street culture (Jacobs & Wright, 1999; Wright & Decker, 1997). For example, many offenders had no permanent address, and their lifestyles emphasized a perpetual search for good times. As Jacobs and Wright (1999, p. 163) put it:

> The overall picture that emerges from our research is that of offenders caught up in a cycle of expensive, self-indulgent habits (e.g., gambling, drug use, and heavy drinking) that feed on themselves and constantly call for more of the same.

Street culture values the hedonistic pursuit of sensory stimulation, spontaneity, disdain for conventional living, lack of future orientation, and persistent denial of individual responsibility. "Street-corner capitalism" is typified by the need to constantly prove that one is hip, cool, and "in" by conspicuous displays and outlays of cash (Jacobs & Wright, 1999). Naturally, such behaviors create the very reinforcing conditions that drive offenders to rob in the first place (i.e., pressing needs for fast cash), but such financial motivations usually become more a matter of maintaining a certain lifestyle and self-image. That is, few persistent offenders said they robbed to support starving children or a family. This sequence of events is diagrammed in Figure 5.2. We have added corresponding references to the various theories discussed in this section.

FEMINIST THEORY

It is often emphasized that robbery is predominately a male enterprise (e.g., Katz, 1988), but there is growing evidence that a small number of women are heavily involved in violent street crime in ways that go beyond traditional explanations of women using violence for self-defense or self-protection (Miller, 1998, 2008). For both men and women, the

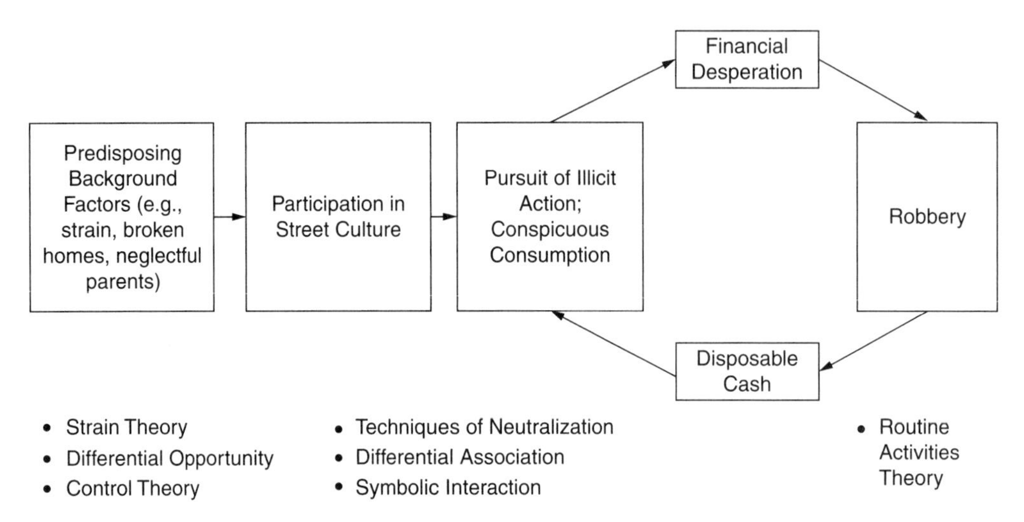

FIGURE 5.2 Cycle of Events Leading to Robbery. *Source*: Adapted with permission from Jacobs and Wright (1999, p. 166).

primary motivation for robbery is to get money or material goods. When asked why they commit robberies instead of other crimes, both women and men say that they choose robberies because it is a fast and easy way to get cash. Many may also derive a psychological or emotional thrill from committing robberies, as Katz (1991) suggests.

While a comparison of women's and men's *motivations* to commit robbery (the "why") reveals gender similarities, how they go about *planning and enacting* robberies (the "how") is quite different. For male robbers, a physical confrontation with a male victim is typical. Respondents in ethnographic studies typically report using violence or the threat of violence (e.g., a gun placed directly against the victim's head) to ensure compliance (Miller, 1998). These male-on-male confrontations both reflect and reinforce widely held views of masculinity in street culture, especially the desire for power and respect (Miller, 1998). Female robbers, in contrast, described three main ways in which they committed robberies: (1) targeting *female* victims in physically confrontational robberies (the most frequent type), (2) targeting *male* victims by appearing sexually available (e.g., creating an opportunity for robbery by feigning sexual interest), and (3) participating *with* male accomplices (usually in a subordinate role) during street robberies of men.

As Miller explains, these differences highlight a clear *gender hierarchy* that exists on the streets. While a small group of women can carve out a niche for themselves in this setting, and even establish partnerships with males, they are still participating in a heavily male-dominated environment, and their actions reflect an understanding of this. One is reminded of Felicia "Snoop" Pearson, a character on the HBO series *The Wire* (HBO, 2014). Snoop was a vicious "hit man" and trusted enforcer in Marlo Stanfield's drug crew, respected and feared on the streets due to her well-deserved reputation for calm ruthlessness. Perhaps Snoop illustrates another emergent type in street culture, a woman who can successfully compete with male peers on their own turf in a dominant rather than subordinate role.

In sum, the differences between male and female robbers may reflect practical choices that are made in the context of a gender-stratified environment.

ROUTINE ACTIVITIES THEORY

Why do robberies occur much more often in some places than in others (i.e., the poorest areas of large cities), and why do both offenders and victims tend to be largely young, minority males? The notion of "place" is important to understanding and explaining these patterns. For our purposes, a place typically refers to a specific address, building, or street corner, but it must always be "a fixed physical environment that can be seen completely and simultaneously, at least on its surface, by one's naked eyes" (Sherman et al., 1989, p. 31).

According to routine activities theory, predatory crimes such as robbery are influenced by the convergence in space and time of three necessary elements: (1) motivated offenders, (2) suitable targets, and (3) the absence of capable guardians. All three must be present for a crime to occur. Conversely, crime can be prevented by removing or altering any of these three elements, especially by reducing the attractiveness of targets (e.g., traveling in pairs rather than alone) or improving supervision, security, or natural surveillance opportunities in specific places. In addition, places, like persons, have their own observable routine activities that are subject to both formal and informal regulation (Sherman et al., 1989). Those places that have unusually high rates of robbery or other predatory crime can be called "hot spots," and we are interested in how such place-specific crime rates can be explained.

In a Minneapolis study of hot spots, Sherman and colleagues (1989) found that 4,166 robbery calls between December 15, 1985, and December 15, 1986, were located in only 2.2% of all definable "places" in the city. There were 113 places with more than five robberies in one year. Not only was robbery highly concentrated in a relatively small number of places, it was even more concentrated than the offenses of auto theft and rape. But do places "cause" crimes? What makes a spot "hot"?

Predatory stranger offenses, such as robbery, seem dependent on places where motivated offenders are especially likely to come into contact with vulnerable victims and low surveillance (Sherman et al., 1989). Such places seem to share common elements. The five hottest of the hot spots in Minneapolis for robberies, rapes, and auto thefts were (1) an intersection that included bars, a liquor store, and a park, (2) a bus depot, (3) an intersection that included homeless shelters and bars, (4) a downtown mall, and (5) an intersection that included an adult bookstore and several bars. Such places are busy (high number of potential targets), and they provide a clientele that may be engaged in legal (e.g., alcohol consumption) or illegal activities (e.g., prostitution, or drug use or sales) that increase their vulnerability and reduce their likelihood of reporting crimes to the police. Police patrols and citizen involvement in crime prevention activities are also less likely in many (but not all) of these hot spots (Sherman et al., 1989).

A research study in Washington DC (Rhodes & Conly, 1991) investigated how offenders actually select targets for certain offenses and how far they travel (i.e., the "criminal commute"). Like everyone else, offenders obtain environmental cues about people and places from their regular, everyday routine activities (e.g., trips to work, school, shopping, recreation). Over time, all people construct "cognitive maps" of the urban areas with which they are most familiar. A person's cognitive map depends on where he or she goes and what he or she does. Implications are that offenders will use cognitive maps (based on their own routine activities) to make decisions about where to commit illegal activities. Offenders will commit offenses near their own homes, because these are the areas they know best. Further, the more instrumental (goal-oriented) the offense (i.e., robbery), the greater the travel. Social disorganization theory has similarly shown us that offenders are clustered in certain areas of the city (i.e., the poorest inner-city neighborhoods with low levels of social cohesion), so it makes sense that crimes such as robbery will also be clustered in certain areas.

In Washington DC, Rhodes and Conly (1991) looked at three types of crime: robbery, burglary, and rape. They matched up land-use data with offender (i.e., residence) and offense (i.e., crime site) data. They examined characteristics of the immediate environment where offenders lived, the surrounding area, the site of the offense, and the distance traveled. Some places indicated "good" targets to offenders, while others did not. The distance traveled to commit a crime was greatest for robbery, then burglary, and the least for rape. The majority of all offenses occurred within two miles of the offender's home. When they looked at the site of the offense, the researchers found that victimized areas for robbery and burglary tended to be more transitional[1] and more heavily used for large business and special purposes. Offenders were most likely to move into "transitional" areas to commit robbery and least likely to move into single residential areas and "mixed-use" areas. There is distinct movement by robbers into transitional areas and large business areas, but for the most part, offenders commit crimes near their homes (consistent with the ideas of routine activities and cognitive maps).

INTERVENTIONS

CRIMINAL JUSTICE APPROACHES

Criminal justice efforts to reduce robbery have often focused on deterrence (i.e., increased law enforcement) and incapacitation (i.e., increased sentences) (Wright & Decker, 1997). *Proactive policing*, in general, refers to the vigorous enforcement of laws against relatively minor offenses to prevent more serious crime. In a recent article, Kubrin, Messner, Deane, McGeever, and Stucky (2010) examined the effect of proactive policing on robbery rates for a sample of large U.S. cities (populations of 100,000+) using Sampson and Cohen's (1988) measure of proactive policing (the sum of the number of arrests for driving under the influence and disorderly conduct, divided by the number of sworn police officers). Their analyses confirmed prior findings (MacDonald, 2002; Sampson & Cohen, 1988) that proactive policing strategies had a significant, downward impact on robbery rates. In addition, they argued that the effects of proactive policing on robbery rates appeared to operate largely through generalized perceptions of greater law enforcement activity, regardless of the actual probability that arrests are made. One of the limitations of their results, as the authors point out, is that many different styles of policing have often been lumped together under the umbrella term "proactive policing." A wide array of different enforcement approaches has in reality been used, and each likely carries different consequences that deserve closer attention (Taylor, 2001).

Other strategies have focused on reducing robberies by increasing law enforcement in specific high-risk places, such as subways, or by targeting situational correlates of robbery (e.g., mandatory sentences for illegal weapon carrying and use of a weapon during a felony). During the years 1965 to 1971, New York City dramatically increased the number of uniformed officers patrolling its subway system. Robberies dropped significantly as a result of the increased police presence, but, as shown in many other studies, robberies were simply displaced to different nearby locations (Chaiken et al., 1974). Studies have failed to consistently demonstrate any clear-cut reduction in crime due to increased police presence alone (e.g., Kelling et al., 1974).

The Bartley-Fox gun law, passed in Massachusetts in 1975, provided for a one-year mandatory minimum sentence for anyone convicted of carrying and possessing a firearm in public without a proper license and gun permit. Originally, the bill was intended to punish offenders more harshly and limit the discretion of sentencing judges. As eventually adopted, however, the law did not prohibit prosecutors from reducing a carrying charge to a simple charge of possession, a crime not covered by the minimum sentence. Two years after the law's passage, researchers found decreased gun assaults, gun robberies, and gun homicides (Pierce & Bowers, 1979). After three years, there was still a slight drop in gun robbery rates but an increase in non-gun armed robberies, suggesting that the law's initial deterrent impact may have been only temporary. Process evaluation also suggested that the law had been vigorously enforced initially, but over the next two years increased confusion by police about its applicability and increased discretion by judges had undercut its intent (Beha, 1977; Rossman et al., 1979).

More recently, some laws have taken aim at repeat offenders, attempting to focus on career robbers. Few robbers specialize, however, making it difficult to predict who will become a high-rate offender. It is instructive to look at three-strikes laws as an example. Such laws are beset with serious weaknesses, including poorly defined target populations, discrimination against minorities, lack of acceptance and use by prosecutors, and lack of prison space (Welsh & Harris, 2013).

It is unlikely that criminal justice responses alone are sufficient to produce a substantial decrease in robbery. As Wright and Decker (1997, p. 133) argue, "Threatened criminal penalties for armed robbery already are severe; there is little reason to believe that increasing them will deter the offenders from committing further stick-ups."

OPPORTUNITY REDUCTION STRATEGIES

Routine activities theory suggests that the number of robberies can be reduced by reducing opportunities to commit robbery. For example, could we reduce robbery by encouraging potential targets to protect themselves: to avoid high-crime areas, to not walk alone at night, to not wear expensive jewelry or clothing, and so forth? Could we reduce robbery by increasing surveillance by citizens and businesses in areas at high risk for robbery?

Evidence suggests that the physical characteristics of stores, buildings, and other places can be manipulated to decrease the risk of robbery. Hunter and Jeffery (1992) reviewed the effects of various measures designed to reduce robbery of convenience stores using a situational strategy called *Crime Prevention through Environmental Design* (CPTED). Four major strategies reduced robbery risk: (1) having two or more clerks on duty (employee surveillance), (2) improving cash-handling techniques (i.e., target removal), (3) improving access control, and (4) increasing natural surveillance. Research methods included physical site assessments, interviews with victims and offenders, and experiments comparing control sites with stores undergoing preventive modifications.

Crow and Bull (1975, cited in Hunter & Jeffery, 1992) examined 349 stores owned by Southland Corporation (i.e., 7-Eleven). A scale of "target attractiveness" was developed based on rankings of different environmental features by former robbers. A field study examined 60 treatment-group stores and 60 matched control stores. Effective prevention strategies included following limits on available cash and posting signs to that effect, enhancing visibility and reducing the obstruction of windows, using of security alarms and surveillance cameras, and providing employee safety training.

Duffala (1976) examined whether spatial attractiveness was associated with robbery. He looked at four features: (1) whether a store was located within two blocks of a major street; (2) whether it was located on a street with light amounts of traffic; (3) whether it was located in a residential or vacant land use area or both; and (4) whether it was located in an area with few surrounding commercial activities. No one variable was significant alone, but all four were significant in interaction with one another.

Jeffery, Hunter, and Griswold (1987, cited in Hunter & Jeffery, 1992) assessed 34 convenience stores in Tallahassee, Florida, from January 1981 to July 1985. Thorough security and environmental assessments were conducted at each store, and records of robberies were obtained from police. Risk of robbery was reduced by the following: a cashier located in the center of the store, more than one clerk on duty, clear visibility within the store and from outside the store, stores located near commercial property, stores located near residential property rather than vacant lots, stores located near other evening activities, location of gas pumps on the property, and good cash-handling policies.

In Gainesville, Florida, city ordinances were passed in 1986 and 1987 requiring various operational procedures for convenience stores (Clifton & Callahan 1987, cited in Hunter & Jeffery, 1992). In 1986, ordinances required limitation of cash, a security safe, parking lot lighting, removal of visual obstructions, robbery detection cameras, and training of clerks. Robberies, however, continued at an alarming rate. The 1987 ordinances specified that stores had to either close or else have two clerks on duty between 8 p.m. and 4 a.m. Afterward, a dramatic decline in robberies began, precipitating a decline in convenience store robberies statewide.

Sherman (1995), however, expressed skepticism about the impact of the two-clerk ordinance. A review by the National Academy of Sciences panel on violent crime (Reiss & Roth, 1993) noted that it would be extremely difficult to reliably measure the effect of the two-clerk ordinance in a small city such as Gainesville, and several alternative hypotheses could have accounted for the observed drop in robberies. First, the robbery drop actually began four months prior to the two-clerk law's effective date. The drop occurred about the same time as the arrest of three extremely active robbers in the city and the surrounding area. These arrests may have contributed to the observed decrease in robberies. Second, the larger county experienced the same decline in convenience store robberies as Gainesville, even though it had enacted no security regulations for convenience stores. This suggests that forces other than the two-clerk ordinance were responsible for the observed decrease. Third, both the city and the county had experienced steep increases in convenience store robberies in 1986, prior to the ordinance. Subsequent reductions could have been due to simple "regression toward the mean"—in other words, a statistical artifact.

State-recommended security procedures were issued in 1989, and in 1990 the Florida legislature enacted the Convenience Store Security Act. The success of prevention still depends mostly on voluntary compliance, however. Corporations sometimes favor and sometimes oppose specific measures, a "contradiction" resulting from the industry's need to provide protection while holding operating costs to a minimum.

CONCLUSIONS

Simple law enforcement or punishment strategies will not have an appreciable impact on reducing robbery. Evidence suggests that robbery is not merely an instrumental (i.e., goal-oriented) crime, as commonly believed, but rather serves offenders' affective (i.e., emotional) needs as well. Robbers often see themselves as "hardmen" or "bad-asses." As such, simple deterrence or incapacitation strategies by themselves are unlikely to work. Broader strategies must focus on reducing the opportunity for robbery, both by increasing awareness of routine activities as they relate to risk and by altering the physical design of places when such policies can be implemented cost-effectively. Social and cultural correlates of robbery (e.g., growing up in crime-ridden, poverty-stricken neighborhoods with attendant consequences for formative values and behavior) might also be partially addressed by broader social policies including education, job training, and welfare reform. These will be addressed in more detail in the concluding chapter of this book.

DISCUSSION QUESTIONS

1. Answer these questions about robbery *patterns*: (a) How common is *injury* in a robbery? (b) How common is the *death* of the victim? (c) Does victim resistance *increase or decrease* the likelihood of injury? (d) What are the most common offender *motivations for using a weapon*? (e) How often are *guns* used in robberies? (f) What is the average *"take"* in a robbery? (g) Do *drug users* account for a large portion of robberies?
2. Discuss evidence for each of the following *explanations of robbery*: (a) strain theory, (b) control theory, (c) differential association theory, (d) symbolic interaction theory, (e) routine activities theory, and (f) feminist theory. Which explanation do you think is most relevant, and why?
3. Describe each of the following *intervention strategies* and discuss its *effects* on robbery (give specific evidence and examples): (a) criminal justice approaches and (b) opportunity reduction strategies.

SUGGESTED READINGS

Jacobs, B. A. (2000). *Robbing drug dealers: Violence beyond the law*. New York: Walter de Gruyter.

Wright, R. T., & Decker, S. H. (1997). *Armed robbers in action*. Boston: Northeastern University Press.

NOTE

1. Consistent with Shaw and McKay's (1942) formulation of social disorganization theory, "transitional" areas had high rates of instability and population turnover, such as high rates of temporary lodging, construction, and demolition.

REFERENCES

Agnew, R. (2007). *Pressured into crime: An overview of general strain theory*. New York: Oxford University Press.

Akers, R. L., & Sellers, C. S. (2012). *Criminological theories* (6th ed.). New York: Oxford University Press.

Beha, J. A., III. (1977). And nobody can get you out: The impact of a mandatory prison sentence for the illegal carrying of a firearm on the use of firearms and the administration of criminal justice in Boston. *University Law Review, 58*, 106–208.

Block, R. (1977). *Violent crime*. Lexington, MA: Lexington.

Bureau of Justice Statistics (BJS). (2006). *Criminal victimization in the United States—Statistical tables index. Robbery*. Retrieved July 24, 2006, from http://www.ojp.usdoj.gov/bjs/abstract/cvus/robbery.htm#top.

Bureau of Justice Statistics (BJS). (2013a). Number of robberies by injury and medical treatment for physical injuries, 2012. Generated April 22, 2014, using the NCVS Victimization Analysis Tool at http://www.bjs.gov.

Bureau of Justice Statistics (BJS). (2013b). Percent of robberies by weapon use and weapon category, 2012. Generated April 22, 2014, using the NCVS Victimization Analysis Tool at http://www.bjs.gov.

Bureau of Justice Statistics (BJS). (2013c). Rates of robberies by age, 2012. Generated April 22, 2014, using the NCVS Victimization Analysis Tool at http://www.bjs.gov.

Bureau of Justice Statistics (BJS). (2013d). Rates of robberies by sex, 2012. Generated April 22, 2014, using the NCVS Victimization Analysis Tool at http://www.bjs.gov.

Bureau of Justice Statistics (BJS). (2013e). Rates of robberies by race, 2012. Generated April 22, 2014, using the NCVS Victimization Analysis Tool at http://www.bjs.gov.

Bureau of Justice Statistics (BJS). (2013f). Rates of robberies by household income, 2012. Generated April 22, 2014, using the NCVS Victimization Analysis Tool at http://www.bjs.gov.

Bureau of Justice Statistics (BJS). (2013g). Number of rape/sexual assaults, and robberies by sex and victim-offender relationship, 2012. Generated April 22, 2014, using the NCVS Victimization Analysis Tool at http://www.bjs.gov.

Bureau of Justice Statistics (BJS). (2013h). Percent of rape/sexual assaults, and robberies by reporting to the police, 2012. Generated April 22, 2014, using the NCVS Victimization Analysis Tool at http://www.bjs.gov.

Chaiken, J. M., & Chaiken, M. R. (1982). *Varieties of criminal behavior*. Santa Monica, CA: Rand.

Chaiken, J. M., Lawless, M., & Stevenson, K. A. (1974). *The impact of police activity on crime: Robberies on the New York City subway system* (R-1424-NYC). Santa Monica, CA: Rand.

Clifton, W., Jr., & Callahan, P. T. (1987). *Convenience store robberies in Gainesville, Florida: An intervention strategy by the Gainesville Police Department.* Gainesville, FL: Gainesville Police Department.

Cloward, R., & Ohlin, L. (1960). *Delinquency and opportunity.* Glencoe, IL: Free Press.

Cohen, L., & Felson, M. (1979). Social change and crime rate trends: A routine activity approach. *American Sociological Review, 44,* 588–608.

Conklin, J. E. (1972). *Robbery and the criminal justice system.* Philadelphia: Lippincott.

Cook, P. (1983). *Robbery in the United States: An analysis of recent trends and patterns* (NCJ91149). Washington DC: Department of Justice, National Institute of Justice.

Cook, P. (1986). The relationship between victim resistance and injury in noncommercial robbery. *Journal of Legal Studies, 15,* 405–416.

Cook, P. (1987). Robbery violence. *Journal of Criminal Law and Criminology, 78,* 357–376.

Crow, W. J., & Bull, J. L. (1975). *Robbery deterrence: An applied behavioral science demonstration-final report.* La Jolla, CA: Western Behavioral Sciences Institute.

Duffala, D. (1976). Convenience stores, armed robbery, and physical environment features. *American Behavioral Scientist, 20,* 227–246.

Federal Bureau of Investigation. (2013). *Crime in the United States 2012.* Retrieved April 22, 2014, from http://www.fbi.gov/about-us/cjis/ucr/crime-in-the-u.s/2012/crime-in-the-u.s.-2012/cius_home.

HBO. (2014). *The Wire [Television Series, 2002–2008].* New York: HBO. Retrieved April 24, 2014, from: http://www.hbo.com/the-wire#/.

Hirschi, T. (1969). *Causes of delinquency.* Berkeley: University of California Press.

Hunter, R. D., & Jeffery, C. R. (1992). Preventing convenience store robbery through environmental design. In R. V. Clarke (Ed.), *Situational crime prevention: Successful case studies.* Albany, NY: Harrow & Heston.

Jacobs, B., & Wright, R. T. (1999). Stick-up, street culture, and offender motivation. *Criminology, 37,* 149–173.

Jeffery, C. R., Hunter, R. D., & Griswold, J. (1987). Crime prevention and computer analysis of convenience store robberies in Tallahassee, Florida. *Security Systems,* August, 1987, and *Florida Police Journal*, Spring.

Katz, J. (1988). *Seductions of crime.* New York: Basic Books.

Katz, J. (1991). The motivation of the persistent robber. In M. Tonry (Ed.), *Crime and justice: A review of research* (Vol. 14, pp. 277–306). Chicago: University of Chicago Press.

Kelling, G. L., Pate, T., Dieckman, D., & Brown, C. E. (1974). *The Kansas City preventive patrol experiment: A summary report.* Washington, DC: Police Foundation.

Kubrin, C. E., Messner, S. F., Deane, G., McGeever, K., & Stucky, T. D. (2010). Proactive policing and robbery rates across U.S. cities. *Criminology, 48,* 57–97.

Luckenbill, D. (1981). Generating compliance: The case of robbery. *Urban Life, 10,* 25–46.

MacDonald, J. M. (2002). The effectiveness of community policing in reducing urban violence. *Crime & Delinquency, 48,* 592–618.

Marder, D. (1992, Dec. 6). A new generation of killers, feeling no blame and no shame. *Philadelphia Inquirer,* A01.

Miller, J. (1998). Up it up: Gender and the accomplishment of street robbery. *Criminology, 36,* 37–66.

Miller, J. (2008). *Getting played: African American girls, urban inequality, and gendered violence.* New York: New York University Press.

Petersilia, J., Greenwood, P., & Lavin, M. (1977). *Criminal careers of habitual felons.* Santa Monica, CA: Rand.

Pierce, G. L., & Bowers, W. J. (1979). The impact of the Bartley-Fox gun law on crime in Massachusetts. Unpublished manuscript. Boston: Northeastern University, Center for Applied Social Research.

Prothrow-Stith, D. (1991). *Deadly consequences.* New York: Harper Collins.

Prothrow-Stith, D., & Spivak, H. (2004). *Murder is no accident: Understanding and preventing youth violence in America.* San Francisco: Jossey Bass.

Reiss, A. J., Jr., & Roth, J. A. (Eds.). (1993). *Understanding and preventing violence.* Washington, DC: National Academy Press.

Rhodes, W. M., & Conly, C. (1991). Crime and mobility: An empirical study. In P. J. Brantingham & P. L. Brantingham (Eds.), *Environmental criminology* (pp. 167–188). Prospect Heights, IL: Waveland.

Rosenfeld, R., & Fornango, R. (2007). The impact of economic conditions on robbery and property crime: The role of consumer sentiment. *Criminology, 45,* 735–769.

Rossman, D., Floyd, P., Pierce, G. L., McDevitt, J. L., & Bowers, W. (1979). *The impact of the mandatory gun law in Massachusetts.* Boston: Boston University School of Law, Center for Criminal Justice.

Sampson, R. J., & Cohen, J. (1988). Deterrent effects of the police on crime: A replication and theoretical extension. *Law & Society Review,* 22, 163–89.

Shaw, C. R., & McKay, H. D. (1942). *Juvenile delinquency and urban areas.* Chicago: University of Chicago Press.

Sherman, L. W. (May, 1995). Reactions to crime and violence. *Annals of the Academy of Political and Social Science, 539,* 102–113.

Sherman, L., Gartin, P., & Buerger, M. (1989). Hot spots of predatory crime: Routine activities and the criminology of place. *Criminology, 27,* 27–55.

Sykes, G., & Matza, D. (1957). Techniques of neutralization: A theory of delinquency. *American Journal of Sociology, 22,* 664–670.

Taylor, R. B. (2001). *Breaking away from broken windows: Baltimore neighborhoods and the nationwide fight against crime, grime, and decline.* Boulder, CO: Westview.

Truman, J., Langton, L., & Planty, M. (2013). *Criminal victimization,* 2012 (NCJ-243389). Washington, DC: U.S. Department of Justice, Office of Justice Programs.

Welsh, W. N., & Harris, P. W. (2013). *Criminal justice policy and planning* (4th ed.). Waltham, MA: Elsevier/Anderson.

Wish, E. D., & Johnson, B. D. (1986). Impact of substance abuse on criminal careers. In A. Blumstein, J. Cohen, J. A. Roth, & C. A. Fisher (Eds.), *Criminal careers and career criminals, Vol. II.* Washington, DC: National Academies Press.

Wright, J. D., & Rossi, P. H. (1994). *Armed and considered dangerous.* New York: Aldine de Gruyter.

Wright, J. D., Rossi, P. H., & Daly, K. (1983). *Under the gun: Weapons, crime, and violence in America.* Hawthorne, NY: Aldine de Gruyter.

Wright, R. T., & Decker, S. H. (1997). *Armed robbers in action.* Boston: Northeastern University Press.

CHAPTER 6

RAPES AND SEXUAL ASSAULTS

Rapes and sexual assaults take many different forms. Victims are young as well as old, male as well as female, and from various racial backgrounds and income levels. Definitions of rape and sexual assault have changed substantially over time in response to criticism and advocacy by women's groups. Rape at one time was commonly (but mistakenly) assumed to be caused by sexual desire alone. This assumption caused various misconceptions about the offender, the offense, and the victim, and it failed to distinguish among different types of rape and sexual assault. In the first section of this chapter, we examine important definitions, patterns, and trends in rape and sexual assault. We then turn to explanations and interventions informed by current knowledge.

We begin with five examples that illustrate the diversity of sexual assault incidents, offenders, and victims.

1. On March 2, 2005, L.A. Lakers basketball star Kobe Bryant and the 20-year-old woman who accused him of rape settled her civil lawsuit against him (Sarche, 2005). Terms were not released, and both parties agreed to comment no further. The lawsuit sought unspecified damages for mental injuries, public scorn, and humiliation the woman said she had suffered since their June 2003 encounter at the Vail, Colorado, hotel where she worked. After a tour of the hotel and spa, the two ended up in his room. They began to kiss and Bryant became more aggressive, finally holding her by the throat while he raped her, the lawsuit said. Shortly after jury selection began in the criminal case, prosecutors dropped charges after the woman told them she could not take part in a trial. Prosecutors said they were confident they could win a conviction, but only with her cooperation. Bryant apologized for his conduct, but maintained that the sex was consensual.
2. A "Code R" (sexual assault victim) comes into a hospital emergency room for help. The young teenager was abducted by a stranger, tied up, and held for many hours. The ER is busy, so she has to wait many hours for a physical exam (required for legal purposes); until she has the exam, she is not allowed to eat or drink. A family member asks if the girl's story will be on the news (Philadelphia Inquirer, 1997).
3. A woman comes into a busy rape crisis center for help in coping with her assault of a few months ago. Her biggest concern is how to tell her husband. The couple is from a country where sexual assault is shameful and can permanently scar the family's name. Not only does the woman fear retaliation by the rapist, a family friend, but she dreads her husband's response (Philadelphia Inquirer, 1997).
4. It is a typical day in Family Court. A number of child sex abuse cases are being heard. Similarities in these cases become apparent—the accused is a parent, stepparent, cousin, or the mom's boyfriend. The incident happened in

(continued)

(*continued*)

the living room, near the bed, at the video store, or at grandma's or grandpa's house. The child is asked to describe, in court terms, what happened—which part of the perpetrator touched him or her and how (Philadelphia Inquirer, 1997).

5. According to police reports, two 15-year-old girls went to an apartment complex to visit a friend. When the two did not come home that night, their parents called the police. Police entered an apartment inhabited by two young men known to be acquainted with the missing girls. Police found the two teenagers, a suspect, and the drug Rohypnol ("roofies," the so-called date-rape drug). Rohypnol, an illegal sedative, is about 10 times the strength of Valium and has no taste or odor when dissolved in drinks. The girls said they were drinking soda and then couldn't remember anything until about 5 the following morning. Police believe the girls were given the drug and then raped (KRON-TV, 1996).

DEFINITIONS

The National Crime Victimization Survey (NCVS) (see Chapter 2) currently provides the most detailed data on rape and sexual assaults. *Rape* is defined in the NCVS as forced sexual intercourse including both psychological coercion and physical force (Bureau of Justice Statistics [BJS], 2014a). Forced sexual intercourse refers to any vaginal, anal, or oral penetration by the offender(s). The NCVS counts attempted as well as completed rapes, male as well as female victims, and both heterosexual and homosexual rape. In contrast, *sexual assault* refers to a wide range of victimizations, separate from rape or attempted rape. These crimes include attacks that involve unwanted sexual contact between victim and offender (e.g., grabbing, touching, fondling). Victims interviewed by the NCVS must be at least 12 years old; victims younger than 12 are excluded from all estimates.

As of January 1, 2013, the Federal Bureau of Investigation (FBI) revised the Uniform Crime Reports (UCR) definition of "rape" as follows: "Penetration, no matter how slight, of the vagina or anus with any body part or object, or oral penetration by a sex organ of another person, without the consent of the victim" (FBI, 2013b). The UCR had formerly defined *forcible rape* as "the carnal knowledge of a female forcibly and against her will." The revised definition clarifies three critical points: (a) rape includes either male or female victims or offenders; (b) it includes instances in which the victim is incapable of giving consent because of temporary or permanent mental or physical incapacity (e.g., due to the influence of drugs or alcohol or because of age); and (c) it reflects the various forms of sexual penetration usually understood to be rape. The UCR definition includes attempts as well as completed rapes. In contrast to the NCVS and the National Incident-Based Reporting System (NIBRS), the UCR excludes statutory offenses, in which either no force is used or the victim is under the age of consent. Rape is a Part I offense (see Chapter 2).

As noted in Chapter 2, the NIBRS was designed to improve the definition, accuracy, and measurement of crime reported by police authorities. The NIBRS (FBI, 2013b), in contrast to the UCR, separates sex offenses into two categories: *forcible* (rape, sodomy, sexual assault with an object, and fondling) and *nonforcible but unlawful* (incest and statutory rape). *Rape* is defined in NIBRS as "the carnal knowledge of a person, without the consent of the victim, including instances where the victim is incapable of giving consent because of his/her age or because of his/her temporary or permanent mental or physical incapacity."

Sodomy refers to "oral or anal sexual intercourse with another person, without the consent of the victim, including instances where the victim is incapable of giving consent because of his/her age or because of his/her temporary or permanent mental or physical incapacity." *Sexual assault with an object* means "to use an object or instrument to unlawfully penetrate, however slightly, the genital or anal opening of the body of another person, without the consent of the victim, including instances where the victim is incapable of giving consent because of his/her age or because of his/her temporary or permanent mental or physical incapacity." *Fondling* refers to "the touching of the private body parts of another person for the purpose of sexual gratification, without the consent of the victim, including instances where the victim is incapable of giving consent because of his/her age or because of his/her temporary or permanent mental or physical incapacity." Fondling is the only "forcible" offense in NIBRS that is not counted as "rape" in the UCR (because no penetration occurred). *Incest* is defined as "nonforcible sexual intercourse between persons who are related to each other within the degrees wherein marriage is prohibited by law." *Statutory rape* is "nonforcible sexual intercourse with a person who is under the statutory age of consent."

Although we focus mainly on rape in this chapter, it is clear that sex offenses cover a wide variety of behaviors. We reiterate that definitions are critical in the social construction of a crime (see Chapter 1): They influence statistical estimates of a crime, perceptions of causes, and official responses to it. The question of consent has been especially controversial in defining rape, and we will examine in this chapter how that issue has been addressed by criminal justice legislation and policy.

PATTERNS AND TRENDS

Rape and sexual assault victimization rates have fluctuated over time but have generally decreased since 1993 (Fig. 6.1). Although a slight upward tick in 2006 is visible, methodological changes in the NCVS in 2006 require caution when comparing 2006 criminal victimization estimates to other years (Truman et al., 2013). Although another slight increase is apparent from 2011 to 2012, this change was not statistically significant (Truman et al., 2013).

If we look at offenses known to police over time (collected through UCR data), similar patterns emerge (Fig. 6.2). The conclusion that rape has been declining gradually since 1993 is basically the same. The UCR data, however, suggest a fairly steady increase in rape from 1973 to 1991. As we saw in Chapter 2, offenses known to police may reflect a number of forces besides actual crimes (e.g., reporting by victims and witnesses, accuracy of police record systems, and reporting of crime data to the FBI by local and state law enforcement agencies).

CHARACTERISTICS OF VICTIMS, OFFENDERS, AND OFFENSES

According to NCVS estimates, 346,830 people aged 12 or older were victims of rapes or sexual assaults in 2012 (Truman et al., 2013). It is the norm rather than the exception that sex offenders and victims know one another. In 75.1% of rape and sexual assault incidents

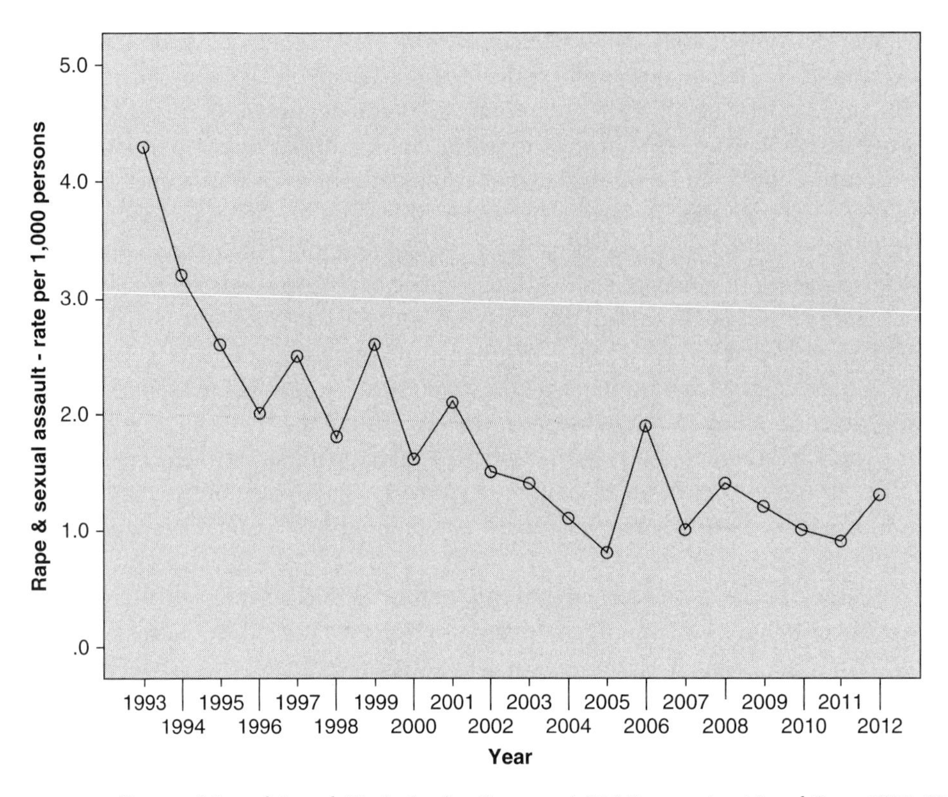

FIGURE 6.1 Rape and Sexual Assault Victimization Rates per 1,000 Persons Age 12 and Over, 1993–2012.
Note: Due to methodological changes in the 2006 NCVS, use caution when comparing 2006 criminal victimization estimates to other years. See Criminal Victimization, 2007, NCJ 224390, BJS website, December 2008, for more information.
Source: Bureau of Justice Statistics, National Crime Victimization Survey, 1993–2012. Retrieved April 22, 2014, from the BJS website at http://www.bjs.gov/index.cfm?ty=pbdetail&iid=4781.

reported by victims over the age of 12, the offender was not a stranger (BJS, 2014b). Victim and offender were likely to have had a prior relationship as family members, intimates, or acquaintances (especially the latter).

Only 28.2% of victims reported their rapes or sexual assaults to the police in 2012 (BJS, 2014c), making rape the most underreported of all violent crimes. The reasons most frequently given by victims for not reporting the incident to police (Table 6.1) were because it was a personal or private manner (22%), it was reported to another official (19.5%), the offender was unsuccessful (15.8%), or fear of reprisal (11.3%). In contrast, the most common reasons victims gave for reporting the crime to the police were to prevent further crimes by the offender against themselves or others, and "because it was a crime" (BJS, 2011).

Overall, an estimated 62% of the victims of rape and sexual assault in 2012 were female (BJS, 2014d). Like victims of other types of violent crime, rape and sexual assault victims were disproportionately low-income urban residents of the same race as their attackers (BJS, 2014e). Young adults aged 18 to 20 reported the highest per capita rate (4.7 per 1,000)

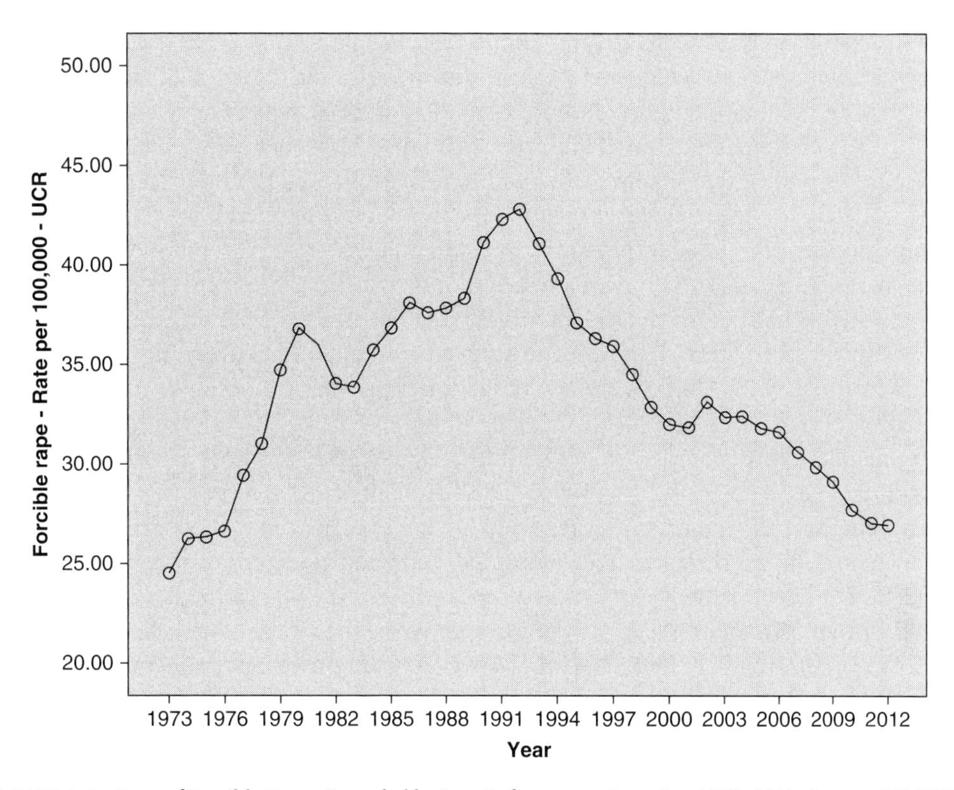

FIGURE 6.2 Rate of Forcible Rapes Recorded by Law Enforcement Agencies, 1973–2012. *Sources*: FBI, UCR, prepared by the National Archive of Criminal Justice Data. Retrieved May 1, 2014, from the UCR website at http://www.ucrdatatool.gov/Search/Crime/Crime.cfm

Table 6.1 Reasons for Not Reporting Rape/Sexual Assault to the Police

Reason for Not Reporting	Percent
Private or personal matter	22.4%
Reported to another official	19.5%
Offender unsuccessful	15.8%
Fear of reprisal	11.3%
Police inefficient, ineffective, or biased	4.2%
Police would not want to be bothered	2.4%
Lack of proof	2.3%
Other/unknown	22.1%
Total	100%

Note: Details may not add to total shown because of rounding. Some respondents may have reported more than one reason for not reporting victimization to police. Numbers shown are estimates based on percentages reported by the Bureau of Justice Statistics.

Source: Bureau of Justice Statistics. (2011). *Criminal victimization in the United States—statistical tables index. Table 102: Percent of reasons for not reporting victimizations to the police, by type of crime.* Retrieved May 1, 2014, from http://www.bjs.gov/content/pub/html/cvus/reasons_for_not766.cfm

of victimization in 2012 (BJS, 2014f). About 42% of rape victims reported some kind of injury, although only 19% required medical treatment for the injury (BJS, 2014g).

Only 40% of all rapes reported to police in 2012 were cleared by an arrest (FBI, 2012). In 2012, 99% of offenders arrested for rape were male; 65% were white, and 86% were over the age of 18 (FBI, 2012). Rapists rarely murder their victims (1.9 murders per 100,000 rapes), contrary to media stereotypes and popular fiction (FBI, 2012).

Rape occurs more frequently at certain times and places. In summer months, for example, more rapes occur when people are outdoors and moving around (FBI, 2009). Rape is also more likely to occur during the times when most people are off work, during the hours from 6 p.m. to 6 a.m. Rape occurs much more frequently in urban rather than rural areas. According to the FBI (2012), 74% of forcible rapes in 2012 occurred in cities with a population of more than 50,000.

In one of the most comprehensive studies of date rape so far, Koss and her colleagues (Koss, 1988; Koss et al., 1987) surveyed 6,000 students at 32 colleges across the United States. A majority of women (53%) reported having experienced some kind of unwanted sexual contact during their lifetime. Fifteen percent had been victims of completed rapes and 12% had been victims of attempted rapes, where rape was defined as "penetration against consent through force, threat of force, or when the victim was incapacitated with alcohol or other drugs." Fully 83% of the victims of completed rapes knew their attacker, and 57% of the victimizations occurred while on dates. While only 10% of the victims reported the assault to police or rape crisis centers, Koss (1992, p. 124) puts these figures into context: "the great majority of rape victims conceptualized their experience in highly negative terms and felt victimized whether or not they realized that legal standards for rape had been met."

The frequency of date rape on college campuses is surprisingly high (Humphrey & Kahn, 2000; Koss, 1993; Michael et al., 1994; Sanday, 1996). Since starting college, 26.1% of female seniors report being victims of either an attempted or completed sexual assault (Krebs et al., 2007, 2009). Victimization occurs most frequently during the freshman or sophomore years, and in the majority of cases (75% to 80%), the victim knows the attacker—usually an acquaintance, classmate, friend, or boyfriend. Athletes and fraternity members tend to commit sexual assaults on campus at higher rates than the rest of the male college population (Jackson et al., 2004). While acknowledging these patterns, Sanday (1990, p. 90) cautions about making overgeneralizations:

> The sexual aggression evident in these particular cases does not mean that sexual aggression is restricted to fraternities or that all fraternities indulge in sexual aggression. . . . Male bonding that rejects women and commodifies sex is evident in many other social contexts outside of universities. Thus, it would be wrong to place blame solely on fraternities. However, it is a fact also that most of the reported incidents of "pulling train" on campus have been associated with fraternities.

Attitudes, beliefs, norms, and behaviors can vary across different groups, campuses, workplaces, regions, and even societies, and can tolerate, facilitate, or discourage sexual assault. Cultural theories of rape are discussed in the next section.

EXPLANATIONS

Over the years, many people assumed that rape was motivated *solely* by sexual desire. If this explanation is incorrect, as now seems to be the case, then many interventions intended to reduce sexual desire (e.g., chemical castration, censorship of pornography) are unlikely to affect the incidence of rape. Identifying the relevant causes of this behavior is a prerequisite for doing something about it.

PSYCHIATRIC PERSPECTIVES

Psychiatric explanations of rape often examine unresolved needs and conflicts in the offender's past: "His unfulfilled needs for acceptance, affection, and intimacy result in depression" (Groth, 1990). Many rapists have episodic careers in which particular incidents often seem related to negative life events and feelings of helplessness. A majority of adult rapists reported committing their first offense by the age of 16, although most incidents go undetected or are not treated as serious crimes (Groth, 1990).

A number of background characteristics significantly increase the *likelihood* of a person becoming a rapist. These *risk factors* include experiencing sexual trauma as a child or being victimized sexually. Although only one third of sexual assault offenders reported that they had ever been physically or sexually abused while growing up, these offenders were substantially more likely than any other category of offenders to report such abuse (Greenfeld, 1997).

Insecurity about masculine identity is not uncommon. Often, failures in multiple areas of life make the rapist experience doubts about his manhood. He may compensate by attempting to aggressively display his masculinity. He often has poor social relationships, poor social skills, and high anxiety in dealing with other people. As a result, the rapist fails to develop successful interpersonal relationships. He is frequently detached or self-centered in interactions with others. Convicted rapists often report chronic unhappiness due to a sense of inadequacy and a feeling of isolation from others (Groth, 1990).

Alcohol and drug use are common among rape offenders, symptomatic of attempts to cope with high levels of anxiety and distress. Although substance abuse may lower inhibitions against committing acts of violence, it is not necessarily a causative factor.

Clinical studies illustrate that rape serves nonsexual needs of offenders, not just sexual desires. In particular, strong needs for control and high levels of hostility have been observed (Groth & Binbaum, 1979). Rape may symbolize an offender's attempt to regain control, to punish someone, or do both of these for his perceived mistreatment (i.e., a victim identifies with the role of aggressor to overcome a sense of powerlessness and helplessness). In fact, many rapists report difficulty in maintaining an erection during the offense.

A typology of rape originally developed by Groth (Groth, 1990; Groth & Binbaum, 1979) has since been adapted and modified by the FBI's National Center for the Analysis of Violent Crime as part of the FBI's *Crime Classification Manual* (Douglas et al., 1997; Hazelwood & Burgess, 2001). Although any one rape may contain elements of more than one type, one often tends to predominate. Offender behavior can be classified into one of five categories according to this model:

1. *Power Reassurance:* Also known as "compensatory," this type of offender behavior suggests an underlying lack of confidence and inadequacy and a misguided belief that the sex act is consensual, expressed through minimal force and low confidence. This type of offender does not wish to hurt the victim.
2. *Power Assertive:* Also known as "exploitative," this type of offender behavior suggests an underlying lack of confidence and inadequacy, expressed through a need for control, mastery, and humiliation of the victim, while demonstrating authority. Unlike the power reassurance type, the power assertive offender has no fantasies of victim consent or participation: He seeks to dominate the victim completely.
3. *Anger Retaliatory:* Offender behaviors suggest a great deal of displaced rage and violence, toward a specific person, group (women), institution, or a symbol of either. This type of offender is punishing the victim for real or perceived wrongs he has suffered early in life; he is taking revenge on a victim who is symbolic of those who have hurt him in the past. In this sense, his anger toward other women is *displaced* onto the victim.
4. *Anger Excitation:* Also known as "sadistic," this type of offender behavior implies that the offender gets sexual gratification or excitement from inflicting pain and suffering on the victim. The attack often involves torture or mutilation. This offender is at the opposite end of the continuum from the power reassurance type. Thankfully, such types are relatively rare.
5. *Opportunistic:* This type of offender behavior suggests an offender who is out to satisfy immediate sexual impulses, often while committing another crime, such as burglary. The offender's primary motivation in this case is sexual in nature rather than anger or a desire for power.

FEMINIST THEORIES

Although psychiatrists focus on individual offender characteristics, we also need to consider sociocultural aspects (e.g., norms and values regarding sexuality and attitudes toward women). The causes of rape, according to feminists, lie deep within a society and culture dominated by male attitudes, values, and beliefs. Male-dominated culture, in many ways, objectifies relationships with women, eschews female value and belief systems, and limits females' rights and opportunities. Feminists argue that, historically, rape has been inappropriately defined, investigated, prosecuted, and punished by male-dominated legislative and justice systems. Rape law reform thus became a major research and policy agenda for feminists.

Susan Brownmiller (1975), one of the best-known early feminist theorists, focused her analysis on the historical power advantage that men have enjoyed over women, resulting in the unequal status and unfair treatment of women in our society. Traditional socialization patterns have encouraged men to associate masculinity with power, dominance, strength, virility, and superiority, and femininity with submissiveness, passivity, and weakness. Various cultural expectations, including those embodied in male-dominated legislative and justice systems, historically tended to view women as little more than male property.

Research has been largely supportive of the sociocultural view of rape. Sanday (1981) conducted a cross-cultural study of 156 tribal societies existing between 1750 B.C. and 1960. At the extremes of her sample, she found that rape was rare or absent in 47% of the societies studied, but a frequent and accepted practice against women in 18% of the societies. In the most rape-prone societies, female authority and power were low, and masculinity was frequently expressed by interpersonal violence and toughness.

Scully and Marolla (1985) conducted interviews with 114 convicted rapists in a Virginia prison. Rewards or justifications for rape perceived by offenders included a means of exacting revenge or punishment, achieving a "bonus" while committing another crime (such as burglary or robbery), obtaining sexual access to women who would otherwise be unavailable, exercising sexual power and control, and participating in an "adventure." Supporting a sociocultural interpretation, the authors warned that rape could not be seen as merely the act of a few sick men. Rather, "rape can be viewed as the end part in a continuum of sexually aggressive behaviors that reward men and victimize women" (Scully & Marolla, 1985, p. 262).

Malamuth (1981, 1984) conducted studies to assess male views associated with sexual aggression. He asked different male samples (mostly college students) to determine the likelihood that they would commit a rape if they could be assured of not being caught and punished. Responses to various questions were given on five-point scales ranging from very likely (5) to not likely at all (1). On average, about 35% of respondents across samples indicated some likelihood of raping by scoring a 2 or higher. A high likelihood was associated with callous attitudes toward rape and belief in various rape myths (e.g., that women really enjoy rape despite their protests).

Although supportive of sociocultural theories of rape, research studies have not yet adequately answered the question of why most men do *not* rape or commit other sexual offenses in a society and culture that is, to some degree, accepting of rape myths and aggressive male sexual behavior. The samples used in many studies are unrepresentative of the male population and may in fact target those with more aggressive sexual attitudes and behaviors. Sociocultural views also do not fully explain sexual violence directed against children or adult males. More interdisciplinary perspectives are needed that incorporate individual as well as sociocultural views. Although certain cultures may be "rape-prone" to varying degrees, the individual offender must still have a motivation to commit sexual aggression, must overcome internal and external inhibitors against sexual aggression, and must formulate a strategy to overcome victim resistance (Finkelhor, 1984).

SOCIAL COGNITIVE THEORIES

Do men learn to be rapists? Another set of theories, consistent with feminist interpretations but focused more on individual factors, addresses thinking errors and distortions that are supportive of rape. Attitudes and behaviors supportive of rape can be learned and reinforced through social interactions with others, and beliefs may be further reinforced through socialization (e.g., the family, school), membership in various groups, and witnessing media portrayals of coercive male–female relationships (Russell, 1984). Ellis (1989) suggests that four learning processes are facilitated by media portrayals. First, men may imitate witnessed acts of coerciveness or violence toward women. Second, men may increasingly associate sex and violence by viewing material that exhibits sex and violence in the same context. Third, rape myths are perpetuated and reinforced by the media. Fourth, heavy viewers of television may become desensitized to sexual aggression and more tolerant of the pain, fear, and humiliation associated with such acts.

The mythology of rape allows an individual both to engage in illegal sexual behavior and to rationalize and justify it after it occurs (Weis & Borges, 1975). Rape myths can serve to provide men with an ideology that justifies acts of violence toward women (Burt, 1983; Scully & Marolla, 1984). These rationalizations or justifications for deviant behavior are similar to what Sykes and Matza (1957) have referred to as "techniques of neutralization."

One popular rape myth is the belief that "no means yes"—that is, the belief that women make initial protests, but they never really mean it (Koss & Harvey, 1991). Another myth is that women are swept off their feet by sexually forceful men. In reality, women fantasize more frequently about sexual encounters during which they choose their partner as well as the specific acts involved (Koss & Harvey, 1991). Another myth is that "nice girls don't get raped;" in other words, the offender may believe that the victim teased or sexually provoked him, or both. Another myth states that "it is impossible to rape an unwilling woman." This myth perpetuates stereotypes that a woman must have consented unless serious and obvious physical injuries resulted. Evidence for the existence of such myths has been found in samples of convicted rapists (Burt, 1980, 1983; Scully & Marolla, 1985) and noncriminal adult and juvenile males (Burt, 1983; Koss et al., 1987; Muehlenhard & Hollabaugh, 1988).

Although feminist theories argue that rape myths must be addressed through large-scale cultural and social change, including changes in sex role socialization, cognitive-behavioral and social learning theories focus on altering individual, learned patterns of thinking and behavior that increase the likelihood of rape. It is the level of analysis (individual vs. sociocultural) that distinguishes these theories (Gilmartin, 1994).

MULTIFACTOR THEORIES

Single-factor theories (e.g., feminist or social cognitive theories) usually attempt to explain a single underlying cause of sexual aggression. In contrast, multifactor theories attempt to explain how different relationships among underlying causes can interactively shape sexual offending (Ward & Hudson, 1998).

The Confluence Model of Sexual Aggression (Malamuth, 1986, 1996), for example, is based on four core assumptions. First, sexual aggression is seen as the product of a confluence of risk factors that can motivate, disinhibit, or provide the social context for sexual offending to occur. Second, these factors predict aggression against women, but not men (i.e., domain specificity). Third, these factors can explain other aggressive and dominating behaviors toward women (i.e., generalization). Fourth, an individual's likelihood of engaging in sexually aggressive behavior is shaped by both environmental and sociocultural factors.

One of the more intriguing multifactor theories to emerge so far is the Integrated Theory of Sexual Offending (Ward & Beech, 2005; Ward et al., 2006), which argues that sexual aggression stems from three main causal factors that interact continuously throughout the lifespan: *biological factors* (i.e., genetics, evolutionary factors, and brain development), *proximal and distal ecological niche factors* (i.e., the physical, social, and cultural environment and personal context), and three fundamental *neuropsychological systems* associated with different brain structures: (a) motivation–motion, (b) action–control, and (c) memory–perception. For example, for one rapist, a primary causal factor is high impulsivity, which may be related to a brain trauma sustained in infancy but is only activated during times of acute frustration. For another rapist, an aversive event (e.g., death of a family member) may be a primary causal factor, which in turn interacts with other ecological, biological, or neuropsychological mechanisms. A primary strength of the theory is its ability to account for diverse types of offenses and offenders, and its ability to account for different pathways that interact to shape sexually aggressive behavior (Gannon et al., 2008). At the same time, more thorough empirical tests of its validity are needed, and underlying causal mechanisms need further explanation. For example, the theory says little about how neuropsychological deficits emerge, or how such factors may result from complex interactions between biological and environmental influences.

INTERVENTIONS

RAPE LAW REFORM

As seen in Chapter 1, criminal law is a "social construction." In other words, both definitions of illegal behaviors and corresponding penalties result from social processes. Many critics have perceived serious problems with legal definitions of rape and how rape cases are processed in court. Rape law reform proceeded vigorously in the 1970s, initially spurred by the advocacy of women's groups, but joined by researchers and academics. By 1980, almost every state in the United States had passed some form of rape law reform legislation (Bienen, 1980).

Traditional definitions of rape that relied on proof of vaginal penetration, for example, were criticized as inaccurate, incomplete, and unfair to victims. Sexual assault takes many different forms, and serious harm to victims (both female and male, and both children and adults) can occur with or without penetration, often referred to in criminal codes as "carnal knowledge." Rape and different sexual offenses are increasingly defined in gender-neutral terms that attempt to describe the specific behavior involved.

Michigan was one of the earliest states to undergo extensive rape law reform, serving as a model for many other states. In 1975, Michigan legislation abandoned the term *rape* in favor of *criminal sexual conduct*. Four degrees of criminal sexual conduct were established, based on the seriousness of the offense, the amount of coercion used, the infliction of personal injury, and the age and incapacitation of the victim (Marsh et al., 1982). Thus, it was hoped, sexual offenses could be classified using relevant, important legal criteria, displacing a host of outdated, confusing labels that failed to distinguish the actual behavior involved (e.g., "assault with intent to commit rape," "indecent liberties," "carnal knowledge of a female ward by a guardian," and "debauchery of youth").

California adopted a multifaceted approach that included four major elements: (1) sentence enhancements for the use of weapons or violence; (2) a *rape shield law* to constrain the use of prior sexual history by defense attorneys attempting to establish victim consent; (3) gender-neutral language in defining rape; and (4) no spousal exception in cases of rape (Polk, 1985). To determine whether rape law reform in California led to changes in processing or punishment, Polk (1985) examined California data for the years 1977 to 1982. In general, effects were small and were limited more toward the tail end (e.g., sentencing, incarceration) of the criminal justice system. Police were no more likely to make an arrest following rape law reforms, although prosecutors were somewhat more likely to file rape cases as felonies. The felony conviction rate for rape did not increase, however. Even though incarceration rates increased for rape during the period of the studies, they increased at similar rates for other serious felonies as well, reflecting a larger national trend toward tougher penalties.

Similar results were found in Michigan (Caringella-MacDonald, 1985). Sexual assault cases were more likely than nonsexual assault cases to be authorized for prosecution, but offense severity rather than rape law reforms may have confounded these results (i.e., differences in case characteristics were not controlled for in analyses). Among the cases authorized for prosecution, a higher proportion of the sexual assault cases also involved victim credibility problems (e.g., implausible or inconsistent statements). At subsequent stages of criminal justice processing, there were no significant differences in the rate of case convictions or plea bargains for the two types of assaults. Where plea bargains did occur, however, sentences for sexual assaults were reduced to a lesser extent than for other assaults.

Studies of the rape shield law in Indiana (LaFree, 1989) showed similar disappointing results. Based on 38 trials during three years following passage of the law, LaFree examined detailed data including victim, defendant, juror, trial, and courtroom characteristics. In each case, he examined the influence of several types of "nontraditional" victim behavior, including alcohol or drug use (in general, and at the time of the incident), extramarital sexual activity, having illegitimate children, and having a reputation as a partier. The rape shield law appeared to be almost totally ineffective. It was invoked in only one third of the cases examined, and in almost every one of these cases, evidence had already been presented in court (in the presence of jurors) that the victim had allegedly engaged in one or more forms of nontraditional behavior. Further, cases that used a defense based on victim consent were less likely than other cases to result in a guilty verdict. The victim's behavior was important only in those cases in which the defense attempted to prove either that the victim gave consent or that no sex occurred. In such cases, though, interviews revealed that jurors were less likely to perceive that the defendant was guilty when the victim engaged in premarital sex, used alcohol or drugs regularly, knew the assailant, or was black. These are hardly the effects intended by passage of rape reform laws.

Rape shield laws have now been passed in more than 45 states, and the requirement of corroboration of the victim's testimony has been eliminated in all states. Rape law reforms have proved to be quite limited in reducing the role of victim characteristics or increasing conviction rates in sexual assault cases, however. Victim credibility remains a central issue in the processing of sexual assault cases (Kruttschnitt, 1994).

Nowhere was this more evident than in the 2004 Kobe Bryant case, in which Bryant's defense attorneys claimed (but never proved) that his accuser had sex with someone other than Bryant after the alleged rape but before DNA samples were taken from the victim at the hospital. After the accuser refused to go forward with the criminal trial, her attorney said she wanted the case to end because she could not endure any more harassment. The woman, whose name was published in tabloids, listed on websites, and disclosed in documents inadvertently released by court staff, received death threats and moved repeatedly to avoid media pursuers. Her sexual history and mental health had been much discussed, in and out of court, and were certain to have been a major focus of a criminal trial, according to prosecutors (Nussbaum, 2004).

INCARCERATION

Does incarcerating sex offenders reduce recidivism? Langan, Schmitt, and Durose (2003) summarized recidivism findings from a study of 9,691 male sex offenders released from prison in 15 states in 1994. On average, these offenders served only three-and-a-half years of their eight-year sentences before being released in 1994. Most of them had been arrested several times for different types of crimes. The more prior arrests they had, the greater their likelihood of being rearrested for another sex crime after leaving prison. During the three-year follow-up period, released sex offenders were four times more likely than non-sex offenders (5.3% vs. 1.3%) to be rearrested for a new sex crime. Sex offenders had a lower overall rearrest rate compared to non-sex offenders, however. When rearrests for any type of crime (not just sex crimes) were counted, only 43% of the 9,691 released sex offenders were rearrested. The overall rearrest rate for the 262,420 released non-sex offenders was much higher (68%). While recidivism generally speaking is high, it cannot be stated that recidivism for *rape* or *sexual assault* is especially high.

SEX OFFENDER NOTIFICATION AND REGISTRATION LAWS

Sex offender registration and reporting laws have become widespread since the mid-1990s. Such laws stemmed from several highly publicized crimes in which the offender had a prior record of committing sexual offenses against children. Aimed at more closely monitoring the whereabouts of convicted sex offenders in the community, laws usually require released offenders to register with their local law enforcement agency upon their release from prison and allow agencies to publish the addresses of sex offenders. Members of the community may then take measures to protect themselves and their children against potential risks.

The Office of Sex Offender Sentencing, Monitoring, Apprehending, Registering, and Tracking (SMART) (www.smart.gov.) was authorized in the Adam Walsh Child Protection and Safety Act of 2006, and signed into law on July 27, 2006. The SMART Office provides jurisdictions with guidance on the implementation of the Adam Walsh Act and provides technical assistance to states, territories, Indian tribes, local governments, and public and private organizations. The SMART Office also tracks legislative and legal developments related to sex offenders and administers grant programs related to the registration, notification, and management of sex offenders.

Each state has its own distinct sex offender registration and notification system; each makes its own determinations about who is required to register as a sex offender, what information those offenders must provide, which offenders will be posted on the jurisdiction's public registry website, and so forth. Although sex offender registration is not directly administered by the federal government, Congress has enacted various measures that set "minimum standards" for jurisdictions to implement in their sex offender registration or notification systems (U.S. Department of Justice, 2013). The first of these, passed in 1994, is referred to as the "Wetterling Act." This act established a set of minimum standards for registration systems for the states.[1] Two years later, in 1996, "Megan's Law" was passed as a set of minimum standards for community notification. The most recent set of standards can be found in the Sex Offender Registration and Notification Act (SORNA), which was passed in 2006.[2] SORNA currently governs the federal minimum standards for sex offender registration and notification systems.

Little research to date has examined the effects of online registries on public safety, and SORNA continues to face multiple challenges in both federal and state courts (U.S. Government Accountability Office, 2013). In one study, Malesky and Keim (2001) surveyed psychologists, social workers, and counselors who treat sex offenders about their perceptions of SORNA legislation. Nearly 70% of those surveyed felt that Internet sex offender registries created a false sense of security. Among their concerns were that not all offenders are included on every site; sex offenders may move often; and not all sex offenders comply with their registration requirements. More than 80% felt that the sites would not result in a decrease in child sex abuse.

In a meta-analysis (a statistical analysis of a collection of studies), Drake and Aos (2009) analyzed seven studies in selected states that examined the recidivism rates of registered sex offenders released from prison against comparison groups. They found no clear effect on recidivism, either for sex offenses specifically or for other types of crime. One study found increases in recidivism, two found decreases, and four found no statistically significant differences. The small number of available studies and small sample sizes, however, prevented definitive conclusions. Another problem was that different jurisdictions often defined recidivism differently or measured recidivism at different intervals, making comparisons of recidivism rates across jurisdictions difficult. Despite these challenges, there is a clear need for more rigorous evaluations of SORNA policies.

VICTIM RESISTANCE

Does resisting one's attacker decrease or increase the likelihood of rape? Bart and O'Brien (1985) attempted to answer this question by conducting a nonrandom survey of 94 victims solicited through newspaper ads. Their sample was not representative of rape victims nationally: Volunteers for the study were more likely to be young, unmarried, and working or attending school. Offenders in these incidents were also more likely to be strangers than is usually the case. Even though the study did not obtain representative samples of rape victims or offenders, it provided valuable insights about the effects of victim resistance, and its main findings have been fairly well supported (Greenfeld, 1997).

Researchers interviewed victims, asking questions about demographic factors and situational and background variables associated with the rapes. Six possible defense strategies were described: (1) flee or try to flee, (2) scream or yell, (3) beg or plead, (4) "cognitive verbal" techniques (try to reason with offender or con him, or make him see her as a person), (5) take advantage of environmental intervention or opportunity, and (6) respond with physical force.

Study results showed that those who avoided rape used a greater number of strategies than those who did not. *Avoiders* ($n = 51$) were more likely to flee or try to flee, yell or scream, use physical force, and take advantage of environmental opportunity (e.g., a bystander or car passing nearby). *Raped women* ($n = 43$) were more likely to beg or plead. Avoiders and raped women were equally likely to use cognitive strategies (i.e., appealing to the offender's sense of decency or humanity). Avoiders were more likely to experience a gut reaction of rage. Raped women were more likely to think about avoiding death or mutilation (fear). Even for raped women, those who used physical strategies were less depressed than raped women who did not. They were less likely to take the blame for the rape (e.g., attribute it to some personality defect of their own). *There was no evidence that physical resistance significantly increased the use of force by the rapist.*

VICTIM SERVICES

As a result of advocacy by women's groups and increased public awareness of the difficulties faced by rape victims, many victim counseling and assistance programs have been developed since the 1970s. Most of these programs are run by nonprofit groups that rely partially or wholly on grants, charitable contributions, or funding by local, state, or federal government agencies. An excellent example is provided by Philadelphia's Women Organized against Rape (WOAR) (Urban Archives, 1999).

WOAR is a social service and social change organization established as a nonprofit corporation in May 1973 with three major goals: (1) to eliminate rape, (2) to provide needed support and referral to victims of rape, and (3) to empower women to gain control over their lives. Since its inception, WOAR has adopted a feminist interpretation of rape and its effects on victims:

> In short, the socialization of women is a continual exercise in restriction by fear which makes it a struggle for women to fulfill their potential as human beings. WOAR unites women who wish to work actively to eliminate rape and thus help create a healthy and enlightened environment for women. (Urban Archives, 1999)

Rape victims and their families often need specialized support and counseling to deal with the medical, legal, and personal aftermaths of rape. WOAR provides information and support to allow victims to understand the professional and institutional services and processes confronting them and to make informed choices about their options. Services include crisis counseling and support 24 hours a day through a telephone hotline, crisis counseling, and support through hospital emergency room accompaniment, accompaniment and advocacy for survivors at court, and individual and group counseling for survivors and their families.

WOAR staff and experienced volunteers provide counseling and support for victims and survivors receiving medical treatment at Philadelphia hospitals. Because court proceedings can be confusing and upsetting for sexual assault victims and survivors, and especially so for child and adolescent survivors and their families, WOAR staff and experienced volunteers provide accompaniment, information, and support for survivors at preliminary hearings, trials, and sentencings. WOAR provides individual and group counseling services for women, girls, men, and boys who have experienced sexual victimization. WOAR's confidential counseling services are provided free of charge. Support groups are generally conducted for 10 sessions and are led by experienced WOAR counselors. They also offer counseling for the parents and other family members of victims.

One counselor described an individual counseling session with a female client in her mid-30s (Philadelphia Inquirer, 1997). She had been seeing this client for a number of months to help her deal with being sexually abused throughout her childhood and teenage years by an adult male (a family acquaintance). They began with some breathing and relaxation exercises to calm the client. She was able to talk about some images—smells, touches, sounds—that still trigger uncomfortable flashbacks (e.g., seeing a man and a child together, the feel of facial hair, the smell of alcohol on a man's breath). She said her body felt completely numb as she talked about these memories. The counselor remarked how much courage it takes to will oneself to discuss the details of old wounds.

Another counselor described a meeting with a teenage rape victim scheduled to go to court the next day for her preliminary hearing. The girl was so nervous and anxious that the counselor was worried that she might not be able to testify. The victim was terrified of the perpetrator, and the thought of having to see him in court and explain what he did to her made her very scared. The counselor set up a pretend courtroom in the office so that the victim could practice some relaxation techniques to help reduce her anxiety (Philadelphia Inquirer, 1997).

WOAR also brings educational programs about sexual assault and personal safety to children and adults in classrooms, community centers, and workplaces throughout Philadelphia. It distributes brochures and other informational materials on rape and child sexual abuse, available in English and in Spanish. WOAR also provides specific training and information to medical, legal, and counseling personnel who serve rape victims, to improve the timeliness, sensitivity, and substance of these services (Urban Archives, 1999).

SEXUAL VIOLENCE EDUCATION

Based on a public health model, more men have become participants in diverse educational programs aimed at sexual assault prevention. However, such programs still represent only a small minority of all educational programs, and little is known about how effective such programs are in reducing attitudes and behaviors supportive of violence (see also Berkowitz, 2004a, 2004b; Morrison et al., 2004).

One of the more promising efforts involves a research and education project in Australia that seeks positive ways to engage young men in avoiding violence within sexual relationships (Carmody, 2013). The *Sex & Ethics Violence Prevention Program* was designed to assist both young women and men aged 16 to 26 to develop enhanced ethical sexual subjectivity and help them to explore gender attitudes and behaviors in their intimate relationships. The curriculum was based upon reviews of the existing literature and interviews with young people about their needs in relation to both sexuality and violence prevention education (Carmody, 2009a, 2009b).

The program aims to reduce unwanted and pressured sex, without diminishing positive sexual experiences. This alternative approach sees young people as having agency and the ability to negotiate their sexual lives. The program runs for six weeks (two to three hours per week) and locates the individual knowledge and skills that young people learn within a broader sociocultural context of gendered relations. It challenges them to reflect on expectations of sex in their relationships and ways to actively resist dominant beliefs that may promote or condone sexual violence. Participants are given the opportunity to practice and develop knowledge and skills. Topics covered include different cultural perspectives on sexual intimacy; the sexual ethics framework and how people can decide what is right for them and the impact their behavior has on others; how to handle pressures to be sexual; nonverbal communication skills; alcohol and drugs and their impact on sexual decision making; skills in ethical consent and the law; ethical use of social media and technology; negotiating conflicting desires and needs in casual and ongoing relationships; recognizing the signs of abusive relationships; breaking up; and being an ethical bystander and standing up to sexual violence and other gender-based abuse in the community.

Several methods were used to evaluate the program (Carmody, 2013; Carmody & Ovenden, 2013). A short standardized survey was administered at three time periods: (a) before the program, (b) at program completion, and (c) at a follow-up four to six months later. Questions focused on attitudes and behaviors related to both self-care and care for one's partner. The follow-up survey provided an option for open-ended, extended responses to several additional questions. Compared to before the program, at the end of the program and at the follow-up, men indicated a higher level of understanding regarding their own needs in sexual relationships. However, the largest increase was in their understanding of their *partners' needs* in sexual relationships. Findings thus challenged some traditional views of male sexuality as primarily act-driven and self-focused, and provided optimism that many men would be willing to challenge potential sexual aggression by other men. Qualitative data also provided some good examples of effectiveness. For example, men were asked the three most important things in negotiating sex. Responses included: "ensuring that both of us really want to do it;" "respecting the other person's decision;" "both parties know what the other's intentions and feelings are;" and "it's important to check in with the other person to clarify each other's expectations."

A major challenge in preventing sexual violence has been how to engage men as allies rather than treating them solely as potential perpetrators. Many sexuality programs have failed to address what young women and men want and need to know about negotiating sex, dealing with conflicting expectations in relationships, and exploring alternative ways to "express gender." Evaluation results demonstrated significant shifts in attitudes and behaviors over time, and detailed responses to an anonymous e-mail survey six months later suggested that participants were not merely providing researchers with socially desirable responses. At the same time, however, more research is needed with larger and more diverse groups of men to understand how culture, sexuality, socioeconomic status, and other factors may affect men's willingness to address sexual and gendered violence (Carmody, 2013).

A comprehensive community educational and policy strategy to reduce sexual assault on U.S. campuses was announced by a White House Task Force established by U.S. President Barack Obama on January 22, 2014, with a mandate to strengthen federal enforcement efforts and provide schools with additional tools to combat sexual assault on their campuses (White House Task Force to Protect Students from Sexual Assault, 2014). The task force announced a series of actions intended to (1) identify the scope of the problem on college campuses, (2) help prevent campus sexual assault, (3) help schools respond effectively when a student is assaulted, and (4) improve, and make more transparent, the federal government's enforcement efforts. The task force will continue to pursue additional executive or legislative actions in the future. One key feature introduced so far is a dedicated website (www.NotAlone.gov) that makes enforcement data public and provides other resources to students and schools. Students can learn about their rights, search enforcement data, and read about how to file a complaint. The website will also help schools and advocates by making available federal guidance on legal obligations, best available evidence and research, and relevant legislation. The website will also feature resources such as hotline numbers and mental health services locatable by typing in a ZIP code.

SEX OFFENDER TREATMENT PROGRAMS

No unanimous expert opinion exists about the effectiveness of sex offender treatment. Different approaches are used in different states, and different emphases on treatment versus punishment have characterized responses to sex offenders over time. Many research studies have suffered from a shortage of convincing empirical data, inadequate sample sizes and research designs, and inadequate follow-up periods of offenders released back into society (Furby et al., 1989). The better studies, however, suggest promising results (Hanson et al., 2002; Lösel & Schmucker, 2005; Polizzi et al., 1999).

Polizzi and colleagues (1999) used meta-analytic techniques to assess the results of 25 studies that evaluated the effectiveness of various treatment techniques for sex offenders. They found that overall, sex offender treatment resulted in lower posttreatment sex offense rates.

A review by Hanson and colleagues (2002) summarized data from 43 studies examining the effectiveness of psychological treatment for sex offenders. Sexual offenders who received treatment (n = 5,078) were compared to control groups of sexual offenders who received no treatment (n = 4,376). Offenders were tracked for an average of 46 months to examine recidivism. Sex offenders who received some form of psychological treatment had a lower sex offense recidivism rate (12.3%) than offenders who received no treatment (16.8%). Results for general recidivism were similar. Of offenders who received treatment, 27.9% were convicted for subsequent crimes, compared to 39.2% of those who received no treatment.

Using stringent criteria for study inclusion, Lösel and Schmucker (2005) analyzed the results of 69 studies (n = 22,181) and found a 6.4% reduction in sexual recidivism, a 5.2% reduction in violent recidivism, and an 11.1% reduction in general recidivism for treated sexual offenders relative to the comparison group. Cognitive-behavioral treatment was found to be the most effective type of intervention.

Newer programs typically use a combination of cognitive and behavioral approaches, and a consensus is developing that successful treatment models must address deviant sexual interests, social skills deficits, and cognitive distortions about sexual offending (Burdon & Gallagher, 2002; Marques & Nelson, 1992; Polizzi et al., 1999). We will use two examples, from Vermont and California, to illustrate how sex offender treatment programs work.

The Vermont Treatment Program for Sexual Aggressors was created by a special appropriation from the state legislature in 1982 (Pithers et al., 1989). The program includes three residential treatment sites (prison) and 20 outpatient sites (in the community). The program is multimodal, including individual and group psychotherapy, substance abuse counseling, vocational training, behavioral interventions, and psychohormonal therapies. Offenders learn cognitive and behavioral skills to reduce the likelihood of reoffending. One requirement for eligibility is that offenders accept responsibility for their crimes. An extensive battery of psychological and physiological assessment procedures is used to identify and target specific cognitive and behavioral patterns for change.

Treatment generally begins with victim empathy groups, to encourage the offender to acknowledge the harm done to his victim and recognize the victim as a thinking, feeling person. Treatment moves on to training in specific sets of skills, including social skills, sexual knowledge, emotional management skills, and decision-making processes. Treatment then focuses on helping clients recognize the events, emotions, fantasies, and thoughts that typically accompany a relapse to sexual aggression. Offenders learn specific skills and strategies for coping with these triggers and lowering the risk of reoffending. Group therapy focuses on issues of personal victimization (e.g., sexual and/or physical abuse in one's own past), cognitive distortions (e.g., rape myths), behavioral therapies, problem-solving skills, and transition from prison to community life. Individual therapy is also offered on a selective basis.

To qualify for outpatient (i.e., community) treatment, offenders must demonstrate consistent progress in cognitive and behavioral change. Clients must be able to describe the situations that increase their individual risk of reoffending. For each of these situations, clients must be able to verbalize or role-play coping responses that reduce the chance of sexual aggression. They must be able to anticipate new high-risk situations and develop effective coping responses. Clients need to demonstrate that they can perceive, report, and modify an appropriate range of emotions, expressing these emotions verbally and appropriately rather than sexually. Clients must show an understanding and respect that each person has the right to define his or her own sexual role. Finally, they must demonstrate (through physiological measures) a decrease of sexual arousal to deviant sexual stimuli and increased arousal to appropriate stimuli (e.g., consensual sexual behavior between adults). If progress continues in outpatient treatment, the client eventually may qualify for work release, where he is closely monitored and supervised in the community, and, subsequently, parole.

Although strict control groups were not used to evaluate treatment programs, the study's authors report slightly lower rates of relapse compared to less intensive forms of treatment (Pithers et al., 1989).

California's Sex Offender Treatment and Evaluation Project (SOTEP) also uses a relapse-prevention model that emphasizes teaching specific cognitive and behavioral skills to reduce the likelihood of recidivism (Marques & Nelson, 1992). The relapse prevention perspective emphasizes two major steps: (1) identify the steps that increase the risk of relapse and (2) develop, plan, and practice coping responses to the unique factors that increase each offender's risk of reoffending. Multiple risk elements must be identified and addressed for each individual offender. These risk factors may be environmental (e.g., access to potential victims in particular places or at particular times, interpersonal stressors) or intrapersonal (e.g., deviant sexual arousal patterns, negative emotional states, drug or alcohol intoxication, and cognitive distortions and misinterpretations). This program was created in 1985, four years after the state legislature required that all convicted rapists and child molesters be incarcerated by the Department of Corrections rather than face commitment to state hospitals for treatment. According to law, however, offenders can be transferred to a state Department of Health facility during the last two years of their prison terms. The SOTEP treatment project is housed in a 46-bed unit at Atascadero State Hospital.

Evaluations of the SOTEP program were conducted by Marques and Nelson (1992) and Marques, Miederanders, Day, Nelson, and van Ommeren (2005). In the selection phase, project staff screened and recruited inmates who met eligibility criteria. Eligibility was restricted to male inmates convicted of one or more offenses of rape or child molestation and inmates who were between 18 and 30 months of their release from prison, had no more than two felony convictions, admitted their offense, had IQs greater than 80, were between 18 and 60 years of age, spoke English, lacked serious medical or mental illness, and did not present serious management problems in prison. Qualified inmates who volunteered were then matched on the characteristics of type of offense, age, and criminal history, and they were randomly assigned to either the treatment group ($n = 259$) or the volunteer control group ($n = 225$). A third group, the nonvolunteer control group ($n = 225$), consisted of qualified inmates who did not volunteer. Only 20% of eligible offenders actually volunteered for the program (low volunteer rates for sex offender treatment programs typically weaken the generalizability of results to other sex offenders). Volunteers were somewhat more likely than the total population of incarcerated sex offenders to be child molesters rather than rapists, and were slightly younger and less violent.

In an initial evaluation over a one-year period, several in-treatment clinical improvements were observed (Marques & Nelson, 1992): decreases in the use of justifications and cognitive distortions associated with sexual aggression, fewer symptoms of depression and social introversion, and reductions in deviant patterns of sexual arousal. In an eight-year follow-up study, however, no significant effect on recidivism was found overall or for sex offenses specifically. Unlike many other studies, Marques and his colleagues used rigorous experimental procedures to randomly assign subjects to treatment and control groups. While normally the gold standard for evaluation studies, Marshall and Marshall (2007) contend that the use of strict randomization procedures with this population may have resulted in dissimilar comparison groups, and reduced the likelihood of detecting a significant treatment effect. Needless to say, studies that use large samples, rigorous experimental procedures, and long follow-up periods to evaluate the effects of sex offender treatment programs are in short supply.

CONCLUSIONS

Definitions of rape and sexual assault have changed substantially over time, largely in response to advocacy by women's groups. Measurement of these offenses has also improved, although many crimes still go unreported. Rape victims are disproportionately young, while offenders are typically white males between the ages of 18 and 44. Victims and offenders frequently knew one another prior to the offense. Rapes and sexual assaults have decreased gradually over the past 15 years, although rates are still high.

Many different causes have been suggested, but major theories focus either on the individual rapist (e.g., psychodynamic and social learning theories) or the sociocultural forces that maintain or justify coercive male sexual behavior (e.g., feminist theories). Responses to rape and sexual assault have often been contradictory and ambiguous. Changes in legal responses to rape since the 1970s have been most dramatic, although it is not clear that victims have greatly benefited from rape law reforms. Victim assistance and counseling programs are now widespread but often lack stable resources to meet the needs of their clients.

Sex offender treatment programs in recent years show promise, but offenders must be willing to admit responsibility for their offense and demonstrate consistent cognitive and behavioral change prior to release. Comprehensive treatment of sex offenders can significantly lower rates of reoffending and reincarceration, but stronger evaluation research is still needed to determine the range and magnitude of treatment effects over time. There is little doubt that punishment alone provides inadequate protection against sex offenders.

DISCUSSION QUESTIONS

1. Define the following: (a) rape, (b) sexual assault, (c) rape-prone societies, and (d) rape shield laws.
2. Is rape in the United States increasing or decreasing? How can you tell? Give specific evidence to support your argument.
3. Describe major characteristics of rape and sexual assault *offenders, victims,* and *incidents.*
4. Discuss how each of the following explains rape: (a) *psychiatric perspectives,* (b) *feminist theories,* (c) *social cognitive theories, and* (d) *multifactor theories.* In your answer, describe specific *arguments* associated with each theory, and provide specific *evidence* for each theory.

5. Describe each of the following intervention strategies. Explain *how* it attempts to reduce rape or sexual assault, and summarize any *evidence of its effectiveness*: (a) rape law reform, (b) incarceration, (c) sex offender notification and registration laws, (d) victim resistance, (e) victim services, (f) sexual assault education, and (g) sex offender treatment. Give specific examples from course materials to support your answer.

SUGGESTED READINGS

Drake, E. K., & Aos, S. (2009). *Does sex offender registration and notification reduce crime? A systematic review of the research literature*. Olympia, WA: Washington State Institute for Public Policy, Document No. 09-06-1101. Available at http://www.wsipp.wa.gov/ReportFile/1043.

LaFree, G. (1989). *Rape and criminal justice: The social construction of sexual assault*. Belmont, CA: Wadsworth.

Sanday, P. R. (1990). *Fraternity gang rape: Sex, brotherhood and privilege on campus*. New York: New York University Press.

Ward, T., Polaschek, D. L. L., & Beech, A. R. (2006). *Theories of sexual offending*. Chichester, UK: Wiley.

NOTES

1. The Jacob Wetterling Crimes against Children and Sexually Violent Offender Registration Act, Public L. No. 103-322, §170101, 108 Stat. 2038 (1994). See also Final Guidelines for the Jacob Wetterling Crimes against Children and Sexually Violent Offender Registration Act, 61 Fed. Reg. 15110 (April 4, 1996).
2. 42 U.S.C. §16901 (2006), *et. seq.* Two sets of guidelines have been issued to assist in the implementation of SORNA: The National Guidelines for Sex Offender Registration and Notification, 73 Fed. Reg. 38030 (July 2, 2008) and Supplemental Guidelines for Sex Offender Registration and Notification, 76 Fed. Reg. 1630 (Jan. 11, 2011).

REFERENCES

Bart, P. B., & O'Brien, P. H. (1985). *Stopping rape: Successful survival strategies*. New York: Pergamon.

Berkowitz, A. (2004a). *Working with men to prevent violence: An overview (Part One)*. Harrisburg, PA: VAWnet, a project of the National Resource Center on Domestic Violence/Pennsylvania Coalition Against Domestic Violence. Retrieved May 2, 2014, from http://www.vawnet.org.

Berkowitz, A. (2004b). *Working with men to prevent violence against women: Program modalities and formats (Part Two)*. Harrisburg, PA: VAWnet, a project of the National Resource Center on Domestic Violence/Pennsylvania Coalition Against Domestic Violence. Retrieved May 2, 2014, from: http://www.vawnet.org.

Bienen, L. (1980). National developments in rape reform legislation. *Women's Rights Law Reporter, 6*, 171–213.

Brownmiller, S. (1975). *Against our will: Men, women, and rape. New York: Simon & Schuster.*

Burdon, W. M., & Gallagher, C. A. (2002). Coercion and sex offenders: Controlling sex-offending behavior through incapacitation and treatment. *Criminal Justice and Behavior, 29*, 87–109.

Bureau of Justice Statistics (BJS). (2011). *Criminal victimization in the United States—Statistical tables index*. Retrieved May 1, 2014, from http://www.bjs.gov/content/pub/html/cvus/index.cfm.

Bureau of Justice Statistics (BJS). (2014a). *Terms & definitions: Crime type.* Available at http://www.bjs.gov/index.cfm?ty=tdtp&tid=3.

Bureau of Justice Statistics (BJS). (2014b). Number of rape/sexual assaults by victim-offender relationship and sex, 2012. Generated May 1, 2014, using the NCVS Victimization Analysis Tool at http://www.bjs.gov.

Bureau of Justice Statistics (BJS). (2014c). Percent of rape/sexual assaults by reporting to the police, 2012. Generated May 1, 2014, using the NCVS Victimization Analysis Tool at http://www.bjs.gov.

Bureau of Justice Statistics (BJS). (2014d). Percent of rape/sexual assaults by sex, 2012. Generated May 1, 2014, using the NCVS Victimization Analysis Tool at http://www.bjs.gov.

Bureau of Justice Statistics (BJS). (2014e). Rates of rape/sexual assaults by household income and race, 2012. Generated May 1, 2014, using the NCVS Victimization Analysis Tool at http://www.bjs.gov.

Bureau of Justice Statistics (BJS). (2014f). Rates of rape/sexual assaults by age, 2012. Generated May 2, 2014, using the NCVS Victimization Analysis Tool at http://www.bjs.gov.

Bureau of Justice Statistics (BJS). (2014g). Percent of rape/sexual assaults by injury and medical treatment for physical injuries, 2012. Generated May 2, 2014, using the NCVS Victimization Analysis Tool at http://www.bjs.gov.

Burt, M. (1980). Cultural myths and support for rape. *Journal of Personality and Social Psychology, 38*, 217–230.

Burt, M. (1983). Justifying personal violence: A comparison of rapists and the general public. *Victimology, 8*, 131–150.

Caringella-MacDonald, S. (1985). The comparability in sexual and nonsexual assault case treatment: Did statute change meet the objective? *Crime and Delinquency, 31*, 206–222.

Carmody, M. (2009a). *Sex and ethics: Young people and ethical sex.* South Yarra: Palgrave Macmillan.

Carmody, M. (2009b). *Sex and ethics: The sexual ethics education program for young people.* South Yarra: Palgrave Macmillan.

Carmody, M. (2013). Young men, sexual ethics and sexual negotiation. *Sociological Research Online, 18*(2), 22. Available at http://www.socresonline.org.uk/18/2/22.html.

Carmody, M., & Ovenden, G. (2013). Putting ethical sex into practice: Sexual negotiation, gender and citizenship in the lives of young women and men. *Journal of Youth Studies, 16*, 792–807.

Douglas, J. E., Burgess, A. W., Burgess, A. G., & Ressler, R. K. (1997). *Crime classification manual: A standard system for investigating and classifying violent crimes* (rev. ed.). San Francisco: Jossey-Bass.

Drake, E. K., & Aos, S. (2009). *Does sex offender registration and notification reduce crime? A systematic review of the research literature.* Olympia, WA: Washington State Institute for Public Policy, Document No. 09-06-1101. Available at http://www.wsipp.wa.gov/ReportFile/1043.

Ellis, L. (1989). *Theories of rape: Inquiries into the causes of sexual aggression.* New York: Hemisphere.

Federal Bureau of Investigation (FBI). (2009). *Crime in the United States 2008.* Retrieved December 21, 2009, from http://www.fbi.gov/ucr/cius2008/index.html.

Federal Bureau of Investigation (FBI). (2012). *Crime in the United States 2012.* Available at http://www.fbi.gov/about-us/cjis/ucr/crime-in-the-u.s/2012/crime-in-the-u.s.-2012.

Federal Bureau of Investigation (FBI). (2013a). *Frequently asked questions about the change in the UCR definition of rape.* Washington, DC: U.S. Department of Justice, Federal Bureau of Investigation. Available at http://www.fbi.gov/about-us/cjis/ucr.

Federal Bureau of Investigation (FBI). (2013b). *National Incident-Based Reporting System (NIBRS), User Manual Version 1.0.* Washington, DC: U.S. Department of Justice, Federal Bureau of Investigation. Available at http://www.fbi.gov/about-us/cjis/ucr.

Finkelhor, D. (1984). *Child sexual abuse: New theory and research.* New York: Free Press.

Furby, L., Weinrott, M., & Blackshaw, L. (1989). Sex offender recidivism: A review. *Psychological Bulletin, 105,* 3–30.

Gannon, T. A., Collie, R. M., Ward, T., & Thakker, J. (2008). Rape: Psychopathology, theory and treatment. *Clinical Psychology Review, 28,* 982–1008.

Gilmartin, P. (1994). *Rape, incest, and child sexual abuse.* New York: Garland.

Greenfeld, L. A. (1997). *Sex offenses and offenders: An analysis of data on rape and sexual assault* (NCJ-163392). Washington, DC: Department of Justice, Office of Justice Programs.

Groth, A. N. (1990). Rape: Behavioral aspects. In N. A. Weiner, M. A. Zahn, & R. J. Sagi (Eds.), *Violence: Patterns, causes, public policy* (pp. 73–79). San Diego, CA: Harcourt, Brace, Jovanovich.

Groth, A. N., & Binbaum, H. J. (1979). *Men who rape: The psychology of the offender.* New York: Plenum.

Hanson, R. K., Gordon, A., Harris, A. J. R., Marques, J. K., Murphy, W., Quinsey, V. L., & Seto, M. C. (2002). First report of the Collaborative Outcome Data Project on the effectiveness of psychological treatment for sex offenders. *Sexual Abuse, 14,* 169–194.

Hazelwood, R. R., & Burgess, A. W. (Eds.). (2001). *Practical aspects of rape investigation: A multidisciplinary approach* (3rd ed.). Boca Raton, FL: CRC Press.

Humphrey, S. E., & Kahn, A. S. (2000). Fraternities, athletic teams, and rape. *Journal of Interpersonal Violence, 15*(12), 1313–1320.

Jackson, A., Veneziano, L., & Riggen, K. (2004). Sexual deviance among male college students. *Journal of Interpersonal Violence, 19*(1), 72–89.

Koss, M. P. (1988). Hidden rape: Sexual aggression and victimization of students in higher education. In A. W. Burgess (Ed.), *Rape and sexual assault* (Vol. 2, pp. 3–25). New York: Garland.

Koss, M. P. (1992). Defending date rape. *Journal of Interpersonal Violence, 7*(1), 122–126.

Koss, M. P. (1993). Rape: Scope, impact, interventions, and public policy responses. *American Psychologist, 48*(10), 1062–1069.

Koss, M. P., Gidycz, C., & Wisiniewski, N. (1987). The scope of rape: Incidence and prevalence of sexual aggression and victimization in a sample of higher education students. *Journal of Consulting and Clinical Psychology, 55,* 162–170.

Koss, M. P., & Harvey, M. H. (1991). *The rape victim: Clinical and community interventions* (2nd ed.). Newbury Park, CA: Sage.

Krebs, C. P., Lindquist, C. H., Warner, T. D., Fisher, B. S., & Martin, S. L. (2007). *The Campus Sexual Assault (CSA) study: Final report.* Washington, DC: National Institute of Justice (NIJ Grant No. 2004-WG-BX-0010).

Krebs, C. P., Lindquist, C. H., Warner, T. D., Fisher, B. S., & Martin, S. L. (2009). College women's experiences with physically forced, alcohol- or other drug-enabled and drug-facilitated sexual assault before and since entering college. *Journal of American College Health, 57*(6), 639–647.

KRON-TV. (1996). Date rape drug. Aired: June 19, 1996. KRON-TV, Prince William, VA. Available at http://www.kron.com/nc4/use/stories/daterape.htm.

Kruttschnitt, C. (1994). Gender and interpersonal violence. In A. J. Reiss, Jr. & J. Roth (Eds.), *Understanding and preventing violence: Social influences* (Vol. 3). Washington, DC: National Academy Press.

LaFree, G. (1989). *Rape and criminal justice: The social construction of sexual assault.* Belmont, CA: Wadsworth.

Langan, P. A., Schmitt, E. L., & Durose, M. R. (2003). *Recidivism of sex offenders released from prison in 1994* (NCJ 198281). Washington, DC: U.S. Department of Justice, Bureau of Justice Statistics.

Lösel, F., & Schmucker, M. (2005). The effectiveness of treatment for sexual offenders: A comprehensive meta-analysis. *Journal of Experimental Criminology, 1,* 117–146.

Malamuth, N. (1981). Rape proclivity among males. *Journal of Social Issues, 37,* 138–157.

Malamuth, N. (1984). Aggression against women: Cultural and individual causes. In N. M. Malamuth & E. Donnerstein (Eds.), *Pornography and sexual aggression* (pp. 19–52). New York: Academic.

Malamuth, N. (1986). Predictors of naturalistic sexual aggression. *Journal of Personality and Social Psychology, 50,* 953–962.

Malamuth, N. (1996). The confluence model of sexual aggression: Feminist and evolutionary perspectives. In D. B. Buss & N. M. Malamuth (Eds.), *Sex, power, conflict: evolutionary and feminist perspectives* (pp. 269–295). New York: Oxford University Press.

Malesky, A., & Keim, J. (2001). Mental health professionals' perspectives on sex offender registry web sites. *Sexual Abuse, 13*(1), 53–63.

Marques, J. K., Miederanders, M., Day, D. M., Nelson, C., & van Ommeren, A. (2005). Effects of a relapse prevention program on sexual recidivism: Final results from California's Sex Offender Treatment and Evaluation Project (SOTEP). *Sexual Abuse, 17,* 79–107.

Marques, J. K., & Nelson, C. (1992). The relapse prevention model: Can it work with sex offenders? In R. D. Peters, R. J. McMahon, & V. L. Quinsey (Eds.), *Aggression and violence throughout the lifespan* (pp. 222–243). Newbury Park, CA: Sage.

Marsh, J. C., Geist, A., & Caplan, N. (1982). *Rape and limits of law reform.* Boston: Auburn House.

Marshall, W. L., & Marshall, L. E. (2007). The utility of the random controlled trial for evaluating sexual offender treatment: The gold standard or an inappropriate strategy? *Sexual Abuse, 19,* 175–191.

Michael, R. T., Gagnon, J. H., Laumann, E. O., & Kolata, G. (1994). *Sex in America: A definitive survey.* Boston: Little, Brown & Co.

Morrison, S., Hardison, J., Mathew, A., & O'Neil, J., (2004). *An evidence-based review of sexual assault preventive intervention programs* (NCJ 207262). Washington, DC: National Institute of Justice, U.S. Department of Justice. Available at https://www.ncjrs.gov/pdffiles1/nij/grants/207262.pdf.

Muehlenhard, C. L., & Hollabaugh, L. C. (1988). Do women sometimes say no when they mean yes? The prevalence and correlates of women's token resistance to sex. *Journal of Personality and Social Psychology, 54,* 872–879.

Nussbaum, P. (2004, Sept. 2). Bryant rape charge dropped. *Philadelphia Inquirer,* A1.

Philadelphia Inquirer. (1997, March 16). Community voices: Working with WOAR. *The Philadelphia Inquirer,* p. E05.

Pithers, W. D., Martin, G. R., & Cumming, G. F. (1989). Vermont treatment program for sexual aggressors. In D. R. Laws (Ed.), *Relapse prevention with sex offenders* (pp. 292–310). New York: Guilford.

Polizzi, D. M., MacKenzie, D. L., & Hickman, L. J. (1999). What works in adult sex offender treatment? A review of prison- and non-prison-based treatment programs. *International Journal of Offender Therapy and Comparative Criminology, 43,* 357–374.

Polk, K. (1985). Rape reform and criminal justice processing. *Crime and Delinquency, 31,* 191–205.

Russell, D. E. (1984). *Sexual exploitation, rape, child sexual abuse, and workplace harassment.* Beverly Hills, CA: Sage.

Sanday, P. R. (1981). The sociocultural context of rape: A cross-cultural study. *Journal of Social Issues, 37,* 5–27.

Sanday, P. R. (1990). *Fraternity gang rape: Sex, brotherhood and privilege on campus*. New York: New York University Press.

Sanday, P. R. (1996). *A woman scorned: Acquaintance rape on trial*. Berkeley, CA: University of California Press.

Sarche, J. (2005, March 3). Bryant and accuser reach settlement in civil lawsuit. *Philadelphia Inquirer*, p. A02.

Scully, D., & Marolla, J. (1984). Convicted rapists' vocabulary of motive: Excuses and justifications. *Social Problems, 31*, 530–544.

Scully, D., & Marolla, J. (1985). Riding the bull at Gilley's: Convicted rapists describe the rewards of rape. *Social Problems, 32*, 251–263.

Sykes, G., & Matza, D. (1957). Techniques of neutralization: A theory of delinquency. *American Journal of Sociology, 22*, 664–670.

Truman, J., Langton, L., & Planty, M. (2013). *Criminal victimization, 2012* (NCJ-243389). Washington, DC: U.S. Department of Justice, Office of Justice Programs.

Urban Archives, Temple University Libraries. (1999). *Women Organized Against Rape (WOAR). Records, 1972*. Retrieved July 28, 2006, from http://www.library.temple.edu/collections/urbana/woar-tp.jsp?bhcp=1.

U.S. Department of Justice. (2013). *Sex offender registration and notification in the United States: Current case law and issues*. Washington, DC: U.S. Department of Justice, Office of Justice Programs, Office of Sex Offender Sentencing, Monitoring, Apprehending, Registering, and Tracking. Available at http://www.smart.gov/caselaw.htm.

U.S. Government Accountability Office. (2013). *Sex Offender Registration and Notification Act: Jurisdictions face challenges to implementing the act, and stakeholders report positive and negative effects* (GAO-13-211). Washington, DC: Author. Available at http://www.gao.gov/assets/660/652032.pdf.

Ward, T., & Beech, T. (2005). An integrated theory of sexual offending. *Aggression and Violent Behavior, 11*, 44–63.

Ward, T., & Hudson, S. M. (1998). A model of the relapse process in sexual offenders. *Journal of Interpersonal Violence, 13*, 700–725.

Ward, T., Polaschek, D. L. L., & Beech, A. R. (2006). *Theories of sexual offending*. Chichester, UK: Wiley.

Weis, K., & Borges, S. (1975). Victimology and rape: The case of the legitimate victim. In L. G. Schultz (Ed.), *Rape victimology* (pp. 91–141). Springfield, IL: Charles C. Thomas.

White House Task Force to Protect Students from Sexual Assault. (2014, April). *Not alone: The first report of the White House Task Force to Protect Students From Sexual Assault*. Retrieved May 3, 2014, from http://www.whitehouse.gov/sites/default/files/docs/report_0.pdf.

CHAPTER 7

HATE CRIMES

Every year thousands of men and women are targeted and attacked because of their race, religion, ethnicity/national origin, disability, or sexual orientation. A few of these incidents make national headlines, while others are largely ignored by the media. But what is a *hate crime* exactly, and why do people commit such acts? In the examples below, try to find any common elements in regard to the victims, offenders, and incidents.

---

1. On October 6, 1998, two men accompanied 21-year-old University of Wyoming student Matthew Shepard as he left a Laramie tavern. They crushed his skull after beating him with a pistol, and left him strung up on a fence outside town. Shepard, discovered a day later by a passing bicyclist, never regained consciousness and died six days later. Police believed that Shepard was targeted at least partly because he was an openly gay man (Southern Poverty Law Center [SPLC], 1999), although recent evidence strongly suggests that the victim and one of the killers knew each other quite well prior to the attack, and both were heavily involved in the use and trafficking of methamphetamine (Jimenez, 2013).
2. On a November evening in 1988 in Portland, Oregon, Mulugeta Seraw, an Ethiopian graduate student, was being dropped off by two friends. Three skinheads from a group called East Side White Pride spotted them. The skinheads blocked the Ethiopians' path and ordered them to move. When the Ethiopians did not respond immediately, one of the skinheads took a baseball bat and smashed their car windows. Another skinhead attacked Seraw with a bat and crushed his skull with repeated blows. Seraw died on the scene before an ambulance arrived (Dees & Bowden, 2001).
3. On June 7, 1998, a group of white men in Jasper, Texas, abducted black hitchhiker James Byrd Jr., 49, as he walked down the road. They chained him by the ankles to the rear of a pickup truck and dragged him several miles down a country road. What remained of Byrd's body was discovered the next morning. Police arrested Lawrence Russell Brewer, 31, and two 21-year-olds, Shawn Berry and John William King, who reportedly told companions: "We're starting *The Turner Diaries* early." The reference was to a neo-Nazi novel about an impending race war. King and Brewer, both ex-convicts, had white supremacist tattoos on their bodies (SPLC, 1999).
4. On a July evening in 1998, at Hayden Lake, Idaho, Victoria Keenan and her teenage son, Jason, were driving past the 22-acre Aryan Nations compound when their car backfired, a sound that Aryan Nations security guards apparently mistook for a gunshot. A truckload of guards gave chase, firing shots until the Keenans' car went into a ditch. Jesse Warfield, then chief of security, pulled Keenan by the hair and threatened to kill her. The other guards beat her son (Dees & Bowden, 2001).
5. Two black 17-year-olds, Raheem Williams and his cousin Warren, were walking home from the 24-hour Pathmark

(continued)

(continued)

store on Grays Ferry Avenue in Philadelphia just after midnight in February 1997. They encountered a sole white man in a black leather jacket and blue jeans standing on the corner at St. Gabriel's Social Hall, a center of community life for white, Irish-Catholic residents in Grays Ferry. A "beef and beer" party was winding down inside. "Got anything in that bag for me?" Raheem said the man asked. "You're drunk," Raheem said. "Why don't you go home and sleep it off?" Words were exchanged, then shoves and blows. The fight soon involved dozens of whites from inside the hall as well as Raheem's cousin and his mother, Annette Williams, who was punched and kicked on the porch of her home as she tried to intervene. Mrs. Williams was briefly hospitalized; her son and nephew were treated and released. Some whites claimed the incident was retaliation for an attack on a white man by blacks hours earlier; authorities never confirmed the earlier attack. This incident was followed by the March 14, 1997, slaying of white teen Christopher Brinkman (Dawsey et al., 1997). Brinkman was shot as robbers held up Squire Drugs, where he was a clerk. Two black men were arrested and charged with the crime. The funeral was held at St. Gabriel's Church. Over the next six weeks, racial tension threatened to boil over into a riot, with Minister Louis Farrakhan's Nation of Islam calling for a 5,000-man march through Grays Ferry and local white residents dismayed to see themselves labeled as violent racists (Bowden, 1997). In the attack on the Williams family, six white men were convicted on a variety of charges including ethnic intimidation, rioting, and making terroristic threats. The stiffest sentence was nine to 23 months in jail.

DEFINITIONS

A whole new category of crime was created with the passage in 1990 of the Hate Crime Statistics Act (HCSA; Jenness & Grattet, 2001), which for the first time required the collection of nationwide hate crime data. The goals of the HCSA were to gather information on the frequency, location, extent, and patterns of hate crime; increase law enforcement awareness of the problem and responses to it; raise public awareness of the problem; and send a message that the government is concerned about hate crime.

The HCSA requires the Department of Justice (through the Federal Bureau of Investigation [FBI]) to collect and report data on hate crimes involving the *predicate offenses* of murder, nonnegligent manslaughter, forcible rape, aggravated assault, simple assault, intimidation, arson, and vandalism. A predicate offense means two things: (1) a criminal offense has occurred, and (2) the offense was motivated wholly or in part by prejudice (Jacobs & Potter, 1997).[1]

The HCSA (28 U.S.C. § 534) defines hate crimes as "crimes that manifest evidence of prejudice based on race, gender or gender identity, religion, disability, sexual orientation, or ethnicity." *Bias*, according to FBI guidelines, is "a preformed negative opinion or attitude toward a group of persons based on their race, religion, ethnicity/national origin, or sexual orientation" (Jacobs & Potter, 1997). Lawmakers amended the HCSA in 1994 to include bias against persons with disabilities, and in 2009, Congress further amended the HCSA by passing the Matthew Shepard and James Byrd, Jr. Hate Crime Prevention Act (Wilson, 2014). The amendment included the collection of data for crimes motivated by bias against a particular gender and gender identity, as well as for crimes committed by, and crimes committed against, juveniles. The HCSA can be accessed at http://www2.fbi.gov/ucr/hc2009/hatecrimestatistics.html.

The term *hate crime* is somewhat confusing because it refers to criminal behavior motivated by prejudice. This label distinguishes criminal behavior motivated *by prejudice* from criminal behavior motivated by lust, jealousy, greed, and so forth (Jacobs & Potter, 1997). For criminal conduct to be a hate crime, then, it must be motivated by prejudice. The criminal conduct must be *causally related to the prejudice*. But how strong must that relationship be? If the hate crime must be wholly motivated by prejudice, there would be an extremely small number of such crimes. Prejudice is a complex concept, not easy to define in either legal or behavioral terms.

Passage of a new law requiring the collection and reporting of hate crime statistics is not sufficient to ensure reliable or meaningful data, although the FBI has expended considerable effort to train law enforcement agents in definitions and procedures. For example, two manuals were published: *Hate Crime Data Collection Guidelines* (FBI, 1990) and *Training Guide for Hate Crime Data Collection* (FBI, 1991). The training guide instructs police to answer 19 questions about an offense to determine whether to count it as a hate crime or not. Guidelines are often ambiguous, though (Jacobs & Potter, 1997). For example, they do not specify how much weight should be given to each of the 19 questions or how many questions need to be answered affirmatively for an incident to qualify as a hate crime.

Consider the following examples. First, FBI guidelines ask whether the victim is a member of a "target" racial, religious, ethnic or national origin, or sexual orientation group. But are all ethnic and religious groups target groups? Are whites in target groups? Second, guidelines ask whether offenders are of a different group than the victim. What if an offender is from the same group as the victim? Third, guidelines ask whether the incident would have taken place if the victim and offender were of the same group. This judgment seems to rely entirely on subjective perceptions of the police officer rather than objective evidence. Other guidelines ask the police officer to consider whether the neighborhood where the attack occurred has any previous history of such altercations, whether the victim is outnumbered significantly in a specific area, and whether there is any history of negative sentiment against a specific group. Again, such judgments may require historical and sociological analysis, and even affirmative answers beg the question about offender motivation. There remains considerable subjectivity, therefore, as to what gets defined, investigated, or eventually counted as a hate crime (Jacobs & Potter, 1997). It is often difficult to tell whether a given act was a hate crime or a senseless act of violence. Determining this would require one to actually know the motivation of the offender.

PATTERNS AND TRENDS

The Bureau of Justice Statistics' (BJS) National Crime Victimization Survey (NCVS) and the FBI's Uniform Crime Reports (UCR) Hate Crime Statistics Program are the principal sources of information on hate crime in the United States. As noted in Chapter 2, there are differences in how each counts crimes.

The NCVS has been collecting data on crimes motivated by hate since 2003. The NCVS measures crimes perceived by victims to be motivated by an offender's bias against them for belonging to or being associated with a group largely identified by these characteristics. For violent crimes (rape or sexual assault, robbery, aggravated assault, and simple assault) and for personal larceny, the count of hate crime victimizations is the number of individuals who experienced a violent hate crime. For crimes against households (burglary, motor vehicle theft, and other thefts), each household affected by a hate crime is counted as a single victimization. The NCVS collects data on hate crimes both reported and not reported to police and allows the victim to define whether a hate crime occurred.

The FBI's UCR has been collecting data on hate crimes known to the police since 1991. It includes offenses excluded from the NCVS, such as murder or nonnegligent manslaughter, intimidation, arson, vandalism, and crimes against institutions (e.g., churches, synagogues, and businesses). Like other types of crime, UCR estimates of the number of hate crimes reported to police tend to be much lower than NCVS estimates (see Chapter 2), but keep in mind that NCVS estimates are produced by victim perceptions of hate-motivated crimes, and most victims do not necessarily report these crimes to the police.

Many journalists, politicians, and academics have described a "hate crime epidemic," but no reliable empirical data exist to support this conclusion. Until 1990, the only data available were those provided by advocacy groups such as the Anti-Defamation League (ADL), the SPLC, and the Gay and Lesbian Anti-Violence Project. Several problems exist with these data: Each agency pays attention to only limited segments of the population; all lobby for increased attention to the problem; and all compete for scarce government or private funds to support their causes. Further, these agencies use diverse sources of data, including newspaper reports, victim reports to the agency, police data, and so on. There are two main reasons to be skeptical about the existence of an "epidemic": (1) criminologists are familiar with the considerable difficulties of trying to accurately measure crime (see Chapter 2) and (2) there have been numerous, vicious bias-motivated attacks against various groups throughout history (e.g., Native Americans, blacks, ethnic and religious groups, women, and homosexuals), as we saw in Chapter 3.

If we examine hate crimes measured by the FBI since 1990, reported hate crime incidents appear to have increased from 1991 to 2008 (Table 7.1). However, observable increases were due to some extent to an increase in the number of agencies and states reporting rather than a true increase in incidents. There was little change until 2001, when a sharp upward spike was recorded. The sharp 2001 increase in hate crime incidents has been attributed to anti-Muslim and anti-Middle Eastern backlash following the September 11 attacks on the World Trade Center, the Pentagon, and United Airlines Flight 93 (Associated Press, 2003; Disha et al., 2011; Shively, 2005). The number of known incidents targeting people, institutions, and businesses identified with the Islamic faith jumped from 28 in 2000 to 481 in 2001—a more than 1,600% increase. Only 155 such incidents were reported in 2002. Hate crimes directed against people because of their ethnicity or national origin—those not Hispanic and not black—more than quadrupled, from 354 in 2000 to 1,501 in 2001. This category includes people of Middle Eastern descent. This figure went down to 622 in 2002. Hate crimes measured by the UCR dropped sharply in 2002, and declined gradually from 2008 to 2012. According to the NCVS, however, no statistically significant change was observed in either the number of total hate crimes or violent hate crimes that occurred from 2004 to 2012 (Table 7.2).

According to the NCVS (Wilson, 2014), an estimated 293,800 violent and property hate crime victimizations occurred in 2012 against persons age 12 or older residing in U.S.

Table 7.1 Hate Crimes Reported to the FBI by Law Enforcement, 1991–2012

Year	Number of Hate Crime Incidents Reported	Number of States Reporting	Number of Law Enforcement Agencies Participating
1991	4,755	32	2,771
1992	7,466	41 + D.C.	6,181
1993	7,587	46 + D.C.	6,551
1994	5,852	43 + D.C.	7,200
1995	7,947	45 + D.C.	9,500
1996	8,759	49 + D.C.	11,000
1997	8,049	49 + D.C.	11,211
1998	7,755	46 + D.C.	10,730
1999	7,876	48 + D.C.	12,122
2000	8,063	48 + D.C.	11,690
2001	9,730	49 + D.C.	11,987
2002	7,462	49 + D.C.	12,073
2003	7,489	49 + D.C.	11,909
2004	7,649	49 + D.C.	12,711
2005	7,163	49 + D.C.	12,417
2006	7,722	49 + D.C.	12,620
2007	7,624	49 + D.C.	13,241
2008	7,783	49 + D.C.	13,690
2009	6,604	49 + D.C.	14,422
2010	6,628	49 + D.C.	14,977
2011	6,222	49 + D.C.	14,575
2012	5,796	48 + D.C.	13,022

Source: FBI. (2014). *Hate crime statistics (annual reports 1992–2012).* Washington, DC: U.S. Department of Justice. Available at http://www.fbi.gov/about-us/cjis/ucr/ucr-publications#Hate.

households. Victims perceived that 51% of hate crimes were motivated by ethnicity bias in 2012, which was higher than the percentages reported in 2011 (30%) and 2004 (22%). The percentage of hate crimes motivated by religious bias nearly tripled, from 10% in 2004 to 28% in 2012. An estimated 60% of hate crime victimizations were not reported to police in 2012. The offender had a weapon in at least 24% of violent hate crime victimizations in 2012, and the victim sustained an injury in 20% of violent hate crime victimizations.

According to the UCR (FBI, 2013), there were 5,796 single-bias incidents in 2012 (Table 7.3). What is most obvious from Table 7.3, however, is that the NCVS detects a much greater total number of incidents than the UCR (Harlow, 2005). The NCVS also tends to detect higher rates of violent hate crimes. Both find that the most frequently reported motivations for hate crimes are racial and ethnicity bias. Of the 3,968 hate crime offenses

Table 7.2 Hate Crime Victimizations Estimated by the NCVS, 2004–2012

	Total Hate Crimes[a]		Violent Hate Crimes[b]			Property Hate Crimes[c]		
Year	Number	Percent of Total Victimizations[d]	Number	Rate[e]	Percent of Total Violent Victimizations[d]	Number	Rate[f]	Percent of Total Violent Victimizations[d]
2004	281,670	1	220,060	0.9	3.1	61,610	0.5	0.3
2005	223,060	0.9	198,400	0.8	2.9	21,740	0.2	0.1
2006	230,490	0.8	211,730	0.9	2.8	15,830	0.1	0.1
2007	263,440	1	236,860	1	3.1	24,640	0.2	0.1
2008	266,640	1.1	241,800	1	3.7	22,890	0.2	0.1
2009	284,620	1.2	267,170	1.1	4.4	17,450!	0.1	0.1
2010	273,100	1.3	255,810	1	4.8	17,290!	0.1	0.1
2011[g]	218,010	1	195,880	0.8	3.6	22,130	0.2	0.1
2012	293,790	1.2	263,540	1	4.2	30,250	0.2	0.2

! Interpret with caution; estimate based on 10 or fewer cases, or the coefficient of variation is greater than 50%.

[a]Includes violent crimes, personal larceny, and household property crimes.

[b]Includes rape or sexual assault, robbery, aggravated assault, and simple assault.

[c]Includes household burglary, motor vehicle theft, and other theft.

[d]See appendix table 2 for number of total victimizations.

[e]Per 1,000 persons age 12 or older.

[f]Per 1,000 households.

[g]Due to a revision in the public use file, 2011 victimization counts vary slightly from previous publications.

Notes: Hate crime includes incidents confirmed by police as bias-motivated and incidents perceived by victims to be bias-motivated because the offender used hate language or left behind hate symbols. Estimates were based on 2-year rolling averages centered on the most recent year. Numbers rounded to the nearest ten.

Source: Bureau of Justice Statistics. (2014). *Hate crime victimization, 2004–2012—statistical tables.* Available at http://www.bjs.gov/index.cfm?ty=pbdetail&iid=4883.

Table 7.3 Hate Crimes: Incidence and Motivations

	2012	
	UCR	NCVS
Number of hate crimes	5,796	293,800
Percentage of hate crimes involving violence	68	90
Motivation[a]		
Percentage due to ethnicity bias	12	51
Percentage due to race bias	48	46
Percentage due to religious bias	19	28
Percentage due to sexual orientation bias	20	13
Percentage due to disability bias	2	11

[a]Total for NCVS does not sum to 100 because victims could report more than one type of bias that they perceived as a motivation for the victimization.

Sources: FBI Uniform Crime Reports (2012) and National Crime Victimization Survey (2012).

classified by the UCR as crimes against persons in 2012, simple assaults accounted for 39.6%, intimidation for 37.5%, and aggravated assault for 21.5%. Ten murders and 15 forcible rapes were also classified as hate crimes.

Of known offenders in 2012, 54.6% were white and 23.3% were black (FBI, 2013). Race was unknown for 11.5%, and other races accounted for the remainder. Most hate crime incidents (32.6%) occurred in or near homes. About 18% occurred on highways, roads, alleys, or streets; 8.3% occurred at schools or colleges; 5.7% happened at parking or drop lots or garages; and 4.1% took place in houses of worship. The location was unknown for 12.8% of incidents; the remainder took place at other specified or multiple locations. Following routine activities theory, these findings suggests that victims of hate crimes were most likely to be victimized on their way to or from home, work, school, or place of worship.

Per capita rates of violent hate crime victimization varied little by race or ethnicity: about 0.7 per 1,000 for whites, 0.9 per 1,000 for blacks, and 0.6 per 1,000 for Hispanics (Wilson, 2014). Offenders were most likely to be male (61%), but there were few differences by race (34% white and 32% black). About two thirds (64%) of violent hate victimizations involved a lone offender. Men (53%) and women (47%) were about equally likely to have experienced a violent hate crime. Few differences were found by age.

EXPLANATIONS

There are many descriptive studies, debates, typologies, thought pieces, and overviews of prior research on hate crime, but basic research on the etiology of bias-motivated offenses remains underdeveloped (Shively, 2005). We explore three major types of theories in this section, with an eye toward developing further theory in this area.

GROUP CONFLICT THEORIES

A rich tradition of research in social psychology has examined causal explanations of prejudice, although much more focused research on theories of hate crimes is needed (Craig, 2002). We know that the more strongly individuals identify with certain groups they belong to ("in-groups"), the more they experience competition and conflict with other groups ("out-groups"). Such in-group versus out-group conflict, even in childhood and temporary groups, is well documented.

The work of Sherif and his colleagues (Sherif & Sherif, 1953; Sherif et al., 1961) illustrated that group membership serves strong individual needs for affiliation and acceptance, and intergroup conflict strongly facilitates group cohesiveness and identity. In the famous "Robber's Cave" experiments, temporary groups of adolescent campers quickly formed strong in-group attachments and strong dislike of out-group members under conditions of relatively mild competition.

In general, experiments have shown that intergroup competition for scarce resources increases the level of cohesiveness within groups. Members are more likely to report that group membership is important to them under heightened competition with another group. Intergroup competition also increases the rejection of the other group's members, as shown by group members' tendencies to emphasize between-group differences and minimize between-group similarities (Cooper & Fazio, 1979; Coser, 1956). Intergroup conflict facilitates distortions of the other group's intentions and behaviors. The other group is frequently stereotyped, dehumanized, or seen as immoral or malevolent, while one's own group is idealized as moral, powerful, and completely justified in its views and actions toward others (e.g., Linville & Jones, 1980).

Tajfel (1981) argued that all that is necessary for group conflict to occur is individuals' perceptions that they are members of one group and that others are members of a different group, a naturally occurring process he called *social categorization*. Studies have consistently demonstrated systematic in-group preferences and out-group biases, even when the out-group was one with whom in-group members had never met or interacted, and about whom they knew very little (Tajfel, 1981).

STRAIN THEORY

Strain results when individuals experience a gap between culturally emphasized goals (e.g., success, wealth, material possessions) and the legitimate means available to achieve those goals (e.g., access to high-quality education, participation in social networks). Strain is most acutely experienced by lower-income groups, for whom the gap is the largest (Merton, 1957). Although diverse adaptations to strain are possible, violence against perceived competitors might be predicted under the adaptation of *innovation* (i.e., acceptance of cultural goals, but rejection of legitimate means to achieve them).

Intergroup conflict among different ethnic groups may be heightened by the perceived competition for scarce economic resources. According to the "group threat" explanation of hate crime, a narrowing of the economic gap between dominant and subordinate groups can be perceived as a challenge by the dominant group (Blumer, 1958). Similarly, the "defended neighborhood" perspective argues that changes in a neighborhood's racial and ethnic composition can lead to a perceived challenge to one group's dominance, contributing to violent acts against other groups in an attempt to defend their territory (Bergesen & Herman, 1998; Green et al., 1998). According to Danny Welch of the SPLC, "We're seeing more and more of it. Ten years ago you saw classic black-and-white issues . . . nowadays . . . people are struggling for the same jobs—blacks, whites, Asians, Hispanics. It can create problems" (Welch, 1991, p. A04).

Indeed, the U.S. Census has documented a changing racial mix in U.S. society, with large growth in Hispanic and Asian American populations and a relative decline in the majority white population (U.S. Census Bureau, 2011). These demographic shifts may translate into increased racism and resentment of minorities. For example, attacks on Asian Americans may reflect resentment of the economic success of Asia and the attention given to achievements by Asian Americans. Tensions between blacks and Asian American businesspersons, such as Korean grocery store operators in black neighborhoods, have been seen in New York, Los Angeles, Philadelphia, and elsewhere.

Hate crimes cannot be reduced solely to economic frustration, however. An analysis of hate crimes in New York City between 1987 and 1995 found no link between hate crimes and monthly unemployment rates (Green et al., 1998). Instead, researchers concluded that the influx of ethnically diverse people into formerly homogeneous neighborhoods appeared to be the most likely cause of hate-related violence. Although hate-related violence is not the inevitable result of these conditions, it is most likely to occur when prejudice is fueled by perceived competition and a relative sense of deprivation (Craig, 2002).

Such trends are characteristic of Grays Ferry in Philadelphia, an example introduced earlier in this chapter. The neighborhood's physical landscape is dominated by St. Gabriel's Roman Catholic Church, built in 1909 to accommodate the neighborhood's growing number of Irish Catholics. Over the decades, however, the white population began to give way to an increasing influx of African Americans. In 1970, according to U.S. Census Bureau figures, blacks accounted for 27% of the neighborhood and whites 73%. By 1990, whites made up 62% of the community, blacks 36%. The census tracts immediately surrounding Grays Ferry are 76% black. The declining numbers of whites in the area make some feel insecure. Racial tensions between blacks and Irish Catholic Americans in the neighborhood go back a long way, however. In 1832 and 1834, riots took place in the areas south of South Street and east of Grays Ferry. In 1842, the violence moved west and broke out in Grays Ferry and in the neighborhoods to the north. Blacks and Irish lived in the same dilapidated housing in the same alleys and courtyards of South Philadelphia, but they had never blended into a community. The violence persisted throughout the 1800s as each group competed for the same menial jobs and as the Irish tried to maintain a tenuous hold on political power. Even today, it seems, the two groups ignore their similarities (Dawsey et al., 1997, p. A01): "To stroll the streets here, to talk to residents, is to learn that Grays Ferry is a neighborhood of contradictions. Where love and loathing exist in tandem. Where neighbors tolerate poverty but not each other. Where groups of have-nots duel over nothing more than a ratty playground."

SOCIAL LEARNING THEORY

People's attitudes, values, and beliefs about individuals who belong to specific groups do not surface in a vacuum; they are learned through interaction with others. According to differential association theory (Sutherland, 1947), criminal behavior is learned through interaction with other persons through direct communication. People may learn not only techniques for committing a crime, but also specific motives, drives, rationalizations, and attitudes associated with the act. They learn definitions of certain behaviors as favorable or unfavorable, and they become "free" to commit delinquent or criminal acts when definitions favorable to committing the crime exceed definitions unfavorable to committing the crime (see also Sykes & Matza, 1957).

Differential associations vary in terms of frequency, duration, priority, and intensity. Differential learning of attitudes and behaviors occurs most strongly within primary groups, such as peers and family. Learning of attitudes and behaviors conducive to criminality is subject to all of the mechanisms that are involved in other types of learning. As a result, values and behaviors that are rewarded are likely to increase in frequency, whereas those that are not tend to diminish.

Mistrust, stereotypes, and animosity toward other ethnic groups are learned and reinforced through people's interactions with intimate acquaintances and family members, and those associations provide both justifications and rewards for committing acts of violence or harassment against out-group members. Juvenile perpetrators of hate crimes, for example, often claim they are protecting their neighborhood from the threat of invaders, and the majority of their acts are committed in the company of one or more peers or family members (Levin & McDevitt, 1993).

A British study relates similar factors to individual, group, and community prejudice (Sibbitt, 1997). Case studies were conducted in two London boroughs. Researchers interviewed a wide variety of people in the two areas, including staff in government agencies (police, housing departments, schools, the Youth Service, and the Probation Service) as well as victims, perpetrators, and residents of local communities. Perpetrators of racial harassment and violence frequently acted together as friends or even families. Views held by perpetrators toward ethnic minorities tended to be shared by the wider communities to which they belong. For perpetrators and community residents expressing racist views, racism served to divert attention from underlying problems and a sense of powerlessness in their lives. In this sense, ethnic minorities may serve as scapegoats for some segments of the population, especially in times of economic hardship (Allport, 1954).

INTERVENTIONS

LAW ENFORCEMENT RESPONSES

Many cities have formed police *bias units* to investigate possible bias crimes. One study examined police responses in two departments recognized as leaders in formulating responses to hate crimes: New York City and Baltimore County, Maryland (Martin, 1996). In New York, the Bias Incident Investigating Unit (BIIU) consisted of 18 investigators citywide. The procedure for investigating bias crimes was as follows. Initially, if the first officer on the scene suspects bias, he or she notifies a shift sergeant, who contacts the precinct commander. Both officials respond, as well as a BIIU officer. Then, BIIU decides whether the crime was likely motivated by bias or not. At this point, BIIU becomes responsible for the case, and a special review is needed to reclassify the case as not a hate crime. Thus, the first officer on the scene has enormous influence in determining whether an incident is labeled as a bias crime or not. In New York, bias need only be responsible in part for the offense. Factors considered in the determination of bias include display of offensive symbols, date and time of occurrence, and statements by the suspect at time of attack (e.g., racial epithets). The duties of BIIU officers include working closely with precinct detectives, paying special attention to victims (e.g., reassure, link with neighbors, and refer to organizations and agencies who can help), and monitoring the progress of cases through the criminal justice system.

In Baltimore County, where the population was 85% white, the department initiated a special approach to bias crimes following several reported Ku Klux Klan incidents. Unlike New York City, there is no special bias investigation unit; responsibility for investigating bias cases rests with individual beat officers, precinct supervisors, and Community Service Officers (CSOs). If organized hate groups are involved, precinct officers may request assistance from the department's Community Relations Division (CRD) or from its Intelligence Division. This approach has grown with the department's emphasis on community-oriented policing in general. Between 1981 and 1986, one detective was assigned to bias crime investigations. In 1986, verification criteria were modified, investigative responsibility was shifted to precinct personnel, and oversight and recordkeeping were shifted to CRD. CRD monitors cases and maintains close ties with community groups and with each precinct's CSO. Cases are handled according to department procedures and then reviewed at monthly meetings attended by officers from CRD, a representative from the state Human Relations Commission, the county executive's minority affairs specialist, and at least one precinct CSO. Based on FBI guidelines, all cases are reviewed and classified as verified, unverified (i.e., not enough evidence to determine), or unfounded (i.e., clearly not a bias incident).

In another example, the Metropolitan Police Department in Washington DC established a unit to deal specifically with issues affecting the gay, lesbian, bisexual, and transgender (GLBT) community (Bune, 2004). The unit educates police officers and community members about hate crimes and attempts to build trust between the police and the GLBT community. One focus was the increased risk of victimization associated with victims' alcohol or drug abuse. As Bune argues, an effective response to hate crimes requires that the police cooperate with other criminal justice agencies and community organizations to ensure a coordinated response to hate crimes.

These are examples of diverse policing strategies. None are cheap, and all require some reallocation of police resources. Further, jurisdictions differ considerably, and an appropriate intervention strategy needs to take into consideration relevant community characteristics, such as demographic makeup, needs, priorities, histories, and so on. As Shively (2005, p. 73) notes, it is difficult at this time to assess the quality, impact, or level of innovation of criminal justice responses to hate crime: "Given the lack of evaluations of interventions, the question of 'what works' in preventing and effectively responding to hate crime cannot be answered with more than anecdotal evidence or opinion."

HATE CRIME LEGISLATION

Forty-six states and the District of Columbia have now enacted some kind of hate crime legislation (Shively, 2005). Common types of state legislation include institutional vandalism in 36 of the 47 (e.g., vandalism against churches, synagogues, and schools), bias-motivated violence and intimidation (29), and interference with religious worship (18), such as crimes that disrupt religious services or desecrate religious symbols (Levin & McDevitt, 1993). Because individual states have the constitutional authority to develop their own criminal laws, hate crime legislation varies a great deal from one state to another.

Three major types of hate crime laws exist (Jacobs & Potter, 1997). Each has different functions, and each provides important options for law enforcement and courts. The first type, *substantive laws*, is largely based on the ADL's Model Hate Crime Law (ADL, 1992), which establishes a separate *intimidation* offense. State laws vary a great deal in designating which offenses are predicate crimes.[2] *Most hate crime laws do not use the word "motivation."* Instead, they refer to a person who commits an offense *because* of or by *reason of*. Nevertheless, state courts have generally interpreted hate crime statutes to require proof of a prejudiced motive (Jacobs & Potter, 1997).

The second type, *sentence enhancements*, involves statutes that either upgrade an existing offense or increase the maximum penalty for offenses motivated by prejudice. In Pennsylvania, for example, an offender is charged with a crime one degree higher than the predicate offense (thus allowing stronger penalties). State laws vary greatly in regard to the magnitude of the enhancement for bias motivation. In federal law, the 1994 Crime Bill mandated a revision of the U.S. sentencing guidelines to allow enhancements for hate crimes of three offense levels (sentencing guidelines depend on offense level and previous record) above the base level for the underlying offense (Jacobs & Potter, 1997).

The third type, *reporting statutes*, refers to laws that specify requirements for hate crime data collection and reporting. The exemplar is the HCSA of 1990 (mentioned earlier), which required the collection of nationwide hate crime data for the first time. The prosecution of hate crimes, unfortunately, remains relatively rare, although defendants charged with criminal acts (e.g., assault) have been and continue to be prosecuted under other criminal laws. The prosecutor faces a considerable burden in trying to prove that the person was motivated by hate. A Catch-22 exists: A hate crime is very difficult to prosecute successfully, but failure to pursue criminal charges could result in anger and retaliation in the victim's community. At the same time, prosecution may anger those in the alleged offender's group or community. Either way, the prosecutor risks the possible escalation of community tensions, and selecting an impartial jury is often extremely difficult (Jacobs & Potter, 1997).

For laws to be effective, police must arrest, prosecutors must charge, juries must convict, and judges must sentence. For various reasons, hate crimes (like all crimes) undergo much case attrition: Cases are filtered out of the criminal justice system as they are processed (Levin & McDevitt, 1993). In Boston, of 452 cases reported to police, only 60 resulted in arrests, 38 were charged (in the other 22 cases, there was insufficient evidence or diversion), 30 defendants were convicted, and five were incarcerated. Numerous difficulties explain such attrition. For example, prosecutors may be hesitant to pursue charges vigorously. There are relatively few arrests, and most offenders are strangers to the victim. The evidence is often insufficient to sustain conviction (e.g., offender motivations of bias are difficult to prove), and judges may not be sure how to proceed with punishment (e.g., specialized sentencing enhancements further complicate existing state sentencing guidelines).

Some cases are prosecuted under the Federal Civil Rights Act (e.g., fair housing laws, fair hiring practices), although a much larger number of prosecutions occur at the state level (Levin & McDevitt, 1993). There are four main types of federal legislation: (1) *civil rights protections against conspiracies* (e.g., neighbors conspiring to keep out certain ethnic groups), (2) *forcible interference with civil rights* (e.g., preventing someone from eating in a public restaurant or enrolling in school), (3) *deprivations of civil rights under color of law* (i.e., actions committed by public officials, especially police, who intentionally deprive an individual of his or her constitutional rights),[3] and (4) *willful interference with civil rights under the Fair Housing Act* (i.e., interference with an individual's rights to buy, rent, or live in a home; includes incidents of firebombing and harassment).

Like state laws, however, federal statutes are only rarely enforced (Levin & McDevitt, 1993). At least two main explanations have been offered. First, a markedly reduced emphasis on civil rights since 1980 has been reflected by conservative nominees to the U.S. Supreme Court and a lack of federal funding for enforcement of civil rights legislation. Second, the remedies available under federal law are extremely limited. They only protect citizens who are threatened or attacked while exercising a federally protected right (e.g., buying a home). This would exclude a majority of victims.

CIVIL LAWSUITS

Both the Seraw and Aryan Nations incidents described at the beginning of this chapter resulted in major civil lawsuits by the SPLC that intentionally bankrupted two of the most notorious white supremacist organizations in the United States. The SPLC, founded in 1971, is a nonprofit organization that combats hate, intolerance, and discrimination through education and litigation. Its programs include Teaching Tolerance (see following section) and the Intelligence Project, which collects and disseminates detailed information about the location, operations, and activities of major hate groups operating in the United States. The organization and its founder, attorney Morris Dees, are probably best known for winning several major lawsuits against organized hate groups (Dees & Bowden, 2001).

In the *Seraw* case, Dees and the SPLC won $12,500,000 in damages against the defendants, Tom Metzger and his son John, leaders of the White Aryan Resistance (WAR) movement. Dees proved that the Metzgers, by their actions in sending skinheads to Portland to propagate the racist and violent mission of WAR, and by inciting youth to commit acts of violence against minorities and foreigners, were legally liable for Seraw's death, even though the Metzgers were 1,500 miles away when the crime occurred. The *Seraw* case established a strong precedent for future litigation based on the legal principle of *vicarious liability*. That is, hate groups can be held legally liable for spawning violence even when they do not directly participate in the actual crimes. The U.S. Supreme Court refused to hear Metzger's appeal, and the judgment stood.

In the other verdict, an Idaho jury on September 7, 2000, returned a $6,300,000 civil judgment against the Aryan Nations; its founder, Richard Butler (1918–2004); and former security guards. Butler, an 82-year-old rural Idaho pastor often called the elder statesman of American hate, was held liable for the actions of his security force. Dees established that the Aryan Nations guards were poorly trained, guards were hired without any background checks, and the organization attempted to cover up a lack of proper procedures after the lawsuit was filed. Further, Dees convincingly demonstrated that the Aryan Nations had a long history of promoting violent racism. Through an extensive publishing network and a prison outreach program, Aryan Nations had for years promoted the supremacy of the white race and the notion of a separate white homeland. Its annual summer conferences in

Idaho were well known as the largest and most visible meetings for white supremacists in the United States. In a final insult to Butler, the entire 20-acre Aryan Nations compound was seized and awarded to the plaintiffs. In sum, civil lawsuits provide important strategic weapons to reduce hate-related violence.

EDUCATIONAL STRATEGIES

If values and attitudes conducive to committing hate crimes can be learned, as suggested by social learning theories, then it is possible that they can be unlearned. In-group biases and stereotypes can potentially be reduced through regulated contact between persons from each group, especially if the contact is between persons of equal status, the contact is in-depth and not superficial, the social climate for contact is friendly, the behavior during such contact challenges previously formed stereotypes, and the contact occurs within an environment favoring cooperation rather than competition. Such principles have been used effectively to reduce conflict between various adversarial groups, such as members of different ethnicities and nationalities (e.g., Amir, 1969; Foley, 1976).

Various curricula have also been designed to dispel stereotypes and increase tolerance among different groups. The SPLC (2014) offers free or low-cost resources to educators at all levels. The SPLC began the Teaching Tolerance project in 1991 as an extension of the center's various legal and educational efforts (http://www.tolerance.org). The Teaching Tolerance curriculum resources include two video-and-text teaching kits, *America's Civil Rights Movement* and *The Shadow of Hate*, which chronicle the history of hatred and intolerance in America and the struggle to overcome prejudice. A third kit, *Starting Small*, is a teacher-training package for early childhood educators. Other resources include a set of "One World" posters, accompanied by a 12-page teacher's guide and grants of up to $2,000 for K–12 teachers. The program also offers a one-year research fellowship for educators with strong writing skills and an interest in equity issues. A magazine titled *Teaching Tolerance* is distributed free twice a year to a half-million educators throughout the United States and 70 other countries. It features writing and artwork that address classroom themes of tolerance, respect, and community building.

Other strategies have combined school curricula with broad-based school–community partnerships to reduce hate crimes. In Massachusetts, the Student Civil Rights Project attempts to reduce hate through several initiatives (Mahoney, 1999). First, a summer internship program brought together a diverse group of college and high school students from across the state to explore, identify, review, and recommend curricula and resources that school communities could implement to prevent hatred and prejudice in schools. Students had to confront their own feelings and attitudes toward different groups, as well as their own experiences with victimization and discrimination. Interns received training in civil rights laws and history from legal experts and civil rights organizations.

A centerpiece of the internship program was the creation of a youth-focused website, an educational-reporting mechanism designed to provide students, teachers, and administrative professionals with tools and resources to combat and reduce bias within schools. The site provides information on victim assistance, diversity awareness training, and peer mediation as strategies to reduce bias-related incidents. A history section features information on the Holocaust and the Civil Rights Movement. An online bulletin board is featured. Students can use the site's reporting form to report incidents of hate-motivated harassment or violence. These reports are received by a student civil rights director, who may then establish contact with school officials or law enforcement, or both. The student site is linked to the Governor's Task Force on Hate Crimes website.

The project developed a resource manual called the *Educator's Resource Manual*, containing a comprehensive overview of hate crime laws and prevention steps for schools and communities, as a well as the *Hate Crimes Resource Manual for Law Enforcement and Victim Assistance Professionals*. The project also focused on raising student awareness about hate crimes through distribution of pamphlets and posters as well as its website. The project provides extensive community outreach, mainly through designing and offering collaborative training symposia for schools, educators, and law enforcement. In collaboration with a local UPN television station, the group also works on strengthening media resources to raise awareness about issues and resources to prevent hate crimes. A one-hour special, *The Teen Files: The Truth about Hate*, was created and produced, and a diversity awareness curriculum was designed to complement the television special and integrate with online resources.

The project requested through the governor's office that all Massachusetts high schools designate a civil rights coordinator to serve as a contact for the student civil rights director in the event of a hate-related incident; the coordinator also acts as a liaison between the school and local law enforcement. The project is expanding its efforts throughout the state, including creation of pilot civil rights teams in 10 to 15 high schools.

CONCLUSIONS

Creating a new crime category may serve important symbolic and political functions. Hate crime laws attempt to rectify past wrongs by translating civil rights into the criminal law (Jacobs & Potter, 1997). Passing new laws does not necessarily improve crime control, however. Defining and measuring hate crimes remain problematic; gathering data from police agencies has been difficult; and enforcement and prosecution have been minimal. Efforts aimed at providing better training for criminal justice personnel may help in the future. Civil lawsuits have provided an important weapon against hate crime, as witnessed by major lawsuits won by the SPLC.

At the very least, the ability of laws to change human behavior is limited. We still need to address the individual and social causes that underlie hate and prejudice. It is unlikely that legal strategies alone will suffice. Well-designed educational and social learning strategies aimed at promoting and assessing tolerance must be part of a multifaceted strategy to reduce hate crime. While a number of promising prevention and intervention strategies have been developed, evaluations of their effectiveness are so far scarce (Shively, 2005).

DISCUSSION QUESTIONS

1. Define the following: (a) hate crime, (b) predicate offense.
2. (a) Describe the Hate Crime Statistics Act of 1990. What were its goals? What actions did it require? What revisions have occurred since 1990? (b) Discuss problems involved with determining whether a particular incident is or is not a "hate crime."
3. Are hate crimes in the U.S. *increasing, decreasing,* or *staying the same*? How can you tell? Give specific evidence to support your answer.
4. Describe major characteristics of hate crime *offenders, victims, and incidents.*
5. Discuss each of the following *explanations* of hate crimes, including available *evidence* for each: (a) group conflict theories, (b) strain theory, and (c) social learning theory.
6. Describe how each of the following *interventions* attempts to reduce hate crimes: (a) police bias units, (b) hate crime legislation, (c) civil lawsuits, and (d) educational strategies. Give specific evidence and examples from course materials to illustrate your answer (e.g., what is done, where, how, and by whom).

SUGGESTED READINGS

Dees, M., & Bowden, E. (2001). *Courtroom victories: Taking hate groups to court.* Montgomery, AL: Southern Poverty Law Center (SPLC). Retrieved December 22, 2009, from http://www.splcenter.org/pdf/static/courtroom_victories.pdf.

Shively, M. (2005). *Study of literature and legislation on hate crime in America* (NCJ 210300). Washington, DC: U.S. Department of Justice, National Institute of Justice. Retrieved December 21, 2009, from http://www.ncjrs.gov/pdffiles1/nij/grants/210300.pdf.

NOTES

1. As an analogy, consider the predicate in a written sentence. The predicate (some specific action) depends on (requires) the subject (some specific actor, place, or object). The predicate cannot exist alone (in a proper sentence) without the existence of a subject. In predicate *crimes*, similarly, the bias statute depends on an already existing criminal statute.
2. FBI data do not provide very much data on offenders. See Martin (1996) and Jacobs and Potter (1997) for further discussion.
3. The federal civil rights convictions of police officers in the Rodney King case in Los Angeles certainly provide the best-known example, although successful prosecutions under these provisions are extremely rare; in fact, charges are rarely even initiated.

REFERENCES

Allport, G. (1954). *The nature of prejudice.* Cambridge, MA: Addison-Wesley.

Amir, Y. (1969). Contact hypothesis in ethnic relations. *Psychological Bulletin, 71,* 319–342.

Anti-Defamation League (ADL). (1992). *Hate crimes statutes: A 1991 status report.* New York: Anti-Defamation League.

Associated Press. (2003, Nov. 13). FBI sees drop in hate crimes after rise in 2001. *Philadelphia Inquirer,* p. A02.

Bergesen, A., & Herman, M. (1998). Immigration, race, and riot: The 1992 Los Angeles uprising. *American Sociological Review, 63,* 39–54.

Blumer, H. (1958). Race prejudice as a sense of group position. *Pacific Sociological Review, 1,* 3–7.
Bowden, M. (1997, April 13). How a Grays Ferry street fight became a racial crisis. *Philadelphia Inquirer,* p. A01
Bune, K. L. (2004). Law enforcement must take lead on hate crimes. *Police Chief, 71*(4), 41–42, 44.
Cooper, J., & Fazio, F. H. (1979). The formation and persistence of attitudes that support inter-group conflict. In W. G. Austin & S. Worchel (Eds.), *The social psychology of intergroup relations.* Pacific Grove, CA: Brooks/Cole.
Coser, L. A. (1956). *The functions of social conflict.* Glencoe, IL: Free Press.
Craig, K. M. (2002). Examining hate-motivated aggression: A review of the social psychological literature on hate crime as a distinct form of aggression. *Aggression and Violent Behavior, 7,* 85–101.
Dawsey, D., Giordano, R., Fish, L., & Rhor, M. (1997, March 23). Grays Ferry: Decades of racial divide. *Philadelphia Inquirer,* p. A01.
Dees, M., & Bowden, E. (2001). *Taking hate groups to court.* Montgomery, AL: Southern Poverty Law Center (SPLC). Retrieved August 1, 2006, from http://www.splcenter.org/legal/publications/pub.jsp.
Disha, I., Cavendish, J. C., & King, R. D. (2011). Historical events and spaces of hate: Hate crimes against Arabs and Muslims in post-9/11 America. *Social Problems, 58,* 21–46.
Federal Bureau of Investigation (FBI). (1990). *Hate crime data collection guidelines.* Washington, DC: Government Printing Office.
Federal Bureau of Investigation (FBI). (1991). *Training guide for hate crime data collection.* Washington, DC: Government Printing Office.
Federal Bureau of Investigation (2013). *Crime in the United States 2012.* Retrieved May 14, 2014, from: http://www.fbi.gov/about-us/cjis/ucr/crime-in-the-u.s/2012/crime-in-the-u.s.-2012.
Foley, L. A. (1976). Personality and situational influences on changes in prejudice. *Journal of Personality and Social Psychology, 34,* 846–856.
Green, D. P., Strolovitch, D. Z., & Wong, J. S. (1998). Defended neighborhoods, integration, and racially motivated crime. *American Journal of Sociology, 104,* 372–403.
Harlow, C. W. (2005). *Hate crime reported by victims and police* (NCJ 209911). Washington, DC: Department of Justice, Bureau of Justice Statistics.
Hate Crime Statistics Act (HCSA). (1992). 28 U.S.C. § 534 (Supp. IV).
Jacobs, J. B., & Potter, K. A. (1997). Hate crimes: A critical perspective. In M. Tonry (Ed.), *Crime and justice, a review of research* (Vol. 22, pp. 1–50). Chicago: University of Chicago Press.
Jenness, V., & Grattet, R. (2001). *Making hate a crime: From social movement to law enforcement.* New York: Russell Sage Foundation.
Jimenez, S. (2013). *The book of Matt: Hidden truths about the murder of Matthew Shepard.* Hanover, NH: Steerforth.
Levin, J., & McDevitt, J. (1993). *Hate crimes: The rising tide of bigotry and bloodshed.* New York: Plenum.
Linville, P. W., & Jones, E. E. (1980). Polarized appraisals of out-group members. *Journal of Personality and Social Psychology, 38,* 689–703.
Mahoney, J. (1999, August). Stop the hate: Massachusetts task force creates student civil rights project to combat problem. *Corrections Today,* 82–86.
Martin, S. (1996). Investigating hate crimes: Case characteristics and law enforcement responses. *Justice Quarterly, 13,* 455–480.
Merton, R. K. (1957). *Social theory and social structure.* Glencoe, IL: Free Press.

Sherif, M., Harvey, O. J. White, B. J., Hood, W. R., & Sherif, C. W. (1961). *Intergroup conflict and cooperation: The Robber's Cave experiment.* Norman, OK: Institute of Group Relations.

Sherif, M., & Sherif, C. W. (1953). *Groups in harmony and tension.* New York: Harper & Row.

Shively, M. (2005). *Study of literature and legislation on hate crime in America* (NCJ 210300). Washington, DC: Department of Justice, National Institute of Justice. Retrieved August 1, 2006, from http://www.ncjrs.gov/pdffilesl/nij/grants/210300.pdf.

Sibbitt, R. (1997). *Perpetrators of racial harassment and racial violence.* London: Great Britain Home Office Research and Statistics Directorate.

Southern Poverty Law Center (SPLC). (1999). *The toll of hate. Intelligence Report,* Winter. Retrieved August 3, 2006, from http://www.splcenter.org/intel/intelre *port/article.jsp?aid-357.*

Southern Poverty Law Center (SPLC). (2014). *Teaching Tolerance.* Retrieved May 14, 2014, from http://www.tolerance.org/.

Sutherland, E. H. (1947). *Principles of criminology* (4th ed.). Philadelphia: Lippincott.

Sykes, G., & Matza, D. (1957). Techniques of neutralization: A theory of delinquency. *American Journal of Sociology, 22,* 664–670.

Tajfel, H. (1981). *Human groups and social categories: Studies in psychology.* New York: Cambridge University Press.

U.S. Census Bureau. (2011). *2010 Census shows America's diversity.* Retrieved May 14, 2014, from http://www.census.gov/newsroom/releases/archives/2010_census/cb11-cn125.html.

Welch, W. M. (1991, Sept. 10). New racial diversity fuels hate-crime wave. *Philadelphia Inquirer,* p. A04.

Wilson, M. M. (2014). *Hate crime victimization, 2004–2012—statistical tables* (NCJ 244409). Washington, DC: U.S. Department of Justice, Office of Justice Programs, Bureau of Justice Statistics. Available at http://www.bjs.gov/content/pub/pdf/hcv0412st.pdf.

SECTION IV

VIOLENCE IN SPECIFIC SETTINGS AND CONTEXTS

CHAPTER 8

INTIMATE VIOLENCE

"PEOPLE HIT FAMILY MEMBERS BECAUSE THEY CAN"

Gelles and Straus (1988), from whom the quotation was taken, describe the 10-year marriage of Chet and Marjorie, in which Chet beats his wife every couple of months because she does a poor job of keeping the house neat. The other case described is David and Marie and their 3-year-old son, Peter, who was being x-rayed for a possible skull fracture given to him by his father because he knocked over the new television set and shattered the picture tube.

In the next paragraph, the authors ask whether Chet would feel free to beat up the janitor if he failed to keep his office clean. What would happen to David if he had a new television in his automobile showroom and a 3-year-old son of a customer overturned it? Obviously, the outcomes would be quite different if Chet and David behaved toward strangers as they behaved toward their wife and son. If they attacked the janitor and the 3-year-old, both would be facing arrest and prosecution for assault and battery. Why should hitting loved ones be any different?

This chapter is an examination of how our attitudes toward hitting or expressing other kinds of violence toward loved ones have changed. When Gelles and Straus wrote their book in 1988, widespread changes in the treatment of intimate partner and family violence were occurring in the form of legislation, criminal justice practices, and treatment of victims and perpetrators. This chapter looks not only at violence between intimate partners, but also violence between parents and children. Although the changes have been enormous, the results have been less effective than hoped. In short, people still hit family members because they can. Before considering these trends, however, let us examine the patterns and risks of violence toward intimate partners and other family members.

PATTERNS AND RISKS

INTIMATE PARTNER VIOLENCE

This section will draw upon the very detailed nationwide study of intimate partner violence provided by the National Intimate Partner and Sexual Violence Survey (NISVS; Black et al., 2011). The report provides detailed information on the prevalence and characteristics of intimate partner violence, stalking, and sexual violence; who is most likely to experience these forms of violence; the patterns and impact of violence experienced by specific perpetrators; and the health consequences of these forms of violent threats of physical or sexual violence, stalking, and psychological aggression (including coercive tactics) by a current or former intimate partner. Intimate partner violence may occur between spouses, between cohabitating or noncohabiting romantic or sexual partners, and between opposite-sex or same-sex couples (Basile & Saltzman, 2002; Black et al., 2011).

NISVS measured intimate partner violence involving the following types of behavior:

- *Rape*: any completed or attempted unwanted vaginal, oral, or anal penetration through the use of physical force (such as being pinned or held down, or by the use of violence) or threats to physically harm and includes times when the victim was drunk, high, drugged, or passed out and unable to consent
- *Physical violence*: ranging from slapping, pushing, or shoving to severe acts such as beating, burning, or choking
- *Stalking victimization*: involves a pattern of harassing or threatening tactics used by a perpetrator that is both unwanted and causes fear or safety concerns in the victim. These include unwanted phone calls and computer-generated messages; unwanted cards, letters, or presents; watching or following from a distance with devices such as a listening device, camera, or GPS; showing up unwanted at the victim's home, workplace, or school; or leaving items at the victim's home or car to let the victim know of the stalker's presence.

One type of behavior included in the NISVS report but not discussed here is psychological aggression such as name calling, insulting, or humiliating an intimate partner. Another type is control of reproductive or sexual health, such as refusing to use a condom or trying to get a woman pregnant when she does not want to become pregnant.

More than a third of U.S. women (35.6%) have experienced one or more rapes or incidents of physical violence or stalking by an intimate partner at some time in their lifetime. Almost a third of the women (32.9%) have experienced physical violence and nearly 1 in 10 (9.4%) have been raped by an intimate partner at some time in their lifetime. Approximately 5.9% of women reported that these forms of violence by an intimate partner occurred in the 12 months prior to the survey.

Comparing the lifetime and 12-month percentages side by side provides some sense of the frequency of these cases. Rape, for example, is a very serious crime but is infrequent. Physical violence, on the other hand, can be the most serious and, as Table 8.1 indicates, it is also the most common form.

The NISVS does not provide information on intimate partner homicides. In 2007, the rates of homicide for female victims in an intimate relationship were four to five times higher than the rate for male victims. Using data from the Federal Bureau of Investigation (FBI), approximately 30% of female murder victims are killed by a husband, ex-husband, or boyfriend. In comparison, 5.5% of male murder victims killed by female intimate partners.

Table 8.1 Lifetime and 12-Month Prevalence of Rape, Physical Violence, and/or Stalking Victimization by an Intimate Partner, U.S. Women

Event	Lifetime Prevalence (weighted %)[1]	12-Month Prevalence (weighted %)[1]
Rape	9.4	0.6
Physical violence	32.9	4.0
Stalking	10.7	2.8
Three forms	35.6	5.9

[1]Percentages of completed interviews are weighted by sex, race/ethnicity, and age of respondents.
Source: NISVS (2010, p. 38).

Table 8.2 Lifetime Prevalence of Rape, Physical Violence, and/or Stalking by an Intimate Partner, by Race/Ethnicity, U.S. Women[1]

			Black	White	Asian or Pacific Islands	Native Amer.	Multiracial
Rape	Weighted %	8.4	12.2	9.2	#	#	20.1
Physical Violence	Weighted %	35.2	40.9	31.7	#	45.9	50.4
Stalking	Weighted %	10.6	14.6	10.4	#	#	18.9
All Forms	Weighted %	37.1	43.7	34.6	19.6	46.0	53.8

[1] Percentages of completed interviews are weighted by sex, race/ethnicity, and age of respondents.
Race/ethnicity was self-described. The American Indian or Alaska Native designation does not indicate being enrolled or affiliated with a tribe.
Source: NISVS (2010, p. 40).

With a focus on heterosexual intimate partners, the percentage of women killed by intimate partners increased to between 40% and 50%. In a later section we will discuss the decline in intimate partner homicides (Campbell et al., 2007).

Race/Ethnicity

The largest single category in Table 8.2 is physical violence. The weighted percentages range from 31.7% for white women to 50.4% for the multiracial category. The percentage of women of all race/ethnic groups who experience rape, physical violence, or stalking in their lifetime is very large. According to the NISVS (2010, p. 39):

> Approximately 4 out of every 10 non-Hispanic Black women, 4 out of every 10 American Indian or Alaska Native women (43.7% and 46.0%, respectively), and 1 in 2 multiracial non-Hispanic women (53.8%) have been the victim of rape, physical violence, and/or stalking by an intimate partner in their lifetime.

One of the more interesting studies of intimate partner homicide not only examined racial/ethnic variations but also included the number of corollary victims. Smith, Fowler, and Niolon (2014) analyzed 4,470 homicides, 2,903 of which were classified as intimate

Table 8.3 Characteristics of Intimate Partner and Corollary Homicide Victims

Characteristic	Total Homicides (N = 4,470)	Intimate Partner Homicides (N = 2,903)	Corollary Victims (N = 718)	Perpetrator Victims (N = 849)
Gender				
Female	55.1	77.1	27.3	3.5
Male	44.9	23.0	72.7	96.1
Race/Ethnicity				
White	53.0	52.0	49.3	59.1
Black	33.0	35.3	33.3	24.7
Hispanic	9.0	9.0	12.1	10.4
Other, unknown	5.0	5.0	5.3	5.2

Source: (Smith, Fowler, & Niolon, 2014 p. 463).

partner homicides. The data were taken from 16 states in the National Violent Death Reporting System for the years 2003 to 2009.

Intimate partner homicides account for 80% of total homicides, of which 77.1% are female victims. For racial/ethnic groups, 52% of victims were white, 33% black, 9% Hispanic, and 5% other or unknown. It is important to note that these are percentages and not rates. Rates take into account differences in the size of the population, and when they are used black homicide rates are much higher than for other racial/ethnic groups (Smith, Fowler, & Niolon, 2014).

Homicides of corollary victims are "the murder of other people that occurs in the context of a domestic violence incident (such as new intimate partners, intervening friends, family or strangers, or responding law enforcement officers" (Smith et al., 2014, p. 462). The authors state this was the first study of intimate partner homicides and corollary victims.

Table 8.3 shows that the percentage of corollary victims for white victims is higher (49.3%) than for black victims (33.3%). Corollary victims were predominantly male (72.7%), and a quarter (24.5%) of the corollary victims were aged 17 or younger. Although detailed information about racial differences is not available, one of the reasons many of the corollary victims are young is because many of the homicides occurred in the home; more incidents involving nonwhite victims may occur outside the home.

The authors give an example:

> Victim 1 (male, aged 14 years) was killed during a domestic incident between his mother and father (suspect). The suspect was drinking throughout the day and got into an argument with his wife. The argument became physical, and the suspect pulled out a gun and began threatening his wife; he then shot and wounded her. Victim 1 tried to grab the gun and was shot in the process. (Smith, Fowler, & Niolon, 2014, p. 464)

Eight hundred forty-nine "perpetrator victims" committed suicide during a homicide/suicide incident or were killed by police in a legal intervention. As Table 8.3 indicates, almost all (96.1%) of the perpetrator victims were male. The high percentage of perpetrator victims for white intimate partner homicides reflects the fact that about 75% of homicide/suicides are committed by whites (Riedel, 2010).

Intimate Partner Violence in Other Countries

The World Health Organization (WHO) did a multicountry study on women's health and domestic violence. The 24,000 respondents came from the following countries: Bangladesh, Brazil, Ethiopia, Japan, Namibia, Peru, Samoa, Serbia and Montenegro, Thailand, and the United Republic of Tanzania. Participating countries were chosen according to specified criteria, including the presence of local antiviolence groups able to use the data for advocacy and policy reform, absence of existing data, and a political environment receptive to tackling the issue.

The survey questionnaire was constructed and pretested in the subject countries. The WHO study used female interviewers and supervisors who were selected according to criteria such as emotional maturity, ability to engage with people of different backgrounds in an empathetic and nonjudgmental manner, and skills in dealing with sensitive issues. All were trained using a standardized three-week curriculum designed for the study (García-Moreno et al., 2005; WHO, 2005).

Questions asked about the prevalence of physical and sexual violence. Physical violence was defined as

- slapping the woman, or throwing something at her that could hurt her;
- pushing or shoving her;
- hitting her with a fist or something else that could hurt;
- kicking her, dragging her or beating her up;
- choking or burning her on purpose;
- threatening her with, or actually using a gun, knife or other weapon against her.

Sexual violence was defined as

- being physically forced to have sexual intercourse against her will;
- having sexual intercourse because she was afraid of what her partner might do;
- being forced to do something sexual she found degrading or humiliating. (WHO, 2005, p. 5)

Severity and Frequency of Violence

The most common act of violence was being slapped by an intimate partner; rates ranged from 9% in Japan to 52% in Peru. This was followed by being hit with a fist; the two countries were also similar in extremes (2% vs. 42%).

Being hit with a fist, kicked, dragged, threatened with a weapon, or having a weapon used against her was defined as severe physical violence. According to these criteria, rates for severe physical violence ranged from 4% in Japan to 49% in provincial Peru. Most women responded affirmatively when asked if they had ever experienced severe physical violence. In only three countries—Bangladesh, Japan, and Serbia and Montenegro—had a greater proportion of women experienced moderate violence than the severe kind.

Moreover, the physical violence experienced was not an isolated event; intimate partner violence represented a continuing pattern of abuse. Excluding severe physical violence, over half the women who reported a violent act in the past 12 months had experienced that act more than once.

Sexual Violence

The proportion of women physically forced into intercourse ranged from 4% in Serbia and Montenegro to 46% in provincial Bangladesh and Ethiopia. The high rate of forced sex is particularly disturbing in the light of the AIDS epidemic and the difficulty women have in protecting themselves from HIV infection.

About half of the respondents reported sexual violence out of fear of what their partners might do if they refused. In all settings, some women reported being forced into sexual behavior they found degrading or humiliating (WHO, 2005).

Women's Attitude Toward Violence

The WHO survey also asked respondents to give circumstances under which a man is justified in beating his wife, and whether and when women may refuse to have sex with their intimate partner. The respondents were given six situations that would justify beatings, such as not completing housework adequately, refusing to have sex, disobeying their husband, and being unfaithful.

The most dramatic differences were between urban industrialized areas and rural and traditional ones. Three fourths of the respondents in the urban settings of Brazil, Japan, Namibia, and Serbia and Montenegro felt that violence was never justified, but one fourth of the respondents in provincial settings of Bangladesh, Ethiopia, Peru, and Samoa thought so.

In all settings, the most frequent reason justifying beating was infidelity. Disobeying a husband was the next most common reason.

The authors of the study noted that acceptance of wife beating was higher among women who had experienced abuse than among those who had not. They hypothesized that these women may find violence more acceptable and "normal" when they themselves are victims.

The respondents were also asked whether they had a right to refuse sex with their husbands if they are sick or do not want to have sex, or if the husband is drunk or has been mistreating them. Fewer women thought they could refuse sex if they didn't want it than if they were ill or if the partner was drunk or abusive. Between 10% and 20% of the women in the provincial sites of Bangladesh, Peru, the Republic of Tanzania, Ethiopia, and Samoa felt that women did not have the right to refuse sex under any circumstances (García-Moreno et al., 2005).

Risk Factors

Except for Japan and Ethiopia, 15- to 19-year-old girls and women were at greater risk for physical or sexual violence in the past 12 months. In urban Peru, for example, 41% of the

15- to 19-year-old girls and women were victimized, compared to 8% of the 45- to 49-year-old respondents.

In nearly all the countries, women who were divorced or separated during their lifetimes reported more violent victimization than currently married women. In almost half the settings, there was more intimate partner violence among women who were cohabiting with their partners rather than married.

The WHO study also found that women with higher education are less likely to experience intimate partner violence. Women with higher education may have a greater choice of partners, may be able to choose to marry or not, or may be able to negotiate with greater autonomy and control of resources (García-Moreno et al., 2005).

VIOLENCE TOWARD FAMILY MEMBERS

As part of *Crime in the United States 2004* (FBI, 2006), a special report on victimization of children under age 18 was published using National Incident-Based Reporting System (NIBRS) data for 2001 to 2003. The study focused on crimes against the person, including murder and nonnegligent manslaughter, negligent manslaughter, aggravated assault, simple assault, intimidation, forcible rape, forcible sodomy, sexual assault with an object, forcible fondling, and kidnapping/abduction. In Table 8.4, infants are defined as under 1 year of age; victims aged 1 to 11 are classified as young children; 11- to 17-year-old victims are listed as such; and victims aged 18 and older are excluded.

As noted in Chapter 2, NIBRS coverage is not nationwide, so the results in Table 8.4 should be viewed with caution. Where it is possible to compare NIBRS data with other sources, we have done so.

Table 8.4 Victim–Offender Relationships for Victims Under Age 18

	Victims					
Offenders	**Infants**	**%**	**Young Children**	**%**	**11 to 17 Years Old**	**%**
Intimate partners	0	0.0	0	0.0	39	14.1
Parental roles	0	0.0	0	0.0	1	0.4
Dependents in household	2095	57.9	398	50.8	44	15.9
Siblings	59	1.6	22	2.8	10	3.6
Other family	169	4.7	62	7.9	8	2.9
Acquaintances	55	15.3	109	13.9	97	35.0
Babysitter	103	2.8	10	1.3	1	0.4
Unknown	404	11.2	95	12.1	46	16.6
Stranger	232	6.4	90	11.5	31	11.2
Sum	3617	100.0	786	100.0	277	100.0

Source: Adapted from *Infant Victims: An Exploratory Study* (FBI, 2006).

There is little doubt that there is underreporting of violence against children because child homicides, the most serious and reliably reported, are undercounted. Research indicates a substantial amount of underreporting by official reporting agencies (Chew et al., 1999; Crittenden & Craig, 1990; Crume et al., 2002; McClain et al., 1993). For example, Ewigman, Kiviahan, and Land (1993) studied 384 Missouri children younger than 5 who died from 1983 to 1986 and whose death had been classified as due to an external cause or abuse or neglect. Of the 121 cases classified as definite maltreatment, only 38.8% were reported in the Supplementary Homicide Reports. Similarly, Herman-Giddens and colleagues (1999) reviewed 259 cases of homicide reported to the North Carolina medical examiner from 1985 to 1994. On the basis of additional information obtained through the efforts of the North Carolina child death review organization, the authors concluded that abuse homicides were underestimated in vital statistics records by 61.5%.

A major reason for underreporting is that homicides of young children are difficult to document because they often resemble deaths from accidents or other causes. For example, one of the more common expressions of child abuse is shaken baby syndrome. This occurs when the baby's body is vigorously shaken so that the head is repeatedly jerked back to front. This causes severe internal bleeding and swelling in the brain, brain stem, or spinal cord. The result is neurological damage and, in some cases, death (Ewing, 1997).

Another example is deaths from sudden infant death syndrome. As Finkelhor (1997, p. 22) noted:

> [It] is difficult to distinguish children who are suffocated from those who die from sudden infant death syndrome (SIDS). It is difficult to distinguish young children who are dropped, pushed, or thrown from those who die from falls. Even in many so-called accidental deaths, such as falls or auto fatalities, there may be a major component of willful parental negligence that is difficult to establish.

It is useful to examine the wide variety of offenses involving infants covered by the classification in Table 8.4. Among the 2,917 offenses covered by the NIBRS report, the most frequent violent offense was simple assault (48.1%), followed by aggravated assault (35.1%), kidnapping/abduction (7.4%), and murder/negligent manslaughter (3.2%). Given the physical vulnerability of infants, it is no surprise that the most commonly used weapon was "personal weapons" (hands, feet, teeth, etc.), which represented 55.9% of the 2,917 offenses. Information for other age groups were not given in detail.

Several characteristics in Table 8.4 help provide a general picture of violence toward other family members. In general, the older the victim, the more socially distant the relationship between victim and offender. For example, 57.9% of the infant victims had offenders who were members in the household, such as parents or primary caregivers. On the other hand, among 11- to 17-year-old victims, only 15.9% were dependents in the household. Only 6.4% of the infant victims had strangers as offenders, while almost double that percentage (11.2%) of 11- to 17-year-olds were victims of strangers. Similarly, among infants, only 15.3% were victims of acquaintances, while among 11- to 17-year-olds, 35% were victims of acquaintances.

Parental Homicide

The killing of a child by parents is also called filicide, neonaticide, or infanticide. The term *filicide* refers to the murder of a child up to age 18 by the parent. *Neonaticide* refers to the killing of a child on the day of birth, while *infanticide* refers to the killing of a child under one year of age, although the terms are used interchangeably in the literature (Bourget et al., 2007; West, 2007).

There have been a number of classifications of filicides (West, 2007). Resnick (1970) classified 131 cases into five categories:

- *Altruistic Filicide*: The parents kill the child to relieve him or her of imagined or real suffering.
- *Acute Psychotic Filicide*: The parent, responding to severe mental illness, kills the child for no rational reason.
- *Unwanted Child Filicide*: The parents kill the child because he or she is a hindrance or because they benefit from his or her death (e.g., financially, or being able to marry someone who does not want children).
- *Accidental Filicide*: The parent unintentionally kills the child as a result of abuse.
- *Spouse Revenge Filicide*: Murder of the child is a means of revenge against the spouse because of infidelity or abandonment.

According to Resnick (1970), the most frequent form of filicide is the first, altruistic filicide. An example is Andreas Yates, who on June 20, 2001, drowned her five children, ranging in age from six months to seven years, in a bathtub. Prior to this, she displayed symptoms of depression that increased during periods following the birth of a child. She had been hospitalized four times prior to the homicides. Following her arrest, she stated that she believed she was a bad mother and the children would subsequently not grow up properly. She killed the children to save them from damnation. When Yates went to trial in 2001, she entered a plea of not guilty by reason of insanity. The jury, who could have sentenced her to death, instead rejected the plea, found her guilty, and sentenced her to life in prison. Due to an error by a prosecution witness, in 2005 the case was brought back to the trial count. Yates entered the same plea, and this time it was accepted (it is not known why the jury in the second trial accepted the plea). Yates is most likely to spend the remainder of her life in a maximum-security hospital in north Texas (West, 2007).

Kunz and Bahr (1996) provided a profile of parental homicide against children using Uniform Crime Report data or data from *Crime in the United States* for all familial homicide incidents from 1976 to 1985 in which the son or daughter was the victim. Table 8.5 provides the age, gender, and race of child homicide victims.

More than one third (39.4%) of the homicide victims were less than 1 year old; 38.9% were age 1 to 4. In other words, in the first year, both percentages and rates are extremely high; they decline progressively to age 4. From ages 5 to 12, the homicide rates and percentages are extremely low, lower than at any other time during the human lifespan.

The reasons for the low percentages in the 5- to 12-year-old group are twofold. The child is interacting with many other people outside of the household, and the people the

Table 8.5 Age and Gender of Child Homicide Victims

Variable	Percentage
Age of Victim	
Birth–1 week old	9.4
1 week–1 year old	30.0
1–4 years old	38.9
5–12 years old	13.9
13–18 years old	7.8
Gender of Victim	
Female	44.7
Male	55.3
Sample Size	3,459

Source: Adapted from Kunz and Bahr (1996, p. 323).

child is interacting with are concerned with protecting him or her (e.g., teachers and secondary caregivers). It is difficult to underestimate the power that parents have infants: *"Children have comparatively little choice over whom they associate with, less choice perhaps than any segment of population besides prisoners"* (Finkelhor, 1997; emphasis in the original). Not surprisingly, most homicides in the 0-to-4 age group are committed by parents.

For the 5- to 12-year-old group, the low homicide rates are a result of the increased surveillance in general for this age group. While the family retains responsibility for the child, the school provides an added layer of protection. For example, schools have clear rules about who has contact with the child during school hours and who picks the child up at the end of the school day.

Boudreaux, Lord, and Dutra (1999) analyzed 550 child abduction cases from FBI files. Although there are cases of alleged child abduction in all age groups under 17, the largest number (165) were found in ages 6 to 11. "Sexually motivated crimes dominated this age group" (Boudreaux et al., 1999, p. 541). In these abductions, 88% of the victims were female and 80% were Caucasian. While the offender's race typically followed national demographic distributions, male offenders predominated. Strangers were the most common offenders (51%), followed by acquaintances (40%) and family members (9%).

The low percentage in Table 8.5 of 7.8% for 13- to 18-year-old victims is somewhat misleading in that it *only reflects parental killing* of children in this age range. In fact, if we look at the victimization rates from *all types* of offenders for 1996 to 2000, the rate increases from 0.89 per 100,000 at age 12 to 11.66 per 100,000 at age 17, indicating that juveniles in that age range are also victimized by other juveniles and gangs.

According to Kunz and Bahr (1996), of infants killed in the first week of life, 90.5% were killed by their mothers. From 1 week to 12 years, there were about equal numbers killed by mothers and father (Boudreaux et al., 2001). Beyond 1 year, offenders shift to a variety of caregivers and adults in the household. When children are murdered, there is typically a long history of abuse by caregivers. For small children, the most frequent occasions for abuse are toilet training and colic among infants. Toilet training a toddler requires large amounts of patience and perseverance. Colic in infants leads to crying without apparent reason and causes great distress among parents. In either case, caregivers lose patience and physically abuse the child. Adults other than parents, not biologically related to the child, may find that repetitive and fatal violence can be a way of dealing with a frustrating and largely unwanted child.

A study was done in Missouri in which deaths due to maltreatment were compared to deaths due to natural causes from 1992 to 1994. The authors found the following:

> Children residing in households with adults unrelated to them were 8 times more likely to die of maltreatment than children in households with 2 biological parents . . . Risk of maltreatment death was elevated for children residing with step, foster, or adoptive parents . . . and in households with other adult relatives present . . . Risk of maltreatment death was not increased for children living with only 1 biological parent. (Stiffman et al., 2002, p. 617)

During the first year of life, slightly more boys than girls are victimized, but overall Table 8.5 shows that 55.3% of boys were victimized compared to 44.7% of girls. Child Trends Data Bank (2002) reports that during the first year of life homicide rates were 10.2 per 100,000 for boys and 7.9 for girls. According to the latter source, non-Hispanic blacks are more at risk than other races of being killed during the first year of life. In 2000, blacks had an infant homicide rate of 25.6 per 100,000, non-Hispanic whites had a rate of 6.0, and Hispanics had a rate of 7.3.

Parricides—Children Killing Parents

Nothing shocks our society as much as a child killing a parent or stepparent. Following an earlier study of parricides, Heide (1992) examined parricides using FBI data from 1976 to 1999 (Heide & Petee, 2007).

It appears that the most common circumstance or motive for parricides among the six categories used are "other reasons" and arguments. "Other reasons" are not defined further in FBI data except that the category does not include felonies. There is a statistically significant difference between father and mother victims: "other reasons" and arguments are cited as motives or circumstances in 58.5% of the cases in which the father is the victims but only 44.5% where the mother is the victim.

Table 8.6 gives some of the victim characteristics for father and mother victims as well as offender characteristics. Different totals are given for victim and offender datasets and for variables where there are missing values, although in some cases the percentage differences are small.

Table 8.6 shows that the median age for father victims was 53 and the median age for mother victims was 57. Parricide is clearly a white crime, although there was a difference between mother and father victims: 67.6% of the father victims and 75.3% of the mother victims were white; 30.1% of the father victims and 22.6% of the mother victims were black. (The remaining races of victims accounted for around 2% of cases.)

Table 8.6 Characteristics of Parricides by Offenders and Mother and Father Victims

	Victims		Offenders	
Characteristic	**Father**	**Mother**	**Father Victim**	**Mother Victim**
Median age	53	57	23	27
Total	3,173	2,578	3,122	2,436
Race				
White	67.6	75.3	67.2	24.1
Black	30.1	22.1	30.4	1.1
Oriental	1.0	1.1	1.0	0.6
Indian	0.8	0.5	0.9	0.1
Other	0.1	0.2		
Unknown	0.4	0.3	0.4	0.3
Total			2,716	2,034
Gender				
Male			87.0	83.5
Female			13.0	16.5

Source: Table adapted from Heide and Petee (2007, pp. 1387 & 1389).

The right side of Table 8.6 gives offender characteristics for parricides from 1976 to 1999. Offenders who killed their fathers had a younger median age (23) than those who killed their mothers (27). The racial profiles for offenders are very similar to those for victims.

In addition to being a white crime, parricides are a male crime. Table 8.6 shows that 87.0% of the offenders who killed their fathers were male, while 83.5% of the matricides were committed by males.

A more refined age classification indicates that father victims are killed by younger offenders than mother victims. By age 18, 25.4% of the offenders had killed their father, while only 17% had killed their mother. By age 29, 72.3% of the offenders had killed their father, while only 55.6% had killed their mother.

Very rare (although the media thrives on these kinds of cases) is the dangerously antisocial killer who kills his or her parents without remorse, even where the parents are kind and supportive. The diagnosis of antisocial personality disorder was attributed to Michelle Ann White, age 14, and her 17-year-old brother, John Jr. The father had obtained custody of the children 10 years before the killing, following his divorce. When John Sr. returned home one evening, he was gunned down by a neighborhood boy while Michelle watched. The two children paid the hit man with three $20 bills from their father's wallet. When the two were arrested, they said the motive for killing their father was that he "had not permitted them to do whatever they wanted" (Heide, 1992b).

The common characteristics that emerge from Heide's (1992b) study of more than 50 cases of parricide are the following:

- Evidence of family violence,
- Attempts to get help, which failed,
- Attempts to run away or commit suicide,
- Isolation from peers,
- Increasingly intolerable family situation,
- Children feel helpless to change home situation,
- Inability to cope with what is happening to them,
- No criminal record,
- A gun available in the home,
- Alcoholism present in the parents,
- Amnesia reported after the murder, and
- Victim's death perceived as a relief by all involved.

Murders of parents by children younger than 12 are very rare, but they do occur, and they are diverted very early from the criminal justice process. There is a general legal consensus that a juvenile under the age of 9 cannot form the notion of criminal intent necessary to make the killing a murder (Heide, 1999). Ewing (1997) gives the example of a 3-year-old boy who watched

> as his intoxicated father beat his mother and threatened her with a pistol. When the man laid the pistol on a table, the boy grabbed it and shot him to death. Later, the boy told authorities, "I killed him. Now he's dead. If he would have hit my mother, I would have shot him again."

TRENDS

INTIMATE PARTNERS

Table 8.7 indicates the decline of intimate partner violence and changes in ages, race/ethnicity, and marital status. From 1994 through 2010 male and female intimate partner violence decreased by about 63%. The largest decline was for the age group 12 to 17; this may reflect an increased public concern for violence toward children. The smallest increase (12.8%) was for the age 50 and over group.

Although intimate partner violence declined for whites (60.5%) and blacks (61.6%), the amount of decline was very similar. Intimate partner violence declined by a large amount for Hispanics (78.1%). The largest decline based on marital status was for married people (65.6%) and divorced/widowed people (67.3%). By contrast, the smallest decline was for never-married people (55.9%) and separated people (60.6%). While it is not given in Table 8.7, the amount of total violent crime decreased by 74.0% during this period, and this also contributed to a decline in intimate partner violence.

Figure 8.1 shows the decline in intimate partner homicides from 1976 through 2004. The number has dropped dramatically in the 29-year period. In 1976, there were over

Table 8.7 Intimate Partner Violence by Demographic Characteristics

	Rates			
Demographics	**1994**	**2000**	**2005**	**2010**
Total IPV	9.8	5.1	3.8	3.6
Female	16.1	8.4	5.8	5.9
Male	3.0	1.6	1.1	1.1
12–17	7.4	4.4	2.1	0.9
18–24	33.9	24.3	14.7	9.7
25–34	31.9	17.5	10.5	12.1
35–49	17.9	7.2	7.1	9.6
50 or Older	1.5	0.7	0.9	1.3
White	15.6	8.8	5.4	6.2
Black/African American	20.3	8.5	7.8	7.8
Hispanic/Latina	18.8	6.8	5.9	4.1
Other	6.3	3.9	7.1	3.8
Never Married	18.2	11.4	7.8	8.0
Married	5.9	1.9	1.6	2.0
Divorced or Widowed	19.9	9.6	6.6	6.5
Separated	151.4	95.2	66.6	59.6

Source: Catalano (2012, p. 2).

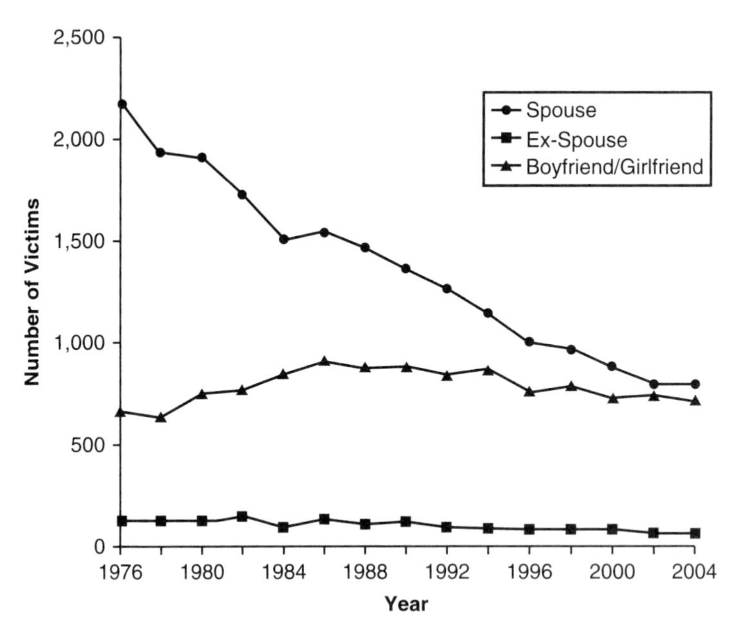

FIGURE 8.1 Homicides of Intimates by Victim–Offender Relationship, 1976–2004. *Source*: Bureau of Justice Statistics, http://www.ojp.usdoj.gov/bjs/homicides/intimtes.htm.

2,000 intimate partner murders, but by 2004, the number intimate partner murders had declined to 784. The number of murders involving boyfriends or girlfriends decreased slightly, from 770 in 1976 to 706 in 2004. Ex-spouse murders declined slightly, from 122 in 1976 to 54 in 2004. Overall, spouse murders decreased by 63.8% from 1976 to 2004.

That was the good news. The bad news is that the decline is lopsided: Far more women are being killed in intimate relationships than are men. Although the number of male murder victims declined from 1,348 to 385, the number of female victims declined from 1,596 to 1,159. This amounts to a 71% decline in male murder victims among intimates and only a 27% decline for female victims. The reasons for this differential decline will be discussed in a later section.

Much of this decline in men's rates is happening among black males. From 1976 to 2004, the number of black male intimate partner victims declined by 81%, dropping from 844 to 152 victims. For black females, the decline was 56%. The declines were 54% for white males and 5% for white females.

CHILD KILLINGS

For homicide victimization by race from 1976 to 2004, black children seem to show the greatest decline. For black children under age 5, the rate was 10.2 per 100,000 in 1976; it climbed to 10.7 in 1978 and then dropped to 8.1 in 1984. After remaining stable, it increased to 11.5 in 1986 and reached a low in 2004. The rates for white children have remained relatively stable, fluctuating between 2.2 and 2.5 per 100,000. Similarly, for children of other races, while the fluctuation has been somewhat greater—ranging between 0.9 and 3.2 per 100,000 in 1982—there has been a gradual decline to 2004.

For ages 0 to 17, the National Clearinghouse on Child Abuse and Neglect (2004) reports that rates of physical abuse of children have declined slightly. In 2000, the rate was 2.4 per 100,000 children; it remained at 2.3 for 2001, 2002, and 2003 and declined to 2.1 in 2004. Of cases of physical abuse, 24.1% were reported by educational personnel, 21.8% by law enforcement, and 11.0% by medical personnel.

EXPLANATIONS

INTIMATE PARTNER VIOLENCE

Research on battered intimate partners has shown there is a cycle of violence consisting of three stages. During the first stage, the *tension-building phase*, there is a gradual increase in tension-inducing activities such as verbal and physical intimidation and physical aggression by the abuser. In the second stage, the *actual battering incident*, the abuser unleashes his aggression and a violent incident occurs. The third stage is one of *loving contrition*, in which the abuser apologizes, shows remorse and numerous kindnesses, and promises that it will never happen again. Unfortunately, because this is a cycle, it simply starts again with the tension-building phase (Walker, 1979).

A single instance of violence toward a wife or an intimate partner may, indeed, be a rare and isolated instance in a relationship. Little is known about these occasions, but

Browne (1997) cites a number of scholars who suggest that once battering occurs, it often becomes chronic. The first battering incident leaves the victim shaken and vulnerable to expressions of remorse, which characterize the third part of the cycle. As the battering is repeated, the battered wife tries to rationalize what is happening to her. She may believe that her husband is under a lot of stress, that she needs to be more understanding, that she is at fault and needs to do a better job as a homemaker, or that she needs to try harder to please her husband—but to no avail. She continues to be battered until she dies of her injuries, the couple splits up, or she kills him (Browne, 1987).

Other theories include the view that intimate violence is caused by mental abnormalities. Makepeace (1986) identified psychological problems that characterize both male abusers and female victims. Generally, alcohol and substance abuse are frequent correlates of intimate partner violence, but the consensus is that neither agent plays a causal role (Browne, 1997; Miller & Wellford, 1997).

Although more research needs to be done, the view that severe physical abuse and neglect in childhood may help to explain intimate violence is supported. Browne, Williams, and Dutton (1999, p. 159) state

> Although later involvement in violence is only one of many potential outcomes of growing up in a violent home, two decades of research on nonlethal assaults by men against female partners documents a sharply increased risk of assaultiveness among men who have experienced or witnessed physical abuse in childhood.

This view receives support from the findings of the National Violence Against Women survey. Statistical examination of a large number of causes of intimate partner victimizations revealed a strong link between child maltreatment and subsequent violence. Both women and men who were physically assaulted as children by adult caretakers were more likely to report being victimized by current intimate partners. More research is needed to determine whether maltreated children are simply more tolerant of violent behavior and are more likely to get involved with abusive adults. Another possibility is that persons who report child maltreatment are more willing to report other types of victimizations.

For cases of violence that end in homicide, the homicide is just the final act. Aware that they are going to be beaten yet one more time, battered wives, victims, may kill because they fear for their lives, because they fear the abuser will harm their children, or simply because, as one woman put it, "I just couldn't take no more beating" (Gillespie, 1989, p. 53). Short of torture in wartime, it is difficult to find any levels of brutality similar to wife battering. The following case is illustrative:

> Betty and Carl Hundley were married for ten years. During that time Carl's abuse of Betty has been constant and severe. He hit her, kicked her, and choked her. He had broken her nose at least five times and had knocked out several of her teeth. He had repeatedly broken her ribs, and he frequently pushed or kicked her down the stairs. She was a diabetic; and a number of times Carl hid her insulin or diluted it with water, causing her to go into a diabetic coma. His pattern was to indulge in this sort of violence whenever he was drunk.

> Betty killed Carl and at her trial her sister testified that she had seen Betty beaten so badly that blood poured from her face and stitches were required. In one instance, Betty hid at her sister's home. Carl found her, dragged her from her hiding place by the hair, threw her on the ground, and kicked her until the police arrived.
>
> Six weeks before Carl was killed, Betty was discharged from the hospital from the latest beating. She decided she could take no more, began carrying a gun, and moved into a motel. Carl found her, beat and raped her and, when he threatened to beat her with a beer bottle, she took out the gun and shot him. She was convicted of involuntary manslaughter and sentenced to serve two to five years in prison. (Gillespie, 1989, p. 73)

The question that frequently arises is this: Why do women stay in relationships where they are repeatedly violently attacked? There are several corollaries that are consistent with the cycle of violence discussed previously. First, battered women become increasingly socially isolated and lose the "reality check" that contact with friends and family can provide. At the outset of the relationship, the abuser wants her to spend time only with him, which she finds flattering and an indication of her importance to him. As time goes on, he gets more and more resentful of any outside contacts with family members, friends, and even eye contact with male strangers. He insists that she not go out shopping or anywhere else without him, and to do so is to risk a beating.

Second, the battered woman may be economically dependent on the offender. Without any economic skills or a college education, which was characteristic of many women in a traditional marriage, what can she do to support herself? This becomes particularly problematic if she has children. Day care is expensive and a minimum-wage job is not going to cover the essential living expenses or even make it possible for her to become more marketable through education.

Finally, our earlier discussion of the constraints that battered women face as well as the description of the cycle of violence implies that the most viable theory for intimate partner violence is one of patriarchy—that is, a view that women are the property of fathers and husbands who may treat them well or badly as they see fit. The central issue is not patriarchy, however, but power and control in a relationship, whether the partners are married or cohabiting or in a same-sex or opposite-sex relationship. Whoever has the greatest amount of power and control can inflict violence on the less powerful partner without fearing retaliation. The reason patriarchy appears so prominently in discussions of intimate partner violence is that norms of traditional marriage and males' generally superior strength and capacity to inflict physical injury give them a distinct advantage in terms of power and control.

While intimate partner violence and homicide are still a problem, rates are declining, largely because increasingly women don't remain in violent relationships. Dugan, Nagin, and Rosenfeld (1999) studied the decline in intimate partner homicides. Based on the fact that female intimate partners kill when they are attacked or believe an attack is imminent, and that male violence toward females is more serious than the reverse, the authors proposed what they called an exposure reduction theory. This states that factors that reduce exposure to violent relationships and provide protective alternatives to violence are more closely related to rates at which women kill their partners than rates at which men kill theirs. The researchers found the following:

- The higher the rate of marriage, the higher the rates of male- and female-perpetrated homicide.
- A higher divorce rate lowers the rate at which wives kill husbands, but not the reverse.
- Declining marriage rates and increased divorce rates are associated with increases in the rate of unmarried males killing their partners.
- The effects of educational and economic status differences between partners were mixed.

Research on the effectiveness of a number of social changes to protect women in a battering relationship suggest that they have a greater effect on whether wives kill husband than on whether husbands kill wives. One of the most persistent problems in the modern setting is that while battered wives successfully use alternatives to escape violent relationships, laws and policies have been less successful at preventing male intimate partners from pursuing and killing them.

VIOLENCE TOWARD CHILDREN

One explanation for parental violence toward children is that the pregnancy is psychologically denied. An example was the so-called prom-mom, Melissa Drexler, who went to her prom, went to the bathroom, delivered a baby, wrapped it in garbage bags, threw it in the garbage can, and returned to the prom (Burns, 2006).

The expectant mother may be fearful and concerned about what her parents and friends will think; overwhelmed by guilt and shame, she denies the pregnancy until she is faced with the newborn child. Kelleher (1998) has suggested that such cases are the result of dissociative disorders. According to Kelleher (1998), dissociative amnesia is an inability to recall important information, usually of a traumatic or stressful nature. Confronted with the undeniable fact of a newborn infant, rather than acknowledging what happened, she disposes of the baby as quickly as possible.

While the latter explains a limited number of neonaticides, a more common reason is that the mother either does not know or is not prepared to accept the dependence imposed by the birth of a child. A study by Overpeck, Brenner, Trumble, Trifiletti, and Berendes (1998) linked together 34,895,000 birth and death certificates for the period 1983 to 1991 to study 2,776 homicides during the first year of life. They found a number of factors indicating that parents, particularly the mother, were simply unprepared to deal with the dependence of an infant a kind of resistance by default. Half the homicides occurred by the fourth month of life. The most important risk factors were a second or subsequent infant born to a mother less than 17 years old (relative risk, 10.9) or 17 to 19 years old (relative risk, 9.3) compared with a first infant born to a mother 25 years old or older; a maternal age of less than 15 years, compared with an age of at least 25 (relative risk, 6.8); no prenatal care as compared with early prenatal care (relative risk, 10.4); and less than 12 years of education among mothers who were at least 17 years old (relative risk, 8.0), compared with 16 or more years of education.

INTERVENTIONS

REDUCING INTIMATE PARTNER VIOLENCE

Beginning in the 1970s and continuing for the past 30 years, the criminal justice system's response to domestic violence has proceeded along three parallel tracks: criminal punishment and deterrence of batterers, treatment programs, and restraining orders designed to protect victims (Fagan, 1996). How successful have these changes been?

The most succinct answer is provided by Fagan (1996, p. 1):

> Thus far, however, research and evaluation on arrest and prosecution, civil or criminal protection orders, batterer treatment, and community interventions have generated weak or inconsistent evidence of deterrent effects on either repeat victimization or repeat offending. For every study that shows promising results, one or more show either no effect or even negative results that increase the risks to victims.

Criminal Legal Sanctions

The simplest answer to the problem of domestic violence is to arrest the offender. In a Minneapolis experiment, police officers responding to a domestic violence call were randomly assigned to pursue one of three courses of action: (1) arresting the suspect, (2) ordering one of the parties out of the residence, and (3) advising the couple. Sherman and Berk (1984) found that the risk of subsequent offending was reduced almost 50% by making an arrest.

However, replications in five other jurisdictions provided conflicting results. One important factor was what was called a "stake-in-conformity" hypothesis. Arrest or the threat of arrest was more likely to have a deterrent effect if the offender was employed or married. In short, a criminal justice sanction is effective if it also means the person will lose something he values highly, like his job. There are relatively few prosecutions of domestic violence, which may also serve to explain why arrest is not very effective (Fagan, 1996).

Batterer Treatment

Treatment programs for batterers vary in their clinical orientation, although most emphasize the need for anger control and attempt to show the batterer the relationship between power and control. Unfortunately, the quality of evaluation research design is such that it is difficult to arrive at any reliable conclusions (Fagan, 1996).

Civil Legal Sanctions

The use of restraining orders for battered women began with Pennsylvania in 1976. Since that time, every state has passed legislation for protection against domestic violence. The advantages are that protective orders are victim-initiated, rely on a relaxed standard of proof, and offer protection for victims.

Unfortunately, they offer relatively little protection. In one study cited by Fagan (1996), 60% of 300 women with protection orders were interviewed twice in one year and suffered abuse at least once. One in five reported receiving murder threats, and severe violence was reported by 29% of them.

What Can Be Done?

Although there is no persuasive evidence to suggest effective responses to the problem of intimate partner violence, the research does offer some useful future avenues. First, the research suggests that legal sanctions are effective when they are reinforced by informal social controls. The "stake-in-conformity" hypothesis suggests that the deterrent effect of arrests is more likely to work if there is a social cost associated with arrest, such as loss of job, relationships, and children, and loss of status in the neighborhood.

The difficulty with the latter is that offenders may have nothing to lose by being arrested. Repeat offenders in the Minneapolis experiment as well as in other replications came from neighborhoods characterized by high unemployment, poverty, and divorce rates.

Second, Fagan (1996) suggests that domestic violence cases are not assigned a high priority for prosecution or court action. If prosecutors and courts assign a higher priority to prosecuting other kinds of cases, any deterrent effects will be lost.

Finally, the deterrence logic of criminalization assumes a rational actor—someone who weighs the costs of violence in the form of legal sanctions. In a study of batterers, Dutton (1995) suggested that batterers may have impaired cognition or mental disorders. Clearly, this may be a problem with offenders who pursue their intimate partners after they have left the relationship and kill them. The behavior may be purposeful but it is not rational, which compromises the logic of deterrence.

REDUCING FAMILY VIOLENCE

Legislation has been passed to encourage and sometimes require reporting of child abuse by social workers, law enforcement, medical personnel, and educators. Treatment and prevention programs and agencies are also available. Websites such as the National Clearinghouse for Child Abuse and Neglect Information (http://www.childwelfare.gov) provide an abundance of information on how and where to report abuse and neglect as well as publications on various aspects of the problem. Like intimate partner violence, reducing nonlethal violence will help prevent lethal violence.

The legal system has been active in the more traditional role of providing punishment and deterrence for juvenile homicide offenders, including those who kill their parents. In recent decades, the public has become outraged at the leniency extended to murderers under the age of 18. The response has been laws in every state that provide for the prosecution of some juveniles as adults, including the imposition of the death penalty. These laws require that older juveniles who commit the most serious violent crimes—such as homicide, rape, kidnapping, armed robbery, and sodomy—may be prosecuted, convicted, and sentenced to long prison terms and, in some jurisdictions, receive a death sentence. In the 2005 session, however, the U.S. Supreme Court, by a vote of 5–4, held that the Eighth and Fourteenth Amendments forbid the execution of offenders who were under the age of 18 when their crimes were committed (*Roper v. Simmons*, 2005).

Between 1985 and 1993, nine adults were executed who were juveniles at the time of their crimes (Kelleher, 1998). There is little evidence that changes in the law or the imposition of the death penalty accounted for the decline in juvenile homicides from 1993 to 1997—or on the juvenile homicide rate in general. There is no evidence that the death penalty is a deterrent, and its discriminatory application has been repeatedly demonstrated (Bailey & Peterson, 1998; Bedau, 1982). With respect to changing laws to treat juveniles as adults, harsher punishments have not had a positive effect on adults, and there is no reason to believe they will be more effective with juveniles (Kelleher, 1998).

Finally, policies to reduce access to firearms have been largely unsuccessful. In their study of inner-city youth and guns, Sheley and Wright (1995) pointed out, first, that there are simply too many juveniles carrying weapons or having access to them to believe that current policies will have any effect. Second, the authors found that self-protection was the most important reason for carrying a weapon. Inner-city dwellers live in a truly dangerous environment, and many inner-city juveniles interact daily with a demographic group characterized by high rates of violence.

CONCLUSION: IS IT TIME FOR ANOTHER LOOK?

The problem of intimate and family violence has been addressed in a typically American fashion: We made laws against it. Although the criminalization of family violence may be an appropriate response, its effectiveness can be questioned. Arresting batterers has been shown to be of limited value; protection orders are not effective; intimate partner violence does not receive the same kind of attention from the courts as other kinds of crimes; and battering husbands can still hunt down the wives who have left and kill them.

Other kinds of family violence, although less common, are better recorded but not more effectively treated. Child abuse continues to be a major problem, and the consequences of child abuse are lifelong and continue the cycle of violence. Research and evaluation studies in this area are spotty. We don't have adequate knowledge of what works and what does not, and we don't know what works under what kinds of circumstances. What is needed is not only more research, but a better integration between research and policy. Research on various programs and policies is not organized in a way that can be applied usefully. Although many alternatives have been developed to reduce intimate partner and family violence, they are not evaluated in a way that meets minimum methodological standards. Further, continued resources for these programs are made available on the basis of purely political decisions in which evaluations play little or no part.

Finally, intimate partner violence and family violence occur in what are traditionally and legally viewed as private settings. Even though privacy and intimacy are important, due to the prevalence of these types of violence, the government has a clear and legitimate interest in intervening to protect its citizens; the state has a right and obligation to protect its citizens even in private settings. The challenge is how to reduce intimate partner and family violence without intruding on socialization processes that are central to making us humans.

DISCUSSION QUESTIONS

1. Describe the cycle of violence.
2. Discuss research support for the view that the greater the inequality between intimate partners, the greater the risk for violence.

3. What is meant by the statement that intimate partner violence is "chronic"? Is that supported by research on intimate partner violence in other countries.

SUGGESTED READINGS

Browne, A. (1987). *When battered women kill.* New York: Free Press.

Sherman, L. W., & Berk, R. A. (1984). The specified deterrent effects of arrest for domestic assault. *American Sociological Review, 49,* 261–272.

Ewing, C. P. (1990). *When children kill: The dynamics of juvenile homicide.* Lexington, MA: Lexington Books.

REFERENCES

Bailey, W. C., & Peterson, R. D. (1998). Capital punishment, homicide, and deterrence: An assessment of the evidence and extension to female homicide. In M. D. Smith & M. A. Zahn (Eds.), *Homicide: A sourcebook of social research* (pp. 257–276). Thousand Oaks, CA: Sage.

Basile, K. C., & Saltzman, L. E. (2002). *Sexual violence surveillance: Uniform definitions and recommended data elements.* Atlanta, GA: National Center for Injury Prevention and Control, Centers for Disease Control and Prevention.

Bedau, H. A. (1982). *The death penalty in America* (3rd ed.). Oxford: Oxford University Press.

Black, M. C., Basile, K. C., Breiding, M. J., Smith, S. G., Walters, M. I., Merrick, M. T., . . . & Stevens, M. R. (2011). *The national intimate partner and sexual violence survey: 2010 summary.* Atlanta, GA: National Center for Injury Prevention and Control, Centers for Disease Control and Prevention.

Boudreaux, M. C., Lord, W. C., & Dutra, R. L. (1999). Child abduction: Aged-based analyses of offender, victim, and offense characteristics in 550 cases of alleged child disappearance. *Journal of Forensic Sciences, 44,* 539–553.

Boudreaux, M. C., Lord, W. C., & Jarvis, J. P. (2001). Behavioral perspectives on child homicides: The role of access, vulnerability, and routine activities theory. *Trauma, Violence, & Abuse, 2,* 56–78.

Bourget, D., Grace, J., & Whitehurst, L. (2007). A review of maternal and paternal filicide. *Journal of the American Academy of Psychiatry and Law, 35,* 74–82.

Browne, A. (1987). *When battered women kill.* New York: Free Press.

Browne, A. P., Williams K. R, & Dutton D. G., (1999). Homicide between intimate partners: A 20-year review. In M. D. Smith & M. A. Zahn (Eds.), *Homicide: A sourcebook of social research* (pp. 149–164). Thousand Oaks, CA: Sage.

Burns, K. S. (2006). Infanticide: Melissa Drexler. Retrieved from http://www.karisable.com/drexler.html.

Campbell, J. C., Glass, N., Sharps, P. W., Laughon, K., & Bloom, T. (2007). Intimate partner homicide: Review and implications of research and policy. *Trauma Violence & Abuse, 8,* 246–269.

Catalano, S. (2012). *Intimate partner violence, 1993–2010.* Washington, DC: Bureau of Justice Statistics.

Chew, K. S. Y., McCleary, R., Lew, M. A., & Wang, J. C. (1999). The epidemiology of child homicide in California, 1981 through 1990. *Homicide Studies, 3,* 151–169.

Child Trends Data Bank. (2002). Infant homicide. Retrieved March 12, 2009, from http://www.childtrendsdatabank.org/pdf/72_PDF.pdf.

Crittenden, P. M., & Craig, S. E. (1990). Developmental trends in the nature of child homicide. *Journal of Interpersonal Violence, 5,* 202–216.

Crume, T. L., DiGuiseppi, C., Byers, T., Sirotnak, A. P., & Garrett, C. J. (2002). *Under ascertainment of child maltreatment fatalities by death certificates, 1990–1998.* Retrieved March 15, 2009, from http://www.pediatrics.org/cgi/content/full/110/2/el 8.

Dugan, L., Nagin, D. S., & Rosenfeld, R. (1999). Explaining the decline in intimate partner homicide: The effects of changing domesticity, women's status, and domestic violence resources. *Homicide Studies, 3,* 187–214.

Dutton, D. G. (1995). *The domestic assault of women* (2nd ed.). Boston: Allyn-Bacon.

Ewigman, B., Kiviahan, C., & Land, G. (1993). The Missouri child fatality study: Underreporting of maltreatment fatalities among children younger than five years of age, 1983 through 1986. *Pediatrics, 91,* 330–337.

Ewing, C. P. (1997). *Fatal families: The dynamics of intrafamilial homicide.* Thousand Oaks, CA: Sage.

Fagan, J. (1996, January). The criminalization of domestic violence: Promises and limits. Paper presented at the 1995 Conference on Criminal Justice Research and Evaluation, Washington, DC.

Federal Bureau of Investigation (FBI). (2006). *Crime in the United States 2004.* Retrieved June 2006 from http://www.fbi.gov/ucr/cius_04/.

Finkelhor, D. (1997). The victimization of children and youth: Developmental victimology. In R. C. Davis, A. J. Lurigio, & W. G. Skogan (Eds.), *Victims of crime* (2nd ed., pp. 86–107). Thousand Oaks, CA: Sage.

García-Moreno, C., Jansen, A. F. M., Ellsberg, Heise, M. L., & Watts, C. (2005). *WHO multi-country study on women's health and domestic violence against women: Initial results on prevalence, health outcomes and women's responses.* Geneva: World Health Organization.

Gelles, R. J., & Straus, M. A. (1988). *Intimate violence.* New York: Simon and Schuster.

Gillespie, C. K. (1989). *Justifiable homicide:Battered women, self-defense, and the law.* Columbus: Ohio State University Press.

Heide, K. M. (1992). *Why kids kill parents: Child abuse and adolescent homicide.* Columbus: Ohio State University Press.

Heide, K. M. (1999). Youth homicide: An integration of psychological, sociological, and biological approaches. In M. D. Smith & M. A. Zahn (Eds.), *Homicide: A sourcebook of social research* (pp. 221–238). Thousand Oaks, CA: Sage.

Heide, K. M., & Petee, T. A. (2007). Parricide: An empirical analysis of 24 years of U.S. data. *Journal of Interpersonal Violence, 22,* 1382–1399.

Herman-Giddens, M. E., Brown, G., Verbiest, S., Carlson, P. J., Hooten, E. G., Howell, E., & Butts, J. D. (1999). Underascertainment of child abuse mortality in the United States. *Journal of the American Medical Association, 281,* 463–467.

Kunz, J., & Bahr, S. J. (1996). A profile of parental homicide against children. *Journal of Family Violence, 11,* 347–362.

Makepeace, J. (1986). Gender differences in courtship violence victimization. *Family Relations, 35,* 383–388.

McClain, P. W., Sacks, J. J., Froehlke, R. G., & Ewigman, B. G. (1993). Estimates of fatal child abuse and neglect, United State, 1979 through 1988. *Pediatrics, 91,* 338–343.

Miller, S. L., & Wellford, C. F. (1997). Patterns and correlates of interpersonal violence. In A. P. Cardarelli (Ed.), *Violence between intimate partners: Patterns, causes, and effects* (pp. 19–26). Boston: Allyn and Bacon.

National Clearinghouse on Child Abuse and Neglect. (2004). *Child maltreatment*. Washington, DC: Author.

Overpeck, M. D., Brenner, R. A., Trumble, A. C., Trifiletti, L. B., & Berendes, H. W. (1998). Risk factors for infant homicide in the United States. *New England Journal of Medicine, 339*, 1211–1216.

Resnick, P. J. (1970). Child murder by parents: A psychiatric review of filicide. *American Journal of Psychiatry, 126*, 325–334.

Riedel, M. (2010). Homicide-suicides in the United States: A review of the literature. *Sociology Compass, 4*, 430–441.

Sheley, J. F., & Wright, J. D. (1995). *In the line of fire: Youth, guns, and violence in urban America*. New York: Aldine de Gruyter.

Sherman, L. W., & Berk, R. A. (1984). The specified deterrent effects of arrest for domestic assault. *American Sociological Review, 49*, 261–272.

Smith, S, G., Katherine A. Fowler, K. A., & Niolon, P. H. (2014). Intimate partner homicide and corollary victims in 16 states: National Violent Death Reporting System, 2003–2009. *American Journal of Public Health, 104*, 461–466.

Stiffman, M. N., Schnitzer, P. G., Adam, P., Kruse, R. L., & Ewigman, B. (2002). Household composition and risk of fatal child maltreatment. *Pediatrics,109*, 615–621.

Walker, L. E. (1979). *The battered woman*. New York: Harper and Row.

West, S. G. (2007). An overview of filicide. *Psychiatry, 4*(2), 48–57.

World Health Organization. (2005). *WHO multi-country study on women's health and domestic violence against women: summary report of initial results on prevalence, health outcomes and women's responses*. Geneva: Author.

CHAPTER 9

WORKPLACE VIOLENCE

INTRODUCTION

Workplace violence has existed whenever people have worked. It is has only been since the 1960s and 1970s, however, that it has become an area of concern for researchers, governments, and employers (Bowie, 2002). According to Henson (2010), 5.3% of industries reported as least one incident of workplace violence in 2005, with 62.7% of industries in which employees work directly with the public experiencing violence in the workplace. The most common forms of violence were simple and aggravated assault, which accounted for 93.8% of all violent crime in the United States.

Workplace violence imposes a significant cost on employers. According to Perone (1999), it costs American employers between $4 billion and $6 billion annually. According to Philbrick, Sparks, Hass, and Arsenault (2003), the average financial cost to employers of a serious workplace violence incident is $250,000, while a less serious incident is estimated to cost as much as $25,000.

There are major difficulties in defining what is meant by violence, the workplace, and the relationship between the two. If we put aside behaviors related to physical harm for the moment, however, Chappell and Di Martino (1999) list a large variety of workplace behaviors that are psychologically violent: ostracism, leaving offensive messages, aggressive posturing, rude gestures, swearing, shouting, name calling, innuendo, and deliberate silence.

There are problems establishing the work-relatedness of the violent incident, as Perone (1999) indicates. In the United States, any employee "includes paid and unpaid family workers, and may include owners of incorporated businesses, or members of partnerships" (Toscano & Weber, 1995). This excludes voluntary workers as well as former employees who attack an organization's employees. Is an employee who is attacked en route to and from the office included as a victim of occupational violence?

As an instance of the measurement problems, Davis (1988) gathered death certificates on homicides from five populous Texas counties in which the victim was classified as having died at work. He compared these cases to medical examiners' records to determine to what extent the death certificates agreed with medical examiners' judgments of workplace homicides. Of the 533 confirmed cases in the analysis, 386 had accurate classification of workplace homicides. What Davis found is that if the victim was working in a high-risk industry (taxi driver, waiter or waitress, police officer) at the time the injury occurred, the death certificate had high levels of agreement. If the victim was classified as belonging to a low-risk industry (student or housewife) *but was working in a high-risk industry at the time of the workplace homicide,* the homicide was frequently misclassified.

MULTIPLIER EFFECTS

Citing a large number of other researchers, Perone (1999) points out that workplace violence has multiplier effects that extend beyond the financial costs to the employers. Thus, in the case of a homicide and the obvious costs to the victim's family, there is a cost to other people working in the same organization. If the violent event is not fatal, there are effects on the victim. While other crimes have multiplier effects, this may be more pronounced in the case of workplace violence because the victim and the victim's coworkers generally return to the same location where the crime occurred to continue their work.

Costs for the Victim

The following are the victim's costs:

- Immediate and future medical expenses
- Short- and long-term psychological stress (possibly leading to posttraumatic stress disorder, substance abuse, and stress-related disorders)
- Opportunity costs if the victim's employability is reduced
- Job displacement if the victim refuses to work in conditions that are similar to prior victimization
- Increased fear of crime.

Costs for the Employer

The following are possible costs for the employer:

- Loss of property and property damage through robbery
- Increased insurance premiums
- Legal expenses incurred with liability actions
- Absenteeism and loss of work quality
- Loss of clients through failure to meet production orders
- Premature staff turnover and increased costs of training
- Costs of prevention efforts.

Costs for Society

The following are possible costs to society:

- Stress, trauma, and financial costs to the victim's support network
- Interpersonal difficulties between the victim and his or her intimate partner
- Elevated costs borne by government health care systems
- Loss of business confidence (Perone, 1999).

From a broad perspective, an appropriate definition is essential to sound policy and practice. Perone (1999, p. 18) summarizes the difficulties:

> If the definitional parameters of violence are drawn too narrowly, there is a risk of over-concentrating on what are the essentially sensational, though rarely enacted, forms of occupational violence, while overlooking the more prevalent, though insidious, manifestations which may have longer lasting effects, and which represent more of a financial drain on our health system, and our economy generally (for example, occupational diseases, stress, and stress-related illnesses).
>
> On the contrary, if the term "violence" is defined too broadly, then it is important to question the value of treating violence in the workplace as a phenomenon separate from the larger universe of violence.

While it is important to be aware of the larger issues involved in workplace violence, in this chapter we will use the following definition: "violent acts, including physical assaults and threats of assault, directed toward persons at work or on duty" (National Institute for Occupational Safety and Health, 1996, p. 1).

PATTERNS AND TRENDS

TYPES OF WORKPLACE VIOLENCE

If there is little consensus about the definition of workplace violence, it should not be surprising there are multiple classifications of types of workplace violence. One widely used threefold classification of workplace violence has been developed by the California Division of Occupational Safety and Health (Cal/OSHA, 1995). In type I offenses, the offender has no legitimate business relationship with the workplace but enters to commit a robbery or other criminal act. For example, in California, 60% of offenders in workplace homicides enter a small late-night establishment, such as a liquor or convenience store, to commit a robbery. Type II events involve an assault by someone who is either a recipient or the object of a service provided by the victim or the workplace. About 30% of workplace homicides in California fit in this category, and they include people such as police or correctional personnel; bus, taxi, or railway drivers; and health care providers. Type III workplace violence events involve persons who have some employment-related involvement with the location (e.g., a current or former employee, or supervisor). These events account for only 10% of workplace homicides in California.

In 2001, the University of Iowa Injury Prevention Center held a workplace violence intervention workshop, and their final report described four types of workplace violence. The report represents a synthesis of 37 invited participants from within industry; organized labor; municipal, state, and federal governments;, and academia.

Type I, Criminal Intent

In type I offenses, the offender does not have any legitimate business relationship with the workplace. The primary motive is theft, with the use of deadly weapons resulting increasingly in fatal injury. High-risk targets are workers who exchange cash as part of the job and/or work alone. Hendricks, Jenkins, and Anderson (2007) analyzed workplace fatalities from the Bureau of Labor Statistics for 1993 to 2002. Table 9.1 gives the national breakdown of workplace homicides.

Type II, Customer/Client

As with type II in the Cal/OSHA classification, the offender is a customer or client of the victim. The violent act occurs in conjunction with the normal duties that occur in the workplace. Unlike in California, 3.8% of workplace homicides nationwide are in this category (see Table 9.1). The following is an example of Type II workplace violence:

> Rhonda Bedow, a nurse who works in a state-operated psychiatric facility in Buffalo, New York, was attacked by an angry patient who had a history of threatening behavior, particularly against female staff. He slammed Bedow's head down onto a counter after learning that he had missed the chance to go outside with a group of other patients. Bedow suffered a concussion, a bilaterally dislocated jaw, an eye injury, and permanent scarring on her face from the assault. She still suffers from short-term memory problems resulting from the attack. When she returned to work after recuperating, the perpetrator was still on her ward, and resumed his threats against her. (University of Iowa Injury Prevention Center, 2001, p. 7)

Type III, Worker on Worker

Type III violence occurs when a former or present employee attacks coworkers. This kind of workplace violence may be the culmination of a series of increasingly hostile behaviors from the offender. This type of workplace violence is best known to people as "going postal," where an offender attacks coworkers. In a subsequent section, we will show that the postal service is no more likely than any other industry to be victimized, as this type of violence is not limited to any specific occupation. Table 9.1 indicates that type III violence accounts for about 8.2% of workplace homicides nationwide.

The following is an example of type III workplace homicide.

> On the day of the shooting Williams had to attend a mandatory ethics and diversity class together with 13 others. According to some colleagues Williams arrived at the plant in a very agitated state and made threats to kill workers, though others who had talked to him prior to

Table 9.1 Workplace Homicides by Type, Frequency, and Percentage in the U.S., 1993–2002

Workplace Violence Types	Total Homicides	Percentage
Type I, Robberies and other crimes	6,682	82.4
Type II, Customer/client	313	3.8
Type III, Coworker/former coworker	669	8.2
Type IV, Relatives/other personal acquaintances	447	5.5
Total	8,111	100.0

Source: Hendricks, Jenkins, and Anderson (2007, p. 121).

the shooting stated that he "gave no indications that anything was wrong."[3] At the meeting Williams stayed only for a few minutes. After having a normal conversation with his colleague Al Collier, who described it as a "friendly littletalk", he suddenly stormed out of the room with the words "Y'all can handle this."[3] Telling his supervisor, Jeff McWilliams, that he would take the matters into his own hands Williams went to retrieve several guns from his pick-up truck. Armed with a 12 gauge Winchester 1200 shotgun On the day of the shooting Williams had to attend a mandatory ethics and diversity class together with 13 others. According, a Ruger Mini-14 on his back, bandoliers with ammunition draped across his chest and a bandana on his head he returned to the annex, where the meeting was held.

At approximately 9:30 a.m. Williams entered the room, yelling "I told y'all to stop fucking with me! Didn't I tell y'all not to fuck with me?,"[3] and began shooting. He first killed Mickey Fitzgerald, who tried to calm him down, with a shot in the face, before turning his attention towards a group of four workers cowering on the floor. Remarking "There's four right there." Williams killed Sam Cockrell, whom he believed to have made complaints about him to the management, wounded Al Collier, who was shot in the back and right hand, as well as Charles Scott, and fatally wounded DeLois Bailey, when she was trying to run out of the room. Steve Cobb, the plant manager, as well as Brad Bynum, Chuck McReynolds and Brenda Dubose, whose head and hand were grazed by bullet fragments, were also wounded by ricochet. Williams then went out of the room, but returned after a short while and, searching and calling for Jack Johns, the production manager, he continued shooting. Williams eventually left the annex and headed for the main factory, searching for other employees who had reported him to the management for making racist threats. There he was apprehended by his colleague Pete Threatt, who tried to take away his gun, but Williams pushed him out of the way, lowered the shotgun with the words "Get out of my way or I'll kill you, too." and moved on. While Threatt tried to make the others aware of the gunman, screaming for people to take cover, Williams walked through the plant and shot five other people, most of them at point blank range. He killed Charles J. Miller, Thomas Willis and Lynette McCall at their work stations and wounded Henry Odom and Randy Wright, before his girlfriend and co-worker, Shirley J. Price, began pleading with him to stop shooting. Williams then committed suicide in front of her by shooting himself in the torso, thus ending his rampage which had lasted approximately ten minutes. (Wikipedia, 2014)

Type IV, Personal Relationship

In type IV workplace violence, the offender generally has a relationship with the victim but not with anyone else in the workplace. While the previous three types were the same as those given by Cal/OSHA, this type is added by the Iowa report because of the insidious nature of domestic violence. Victims are disproportionately female and represent a continuation of domestic conflicts carried to the workplace. Table 9.1 shows that 5.5% of workplace homicides were in the type IV category (Hendricks, Jenkins, & Anderson, 2007).

A typical case of this type of workplace violence involves an estranged husband who follows his wife to her workplace and kills her. Frequently, other employees are killed as well.

The different classifications provide illustrations of the different types of workplace violence, victim–offender relationships, occupations at risk, and their relative proportions. Unfortunately, there is not sufficient consensus over type of classification to justify using one or the other as a basis to gather data on workplace violence. In what follows, we will first consider nonfatal forms of workplace violence, followed by workplace homicide

NONFATAL WORKPLACE VIOLENCE

According to the National Crime Victimization Survey (NCVS), in 2009, 572,000 nonfatal violent crimes (rape/sexual assault, robbery, and aggravated and simple assault) occurred against persons age 16 older while they were at work or on duty. This accounted for about 24% of cases of nonfatal violence against employed persons age 16 or older.

From 2005 to 2009, the most common form of nonfatal workplace violence victimization was simple assault (with a rate of 4.0 per 1,000), followed by aggravated assault (0.9), robbery (0.2), and rape/sexual assault (0.1). Workplace violence declined by 35% from 2002 (6 per 1,000) to 2009 (4 per 1,000). This compares to a 37% decline for non-workplace violence for the same period. From 1993 to 2002, a longer period of time, the rate of workplace violence declined by 62%; for the same period, non-workplace violence declined 51% (Harrell, 2011).

Demographic Characteristics of Workplace Violence Victims

Males were more likely to be victims of workplace violence (5.9 per 1,000) than females (4.1) (Table 9.2). For comparison, the rates for non-workplace violence were 17.2 for males and 15.5 for females.

Table 9.2 Percentage of Workplace and Non-Workplace Violence, by Race and Age

	Percent of Nonfatal Violence Victimization	
Victim Characteristic	**Workplace**	**Non-Workplace**
White	47.6	50.3
Black	47.5	58.4
Hispanic	33.9	51.7
Native American	61.5	62.6
Asian/Pacific Islander	41.7	51.0
Other	64.5	39.9
Age 16–19	28.3	3[illegible].8
20–24	38.1	48.1
25–34	56.3	53.5
35–49	47.4	57.2
50–64	40.5	52.7
65 & older	33.1	71.5

Source: Adapted from Harrell (2011, p. 8).

Table 9.2 shows that whites (47.6%) were more likely to report workplace violence than blacks (47.5%), while blacks had a higher percentage of non-workplace violence (58.4%). While Native Americans had a higher percentage (61.5%) than whites (47.6%), the difference was not statistically significant. Hispanics experienced lower percentages of workplace violence (33.9%) than Asian/Pacific Islanders (41.7%), but the two groups had the same percentages of non-workplace violence (51.7%). Asian/Pacific Islanders experienced the lowest rate (8.6%) of non-workplace violence.

While 16- to 19-year-old victims had the lowest percentage of reporting workplace violence (28.3%) and the lowest percentage of non-workplace violence (39.8%), it is important to note that only 4.8% of people in this age group were employed. Among employed persons, those aged 25 to 34 experienced the highest percentage of reporting workplace violence, while older groups had much higher percentages of non-workplace victimization.

Table 9.3 shows that most cases of workplace violence are committed by strangers. This represents primarily type I workplace violence (i.e., "Robberies and Other Crimes").

The three types of relationships included under "Current or Former" in Table 9.3 (supervisors, employee, coworker) are very similar to type III, workplace violence among workers and coworkers. Table 9.3 shows that workplace violence committed by coworkers is most common type of workplace violence (16.3%) committed by "current or former" employees.

Excluding coworkers and strangers, workers who deal with customers/clients (e.g., taxi drivers, police officers, and gas station attendants) or patients (e.g., nurses and mental health occupations) have the highest risk of workplace violence.

Table 9.3 Victim–Offender Relationship for Victims of Workplace Violence

	Percentage of Workplace Violence	
Victim–Offender Relationship	**Male**	**Female**
Total	100.0%	100.0%
Intimate Partner	0.8	1.7
Other relatives	0.6	0.7
Well-known/casual acquaintances	11.7	18.9
Work relationships	25.5	31.7
Customer/client	3.9	6.5
Patient	1.5	6.0
Current or former—		
Supervisor	1.2	3.3
Employee	2.6	1.7
Coworker	16.3	14.3
Do Not Know	8.5	6.1
Stranger	52.9	40.9

Source: Adapted from Harrell (2011, p. 6).

The first group in Table 9.3 includes interpersonal relationships that intrude on the workplace. Examples can include violent intimate partner relationships where one of the partners goes to the workplace and is involved in a violent conflict.

Dangerous Jobs

NCVS used a different classification of occupations from that used by the Bureau of Labor Statistics in discussing workplace homicides. The types of jobs that present high risks for workplace victimization are very similar for both types of workplace violence, however. NCVS divides occupations into medical, mental health, teaching, law enforcement, retail sales, transportation, and others (Duhart, 2001).

Although workplace nonfatal victimizations fell between 2005 and 2009, law enforcement occupations had the highest average rates per 1,000 workers. These included police (47.7), corrections (77.8), private security (65.0), and other (17.5). Retail sales also had very high rates of victimization, led by bartenders (79.9) and gas station attendants (30.2). Medical and mental health personnel, but especially the latter, had high rates of victimization.

In general, the lowest rates of workplace victimization were found in teaching occupations. Except for technical/industrial teachers (54.9), special education teachers (17.8) and high school teachers (13.5), all other categories had rates lower than 9 per 1,000 workers (Harrell, 2011).

WORKPLACE HOMICIDES

The number of people aged 16 or older who died from workplace homicides declined by 39% from 1993 to 1999. In 1993, the number of workplace homicides was 1,068; by 1993, it had declined to 648. The number decreased again by 2009, for which preliminary data placed the number of workplace homicides at 521 (Harrell, 2011). This number represents about 10% of occupational fatalities from all causes (5,071) (Bureau of Labor Statistics, 2009). Workplace homicides represent only 0.1% of all workplace victimizations (Duhart, 2001).

Demographic Characteristics of Workplace Homicide Victims

As was the case for nonfatal workplace victimizations, males are more likely to be victims of workplace homicide than females (81.6%). Whites represent 48.9% of victims, blacks 21.7%, Hispanics 16.2%, Asian/Pacific Islanders 11.2%, and Native Americans 0.4% (Table 9.4).

Table 9.5 breaks down workplace homicides by offender. Robbers and assailants make up the largest category; together they are responsible for 70% of workplace homicides. Work associates, including coworkers and former coworkers, customers, and clients, are responsible for 21.4% of the homicides. Relatives committed 4.0% of the workplace homicides, personal acquaintances 4.3%. In these latter offenses, conflict from outside the workplace spills over into the workplace—for example, if a wife discovers her husband is having an affair with a coworker, a lethal confrontation may occur in the workplace.

Table 9.4 Workplace Homicides by Sex, Race/Ethnicity, and Age

Victim Characteristic	Percent Workplace Homicides
Male	81.6%
Female	18.4
White	48.9
Black	21.7
Hispanic	16.2
Native American	0.4
Asian/Pacific Islander	11.2
Other	1.4
Age 16–19	2.2
20–24	7.4
25–34	21.0
35–49	25.4
50–64	22.6
65 & older	14.8

Source: Adapted from Harrell (2007, p. 10).

Table 9.5 Workplace Homicides by Offender Type

Type of Workplace Offender	Percent of Homicide Victims
Total	100.0%
Robbers & Assailants	70.3
Robbers	38.3
Other Assailants	32.0
Work Associates	21.4
Coworker, former coworker	11.4
Customer, client	10.0
Relatives	4.0
Spouse	0.8
Other relatives	0.8
Other Personal Acquaintances	4.3
Former or current boyfriend or girlfriend	2.0
Other acquaintances	2.3

Source: Adapted from Harrell (2011, p. 11).

Dangerous Jobs

Surprisingly, about 33% of workplace homicide victims worked in a sales or office occupation. Sales-related occupations represented 27.9% of workplace homicides, while protective services constituted 17.2%. The smallest percentage of workplace homicides occurred in natural resources, construction, and maintenance occupations (6.5%). These included farming, fishing, and forestry (0.8%), construction (3.0%), and installation, maintenance, and repair (2.7%).

"GOING POSTAL"

No discussion of workplace violence would be complete without a discussion of a form that has captured the media and popular discussion. "Going postal" has become a pejorative term for employee violence. The term may have originated with the 1986 murders in an Edmond, Oklahoma, post office; certainly the event heightened public concern about workplace violence:

> Patrick Henry Sherrill was a mediocre postman. After 16 months as a part-time letter carrier for the post office in Edmond, Okla. (pop. 47,000), Sherrill was still receiving complaints from his managers about misdirected mail and tardy performance. Last week, after two supervisors reprimanded him, Sherrill told a local steward for the American Postal Workers Union that he was being mistreated. "I gotta get out of here,"he said.
>
> Instead, the angry mailman returned the next morning with a vengeance. At about 7 a.m. he strode into the post office in his blue uniform, toting three pistols and ammunition in a mailbag slung over his shoulder. Without a word, he gunned down Richard Esser, one of the supervisors who had criticized him, and fellow Postman Mike Rockne, grandson of the famous Notre Dame football coach Knute Rockne.
>
> The gunman then chased a group of fleeing employees through a side exit, shooting one man, who later died in the parking lot. Bolting several doors, he sought out workers cowering under tables and in cubicles, killing three people in one work station, five in another. Debbie Smith was sorting letters when the shooting started. "I froze. I couldn't run. He came to shoot the clerks in the box section next to mine. I just knew I was next." But as she hid, Sherrill passed her by and opened fire on the next section. As Smith ran for the front door, she said, "I could hear all the clerks screaming as they were shot." Another employee escaped by locking herself in a vault where stamps are kept. Two other survivors hid in a broom closet.
>
> Minutes after the shooting started, police arrived outside the post office. For 45 minutes they tried to communicate with the gunman by telephone and bullhorn. There was no response. When an Edmond SWAT team finally stormed the building at 8:30 a.m., they found Sherrill's body amid the carnage. After killing 14 people and wounding six, he had pumped a bullet into his own head. (Time, 2001)

These and other homicides by postal employees generated massive media coverage and a special niche in public awareness. In 1995, the American Dialect Society selected "going postal" as its word of the year. There was a movie called *Going Postal* and a computer game, *Postal*. Journalists and comedians have made liberal use of the phrase in jokes and stereotypes (National Center on Addiction and Substance Abuse, 2000).

To address the problem and obtain a more objective view, William J. Henderson, the Postmaster General, established the U.S. Postal Service Commission on a Safe and Secure Workplace in 1998 and charged it to "detail concrete steps which the Postal Service can take to make its 38,000 post offices and related facilities the safest possible environment for its employees." The resulting report was prepared by the National Center on Addiction and Substance Abuse (2000).

Data for the report came from several sources. The commission surveyed almost 12,000 postal employees and 3,000 employees in the national workforce from July to December 1999. The survey included topics on workplace physical assault, sexual harassment, and verbal abuse. The survey also included questions potentially related to violence, such as attitudes about work, psychological conditions, and substance abuse.

The commission also held focus groups with more than 350 postal employees throughout the nation and conducted interviews with more than 300 members of the Postal Service Union. The commission met with management officials at the national level and in the field. Finally, it reviewed postal policies and practices in addition to conducting an intensive review of every post office workplace homicide since 1986.

The results indicated that of the 6,179 workplace homicides from 1992 to 1998, only 16 victims were postal employees. Postal employees are only about a third as likely as people in the national workforce to be homicide victims (0.26 vs. 0.77 per 100,000 workers). Employees in the retail trade are eight times more likely to be workplace homicide victims; cab drivers are 150 times more likely to be workplace homicide victims. Of the 15 postal employees who were perpetrators, 14 had troubled histories of mental problems, violence, substance abuse, and criminal convictions that should have excluded them from being hired.

In terms of nonfatal workplace violence, postal service employees are no more likely to be the victims than members of the national workforce. Five percent of both postal employees and members of the national workforce reported being physically assaulted during 1998. Assaults include "throwing something, pushing, grabbing, slapping, hitting or kicking, hitting with an object, beating, rape or attempted rape, and the threat or use of weapons" (National Center on Addiction and Substance Abuse, 2000).

What is noteworthy, possibly because of the media attention to the problem, is that postal employees are more fearful of the workplace than persons in the national workforce. Despite evidence to the contrary, postal employees are six times more likely to believe they will be victimized by coworkers in comparison to the national workforce (17% vs. 3%). Postal employees are less likely to believe their employers will take action to protect them and more likely to say they fear being robbed or attacked at work compared to the national workforce sample.

The conclusions of the commission were, first, that "'Going postal' is a myth, a bad rap. Postal workers are no more likely to physically assault, sexually harass, or verbally abuse their coworkers than employees in the national workforce." Second, "Postal employees are only a third as likely as those in the national workforce to be victims of homicide at work" (National Commission on Addiction and Drug Abuse, 2000, p. 4).

EXPLANATIONS

ROUTINE ACTIVITIES

The most frequently used sociological explanation of workplace violence is routine activities theory. Routine activities theory posits that crime occurs when there is a conjunction of suitable targets and likely offenders and an absence of suitable guardians. As Felson and

Cohen (1980) stated, routine activity theory assumes that everyone has a routine range of behavior: People get up, have breakfast, and usually go to work in the morning. In most cases, children go to school while both parents head off to work. In the evening, the house and the neighborhood are populated once more as parents and children return for dinner and the round of evening routine activities.

Suitable targets for crime can include either human beings or objects that can be easily stolen and resold illegally. For example, it's unlikely that refrigerators would be stolen in a burglary, but electronics are likely to be stolen because (1) they are light in weight and easily carried; (2) they are easily concealed; and (3) there is a market for them.

The second component is the absence of a capable guardian. While police officers are not excluded as capable guardians, Felson and Cohen attach a much broader meaning to the term: A capable guardian is basically anyone who is present to prevent a crime. Suppose you are waiting in the ticket line at an airport with a friend and a suitcase. You want to go to the bathroom, so you tell your friend to watch your suitcase in your absence. In that instance, your friend is acting as a capable guardian.

The third component in routine activity theory is a likely offender. The term means there is an offender available to exploit the situation of a suitable target in the absence of a capable guardian.

It would be difficult to imagine a more routine set of activities than work and a workplace. Lynch (1987, p. 287) pointed out that routine activities theory would benefit by focusing on the distinct domains of work, school, home, and leisure because violence may be a very different phenomenon in each domain. With respect to work, he tested routine activities theory by using four concepts consistent with the theory:

- Exposure: The "visibility of or physical access to victims by potential offenders." The concept is directed toward measuring conjunction of victims and offenders.
- Guardianship: The "presence of persons or devices that can prevent or inhibit victimization."
- Perceived dangerousness: As a measure of likely offenders, perceived dangerousness refers to proximity to a dense pool of offenders. The concept is directed toward measuring the nearness of likely offenders.
- Attractiveness: The suitability of a target was measured by the extent to which the victim handled money as part of the job.

Data used in the study were the Victim Risk Supplement taken from the NCVS. The social and demographic characteristics of victims were not as important as activity at work. Lynch (1987, p. 295) summarizes the results:

> This analysis tells us many useful things about the risk of victimization at work, beyond a simple taxonomy of risky and safe occupations. What you do at work affects your chances of being victimized while at work. If your employment involves face-to-face contact with large numbers of persons on a routine basis, your risk of victimization is greater than those who are less accessible to the public. If you handle money as part of your job, you are at greater risk than people who do not. Jobs that involve more than a single work site or routine travel (local

> and extra local) expose those who occupy these roles to a greater risk of victimization than persons working at a single location. People whose occupation involves all of these features—public accessibility, mobility, and handling money—run the greatest risk of victimization.

Lynch tested routine activities theory with respect to the general domain of work. Wooldredge, Cullen, and Latessa (1992) extended the research by examining victimization in a specific occupation: the faculty at the University of Cincinnati. Their subjects were faculty members who were employed on one of the campuses between September 1, 1989, and December 31, 1990. The faculty members were asked to respond to a questionnaire about personal and property victimization that included measures of the four concepts used by Lynch. Personal victimizations included robbery, aggravated assault, sexual assault, and assault with a deadly weapon. Of the 442 faculty member respondents, 116 were the victims of property crimes and 21 were the victims of personal crimes.

Consistent with Lynch's study, none of the demographic characteristics (age, race, gender) was a predictor of property or personal crimes. Three of the five exposure variables (on campus after hours, walking alone on campus, socializing with students outside class) were significant predictors of personal victimization. Perceived dangerousness was negatively related; that is, the less the faculty member felt safe on campus, the more likely he or she was to be victimized. None of the guardian or target attractiveness measures was related to victimization.

Fisher and colleagues (1998) looked at another occupation in the work domain: college students. They also used the four concepts given by Lynch to test routine activities theory. They interviewed 3,472 students at 12 colleges and universities, asking them whether they had been the victims of personal or property crimes, as well as various characteristics surrounding their victimization. The personal crimes were rape, sexual assault, robbery, and aggravated and simple assaults. Simple assaults were the most common form of personal victimization; rape was comparatively prevalent.

Unlike in previous studies, the only variable that was statistically significantly increasing was attending a nonmandatory crime prevention or awareness meeting during the school term, a measure of guardianship. The only other measures that were significantly increasing were those in which the student engaged in a lifestyle that has been reported in previous research as increasing the chances of violent victimization. Students who reported frequent partying on campus and regularly used recreational drugs had an increased risk of experiencing a violent victimization.

Hopkins (2002) applied routine activities theory to data obtained from the Scottish Business Crime survey. He reported that businesses with the highest turnover and those with the highest risk for shop theft had the highest average incidence of violent victimizations. These include off-license establishments and those providing motor fuels and parts. Off-license establishments sell liquor for consumption off the premises. The lowest risk of violence was found in food shops and clothing stores. Among businesses in the service sector, bookmakers, postal services, and public houses had the highest average, while hotels and eating places had the lowest average.

Male workers are at a higher risk of abuse and violence than female workers. Hopkins attributed this difference to the fact that 60% of the female workforce were employed in low-risk occupations such as manufacturing and wholesale. Hopkins also suggested that females may manage their work schedules to avoid working at high-risk times such as late at night. Males, on the other hand, may also be less willing to back down from a violent situation than females.

Routine activities theory has benefited from dividing possible conjunctions of victims and offenders into domains. The research seems to indicate that routine activities theory is best supported where the routine is more or less predictable, such as full-time occupations. Where the victims have more control over their daily activities, such as college students, routines lose their predictability and, at the same time, lessen the opportunities for victimization based on occupational routines. Victimization does, however, occur with other kinds of routines such as, for students, habitual partying and drug use.

RATIONAL CHOICE AND AGGRESSION IN THE WORKPLACE

In discussing his view of workplace violence from a rational choice perspective, Felson (2006, p. 7) opened by saying

> Violence is violence, whether it occurs in the home, on the street, or in the workplace . . . For example, the motivation to assault a coworker should not be all that different from the motivation to assault a family member or stranger.

All aggression is instrumental behavior. Aggressive behavior has a purpose in that people will use aggression to achieve an outcome they value if the costs are not too high. Rational choice actors assess the payoffs and costs; in some cases, the decisions may be careless in that aggression results in payoffs that are disastrous for the individual. Be that as it may, the behavior is goal oriented and the actor is still making decisions. Aggression that involves the threat or use of physical force to achieve goals is violence.

Felson (2006) distinguished between whether the harm is incidental to achieving the goal or the harm is the actor's desired outcome. Where harm is incidental to achieving the goal, there is a further distinction between predatory violence and nonviolent predation.

Most robberies, which are one of the most common forms of workplace violence, represent incidental harm and predatory violence. The reason harm is incidental is that the victims are interchangeable. For example, in their study of robbery offenders, Wright and Decker (1997) found that offenders could not agree whether whites or blacks were preferred victims. Nonviolent predation involves mostly theft.

When harm is the intended goal, disputes may be violent or nonviolent. In dispute-related violence, the actors have a grievance with their victims, they are angry, and they want to see their victims suffer in some way. As previous chapters indicated, this can include robberies, rapes, thefts, and frauds. Although violence is rare, an experiment by Greenberg (1993) using 102 undergraduates found that if the subjects believed they were unfairly underpaid, they stole more of the pay for the experimental task than subjects who believed they were equitably paid for the task. Nonviolent dispute-related aggression involves insults.

Felson (2006) focused on the kinds of conditions that lead actors to decide to harm someone. The most obvious reason to decide to harm someone is to "get your way"—that is, to achieve the intended goal. Robbery offenders use the threat to harm someone to gain compliance. Aggression can be used to deter someone from behavior that is not desired by the actor. Managers and supervisors use aggression to punish workers who are consistently tardy. Such applications by managers and supervisors, however, frequently lead to conflict, which can lead to more aggression and violence.

For example, on December 18, 1997, "Arturo Reyes Torres, 43, walks into a maintenance yard in Orange, Calif., with an AK-47 and kills his former boss and three others. Torres, who blamed the supervisor for getting him fired, is later shot by police" (*Workplace Shootings, 1997;* National Institute for the Prevention of Workplace Violence, 1997, p. 253).

Another reason that aggression may lead to workplace violence is the desire for justice. People who feel that they have been wronged have a grievance, and a punishment is needed to restore justice. Drawing from a paper by Mikula, Petri, and Tanzer (1989), Felson (2006) described three basic types of justice. An effort at *distributive justice* occurs when an employee becomes angry and aggressive because he or she feels overworked and underpaid, for example. *Procedural justice* refers to the fairness of the method used to determine outcomes. Employees may become angry and aggressive when they feel that the method for giving raises is unfair and they have no opportunity to complain. *Interactional justice* involves situations of showing respect for others. The absence of courtesy and respect for others in the workplace may make the offended employee angry and aggressive.

Expressing grievances may be a problem in the workplace, leading to greater aggression and violence. Most employees with grievances are reluctant to become involved in altercations, possibly because of the possible costs: Conflict with others, particularly supervisors, may lead to termination or some other form of administrative punishment. However, these grievances accumulate and may be expressed outside of the workplace, such as at home with family members.

Felson's theory on instrumental aggression covers a much wider span of conflicts in the workplace than violence. Some scholars distinguish between aggression and violence as act and consequences; others see the two as positions on a continuum of undesirable behavior. The violence that the media report represents only a small part of workplace violence. For example, in 1994, there were only 650 workplace homicides (Kelley & Mullen, 2006). Because other forms of violence and abuse are more common problems in the workplace, a theory that focuses on aggression, which subsumes violence, is a useful approach.

INTERVENTIONS

It might be supposed that with the overwhelming amount of evidence about workplace violence and the negative impact it has on organizations, employers would be very concerned. When, in addition, there is an increasing legal obligation for employers to provide a safe workplace, it might be expected that they would put into place programs and policies to prevent violence and would know what to do should it occur. However, most employers don't have policies or practices in place to prevent violence and are not prepared to respond to it should it occur (Kelley & Mullen, 2006).

Little is known about effective organizational responses to workplace violence. As Kelley and Mullen (2006, p. 292) note, "books and articles on the topic have grown 'exponentially in recent years,' but the majority of these publications are prescriptive. There has been very little research exploring short- or long-term organizational responses to workplace violence. Whatever the reason, there has been little progress in empirically demonstrating which, if any, specific organizational responses to workplace violence are most effective in mitigating its effects and preventing its recurrence" (Kelley & Mullen, 2006).

Before turning to the results of two studies that empirically examine organizational responses to workplace violence, let us examine the kinds of policies and procedures that can be put into place. Although most of the literature on ways of preventing workplace violence offers little or no supporting evidence, it does provide a considerable amount of conventional wisdom (Howard, 2001).

PREVENTION POLICIES AND STRATEGIES

The National Institute for Occupational Safety and Health (NIOSH) (1996) has developed a number of prevention strategies that are particularly appropriate for instances of type I and type II workplace violence. NIOSH lists the following characteristics of those types of workplace violence:

- Contact with the public
- Exchange of money
- Delivery of passengers, goods, or services
- Having a mobile workplace, such as a taxicab or police cruiser
- Working with unstable or volatile persons in health care, social service, or criminal justice settings
- Working alone or in small numbers
- Working late at night or during early-morning hours
- Working in high-crime areas
- Guarding valuable property or possessions.

Environmental Designs

Cash-handling policies in retail settings should include such procedures as making accessible only small amounts of cash, using locked drop safes, and posting signs stating that only small amounts of money are accessible. The NIOSH bulletin (1996) also suggests exploring the feasibility of cashless transactions in taxicabs and retail settings where account or debit cards could be used.

NIOSH further suggests using bullet-resistant barriers or enclosures for gas stations, convenience stores, hospital emergency departments, and social service claims areas. Counters can be designed to increase the physical distance between workers and potential attackers. The number of entrances and exits in the workplace should be examined, as well as the ease with which nonemployees can gain access to work areas because of unlocked doors. Workplaces should minimize the number of places attackers can hide both inside and near the building, such as garbage storage areas, outdoor refrigeration areas, and other storage facilities that workers must use during their shift.

Environmental design includes security devices such closed-circuit cameras, alarms, two-way mirrors, card-key access systems, panic-bar doors locked from the outside only, trouble lights, and GPS devices for taxis and mobile workplaces. Body armor, such as Kevlar vests, has been used effectively by public safety personnel.

Administrative Controls

These include activities such as plans and policies for escorting patients and prohibiting movement between and within clinic areas. Another suggestion is to increase the number of staff on duty in service and retail businesses. NIOSH (1996) also suggested the use of security guards to screen people entering work areas and controlling access to work areas. Work practices and staffing need to be reviewed for times such as the opening and closing of establishments, during money drops and pickups, and when workers take out garbage, dispose of grease, and store food and other items in storage areas.

Screening and Selection

Howard (2001) discussed a number of policies and procedures to reduce workplace violence. One of the most effective ways is to identify potential offenders during the application process. Organizations should do more thorough background checks on the work history of applicants. Applicants who have a history of workplace violence may be a risk to safety. As noted before, postal authorities ignored red flags in the background of Patrick Henry Sherrill, who went on to murder 14 coworkers.

Unfortunately, many organizations do not provide information to hiring organizations about an individual's violent propensities because they fear being sued for defamation of character. The fear of lawsuits plus the ability of applicants to present the most desirable image of themselves to the hirer makes it likely that any danger signs will be missed or ignored.

Policies and Procedures

What is needed to prevent workplace violence is an overall policy that no violence of any type will be tolerated. Coupled with this policy should be disciplinary procedures that spell out severe costs for violators.

Harassment is a less severe form of workplace violence, but it should be addressed. An employee who is repeatedly threatened by another might decide to retaliate, escalating the problem to the point where violence occurs.

As part of their policies and procedures, organizations should foster an atmosphere of open communication with employees. When organizations do not openly communicate, employees may take actions to further their personal interests. This may result in not only losing good employees but also other forms of action, including violence.

As part of this open communication with employees, the organization should make certain that it does not punish employees too harshly. The disciplinary procedure should allow the employee to respond to the charges. Organizations must realize that punishment may generate violent responses (Howard, 2001).

Training for Supervisors/Employees

It is important to train both supervisors and employees to recognize warning signs of violence. Belligerent, intimidating, or threatening behavior may be an early indication of an individual's willingness to commit a violent act in the future (Cal/OSHA, 1995).

Training should go beyond identifying warning signs of potential problems, however. Supervisors and employees need to receive training on what to do in the event of a problem. Cal/OSHA (1995), for example, provides instructions as well as reporting forms to be used in the event of workplace violence.

Employee Assistance Programs

Another way of preventing workplace violence is through providing counseling services to employees. Employee assistance programs generally involve professional counselors who can address the problems of troubled individuals. The counselors can address problems that begin to appear at work because of problems at home. In some cases, the employee assistance program may include counseling for both the employee and family members in an effort to keep domestic problems from spilling over to the workplace (Howard, 2001). A case in which counseling would have been applicable involved Carrie Byrd:

> Carrie Byrd had won a temporary restraining order against her husband after she alleged in court paperwork that he assaulted and verbally abused her, forcing her to leave their home. Under the order, Byrd also was awarded temporary custody of their 3- and 4-year-old sons and use of their Pisgah Forest home.
>
> The day before a hearing on the restraining order, Byrd, 32, was in Mission Hospital in critical but stable condition. She was shot in the head with a 22-caliber rifle at her workplace, Olsten Staffing Services. Her husband, Billy Ray Byrd, also 32, was charged with shooting her the day before the couple were scheduled to appear in a Transylvania County court for a hearing on the restraining order.
>
> She had first requested a domestic violence protective order against her husband a year ago. "He chased me as I ran to my truck and grabbed my hair and jerked me out and down to the ground, then hit me again on the head," she wrote in court documents. Billy Ray Byrd was later charged with violating the domestic violence protective order issued in that case, but the matter was dismissed when his wife did not appear to testify, according to court paperwork. (National Institute for the Prevention of Workplace Violence, 1997)

Outplacement Services

The manner in which employees are released from organizations has led to a number of highly publicized workplace violence events. Employees who feel they have been unjustly disciplined or dismissed may turn to violence against their employers to correct the inequities. Helping employees find other jobs through outplacement services promotes an atmosphere of fairness and equity (Howard, 2001).

EMPIRICAL EVIDENCE

How Many Organizations Have Workplace Violence Prevention Programs?

The study by Howard (2001) drew on a sample of 2,000 corporations from all the corporations in the United States given Standard Industrial Classifications. Howard (2001) sent questionnaires on workplace violence to the heads of the human resources department in each corporation. The return rate was 21%, which is within the expected range for surveys targeting organizational leaders.

Howard (2001) found that only 8.75% of 423 respondents had *implemented* a workplace violence policy. In other words, only a minority of organizations had done a formal assessment of the potential for workplace violence, and fewer than 10% had actually implemented a policy. The author suggested that this neglect reflects that workplace violence does not occur with high frequency and that executives have more immediate and pressing concerns. Howard suggested, in addition, that organizations tend to take a reactive rather than a proactive view: "Workplace violence is a problem for other organizations, not ours."

Specific Policies

Although only a few organizations had comprehensive prevention programs, many organizations had components in place that could serve as a foundation for a comprehensive policy. Howard (2001) compared organizations with and without workplace violence policies (Table 9.6). Those without a formal policy tended to lack guidelines about the use of discipline following workplace violence, procedures to address workplace violence incidents, termination procedures, and counseling after workplace violence.

Howard also tested a number of hypotheses about workplace violence. For instance, if an organization had a workplace violence prevention policy, was that related to whether it had a workplace violence incident? Howard found that the number of organizations with incidents of workplace violence was not statistically significantly related to the presence of a policy. On the other hand, for organizations with a stress management plan in effect, a significantly greater number of them had experienced workplace violence events. Similarly, for organizations with grievance procedures, a significantly greater number of them, too, had experienced a workplace violence event. This suggests that organizations react to workplace violence by putting into place some specific policies, but that the presence of a general policy seems unrelated to workplace violence events.

Consistent with other studies was the finding about what organizational conditions lead to a greater or lesser incidence of workplace violence. Howard (2001) found that organizations working with unstable individuals and organizations involved in guarding property had significantly greater levels of workplace violence.

Also, organizations with workplace violence policies were more likely than organizations without workplace policies to have additional policies. In short, organizations with workplace violence policies were significantly more likely to also have prevention plans, stress management plans, employee assistance plans, and harassment policies,

Table 9.6 Elements of Workplace Violence (WPV) Policies

Organizations with Formal WPV Policies	**N**
Harassment policies	34
Use of discipline following WPV	33
Screening of potential employees	33
Procedures to address WPV incidents	31
Termination procedures	29
Employee assistance plans	28
Grievance procedures	27
WPV prevention plans	26
Communication training	24
Crisis plans	20
Outplacement services	17
Training to identify threats	17
Counseling required following WPV	16
Stress management plans	9
Organizations without Formal WPV Policies	
Screening of potential employees	17
Harassment policies	16
Grievance procedures	12
Employee assistance plans	10
Communication training	9
Outplacement services	9
Training to identify threats	7
Crisis plans	6
WPV prevention plans	5
Regular meeting between managers and employees	5
Stress management plans	1

Source: Adapted from Howard (2001, p. 67).

Most of the suggestions for policies and procedures to prevent workplace violence have a strong element of common sense. These involve taking necessary security steps to control access and egress from the workplace, using strategies to protect employees while at work, developing procedures to inform employees what should be done in the event of threatened or actual workplace violence, and treating employees with fairness and equity.

However, what is obvious is not always true in the study of criminal violence: More research is needed to determine the level of effectiveness of these "obvious" steps.

DISCUSSION QUESTIONS

1. Define and discuss the concepts of routine activities theory.
2. How did the term, "Going Postal" originate and what were some of its consequences?
3. Define and discuss the application or rational choice and aggression theory on workplace violence.

SUGGESTED READINGS

Gill, M., Fisher, B., & Bowie, V. (Eds.). (2002). *Violence at work: Causes, patterns, and prevention.* Portland, OR: Willan.

Janicak, C. A. (2001). Racial differences in occupational firearm homicides, 1993–1997. *Compensation and working conditions, Spring,* 22–26.

Federal Bureau of Investigation (FBI). (2002). *Workplace Violence: Issues in response.* Quantico, VA: FBI Academy.

Felson, R. B. (2006). Violence as instrumental behavior. In E. K. Kelloway, J. Barling, & J. J. Hurrell, Jr. (Eds.), *Handbook of workplace violence* (pp. 7–28). Thousand Oaks: Sage Publications.

REFERENCES

Bowie, V. (2002). Defining violence at work: A new typology. In M. Gill, B. Fisher, & V. Bowie (Eds.), *Violence at work: Causes, patterns, and prevention* (pp. 1–20). Portland, OR: Willan Publishing.

California Department of Industrial Relations (Cal/OSHA). (1995). *Cal/OSHA guidelines for workplace security.* Retrieved July 2005 from http://www.dir.ca.gov/dosh/dosh%5F*publications/worksecurity.html.*

Chappell, D., & Di Martino, V. (1999). Violence at work. *Asian-Pacific Newsletter on Occupational Health and Safety, 6,* 7–9.

Davis, H. (1988). The accuracy of industry data from death certificates for workplace homicide victims. *American Journal of Public Health, 78,* 1579–1581.

Duhart, D. T. (2001). *Violence in the workplace, 1993–1999* (NCJ 190076). Washington, DC: Bureau of Justice Statistics.

Felson, R. B. (2006). Violence as instrumental behavior. In E. K. Kelloway, J. Barling, & J. J. Hurrell, Jr. (Eds.), *Handbook of workplace violence* (pp. 7–28). Thousand Oaks, CA: Sage.

Felson, M., & Cohen, L. E. (1980). Human ecology and crime: A routine activity approach. *Human Ecology, 8,* 389–406.

Fisher, B., Sloan, J. J., Cullen, F. T., & Lu, C. (1998). Crime in the ivory tower: The level and sources of student victimization. *Criminology, 36,* 671–710.

Greenberg, J. (1993). Stealing in the name of justice: Informational and interpersonal moderators of theft reactions to underpayment inequity. *Organizational Behavior and Human Decision Processes, 54,* 81–103.

Harrell, E. (2011). *Workplace violence, national crime victimization 1993–2009.* Washington, DC: Bureau of Justice Statistics.

Hendricks, S. A., Jenkins, E. L., & Anderson, K. R. (2007). Trends in workplace homicides in the U.S., 1993–2002: A decade of decline. *American Journal of Industrial Medicine, 50,* 316–325.

Henson, B. (2010). Preventing interpersonal violence in emergency departments: Practical applications of criminology theory. *Violence and Victims, 25,* 553–565.

Hopkins, M. (2002). Developing a framework for understanding patterns of abuse and violence against businesses. In M. Gill, B. Fisher, & V. Bowie (Eds.), *Violence at work: Causes, patterns, and prevention* (pp. 59–75). Cullompton, Devon, UK: Willan Publishing.

Howard, J. (2001). Workplace violence in organizations: An exploratory study of organizational prevention techniques. *Employees Responsibilities and Rights Journal, 13*, 57–75.

Kelley, E., & Mullen, J. (2006). Organizational response to workplace violence. In E. K. Kelloway, J. Barling, & J. J. Hurrell, Jr. (Eds.), *Handbook of workplace violence* (pp. 493–515). Thousand Oaks, CA: Sage.

Lynch, J. P. (1987). Routine activity and victimization at work. *Journal of Quantitative Criminology, 3*, 283–300.

Mikula, G., Petri, B., & Tanzer, N. (1989). What people regard as unjust: Types and structures of everyday experiences of justice. *European Journal of Social Psychology, 20*, 133–149.

National Center on Addiction and Substance Abuse. (2000). *Report of the United States Postal Commission on a Safe and Secure Workplace.* Retrieved January 2006 from http://www.casacolumbia.org/ Absolutenm/articlefile/s/33994.pdf.

National Institute for Occupational Safety and Health (NIOSH). (1996). *Violence in the workplace.* Retrieved July 2005 from http://www.cdc.gov/niosh/violpurp.html.

Perone, S. (1999). *Violence in the workplace* (Research and Public Policy Series No. 22). Canberra: Australian Institute of Criminology.

Philbrick, J. H., Sparks, M. R., Hass, M. E., & Arsenault, S. (2003). Workplace violence: The legal costs can kill you. *American Business Review, 21*, 84–91.

Time Magazine. (2001). Crazy Pat's revenge. Retrieved December 2014 from http://content.time.com/time/magazine/article/0,9171,144859,00.html

Toscano, G. A., & Weber, W. (1995). Violence in the workplace. Retrieved March 2003 from http://www.bls.gov/oshwc/cfar0005.pdf.

University of Iowa Injury Prevention Center. (2001). *Workplace violence: A report to the nation.* Washington, DC: University of Iowa Injury Prevention Center.

Wooldredge, J. D., Cullen, F. T., & Latessa, E. J. (1992). Research note: Victimization in the workplace: A test of routine activities theory. *Justice Quarterly, 9*, 325–335.

Workplace Shootings. (1997). Retrieved May 2006 from http://www.workplaceviolence911.com/Articles/articles,jsp?listType=1015.

Wright, R. T., & Decker, S. H. (1997). *Armed robbers in action: Stickups and street culture.* Boston: Northeastern University Press.

CHAPTER 10

SCHOOL VIOLENCE

Throughout the United States, shootings in and around schools have fueled a national debate about school violence. Increased attention is being devoted to measuring, explaining, and preventing school violence, often in response to new dramatic, bloody incidents. While public perceptions of any social problem are frequently driven by rare and tragic incidents (Welsh & Harris, 2012), the examples below suggest that there is ample cause for concern.

---

1. On April 20, 1999, Dylan Klebold, 17, and Eric Harris, 18, entered Columbine High School in Littleton, Colorado, armed with assault rifles, grenades, and explosives. One teacher and 14 students were killed. The two assailants, who committed suicide after their rampage, were known to hate jocks, minorities, rich kids, and fancy cars (National School Safety Center, 2009).
2. On April 16, 2007, Seung-Hui Cho killed 32 people and wounded 69 in two separate attacks two hours apart at Virginia Polytechnic Institute and State University in Blacksburg, Virginia. Before taking his own life, Cho, 23, a senior English major, sent a large multimedia package outlining his grievances against religion and the wealthy to NBC News. The material bristled with hatred toward unspecified people whom Cho, a South Korean immigrant, accused of having wronged him. Investigations revealed a portrait of an angry, solitary young man who was ridiculed by others for his shyness and the strange way he talked (Begley, 2007).
3. Music teacher Ed Klein, 55, suffered a broken jaw and concussion when a 16-year-old student punched him in his West Philadelphia High School classroom. The incident followed a week of harassment and threats that began after Klein called several parents about students' misbehavior in his class. He had also reported the incidents to the school security office (Gammage, 2007).
4. A group of high school girls was smearing Vaseline on their faces and tying scarves on their heads, a prefight ritual intended to keep skin from scarring and hair from getting ripped out. As Teshada, 15, passed the group on her way to class, she recalled the fight she had witnessed, the Facebook posts warning that someone would be attacked, and a threatening text message to her phone. A few minutes later, while she was taking an algebra test, a band of more than a dozen girls and boys—captured on video roaming the halls and looking into classrooms—barged through the door, converged on Teshada, and began to beat her. In less than a minute, they vanished. "It was like a tornado," her teacher said afterwards (Sullivan et al., 2011).

PATTERNS AND TRENDS

Terms like "school violence" have often been used indiscriminately by researchers, education professionals, and the media to refer to quite diverse phenomena, including school shootings, deaths and injuries; student, teacher, and administrator perceptions of disorder; school security responses and disciplinary data; student and teacher self-reported victimizations; and self-reported measures of serious offending or misconduct by students (Welsh, 2001). Because different statistics carry different messages about school violence, it is important to distinguish among different sources of data.

Following the public health approach (see Chapter 1), an inspection of multiple indicators of school violence across different levels of analysis (e.g., individual, school, and community) helps inform causal explanations and interventions to reduce school violence. *Indicators of School Crime and Safety* is an annual report jointly produced by the U.S. Department of Education and the Bureau of Justice Statistics (BJS) (Robers et al., 2013). This report provides the most comprehensive data available on school crime and safety. Indicators are based on several different data sources, including national surveys of students, teachers, and principals, and data collected by federal agencies including the BJS, the National Center for Education Statistics, the Federal Bureau of Investigation (FBI), and the Centers for Disease Control and Prevention (CDC). Key findings are described below.

FEAR AND AVOIDANCE

Student perceptions and fear of violence are important to the degree that they influence student behavior. As student fear increases, confidence in school administrators and/or teachers diminishes, and informal social controls against violence weaken. Resultant behaviors may include choices to carry weapons to school, to manage impressions by fighting or putting on a tough front, or to retaliate against perceived transgressors (Lockwood, 1997).

In 2011, a higher percentage of students ages 12 to 18 reported that they were afraid of attack or harm at school (4%) than away from school (2%) during the school year (Robers et al., 2013). Between 1995 and 2011, the percentage of students who reported being afraid of attack or harm at school decreased from 12% to 4%. A lower percentage of white students (3%) than black (4.9%) or Hispanic students (4.8%) reported being afraid of attack or harm at school. A higher percentage of students in public schools (4%) than in private schools (2%) reported being afraid of attack or harm at school. Between 1995 and 2011, the percentage of students who reported being afraid of attack or harm at school decreased from 12% to 4%.

Students may deliberately alter their behavior so as to reduce their perceived risk of victimization. In 2011, about 6% of students ages 12 to 18 reported that they avoided school activities or one or more places in school because they thought someone might attack or harm them (Robers et al., 2013). Places most frequently avoided included school entrances, stairs or hallways, the school cafeteria, and restrooms.

Students may engage in less benign behavior to protect themselves. Between 1993 and 2011, the percentage of students in grades 9 to 12 who reported carrying a weapon on school property declined from 12% to 5% (Robers et al., 2013). In 2011, 8% of males and 2% of females reported carrying a weapon on school property.

SCHOOL SECURITY RESPONSES

School security responses reflect *reactions* to perceived disorder; they do not necessarily correspond to measures of victimization or offending in and around the school. Security responses reflect concerns not only about student safety, but also about the school's potential legal liability.

In the 2009–10 school year, nearly all public schools (99%) reported that they required visitors to sign in or check in (Robers et al., 2013). Other frequently reported safety and security measures included limiting access to social networking websites from school computers (93%), controlling access to school buildings by locking or monitoring doors during school hours (92%), and prohibiting the use of cell phones and text messaging devices during school hours (91%). In addition, 63% of public schools reported that they had an electronic notification system for a school-wide emergency, and 36% reported that they had a structured, anonymous threat-reporting system in place. Sixty-one percent of public schools reported the use of one or more security cameras to monitor school activities; 1.4% of public schools required students to pass through metal detectors daily.

SCHOOL INCIDENTS AND DISCIPLINARY ACTIONS

Data on school disciplinary actions, including school records of incidents, suspensions, and other actions, are limited by several sources of unreliability (Welsh, 2001). Because recordkeeping is typically low on the list of school district priorities, school disciplinary records often contain significant errors in teacher reporting and/or administrative recording. Disincentives to report violent incidents include fear of appearing incompetent, legal liability, and potential loss of local and state political support. Disciplinary records thus reflect individual teacher, school, and/or district policies, not necessarily actual rates of incidents.

During the 2009–10 school year, 39% of public schools took at least one serious disciplinary action against a student for specific offenses, including suspensions lasting five days or more, expulsions, and transfers to specialized schools for specific offenses (Robers et al., 2013). A total of 433,800 serious disciplinary actions were taken by public schools during this period. Disciplinary actions were most commonly taken in response to a physical attack or fight (29% of schools).

In the School Survey on Crime and Safety, public school principals were asked to provide the number of serious violent incidents (rape, sexual battery other than rape, physical attack or fight with a weapon, threat of physical attack with a weapon, and robbery with or without a weapon); violent incidents (serious violent incidents plus physical attack or fight without a weapon and threat of physical attack without a weapon); thefts valued at $10 or more; and other incidents that occurred at their school, as well as the number of incidents reported to the police. During the 2009–10 school year, 74% of schools recorded one or more violent incidents of crime, and 16% recorded one or more serious violent incidents (Robers et al., 2013). Only a portion of those incidents were reported to police: 40% of public schools reported at least one violent incident to police, and 10% reported at least one serious violent incident to police. Violent incidents were more concentrated in city schools; 25% of city schools recorded 20 or more violent incidents, compared to 19% of suburban schools and 14% of rural schools.

STUDENT VICTIMIZATION

Fortunately, violent deaths occurring on school property are extremely rare compared to other indices of school disorder. From July 1, 2010, through June 30, 2011, there were 31 school-associated violent deaths in elementary and secondary schools in the United States (Robers et al., 2013). Over all available survey years, the percentage of youth homicides occurring at school remained at less than 2% of the total number of youth homicides, and the percentage of youth suicides occurring at school remained at less than 1% of the total number of youth suicides.

Unfortunately, school is the most common setting for nonfatal violent victimizations (rape, sexual assault, robbery, aggravated assault, or simple assault) of youths aged 12 to 17 (Snyder & Sickmund, 2006). The 2011 victimization rates for violent crimes (primarily simple assaults) were 24 per 1,000 students at school and 17 per 1,000 students away from school (Robers et al., 2013). In 2011, approximately 4% of students ages 12 to 18 reported being victimized at school during the previous six months. Three percent of students reported theft, 1% reported violent victimization, and one-tenth of 1% reported serious violent victimization.

Violent victimization rates at school in 2011 varied by age, gender, and race (Table 10.1). Violent victimization rates were higher for students aged 12 to 14 (34.1 per 1,000 students) than for students aged 15 to 18 (14.3 per 1,000). Females had lower rates of violent victimization (19 per 1,000) than males (28 per 1,000). Whites had lower rates of violent victimization (22.5 per 1,000) than blacks (30.1 per 1,000) or Hispanics (23.8 per 1,000). Higher percentages of black and Hispanic students (9% each) reported being threatened or injured with a weapon on school property than white students (6%).

Bullying is another important indicator of victimization. In 2011, about 28% of 12- to 18-year-old students reported being bullied at school, and 9% reported being cyber-bullied

Table 10.1 Number of Nonfatal Victimizations Against Students Ages 12 to 18 and Rate of Victimizations per 1,000 Students at School, by Type of Victimization and Selected Student Characteristics: 2011

	Number of Victimizations				Rate of Victimizations Per 1,000 Students			
Student Characteristic	Total	Theft	Violent	Serious Violent[1]	Total	Theft	Violent	Serious Violent[1]
At school								
Total	1,246,000	648,600	597,500	89,000	49.2	25.6	23.6	3.5
Sex								
Male	746,600	376,000	370,600	55,600	57.1	28.8	28.3	4.3

(Continued)

Table 10.1 *Continued*

Female	499,400	272,500	226,900	33,400 !	40.9	22.3	18.6	2.7 !
Age								
12–14	654,600	248,500	406,200	65,900	55.0	20.9	34.1	5.5
15–18	591,400	400,100	191,300	23,000 !	44.2	29.9	14.3	1.7 !
Race/ethnicity[2]								
White	657,800	337,500	320,300	36,100	46.2	23.7	22.5	2.5
Black	265,300	151,000	114,300	42,600 !	69.8	39.7	30.1	11.2 !
Hispanic	243,700	114,800	128,800	10,400 !	45.1	21.3	23.8	1.9 !
Other	79,300	45,300	34,000	‡	42.7	24.4	18.3	—
Urbanicity[3]								
Urban	469,600	221,800	247,800	55,800	60.9	28.8	32.1	7.2
Suburban	619,300	350,300	269,000	26,500 !	45.3	25.6	19.7	1.9 !
Rural	157,200	76,400	80,700	6,600 !	40.0	19.5	20.6	1.7 !
Household income								
Less than $15,000	163,600	49,300	114,300	3,000 !	86.7	26.1	60.6	1.6 !
$15,000–29,999	146,900	68,600	78,300	13,800 !	47.1	22.0	25.1	4.4 !
$30,000–49,999	194,500	116,400	78,100	22,300 !	48.0	28.7	19.3	5.5 !
$50,000–74,999	182,700	114,500	68,200	7,000 !	53.6	33.6	20.0	2.0 !
$75,000 or more	288,900	191,100	97,800	10,000 !	42.1	27.9	14.3	1.5 !
Not reported	269,500	108,700	160,800	33,000 !	45.1	18.2	26.9	5.5 !

— Not available.

! Interpret data with caution. Estimate based on 10 or fewer sample cases, or the coefficient of variation is greater than 50%.

‡ Reporting standards not met. There are too few cases for a reliable estimate.

[1] Serious violent victimization is also included in violent victimization.

[2] "Other" includes Asians, Pacific Islanders, and American Indians (including Alaska Natives). Race categories exclude persons of Hispanic ethnicity.

[3] Refers to the Standard Metropolitan Statistical Area (MSA) status of the respondent's household as defined in 2000 by the U.S. Census Bureau. Categories include "central city of an MSA (Urban)," "in MSA but not in central city (Suburban)," and "not MSA (Rural)."

Note: "Serious violent victimization" includes rape, sexual assault, robbery, and aggravated assault. "Violent victimization" includes serious violent crimes and simple assault. "Theft" includes attempted and completed purse-snatching, completed pickpocketing, and all attempted and completed thefts, excluding motor vehicle theft. Theft does not include robbery in which threat or use of force is involved. Robbery is classified as a violent crime. "Total victimization" includes violent crimes and theft. "At school" includes inside the school building, on school property, or on the way to or from school. Although Indicators 2 and 3 present information on similar topics, the survey sources for these two indicators differ with respect to time coverage and administration. For more information on these two surveys, please see Robers et al. (2013, appendix A). Population size is 25,302,000 students ages 12–18 in 2011. Detail may not sum to total due to rounding and missing data on student characteristics. Estimates of number of crimes are rounded to the nearest 100.

Source: Robers, S., Kemp, J., & Truman, J. (2013). *Indicators of school crime and safety: 2012* (NCES 2013-036/NCJ 241446), Table 2.2, p. 101. Washington, DC: National Center for Education Statistics, U.S. Department of Education, and Bureau of Justice Statistics, Office of Justice Programs, U.S. Department of Justice.

during the school year (Robers et al., 2013). Eighteen percent of students said they had experienced bullying that consisted of being made fun of; 18% reported being the subject of rumors; 8% said they were pushed, shoved, tripped, or spit on; 5% said they were threatened with harm; 6% said they were excluded from activities on purpose; and 3% each said that someone tried to make them do things they did not want to do or that their property was destroyed on purpose.

TEACHER VICTIMIZATION

The National Crime Victimization Survey also provides information about teacher victimization by collecting data on the occupations of respondents. In addition to personal safety concerns, victimization interferes with teachers' ability to teach. Such concerns may cause many qualified teachers to leave the profession (Ingersoll, 2001; Scheckner et al., 2002).

During the 2007–08 school year, 7% of teachers were threatened with injury by a student from their school; the figure was 12% in 1993–94. The percentage of teachers reporting that they had been physically attacked by a student from their school, 4%, was not measurably different in 2007–08 than in any previous survey year. The rate of victimization was higher, however, for male than female teachers, teachers in city rather than suburban or rural schools, and teachers in public rather than private schools (Robers et al., 2013).

SELF-REPORTED SCHOOL VIOLENCE

While self-report measures of offending have been widely used in delinquency research (Farrington, 1973; Farrington et al., 1996; Hindelang et al., 1981; Huizinga & Elliott, 1986), self-reported measures of violent offending *in school* are rare (D. C. Gottfredson et al., 1993; Jenkins, 1997; Welsh et al., 1999a). Only limited information on violent offending is available through annual reports. For example, the percentage of students in grades 9 to 12 who reported being in a physical fight on school property decreased from 16% in 1993 to 12% in 2011. In 2011, 16% of males and 8% of females said they had been in a fight on school property (Robers et al., 2013).

EXPLANATIONS OF SCHOOL DISORDER

INDIVIDUAL EXPLANATIONS

Control theorists contend that delinquency is the result of a weakening of effective social and cultural constraints, especially via weakened transmission of values through institutions such as the family and the school. Social bonding is the mechanism by which effective controls and constraints are learned. In the original formulation of the theory, Hirschi (1969) identified four major elements of social bonding: (1) commitment to conventional goals: perceived costs and risks of investing time, energy, and self in conventional behavior, (2) attachment to prosocial others—that is, the extent to which one cares about others and their expectations and opinions, (3) involvement in conventional activities: participation in conventional activities as opposed to delinquent activities, and (4) belief in conventional rules: the degree of moral validity that youths do or do not attach to conventional values.

Schools provide a central venue for social bonding (or failure). Those with poor academic or interpersonal skills are likely to experience failure and alienation in school. They do not become attached to school because social interaction is unrewarding. They do not become committed to educational goals because they view them as unrealistic. They do not become involved in conventional social activities either because they are denied access or because meaningful activities are lacking. They do not come to believe in conventional rules because they do not perceive meaningful present or future rewards for compliance. An essay written by the mother of one of the Columbine shooters suggests that such factors may have played a role in her son's development (Klebold, 2009).

Relationships between bonding and delinquency have been generally supported by research (Akers & Sellers, 2012; Bernard, Snipes, & Gerould, 2009; M. Gottfredson & Hirschi, 1990). While relationships between school bonding and general delinquency have been demonstrated (Cernkovich & Giordano, 1992; Hagan & Simpson, 1978; Hindelang, 1973; Krohn & Massey, 1980; Liska & Reed, 1985; Thornberry et al., 1991), studies of relationships between school bonding and *school* misbehavior are rare (D. C. Gottfredson, 1986; Jenkins, 1997; Welsh et al., 1999a).

Other individual predictors of school disorder include gender, age, and race. Girls have generally evidenced lower rates of delinquency and school misconduct than boys (G. D. Gottfredson, 1984; Kazdin, 1987; Lawrence, 2006), although the gender gap has narrowed in recent years (Chesney-Lind & Shelden, 2003). Older teenagers, on average, are at higher risk of being involved in both minor and serious delinquent acts (Farrington, 1986; Hirschi & Gottfredson, 1983; Steffensmeier et al., 1989). The effects of race are not entirely clear. Although minorities are overrepresented in official (police or court) statistics, self-report measures of delinquency have generally revealed much smaller racial differences (Farrington et al., 1996). At least three reasons for this discrepancy have been suggested: police and courts are biased against minorities, minorities are underrepresented in survey samples, and the validity of self-reported delinquency may vary across ethnic groups.

Although school shootings are rare, concern about tragedies such as Columbine has led to attempts to develop screening tools that might identify potential shooters before they act. An investigation of school shootings from 1992 to 1999 found that no well-defined profile of school shooters exists (U.S. Secret Service, 2000). Offenders ranged in age from 11 to 21 and came from a variety of racial and ethnic backgrounds and family situations. Their academic performance ranged from excellent to failing, and prior behaviors ranged from no observed behavior problems to a clear history of violence and weapon use. Identification of the characteristics of potential school shooters, however, is difficult due to the low base rate of school shootings and because these events are usually embedded in social contexts not captured by the assessment of individual characteristics alone (Mulvey & Cauffman, 2001).

SCHOOL-LEVEL THEORIES

According to school climate theorists, schools have their own characteristic "personalities," just as individuals do. School climate includes factors such as communication patterns, norms about what is appropriate behavior and how things should be done, role relationships and role perception, patterns of influence and accommodation, and rewards and sanctions (D.C. Anderson, 1998; Fox et al., 1979; Welsh et al., 2000). Organizational climate, in general, is the "study of perceptions that individuals have of various aspects of the environment in the organization" (Owens, 2003, p. 168). In an education context, it is the "feel" of a school as perceived by students and employees; it is the general "we feeling" and interactive life of a school (C. S. Anderson, 1982). Perceptual measures are generally used to assess different aspects of organizational climate (Hellriegel & Slocum, 1974; Lawler & Oldham, 1974).

In an analysis of national data, schools with the worst discipline problems were

- Those in which the rules were unclear, unfair, or inconsistently enforced
- Those that used ambiguous or indirect responses to student behavior (e.g., lowered grades in response to misconduct)
- Those in which teachers and administrators did not know the rules or disagreed on responses to student misconduct
- Those that ignored misconduct
- Those in which students did not believe in the legitimacy of the rules (D. C. Gottfredson, 1989, 2001; G. D. Gottfredson & D. C. Gottfredson, 1985).

A Philadelphia study based on survey responses from 5,203 middle school students explored the effects of school climate (e.g., clarity and fairness of rules) and individual student characteristics (e.g., age, sex, race, and dimensions of bonding) on two different measures of school disorder: students' self-reported offending and less serious misconduct at school (Welsh, 2003; Welsh, Jenkins, & Greene, 1997). Between-school factors and individual factors were examined using Hierarchical Linear Modeling techniques. Schools varied significantly on both measures of disorder, but school climate variables explained a larger percentage of variance in misconduct than offending (10% vs. 2%). The strongest predictors of both offending and misconduct were measures of positive peer associations, belief in rules, and school effort. Older, nonwhite, and male students displayed higher levels of both offending and misconduct.

In a nationally representative study of 254 U.S. secondary schools (G. D. Gottfredson et al., 2005), researchers examined relationships among numerous indicators of school climate and disorder (e.g., self-reported victimization and delinquency). School climate explained a substantial percentage of the variance in school disorder, even when controlling for the effects of community characteristics and school student composition. Schools in which students perceived greater fairness and clarity of rules had lower rates of delinquent behavior and student victimization, although rule fairness and clarity did not influence teacher victimization. Schools with a more positive climate overall had lower teacher victimization, but this more general measure of school climate did not influence student victimization or delinquent behavior.

COMMUNITY AND MULTILEVEL EXPLANATIONS OF SCHOOL DISORDER

Schools, of course, are embedded in communities. In addition to school characteristics, high levels of crime, poverty, and unemployment in the community surrounding the school have occasionally been associated with higher levels of school victimization (G. D. Gottfredson & Daiger, 1979; Rubel, 1978; Toby, 1983).

Social disorganization describes the inability of a neighborhood to "control itself" by monitoring and managing its boundaries, socializing its youth, and exerting control over the behavior of those who live there. A major premise of social disorganization theory is that crime rates vary with the capacity of a community to control the behavior of its members. In fact, social disorganization theory is the macro-level precursor to Hirschi's (1969) micro-level control theory (Messner & Rosenfeld, 2012). The classic work of Shaw and McKay (1942) found that three major structural factors—low economic status, ethnic heterogeneity, and high residential mobility—led to the disruption of community cohesion and organization, and subsequently to higher rates of delinquency. These disruptions in the social metabolism of a community made it difficult for residents to form close ties, to maintain kin and friendship networks, and to exert collective control over norms and behaviors. These conditions impaired the ability of local institutions of socialization, including the family, school, churches, and businesses, to transmit proper rules of behavior and to control the behavior of juveniles.

Associations between socioeconomic status and violence have been well established, although the exact causal mechanisms are not entirely clear. Recent research has uncovered complex links between poverty and crime, and between social disorganization and violence. Researchers studying community-level variations have found relationships between poverty and high rates of delinquency, and between poverty and high homicide rates (Reiss & Roth, 1993). Community characteristics found to relate to violence have included the following:

- Concentrations of poverty
- High residential mobility and population turnover
- Family disruption
- High density in housing and population
- Weak local social organization, such as low density of friends and acquaintances
- Few social resources
- Weak intergenerational ties in families and communities
- Weak control of street-corner groups
- Low participation in community events and activities
- Opportunities associated with violence.

Although such relationships are complex, it can safely be said that community influences often combine with poverty and with one another to affect crime rates (Sampson & Lauritsen, 1993; Sampson et al., 1997).

Community characteristics can affect levels of school violence in complex ways: by heightening exposure to risk coming to and from school, by modeling norms and behaviors conducive to the use of violence to resolve disputes, and by weakening effective community controls over the behavior of children who attend school in a specific neighborhood (Hellman & Beaton, 1986; Pearson & Toby, 1991). Poverty and unemployment in the surrounding community are often linked to violence in schools, although the exact chain of causality is rarely articulated or explored (G. D. Gottfredson & Daiger, 1979).

In a study of more than 7,000 middle school students and 400 teachers, researchers examined multilevel predictors (individual, neighborhood, and school characteristics) of school violence in Philadelphia (Welsh, 2000, 2001, 2003; Welsh et al., 1999a, 2000). Significant predictors of school disorder were found at the community level (poverty), the school level (fairness of rules, respect for students), and the individual level (belief in conventional rules, positive peer associations, age, race, sex). Models examining multiple indicators of school violence suggested that individual-level theories (e.g., control theory) did a better job of explaining more serious types of school violence (e.g., assault), while school climate theories better accounted for more pervasive but less serious forms of misconduct such as classroom misbehavior (Welsh, 2001, 2003).

Although community effects on school disorder were statistically significant, community-level factors in large, urban school districts offered little additional explanatory power beyond that afforded by individual and school variables (Welsh et al., 1999a). Researchers carefully distinguished between local versus "imported" (students attending school from other parts of the city) community characteristics. In general, local community variables explained school disorder slightly better than imported community characteristics, although neither one provided a strong explanation by itself. Poverty in the local community, however, was significantly associated with higher rates of student misconduct.

Welsh, Stokes, and Greene (2000) found that school climate (measured by student attendance and turnover) strongly mediated the effects of community variables (poverty, residential stability, and community crime rates) on school disorder (as measured by school incident and dismissal rates). Poverty retained a significant but indirect effect through its influence on school climate. A school, then, is neither blessed nor doomed entirely on the basis of where it is located, nor on the basis of its student demographics.

A nationally representative sample of 254 public, nonalternative, secondary schools (National Study of Delinquency Prevention in Schools) was used to examine relationships among communal school organization, student bonding, and school disorder (Payne et al., 2003). Communal school organization refers to supportive relationships between and among teachers, administrators, and students; a common set of goals and norms; and a sense of collaboration and involvement. Schools that were more communally organized had lower levels of school disorder, although the effects were small and statistically significant only for a measure of student delinquency, but not for student or teacher victimization. Levels of student bonding mediated the relationship between communal school organization and student delinquency, but not the relationship between communal school organization and teacher victimization.

Further analyses of results from the National Study of Delinquency Prevention in Schools showed that relatively small but significant portions of the variance in student delinquency and victimization were attributable to differences between schools as opposed to individuals (G. D. Gottfredson et al., 2005). Schools in areas of high residential crowding and concentrated poverty, and schools serving high percentages of African American students and teachers, had higher levels of school disorder.

Misbehavior of low-income African American children may partially represent reactions to oppressive life experiences and standards perceived as unfair and unobtainable, resulting in attempts to recapture feelings of self-worth, identity, and respect by adopting norms of social distancing and physical toughness (E. Anderson, 1990, 1999; Hanna,

1988). Beliefs in materialistic values combined with experience that the legitimate means required for success (e.g., a good-quality education in a safe environment) are blocked may produce alienation, anger, and aggression (Agnew, 1993; Brezina et al., 2001; Cernkovich & Giordano, 1992; Messner & Rosenfeld, 2012).

In a study of Chicago middle schools, Kirk (2009) examined the effects of five types of social control (parental supervision, student–teacher trust, school collective efficacy, parent–teacher trust, and neighborhood collective efficacy) on suspensions and juvenile arrests. Social controls within schools were loosely coupled with social controls in neighborhoods and families. Neighborhoods characterized by concentrated poverty and low collective efficacy did not necessarily contain dangerous schools or unstable families. However, school-based and family-based informal social controls *additively* combined to influence the likelihood of suspension and arrest. A multicontextual approach is thus warranted to understand school delinquency and violence (Kirk, 2009).

INTERVENTIONS

Schools, as sites where juveniles spend a majority of their weekday time, offer primary opportunities for violence prevention and intervention efforts, but not in isolation from concerned citizens, communities, and other agencies. Despite resource constraints and other problems facing public schools in the 21st century, it is possible to implement positive change. Student misconduct can be shaped by conscious efforts by school administrators, teachers, parents, students, and others involved in the task of facilitating the healthy development of children (D. C. Gottfredson, 1989; Owens, 1987; Welsh et al., 1999b). School-based violence-prevention efforts that attempt to raise children's school effort, encourage positive associations, and demonstrate that obeying the rules will result in valued rewards may provide critical foundations for reducing student misconduct (D. C. Gottfredson, 1986).

While violence-prevention programs are ubiquitous in U.S. schools, this terminology can be misleading. Many of these programs do not directly target violence but rather seek to change potential mediators of violence, such as social and communication skills (S. J. Wilson & Lipsey, 2005). Because extreme violence is rare in schools, prevention programs typically focus on common forms of aggressive behavior such as fighting, name calling, bullying, verbal conflict, intimidation, and disruptive behavior. These behaviors, however, may inhibit learning, create interpersonal problems, and escalate into more serious altercations.

SCHOOL-BASED VIOLENCE PREVENTION: WHAT WORKS?

One way to categorize school-based prevention programs is in terms of their reach and focus (Greenberg, 2010). In two large meta-analyses, S. J. Wilson and Lipsey (2005, 2007) grouped interventions into four main formats: *universal, selected/indicated, special schools or classes,* and *comprehensive/multimodal programs.*

Universal programs are delivered to an entire classroom or an entire school. Such programs aim to improve resilience and coping and social skills. Universal strategies are the most commonly used in practice and are often relatively inexpensive to implement

(Greenberg, 2010; Hahn et al., 2007). Universal interventions incorporate various foci, including teachers' classroom management skills and communal school organization. Curricula that teach students new skills have received the most empirical attention (Greenberg, 2010; Hahn et al., 2007). These programs often focus on "social and emotional learning" (Elias et al., 1997, 2000), including improved social skills and self-control (Greenberg, 2010; Hahn et al., 2007). In a recent meta-analysis, S. J. Wilson and Lipsey (2007) reported a weighted mean effect size of 0.21 for universal interventions in schools (n = 77).

Common treatment modalities within universal programs include cognitively oriented programs, social skills programs, behavioral strategies, and counseling or talk therapy (S. J. Wilson & Lipsey, 2005). The most common modality was cognitively oriented approaches, which also had the largest mean effect size (0.33). Social skills programs were a close second, with an overall mean effect size of 0.30. The mean effect size for counseling was 0.16, although only one program was included in this category (S. J. Wilson & Lipsey, 2005). Behavioral programs had an overall mean effect size of 0.16 using student and teacher self-report measures. Younger students and students of low socioeconomic status benefited the most from universal strategies (S. J. Wilson & Lipsey, 2005).

Despite generally positive effects, universal interventions also have limitations. First, they are often low in "dosage;" high-risk students may require a higher dosage (Greenberg, 2010). Second, universal programs often require the participation of an entire school system. Given budget constraints and the pressures to improve academic performance, it may be difficult to convince an entire school district to implement a program with a non-academic focus.

Selected/indicated programs are delivered to specific groups of students who have been selected for participation because they are at an elevated risk for future delinquent behavior (Greenberg, 2010). Most of the selected/indicated programs were "pull-out" programs delivered to students outside of the primary classroom in either small groups or one on one. Students can be chosen because they have already begun exhibiting high levels of aggression, depression, or other maladjustment (indicated programs), or because of an experience that puts them at a higher risk for problem behavior in the future (selected programs). Selected and indicated interventions, like universal ones, can often be characterized as social and emotional learning (Greenberg, 2010). Such skills are taught and reinforced in special group settings with an emphasis on skill learning and maintenance.

S. J. Wilson and Lipsey (2005, 2007) found an overall mean effect size of 0.29 for selected/indicated programs. Differences in mean effect sizes across treatment modalities (social skills training, counseling, cognitively oriented approaches, behavioral programs implemented in small groups, and peer mediation) were small and statistically nonsignificant (S. J. Wilson & Lipsey, 2005). Similarly, there were no significant differences across different types of personnel who delivered the services or across different session formats (i.e., one on one vs. group) (S. J. Wilson & Lipsey, 2005). Selected/indicated programs were more effective for those exhibiting a higher risk (S. J. Wilson & Lipsey, 2005).

Special schools or classes are delivered in schools or classrooms outside of a mainstream school setting. An academic curriculum is provided in addition to programming that targets social skills and/or aggressive behavior (S. J. Wilson & Lipsey, 2005). Typically such programs serve youth with serious behavioral or academic difficulties. S. J. Wilson and Lipsey (2007) reported a nonsignificant ($p < 0.10$) mean effect size of 0.11 for programs in this category. Moderators of effect size included method of group assignment, level of risk of students, and quality of program implementation (S. J. Wilson & Lipsey, 2005, 2007).

Comprehensive/multimodal programs include multiple treatment elements and formats within the same intervention (S. J. Wilson & Lipsey, 2005, 2007). Comprehensive programs typically use three or more formats or modalities simultaneously. These strategies use classroom-based and pull-out components (removing targeted children from their primary classrooms for specialized programming). In addition to student-focused learning, these programs may also incorporate parent training, family involvement, capacity building among administrators, or teacher training. Comprehensive/multimodal programs were found to be surprisingly ineffective, with a nonsignificant mean effect size of 0.05 across 21 different programs (S. J. Wilson & Lipsey, 2007). In practice, however, multiple interventions are often implemented in the same school, and it becomes difficult to parse out which program components produce positive or negative results (D. B. Wilson et al. 2001). Identifying which specific components contribute to the success of some approaches over others would be of great benefit to practitioners.

THE NATIONAL STUDY OF DELINQUENCY PREVENTION IN SCHOOLS

A substantial amount of federal, state, local, and private funding in recent years has been devoted to school-based prevention programs (D. C. Gottfredson & G. D. Gottfredson, 2002). One of the largest funders is the U.S. Department of Education's Safe and Drug Free Schools and Communities program, which provides about $566 million to states each year for local drug- and violence-prevention activities. Research raises questions about the implementation and efficacy of many of these programs.

The National Study of Delinquency Prevention in Schools was a survey conducted during the 1997 and 1998 school years to collect information about programs and practices intended to improve school safety (D. C. Gottfredson & G. D. Gottfredson, 2002; G. D. Gottfredson et al., 2004). The study used a national probability sample of public, private, and Catholic schools, stratified by location (urban, suburban, and rural) and level (elementary, middle, and high). Principals were asked to identify activities their schools had in place to prevent or reduce delinquency, drug use, or other problem behaviors. Responses were obtained about 3,691 prevention activities in 848 schools. Researchers classified these diverse activities into three broad categories (Table 10.2):

1. *Direct services to students, families, or staff.* Activities included group instruction, provision of instructional materials, and interventions aimed at preventing problem behavior, promoting school orderliness, and counseling students or their families. Interventions such as community service, peer mediation, and student courts were rarely used compared to other responses to misconduct. Schools used very few of the possible methods of influencing student behavior, such as rewards for desirable behavior.

Table 10.2 Prevention Activities to Reduce Problem Behavior or Promote School Safety

Prevention Activity	Percentage of Schools Using Activity
Direct services to students, families, and staff	
Provision of isolated information (e.g., pamphlets about alcohol, tobacco, drug use, or risky sexual behavior)	90
Prevention curriculum, instruction, or training	76
Counseling, social work, psychological/therapeutic interventions	75
Behavioral or behavior modification interventions	64
Recreational, enrichment, and leisure activities	64
Individual attention, mentoring, tutoring, or coaching	58
Services to families	55
Treatment or prevention interventions for administrators, faculty, or staff	49
Organizational and environmental arrangements	
Reorganization of grades, classes, or school schedules	81
Architectural features of the school	76
Use of external personnel resources in classrooms	72
Distinctive culture or climate for interpersonal exchanges	66
Improved instructional methods or practices	62
Improved classroom organization and management methods or practices	57
School planning structure or process, or management of change	57
Improved intergroup relations or interaction between school and community	57
Altered school composition	32
Discipline and safety management	
Rules, policies, regulations, laws, or enforcement	100
Security and surveillance	55
Youth roles in regulating and responding to student conduct	40

Source: Gottfredson, G. D., Gottfredson, D. C., Czeh, E. R., Cantor, D., Crosse, S. B., & Hantman, I. (2004). *Toward safe and orderly schools—the national study of delinquency prevention in schools* (NCJ 205005). Washington, DC: U.S. Department of Justice, Office of Justice Programs, National Institute of Justice.

2. *Organizational and environmental arrangements*. Schools made substantial use of architectural and structural arrangements to prevent problem behavior and promote school safety. Urban schools were more likely than schools in other locations to use gates, fences, walls, and barricades, and to physically block off sections of the building.

3. *Discipline or safety management activities*. Virtually all schools had strict rules about dangerous behavior and the possession of weapons, and virtually all principals reported that they communicated those rules. Most schools reported that they applied severe

consequences when rules were broken. Schools were very likely to suspend or expel a student for possession of a gun, knife, or alcohol or other drugs. Suspension or expulsion for physical fighting, possession of tobacco, and use of profane or abusive language was also common.

For each activity for which a research base (e.g., prevention curriculum, classroom management) or a basis of informed professional opinion (e.g., counseling) was available, researchers developed "best practices" scales to assess program content and methods. Indicators of program *intensity* included level of use by school personnel, frequency of operation, duration, number of sessions, frequency of student participation, ratio of providers to students in the school, and proportion of students involved in the activity. Indicators of *fidelity* included organizational capacity (school amenability to program implementation, turnover in implementing staff), organizational support (amount of training in activity/program, quality of training in activity/program, supervision or monitoring of implementation of program), and program structure (e.g., standardization, local responsibility, amount of providers job related to the program, whether the activity was a regular, required activity in the school). Scales were scored by calculating the proportion of the identified best practices with respect to content or methods that were used in a particular activity or program.

Results indicated a low quality of implementation in the typical school. Programs tended to have far fewer sessions and to last for much shorter periods than research-based programs suggested as optimal. The typical prevention activity used 71% of the identified best practices with respect to content and only 50% of the best practices with respect to methods. Although somewhat subjective, ratings of program quality based on best practices were unimpressive. For example, only 10% of the nation's schools reported using what researchers considered to be minimally adequate discipline practices. The majority of schools either did not use available methods of influencing behavior or did not apply consistent disciplinary responses.

Researchers concluded that several approaches would improve the quality of prevention programming, including better integration of prevention activities into normal school operations; more extensive local planning and involvement in decisions about what to implement; greater organizational support in the form of high-quality training, supervision, and principal support; and greater standardization of program materials and methods (D. C. Gottfredson & G. D. Gottfredson, 2002; G. D. Gottfredson et al., 2004).

EXAMPLES OF SCHOOL-BASED PREVENTION PROGRAMS

Studies have indicated potential positive benefits from *well-designed* school-based programs such as conflict resolution, social skills, life skills, after-school programs, and other violence-prevention offerings. Empirical research suggests that many such programs are targeting appropriate causal factors (Welsh et al., 1999a, 1999b), although further tests of their effectiveness are needed. Below, we briefly describe examples of three popular program types: (1) *conflict resolution,* (2) *peer mediation,* and (3) *school organization and climate strategies.*

Conflict resolution training programs for juveniles are based on research findings that violent juveniles often display impulsivity and poor decision-making skills that contribute to violence in their daily, routine interactions with others (J. J. Wilson & Howell, 1994). By teaching youths how to effectively manage conflict and develop lifelong decision-making skills, it is hoped that juvenile violence can be reduced. Youths involved in disputes learn how to identify their interests in a specific interaction, express their views, listen attentively, and seek mutually acceptable solutions. One of the most common approaches is the process curriculum: Educators teach the principles and processes of conflict resolution as a distinct lesson or course.

Examples include the widely used Violence Prevention Curriculum for Adolescents, developed by Deborah Pothrow-Stith, and the Program for Young Negotiators, based on the Harvard Negotiation Project. In general, lessons concentrate on active listening, assertiveness (not passivity or aggressiveness), expression of feelings, perspective taking, cooperation, and negotiation. An initial evaluation of the Harvard Negotiation Project suggested that participating youths were more successful in discussing disputes and avoiding fights with their peers (LeBoeuf & Delany-Shabazz, 1997). Parents and teachers reported less need to intervene and general improvement in students' communication skills. In an evaluation of Pothrow-Stith's curriculum, experimental teachers from four inner-city high schools received one day of training to use the curriculum. Teachers then assigned tenth-grade classes to an experimental or comparison group (no curriculum). Teachers administered pretests two weeks before the lessons began and one month after the curriculum ended. Evaluators found no significant differences between experimental and control groups on knowledge about violence, attitudes about how to handle conflict, acceptance of violence, self-esteem, or weapon carrying (Howell, 1995). A marginal decrease was found for self-reported fighting.

Conflict resolution curricula, in general, have proven successful in improving social skills but only somewhat effective in changing attitudes toward violence and self-reported fighting. Programs are most effective when they involve the entire institution or school, when they are integrated into the educational curriculum, and when they are linked with supportive family and community mediation initiatives (LeBoeuf & Delany-Shabazz, 1997). Evaluations, though, have often been weakened by small samples, scarce information about successful program implementation, and inadequate research designs (Howell, 1995).

Another widely used approach is *peer mediation*: Trained youth mediators work with their peers to find resolutions to specific disputes. An evaluation of a comprehensive school-based mediation program for 2,500 students at one middle school and three elementary schools in Las Vegas, Nevada, found that peer mediators resolved 86% of the disputes they mediated, and there were fewer fights on school grounds. An evaluation of a peer-mediation program in Hawaii found it to be the best of 14 programs reviewed (Howell, 1995). That evaluation indicated favorable program assessments by participants but no consistent program effects on school climate or rates of student retention, suspension, dismissal, or attendance. In a study by Tolson, McDonald, and Moriarty (1992, cited in Howell, 1995), high school students were referred to assistant deans for interpersonal conflicts. They were then randomly assigned to either peer mediation or traditional discipline (warnings, demerits, or suspensions). Peer-mediation participants were significantly less likely to be referred again in two-and a-half months.

Although peer-mediation programs hold promise, their impact is often less well documented than advocates claim. Lam (1989, cited in Howell, 1995) reviewed 14 evaluations of peer-mediation programs. Numerous problems were found: None used a randomized experimental design (the preferred approach); only three had acceptable quasi-experimental designs; many evaluations had short observation periods; many used poorly conceived measures; follow-up periods were too brief to measure impact; and objective indicators of impact were lacking. Similar observations were echoed in earlier reviews by G. D. Gottfredson (1987) and Wilson-Brewer and colleagues (1991).

Other interventions have focused on changing *school organization and climate*. Project PATHE (Positive Action Through Holistic Education), for example, was implemented at four middle schools and four high schools in low-income, predominantly African American urban and rural areas in Charleston County, South Carolina (D. C. Gottfredson, 1986). The program contained six main components: (1) teams of teachers, students, parents, and community members designed and implemented school improvement programs, (2) curriculum and discipline policy review and revision, (3) school-wide academic innovations, such as study skills programs and cooperative learning techniques, (4) school climate interventions, including expanded extracurricular activities, peer counseling, and a school pride program, (5) career-oriented activities, and (6) special academic and counseling services for low-achieving and disruptive students.

Although experimental and comparison schools were not directly compared in statistical models, descriptive results suggested that the PATHE program produced several favorable outcomes. Experimental schools reported less delinquency, less drug involvement, and fewer suspensions or other punishments. Students in experimental schools who received special academic and counseling services scored significantly higher on standardized tests and were less likely to report drug involvement or repeat a grade than control-group students. Although school-based interventions appear promising, future evaluations should use more rigorous research designs to determine treatment effects (Howell, 1995).

CONCLUSIONS

Although school and community factors play a significant role in school violence, individual-level factors appear to offer stronger explanations for serious student misbehavior (G. D. Gottfredson et al., 2005; Welsh et al., 1999a). School climate factors seem to better explain the more common but less serious forms of student misconduct in schools (Welsh, 2001, 2003). Close scrutiny of school climate should be included in any school-based program designed to reduce violence. Efforts to change individuals, in the absence of attention to school policies that may be contributing to high levels of disorder, are likely to be unproductive or even counterproductive. Community factors such as poverty and instability should also be carefully assessed when designing or evaluating any school-based prevention program.

Further research on school violence should continue to sort out the interactive influences of individual-, school-, and community-level variables on behavior, and inform the development of effective strategies for violence prevention. Interventions must address multiple causes, and success will likely require greater cooperation between school officials, students, parents, community members, police, and other government agencies. Better implementation of violence-prevention programs is needed, as are stronger evaluations of their impacts.

DISCUSSION QUESTIONS

1. What do we know about the characteristics of *school shooters*? Give specific evidence from course materials.
2. *How much* violence occurs at school? How do we know? Describe at least two specific measures of school violence discussed in the text and give examples.
3. How does each of the following theories *explain* school violence: (a) control theory, (b) school climate theory, and (c) social disorganization theory? Describe the specific arguments of each theory as it relates to school violence.
4. (a) Describe the *four basic types* of school-based prevention programs, and describe one specific example of each. (b) Discuss *evidence* for the effectiveness of each of the four types. (c) What were some of the major *weaknesses* of school-based prevention programs?

SUGGESTED READINGS

Klebold, S. (2009, Oct. 13). I will never know why. *O, the Oprah Magazine*. Retrieved January 14, 2010, from http://www.oprah.com.

Robers, S., Kemp, J., & Truman, J. (2013). *Indicators of school crime and safety: 2012* (NCES 2013-036/NCJ 241446). Washington, DC: National Center for Education Statistics, U.S. Department of Education, and Bureau of Justice Statistics, Office of Justice Programs, U.S. Department of Justice.

REFERENCES

Agnew, R. (1993). Why do they do it? An examination of the intervening mechanisms between "social control" variables and delinquency. *Journal of Research in Crime and, Delinquency, 30*, 245–266.

Akers, R. L., & Sellers, C. S. (2012). *Criminological theories* (6th ed.). New York: Oxford University Press.

Anderson, C. S. (1982). The search for school climate: A review of the literature. *Review of Educational Research, 52*, 368–420.

Anderson, D. C. (1998). Curriculum, culture, and community: The challenge of school violence. In M. Tonry & M. H. Moore (Eds.), *Youth violence. Crime and Justice* (Vol. 24, pp. 317–363). Chicago: University of Chicago Press.

Anderson, E. (1990). *Streetwise: Race, class, and change in an urban community*. Chicago: University of Chicago Press.

Anderson, E. (1999). *Code of the street: Decency, violence, and the moral life of the inner city*. New York: W. W. Norton.

Begley, S. (2007). The anatomy of violence. *Newsweek, 149*(18), 40–46.

Bernard, T. J., Snipes, J. B., & Gerould, A. L. (2009). *Vold's theoretical criminology* (6th ed.). New York: Oxford University Press.

Brezina, T., Piquero, A., & Mazerolle, P. (2001). Student anger and aggressive behavior in school: An initial test of Agnew's macro-level strain theory. *Journal of Research in Crime and Delinquency, 38*, 362–386.

Cernkovich, S. A., & Giordano, P. C. (1992). School bonding, race, and delinquency. *Criminology, 30*, 261–291.

Chesney-Lind, M., & Shelden, R. G. (2003). *Girls, delinquency, and juvenile justice* (3rd ed.). Pacific Grove, CA: Wadsworth.

Elias, M. J., Tobias, S. E., & Friedlander, B. S. (2000). *Emotionally intelligent parenting: How to raise a self-disciplined, responsible, socially skilled child.* New York: Random House/Three Rivers Press.

Elias, M. J., Zins, J. E., Weissberg, R. P., Frey, K. S., Greenberg, M. T., Haynes, N. M., et al. (1997). *Promoting social and emotional learning: Guidelines for educators.* Alexandria, VA: Association for Supervision and Curriculum Development.

Farrington, D. P. (1973). Self-reports of deviant behavior: Predictive and stable? *Journal of Criminal Law and Criminology, 64*, 99–110.

Farrington, D. P. (1986). Age and crime. In M. Tonry & N. Morris (Eds.), *Crime and justice, an annual review of research* (Vol. 7, pp. 189–250). Chicago: University of Chicago Press.

Farrington, D. P., Loeber, R., Stouthamer-Loeber, M., Van Kammen, W., & Schmidt, L. (1996). Self-reported delinquency and a combined delinquency seriousness scale based on boys, mothers, and teachers: Concurrent and predictive validity for African-Americans and Caucasians. *Criminology, 34*, 493–517.

Fox, R. S., Schmuck, R., Van Egmond, E., Rivto, M., & Jung, C. (1979). *Diagnosing professional climates of schools.* Fairfax, VA: Learning Resources Corporation.

Gammage, J. (2007, March 11). Music teacher Ed Klein is still recuperating from a broken jaw. *Philadelphia Inquirer.* Available at: http://www.philly.com/philly/news/special_packages/inquirer/20070311_Music_teacher_Ed_Klein_is_still_recuperating_from_a_broken_jaw_and_concussion_suffered_when_a_student_slugged_him_Nov__3_in_his_West_Philadelphia_High_School_classroom_.html#l2ixq8liUIDxtP3Z.99.

Gottfredson, D. C. (1986). An empirical test of school-based environmental and individual interventions to reduce the risk of delinquent behavior. *Criminology, 24*, 705–731.

Gottfredson, D. C. (1989). Developing effective organizations to reduce school disorder. In O. C. Moles (Ed.), *Strategies to reduce student misbehavior.* Washington, DC: U.S. Department of Education, Office of Educational Research and Improvement.

Gottfredson, D. C. (2001). *Schools and delinquency.* New York: Cambridge University Press.

Gottfredson, D. C., & Gottfredson, G. D. (2002). Quality of school-based prevention programs: Results from a national survey. *Journal of Research in Crime and Delinquency, 39*, 3–35.

Gottfredson, D. C., Gottfredson, G. D., & Hybyl, L. G. (1993). Managing adolescent behavior: A multiyear, multischool study. *American Education Research Journal, 30*, 179–215.

Gottfredson, G. D. (1984). *The effective school battery.* Mairiottsville, MD: Gottfredson Associates, Inc. Retrieved August 14, 2006, from *http://www.gottfredson.com/esb.htm*.

Gottfredson, G. D. (1987). Peer group interventions to reduce the risk of delinquent behavior: A selective review and a new evaluation. *Criminology, 25*, 671–714.

Gottfredson, G. D., & Daiger, D. (1979). *Disruption in six hundred schools: The social ecology of personal victimization in the nation's public schools.* Baltimore: Johns Hopkins University.

Gottfredson, G. D., & Gottfredson, D. C. (1985). *Victimization in schools.* New York: Plenum.

Gottfredson, G. D., Gottfredson, D. C., Czeh, E. R., Cantor, D., Crosse, S. B., & Hantaan, I. (2004). *Toward safe and orderly schools—The National Study of Delinquency Prevention in Schools* (NCJ

205005). Washington, DC: U.S. Department of Justice, Office of Justice Programs, National Institute of Justice.

Gottfredson, G. D., Gottfredson, D. C., Payne, A. A., & Gottfredson, N. C. (2005). School climate predictors of school disorder: Results from a national study of delinquency prevention in schools. *Journal of Research in Crime and Delinquency, 42*, 412–444.

Gottfredson, M., & Hirschi, T. (1990). *A general theory of crime.* Stanford, CA: Stanford University Press.

Greenberg, M. T. (2010). School-based prevention: Current status and future challenges. *Effective Education*, 2(1), 27–52.

Hagan, J., & Simpson, J. (1978). Ties that bind: Conformity and the social control of student discontent. *Sociology and Social Research, 61*, 520–536.

Hahn, R., Fuqua-Whitley, D., Wethington, H., Lowy, J., Crosby, A., Fullilove, M., et al. (2007). Effectiveness of universal school-based programs to prevent violent and aggressive behavior: A systematic review. *American Journal of Preventive Medicine*, 33(2 Suppl.), S114–129.

Hanna, J. L. (1988). *Disruptive school behavior: Class, race, and culture.* New York: Holmes and Meier.

Hellman, D. A., & Beaton, S. (1986). The pattern of violence in urban public schools: The influence of school and community. *Journal of Research in Crime and Delinquency, 23*, 102–127.

Hellriegel, D., & Slocum, J., Jr. (1974). Organizational climate: Measures, research and contingencies. *Academy of Management Journal, 17*, 255–280.

Hindelang, M. (1973). Causes of delinquency: A partial replication and extension. *Social Problems, 20*, 471–487.

Hindelang, M. J., Hirschi, T., & Weis, J. G. (1981). *Measuring delinquency.* Beverly Hills, CA: Sage.

Hirschi, T. (1969). *Causes of delinquency.* Berkeley: University of California Press.

Hirschi, T., & Gottfredson, M. (1983). Age and the explanation of crime. *American Journal of Sociology, 89*, 522–584.

Howell, J. C. (Ed.). (1995). *Guide for implementing the comprehensive strategy for serious, violent, and chronic juvenile offenders* (NCJ 153681). Washington, DC: U.S. Department of Justice, Office of Justice Programs, Office of Juvenile Justice and Delinquency Prevention.

Huizinga, D., & Elliott, D. (1986). Reassessing the reliability and validity of self-report measures. *Journal of Quantitative Criminology, 2*, 293–327.

Ingersoll, R. (2001). Teacher turnover and teacher shortages: An organizational analysis. *American Educational Research Journal, 38*, 499–534.

Jenkins, P. (1997). School delinquency and the school social bond. *Journal of Research in Crime and Delinquency, 34*, 337–367.

Kazdin, A. E. (1987). *Conduct disorders in childhood and adolescence.* Newbury Park, CA: Sage.

Kirk, D. S. (2009). Unraveling the contextual effects on student suspension and juvenile arrest: The independent and interdependent influences of school, neighborhood, and family social controls. *Criminology, 47*, 479–517.

Klebold, S. (2009, October 13). I will never know why. *O, the Oprah Magazine*. Retrieved January 14, 2010, from: http://www.oprah.com.

Krohn, M., & Massey, J. (1980). Social control and delinquent behavior: An examination of the elements of the social bond. *Sociological Quarterly, 21*, 529–543.

Lam, J. A. (1989). *The impact of conflict resolution programs on schools: A review and synthesis of the evidence.* Amherst, MA: National Association for Mediation in Education.

Lawler, E., Hall, D., & Oldham, G. (1974). Organizational climate: Relationship to organizational structure, process and performance. *Organizational Behavior and Human Performance, 11*, 139–155.

Lawrence, R. A. (2006). *School crime and juvenile justice* (2nd ed.). New York: Oxford University Press.

LeBoeuf, D., & Delany-Shabazz, R. V. (1997). *Conflict resolution. Fact Sheet #55*. Washington, DC: U.S. Department of Justice, Office of Justice Programs, Office of Juvenile Justice and Delinquency Prevention.

Liska, A., & Reed, M. (1985). Ties to conventional institutions and delinquency: Estimating reciprocal effects. *American Sociological Review, 50*, 547–560.

Lockwood, D. (1997). *Violence among middle school and high school students: Analysis and implications for prevention* (NCJ-166363). Washington, DC: U.S. Department of Justice, Office of Justice Programs, National Institute of Justice.

Messner, S. F., & Rosenfeld, R. (2012). *Crime and the American dream* (5th ed.). Belmont, CA: Wadsworth.

Mulvey, E. P., & Cauffman, E. (2001). The inherent limits of predicting school violence. *American Psychologist, 56*, 797–802.

National School Safety Center. (2009). *School-associated violent deaths.* Retrieved Jan. 11, 2009, from http://www.schoolsafety.us.

Owens, R. G. (2003). *Organizational behavior in education* (8th ed.). Boston: Allyn & Bacon.

Payne, A. A., Gottfredson, D. C., & Gottfredson, G. D. (2003). Schools as communities: The relationships among communal school organization, student bonding, and school disorder. *Criminology, 41*, 749–778.

Pearson, F. S., & Toby, J. (1991). Fear of school-related predatory crime. *Sociology and Social Research, 75*, 117–125.

Reiss, A. J. Jr., & Roth, J. A. (Eds.). (1993). *Understanding and preventing violence (Vol. 1)*. Panel on the Understanding and Control of Violent Behavior, National Research Council. Washington, DC: National Academy Press.

Robers, S., Kemp, J., & Truman, J. (2013). *Indicators of school crime and safety*: 2012 (NCES 2013-036/NCJ 241446). Washington, DC: National Center for Education Statistics, U.S. Department of Education, and Bureau of Justice Statistics, Office of Justice Programs, U.S. Department of Justice.

Rubel, R. J. (1978). Analysis and critique of HEW's safe school study report to Congress. *Crime and Delinquency, 24*, 257–265.

Sampson, R. J., & Lauritsen, J. L. (1993). Violent victimization and offending: Individual, situational, and community-level risk factors. In Reiss, A. J., Jr., & Roth, J. A. (Eds.), *Understanding and preventing violence: Social influences* (Vol. 3). Washington, DC: National Academy Press.

Sampson, R. J., Raudenbush, S. W., & Earls, F. (1997). Neighborhoods and violent crime: A multilevel study of collective efficacy. *Science, 277*, 918–924.

Scheckner, S., Rollins, S. A., Kaiser-Ulrey, C., & Wagner, R. (2002). School violence in children and adolescents: A meta-analysis of effectiveness. *Journal of School Violence, 1*, 5–34.

Shaw, C. R., & McKay, H. D. (1942). *Juvenile delinquency and urban areas.* Chicago: University of Chicago Press.

Snyder, H. N., & Sickmund, M. (2006). *Juvenile offenders and victims: 2006 national report* (NCJ 212906). Washington, DC: U.S. Department of Justice, Office of Justice Programs, Office of Juvenile Justice and Delinquency Prevention.

Steffensmeier, D., Allen, E., Harer, M., & Streifel, C. (1989). Age and the distribution of crime. *American Sociological Review, 94*, 803–831.

Sullivan, J. Snyder, S., Graham, K. A., & Purcell, D. (2011, March 27). Climate of violence stifles city schools: Efforts by Phila. administrators to stem the complex problem have fallen short.

Philadelphia Inquirer. Retrieved from http://www.philly.com/philly/news/special_packages/inquirer/school-violence/118812644.html.

Thornberry, T., Lizotte, A., Krohn, M., Farnsworth, M., & Jang, S. (1991). Testing interactional theory: An examination of reciprocal causal relationships among family, school, and delinquency. *The Journal of Criminal Law and Criminology, 82,* 3–35.

Toby, J. (1983). Violence in school. In M. Tonry & N. Morris (Eds.), *Crime and justice: An annual review of research. Vol. 4.* Chicago: University of Chicago Press.

Tolson, E. R., McDonald, S., & Moriarty, A. R. (1992). Peer mediation among high school students: A test of effectiveness. *Social Work in Education, 14,* 86–93.

U.S. Secret Service National Threat Assessment Center.(2000). *Safe school initiative: An interim report on the prevention of targeted violence in schools.* Washington, DC: U.S. Secret Service.

Welsh, W. N. (2000). The effects of school climate on school disorder. *Annals of the American Academy of Political and Social Science, 567,* 88–107.

Welsh, W. N. (2001). Effects of student and school factors on five measures of school disorder. *Justice Quarterly, 18,* 401–437.

Welsh, W. N. (2003). Individual and institutional predictors of school disorder. *Youth Violence and Juvenile Justice, 1,* 346–368.

Welsh, W. N., Greene, J. R., & Jenkins, P. H. (1999a). School disorder: The influence of individual, institutional and community factors. *Criminology, 37,* 73–115.

Welsh, W. N., & Harris, P. W. (2012). *Criminal justice policy and planning* (4th ed.). Waltham, MA: Elsevier/Anderson.

Welsh, W. N., Jenkins, P. H., & Greene, J. R. (1997). *Building a culture and climate of safety in public schools in Philadelphia: School-based management and violence reduction.* Final report to the National Institute of Justice. Philadelphia: Center for Public Policy, Temple University.

Welsh, W. N., Jenkins, P. H., & Harris, P. W. (1999b). Reducing minority over-representation in juvenile justice: Results of community-based delinquency prevention in Harrisburg. *Journal of Research in Crime and Delinquency, 36,* 87–110.

Welsh, W. N., Stokes, R., & Greene, J. R. (2000). A macro-level model of school disorder. *Journal of Research in Crime and Delinquency, 37,* 243–283.

Wilson, D. B., Gottfredson, D. C., & Najaka, S. S. (2001). School-based prevention of problem behaviors: A meta-analysis. *Journal of Quantitative Criminology,* 17(3), 247–272.

Wilson, J. J., & Howell, J. C. (1994, December). Comprehensive strategy for serious, violent, and chronic juvenile offenders. Program Summary. Washington, DC: U.S. Department of Justice, Office of Justice Programs, Office of Juvenile Justice and Delinquency Prevention.

Wilson, S. J., & Lipsey, M. W. (2005). *The effectiveness of school-based violence prevention programs for reducing disruptive and aggressive behavior* (NCJ 211376). Washington, DC: U.S. Department of Justice, National Institute of Justice.

Wilson, S. J., & Lipsey, M. W. (2007). School-based interventions for aggressive and disruptive behavior: Update of a meta-analysis. *American Journal of Preventive Medicine,* 33(2), S130–S143.

Wilson-Brewer, R., Cohen, S., O'Donnell, L., & Goodman, I. (1991). *Violence prevention for young adolescents: A survey of the state of the art.* Washington, DC: Carnegie Council on Adolescent Development.

CHAPTER 11

GANGS AND GANG VIOLENCE

PATTERNS AND TRENDS

The topic of gang violence poses some challenges in a book devoted to understanding criminal violence. There is a wide variety of what are called "gangs"; they include youth gangs, street gangs, delinquent gangs, prison gangs, taggers, skinheads, bikers, stoner and punk groups, and even terrorist groups. Because we cannot discuss each, what we will discuss in this chapter is youth or street gangs using a definition provided by the National Gang Center. The following criteria are widely to classify groups as gangs:

- The group has three or more members, generally aged 12 to 24.
- Members share an identity, typically linked to a name and often other symbols.
- Members view themselves as a gang and are recognized by others as a gang.
- The group has some permanence and a degree of organization.
- The group is involved in an elevated level of criminal activity.

Much of what we know about gangs has come from the National Youth Gang Survey (NYGS), which has been conducted annually since 1996 by the National Gang Center. The NYGS is based on a nationally representative sample of more than 2,500 law enforcement agencies serving larger cities, suburban counties, smaller cities, and rural counties. The average annual response rate is high, approximately 85% for the sample. At least 95% of the agencies surveyed have reported gang-related activity at least once of three survey cycles.

To understand gang violence it is important to have a uniform definition over all jurisdictions. First, how gangs are defined has substantial research and, ultimately, policy consequences. Maxson and Klein (1990, 1996) noted that Los Angeles uses a different definition of gangs from Chicago. In Los Angeles, police record that the event is gang related by, for example, the homicide victim's appearance, dress, vehicle, or known gang associations. In contrast to the latter *gang member* definition, the Chicago police use a *gang motive* definition. The gang motive definition is more stringent; there must be evidence that gang membership or gang activity was the motive for the homicide. Examples are retaliation, territory conflicts, and recruitment.

Maxson and Klein then applied the more restrictive gang motive definition to the Los Angeles data to see what difference it would make in terms of the number of gangs and the characteristics of the more "purified" Los Angeles sample. They found that using the narrower definition on the Los Angeles data reduced the number of gang homicides by about half.

The possibility of underestimating or overestimating gang membership has serious consequences on resource allocation, as well as on public fear of crime. For example, estimates of gang members in the United States in the mid-1990s ranged from 660,000 to 1,500,000 (Esbensen et al., 2001).

Second, the importance of a uniform consistent definition of the gang problem has political consequences. Many jurisdictions deny there is a gang problem in their community for political and social reasons. At the beginning of his study of gangs in San Diego, Sanders (1994) found the police department claimed there were no gangs. The official policy that San Diego had no gangs may have been a way of protecting its multimillion-dollar tourist industry. Further, city officials believed that any publicity about gangs would encourage gang activity. Partly as a result of media accounts of gang violence, the city police department formed a gang detail unit a few years later.

Hagedorn (1990) gives the example of a public official in Indianapolis who, after repeated denials of gangs in the city, said, "Look, we do not have a gang problem here. We do have a slight problem in the summer with groups of youths running around with shotguns, but we don't have a gang problem." The official said that the city could not admit to a gang problem because it was preparing to host the Pan American Games.

When asked to rank the definitional characteristics of gangs from 1 = least important to 6 = most important, the survey respondents rated "commits crimes together" highest (mean rank = 4.7) followed by gang "has a name" (mean rank = 3.6). The characteristics "displays colors or other symbols," "hangs out together," "claims turf or territory," and "has a leader" all had a mean rank of 3.2 or less. In general, for law enforcement, group criminality is more important and leadership is least important.

Table 11.1 gives the criteria used to designate that gang members belong to a gang. The table shows that in larger and small cities and suburban counties, from 68% to 79% emphasize the use of self-nomination techniques. The figure is 47.8% for rural counties, which show a preference for the display of tattoos, colors, or other symbols for designation as gang membership. In short, law enforcement, except for that in rural areas, seems to rely on crimes committed together and self-nomination as an operational definition of gang membership (National Gang Center, 2011).

Table 11.1 Designating Gang Membership

Individual Claims Membership	Larger Cities	Suburban Counties	Smaller Cities	Rural Counties
Frequently used	78.7%	69.3%	67.8%	47.8%
Infrequently used	21.3%	30.7%	32.2%	52.2%

Source: National Gang Center. (2011). *National Youth Gang Survey Analysis*. Retrieved June 2, 2014, from http://www.nationalgangcenter.gov/Survey-Analysis.

GROWTH AND CHANGE IN GANGS

One of the best ways to understand gangs and gang-related violence is to examine the growth of gangs in the past decades. In the 1960s, there was a period of great concern about violence. The government responded by forming three commissions: the President's Commission on Law Enforcement and the Administration of Justice (1967), the National Commission on the Causes and Prevention of Violence (1969), and the National Advisory Commission on Criminal Justice Standards and Goals (1973). As Miller (2001) noted, while gangs were mentioned in each of the commissions, they were not the subject of any special report, nor was the possibility of violence by gangs given much attention.

In the 1980s and 1990s, however, the government as well as the general public came to view gangs as dangerous, violent, and on the increase. Once cities and police departments acknowledged that a gang problem existed, departments established gang control units. At the conclusion of his national assessment of the gang problem, Miller (1982) concluded that any significant reduction in gang and collective youth crime would require a major federal initiative. This federal involvement began to be implemented in the 1980s and 1990s. Some types of federal involvement are as follows:

- The Department of Health and Human Service's Youth Gang Drug Prevention Program (1989)
- The National Institute of Justice Gang Research Initiative (1991)
- The Office of Juvenile Justice and Delinquency Prevention Comprehensive Response to America's Gang Problem (1988)
- Gang Resistance Educational Assistance and Training (1994)
- The Community Oriented Police Service Anti-Gang Initiative (1996).

Because the NYGS (2009) was interested in the prevalence and extent of gangs—that is, how and whether gangs had spread to smaller jurisdictions—the survey focused on the following:

- *Larger cities*: 624 police departments in jurisdictions with populations of 50,000 or more
- *Suburban counties*: All suburban police and sheriff's departments ($N = 739$)
- *Smaller cities*: 543 randomly selected sample of police departments in cities with populations between 2,500 and 49,999
- *Rural counties*: 492 randomly selected samples of rural county police and sheriff's departments.

Demographics

Table 11.2 shows that the percentage of gang members over the age of 18 has consistently increased from 1996 to 2011. In 1998, there was an equal percentage of gang members under and over age 18, but by 2011, older gang members predominated (65.0%). Larger cities and suburban counties report a higher percentage of gang members over the age of 18 than small cities and rural counties. This may be due to the fact that larger cities and suburban counties have longstanding gang problems and are more likely to report older gang

Table 11.2 Age of Gang Members

	Juvenile (Under 18)	Adult (18 and Over)
1996	50.0	50.0
1998	40.1	59.9
1999	37.3	62.7
2001	33.2	66.8
2002	38.0	61.9
2004	41.1	58.9
2005	38.9	61.1
2006	36.5	63.5
2008	41.4	58.6
2011	35.0	65.0

Source: National Gang Center. (2011). *National Youth Gang Survey Analysis.* Retrieved June 2, 2011, from http://www.nationalgangcenter.gov/Survey-Analysis/Demographics#anchorage.

members. Smaller cities and rural counties with more recent gang problems are more likely to report younger gang members.

According to the 2007 NYGS, gangs are overwhelmingly and consistently male. The percentage of males ranged from 92.3% in 1998 to 93.9% in 2004. While there are few females found in law enforcement records, the survey by Esbensen and Winfree (2006) found that 38% of gang members were females. This is consistent with earlier studies using self-reported gang membership (Bjerregard & Smith, 1993; Esbensen & Huizinga, 1993; Maxson & Whitlock, 2002; Moore & Hagedorn, 2001).

Esbensen and Winfree (2006) suggest there are two reasons females have been excluded from earlier research. Early research relied on males nominating other persons as gang members, and they may have failed to nominate female gang members. In addition, early research relied on older gang members, and females age out of gangs at an earlier age. The older view, that female gang members are mere sex objects with no involvement in the violent acts gang males commit, receives no support. Gang girls commit the same variety of acts as gang boys, but at a slightly lower frequency (Esbensen & Winfree, 2006; Maxson & Whitlock, 2002).

The percentage of various race/ethnic groups changed little over the period from 2008 to 2011. Hispanic or Latino gangs ranged from 45.2% of the total in 1996 to 50.2% in 2010. African American gangs ranged from 31.8% of the total in 2008 to 35.3% in 2011. White gangs ranged from 5.7% in 2004 to 7.7% one year later.

GANG ORGANIZATION AND VIOLENCE

On the basis of their research, Klein and Maxson (2006) described five different types of street gangs:

- *The Traditional Gang*: Traditional gangs have been around for 20 years or more and keep generating themselves. They number 100 or more members, they are territorial, and they have several internal cliques based on age or area. Their members vary widely in age (the oldest members may be 9 to 10 years older than the youngest).
- *The Neotraditional Gang*: Resembles the traditional gang but has not been in existence as long. The neotraditional gang is of medium size (50 to 100 members) and is territorial.
- *The Compressed Gang*: The age span of members is less (10 years or less between oldest and youngest members), and there are up to 50 members. The gang has been in existence for 10 years or less and its future is unclear. Some of these gangs are territorial.
- *The Collective Gang*: Like the compressed gang, but larger and has been around longer. Described as a "shapeless" mass that has not developed distinguishing characteristics.
- *The Specialty Gang*: Unlike other gangs that may engage in a variety of criminal offenses, the specialty gang is narrowly focused. The principal purpose is criminal, with a well-defined territory and a narrow age range. Drug gangs are an example of a specialty gang.

Gang Violence

The 2011 NYGS reported striking changes in gang-related crime in 2010 and 2011: a 48% increase in violent crimes, a 51.5% increase in property crimes, and a 32.7% increase in drug sales in one year.

In a study of Rochester, Seattle, and Denver, Thornberry (1998) found that gang members were responsible for 85% of all robberies reported in Seattle, 79% of all serious violent crimes and 87% of all drug sales in Denver, and 86% of all serious offenses and 70% of all drug sales in Rochester.

The National Crime Victimization Survey (NCVS) avoids some of the problems of collecting data on gangs from a law enforcement perspective because it is a national survey of victims. Victims were asked whether any of the offenders were members of a gang. Victims in about 6% of all violent crimes believed the offenders were gang members. According to the NCVS, completed violent crimes include rape, robbery, and simple and aggravated assault. Homicides are taken from the Supplementary Homicide Report.

Gang violence declined from 1993 to 2003. The peak was in 1996, when gang members were responsible for 10% of all violent crimes. The figure declined to about 6% in 1998 and did not significantly change thereafter. For this 11-year period, Hispanic victims of violence identified gang offenders at a higher rate than non-Hispanic victims; similarly, black victims identified more gang offenders than whites.

Victimization by gang members was highest for aggravated assault (12%), followed by robberies (10%), simple assaults (6%), and rapes (4%). For the period 1993 to 1996, the Federal Bureau of Investigation (FBI) reported that 5% to 7% of homicides were gang related, and 8% to 10 % were firearm homicides.

While the number of respondents was small, younger victims were more likely to identify offenders as gang members than older victims. For victims aged 12 to 19, 12% of violent victimizations were reported to be by gang members. This compares with 6% of violent victimizations for subjects aged 20 to 49. For the 11-year period, a lone offender was named in 54% of the violent victimizations and more than one offender in 46% of the cases (Harrell, 2005).

Gang Homicides

Because gang homicides are difficult to classify and report, 79.6% of the agencies surveyed provided homicide data. According to the NYGS sample, there were more than 1,900 gang-related homicides from 2007 to 2011. Nationally, the FBI estimated more than 15,500 homicides, which means that gang-related homicides account for about 12% of all homicides annually.

Gang-related homicides are concentrated in large cities. In the so-called gang capitals of Chicago and Los Angeles, about half of all homicides are gang related. These two cities accounted for approximately 20% of gang homicides in 2010 and 2011. More than 80% of smaller cities and rural counties reported no gang-related homicides.

EXPLANATIONS

STRAIN THEORIES

Strain theory argues that most people are law-abiding but become criminal under pressure. The task is to explain what is meant by pressure or strain. Merton (1957) believed that the disparity between cultural goals and institutionalized means leads to a number of adaptations. Merton's theory has been called by one writer the "most influential single formulation in the sociology of deviance in the last twenty-five years" (Clinard, 1964, p. 10). Because it has heavily influenced other theories that explain gang violence, we will summarize it here.

Merton first distinguished between cultural goals and institutionalized means. Every culture has goals that are considered desirable and important. In the United States, a major cultural goal is success, primarily economic success or wealth. Because it is an egalitarian society, the United States encourages everyone to pursue this goal and praises the few who reach it. Those who do succeed become the stuff of legend, the Horatio Alger story of "poor boy makes it big," but those who do not even try are characterized as "lazy" or "unambitious."

In a well-integrated society, the people also prescribe institutionalized means to reach these goals. In U.S. society, the institutionalized means to reach the success goal consist of such elements as willingness to work hard, to be honest, to get an education, and to defer gratification (things like purchasing an expensive automobile or house or taking an expensive vacation).

Where these two components are well integrated, the mode of adaptation is described as "conformity." There are several other adaptations, however, which have implications for crime and violence (Table 11.3). A disjunction between goals and means gives rise to anomie, or "normlessness." In short, Merton thought that without the guidelines provided by culture, behavior would arise that culture was designed to prevent, like crime.

Criminological theorists interested in explaining crime and violence drew upon the second adaptation, innovation. In this adaptation, the cultural goal of success is accepted, but criminal and deviant means are used to reach it. Innovation occurs when the goal is emphasized at the expense of the institutionalized means. The culturally approved version of institutionalized means states that "It's not whether you win or lose, it's how you play the game." Merton claims that the goal has become more important than the means:

Table 11.3 Typology of Individual Adaptations

Modes of Adaptation	Cultural Goals	Institutionalized Means
I. Conformity	+	+
II. Innovation	+	−
III. Ritualism	−	+
IV. Retreatism	−	−
V. Rebellion	±	±

+Accepts cultural goals or institutionalized means.
−Rejects cultural goals or institutionalized means.
±Rejects cultural goals and institutionalized means but wishes to replace with new goals and means.

Source: Merton (1957, p. 140).

"It's not how you play the game, it's whether you win." With an undue emphasis on the goal, we realize that institutionalized means offer little intrinsic satisfaction.

Consider two types of individuals. Individual 1 has been working hard, is honest, has struggled to get an education, and has saved her money. She receives little social reward for her efforts and, unless she was prudent in providing for herself, may well have financial difficulties when she retires.

Individual 2 does none of these things: He has been a gambler, has moved from job to job, and has a reputation for legal and moral "corner cutting," but he is wealthy. He will receive more rewards of prestige and social status than Individual 1, even though his wealth may not have been achieved by approved means. Individual 2 is rich, and according to Merton, that is really what counts when the innovation adaptation is used. Consequently, crime is another way of being successful.

This strain, or disparity, tends to be concentrated in the lower class, because the ability to achieve wealth is limited by the social structure itself. Because of income and education differentials, it is the lower class that does the worst job of preparing children to achieve success goals. On the other hand, strain is least apparent in the upper and middle classes, because members of these strata can achieve wealth with only a reasonable effort.

Consider the third adaptation, ritualism, which does not generate criminality (see Table 11.3). In this adaptation, the cultural goals are rejected while the institutionalized means are accepted. This is demonstrated by people who "go through the motions" but feel there is little hope of achieving higher goals; they are satisfied with a modest level of achievement.

"Retreatism" refers to people who reject both means and goals. They are best described as dropouts from society such as drug addicts, alcoholics, and vagrants. "Rebellion," the last of the adaptations, is what the name implies: These people reject the current culture and structure and want to replace it with something new.

Cohen's *Delinquent Boys* (1955) offered one of the earliest strain theories. Cohen's gangs were not particularly violent; they were involved in activities that were "malicious, non-utilitarian, and negativistic." According to Merton's theory, gang members were unhappy and frustrated by being subjected to middle-class measures of "good boys," such as achievement, deferred gratification, and ability to control aggression. These young males found other like-minded young males and formed groups that behaved exactly opposite to what was expected of nice middle-class children. Such behavior could include such crimes as vandalism but not drug selling, drive-by shootings, or attacks on rival gangs.

Also drawing on Merton's strain theory, but in a different way, Cloward and Ohlin (1960) argued that crime occurred because opportunities to achieve success were blocked for lower-class youth. What makes the Cloward and Ohlin theory an extension of Merton's work is that the authors argued that there are illegitimate opportunity structures as well as legitimate ones. Thus, in areas where there is a *criminal subculture*, older criminals teach young criminals and act as role models.

A second adaptation to illegitimate opportunity was the *retreatist subculture*. These are gangs who are double failures: They are not successful in either the legitimate opportunity structure or in the illegitimate structure. They retreat into a world of drugs, alcohol, and atypical sexual experiences, or a combination of all three.

In addition to the criminal subculture adaptation, there was the *conflict subculture* that occurred in neighborhoods characterized by high turnover of residents, high unemployment, and low home ownership. This adaptation seems most relevant to contemporary gang violence. Gang violence occurs when the members protect their turf, and gang membership is a means of achieving status in the neighborhood.

While the preceding theories may appear to have limited relevance to the contemporary scene, they played an extremely important role in shaping public and criminological images of gangs and gang violence. With the cooperation of and funds from the Ford Foundation and the political support of President John F. Kennedy's Committee on Juvenile Delinquency and Youth Crime, chaired by Attorney General Robert Kennedy, well-funded projects in New York, Chicago, and Los Angeles focused on community intervention to reduce gang crimes by using street workers. Theoretically, the programs were based on Lloyd Ohlin's view of legitimate and illegitimate opportunity structures (Klein, 1995).

CULTURAL DEVIANCE

Walter Miller (1958) advanced the view that the lower class had "focal concerns," very similar to social values. These focal concerns shaped the behavior of young people in ways that led to delinquent behavior. The focal concerns are as follows:

1. *Trouble.* Getting into and out of trouble: Such activities as fighting, drinking, and sexual misbehavior are a daily part of lower-class life.
2. *Toughness.* This focal concern refers to a show of masculinity and a denial of sentimentality. Miller argued that this focal concern results from many lower-class males growing up in female-dominated households.
3. *Smartness.* Street smarts: the ability to get something by outwitting or conning another person.
4. *Excitement.* A focal concern expressed by fighting, getting drunk, or using drugs; anything to break up a monotonous existence.

5. *Luck.* People believe that life is subject to forces over which they have little control. The focal concern of luck expresses itself in a belief in lucky numbers, whether the cards are right, or whether the dice are good to them.
6. *Autonomy.* The last focal concern is expressed in the lower-class person's resentment of authority and its rules.

The fact that these values conflict with middle-class values is the basis of the problem. These focal concerns generate the kind of behavior that gets juveniles and gang members in trouble and arrested. Thus, in Miller's view, gang violence is not a reaction to middle-class values; it is a consequence of lower-class values that coincidentally conflict with middle-class authority.

Wolfgang and Ferracuti's (1967) subculture of violence theory is similar to Miller's theory in thinking that cultural beliefs cause crime. The difference is that the focus is on one set of norms, values, and social expectations that define the behavior of lower-class individuals with respect to the expression of violence. For instance, a man in a bar makes a disparaging remark to another person about some subject that he has firm beliefs about—say, a sports team or a religious or political group. This starts a chain of escalating insults and counter-insults; the situation quickly becomes physical and can end in homicide. Much the same process can occur with gangs. Rival gang members can invade another gang's neighborhood or "diss" them in a variety of settings. This behavior is construed as an insult and justifies a violent response. Put another way, violence is seen as problem-solving behavior.

SOCIAL CONTROL

The traditional version of social control theory (Hirschi, 1969) took the view that criminality did not depend on biological, psychological, or sociological causes that drove offenders to commit crimes. Instead, criminality is part of human nature and, left to their own devices, all individuals would commit crimes.

The problem is to explain why people *do not* commit crimes. What are the social forces and institutions that "keep people in line"? Hirschi discussed various aspects of the social bond, but contemporary writers argue that applying social control to gangs and gang violence requires an integration of social control theory with ecological and other perspectives such as multiple marginality (Vigil & Yun, 2002).

The concept of multiple marginality began with Vigil's (1990) study of the growth of gangs that resulted from Mexican immigration. The term *cholo* meant a person marginalized in terms of his ethnic background and social status. Vigil traced the history of Mexican immigration and found that many individuals who turn to gangs do so because of racism, poverty with little chance of mobility, and the general problems associated with school and employment. These, Vigil claimed, are the end product of *choloization*, and *cholos* are drawn to gangs in which drug dealing and intergang violence occurs.

Multiple marginality means what is happening to one ethnic group is happening to others. Vigil and Yun (1990) found that Vietnamese gangs originated from two immigrations. The first, in 1975, consisted of well-educated, highly urbanized, relatively wealthy young people. President Gerald Ford attempted to disperse these people throughout the United States, but they returned to communities in Southern California. The second immigration was that of the "boat people," who were poorer and generally less prepared to live in the United States than the first wave.

Both waves were greeted with hostility by Americans, and the immigrant children were not prepared to succeed in U.S. schools, mainly because of their lack of English. The stability of the Vietnamese family was marred by conflict. Children were learning about wealth and U.S. lifestyles while their parents worked long hours at low-paying jobs and left the children unsupervised. Thus, the parental values of hard work, self-sacrifice, and patience were largely lost on their children.

> Vietnamese gangs stole automobiles initially, not for joyriding but to sell. However, according to Vigil and Yun, this was not sufficient to support gang members' lifestyles. Vietnamese Americans traditionally do not trust banks and therefore keep large amounts of gold and cash in their homes. Thus, one of the most important criminal activities for Vietnamese gangs was home invasion robberies. The victims had little faith in the police and typically would not report the crimes.

Because of the difficulty of acculturation and assimilation, socialization of young people on the streets becomes the most important feature of multiple marginality. This street socialization blurs ethnic lines, because similar things are learned. Fear and vulnerability generate the need for protection, friendship, and loyalty—hallmarks of gangs. Because other institutions have been undermined and fragmented, the street gang begins to dominate members' lives (Vigil & Yun, 2002).

Much of what we have discussed has received support from research on structural explanations. Curry and Spergel (1988) concluded that gang homicides are different from nongang homicides and that the former occur in areas of high poverty and social disorganization.

INTERACTIONAL THEORY

Interactional theory, a theory of delinquency developed by Thornberry (1987), has been described as an integrated life course theory (Ontario Ministry of Children and Youth Services, 2008). A life course perspective means that delinquency involves processes that unfold over time; each has an onset, duration, and termination. Different processes become important at different stages.

During childhood, attachment to the family is the single most important determinant as to whether the youth will adjust to conventional society and will be shielded from delinquency. By adolescence, the family is replaced by friends, school, and youth culture. By adulthood, the person's behavior is shaped by his or her place in conventional society.

The second premise is that delinquency and its causes interact with each other, which affects the level of offending. For example, ineffectual parenting may increase the risk of delinquency, but further parental response may increase it even more.

The third premise is that multiple causes of delinquency vary in magnitude across persons. Thus, as causal forces become more pronounced, a person's involvement in crime increases in severity.

Interactional theory includes hypotheses derived from these premises. For instance, a childhood onset of delinquency is associated with families and neighborhoods characterized by poverty and social disorganization. In contrast, those who begin offending at a later age are hypothesized to have lower intelligence and academic capabilities but were not affected by traits that affected other members of their age group because of a strong school environment and a supportive family.

INTERVENTIONS

Spergel and Curry (1995) described a typology of five different intervention strategies based on a survey of 254 criminal justice and community service agencies. Suppression was the most common type of intervention (44.0% of the respondents). According to Spergel and Curry (1995, p. 258), suppression "includes arrest, incarceration, and other forms of criminal justice, along with youth agency or community group supervision."

Social intervention was the second most common type (31.5% of respondents). This strategy involves converting or redirecting gangs to conventional organizations or legitimate groups. It consists of all psychological and social work approaches, street worker efforts, religious conversions, and so forth.

The problem with suppression and detached street-based worker programs is that they actually increase the amount gang crime. It is certainly true that detached workers have been able to connect with seriously alienated young people and have been successful in finding them jobs, tutoring, family intervention, counseling, and so forth. Unfortunately, this has not led to crime reduction at the individual level.

Klein (1995, p. 233) goes on to say:

> Suppression programs also are short term. They do little to nothing about the forces that foster gang development. But by focusing on gang-qua-gang problems, they can and—I'm convinced—do serve to reinforce gang identity.

The third most common intervention strategy was organizational change and development (10.9% of respondents). This strategy includes organizational changes that make it easier to put into place other interventions—for instance, a police department that starts a special gang unit (Spergel & Curry, 1995). Other examples include advocacy for legislation and the use of media.

Community organization, chosen by 8.95% of the respondents, refers to efforts to bring about change among groups or organizations to address social problems. Examples include cleaning up the community, involving parents and families, and building community trust.

Opportunities provision, which was ranked the lowest of the strategies (4.8%), involves job preparation, development, training, and placement, assistance with school, and tutoring (Spergel & Curry, 1995).

REDUCING GANG VIOLENCE IN BOSTON

One of the best-known gang violence interventions began in 1995 when an interagency working group of Harvard University researchers, members of the Boston Police Department, and other community agencies did research and analysis on Boston's youth violence problem (Braga & Kennedy, 2002). The research showed that youth violence was concentrated among a small number of serially offending, gang-involved youths. The study also showed that Boston had 61 gangs, with 1,300 gang members; most gang members were between 14 and 24 years of age. Many of the gang members were known to police and street workers and were known to have extensive and varied criminal histories. Gang membership in Boston, like gang membership elsewhere, increases the amount of delinquent and criminal behavior.

Boston gangs congregated in and defended their "turf" (well-defined areas in their neighborhoods). While disputes over turf, drugs, and money led to gang violence, the majority of gang-related homicides were personal and resembled vendettas. The conflict might have started over drugs or money, but it tended to take on a life of its own.

Related research indicates that gang violence frequently involves the use of firearms (Decker & Van Winkle, 1996). Contrary to the popular image of cheap handguns and "Saturday Night Specials," however, gangs, including those in Boston, preferred new semiautomatic pistols that had been diverted from retail or smuggled in from out of state (Sheley & Wright, 1995). Braga and Kennedy (2002) point out that gang members not only try to increase the number of weapons but seek more sophisticated and powerful weaponry than their rivals. Gang members believe this "arms race" will increase personal protection and decrease the risk of victimization.

The problem-solving intervention implemented in 1996 involved a Working Group that included a large number of Massachusetts criminal justice agencies, such as the Boston Police Department, the Suffolk County District Attorney, the Boston School Police, street workers attached to the Boston Community Centers Program, the Massachusetts Attorney General's office, the Department of Youth Services (DYS), and the State Police. Other participants included the U.S. Attorney's office, the Drug Enforcement Administration (DEA), the Bureau of Alcohol, Tobacco, Firearms and Explosives (ATF), and the Ten Point Coalition of activist black clergy.

The plans of the Working Group led to the "Operation Ceasefire" intervention, which had two components. The first focused law enforcement attention on gun trafficking within the state, the type of guns used by gangs, and the guns that were most likely to be trafficked (i.e., new guns and guns with obliterated serial numbers). The second component, "pulling levers," focused on a deterrence strategy: The message was sent that violence would no longer be tolerated, and when it did occur, every available legal "lever" was pulled to back up the prohibition on violence. In other words, gangs were not subject to increased law enforcement attention arbitrarily, nor did the Working Group develop a "hit list" of members. Rather, by engaging in violence, gang members selected themselves for a large amount of extra attention from law enforcement and others. Police officers, DYS caseworkers, probation officers, street workers, and members of the Ten Point Coalition flooded gang turf and communicated that the violence was to stop and that law enforcement efforts were supported. The Ten Point Coalition also offered services and opportunities to gang members, such as health and social services, educational programs, substance abuse interventions, and food and shelter.

Operation Ceasefire tailored its "lever pulling" to stop violent activity. Enforcement responses were configured to the particular gang and included such actions as conducting probation checks, changing community supervision conditions, serving outstanding arrest warrants, and disrupting street-level drug markets. The enforcement actions were only as harsh as they needed to be to stop the violence, and most of the time these enforcement responses were sufficient. With hardcore gang members, however, federal authorities were brought in. ATF, DEA, and FBI investigations, prosecutions by the U.S. Attorney's office, and the prospect of serving an additional term in federal prison were extra deterrents.

While these enforcement actions were going on, the Working Group members continued communicating with gang members that violent behavior would no longer be tolerated. They also disseminated fliers and held public forums that gang members under supervision were required to attend.

Evaluating Operation Ceasefire

The most immediate effect of the program was a marked decline in youth homicides. From 1991 to 1996, the mean number of youth homicides was about 44. The figure was 26 in 1996, 15 in 1997, 18 in 1998, and 15 in 1999 (Braga & Kennedy, 2002).

Was Operation Ceasefire responsible for this decline? To test this, Braga and colleagues (2001) used time-series modeling and found a 63% decrease in youth homicides and a 25% decrease in Boston's gun assaults in one high-risk district. The evaluators then added variables such as changes in the unemployment rate for young people, changes in the violence crime index, older homicide victimizations, and changes in street-level drug activity; adding these variables did not substantively change the results.

Why Was Operation Ceasefire Effective?

Braga and his associates were not able to construct a classic experiment with before-and-after measures to determine what accounted for the success of Operation Ceasefire. To explore the effectiveness of the program further they drew on Spergel and Curry's (1995) model to discuss four of the typologies of intervention: suppression, social intervention, opportunity provision, and community organization.

Suppression. Suppression approaches are built on deterrence theory. Through such activity as street sweeps, law enforcement hopes to deter gang activity and remove gangs from the street. This process is continued at the subsequent levels of the criminal justice process by greater surveillance of gang members through probation and parole caseloads and prosecution programs that target gang leaders and members.

Police cannot remove all gangs from the community, however, nor can they respond powerfully in all gang jurisdictions. The result may be that suppression increases gang cohesion, as Klein (1995, p. 163) points out:

> Now he [the gang member] returns to his neighborhood and encounters or seeks out his homies. Does he say to them, "Oh, gracious, I've been arrested and subject to deterrence; I'm going to give up my gang affiliation." Or does he say, "Shit, man, they're just jivin' us—can't hold us on any changes, and gotta let us go." Without hesitation, the gangbanger will turn the experience to his and the gang's advantage. Far from being deterred from membership or crime, his ties to the group will be strengthened when the members group together to make light of the whole affair and heap ridicule on the police. It does, indeed, become good laughing material.

But the approach in Operation Ceasefire was different. The deterrence efforts were delivered to the door of the offending gang rather than to a whole area—as Braga and Kennedy (2002) put it, "retail deterrence." In addition, the suppression component was supplemented by messages from the Working Group that the strategy was designed to protect both gang members and the community.

Operation Ceasefire also provided gang youth with a way to save face. Previously, when a gang member was killed, the victim gang had to respond or it would lose status and respect on the street. With Operation Ceasefire in place, however, victimized gang youths could argue that authorities had removed the offending youth and that a violent response was unwise.

Social Intervention and Opportunity Provision. Operation Ceasefire made use of street workers to provide services such as job skills training and substance abuse counseling, as well as attempting to prevent violence by mediating disputes among gang members. What made the efforts of street workers more effective was that they were able to pair criminal justice sanctions or the threat of sanctions with help and services. Thus, the opportunity for legitimate jobs became more appealing as the risk for drug dealing was increased.

Community Organization. One of the most important players with respect to community organization was the Ten Point Coalition of activist black clergy. The coalition formed after rival gang members invaded the Morningstar Baptist Church during the memorial service of a slain gang member and attacked mourners with knives and guns. Initially, the coalition began working with the Boston Community Center's street workers program and was highly critical of Boston law enforcement. Once the Operation Ceasefire intervention strategy was implemented, however, the coalition forged a strong relationship with the Working Group and the Boston Police Department.

The coalition's contribution consisted of providing an umbrella of legitimacy for police actions. Coalition members would accompany police on home visits to families of gang youths and would act as advocates for youths in the criminal justice system. The coalition had condemned the indiscriminate, highly aggressive law enforcement sweeps of neighborhoods, but they did support Operation Ceasefire's tight focus on violent youth. Because of coalition support, Boston's black community ceased to see law enforcement action as harassment and supported Operation Ceasefire as a legitimate youth violence prevention campaign (Braga & Kennedy, 2002).

There seems little doubt that Operation Ceasefire was successful. McDevitt and colleagues (2003) note, however, that traditional gangs still exist, and formerly incarcerated gang members are now being released from prison. Two new groups have become more involved with gang violence in Boston: females and young males who identify themselves with national gangs.

While the majority of female gangs are of mixed gender, some 25% are independent, all-female groups. Female gangs in Boston have arrest rates similar to those of male gangs. Their criminality tends to be more group-oriented than males. Fighting occurs frequently, in response to disrespect to either the individual or to the group.

Young male groups take on the name and symbols of "Bloods" or "Crips," but there is no known connection to the national groups. These groups do not seem to be as involved in drug sales or territorial disputes. The Boston School Police have documented an increase in school assaults, including stabbings and other weapons attacks with hammers, machetes, and cleavers. Thus, while Operation Ceasefire was designed to deal with a relatively small number of gang-involved violent offenders, the nature of gang violence in Boston has evolved, and it is unclear whether the techniques used by Operation Ceasefire would be effective with the new groups that have emerged (McDevitt et al., 2003).

PULLING LEVERS IN OTHER JURISDICTIONS

Following the pioneering work in Boston, a number of other jurisdictions have focused on a deterrence strategy for chronic offenders; developed an interagency working group of criminal justice and social service personnel; conducted a jurisdiction-specific assessment of violence, victims, and offenders; and examined drug market characteristics and weapons use and acquisition. Programs were started in Minneapolis, Baltimore, Los Angeles, and five medium-size cities: Indianapolis, Memphis, New Haven, Portland (Oregon), and Winston-Salem (Braga et al., 2002).

The Indianapolis Violence Reduction Partnership was patterned after the Boston project, using a problem-solving approach to reducing homicide. The response to homicide was having multiple agencies respond, directing resources toward chronic offenders, and having lever-pulling meetings with high-risk probationers and parolees. The number of homicides declined after the intervention began. There were 155 homicide recorded in 1997 and 115 in 2001. Fifty-six percent of the homicide victims were described as members of gangs or groups of known chronic offenders. After the intervention period, this figure dropped to 44%. For homicide suspects, the corresponding numbers were 54% and 39%. After the notification or lever-pulling meetings, the arrestees thought the criminal justice system was more effective responding to crime. However, probationers/parolees were not less likely to recidivate compared to a control group (Chermak & McGarrell, 2004).

In a lengthy and critical discussion of gang control patterns and policies, Klein and Maxson (2006, pp. 258–259) compared a suppression program, Operation Hardcore, to Operation Ceasefire and said that it seemed more promising, despite controversy over some outcomes, for several reasons:

> First, it undertook explicit procedures to produce general as well as special deterrence, thus expressing a far broader goal. Second, it engaged not only the local criminal justice agencies but also local community agencies. Third, it placed a major emphasis on relevant data collection prior to launching the program. Included in these data were gun locations, gun sources inside and outside of the community, and information about the most active and pivotal street gangs involved in gun-related serious violence. Fourth, although given less emphasis, there was some offering of alternative activities through social service, drug rehab, and the like.

CONCLUSIONS

Several conclusions can be drawn from this survey of gangs and gang violence. There seems to be no settled definition of a gang, although the definitions of street or youth gangs have considerable overlap and are used to generate most of the research.

One of the most disturbing of recent trends is the spread of gangs to small and medium-size cities. At first, many cities attempted to deny the presence of gangs, but most have now awakened to the new reality, as evidenced by their efforts at suppression.

There is little doubt that gang members are more frequently involved in delinquent and criminal activities than nongang members. Gang members sell drugs and commit violent acts, although, for many gangs, this is a small part of their daily activity. Violence is a response to a threat that is based on an underclass of poverty, unemployment, and omnipresent violence in daily life. There are drug gangs, but selling drugs is predominantly a money-making activity of individual members.

One of the most successful forms of intervention has been the Boston Gun Project, or Operation Ceasefire. In addition to tracking the use of weapons, the Working Group of the project engages in what is described as "pulling levers." If a homicide occurs, there is a wide range of responses from social service, community, and criminal justice groups. Part of what makes it effective is the delivery of an extensive and coordinated response to the offending gang rather than to an area; it is "retail deterrence." The Boston model has been implemented in other jurisdictions and shows success where evaluations have occurred. However, it is not clear whether, as female gangs and younger male gangs appear, the techniques used in Operation Ceasefire will be as effective.

DISCUSSION QUESTIONS

1. Discuss the relationship between Merton's strain theory and that of Cohen and Cloward and Ohlin.
2. Describe the self-nomination technique in studying gang membership and discuss its strengths and limitations.
3. Why are gangs growing in rural areas?

SUGGESTED READINGS

Egley, A., Jr., Maxson, C. L., Miller, J., & Klein, M. W. (Eds.). (2006). *The modern gang reader* (3rd ed.). New York: Oxford University Press.

Klein, M. W., & Maxson, C. L. (2006). *Street gang patterns and politics*. New York: Oxford University Press

National Gang Center. (2009). National Youth Gang Survey Analysis. Retrieved January 2009, from http://www.nationalgangcenter. gov/Survey-Analysis/.

REFERENCES

Braga, A. A., & Kennedy, D. M. (2002). Reducing gun violence in Boston. In W. L. Reed & S. H. Decker (Eds.), *Responding to gangs: Evaluation and research* (National Institute of Justice NCJ 190351, pp. 265–288). Washington, DC: U.S. Government Printing Office.

Braga, A. A., Kennedy, D. M., & Tita, G. E. (2002). New approaches to the strategic prevention of gang and group-involved violence. In C. R. Huff (Ed.), *Gangs in America III* (pp. 271–285). Thousand Oaks, CA: Sage Publications.

Braga, A. A., Kennedy, D. M., Waring, E. J., & Piehl, A. M. (2001). Problem-oriented policing, deterrence, and youth violence: An evaluation of Boston's Operation Ceasefire. *Journal of Research in Crime and Delinquency, 38*, 195–225.

Bjerregaard, B., & Smith, C. (1993). Gender differences in gang participation, delinquency and substance use. *Journal of Quantitative Criminology, 9*, 329–355.

Chermak, S., & McGarrell, E. (2004). Problem-solving approaches to homicide: An evaluation of the Indianapolis violence redeuction partnership. *Criminal Justice Policy Review, 15*, 161–192.

Clinard, M. B. (1964). The theoretical implications of anomie and deviant behavior. In M. B. Clinard (Ed.), *Anomie and deviant behavior* (pp. 1–56). New York: Free Press.

Cloward, R. A., & Ohlin, L. E. (1960). *Delinquency and opportunity: A theory of delinquency gangs*. New York: Free Press.

Cohen, A. K. (1955). *Delinquent boys: The culture of the gang*. Glencoe, IL: Free Press.

Curry, G. D., & Spergel, I. A. (1988). Gang homicide, delinquency, and community. *Criminology, 26*, 381–405.

Decker, S. H. (2002). A decade of gang research: Findings of the National Institute of Justice gang portfolio. In W. L. Reed & S. H. Decker (Eds.), *Responding to gangs: Evaluation and research* (Vol. National Institute of Justice, NCJ 190351, pp. 2–24). Washington: U.S. Government Printing Office.

Decker, S. H., & Van Winkle, B. (1996). *Life in the gang: Family, friends, and violence*. Cambridge: Cambridge University Press.

Esbensen, F. -A., & Huizinga, D. (1993). Gangs, drugs, and delinquency in a survey of urban youth. *Criminology, 31*, 565–587.

Esbensen, F., & Winfree, L. T. Jr. (2006). Race and gender differences between gang and nongang youths: Results from a multi-site study. In A. Egley, Jr., C. I. Maxson, J. Miller, & M. W. Klein (Eds.), *The modern gang reader* (pp. 162–175). New York: Oxford University Press.

Esbensen, F., Winfree, L. T. Jr., Ni, H., & Terrance, J. T. (2001). Youth gangs and definitional issues: When is a gang a gang, and why does it matter? *Crime and Delinquency, 47*, 105–130.

Hagedorn, J. (1990). Back in the field again: Gang research in the 1990s. In C. R. Huff (Ed.), *Gangs in America: Diffusion, diversity and public policy* (pp. 240–259). Newbury Park, CA: Sage.

Harrell, E. (2005). *Violence by gang members, 1993–2003* (Crime Data Brief). Washington, DC: Bureau of Justice Statistics.

Hirschi, T. (1969). *Cause of delinquency*. Berkeley: University of California Press.

Klein, M. W. (1995). *The American street gang: Its nature, prevalence and control*. New York: Oxford University Press.

Klein, M. W., & Maxson, C. L. (2006). *Street gang patterns and policies*. New York: Oxford University Press.

Maxson, C. L., & Klein, M. W. (1990). Street gang violence: Twice as great, half as great? In C. R. Huff (Ed.), *Gangs in America* (pp. 71–100). Newbury Park, CA: Sage.

Maxson, C. L., & Klein, M. W. (1996). Defining gang homicide: An updated look at member and motive approaches. In C. L. Huff (Ed.), *Gangs in America* (2nd ed., pp. 3–20). Thousand Oaks, CA: Sage.

Maxson, C., & Whitlock, M. L. (2002). Joining the gang: Gender differences in risk factors for gang membership. In C. R. Huff (Ed.), *Gangs in America* (3rd ed., pp. 19–35). Newbury Park, CA: Sage.

McDevitt, J., Braga, A. A., Nurge, D., & Buerger, M. (2003). Boston's youth violence prevention program: A comprehensive community-wide approach. In S. H. Decker (Ed.), *Policing gangs and youth violence* (pp. 53–76). Belmont, CA: Thomson Wadsworth.

Merton, R. K. (1957). *Social theory and social structure*. New York: Free Press.

Miller, W. B. (1958). Lower class culture as a generating milieu of gang delinquency. *Journal of Social Issues, 14*, 5–19.

Miller, W. B. (1982). *Crime by youth gangs and groups in the United States*. Washington, DC: National Institute of Juvenile Justice and Delinquency Prevention.

Miller, W. B. (2001). *The growth of youth gang problems in the United States: 1970–1998*. Washington, DC: Office of Juvenile Justice and Delinquency Prevention.

Moore, J., & Hagedorn, J. (2001). *Female gangs: A focus on research*. Washington, DC: Office of Juvenile Justice and Delinquency Prevention.

National Advisory Commission on Criminal Justice Standards and Goals. (1973). *Report on community crime prevention*. Washington, DC: U.S. Government Printing Office.

National Commission on the Causes and Prevention of Violence. (1969). *Crimes of Violence*. Washington, DC: U.S. Government Printing Office.

National Gang Center. (2011). *National Youth Gang Survey Analysis*. Retrieved June 3, 2014, from http://www.nationalgangcenter.gov/Survey-Analysis.

Ontario Ministry of Children and Youth Services. Review of the roots of youth violence. Retrieved June 3, 2014, from http://www.children.gov.on.ca/htdocs/English/topics/ youthandthelaw/roots volume5/chapter13_life_theories.aspx.

President's Commission on Law Enforcement and the Administration of Justice. (1967). *The challenge of crime in a free society*. Washington, DC: U.S. Government Printing Office.

Sanders, W. B. (1994). *Gangbangs and drive-bys: Grounded culture and juvenile gang violence*. New York: Aldine de Gruyter.

Sheley, J. F., & Wright, J. D. (1995). *In the line of fire: Youth, guns, and violence in urban America*. New York: Aldine de Gruyter.

Spergel, I. A., & Curry, G. D. (1995). The national youth gang survey: A research and development process. In M. W. Klein, C. L. Maxson, & J. Miller (Eds.), *The modern gang reader* (pp. 254–265). Los Angeles: Roxbury Publishing Co.

Thornberry, T. P. (1987). Toward an interactional theory of delinquency. *Criminology, 25*, 863–891.

Thornberry, T. P. (1998). Membership in youth gangs and involvement in serious and violent offending. In R. Loeber & D. P. Farrington (Eds.), *Serious and violent juvenile offenders: Risk factors and successful intervention* (pp. 147–166). Thousand Oaks, CA: Sage.

Vigil, J. D. (1990). Cholos and gangs: Culture change and street youth in Los Angeles. In C. R. Huff (Ed.), *Gangs in America* (pp. 116–128). Newbury Park, CA: Sage.

Vigil, J. D., & Yun, S. C. (1990). Vietnamese youth gangs in southern California. In C. R. Huff (Ed.), *Gangs in America* (pp. 146–162). Newbury Park, CA: Sage.

Vigil, J. D., & Yun, S.C. (2002). A cross-cultural framework for understanding gangs. In C. R. Huff (Ed.), *Gangs in America* (3rd ed., pp. 161–174). Thousand Oaks, CA: Sage.

Wolfgang, M. E., & Ferracuti, F. (1967). *The subculture of violence: Towards an integrated theory in criminology*. London: Tavistock Publications.

CHAPTER 12

THE ROLE OF FIREARMS IN VIOLENCE

Violent mass shootings such as the 1999 Columbine High School incident, the 2007 Virginia Tech shootings, the 2012 Aurora, Colorado, theater shootings, and the 2012 Sandy Hook Elementary School shootings in Newtown, Connecticut, have once again renewed interest and debate about gun control legislation and other strategies to reduce firearm violence. A major challenge in the current climate is to learn what we can from available scientific evidence about works and what doesn't to reduce firearm violence.

---

1. On Friday, Dec. 14, 2012, a lone police cruiser stood outside Columbine High School in Littleton, Colorado, following news of a deadly attack at Sandy Hook Elementary School in Newtown, Connecticut, where 26 people, including 20 children, were murdered (Peipert, 2012). In Colorado, a state shocked by the 1999 Columbine school massacre and the 2012 Aurora movie theater shootings, the Newtown shootings soon renewed debate over why mass shootings keep occurring and whether gun control can stop them. "Until we get our acts together and stop making these . . . weapons available, this is going to keep happening," said an angry Tom Teves, whose son Alex was killed in the Aurora shooting (Peipert, 2012). Colorado Governor John Hickenlooper said that it was time to start talking about gun control measures: "We can't postpone the discussion on a national level every time there's a shooting. They're too often." A visibly shaken President Obama called for "meaningful action" to prevent similar shootings. New York Mayor Michael Bloomberg stated: "Calling for 'meaningful action' is not enough. We need immediate action. We have heard all the rhetoric before." Mark Kelly, the astronaut husband of former U.S. Rep. Gabrielle Giffords, who was shot in the head during a 2011 attack that killed six people in Tucson, Arizona, said the Newtown shootings should "sound a call for our leaders to stand up and do what is right . . . This time our response must consist of more than regret, sorrow, and condolence." Kelly called for "a meaningful discussion about our gun laws and how they can be reformed and better enforced to prevent gun violence and death in America" (Peipert, 2012).
2. On April 20, 1999, two teenage gunmen stormed Columbine High School in suburban Littleton, Colorado, killing 12 fellow students and a teacher before committing suicide. Colorado Governor Bill Owens was sitting in his office, ready to sign legislation to expand the right to carry concealed firearms, when gunshots rang out at Columbine High (Paulson, 2000). Instead, the Republican governor refused to sign the measure and asked lawmakers to take all gun legislation off the table pending further review. Owens admitted that he was previously unaware of straw purchases or the ease of acquiring a weapon at gun shows. A straw purchase refers to the practice of a "clean" buyer (e.g., no criminal record) buying a gun for someone who legally cannot do so. Owens was

(continued)

(continued)

also surprised to discover that many guns were sold by unlicensed gun dealers at gun shows, where no background checks are conducted. In fact, the two Columbine assassins had purchased one of their weapons at a gun show. Nine months after the Columbine murders, Gov. Owens voiced support for gun control measures (e.g., banning straw purchases, requiring safe storage of firearms, raising the age for buying a handgun from 18 to 21, adding juvenile records to background checks, and requiring criminal background checks at gun shows).

PATTERNS AND TRENDS

As a review by the National Research Council (NRC, 2005) attests, the available data on gun-related violence are somewhat thin: "No authoritative source of information exists to provide representative, accurate, complete, timely, and detailed data on the incidence and characteristics of firearm-related violence in the United States." Instead, a patchwork of different data sources exists. Useful data sources (see Chapter 2) include the National Crime Victimization Survey, Uniform Crime Reports, and gun trace data from the Bureau of Alcohol, Tobacco, Firearms and Explosives (ATF). A variety of one-time surveys and various experiments add to this scattered knowledge base. In this section, we discuss major patterns and trends, noting sources and limitations where appropriate.

CRIMES INVOLVING FIREARMS

In any given year, firearms are involved in more than half of all known suicides and two thirds or more of homicides (NRC, 2005). In 2011, about 70% of all homicides and 8% of all nonfatal violent victimizations (rape, sexual assault, robbery, and aggravated assault) were committed with a firearm (Planty & Truman, 2013). About 26% of robberies and 31% of aggravated assaults in 2011 involved a firearm. A handgun was used in about 7 out of 10 firearm homicides and about 9 out of 10 nonfatal firearm violent crimes in 2011.

These numbers are certainly cause for concern, although recent declines in felony gun use are encouraging. The rate of homicides (Fig. 12.1) and nonfatal crimes committed with firearms (Fig. 12.2) both declined from 1993 to 2011 (Planty & Truman, 2013). Firearm-related homicides declined 39% (from 18,253 homicides in 1993 to 11,101 in 2011), and nonfatal firearm crimes declined 69% (from 1.5 million in 1993 to 467,300 in 2011).

In 2011, the rate of nonfatal firearm victimization for males (1.9 per 1,000) was not significantly different than the rate for females (1.6 per 1,000). Non-Hispanic blacks (2.8 per 1,000) and Hispanics (2.2 per 1,000) had higher rates of nonfatal firearm victimization than non-Hispanic whites (1.4 per 1,000). Persons aged 18 to 24 had the highest rates of nonfatal firearm violence (5.2 per 1,000) compared to 1.4 per 1,000 for ages 12 to 17, 2.2 per 1,000 for ages 25 to 24, 1.4 per 1,000 for ages 35 to 49, and 0.7 per 1,000 for ages 50 and over.

VICTIMS

Death is a rare outcome of violent crime. About 5.7 nonfatal gunshot injuries occur for every homicide, but the risk of death is highly elevated for young people (ages 15 to 34), particularly black males (Cook, 1991; NRC, 2005). Homicide is the leading cause of death

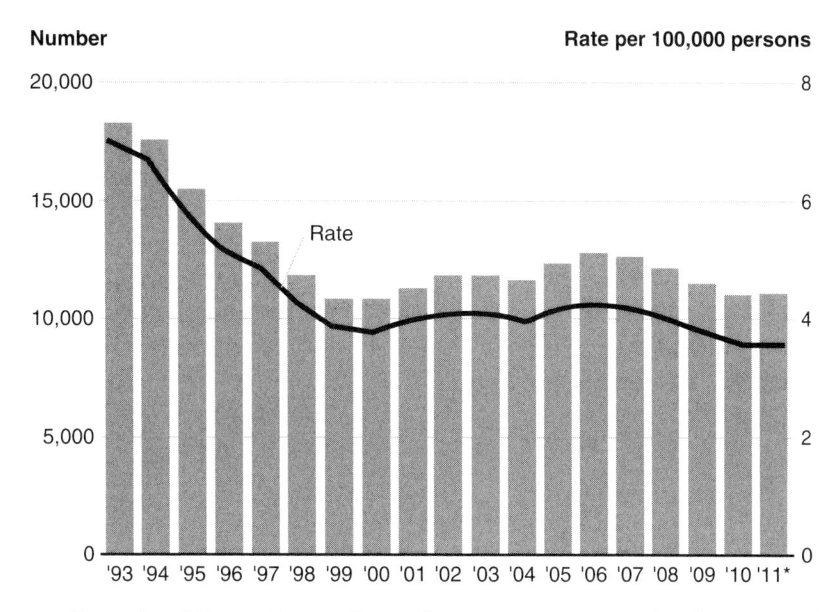

FIGURE 12.1 Firearm homicides, 1993–2011. *Source:* Planty, M., & Truman, J. L. (2013). *Firearm Violence, 1993–2011* (NCJ-241730). Washington, DC: U.S. Department of Justice, Office of Justice Programs, Bureau of Justice Statistics.

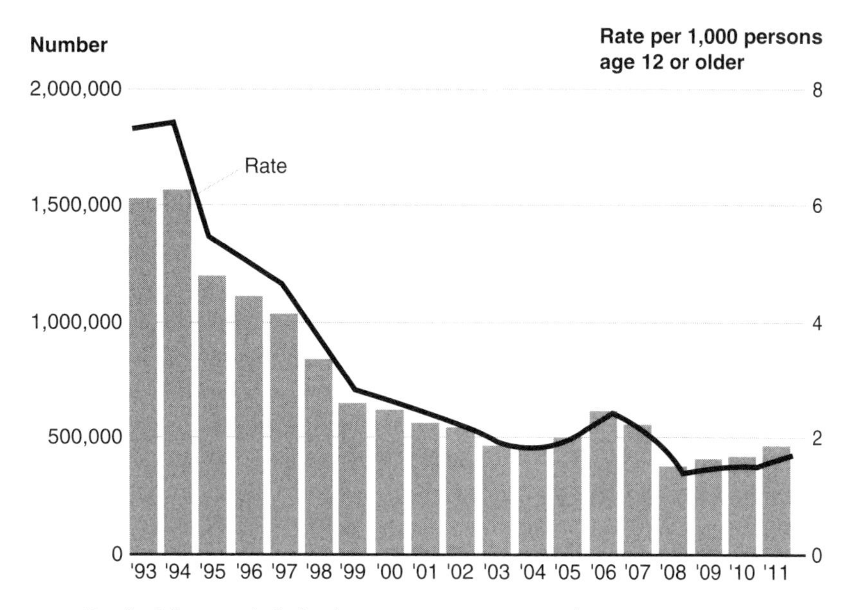

FIGURE 12.2 Nonfatal firearm victimizations, 1993–2011. *Source:* Planty, M., & Truman, J. L. (2013). *Firearm Violence, 1993–2011* (NCJ-241730). Washington, DC: U.S. Department of Justice, Office of Justice Programs, Bureau of Justice Statistics.

for blacks ages 15 to 24 and 25 to 34, and it is the sixth leading cause of death for blacks at all ages (NRC, 2005). In 2010, the rate of firearm homicide for blacks was 14.6 per 100,000, compared to 1.9 for whites, 2.7 for American Indians and Alaska Natives, and 1.0 for Asians and Pacific Islanders (Planty & Truman, 2013).

Injuries are more common. In the period from 2007 to 2011, about 23% of all nonfatal firearm victims were physically injured during the incident (Planty & Truman, 2013). About 7% suffered serious injuries (e.g., a gunshot wound, broken bone, or internal injuries), while 16% suffered minor injuries (e.g., bruises or cuts). Of the nonfatal firearm victims who were injured, 72% received some type of care, with about 82% receiving care in a hospital or medical office.

Some researchers have argued that the use of a gun during a crime, such as robbery, enables the perpetrator to achieve his or her goals without firing the weapon, and thus the risk of physical harm due to an attack may actually be reduced (Kleck, 1991). Escalation from threat to attack was less likely when the offender was armed with a gun (probability = 0.14) than when he or she was unarmed (0.30), was armed with a knife (0.25), or was armed with another weapon (0.45) (Reiss & Roth, 1993). It is equally likely, however, that possession of a gun may encourage perpetrators to challenge potential victims they might otherwise have avoided (Cook, 1981). Fully 55% of commercial robberies involve guns; only 13% of personal robberies involve guns. Guns may also be fired impulsively (e.g., conflicts between intimates and acquaintances). Between 1976 and 1987, twice as many women were shot and killed by their partners as by strangers (Reiss & Roth, 1993).

CHARACTERISTICS OF OFFENDERS

Ninety percent of firearm-related homicides are committed by males (NRC, 2005). The highest concentrations of involvement in handgun homicides have been among young black males (Blumstein, 2000).

Reliable long-term statistics on juvenile gun use are scarce, but official statistics suggest escalation during a fairly brief time period. Juvenile arrests for weapons law violations doubled from 1987 to 1993 (Snyder, 1998). Gun homicides by juveniles in the United States tripled from 1983 to 1997, while homicides involving other weapons declined. From 1983 through 1995, the proportion of homicides in which a juvenile used a gun increased from 55% to 80% (Greenbaum, 1997). In fact, the *overall increase in juvenile homicide witnessed in the mid-1980s was entirely related to firearms* (Snyder et al., 1996). Likewise, decreases in juvenile homicides since 1993 are entirely attributable to decreases in murders committed with firearms (Snyder, 1998).

Juveniles report having easy access to guns. In a survey of 758 male students in inner-city high schools and 835 male serious offenders incarcerated in six different detention facilities, Sheley and Wright (1993) found that 83% of inmates and 22% of students possessed guns. These firearms tended to be high-quality, powerful revolvers. Most detainees and students stated it was easy to acquire a gun; only 35% said it would be difficult. Fifty-three percent of students said they would "borrow" a gun if they needed one (from family members or friends); 37% of students and 54% of detainees said they would get one off the street. Although involvement in drug sales was more common among those reporting that they carried a gun, the main reason given for carrying a gun was self-protection.

FIREARM ACQUISITION, OWNERSHIP, AND USE

How many firearms are there in the United States? The two major methods of measuring gun ownership in the United States are (1) production-based data and (2) survey-based data (NRC, 2005). Production-based estimates suggest that there were an estimated 258 million firearms in the United States as of 1999. Surveys show wide disparities in the percentage of households with a firearm, although the mean estimate is around 43%. However we look at it, there are a lot of guns in the United States.

An important question concerns a person's motivation for using a gun: What situations increase the likelihood of one person using a firearm against another? According to the NRC (Reiss & Roth, 1993, p. 262), "establishing the motive for an instance of gun use is a formidable, time-consuming, judgmental task, often with an uncertain outcome." Available evidence, however, provides some interesting results. In a survey of 1,874 incarcerated felons interviewed during 1982 by Wright and Rossi (1985), 184 reported firing a gun while committing an offense. Of these, the most commonly reported motivations for using a gun included "to protect myself" (48%), "to scare the victim" (45%), and to "kill the victim" (36%) (categories are not mutually exclusive). Fully 76% of the felons who used a gun during an offense claimed that they had no prior intent to fire the gun, suggesting that the presence of a gun alone greatly increases the chances of using it. The 1991 Survey of State Prison Inmates (Beck et al., 1993), based on interviews with a representative national sample of 14,000 inmates, found similar results. The most frequently reported reasons for using a gun were to scare the victim (54%), for protection (30%), to kill the victim (14%), and to get away (12%). The conclusion to be drawn is that many criminals who use guns do so for instrumental reasons (i.e., to expedite commission of the offense or the escape, or both).

Inmates were also questioned about the sources (i.e., from whom) and means (i.e., what type of transaction) of gun acquisitions (Wright & Rossi, 1985). The most common source was family or friends (44%), followed by illegal gun markets (26%), retail outlets (21%), and other (9%). The most common means or type of transaction was a cash purchase (43%), followed by theft (32%), a loan (9%), a gift (8%), or trade (7%). The 2004 Survey of Inmates in State and Federal Correctional Facilities found similar results. Among state prison inmates who possessed a gun at the time of the offense, fewer than 2% bought their firearm at a flea market or gun show (Planty & Truman, 2013). About 10% of state prison inmates said they purchased it from a retail store or pawnshop, 37% obtained it from family or friends, 40% obtained it from an illegal source, and 11% obtained it from another (unspecified) source.

The most criminally active offenders are especially likely to obtain guns from nonretail sources (Wright & Rossi, 1985), suggesting the limitations (but not necessarily the futility) of prevention strategies aimed at regulating retail sales (see the following). Even legitimately purchased guns can end up being used in violent crimes. In one study, Cook (1981) found that of each new cohort of handguns sold, about one third are involved in a crime at least once in their lifetimes.

Motivations by law-abiding citizens to use a gun, not surprisingly, are different. Self-defense is often reported as a primary motive for gun ownership, although the actual frequency of self-defense incidents is a point of considerable disagreement among researchers (NRC, 2005). For example, Kleck (1991) estimates incidents of self-defense gun use at between 700,000 and 1 million times per year, about 10 times higher than estimates obtained by Cook (1991). To interpret such findings, however, numerous questions must be asked about the reliability of different data sources (e.g., self-report surveys vs. arrest statistics), problems associated with definitions and measurement of self-defense, and how researchers adjust data to address possible alternative explanations of results. Often simple bivariate correlations are used without controlling for potential confounding factors. Overall, available evidence that self-defense deters gun-related crimes or reduces harm to victims is ambiguous (NRC, 2005).

EXPLANATIONS

Based on the data reviewed so far, it is tempting to conclude that gun availability is responsible for much of the violent crime in the United States. Such a conclusion would be premature, however. International comparisons show that homicide rates in the United States are two to four times higher than in countries at similar rates of development and democracy. However, the United States is a world leader in nongun homicides, not just gun homicides (NRC, 2005). For example, there are three times as many nongun homicides in the United States as in England. While guns clearly play an important role, they are not the only factor explaining the high rates of homicide in the United States.

SYMBOLIC INTERACTION THEORY

A landmark study by Luckenbill (1977) illustrated how disputes become violent through a series of interpersonal exchanges. The concept of a situated transaction refers to a series of interactions between people in a specific setting, time, and social context. The presence of a weapon during such a dispute greatly increases the likelihood of its use. Luckenbill examined 71 homicide cases drawn from one county over a 10-year period. Data included police, probation, psychiatric, and witness reports; offender interviews; victim statements; and grand jury and court testimony. Luckenbill illustrated that criminal homicide frequently resulted from some conflict between offender and victim that escalated over time, resulting in attempts by one or both parties to "save face" at the other's expense. In 36% of the cases examined by Luckenbill, offenders had carried weapons into the setting. In 64% of the cases, the offender either left to get a weapon or used an existing prop as a weapon (e.g., a knife, baseball bat, beer bottle, or glass).

Luckenbill's research showed that murder is often the result of an intense two-way interchange among offenders, victims, and bystanders in particular settings. The availability and presence of guns in situated transactions greatly increased the likelihood of their use. The 1991 Survey of Prison Inmates (Beck et al., 1993) confirmed that 90% of offenders who carried a weapon into a particular setting to commit a crime actually used it. More than half of the inmates who committed murder (64%), robbery (51%), and assault (57%) regularly carried a weapon.

ROUTINE ACTIVITIES AND ILLEGAL MARKETS

Is gun crime more concentrated in some places than others? Evidence suggests that focusing on the specific places and activities where gun crime is the most common may provide promising explanations and strategies for the prevention of gun violence.

Routine activities refer to recurrent and prevalent activities that provide for basic population and individual needs, including work, food, shelter, recreation, socializing, learning, and raising a family (Cohen & Felson, 1979). According to the theory, offenders commit offenses near places where they spend most of their time, and major pathways in between. Likewise, individuals are victimized near places where they spend most of their time, and major pathways in between. Routine activity patterns influence crime rates by affecting the convergence in space and time of the three elements required for direct personal victimization to occur: (1) motivated offenders, (2) suitable targets, and (3) the absence of capable guardians.

Cohen and Felson used national data to describe population routine activities and crime rates, but others have argued that a smaller, more appropriate unit of analysis is *places*: "fixed physical environments that can be seen completely and simultaneously, at least on surface, by one's naked eyes" (Sherman et al., 1989, p. 31). Places, like people, have their own routine activities that partially explain the different frequencies and types of crime. Although the population in certain places may be transient (people come and go), the *activities* that occur there are often patterned in regular (routine) ways. Examples of routine activities in specific places include typical types of social and economic interactions, the relative wealth or poverty of participants, approved and disapproved activities, and typical moral values. Places, like people, then, have their own distinct "characters."

Sherman and colleagues (1989) found that specific crimes in Minneapolis during 1985 and 1986 were heavily concentrated in specific places. More than half of all calls to police were to only 3.3% of all places, and the top 5% of all locations generated an average of 24 calls each (i.e., nearly one every two weeks). When researchers focused on specific crimes, hot spots became even more concentrated: 4,166 robberies were reported in only 2.2% of places; 3,908 auto thefts were reported in only 2.7% of places; and 1,729 sex crimes were reported in only 1.2% of places. The hottest spots for robberies, rapes, and auto thefts included an intersection located near bars, a liquor store, a park, a bus depot, an intersection with homeless shelters and bars, a downtown mall, and another intersection near an adult bookstore and bars.

Do places *cause* crimes, however, or merely *host* them? According to Sherman and colleagues (1989), some places actually facilitate crime, especially predatory crime. In particular, robberies (e.g., near 24-hour cash businesses), sex crimes (e.g., in public parks), and stranger violence (e.g., low opportunities for surveillance) were found to be very place-specific. Some illegal market offenses, such as prostitution and drug sales, may create their own routine activities (Sherman et al., 1989). Such activities in and around these specific hot spots tend to overwhelm legitimate activities in the area and increase the likelihood of convergence of motivated offenders, competitors for illegal market sales, and perhaps potential victims (e.g., drug buyers) who, fearing danger, routinely carry firearms in these areas (Decker et al., 1997).

Using data obtained from more than 7,000 arrestees in 11 major urban areas involved in the Drug Use Forecasting Program, Decker and colleagues (1997) found strong evidence relating involvement in illegal markets to gun carrying, gun use, and victimization. They found that a higher percentage of arrestees than in the general population have ever owned a firearm; they acquire firearms easily, and a substantial number have used them to commit crimes. The groups reporting the easiest access to firearms were those most likely to be involved in illegal markets: drug sellers and gang members.

Research findings suggest the existence of a small but violent subculture in which the possession and use of guns is common and tolerated. Gang membership, drug selling, gun carrying, and gun use were all highly related. Among the entire sample of arrestees, gang members (50%) and drug sellers (42%) were much more likely than other arrestees (23%) to use a gun to commit a crime. Both were more likely to be victimized by other gun users as well: 50% of juvenile males and more than 75% of gang members reported being shot at. Similar to other studies (Beck et al., 1993; Sheley & Wright, 1993), reasons most commonly cited by arrestees (two thirds) for carrying a gun were protection or self-defense.

Repeat gun criminals are particularly attracted to gun-carrying hot spots because of illegal market activities, and these high-risk offenders are much more likely to use guns in these high-risk places (Sherman & Rogan, 1995). Gun crimes, unsurprisingly, are highly concentrated in specific areas (Sherman et al., 1995). The good news, if any, is that place-specific opportunities for intervention may also be afforded by such places (see "Interventions" below).

CULTURAL THEORIES AND FIREARM AVAILABILITY

To what degree is the easy availability of firearms partially or largely responsible for high rates of violence in the United States? Does the United States experience higher rates of violent crime (especially homicide) than other countries because of its permissive laws regarding gun ownership and sales? What evidence can we bring to bear on such important questions?

A comparison of Seattle and Vancouver, British Columbia (two cities that are similar in demography, geography, and socioeconomic status, but located in different countries), showed that gun ownership had no effect on the prevalence of robbery rates, but Seattle had an overall homicide rate 60% higher and a firearm homicide rate that was 400% higher (Sloane et al., 1988). More permissive gun laws in Seattle were implicated by the researchers as the major explanation for these dramatic differences.

No precise gun count exists, but the ATF estimated there were 258 million firearms in the United States as of 1999 (NRC, 2005). The proportion of households owning any gun has remained stable at about 50% for three decades. The biggest increase in gun ownership occurred from 1959 to 1978, when the portion of citizens owning handguns increased from 13% to 25%. Rates of gun ownership are generally highest in rural areas and small towns, higher for whites than blacks, highest in the South, and higher for high-income households (Reiss & Roth, 1993). Simple subcultural interpretations suggesting that some groups are more predisposed toward owning and using guns than others are thus not easy to support; there is considerable diversity in gun owners.

Reviews of studies using cross-national, interjurisdictional, and longitudinal analyses to examine the relationship between gun availability and violence found no relationship between gun availability and the number of nonfatal gun crimes (Cook, 1991; NRC, 2005). For crimes that ended in death, greater gun availability was associated with somewhat higher rates of felony murder, but this factor did not account for a large proportion of total violence.

Many researchers have used comparisons between the United States and other nations to assess the relationship between firearm-related homicides and firearms availability. While the majority of studies conclude that homicides and gun availability are closely associated, various methodological problems weaken conclusions that can be drawn. For example, measurement of key variables is of questionable validity; the use of nation-states as the unit of analysis may mask substantial regional variation within nations; and the statistical models tested are often poorly specified (NRC, 2005).

Available evidence, although not entirely conclusive, suggests that gun availability alone cannot explain the high rates of violent crime in the United States. The *direction of causality* in such studies is not always clear (NRC, 2005; Reiss & Roth, 1993). For example, in household surveys, some respondents who report owning guns may be arming themselves in response to higher crime rates in their communities, producing a spurious correlation between gun ownership and violence rates. Differences may also reflect regional differences in culture and attitudes, which are difficult to measure and control for in cross-jurisdictional studies. Research is further complicated by the lack of a national data system to track unique identifiers of firearms, and by their frequent movement, through burglary, unregulated sales, and simple carrying from one situation to another (NRC, 2005).

MEDIA VIOLENCE

Sandy Hook shooter Adam Lanza frequently played violent video games. Aurora theater shooter James Holmes dressed up as Batman's nemesis "The Joker." Columbine shooters Eric Harris and Dylan Klebold played violent video games, worshipped the movie "Natural Born Killers," and dressed as "the trench coat mafia" in reference to a graphic classroom shooting portrayed in the movie "The Basketball Diaries." But is there a connection between viewing media violence and later acting it out, with or without guns? After hundreds of studies since the early 1960s, the consensus by researchers and health professionals is: Yes, there is.

Hundreds of studies have demonstrated the impact of media violence on children's aggressive behavior (e.g., Anderson et al., 2003, 2010; Bushman & Huesmann, 2006; Comstock & Paik, 1994; Subra et al., 2010). In 2000, six major medical associations (American

Academy of Pediatrics, American Academy of Child and Adolescent Psychiatry, American Psychological Association, American Medical Association, American Academy of Family Physicians, and American Psychiatric Association) issued a joint statement to Congress concluding that viewing media violence can increase aggressive attitudes, values, and behaviors, especially in children (Cook et al., 2000).

Social cognitive theory, a variant of social learning theory, suggests that children can learn ideas, values, emotions, and behaviors by observing others in their social environment (Bandura, 1986). Children can imitate people in their immediate environment or they can imitate characters they see in movies or on TV (Bandura, 1986; Barr et al., 2007). Children are more likely to imitate observed behaviors that are rewarded than those that are punished (Bandura, 1965; Bandura et al., 1963).

Information processing theory (Huesmann, 1986) helps explain the long-term effects of media exposure to violence. Huesmann states that children develop and learn routine "scripts" for all sorts of things: for bedtime routines, for going to the doctor, for getting ready for school. Scripts, then, are mental routines for familiar events that are stored in a person's memory. Such scripts can be learned either through direct experience or by observing others (as in movies) (Huesmann, 1988). As we observe others over time, we accumulate a set of scenarios or scripts in our head that allow us to recount the actions taken by others to solve problems (Schank & Abelson, 1977). A child who is exposed to a great deal of violence, either in real life or through the media, is more likely to acquire scripts that promote aggression as a way of solving problems. Once learned, these scripts can easily be retrieved from memory, especially when an immediate situation resembles features of the script. The more often an aggressive script is retrieved, the more it is reinforced and generalizes to a wider set of circumstances. Thus, children who are repeatedly exposed to media violence develop a stable set of aggressive scripts that are easily activated and serve as a guide in responding to social situations.

But viewing media violence is only one risk factor for aggression: It doesn't mean that *everyone* who witnesses *any* media violence becomes a "natural born killer." One variable that modifies the influence of viewing violent media is the age or developmental level of the child. Television violence has the strongest impact on preschool children, partly because they are still learning social norms about how to behave. Children also pay closer attention when they perceive that what they are watching is realistic, and are more likely to remember such scenes (Huesmann, 1986; Wright et al., 1994). Another variable is the extent to which children identify with characters featured in a show. Children are more likely to imitate those whom they perceive as attractive role models. Strongly identifying with violent characters makes children more likely to imitate aggression (Bandura, 1986; Huesmann, 1986).

Other important risk factors include the presence of weapons and the amount of violence viewed (Bushman et al., 2013). Social learning researchers have demonstrated in numerous studies that simply seeing a weapon can increase aggression, a phenomenon known as the *weapons effect* (Berkowitz & LePage, 1967). More than 50 studies have replicated the weapons effect, both inside and outside the laboratory, and in both angered and nonangered individuals (Carlson et al., 1990), suggesting that there is a strong link between weapons and aggression in memory. The abundant presence of guns in the media, therefore, may strengthen the weapons effect by providing youth with acceptable scripts for using guns (Bushman et al., 2013).

In sum, unequivocal evidence shows that media violence, especially when guns are present, increases the likelihood of aggressive and violent behavior in both immediate and long-term contexts (Anderson et al., 2003). The research base is large and consistent in overall findings. The evidence is clearest within the most extensively researched domains, television and film violence, although a growing body of video game research yields essentially the same conclusions. Additional laboratory and field studies are still needed, however, to better understand underlying psychological processes and help develop more effective interventions (Anderson et al., 2003).

INTERVENTIONS

As we have seen so far, explaining violent injuries or deaths is a difficult business. Multiple influences include personal temperament, different motivations, law enforcement policies, social setting (e.g., nature of the interaction), situational variables, and accidental circumstances (NRC, 2005). Even if firearms are one significant cause among many, any effective prevention strategy would have to address multiple factors. Fortunately, some research points to promising solutions.

DISRUPTING ILLEGAL GUN MARKETS

As already noted, some evidence indicates that gun availability is related to gun homicide rates. However, some researchers (e.g., Sherman et al., 1995) argue that it is not simply the total number of guns in circulation that increases gun violence, but the carrying of guns in high-risk places at high-risk times. If this is true, then greater enforcement of existing laws against carrying concealed weapons might reduce gun crime.

The Kansas City Gun Experiment

If police could get more guns off the street, would there be fewer gun crimes? This was the question posed by the Kansas City Gun Experiment, an evaluation of a police patrol project to reduce gun violence. The experiment developed out of a federal grant awarded to the Kansas City (Missouri) Police Department (KCPD) under the Bureau of Justice Assistance "Weed and Seed" program in 1991. The intervention was based on the theory that additional, proactive police patrols to detect gun violations would increase gun seizures, which in turn would reduce gun crime either by deterring potential offenders or by incapacitating greater numbers of gun-using criminals.

The target beat was an 80- by 10-block area with a 1991 homicide rate of 177 per 100,000 persons, about 20 times the national average. The population was almost entirely nonwhite; the area had very low property values and consisted predominantly of single-family detached homes. A comparison beat with very similar population demographics and similar crime rates (e.g., total firearm-related crimes, shots fired per incident, drive-by shootings, and homicides) was chosen. For 29 weeks, from July 7, 1992, to January 27,

1993, the KCPD focused extra patrol attention on gun crime "hot spots" in the target area. The actual techniques the officers used to find guns included stop-and-search frisks based on reasonable suspicion, searches incident to an arrest on other charges (i.e., the basis for a legitimate arrest had already been established), and safety frisks associated with car stops for traffic violations. No special efforts were made to limit police activities in the comparison beat, but neither were special funds available for extra patrol time in that area. The hot spot locations were identified by a computer analysis of all known gun crimes.

The extra patrol was provided in rotation by officers from Central Patrol in a pair of two-officer cars; overtime was funded under the federal Weed and Seed program. Four officers thus worked six hours of overtime each night, from 7 p.m. to 1 a.m., seven days a week, for a total of 176 nights, with two officers working an additional 24 nights, for a total of 200 nights, 4,512 officer hours, and 2,256 patrol car hours. They focused exclusively on gun detection through proactive patrol and did not respond to calls for service. Because the extra patrol hours were federally funded, separate bookkeeping was required to document the time. In addition, an evaluator accompanied the officers on 300 hours of hot spot patrol and coded every shift activity narrative for patrol time and enforcement in and out of the area. Property room data on guns seized, computerized crime reports, calls for service data, and arrest records were analyzed for both areas under the study.

The primary data analyses compared all 29 weeks of the Phase I patrol program (July 7, 1992, through January 25, 1993, when the Phase 1 funding for the special patrols expired) to the 29 weeks preceding Phase 1. Other analyses added all of 1991 and 1993. The 1993 data included six months with no overtime patrols and Phase 2 overtime patrols for six months in the second half of 1993. Analyses thus covered six six-month periods, two of which had the program and four of which did not.

The officers generated a lot of activity. Both in and out of the target beat, the directed patrols issued 1,090 traffic citations, conducted 948 car checks and 532 pedestrian checks, and made 170 state or federal arrests and 446 city arrests, for an average of one police intervention for every 40 minutes per patrol car.

The results of the evaluation indicated that directed police patrols in gun crime hot spots reduced gun crimes by increasing the seizures of illegally carried guns. *Gun seizures* by police in the target area increased significantly, from 46 before the intervention to 76 afterward (an increase of 65%), while *gun crimes* declined significantly, from 169 to 86 (a decrease of 49%). Traffic stops were the most productive method of finding guns, with an average of one gun found in every 28 traffic stops. The number of guns found during car checks tripled. During the same time period, neither gun crimes nor guns seized changed significantly in the comparison beat several miles away. If anything, the number of guns seized in the comparison beat dropped slightly, from 85 to 72, and the number of gun crimes increased very slightly, from 184 to 192. Further, drive-by shootings dropped from seven to one in the target area, doubled from 6 to 12 in the comparison area, and showed no displacement to adjoining beats. Homicides decreased significantly in the target area but not in the comparison area.

Data analyses ruled out several alternative hypotheses. First, only gun crimes were affected by the directed patrols, with no changes in the number of calls for service or in the total number of violent or nonviolent crimes reported. Second, there was no measurable displacement of gun crimes to patrol beats surrounding the target area, as gun crimes remained stable in the seven contiguous beats. Before-and-after surveys of citizens showed that respondents in the target area became less fearful of crime and more positive about their neighborhood than respondents in the comparison area. Replications in Indianapolis and Pittsburgh supported the major findings of this study (NRC, 2005).

Although the before-and-after study of the target beat and the comparison beat could not eliminate all possible competing explanations for the results, the inverse correlation between gun seizures and gun crime suggested that proactive policing of gun crimes in high-risk places is a promising strategy deserving of further research (NRC, 2005). Gun violence may be reduced through tactics that police already apply in illegal drug markets, including buy-bust operations, high-priority investigation and prosecution of unregulated gun dealers, use of minors as informants against illegal dealers, phony fencing operations for illegal guns, high-priority investigation and prosecution of felonies in which guns are stolen, and high mandatory minimum sentences for those who steal or illegally sell guns (Reiss & Roth, 1993).

Stop-and-Frisk

Since the Supreme Court decision in *Terry vs. Ohio* (392 US 1, 1968), police officers have been permitted to stop, question, and search (depending on circumstances) persons on the basis of "reasonable suspicion" that they have committed or are about to commit a crime. Stop, question, and frisk (SQF) is a crime prevention tactic whereby a police officer may stop a person based on "reasonable suspicion" of criminal activity and perhaps conduct a "frisk" or pat-down when based on reasonable suspicion that the person is armed and dangerous (Rudovsky, 2013). In recent years, the policy of SQF has been criticized as unfairly targeting innocent persons, racially biased, and ineffective in reducing crime (Rosenfeld & Fornango, 2014).

But does SQF work, and if so, at what cost? Comprehensive records on SQF activity in New York have been publicly available only since 2003, following a settlement reached in *Daniels et al. vs. City of New York et al.* (http://ccrjustice.org/ourcases/past-cases/daniels,-et-al.-v.-city-new-york). A similar settlement was reached in a Philadelphia lawsuit by the ACLU in 2011, although data and analyses are not yet available (Gregg, 2014). Over the period from 2003 to 2010, police stops were increasing in New York City at the same time that crime rates were falling (Rosenfeld & Fornango, 2014). But is there any causal relationship? Did the increased police stops contribute to observed decreases in robbery and burglary, for instance?

Critics point out that few arrests result from SQF, because the vast majority of persons stopped are innocent of any wrongdoing. Only 6% of all stops in New York resulted in an arrest; an additional 6% resulted in a summons; the remaining 88% resulted in no further law enforcement action (Rudovsky, 2013). Only a small fraction of stops yielded a weapon (about 1.5%). Police officials argue the opposite: The fact that few arrests are made reflects the deterrent value of the policy. Knowing there is a strong likelihood they will be stopped by the police, potential offenders are deterred from carrying weapons or otherwise engaging in criminal activity (Rosenfeld & Fornango, 2014).

In one study, Smith and Purtell (2008) investigated monthly time series of police stops and precinct crime rates in New York for the period February 1997 through December 2006. Results were mixed. They found statistically significant and negative effects of police stops on rates of robbery, burglary, motor vehicle theft, and homicide, but no significant effects on rates of assault, rape, or grand larceny. This study was criticized for its methodological weaknesses, however, including lack of statistical controls for other precinct conditions, including economic disadvantage, immigration, residential instability, racial composition, vacant housing, and precinct divorce rates (Rosenfeld & Fornango, 2014).

Rosenfeld and Fornango (2014) addressed these issues in their analysis of New York police stops and crime rates for the period from 2003 to 2010, and they controlled for the spatial dependence of precinct crime rates on those of nearby precincts. Researchers found no significant effects of police stops on precinct robbery and burglary rates, with the exception of a small, marginally significant, negative effect of police stops that lagged two years behind the burglary rate. No significant effects of police stops were found for precinct robbery rates. They also found no significant effects of SQF arrests or misdemeanor arrests on robbery or burglary.

According to Rosenfeld and Fornango (2014), the police must find ways to reduce crime that safeguard the rights and liberties of those they suspect of criminal activity. As currently practiced in New York or elsewhere, SQF may or may not meet this difficult policy challenge. Research that examines both the crime reduction effects and possible collateral consequences of SQF should help law enforcement agencies, city officials, and the public decide whether to retain the policy, expand it, modify it, or abandon it.

The Boston Gun Project and Operation Ceasefire

Along with other efforts launched concurrently, the National Institute of Justice supported a problem-solving project to devise, implement, and evaluate strategic interventions to reduce youth homicide rates (Kennedy, 1997). The Working Group for the Boston Gun Project thus included representatives from Harvard University, the Boston Police Department, the ATF, the U.S. Attorney's office, the Suffolk County District Attorney's Office, the Massachusetts Department of Probation, and city-employed gang outreach and mediation specialists, known as street workers.

The group focused first on analyzing the supply and demand for guns and then on trying innovative methods to disrupt illegal firearm markets and deter youth violence. Researchers found that both victims and offenders typically had histories of gang membership and high rates of offending. For example, 75% of offenders and victims had been arraigned for some offense and 55% had been on probation. Twenty-five percent of the offenders were on probation at the time they committed murder. Further, youth homicides were concentrated in neighborhoods that hosted an estimated 61 gangs involving about 1,300 juveniles.

Intervention strategies focused on both supply and demand. Operation Ceasefire was a "pulling-levers" strategy designed to deter crime by reaching out directly to gangs, saying explicitly that violence would no longer be tolerated, and backing up that message by "pulling every lever" legally available when violence occurred. First, a stern message was delivered to gang members, warning that continued violence would lead to a comprehensive and intensive system of responses, including severe personal restrictions for those on probation and parole (e.g., bed checks, room searches, and enforcement of warrants), intensive police presence in neighborhoods (e.g., federal agents), search and seizure of unregistered cars, vigorous arrest and prosecution for disorder offenses such as drinking in public, and strict enforcement of curfew laws by probation and police officers. Kennedy (1997) gave one vivid example in which a gang member with a 15-year history of violent felonies was arrested for carrying a single bullet. When his prior convictions were taken into account, he was indicted as an armed career criminal and sentenced to nearly 20 years in prison. As Kennedy (1997, p. 2) stated: "Stunned gang members soon turned over their handguns, and the neighborhood became quiet."

Officials explicitly acknowledged that youth violence is much more than just a law enforcement problem, however. City, state, and federal representatives helped establish and support a large network of community-based job, recreation, and prevention programs for juveniles (Kennedy, 1997).

The evaluation of Operation Ceasefire used a basic one-group time series design to measure the effects of the intervention on youth homicide and other indicators of nonfatal serious violence in Boston. Braga and colleagues (2001a, 2001b) found that Operation Ceasefire was associated with a 63% decrease in monthly youth homicides, a 32% decrease in the monthly number of shots-fired calls, a 25% decrease in the monthly number of firearm-related assaults, and, in one high-risk police district given special attention in the evaluation, a 44% decrease in the monthly number of youth firearm-related assault incidents.

Reductions associated with Operation Ceasefire persisted when control variables—such as changes in Boston's employment trends, youth population, and citywide violence trends—were added to statistical models. The basic qualitative results also held up when youth homicide trends in Boston were compared with youth homicide trends in other large U.S. cities. Boston's significant youth homicide reduction was distinct when compared with youth homicide trends in most major U.S. and New England cities (Braga et al., 2001a, 2001b). It is difficult to specify cause and effect, however, since so many different strategies were used, and no real control group was used (NRC, 2005).

GUN CONTROL LEGISLATION

Three broad strategies of gun legislation are possible (NRC, 2005; Reiss & Roth, 1993): (1) altering gun uses or storage (e.g., rules regulating gun carrying), (2) reducing the lethality of guns (e.g., through technology such as user identification mechanisms and trigger locks), and (3) instituting market-based interventions (i.e., laws regulating who can purchase a gun, where, and under what conditions).[1] We briefly examine each, focusing on interventions for which evaluation research has been conducted.

Altering Gun Uses or Storage

This strategy refers broadly to regulations and policies affecting the legal carrying, storage, and use of a firearm. For example, the Bartley-Fox laws in Massachusetts in 1974 expanded gun licensing procedures and mandated a one-year sentence for unlicensed carrying of a firearm. The law was most effective in the short term because of vigorous law enforcement. Results suggest that the law decreased gun use in assaults and robberies and decreased gun homicides during a two-year evaluation period (Pierce & Bowers, 1981). Researchers concluded that the law, in the short term, may have deterred some individuals from carrying or using their firearms, but it did not prevent them from substituting alternative weapons.

Similarly, an evaluation of sentencing enhancements for the use of a gun during a felony in six jurisdictions showed a decrease in gun homicides, but no change in nongun homicides, and no consistent effect on gun robberies or assaults (McDowall et al., 1992). The available research evidence on the deterrent effects of firearms sentencing enhancements on firearm-related crime is mixed, however (NRC, 2005). City-level studies suggest reductions in firearm-related homicides and possibly other types of firearm-related crime in urban settings (McDowall et al., 1992), but nationwide studies suggest no crime prevention effects at the state level (Marvell & Moody, 1995).

Reducing Lethality of Guns

The second strategy, reducing the lethality of guns, includes measures that designate certain firearms as dangerous because of concealability, firepower, or other risk. It also includes measures that restrict access to certain types of weapons or ammunition by law, or that make weapons less dangerous by requiring specific types of safety technology (e.g., trigger locks). While some of these strategies may eventually be shown to be effective in reducing gun injuries or deaths, little evaluation evidence exists at this time (NRC, 2005).

Market-Based Interventions

A third type of strategy, market-based interventions, attempts to reduce criminals' access to guns. Examples include tougher regulation of federal firearm licensees, limits on the number of firearms that can be purchased in a given time period, gun bans, gun buybacks, and enforcement of laws against illegal gun buyers or sellers. According to the NRC (2005), critical gaps in information and data limit what is currently known about the potential effectiveness of a market-based approach to reducing criminal access to firearms.

Part of the difficulty is that the legal firearms business consists of transactions made in the *primary* firearms market and in the largely unregulated *secondary* firearms market. Acquisitions (other than theft) of new and secondhand firearms from federal firearms licensees (FFLs), whether conducted properly or not, form the primary market for firearms (NRC, 2005). Indeed, as we saw at the beginning of this chapter, a privately owned gun can be transferred in a wide variety of ways not involving FFLs, such as through classified ads in newspapers and gun magazines, and at gun shows (which include both licensed and unlicensed dealers). Transfers of secondhand firearms by unlicensed individuals form the secondary market, for which federal law does not require transaction records or criminal background checks of prospective gun buyers (NRC, 2005). Using household survey data, Cook and Ludwig (2000) estimated that about 2 million transactions per year (30% to 40% of all gun transactions) occur in the secondary market.

States vary greatly in their regulation of secondary firearms market transfers (NRC, 2005). In Massachusetts, for example, all firearms transfers must be reported to the state police, and secondary markets can be regulated through inspection of these transfer records. In neighboring New Hampshire, sales of guns by private citizens are not recorded, and even legitimate transfers in the secondary market cannot be monitored.

Firearms can make their way to prohibited persons, including juveniles and convicted felons, in a variety of ways. A conceptual model of the flow of firearms (Braga et al., 2002) is presented in Figure 12.3. The most important point is that firearms can be diverted to criminals and juveniles at any stage of legitimate business. For example, many guns are stolen from manufacturers, importers, distributors, licensed dealers, and private citizens each year—as many as half a million annually (Cook & Ludwig, 2000).

Prohibited persons can acquire firearms from licensees without theft through three broad mechanisms: (1) a straw purchase, (2) "lying and buying," and (3) buying from a dealer who is willing to ignore regulations (Braga et al., 2002). A straw purchase occurs when the actual buyer, typically someone who is too young or otherwise proscribed, uses another person to complete the purchase and fill out the paperwork. "Lying and buying"

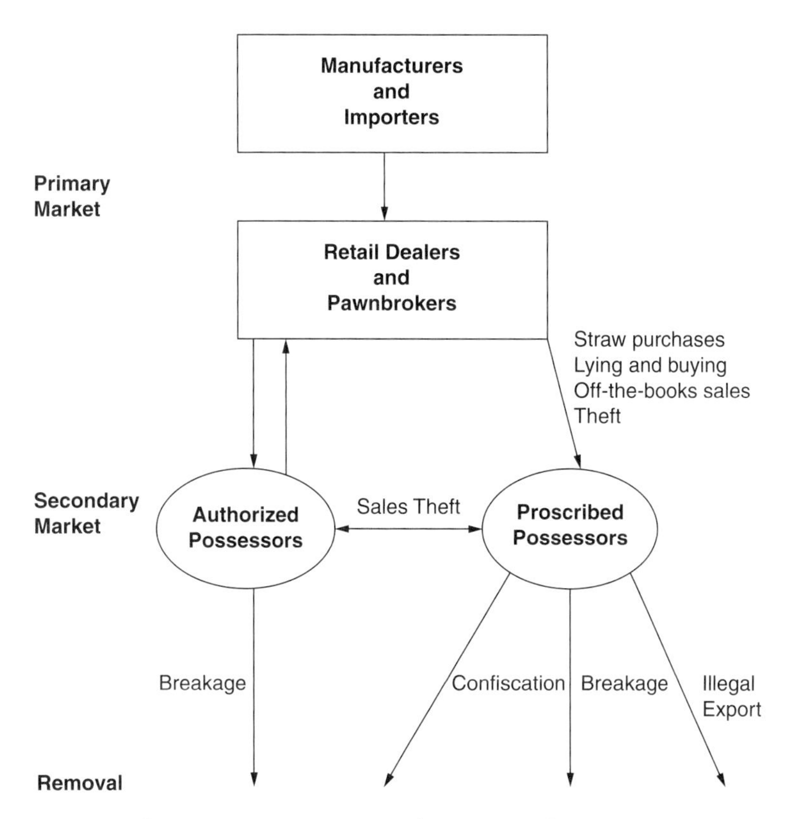

FIGURE 12.3 Firearms flows. *Source:* Braga, A. A., Cook, P. J., Kennedy, D. M., & Moore, M. H. (2002). The illegal supply of firearms. In M. Tonry (Ed.), *Crime and justice: a review of research* (Vol. 29, p. 327). Chicago: University of Chicago Press. Reprinted with permission.

refers to prohibited persons who purchase firearms directly by showing false identification and lying about their status. Finally, the seller may be knowingly involved and may disguise the illegal transaction by falsifying the record of sale or reporting the gun as stolen. A very small number of FFLs generate a large number of crime gun traces (NRC, 2005). Corrupt FFLs accounted for only 9% of gun trafficking investigations conducted by ATF but more than half of all guns diverted to prohibited users.

ATF firearms trace data show that many firearms recovered by law enforcement were illegally diverted from legitimate firearms commerce to criminals and juveniles (NRC, 2005). Gun trace data show that most guns had a "time to crime" (the length of time from the first retail sale to recovery by the police) of only a few months to a few years. As many as 62% of traced firearms were first purchased from licensed dealers in the state where the guns were recovered (NRC, 2005).

Several market-based interventions have been evaluated, but conclusions are often unclear (NRC, 2005). Interventions are rarely independent of other forces influencing gun crime, and it is impossible for researchers to control for everything that might influence gun violence.

Regulating gun dealers. As noted, criminals can acquire guns in the primary market by personally making illegal purchases, arranging straw purchases, or finding corrupt FFLs willing to ignore transfer laws. In 2000, ATF conducted focused compliance inspections on dealers who had been uncooperative in response to trace requests and on FFLs who had 10 or more crime guns (regardless of time-to-crime) traced to them in 1999. These selective inspections disclosed violations in about 75% of the 1,012 dealers inspected (NRC, 2005). Clearly, a strategy of focused inspections should be continued.

Limiting gun sales. Some states have passed laws limiting the number of firearms that an individual may legally purchase during a specific time period (e.g., one per 30 days). The goal is to reduce straw purchases. Some evidence suggests this strategy reduces gun violence, but no controlled studies so far have shown reduced harm due to this intervention. Substitution is another big problem—straw purchasers may simply go to another nearby state or jurisdiction that has less restrictive laws.

Screening gun buyers. The Federal Gun Control Act of 1968 prohibited gun dealers from selling to "dangerous" categories of persons, including juveniles, convicted felons, drug users, and former mental patients. The law also restricted gun imports and retail sales to federally licensed dealers. No significant effect on firearms injuries or deaths was found in an evaluation study (Zimring, 1975), although weak enforcement of the laws may be at least partially responsible for weak effects. In Washington DC, increased enforcement of federal law in 1970 resulted in a six-month decrease in gun homicides but no change in nongun homicides (Reiss & Roth, 1993).

More recently, the Brady Act, in effect since February 1994, mandated background investigations and prohibited retail sales of guns to persons in high-risk categories (identical to the categories specified by the Federal Gun Control Act of 1968). The interim provisions of the Brady Act specified that licensed firearm dealers request a presale check on all potential handgun purchasers from the chief law enforcement officer in the jurisdiction where the prospective buyer resides. That officer must make a reasonable effort to determine whether the purchaser is legally prohibited from possessing a handgun. Unless earlier approval is obtained, the dealer must wait five days before transferring the weapon to the buyer.

This interim system remained in effect until November 30, 1998, when an instant background check became mandatory for purchasers of all firearms. Under the "permanent provisions" of the Brady Act, presale inquiries are now made through the National Instant Criminal Background Check System (NICS) operated by the FBI. The background check determines, based on available records, whether an individual is prohibited under the Federal Gun Control Act or state law from receiving or possessing firearms. As of November 30, 1998, the procedures related to the waiting period of the interim system were eliminated.

From the inception of the NICS on November 30, 1998, to December 31, 2007, a total of 83,274,985 transactions were processed (FBI, 2008). From November 30, 1998, through year-end 2007, the NICS Section denied a total of 610,180 firearm transactions. Of these, the NICS Section rendered 66,817 denial determinations in 2007. The NICS Section's 1.3% denial rate for 2007 remains consistent with the 2006 denial rate of 1.33% (FBI, 2008). Eighty-two percent of rejections in 2007 were due to applicants' criminal histories; 7% were rejected for a domestic violence misdemeanor conviction or restraining order (FBI, 2008). Remaining reasons included state or local law prohibitions, fugitives, mental illness or disability, juveniles, dishonorable military discharge, and illegal aliens.

Few systematic evaluations of the Brady Act have been conducted, and no significant reductions in violence attributable to its influence have yet been found (NRC, 2005). Ludwig and Cook (2000) found no effects comparing pre-Brady (n = 32) with Brady-compliant states (n = 19 states plus the District of Columbia). The only effect was a reduction in gun suicides for persons aged 55 or over. Given the small percentage of refusals relative to applicants, the cost-effectiveness of this measure requires further analysis (Welsh & Harris, 2012).

Gun buybacks. Gun buyback programs usually involve a local government paying individuals to turn in guns they possess. The guns are then destroyed. The programs usually do not require the participants to identify themselves. Advocates of this strategy assume that fewer guns on the streets will result because fewer guns are available for theft or trade, and consequently gun violence will decline. However, the assumptions underlying gun buyback programs are badly flawed (NRC, 2005). First, the guns that are typically recovered are the ones least likely to be used in criminal activities, including many old and inoperative guns. Second, because replacement guns are easily obtained, any decline in the number of guns on the street is likely to be smaller than the number of guns that are turned in. Third, the likelihood that any particular gun will be used in a crime in a given year is low. Available empirical evidence suggests that these programs have no effect on gun-related violence at all (NRC, 2005).

Banning assault weapons. In 1994, Congress enacted the Violent Crime Control and Law Enforcement Act, which banned the importation and manufacture of certain military-style semiautomatic "assault" weapons capable of holding more than 10 rounds. Assault weapons and large-capacity magazines manufactured prior to the effective date of the ban were "grandfathered" and thus were still legal to own and transfer. According to many critics, the legislation was riddled with loopholes that allowed manufacturers to rename their weapons and make minor modifications on copycat models that could then be sold legally. A recent evaluation revealed no clear impacts on gun violence (Koper & Roth, 2001), although the short time period available for analysis (24 months) limits conclusions (NRC, 2005). After congressional leaders failed to reauthorize it, the assault weapons ban expired at midnight on September 14, 2004.

District of Columbia handgun ban. The District of Columbia's Firearms Control Regulations Act of 1975 is probably the most carefully analyzed example of a handgun ban (NRC, 2005). This law prohibited the purchase, sale, transfer, and possession of handguns by District residents other than law enforcement officers or members of the military. However, individuals who had registered handguns prior to the passage of this law were allowed to keep them. During periods of vigorous enforcement in the three years following implementation, the law reduced rates of gun robbery, assault, and homicide (Jones, 1981; Loftin et al., 1991). Increases in gun homicides were noted in 1988, when crack markets exploded, however (Cook, 1991). Empirical evidence for the effectiveness of the ban was mixed, according to the NRC (2005). Although significant effects were discovered, the nonexperimental design could not rule out competing explanations, results were limited to a single city, and it was difficult to draw causal inferences.

On June 26, 2008, the Supreme Court struck down the ban, the strictest in the country, and decided for the first time in the nation's history that the Second Amendment guarantees an individual's right to own a gun for self-defense. Justice Antonin Scalia wrote: "We hold that the District's ban on handgun possession in the home violates the Second Amendment, as does its prohibition against rendering any lawful firearm in the home operable for the purpose of immediate self-defense" (Barnes, 2008).

RIGHT-TO-CARRY LAWS

Some researchers have claimed that increased handgun availability among the population actually provides a deterrent to would-be criminals (Kleck, 1991; Lott, 1998). Right-to-carry-laws allow individuals to carry concealed weapons. Thirty-four states have right-to-carry laws that allow qualified adults to carry concealed handguns. Proponents of these laws argue that criminals are deterred by the knowledge that potential victims may be carrying weapons and that therefore the laws reduce crime. Easy availability may also mean, however, that guns can be used more often in violent crimes, and perpetrators in high-availability jurisdictions may even increase their firepower because of fear that potential victims may be armed (Reiss & Roth, 1993).

Research suggesting that gun availability deters would-be criminals typically suffers from inadequate controls for important cross-jurisdictional variations in poverty rates, gang and drug activity, and local and state gun laws and anticrime programs (Ludwig, 1999; NRC, 2005). Other problems include short time series, a small number of jurisdictions, questionable measurement of key variables, and a lack of individual-level data on actual gun attitudes or use. The NRC (2005) concluded that, in light of (1) the sensitivity of the empirical results to seemingly minor changes in model specification, (2) a lack of robustness of the results to the inclusion of more recent years of data (during which there are many more law changes than in the earlier period), and (3) the imprecision of some results, it is impossible to draw strong conclusions from the existing literature on the causal impact of these laws. One member of the panel wrote a dissenting opinion, however, arguing that the panel treated these studies too harshly (NRC, 2005, Appendix A).

FIREARM INJURY PREVENTION PROGRAMS

The NRC panel (2005) reviewed the research on the effectiveness of primary, secondary, and tertiary programs for the prevention of firearms injury. The prevention of firearms violence has been addressed in a number of ways, from legislative reform, to media campaigns, to educational interventions. Educational interventions are typically employed in school settings, with a focus on modifying the attitudes, knowledge, or behavior of individual children. Most of these programs are centered on educating children themselves about firearms and violence or through programs involving parents or health care providers. Unfortunately, the quality of research is generally poor or nonexistent (NRC, 2005). Problems include weak interventions (often only a few hours total), weak research designs such as a before-and-after design with no control group, and few controls for alternative explanations or variables.

CONCLUSIONS

Because of evidence that felons most frequently obtain their firearms through unregulated sales, the benefits of further federal regulation of guns may be small. This does not mean that such strategies should be abandoned. Quite the contrary, they provide an essential foundation and companion to the other strategies reviewed in this section (e.g., disruption of illegal markets, interagency and community prevention efforts). Indeed, illegal diversions from legitimate gun sellers are important sources of crime guns, and effective strategies to reduce gun violence must address both primary and secondary firearm markets (NRC, 2005).

Although a diverse array of legislation and prevention efforts has been attempted in recent years, much more rigorous, controlled evaluations of different interventions are needed (Cook, 1991; NRC, 2005; Reiss & Roth, 1993). We still know little about the effectiveness of different types of gun legislation and various prevention strategies, and only a few studies adequately control for alternative explanations of results. Among the most promising interventions so far are different types of targeted police intervention that include broad-based community input and interagency cooperation and services.

DISCUSSION QUESTIONS

1. (a) How often are firearms involved in violent crimes? (b) How often are victims injured or killed? Give specific evidence.
2. Is felony gun use in the United States increasing, decreasing, or staying the same? How can you tell? Give specific evidence.
3. (a) What were the most common reasons felons gave for *using a gun* while committing an offense? (b) Where were felons most likely to *get their guns* from? Give specific evidence.

4. How does each of the following *explain* gun-related violence? Give specific examples and evidence from course materials: (a) symbolic interaction theory, (b) routine activities theory, (c) cultural theories, and (d) media violence.
5. Describe how each of the following *interventions* attempted to reduce gun-related violence: (a) Kansas City Gun Experiment, (b) stop-and-frisk, (c) Boston Violence Prevention Project, (d) right-to-carry laws. For each, discuss what was done, how it was done, and any evidence of its effectiveness.
6. The text describes three broad categories of *gun control legislation*. (a) *Describe and explain each*, and (b) *discuss one example of each*. In your examples, discuss what has been done (or suggested), how it was done (or could be done), and any evidence of its effectiveness.

SUGGESTED READINGS

National Research Council. (2005). *Firearms and violence: A critical review*. Committee to Improve Research Information and Data on Firearms. Charles F. Wellford, John V. Pepper, and Carol V. Petrie, Eds. Committee on Law and Justice, Division of Behavioral and Social Sciences and Education. Washington, DC: The National Academies Press.

NOTE

1. Reiss and Roth (1993) originally used four categories: (1) alter gun uses or storage (e.g., carrying); (2) change gun allocation across different user categories (i.e., who can purchase a gun); (3) reduce lethality of guns (e.g., through technology such as user identification mechanisms and trigger locks); and (4) reduce the number of guns (i.e., availability). We find that the second and fourth categories overlap considerably. Following the NRC (2005), we combine these two categories into a single category called "market-based interventions."

REFERENCES

Anderson, C. A., Berkowitz, L., Donnerstein, E., Huesmann, L. R., Johnson, J. D., Linz, D., Malamuth, N., & Wartella, E. (2003). The influence of media violence on youth. *Psychological Science in the Public Interest, 4*(3), 81–110.

Anderson, C. A., Shibuya, A., Ihori, N., Swing, E. L., Bushman, B. J., Sakamoto, A., . . . & Saleem, M. (2010). Violent video game effects on aggression, empathy, and prosocial behavior in eastern and western countries: a meta-analytic review. *Psychological Bulletin, 36*(2), 151–173.

Bandura, A. (1965). Influence of model's reinforcement contingencies on the acquisition of imitative responses. *Journal of Personality and Social Psychology, 36*, 589–595.

Bandura, A. (1986). *Social foundations of thought and action: A social cognitive theory*. Englewood Cliffs, NJ: Prentice Hall.

Bandura, A., Ross, S., & Ross, D. (1963) Vicarious reinforcement and imitative learning. *Journal of Abnormal and Social Psychology, 67*(6), 601–607.

Barnes, R. (2008, June 27). Justices reject D.C. ban on handgun ownership. *Washington Post*. Retrieved from http://www.washingtonpost.com/wp-dyn/content/article/2008/06/26/AR2008062600615.html.

Barr, R., Muentener, P., Garcia, A., Fujimoto. M., & Chávez, V. (2007). The effect of repetition on imitation from television during infancy. *Developmental Psychobiology, 49*(2), 196–207.

Beck, A., Gilliard, D., Greenfeld, L., Harlow, C, Hester, T., Jankowski, L., . . . & Morton, D. (1993). *Survey of state prison inmates, 1991* (NCJ-136949). Washington, DC: U.S. Department of Justice, Office of Justice Programs, Bureau of Justice Statistics.

Berkowitz, L., & LePage, A. (1967). Weapons as aggression-eliciting stimuli. *Journal of Personality and Social Psychology, 7,* 202–207.

Blumstein, A. (2000). Disaggregating the violence trends. In A. Blumstein & J. Wallman (Eds.), *The crime drop in America* (pp. 13–44). New York: Cambridge University Press.

Braga, A. A., Cook, P. J., Kennedy, D. M., & Moore, M. H. (2002). The illegal supply of firearms. In M. Tonry (Ed.), *Crime and justice: A review of research* (Vol. 29, pp. 319–352). Chicago: University of Chicago Press.

Braga, A. A., Kennedy, D. M., Piehl, A. M., & Waring, E. J. (2001a). *Measuring the impact of Operation Ceasefire. Reducing Gun Violence: The Boston Gun Project's Operation Ceasefire.* National Institute of Justice. Washington, DC: U.S. Department of Justice.

Braga, A. A., Kennedy, D. M., Waring, E. J., & Piehl, A. M. (2001b). Problem-oriented policing, deterrence, and youth violence: An evaluation of Boston's Operation Ceasefire. *Journal of Research in Crime and Delinquency, 38*(3), 195–225.

Bushman, B. J., & Huesmann, L. R. (2006). Short-term and long-term effects of violent media on aggression in children and adults. *Archives of Pediatric Adolescent Medicine, 160*(4), 348–352.

Bushman, B. J., Jamieson, P. E., Weitz, I., & Romer, D. (2013). Gun violence trends in movies. *Pediatrics, 132,* 1014–1018. DOI: 10.1542/peds.2013-1600.

Carlson, M., Marcus-Newhall, A., & Miller, N. (1990). Effects of situational aggression cues: A quantitative review. *Journal of Personality and Social Psychology, 58*(4), 622–633.

Cohen, L., & Felson, M. (1979). Social change and crime rate trends: A routine activity approach. *American Sociological Review, 44,* 588–608.

Comstock, G. A., & Paik, H. (1994). The effects of television violence on aggressive behavior: A meta-analysis. *Communications Research, 21,* 516–546.

Cook, D. E., Kestenbaum, C., Honaker, L. M., Anderson, E. R., Jr., American Academy of Family Physicians, & American Psychiatric Association. (2000, July 26). Joint statement on the impact of entertainment violence on children: Congressional public health summit. Available at http://www.aap.org/advocacy/releases/jstmtevc.htm.

Cook, P. J. (1981). Guns and crime: The perils of long division. *Journal of Policy Analysis and Management, 1,* 120–125.

Cook, P. J. (1991). The technology of personal violence. In M. Tonry (Ed.), *Crime and justice: A review of research* (Vol. 14, pp. 1–72). Chicago: University of Chicago Press.

Cook, P. J., & Ludwig, J. (2000). *Gun violence: The real costs.* New York: Oxford University Press.

Decker, S. H., Pennell, S., & Caldwell, A. (1997). *Illegal firearms: Access and use by arrestees* (NCJ-163496). Washington, DC: U.S. Department of Justice, Office of Justice Programs, National Institute of Justice.

Federal Bureau of Investigation. (2008). *National Instant Criminal Background Check System (NICS): Operations 2007.* Retrieved January 15, 2010, from http://www.fbi.gov/hq/cjisd/nics.htm.

Greenbaum, S. (1997). Kids and guns: From playgrounds to battlegrounds. Juvenile justice, *Journal of the Office of Juvenile Justice and Delinquency Prevention, Vol. III, Number 2* (NCJ-165925). Washington, DC: U.S. Department of Justice, Office of Justice Programs, Office of Juvenile Justice and Delinquency Prevention.

Gregg, C. (2014, Jan. 31). Police department rolls out new electronic system to monitor stop and frisks. *Philadelphia Inquirer.* Retrieved from http://philadelphia.cbslocal.com/2014/01/31/police-department-rolls-out-new-system-for-stop-and-frisk-policy/

Huesmann, L. R. (1986). Psychological processes promoting the relation between exposure to media violence and aggressive behavior by the viewer. *Journal of Social Issues, 42*, 125–139.

Huesmann, L. R. (1988). An information processing model for the development of aggression. *Aggressive Behavior, 14*, 13–24.

Jones, E. D., III. (1981). The District of Columbia's firearms control regulations act of 1975: The toughest handgun control law in the United States—Or is it? *Annals of the American Academy of Political and Social Science, 455*, 138–149.

Kennedy, D. M. (1997). *Juvenile gun violence and gun markets in Boston. Research preview.* Washington, DC: U.S. Department of Justice, Office of Justice Programs, National Institute of Justice.

Kleck, G. (1991). *Point blank: Guns and violence in America.* New York: Aldine de Gruyter.

Koper, C. S., & Roth, J. (2001). The impact of the 1994 federal assault weapon ban on gun markets: An assessment of short-term primary and secondary market effects. *Journal of Quantitative Criminology, 18*, 239–266.

Loftin, C., McDowall, D., Wiersema, B., & Cottey, T. (1991). Effects of restrictive licensing of handguns on homicide and suicide in the District of Columbia. *New England Journal of Medicine, 325*, 1615–1620.

Lott, J. R., Jr. (1998). *More guns, less crime: Understanding crime and gun control laws.* Chicago: University of Chicago Press.

Luckenbill, D. (1977). Criminal homicide as a situated transaction. *Social Problems, 25*, 176–186.

Ludwig, J. (1999). Review: More guns, less crime: Understanding crime and gun control laws. *Contemporary Sociology, 28*, 466–467.

Ludwig, J., & Cook, P. J. (2000). Homicide and suicide rates associated with implementation of the Brady handgun violence prevention act. *Journal of the American Medical Association, 284*, 585–501.

Marvell, T., & Moody, C. (1995). The impact of enhanced prison terms for felonies committed with guns. *Criminology, 33*, 247–281.

McDowall, D., Loftin, C., & Wiersema, B. (1992). A comparative study of the preventive effects of mandatory sentencing laws for gun crimes. *Journal of Criminal Law and Criminology, 83*, 378–394.

National Research Council (NRC). (2005). *Firearms and violence: A critical review.* Committee to Improve Research Information and Data on Firearms. Charles F. Wellford, John V. Pepper, and Carol V. Petrie, Eds. Committee on Law and Justice, Division of Behavioral and Social Sciences and Education. Washington, DC: The National Academies Press.

Paulson, S. K. (2000, Jan. 11). Colorado governor changes stance on guns. *Philadelphia Inquirer.* Retrieved from http://www.inquirer.com/.

Peipert, T. (2012, Dec. 15). In Colo., shooting revives debate over gun control. *Philadelphia Inquirer.* Retrieved from http://www.philly.com/philly/news/special_packages/20121215_In_Colo___shooting_revives_debate_over_gun_control.html#BQq7BwuI0Et8q6f0.99.

Pierce, G. L., & Bowers, W J. (1981). The Bartley-Fox gun law's short-term impact on crime in Boston. *Annals of the American Academy of Political and Social Science, 455*, 120–132.

Planty, M., & Truman, J. L. (2013). *Firearm Violence, 1993–2011* (NCJ-241730). Washington, DC: U.S. Department of Justice, Office of Justice Programs, Bureau of Justice Statistics.

Reiss, A. J., Jr., & Roth, J. A. (Eds.). (1993). *Understanding and preventing violence (Vol. 1).* Panel on the Understanding and Control of Violent Behavior, National Research Council. Washington, DC: National Academy Press.

Rosenfeld, R., & Fornango, R. (2014). The impact of police stops on precinct robbery and burglary rates in New York City, 2003–2010. *Justice Quarterly, 31*, 96–122. DOI: 10.1080/07418825.2012.712152.

Rudovsky, D. (2013). Stop-and-frisk: The power of data and the decision in *Floyd v. City of New York.University of Pennsylvania Law Review Online, 162,* 117–126.

Schank, R. C., & Abelson, R. P. (1977). *Scripts, plans, goals, and understanding.* Hillsdale, NJ: Erlbaum.

Sheley, J. K., & Wright, J. D. (1993). *Gun acquisition and possession in selected juvenile samples* (NCJ-145326). Washington, DC: U.S. Department of Justice, Office of Justice Programs, National Institute of Justice.

Sherman, L. W., Gartin, P., & Buerger, M. (1989). Hot spots of predatory crime: Routine activities and the criminology of place. *Criminology, 27,* 27–55.

Sherman, L. W., & Rogan, D. (1995). Effects of gun seizures on gun violence: Hot spots, patrol in Kansas City. *Justice Quarterly, 12,* 673–693.

Sherman, L. W., Shaw, J. W., & Rogan, D. P. (1995). *The Kansas City gun experiment* (NCJ-150855). Washington, DC: U.S. Department of Justice, Office of Justice Programs, National Institute of Justice.

Sloane, J., Kellermann, A., Rey, D., Ferris, J., Koespell, T., Rivara, F., . . . & LoGerfo, J. (1988). Handgun regulations, crimes, assaults, and homicide. *New England Journal of Medicine, 319,* 1256–1262.

Smith, D. C., & Purtell, R. (2008, Nov. 6–8). Does stop and frisk stop crime? Paper presented at the Annual Research Conference of the Association of Public Policy and Management, Los Angeles, CA.

Snyder, H. N. (1998). *Juvenile arrests 1997* (NCJ-173938). Washington, DC: U.S. Department of Justice, Office of Justice Programs, Office of Juvenile Justice and Delinquency Prevention.

Snyder, H. N., Sickmund, M., & Poe-Yamagata, E. (1996). *Juvenile offenders and victims: 1996 update on violence* (NCJ-159107). Washington, DC: U.S. Department of Justice, Office of Justice Programs, Office of Juvenile Justice and Delinquency Prevention.

Subra, B., Muller, D., Bègue, L., Bushman, B. J., & Delmas, F. (2010). Automatic effects of alcohol and aggressive cues on aggressive thoughts and behaviors. *Personality and Social Psychology Bulletin, 36*(8), 1052–1057.

Welsh, W. N., & Harris, P. W. (2012). *Criminal justice policy and planning* (4th ed.). Waltham, MA: Elsevier/Anderson.

Wright, J. C., Huston, A. C., Reitz, A. L., & Piemyat, S. (1994). Young children's perceptions of television reality: Determinants and developmental differences. *Developmental Psychology, 30*(2), 229–239.

Wright, J. D., & Rossi, P. H. (1985, July). *The armed criminal in America: A survey of incarcerated felons.* Washington, DC: National Institute of Justice Research Report (July).

Zimring, F. E. (1975). Firearms and federal law: The Gun Control Act of 1968. *Journal of Legal Studies, 4,* 133–198.

CHAPTER 13

THE ROLE OF DRUGS AND ALCOHOL IN VIOLENCE

The evidence linking drug and alcohol use to violence is striking. For example, prior alcohol use by the victim, perpetrator, or both is found in more than half of all violent events (Reiss & Roth, 1993). Consider each of the following incidents, summarized from a classic study of homicides by Luckenbill (1977). What do these incidents have in common, and how are they different?

- The offender and his friend were sitting in a bar drinking beer. The offender's friend told him that the offender's girlfriend was "playing" with another man (the eventual victim) at the other end of the bar. The offender asked his friend if he thought something was going on. The friend responded that he wouldn't let that guy fool around with *his* girlfriend. The offender agreed, and suggested that his girlfriend and the victim be shot.
- A group of bystanders were watching a fight between a bouncer and a drunken customer on the street outside a bar. The offender was cheering for the bouncer, and the victim was cheering for the customer. The victim turned to the offender and said, "You'd really like to see the little guy have the shit kicked out of him, wouldn't you, big man?" The offender turned toward the victim and asked, "What did you say? You want the same thing, punk?" The victim moved toward the offender. The offender punched the victim, who crashed to the pavement and died a week later.
- The offender, victim, and three friends were driving while drinking beer and wine. The victim started laughing at the offender's car which he, the victim, had scratched a week earlier. The offender asked the victim why he was laughing. The victim responded that the offender's car looked like junk. The offender stopped the car and everyone got out. The offender asked the victim to repeat his statement, and he did. The offender struck the victim, and the ensuing fight led to the victim's death.

High prevalence rates of alcohol- or drug-related violence, however, are insufficient to demonstrate that alcohol or drug use *causes* violence. Problem drinkers are more likely to have previous histories of violence. But how do we make sense of this? Are violent people more likely to drink, or are heavy drinkers more likely to be violent? The two questions are quite different. One requires examination of violent offenders; the other requires examination of problem drinkers. Although these two populations overlap, they are far from identical.

In this chapter, we explore links between alcohol or drugs and violence. As in previous chapters, we examine major patterns, explanations, and interventions. To productively explore this broad, complex, and growing field of knowledge, we integrate relevant material from psychology, sociology, public health, and criminal justice, although violence reduction remains our central goal. In short, broad, interdisciplinary problems of violence require broad, interdisciplinary solutions.

PATTERNS

Offenders who have severe drug problems are responsible for a high proportion of crime (Ball et al., 1983; Chaiken, 1989; Inciardi, 1979). The National Center on Addiction and Substance Abuse (1998) reported that 60% to 80% of all prison inmates (federal, state, and county) have been involved with drug use or drug-related crimes in some fashion.

The Arrestee Drug Abuse Monitoring (ADAM) program tracked drug use among booked arrestees in 35 large urban areas.[1] In 2000, the ADAM program conducted interviews and drug tests with more than 188,000 adult male arrestees (National Institute of Justice [NIJ], 2003). The percentage of adult males arrested for a *violent offense* and who tested positive for one or more drugs[2] varied considerably by city: for example, New York (64%), Philadelphia (58%), Denver (55%), Dallas (42%), and San Antonio (22%). Only rarely did this figure fall below 50%. In 2007, the Office of National Drug Control Policy (2014) initiated ADAM II, where several ADAM sites were selected on the basis of geographical diversity to continue the analysis. Of those arrested for a violent crime, 60.2% in Atlanta tested positive for any drug compared to 75.0% in Chicago, 68.1% in Denver, 49.1% in New York, and 83.9% in Sacramento. Although percentages varied across jurisdictions, the drug most frequently used was marijuana, followed by cocaine (except in Sacramento, where methamphetamine was in second place). Although many arrestees for violent offenses test positive for the use of at least one illegal drug at the time of their arrest, we cannot automatically claim a causal relationship between drug use and violent crime on the basis of drug testing data alone (NIJ, 2003; Wish & O'Neil, 1989).

It is often assumed that drug-using offenders commit violent crimes such as robbery to acquire cash to buy drugs. But do drug users commit more robberies? The answer is not clear, but *seriously addicted* drug users commit robberies at a very high rate. The most predatory offenders (high-rate, heroin-addicted offenders) committed 15 times more robberies, 20 times more burglaries, and 10 times more thefts than offenders who did not use drugs (Chaiken, 1986). Studies conducted among heroin users in Baltimore (Ball et al., 1983) and New York (Johnson et al., 1985) demonstrated that active drug use accelerated the users' crime rate by a factor of four to six, and that the crimes committed while people were on drugs were at least as violent, or more so, than those committed by people who did not use drugs. The Rand Inmate Surveys (Petersilia et al., 1977) showed that among robbers, drug users had an offense rate twice that of nonusers. Studies of crack users show that the robbery rate for this group is as high as or higher than that of heroin users, and their crimes are more violent (Lipton, 1995).

Overall, however, there is a lower rate of drug use among arrestees for violent offenses than arrestees for other types of offenses. Violent offenders in state prison (50%) were less likely than drug (72%) and property (64%) offenders to have used drugs in the month prior to their offense (Mumola & Karberg, 2006). Such evidence argues against the claim that the use of psychoactive drugs directly causes violent behavior.

According to the National Crime Victimization Survey (NCVS), about 27% of victims of violence reported that the offender was using drugs or alcohol at the time of the offense (Bureau of Justice Statistics, 2006). Of violent victimizations in which the offender was perceived to be under the influence, the percentages varied by offense: 43% of rape/sexual assaults, 27% of aggravated assaults, 27% of simple assaults, and 25% of robberies.

Unfortunately, research has not always properly distinguished between three major types of drug-related violence: (1) *pharmacological*, (2) *economic*, and (3) *systemic* (Goldstein, 1989). The nature and frequency of each are different, and the implications for explanation and prevention are also quite different. Remember, there is no automatic connection between drugs and violence. Instead, we must ask: *Under what conditions and in what settings are which individuals more likely to display violent behavior*?

Pharmacological effects refer to the physiological effects of a drug on the body. In some cases, biological effects may help trigger violent behavior, although many interactions involve other factors. For alcohol, no simple dose–response relationship is evident, but low, acute doses are more likely to facilitate aggression, while high doses are more likely to lead to lethargy. For marijuana and opiates, higher doses generally lead to decreased aggression, although opiate withdrawal may lead to increased aggression. For amphetamines, cocaine, LSD, and PCP, increased aggression occurs only inconsistently and occasionally. For example, small doses of amphetamines increase activity levels and competitiveness, but not necessarily violent behavior. Increased activity and competitiveness, however, may create or escalate conflicts with other persons. Thus, interactions with psychological and sociological factors are once again important. Similarly, no direct link has been found between cocaine use and violence.

Economically compulsive violence refers to crimes committed to obtain drugs or money for purchasing drugs. Except during withdrawal, heroin users tend to avoid violent crimes if nonviolent alternatives (e.g., burglary, theft) are available. A classic study by Johnson and colleagues (1985) examined 201 active street opiate users in Harlem. Each subject provided at least 33 consecutive days of data in a storefront ethnographic field station. During the study period, 72% committed no robberies; 23% committed occasional but irregular robberies; and 5% were classified as "high-rate" robbers (i.e., they committed 45% of all reported robberies). The high-rate robbers were more likely to be heroin users. Because the vast majority of heroin users are not robbers, a very small percentage of them, therefore, commit a good deal of robbery. Economically compulsive violence has been less clearly demonstrated among adult users of other illegal drugs.

Systemic violence refers to violence associated with the illegal sale and distribution of drugs. Such disputes include violence associated with gangs or illegal drug organizations (e.g., disputes with rival organizations over territory, enforcement of organizational rules, battles with police, punishment of enemies, protection of drugs or sellers). It includes transaction-related violence (i.e., robberies of drugs or money from the seller or buyer during a drug transaction), assaults to collect debts, and disputes over the quality or quantity of drugs exchanged between buyer and seller. It may also include violence involving third parties: bystanders or participants in related illegal markets (e.g., firearms, hired enforcement, prostitution). One could view the crack problem in the late 1980s and early 1990s as a large industry with a very large supporting or "service" economy (everything that goes with drug use and selling).

How often does each type of drug-related violence occur? Goldstein and colleagues (1989) classified police records of 414 homicides in New York in 1988. They classified 53% of the deaths as drug related. Of these, 39% were systemic, 2% were economic, 8% were pharmacological, and 4% had multiple drug-related causes. Judgments about which incidents are drug related, however, are far from straightforward and objective, especially when multiple causal factors exist in each event. More events were classified as systemic compared to any other category, but officers used the economic category far more often than did the researchers. Researchers classified as economic only crimes in which it was clear that the motive was to finance drug use.

Such research likely understates the role of economics (Reiss & Roth, 1993). For example, the drug motivation for robbery and burglary is often concealed and unknown to police. Second, many crimes classified as systemic may contain economic motives, such as robbery of drugs from a dealer. Third, crimes in which the drug motive was more indirect are likely undercounted (e.g., the original motive for the crime may have been to get money for groceries or some other purpose). The low rate of economic violence reported may also be related to alternative access to other sources of income among users of cocaine and synthetic drugs. For example, dealing cocaine offers an attractive alternative to robbery or burglary as a means of getting drugs directly or getting money to buy drugs. In addition, illegal wholesalers often distribute drugs to street dealers on a consignment basis, and the negotiation often allows for some personal use by the retailer. For many others, part-time drug dealing is a supplement to legal income.

Goldstein's tripartite scheme has proven extremely useful as a descriptive classification scheme, and it has helped to sort out and examine different types of drug-related violence. This scheme, however, does not explain interactions between social context, individuals, and pharmacology (e.g., different drugs). That is a challenge for theoretical explanations of drug-related violent crime.

A CASE STUDY OF SYSTEMIC VIOLENCE: THE MEXICAN DRUG CARTELS

Thousands of people have been killed in drug-related violence in Mexico over the past several years. Much of the violence is attributed to fighting between rival drug gangs or cartels for control of territory and drug shipment routes (BBC News, 2014). The cartels control much of the illegal drug trade in South America and the United States, including the manufacturing and distribution of cocaine, methamphetamine, and marijuana. Cartels are also involved in other crimes, including extortion, kidnappings for ransom, human trafficking, and prostitution (BBC News, 2014).

According to Merriam-Webster (www.merriam-webster.com/dictionary.), a "cartel" is a group of businesses that agree to fix prices so they all will make more money. While cooperation between some of the gangs in Mexico exists, there is also a great deal of violent competition. Analysts suggest that the number of intentional homicides documented by Mexico's National Institute of Statistics, Geography, and Information (INEGI) increased sharply since 2008, with annual increases of more than 58% in 2008, 41% in 2009, 30% in 2010, and 5% in 2011 (Heinle et al., 2014). INEGI estimated 121,669 homicides for the period 2007 to 2012. Appropriate criteria for estimating how many homicides are related to organized crime or gang

(continued)

(continued)

(OGC) activity are subject to debate, but media estimates suggest that between 47,845 (39.3%) and 54,087 (44.4%) of all homicides between 2007 and 2012 were OGC related (Heinle et al., 2014). Characteristics typical of OGC killings include the use of high-caliber automatic weapons, torture, dismemberment, and explicit gang messages.

The largest and most powerful drug gangs are reportedly the Zetas and the Sinaloa cartel (BBC News, 2014). The Zetas' brutal violence may have given the gang an advantage over the Sinaloa cartel, which had traditionally relied more on bribery and corruption. Other influential cartels include the Knights Templar, the Gulf cartel, and the Cartel Jalisco Nueva Generacion. Allegiances shift over time, however, and the emergence of breakaway factions from cartels is not unusual. The Zetas, originally an enforcement branch of the Gulf cartel, later turned on their allies and have been at war with them ever since (BBC News, 2014).

Responses to the violence (and results) so far have varied greatly. Government security forces fight the cartels in an attempt to reestablish law and order, but rival cartels are also at war with each other. Vigilante groups made up of civilians fed up with the ineffectiveness of security forces have also emerged, particularly in the western states of Michoacan and Guerrero. The Knights Templar, the most influential gang in that region, has accused the vigilantes of being in league with their rivals from the Cartel Jalisco Nueva Generacion.

Before taking office in 2013, President Enrique Peña Nieto said he would depart from the approach of his predecessor, President Felipe Calderon, who declared "war" on the drug gangs and relied on the army to go after cartel kingpins. Peña Nieto, in contrast, advocated a strategy that included setting up a national gendarmerie (police force) to take over from the troops. With growing violence, however, Peña Nieto has often been forced to use the army to back up federal and local police forces. He also struck a deal with vigilante groups, allowing them to keep their weapons as long as they agreed to be integrated in the official security forces (BBC News, 2014). Peña Nieto has also begun to emphasize crime prevention and judicial system reform more strongly than in the past. Important initiatives include the creation of a new agency for crime prevention and the introduction of a new, unified federal code of criminal procedure (Heinle et al., 2014). The creation and training of a national gendarmerie and a more unified police command system is ongoing.

Due to the extensive influence of the Mexican cartels on drug trafficking and violence in the United States, cooperation between the governments of the United States and Mexico continues under the Mérida Initiative. The four "pillars" of this initiative are (1) dismantling organized crime groups, (2) strengthening judicial-sector institutions, (3) building a 21st-century border, and (4) fostering resilient communities (Heinle et al., 2014). However, recent shifts in U.S. drug policy make future cooperative efforts somewhat uncertain. Legalization of marijuana in two U.S. states so far—Colorado and Washington—has raised new questions. While public support for legalization of other drugs is very low, over half of U.S. citizens in recent polls now support legalization of marijuana (Heinle et al., 2014). Legalization of marijuana will likely increase its availability and reduce its price, thereby reducing its profitability for the cartels. While this development could diminish the capacity of the Mexican cartels, it could also lead to innovation in other types of drug trafficking and criminal activities to make up for lost revenue.

EXPLANATIONS

Although links between substance abuse (especially alcohol) and violence are well known, these relationships are not easily interpreted as *causal* mechanisms (Denno, 2000; Parker & Auerhahn, 1998). Many, but not all, violent offenders have substance abuse problems. These offenders are likely to be young males. Only small proportions of young males, however, commit acts of serious violence (e.g., robbery, rape, assault, murder). Nor do most substance abusers commit acts of serious violence. For some, however, substance abuse is part of a much broader lifestyle that increases the risk of violent offending or victimization. The challenge is to separate the causal effects of social structural, cultural, and lifestyle factors from individual causes (e.g., psychological and biological).

BIOLOGICAL AND PSYCHOLOGICAL EFFECTS

One thorough review examined animal and human studies of the physiological or pharmacological effects of drugs on violent behavior (Miczek et al., 1993). Thirteen tables (spanning 101 pages) summarize the results of numerous studies examining the effects of drugs (e.g., alcohol, opiates, amphetamines, cocaine, cannabis, and hallucinogens) on both animals and humans. One major conclusion is that the violence-producing effects of drugs are strongest among heavy, chronic users (who make up a small proportion of all users).

There are limitations in our ability to study these effects with human subjects. Animal studies provide the primary means to experimentally investigate the causes of aggressive behavior, whereas studies in humans most often correlate the incidence of violent behavior with past alcohol intake or abuse of other drugs (Miczek et al., 1993). Experimental studies offer the best means of controlling for extraneous variables (i.e., threats to internal validity) but have low external validity (i.e., generalizability). Field studies (i.e., nonexperimental) with humans offer the least control over extraneous variables but have high generalizability. Ethical constraints prevent us from manipulating dosages of different drugs to human subjects at the levels at which effects on violent behavior are most likely. Another common problem is that past and current conditions (individual and social) influence human behavior, in addition to the type of drug and dosage. For example, psychopathology (e.g., psychosis, depression, antisocial personality) often predates and accompanies substance abuse in human research. It is difficult to separate such effects. Despite these limitations, some consistent effects of specific types of drugs have been found.

Alcohol is the drug most consistently linked with aggressive behavior (Denno, 2000; Miczek et al., 1993; Parker & Auerhahn, 1998). Individuals, however, vary considerably in their responses to alcohol (even at high doses), and group-level studies rely mainly on correlational evidence. Alcohol has acute (immediate) and chronic (long-term) biological effects on brain functions, including memory. Alcohol intoxication leads to impaired cognitive skills and interpersonal communication, which in turn increase the risk of violence. It is also difficult to sort out the effects of heavy drinking from the settings in which it occurs. For example, a person who regularly frequents certain bars and drinking parties may be exposed to many opportunities for conflict.

Some researchers argue that there is a remarkable correspondence over a 62-year period (1934 to 1995) between alcohol consumption and homicide rates (Parker & Cartmill, 1998). In fact, even holding poverty, income, and the proportion of males aged 15 to 24 constant, homicide rates for both whites and nonwhites were significantly related to alcohol consumption over this period. Depending on the situation, setting, and people involved, alcohol use can lead to *selective disinhibition*, whereby social norms that normally limit violence are temporarily suspended or neutralized. According to this perspective, alcohol selectively disinhibits violence, depending on contextual factors specific to the situation, the actors involved and their relationships to each other, and the impact of bystanders. Norms that receive the least institutional support are more likely to be disinhibited in a specific situation (e.g., norms governing intimate relationships).

No data suggest a direct pharmacological link between *opiates*, such as heroin, and aggression (Denno, 2000; Parker & Auerhahn, 1998). Where violence occurs, it is more likely to be associated with withdrawal among addicted users, attempts to obtain more of the drug, or both.

Some strong evidence links *amphetamine* abuse to violence in humans, but mainly for heavy, chronic abusers and intravenous users. Chronic amphetamine abuse may increase the likelihood of irritability, psychosis, and communication impairments that increase the risk of violence (Miczek et al., 1993; Parker & Auerhahn, 1998).

Methamphetamine is physically addictive and can be psychologically addictive as well (Center for Substance Abuse Research, 2014). Users experience bursts of energy, talkativeness, and excitement. Users report being able to go for hours or even days without sleep or food. High doses or chronic use have been associated with increased nervousness, irritability, paranoia, and occasionally violent behavior. Chronic abuse produces a psychosis characterized by paranoia, picking at the skin, self-absorption, auditory and visual hallucinations, and sometimes episodes of violence. Violence often occurs when an abuser is severely sleep-deprived, irritable, and paranoid (i.e., "tweaking"). The user craves more of the drug, but it is difficult to achieve the original high, which fuels frustration, unpredictability, and sometimes violent behavior (e.g., domestic disputes, fights, or spur-of-the-moment crimes).

Cocaine is linked to violent behavior primarily through its role in illegal drug markets (sale and distribution). Biological effects on violent behavior are less clear. Violent behavior occurs occasionally (but not consistently among different individuals or different groups), but it seems secondary to the paranoia and psychosis that can be triggered by heavy, chronic cocaine use (Miczek et al., 1993; Parker & Auerhahn, 1998). The route of administration may also be important. Some evidence indicates that users who smoke the drug in the form of crack are more likely to engage in violence; those who snort the drug are less likely to engage in violence. The specific situational circumstances may be as important as the route of administration, however (Giannini et al., 1993).

Most reviews conclude that *cannabis* (e.g., marijuana, hashish) has no discernible effects on aggression or actually decreases aggression (Denno, 2000; Miczek et al., 1993). There is still some concern about the role of these drugs in the violence associated with illegal drug markets, but their use is much more widespread than other drugs, their cost is lower, and profit margins are generally much smaller.

Similarly, the use of *hallucinogens* is only rarely associated with violent behavior. Low, acute doses generally stimulate defensive and timid reactions in animals. Hallucinogens are infrequently associated with human violence, although some evidence suggests that preexisting psychopathology may stimulate hypersensitive or aggressive responses to environmental stimuli (Denno, 2000; Miczek et al., 1993).

The effects of *PCP* are not entirely clear. In animal studies, exposure to PCP leads to very unpredictable results. In human studies, there is no consistent association between PCP intake and violent behavior, contrary to popular stereotypes. In humans, PCP abuse is usually part of a pattern of heavy, polydrug use, making causal inferences difficult. Violence is infrequent, but when it occurs, it is usually associated with the secondary effects of heavy, acute, or chronic exposure (e.g., psychosis) and with preexisting aggressive personality and social background characteristics (Miczek et al., 1993; Parker & Auerhahn, 1998).

Others, noting that men are much more likely to behave violently than women when intoxicated, have suggested that biological differences associated with *gender* are at work. Evidence from biological studies suggests that higher alcohol doses reduce concentrations of the male hormone testosterone. Animal studies show that acute, low alcohol doses increase aggressive behavior in individuals who already had high blood testosterone levels. There is little experimental evidence on endocrinological effects for humans, but available evidence is consistent with animal studies in that alcohol intoxication is more likely to lead to aggression in low doses than high doses (Reiss & Roth, 1993).

The same evidence, however, also implicates the interaction of *psychological, social structural, and cultural factors* (Reiss & Roth, 1993). For example, male drinking patterns are much more likely to include binge drinking and aggressive behavior associated with male peer interactions. Individual histories of aggressive behavior are also a critical determinant of whether drug or alcohol use will lead to violent behavior or not. Men, once again, are much more likely than women to have had aggressive experiences in their development. Emotions also play a role. Male users are more likely to select specific drugs to dampen or intensify certain emotions, such as anger. Such drinking patterns are often related to one's individual developmental experiences or family pathology, or both.

ROUTINE ACTIVITIES

As we saw in Chapter 12, certain types of illegal markets (guns, prostitution, drugs) tend to generate their own routine activities over time (Sherman et al., 1989). Illegal activities in and around these specific hot spots tend to overwhelm legitimate activities in the area and increase the likelihood of convergence of motivated offenders, competitors for illegal market sales, and perhaps potential victims (e.g., drug buyers) who, fearing danger, routinely carry firearms in these areas (Decker et al., 1997). Routine activities may thus explain a good deal of systemic violence.

At the community or neighborhood level, locations with large concentrations of alcohol outlets are often *hot spots* of crime, attracting many visitors who engage in a wide variety of illegal activities (Alaniz et al., 1998, 1999). The spatial distribution of alcohol outlets and the targeted advertising of alcohol to particular communities, especially minority communities, may mediate relationships between alcohol and violence. According to this approach, referred to as the *cultural consequences of availability,* the widespread advertising, sale, and use of alcohol contributes to the construction of a symbolic system that builds alcohol consumption into an idealized life world of its constituents (Alaniz et al., 1998, 1999). The concentration of alcohol outlets may facilitate an atmosphere of "time out" or "anything goes." Combined with the fact that alcohol use and crime rates are already higher in neighborhoods with high concentrations of alcohol outlets, a historical connection between high alcohol use and high homicide rates is plausible (Parker & Auerhahn, 1998; Parker & Cartmill, 1998).

CULTURAL EXPLANATIONS

Social processes (e.g., social structure and culture) also mediate relationships among alcohol use, gender, and violence. These relationships are neither uniform nor unanimous across different cultures. Different cultures or groups may have very different social expectations about the effects of alcohol in different settings (Miczek et al., 1993).

There are different cultural norms and customs regarding the use of alcohol and behavior while intoxicated, different states that MacAndrew and Edgerton (1969) have referred to as *drunken comportment*. The Yuruna Indians in the South American rain forest consistently become withdrawn when drunk, acting as though no one else existed. In a rural Japanese fishing village, drunkenness regularly leads to camaraderie, laughter, jokes, songs, and dances. In a small northern Colombian village, residents remain somber, controlled, and morose, regardless of the degree of intoxication they achieve.

There are also different stresses in different cultures that influence the likelihood of violent behavior under conditions of drunkenness (Fagan, 1990). For example, among the Naskapi Indians of northern Canada, the least successful men (iron miners) were the most aggressive drinkers. Or, in contrast to Guatemalan immigrants to the United States, male Dominican immigrants tended to bring their entire families with them. They also enjoyed greater economic opportunities (perhaps because of more established kinship and cultural networks in the United States) and drank at home more often than in bars. On the other hand, drinking resulted in greater aggression for Guatemalan men, who were more likely to live alone, experience greater economic hardship, and drink at bars rather than at home.

STRUCTURAL EXPLANATIONS

The harsh structural conditions found in many urban areas may promote cultural adjustments that contribute to participation in illegal drug markets and high levels of violence (Bourgois, 2002; Sampson & Wilson, 1995). While the root causes of drug abuse and violence are not completely understood, it is likely that both are intensified if not directly caused by some of the social conditions found in U.S. society: racism, poverty, deindustrialization, unemployment, and dysfunctional families (Denno, 2000).

Because it presents a plausible reason for both the upsurge (1985 to 1993) and downturn (1993 to 2003) of homicide rates in the past two decades, explanations focusing on the proliferation and contraction of crack cocaine markets have received much attention. Few explanations, however, have focused on the structural and cultural factors that may moderate the violence associated with illegal drug markets. Ousey and Lee (2004) used annual data from 122 cities for the period 1984 to 1997 to examine race-specific, within-city relationships between illicit drug markets and homicide rates. Changes in arrest rates for cocaine and opiate distribution corresponded positively with change in both black and white homicide rates over time within cities. Using two different operationalizations of drug markets (drug arrests and percentage of arrestees testing positive), however, the impact of change in the drug market on homicide rates was significantly stronger among blacks than among whites. The connection between illegal drug markets and violence, the authors argue, may vary as a function of preexisting social conditions for both racial groups (Ousey & Lee, 2004). For blacks, key factors influencing the relationship between drug markets and homicide were racial inequality and location in the South; for whites, important factors included resource deprivation and Western location. Although much research has indicated that urban black violence is correlated with resource deprivation, it may be that high levels of disadvantage have become so endemic to many black communities that modest fluctuations are not enough to alter the social context of drug markets.

SITUATIONAL EXPLANATIONS

Fagan's (1990) *situated transaction* framework argues that intoxication has a significant impact on cognitive skills and abilities, but the nature of this impact varies by the substance, the individual, the social setting, and the context (Fig. 13.1). For example, one ethnographic study found that a group of youths was quiet and deferential when drinking among their elders in a neighborhood bar but much more aggressive in other surroundings after they left the elders' company. Repeated observations suggested that the youths occasionally sought out different settings where expression of aggressive behavior was more acceptable. One's company and one's social setting thus strongly influence one's behavior, especially when alcohol or drugs are being used.

Similarly, Goode (2007) argues that three major factors interact to explain how drugs affect behavior: set, setting, and pharmacological effects. *Set* refers to the psychic, mental, or emotional state of the person taking the drug. Set includes the person's expectations, intelligence, personality, imagination, and mood. *Setting* refers to the social and physical environment in which drug use takes place. Setting includes whom one uses drugs with

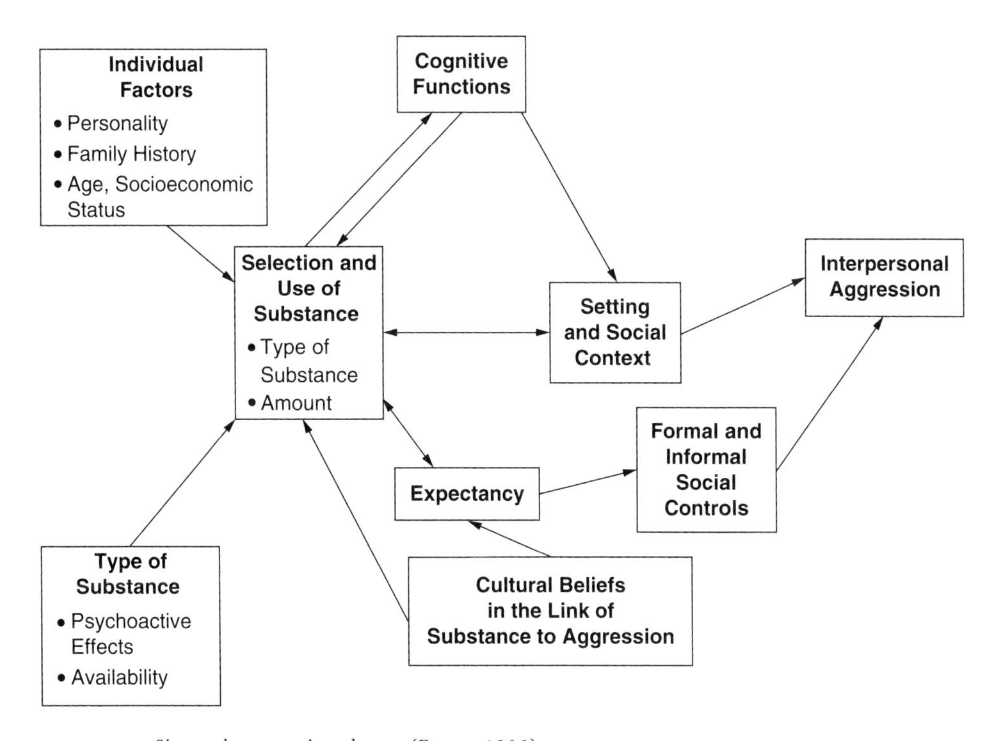

FIGURE 13.1 Situated transaction theory (Fagan, 1990).

and where, such as one's immediate surroundings (e.g., at home, in a car, at a bar, at a party) as well as the larger social and cultural backdrop. Third, as discussed earlier, *pharmacological* effects refer to the physiological effects of drugs (e.g., neurobehavioral changes). Again, we emphasize that these different influences on behavior interact with one another and are not always easy to separate.

INTERVENTIONS

As the preceding discussion illustrates, multiple causes, pathways, and interactions are required to explain drug-related violence. Diverse and complex views on the causes of drug-related violence have led to a lack of agreement among researchers, professionals, and government officials about the best ways to intervene. Discussions surrounding these issues are often politically charged, and good intentions do not necessarily lead to cooperative or productive solutions (Denno, 2000).

Nonetheless, pundits with contrasting views generally agree that an effective strategy to address drug-related violence requires some balance of the two approaches discussed in Chapter 1: the *criminal justice approach*, which emphasizes detecting and punishing offenders, and the *public health approach*, which advocates preventing and treating the drug addiction that contributes to violent crime (Denno, 2000). Indeed, the 2007 National Drug Control Strategy (White House, 2006, p. 1) argued that

> Reducing drug use requires an investment in programs that discourage the use of drugs that help those in need of treatment and law enforcement programs that target those trying to supply illicit drugs to the marketplace.

We review major approaches to drug-related violence below, noting that increased overlap and balance between the two dominant approaches are both feasible and desirable.

CRIMINAL JUSTICE APPROACHES

The War on Drugs

Although the War on Drugs may seem a tired cliché to many, it was a critical flashpoint for the historic mobilization of political and law enforcement resources. The "war" began in 1980 under President Reagan (White House, 2006). To many, the issue became a matter of primary national security and importance (Gates, 1998). The drug problem, like other social problems, is socially constructed, however; it is only partly based in reality (see Chapter 1). In other words, certain social and political dynamics produce social policy and legislation (i.e., the War on Drugs) as well as consequences (e.g., tougher penalties, higher arrest and incarceration rates).

What is meant by the War on Drugs? It included a diverse array of reactions to drug and alcohol abuse: tougher laws aimed at punishing drug users and sellers (e.g., mandatory minimum sentences of up to life imprisonment for trafficking in cocaine), drug interdiction efforts at U.S. borders and overseas (including the use of armed forces and diplomatic initiatives in countries such as Colombia and Mexico), targeted police strikes in neighborhoods where illegal drug markets flourished, mandatory drug testing policies for probationers and parolees as well as employees of government and private corporations, efforts to address presumed social correlates of drug abuse (e.g., chronic poverty, unemployment), drug awareness education in schools, and drug treatment (e.g., in communities and in prison). The major emphases, though, were punishment and interdiction.

There is little disagreement among researchers or politicians that the War on Drugs contributed to longer sentences and increased rates of incarceration for drug-related offenses (Denno, 2000). Much disagreement, however, surrounds views on the *consequences* of those policies. Some have argued that tougher sentencing policies and the incapacitation of violent drug offenders contributed to a downturn in violent crime after 1993 (see also Chapter 15), although it is extremely difficult to parcel out the specific causes for the post-1993 decrease (Blumstein, 2000).

Others are concerned about the unintended consequences of the War on Drugs. For example, minorities were incarcerated in record numbers for drug offenses even as national surveys showed that middle-class, white, employed adults represented the majority of occasional drug users (Heath, 1998). Tougher drug laws, according to some critics, contributed to racial discrimination by mandating tougher sentences for crack cocaine than for powdered cocaine offenses (Jensen & Gerber, 1998). The U.S. Sentencing Commission recommended the repeal of mandatory minimum sentencing statutes because they had more effect on low-end offenders, such as drug carriers ("mules"), than the offenders targeted by the laws—repeat, career, high-end offenders and "kingpins" (Denno, 2000). Both Democrats and Republicans have signed on to federal sentencing reform bills, and 19 states have overhauled mandatory minimum drug laws in recent years (Hoag, 2014).

Many argue that the federal drug budget should be balanced more equally between supply and demand strategies so that adequate resources are available for drug treatment and prevention, including providing young people with good schools, decent housing, recreational programs, and meaningful job prospects (Denno, 2000; Massing, 2000). Others argue that without a continuing, multifaceted War on Drugs, public health and safety will suffer dearly, and hard-fought gains will be quickly lost (Gates, 1998; White House, 2006). Regardless of one's opinions, it is clear that valid information about the problem and its causes is sorely needed, as are sound evaluations of the multitude of programs and policies generated by the War on Drugs (Denno, 2000).

Weed and Seed

Weed and Seed is a federally funded strategy intended to mobilize and coordinate antidrug resources in targeted high-crime communities. Started in 1991, the strategy targets drug trafficking, gang activity, and violence for intervention, enforcement, community policing activities, human services programs, and neighborhood improvement initiatives. Four key components are included in this strategy (Dunworth & Mills, 1999). First, *weeding* refers to concentrated and enhanced law enforcement efforts to identify, arrest, and prosecute violent offenders, drug traffickers, and other criminals operating in the target areas. Second, *seeding* refers to human services, such as after-school, weekend, and summer youth activities; adult literacy classes; parental counseling; and neighborhood revitalization efforts to prevent and deter further crime. Third, *enhanced coordination* refers to coordinated analysis of local problems and developing strategies to address them. The federal oversight responsibility for each participating site rests with the U.S. Attorney's Office for the corresponding district. Fourth, *community policing* refers to proactive police–community engagement and problem solving in which police officers are assigned to specified geographic locations. This effort is seen as the bridge between weeding and seeding. By gaining the trust and support of the community, police engage residents and businesses as problem-solving partners (e.g., neighborhood watches, citizen marches and rallies, and graffiti removal).

A national evaluation of eight case-study cities examined various aspects of program implementation as well as measurable effects on crime and public safety (Dunworth et al., 1999). Although each site had its own distinctive crime problems, they all shared high rates of violent crime related to drug trafficking and drug use. The evaluation included a review of funding applications and other significant program documents; individual interviews with key program administrators, senior law enforcement staff, managers of seeding activities, service providers, and community leaders; analysis of automated, incident-level records of crimes and arrests; group interviews with participants in seeding programs; and two surveys of residents in target areas conducted in 1995 and 1997.

Developing an appropriate seeding strategy was among the greatest challenges for Weed and Seed (Dunworth et al., 1999). Seeding efforts (e.g., youth prevention and recreation programs, family support services, community economic development) required participation and commitment from many diverse organizations with different goals, whereas weeding, operating mainly within the established structures of law enforcement and criminal justice, had a relatively clear mission. For seeding, more time was needed for planning, relationship building, and gaining consensus and commitment from the wide range of participants involved.

Within the target areas of each site, evaluators compared Part 1 crime (see Chapter 2) trends for the year prior to implementation of Weed and Seed and the second year after the program began (Dunworth et al., 1999). Five target areas had double-digit percentage decreases: Stowe Village in Hartford, 46%; Crawford-Roberts in Pittsburgh, 24%; North Manatee, Florida, 18%; the Shreveport target area, 11%; and the Central District in Seattle, 10%. One target area (West Las Vegas) had a single-digit decrease (6%), and three target areas experienced increases in Part 1 crime (South Manatee, 2%; Meadows Village in Las Vegas, 9%; and Salt Lake City, 14%).

As with many other evaluations that attempt to compare crime rates across different communities and time periods, researchers could not state definitively the extent to which different factors contributed to the observed changes in crime (Dunworth et al., 1999). A number of factors appear to be related to observed crime changes, however. Overall crime rates in the surrounding (nontarget) areas of the target sites mirrored increases or decreases in the target areas, suggesting that Weed and Seed had little influence on crime rates. Hartford and Pittsburgh, which experienced the largest Part 1 crime decreases in nontarget areas, are the same two sites whose target areas achieved the largest Part 1 crime decreases. Salt Lake City, the site with the largest Part 1 crime increase in its smaller target area, also exhibited the largest Part 1 crime increase overall.

Changes in drug arrest rates appeared to be associated with changes in the overall Part 1 crime rate. Among the six target areas for which arrest data were available, the four areas reporting decreases in Part 1 crime from the year prior to Weed and Seed through the second year of implementation (Hartford, Pittsburgh, North Manatee, and Shreveport) all experienced initial high rates of drug arrests, suggesting an initial period of intense weeding activities followed by declining drug arrest rates. Assuming the level of law enforcement has remained somewhat constant, this trend may reflect some success in reducing drug activity (Dunworth et al., 1999).

To gain the perspective of community residents whom the seeding programs were intended to benefit, participant interviews and community surveys were also conducted. According to the residents interviewed, the seeding programs provided services that otherwise would not have been available in the target areas. Most of those interviewed indicated that participation in the seeding programs was a positive experience that helped them feel more secure emotionally, physically, or both. Benefits perceived by participants included providing additional structure and discipline in the lives of target area youths and providing opportunities and assistance for adults to work toward personal and professional growth. Community surveys, however, suggested inconsistent impacts. Residents in two areas (Manatee and Pittsburgh) perceived substantial improvements in the severity of crime and police effectiveness in controlling crime. Residents in Akron and Seattle perceived some improvement in drug-related crime; Hartford residents perceived some reduction in violent and gang-related crime. Residents in three areas (Las Vegas, Salt Lake City, and Shreveport) perceived little improvement in general public safety or the severity of specific types of crime.

In conclusion, the effectiveness of weeding and seeding activities varied across the eight sites (Dunworth & Mills, 1999). The evaluation found that preexisting community features may enhance or weaken Weed and Seed efforts. Important factors included the strength of the existing social and institutional infrastructure (e.g., an established network of community-based organizations and community leaders), the severity of crime problems, geographic advantages favoring economic development, and the transiency of the community population. Finding the appropriate mix and sequence of weeding and seeding activities is an important factor in gaining community support for the program.

Disrupting Illegal Drug Markets

In response to high rates of drug-related violence, the Philadelphia Police Department launched *Operation Safe Streets* on May 1, 2002 (Lawton et al., 2005). The program stationed officers at 214 of the highest drug activity locations in the city 24 hours a day, seven days a week. The police department identified these areas with high drug use using crime data, arrest data, firearms seizure data, informant data, and ongoing investigations, and obtained partial funding from the Bureau of Justice Assistance for police overtime pay.

Lawton and colleagues (2005) examined the effects of the program using interrupted time series analyses, focusing on 121 weeks of preintervention and 18 weeks of postintervention data. Results showed no significant impacts on citywide weekly counts for drug crimes, homicides, or total violent crimes. Geographically focused analyses, however, showed significant localized intervention effects for both violent and drug crimes. Comparisons of target sites with nonintervention sites with high drug activity suggested that program effects were not an artifact. Areas within one tenth of a mile of the target site experienced significantly lower weekly crime rates. In this sense, the program was a very limited and very localized success, creating small "bubbles" of relative safety near the target sites. There was a partial, but not total, displacement of drug crime activity. Approximately 23% of the "prevented" weekly drug crimes reappeared slightly further from the intervention sites.

Program tactics have shifted over time in response to serious cost concerns and complaints about police overtime. It was simply not feasible to continue the program in its most intensive form on such a large scale. The authors conclude that crackdowns such as Operation Safe Streets respond to current crises; they cost a lot; they attract attention; and, to at least a limited degree, they get some results. They are rarely sustainable, however, because of high costs (Lawton et al., 2005).

PUBLIC HEALTH APPROACHES

Primary Prevention

Is it possible to reduce eventual drug-related health problems and violent crime by preventing initial experimentation with illegal drugs by high-risk groups? Large-scale reviews of drug abuse prevention programs have examined such effects (Botvin, 1990; Botvin et al., 1995; Dryfoos, 1990; Durlak, 1995; Hansen, 1992; Hawkins et al., 1995; Tobler, 1986, 1992). Relatively ineffective approaches include those based primarily on information dissemination (e.g., different drugs and their effects), fear arousal (e.g., emphasize the risks associated with drug use), moral appeal (e.g., teach students about the evils of drug use), or affective education (e.g., focus on building self-esteem, responsible decision making, and interpersonal growth) (Botvin, 1990). More effective approaches included some kind of resistance skills training—that is, teaching students about the social influences of substance use and specific skills for resisting these pressures, alone or in combination with broader-based life skills training, such as assertiveness.

Prison-Based Drug Treatment

Although two out of three inmates admit drug histories, fewer than 15% receive any systematic treatment while in prison (Mumola, 1999). Many drug-abusing offenders are repeatedly incarcerated but untreated, with the result that a high proportion relapses into drug use and crime after release. The time that drug-involved offenders are incarcerated presents a unique opportunity to provide them with treatment. More than 70% of active street addicts have never been in treatment nor do they intend to enter treatment for their addiction (Lipton et al., 1989). The need for expanding drug abuse treatment was recognized in the Violent Crime Control Act of 1994, which for the first time provided substantial drug treatment resources for federal and state jurisdictions. Studies suggested that in-custody treatment, especially intensive therapeutic community (TC) programming, can be effective in reducing relapse and recidivism rates among seriously drug-involved offenders (Lipton, 1995; Lipton et al., 1992; Simpson et al., 1999).

TC is an intensive, long-term (12 to 18 months), highly structured, residential treatment modality for hard-core drug users. In particular, TC emphasizes the need for the inmate to take responsibility for his or her behavior before, during, and after treatment, and inmates play an important role in structuring group norms and sanctions. Inmates typically move through three phases of treatment in a 12-month program. The first phase consists of orientation, diagnosis, and an assimilation process. In the second phase, lasting five to six months, inmates are expected to take on increased responsibility and involvement in the program. Those who have been in the program longer are expected to share their insights by teaching new members and assisting in the day-to-day operation of the TC. Encounter groups and counseling sessions focus on self-discipline, self-worth, self-awareness, respect for authority, and acceptance of guidance for problem areas. Seminars take on a more intellectual approach. Debate is encouraged as a means of self-expression. During the third phase, preparation for community reentry, which lasts one to three months, inmates strengthen their planning and decision-making skills and design their individual exit plans.

Evaluations of New York's Stay'n Out program (Wexler et al., 1990, 1992), Oregon's Cornerstone Program (Field, 1984, 1989, 1992), Delaware's Key-Crest Programs (Inciardi, 1995; Inciardi et al., 1997), California's Amity Prison TC Program (Wexler et al., 1992, 1999), Pennsylvania's In-Prison TCs (Welsh & Zajac, 2013; Welsh et al., 2014), the Texas In-Prison TC (Knight et al., 1997), and the Federal Bureau of Prisons (1998) Triad program have all demonstrated the effectiveness of prison-based TCs. A *continuum of care* model for offenders that provides primary TC treatment in prison and secondary aftercare in the community is often associated with the greatest reductions in drug use and crime and with improvements in employment and quality-of-life outcomes (Hiller et al., 1999; Inciardi et al., 2004; Knight et al., 1999b; Martin et al., 1999; Prendergast et al., 2004; Wexler et al., 1999).

Although evaluation results are promising, we still need to know more about risk factors that represent barriers to treatment participation and completion (Hiller et al., 1999; Knight et al., 1999a; Welsh et al., 2014) as well as ways to engage inmates in the treatment process more effectively (Blankenship et al., 1999; National Institute on Drug Abuse, 1981; Welsh et al., 2014). Questions remain about what kinds of inmates benefit most from such programs, how treatment needs are assessed, and how treatment processes (e.g., program content, staffing, and policies) influence outcomes (Inciardi et al., 1992; Welsh & Zajac, 2004; Welsh et al., 2014).

CONCLUSIONS

As stated by Reiss and Roth (1993, p. 183): "The link among alcohol, other psychoactive drugs, and violence turns out to be not an example of straightforward causation, but rather a network of interacting processes and feedback loops." Biological effects of drugs on behavior differ considerably according to the specific type of drug and dosage, and biological effects interact with diverse psychological and sociological processes to influence behavior. While most experts agree there is some relationship between drugs and violence, significant issues regarding its causal direction, form, magnitude, and importance remain to be determined (Denno, 2000).

Because potential causal influences connecting drug abuse to violence are complex and diverse, so must be the potential solutions. In this chapter, we focused on both criminal justice (War on Drugs, Weed and Seed, disrupting illegal drug markets) and public health approaches toward prevention and intervention. Comprehensive strategies are needed that target juveniles and adults, demand and supply, and individuals and public policy. Strategies that emphasize punishment and interdiction alone have not yielded productive results in the past, nor should they be expected to do so in the future.

DISCUSSION QUESTIONS

1. To what degree is alcohol and drug use related to violence? Discuss specific evidence.
2. (a) Discuss the *three types* of drug-related violence described by Goldstein, and give an *example* of each. (b) How *often* does each occur? (c) *Why is it important* to distinguish among these three types of violence?
3. Why is it so difficult to precisely determine the effects of alcohol and drug use on violent behavior in humans? Give specific examples and evidence from course materials to illustrate your answer.
4. *How* do the following explain alcohol or drug-related violence: (a) biological and psychological effects, (b) routine activities, (c) cultural explanations, (d) social structural explanations, and (e) situational explanations?
5. Describe how the following *interventions* attempt to reduce drug-related violence, and discuss available evidence for each: (a) Weed and Seed, (b) disrupting illegal drug markets, (c) prison-based drug treatment. Give specific examples from course materials (e.g., what, where, how, with what results).

SUGGESTED READINGS

Goode, E. (2011). *Drugs in American society* (8th ed.). New York: McGraw-Hill.

Heinle, K., Ferreira, O. R., & Shirk, D. A. (2014). *Drug violence in Mexico: Data and analysis through 2013.* San Diego: University of San Diego. Retrieved from http://justiceinmexico.files.wordpress.com/2014/04/140415-dvm-2014-releasered1.pdf

NOTES

1. Following evaluations of Drug Use Forecasting, NIJ strengthened the program by making the sampling procedure more scientifically sound, standardizing data collection, and instituting other changes. After several years of development, the restructured program was fully implemented in 2000 as ADAM. Probability-based sampling was adopted, the interview instrument was enhanced to cover several new areas of drug use and related behavior, and the number of sites was increased.
2. The ADAM report does not give the average or median percentage of adult males who were arrested for a violent offense and who tested positive for one or more illegal drugs, although the report does give site-specific information.

REFERENCES

Alaniz, M. A., Cartmill, R. S., & Parker, R. N. (1998). Immigrants and violence: The importance of neighborhood context. *Hispanic Journal of Behavioral Sciences, 20*, 155–174.

Alaniz, M. A., Trento, A. J., & Saltz, R. F. (1999). Gender, acculturation, and alcohol consumption among Mexican Americans. *Substance Use and Misuse, 34*, 1407–1426.

Ball, J. C, Shaffer, J. W., & Nurco, D. N. (1983). Day-to-day criminality of heroin addicts in Baltimore: A study in the continuity of offense rates. *Drug and Alcohol Dependence, 12*, 119–142.

BBC News. (2014, Feb. 10). *Who is behind Mexico's drug-related violence*? Retrieved from http://www.bbc.com/news/world-latin-america-10681249.

Blankenship, J., Dansereau, D., & Simpson, D. (1999). Cognitive enhancements of readiness for corrections-based treatment for drug abuse. *Prison Journal, 79*, 431–445.

Blumstein, A. (2000). Disaggregating the violence trends. In A. Blumstein & J. Wallman (Eds.), *The crime drop in America* (pp. 13–44). New York: Cambridge University Press.

Botvin, G. J. (1990). Substance abuse prevention: Theory, practice, and effectiveness. In M. Tonry & J. Wilson (Eds.), *Drugs and crime* (pp. 461–519). Vol. 13 in *Crime and justice. A review of research*. Chicago: University of Chicago Press.

Botvin, G. J., Baker, E., Dusenbury, L., Botvin, E., & Diaz, T. (1995). Long-term follow-up results of a randomized drug abuse prevention trial in a white middle-class population. *Journal of the American Medical Association, 273*, 1106–1112.

Bourgois, P. (2002). *In search of respect: Selling crack in el barrio* (2nd ed.). New York: Cambridge University Press.

Bureau of Justice Statistics (BJS). (2006). *Criminal victimization in the United States—Statistical tables index. Alcohol, use by offender.* Retrieved Jan. 18, 2007, from http://www.ojp.usdoj.gov/.

Center for Substance Abuse Research. (2014). *Methamphetamine.* Retrieved from http://www.cesar.umd.edu/cesar/drugs/meth.asp.

Chaiken, M. R. (1986). Crime rates and substance abuse among types of offenders. In B. D. Johnson & E. D. Wish (Eds.), *Crime rates among drug-abusing offenders: Final report to the National Institute of Justice* (pp. 12–54). New York: Narcotic and Drug Research, Inc.

Chaiken, M. R. (1989). *In-prison programs for drug-involved offenders. Research in brief.* Washington, DC: National Institute of Justice.

Decker, S. H., Pennell, S., & Caldwell, A. (1997). *Illegal firearms: Access and use by arrestees* (NCJ-163496). Washington, DC: U.S. Department of Justice, Office of Justice Programs, National Institute of Justice.

Denno, D. W. (2000). When bad things happen to good intentions: The development and demise of a task force examining the drugs-violence relationship. *Albany Law Review, 63*, 749–776.

Dryfoos, J. G. (1990). *Adolescents at risk: Prevalence and prevention*. New York: Oxford University Press.

Dunworth, T., & Mills, G. (1999). *National evaluation of Weed and Seed* (NCJ-175685). Washington, DC: U.S. Department of Justice, National Institute of Justice.

Dunworth, T., Mills, G., Cordner, G., & Greene, J. (1999). *National evaluation of Weed and Seed: Cross-site analysis* (NCJ-176358). Washington, DC: Department of Justice, National Institute of Justice.

Durlak, J. A. (1995). *School-based prevention programs for children and adolescents*. Thousand Oaks, CA: Sage.

Fagan, J. (1990). Intoxication and aggression. In M. Tonry & J. Wilson (Eds.), *Crime and justice: A review of research, drugs and crime* (Vol. 13, pp. 241–320). Chicago: University of Chicago Press.

Federal Bureau of Prisons. (1998). *TRIAD drug treatment evaluation. Six-month report: Executive summary.* Washington, DC: Department of Justice, Federal Bureau of Prisons.

Field, G. (1984). The cornerstone program: A client outcome study. *Federal Probation, 48,* 50–55.

Field, G. (1989). A study of the effects of intensive treatment on reducing the criminal recidivism of addicted offenders. *Federal Probation, 53*(10), 51–56.

Field, G. (1992). Oregon prison drug treatment programs. In C. Leukefeld & F. Tims (Eds.), *Drug abuse treatment in prisons and jails* (pp. 246–260). NIDA Monograph No. 118. Health and Human Services. Rockville, MD: U.S. Government Printing Office.

Gates, D. F. (1998). Some among us would seek to surrender. In J. A. Schaler (Ed.), *Drugs: Should we legalize, decriminalize, or deregulate?* (pp. 80–82). Amherst, NY: Prometheus Books.

Giannini, A. J., Miller, N. S., Loiselle, R. H., & Turner, C. E. (1993). Cocaine-associated violence and relationship to route of administration. *Journal of Substance Abuse Treatment, 10,* 67–69.

Goldstein, P. J. (1989). Drugs and violent crime. In N. A. Weiner & M. E. Wolfgang (Ed.), *Pathways to criminal violence* (pp. 16–48). Newbury Park, CA: Sage.

Goldstein, P. J., Brownstein, H. H. Ryan, P. J., & Bellucci, P. A. (1989). Crack and homicide in New York City, 1988: A conceptually based event analysis. *Contemporary Drug Problems, 16,* 651–687.

Goode, E. (2007). *Drugs in American society* (7th ed.). New York: McGraw-Hill.

Hansen, W. B. (1992). School-based substance abuse prevention: A review of the state of the art of curriculum: 1980–1990. *Health Education Research, 7,* 403–430.

Hawkins, J. D., Arthur, M. W., & Catalano, R. F. (1995). Preventing substance abuse. In M. Tonry & D. Farrington (Eds.), *Building a safer society: Strategic approaches to crime prevention* (pp. 343–427). Vol. 19 of *Crime and justice: A review of research.* Chicago: University of Chicago Press.

Heath, D. B. (1998). War on drugs as a metaphor in American culture. In J. A. Schaler (Ed.), *Drugs: Should we legalize, decriminalize or deregulate?* (pp. 135–154). Amherst, NY: Prometheus Books.

Heinle, K., Ferreira, O. R., & Shirk, D. A. (2014). *Drug violence in Mexico: Data and analysis through 2013.* San Diego: University of San Diego. Retrieved from http://justiceinmexico.files.wordpress.com/2014/04/140415-dvm-2014-releasered1.pdf

Hiller, M., Knight, K., & Simpson, D. (1999). Risk factors that predict dropout from corrections-based treatment for drug abuse. *Prison Journal, 79,* 411–430.

Hoag, C. (2014, Jan. 20). Throw away the key: Why America Is turning away from long drug sentences.Retrievedfromhttp://www.takepart.com/article/2014/01/17/political-will-turning-toward-sentencing-reform-more-needs-be-done.

Inciardi, J. A. (1979). Heroin and street crime. *Crime and Delinquency, 25,* 333–346.

Inciardi, J. A. (1995). The therapeutic community: An effective model for corrections-based drug abuse treatment. In K. C. Haas & G. P. Alpert (Eds.), *The dilemmas of punishment* (pp. 406–417). Prospect Heights, IL: Waveland.

Inciardi, J. A., Martin, S. S., & Butzin, C. A. (2004). Five-year outcomes of therapeutic community treatment of drug-involved offenders after release for prison. *Crime and Delinquency, 50*(1), 88–107.

Inciardi, J. A., Martin, S. S., Butzin, C. A., Hooper, R., & Harrison, L. (1997). An effective model of prison-based treatment for drug-involved offenders. *Journal of Drug Issues, 27,* 261–278.

Inciardi, J. A., Martin, S. S., Lockwood, D., Hooper, R. M., & Wald, B. M. (1992) Obstacles to the implementation and evaluation of drug treatment programs in correctional settings: Reviewing the Delaware KEY experience. In C. G. Leukefeld & F. M. Tims (Eds.), *Drug abuse treatment in prisons and jails* (pp. 176–191). Washington, DC: Government Printing Office.

Jensen, E. L., & Gerber, J. (1998). *The new war on drugs: Symbolic politics and criminal justice policy.* Cincinnati, OH: Anderson.

Johnson, B., Goldstein, P. J., Preble, E., Schmeidler, J., Lipton, D. S., Spunt, B., & Miller, X. (1985). *Taking care of business: The economics of crime by heroin abusers*. Lexington, MA: Lexington Books.

Knight, K., Hiller, M., & Simpson, D. (1999a). Evaluating corrections-based treatment for the drug-abusing criminal offender. *Journal of Psychoactive Drugs,31*(3), 299–304.

Knight, K., Simpson, D., Chatham, L., & Camacho, L. (1997). An assessment of prison-based drug treatment: Texas' in-prison therapeutic community program. *Journal of Offender Rehabilitation, 24*, 75–100.

Knight, K., Simpson, D. D., & Hiller, M. L. (1999b). Three-year reincarceration outcomes for in-prison therapeutic community treatment in Texas. *Prison Journal, 79*(3), 337–351.

Lawton, B. A., Taylor, R. B., & Luongo, A. J. (2005). Police officers on drug corners in Philadelphia, drug crime, and violent crime: Intended, diffusion, and displacement impacts. *Justice Quarterly, 22*, 427–451.

Lipton, D. S. (1995). *The effectiveness of treatment for drug abusers under criminal justice supervision* (NCJ 157642). Washington, DC: U.S. Department of Justice, Office of Justice Programs, National Institute of Justice.

Lipton, D. S., Falkin, G. P., & Wexler, H. K. (1992). Correctional drug abuse treatment in the United States: An overview. In C. G. Leukefeld & F. M. Tims (Eds.), *Drug abuse treatment in prisons and jails* (pp. 8–30). NIDA Monograph No. 118. HHS. Rockville, MD: U.S. Government Printing Office.

Lipton, D. S., Morales, E., & Goldsmith, D. S. (1989). *Pathways into treatment: A study of the drug treatment entry process*. Final Report of NIDA Project 1 R01 DA-03929–01. New York: Narcotic and Drug Research, Inc.

Luckenbill, D. (1977). Criminal homicide as a situated transaction. *Social Problems, 25*, 176–186.

MacAndrew, C., & Edgerton, R. B. (1969). *Drunken comportment*. Chicago: Aldine.

Martin, S. S., Butzin, C. A., Saum, C., & Inciardi, J. A. (1999). Three-year outcomes of therapeutic community treatment for drug-involved offenders in Delaware: From prison to work release to aftercare. *Prison Journal, 79*, 294–320.

Massing, M. (2000). *The fix*. Berkeley: University of California Press.

Miczek, K., DeBold, J. F., Haney, M., Tidey, J., Vivian, J., & Weerts, E. M. (1993). Alcohol, drugs of abuse, aggression, and violence. In A. J. Reiss, Jr. & J. A. Roth (Eds.), *Understanding and preventing violence: Social Influences* (pp. 377–570). Panel on the Understanding and Control of Violent Behavior, National Research Council. Washington, DC: National Academy Press.

Mumola, C. J. (1999, January). *Substance abuse and treatment, state and federal prisoners*, 1997 (Bureau of Justice Statistics Special Report). Washington, DC: U.S. Department of Justice, Office of Justice Programs.

Mumola, C. J., & Karberg, J. C. (2006). *Drug use and dependence, State and Federal prisoners*, 2004. Washington, DC: U.S. Department of Justice, Bureau of Justice Statistics.

National Center on Addiction and Substance Abuse. (1998). *Behind bars: Substance abuse and America's prison population*. New York: Columbia University.

National Institute of Justice. (2003). *2000 arrestee drug abuse monitoring: Annual report* (NCJ 193013). Washington, DC: U.S. Department of Justice, Office of Justice Programs, National Institute of Justice.

National Institute on Drug Abuse. (1981). *Drug abuse treatment in prisons*. Treatment Research Report Series. Washington, DC: National Institute on Drug Abuse, U.S. Government Printing Office.

Office of National Drug Control Policy. (2014). *2013 annual report, Arrestee Drug Abuse Monitoring Program II*. Washington, DC: Executive Office of the President.

Ousey, G. C., & Lee, M. R. (2004). Investigating the connections between race, illicit drug markets, and lethal violence, 1984–1997. *Journal of Research in Crime and Delinquency, 41*, 352–383.

Parker, R. N., & Auerhahn, K. (1998). Alcohol, drugs and violence. *Annual Review of Sociology, 24*, 291–311.

Parker, R. N., & Cartmill, R. S. (1998). Alcohol and homicide in the United States 1934–1995—Or one reason why U.S. rates of violence may be going down. *Journal of Criminal Law and Criminology, 88*, 1369–1398.

Pearson, F., & Lipton, D. (1999). A meta-analytic review of the effectiveness of corrections-based treatments for drug abuse. *Prison Journal, 79*, 384–410.

Petersilia, J., Greenwood, P., & Lavin, M. (1977). *Criminal careers of habitual felons*. Santa Monica, CA: Rand.

Prendergast, M. L., Hall, E. A., Wexler, H. K., Melnick, G., & Cao, Y. (2004). Amity prison-based therapeutic community: 5-year outcomes. *Prison Journal, 84*, 36–60.

Reiss, A. J., Jr., & Roth, J. A. (Eds.). (1993). *Understanding and preventing violence* (Vol. 1). Panel on the Understanding and Control of Violent Behavior, National Research Council. Washington, DC: National Academy Press.

Sampson, R. J., & Wilson, W. J. (1995). Toward a theory of race, crime and urban inequality. In J. Hagan & R. D. Peterson (Eds.), *Crime and inequality* (pp. 37–54). Stanford, CA: Stanford University Press.

Sherman, L. W., Gartin, P., & Buerger, M. (1989). Hot spots of predatory crime: Routine activities and the criminology of place. *Criminology, 27*, 27–55.

Simpson, D., Wexler, H., & Inciardi, J. (1999). Introduction. *Prison Journal, 79*, 291–293.

Tobler, N. S. (1986). Meta-analysis of 143 adolescent drug prevention programs: Quantitative outcome results of program participants compared to a control or comparison group. *Journal of Drug Issues, 16*, 537–567.

Tobler, N. S. (1992). Drug prevention programs can work: Research findings. *Journal of Addictive Diseases, 11*, 1–28.

Welsh, W. N., & Zajac, G. (2004). A census of prison-based drug treatment programs: Implications for programming, policy and evaluation. *Crime and Delinquency, 50*, 108–133.

Welsh, W. N., & Zajac, G. (2013). A multi-site evaluation of prison-based drug treatment: Four-year follow-up results. *Prison Journal, 93*, 251–271.

Welsh, W. N., Zajac, G., & Bucklen, K. (2014). For whom does prison based drug treatment work? Results from a randomized experiment. *Journal of Experimental Criminology, 10*, 151–177. DOI 10.1007/s11292-013-9194-z.

Wexler, H. K., Falkin, G. P., & Lipton, D. S. (1990). Outcome evaluation of a prison therapeutic community for substance abuse treatment. *Criminal Justice and Behavior, 17*(1), 71–92.

Wexler, H. K., Lipton, D., Falkin, G. P., & Rosenbaum, A. B. (1992). Outcome evaluation of a prison therapeutic community for substance abuse treatment. In C. G. Leukefeld & F. M. Tims (Eds.), *Drug abuse treatment in prisons and jails* (pp. 156–175). Washington, DC: U.S. Government Printing Office.

Wexler, H. K., Melnick, G., Lowe, L., & Peters, J. (1999). Three-year reincarceration outcomes for Amity in-prison therapeutic community and aftercare in California. *Prison Journal, 79*, 321–333.

White House. (2006). *National Drug Control Strategy: FY 2007 Budget Summary*. Washington, DC: Office of National Drug Control Policy. Retrieved Jan. 8, 2015, from http://www.whitehouse.gov/sites/default/files/ondcp/Fact_Sheets/FY2007-Budget-Summary-February-2006.pdf.

Wish, E. D., & O'Neil, J. A. (1989, September). *Drug use forecasting* (*DUF*), Research Update, January to March, 1989. Washington, DC: U.S. Department of Justice, National Institute of Justice.

CHAPTER 14

TERRORISM

Shortly after 9/11, it became a truism for many in the United States that "the whole world changed." In reality, terrorism has existed around the world for a long time and will likely continue to do so in the foreseeable future. What is true is that *awareness* of terrorism in the United States increased dramatically. It is critical to examine the use of power and propaganda in such conflicts. Across different nations and time periods, violence has often been used by the powerful to preserve existing power relations, but it has also been used by marginalized groups to challenge the status quo and initiate social change. In this sense, one person's terrorist may be another's freedom fighter, or vice versa.

On a continuum of scale, the most extreme example of group conflict involves open war between opposing political factions or entire nations. It is far beyond the intended scope of this single chapter to offer an examination of international conflicts, wars, or genocide. We do, however, distinguish what we believe to be some of the most important patterns, explanations, and interventions related to terrorism. As you read the three examples below, try to identify any common characteristics and possible explanations of terrorism.

---

1. Fifty-six people, including the four bombers, died in a coordinated series of terrorist attacks on London subways on July 7, 2005. More than 350 were injured. Experts agreed that the attacks were the work of al Qaeda. The attacks were almost certainly timed to disrupt the Group of Eight summit of world leaders being held in Gleneagles, Scotland. Like the coordinated train attacks of March 11, 2004, in Madrid, where 191 were killed, the London attacks targeted the capital of a country that is a member of the U.S.-led coalition in Iraq. As of July 28, 2005, antiterrorism officers in London had arrested 20 suspects in connection with another attempted transit attack, on July 21. No one was killed in those attempted strikes because the bombs did not detonate. In London, thousands of police officers flooded the streets to calm a jittery public as authorities warned that more attacks were possible. Officials said the operation was one of the largest deployments of police officers since World War II (Eggen, 2005).
2. At 8:46 a.m., on September 11, 2001, an airliner carrying some 10,000 gallons of jet fuel plowed into the North Tower of the World Trade Center in Lower Manhattan. At 9:03 a.m., a second airliner hit the South Tower. The Twin Towers, where up to 50,000 people worked each day, both collapsed less than 90 minutes later. At 9:37 a.m. that same day, a third airliner slammed into the western face of the Pentagon. At 10:03 a.m., a fourth airliner crashed in a field in southwestern Pennsylvania. It had been aimed at the U.S. Capitol or the White House and was forced down

(*continued*)

(continued)

by heroic passengers armed with the knowledge that America was under attack. More than 2,600 people died at the World Trade Center; 125 died at the Pentagon; 256 died on the four planes (National Commission, 2004).

3. On Feb. 26, 1993, a huge explosion occurred in the underground garage of the Vista Hotel at the World Trade Center complex in New York City. The bomb, consisting of 1,200 pounds of explosives, caused $500 million in damage, killed six people, and injured more than 1,000 people. According to the Federal Bureau of Investigation (FBI) agent who arrested Ramzi Ahmed Yousef, the convicted architect of the bombing, Yousef proudly admitted to being a terrorist. He stated that his only regrets were that the casualties and destruction had not been greater and that if he had had more money he could have built a bigger, more effective bomb (Kushner, 1998).

DEFINITIONS

Terrorism is a diverse, multifaceted concept that can potentially include many different behaviors and groups (Combs, 1997; FBI, 2014; Hoffman, 2006; Kushner, 1998; Laqueur, 2003; National Consortium for the Study of Terrorism and Responses to Terrorism [START], 2014; Schmid, 1983). Definitions of terrorism commonly include the following elements:

- Violent methods are used, intended to inspire fear and anxiety among a particular group.
- Those carrying out violent acts may include individuals, groups, or state officials.
- The immediate victims of violence are often not the main targets of the immediate act.
- The immediate victims may be chosen randomly or selectively (representative or symbolic targets).
- Violence may be motivated by idiosyncratic, criminal, or political reasons.
- Violence may be a strategy for making demands, gaining attention, or spreading propaganda.

We emphasize once again, however, that definitions of terrorism, like all social problems, are social constructions (Jenkins, 2003; see also Chapter 1). The definitions of terrorism offered by federal government agencies are important because they determine how incidents are measured, counted, and recorded. Section 2656f (d) of Title 22 of the U.S. Code defines two key terms. The term *terrorism* means premeditated, politically motivated violence perpetrated against noncombatant targets by subnational groups or clandestine agents. The term *terrorist group* means any group practicing, or that has significant subgroups that practice, terrorism. Terrorism is either domestic or international, depending on the origin, base, and objectives of the terrorist organization.

Domestic terrorism, according to 18 U.S.C. § 2331, refers to activities with the following three characteristics: (a) involve acts dangerous to human life that violate federal or state law; (b) appear intended (i) to intimidate or coerce a civilian population; (ii) to influence the policy of a government by intimidation or coercion; or (iii) to affect the conduct of a government by mass destruction, assassination, or kidnapping; and (c) occur primarily within the territorial jurisdiction of the United States (FBI, 2014). Well-known examples include Ruby Ridge, Waco, and the Oklahoma City bombings (Hamm, 1997, 2002).

EXAMPLE OF DOMESTIC TERRORISM: THE OKLAHOMA CITY BOMBINGS

On Wednesday, April 19, 1995, a yellow rental van exploded in front of the Alfred Murrah Federal Building in Oklahoma City, killing 168 people and injuring 850 others. Timothy McVeigh was pulled over on Interstate Highway 35 about 75 minutes later for driving without a current registration tag, and he was arrested for carrying a concealed weapon. A search of the car uncovered antigovernment propaganda and other evidence that eventually implicated McVeigh and accomplices as the Oklahoma bombers. The FBI affidavit filed in federal court stated that McVeigh was extremely agitated about the federal government's assault on the Branch Davidian compound near Waco, Texas, exactly two years earlier (Hamm, 1997). McVeigh was sentenced to death and executed on June 11, 2001. For his role in the plot, co-conspirator Terry Nichols was sentenced to 161 consecutive life sentences on August 9, 2004.

International terrorism typically refers to behavior that is directed by specific groups of people at other specific groups, usually with a specific goal or purpose. "International terrorism" is defined by 18 U.S.C. § 2331 as activities with the following three characteristics: (a) involve violent acts or acts dangerous to human life that violate federal or state law; (b) appear to be intended (i) to intimidate or coerce a civilian population; (ii) to influence the policy of a government by intimidation or coercion; or (iii) to affect the conduct of a government by mass destruction, assassination, or kidnapping; and (c) occur primarily outside the territorial jurisdiction of the United States, or transcend national boundaries in terms of the means by which they are accomplished, the persons they appear intended to intimidate or coerce, or the locale in which their perpetrators operate or seek asylum (FBI, 2014). Because such violence is largely but not exclusively a group-level phenomenon, we need to examine the individual, social, political, and historical conditions that can trigger, maintain, or promote violence between specific groups (Gurr, 1989).

PATTERNS AND TRENDS

A BRIEF HISTORY OF TERRORISM

Terrorism is inescapably a political concept—it is about the pursuit of power, the acquisition of power, and the use of power to achieve political change (Hoffman, 2006). The word was first popularized during the French Revolution, when a "reign of terror" referred to revolutionary, antimonarchy, and antigovernment activity before and after the war, resulting in 40,000 or so executions of "traitors" via the guillotine. The French Revolution fueled strong antimonarchy sentiments in Europe.

By the mid-1800s, the term was used to describe violent revolutionaries who revolted against governments. During the U.S. Civil War, civilian targets (e.g., railroads, factories) were attacked by both the Union and Confederate armies. By the end of the 1800s and early 1900s, *terrorism* was used to describe the violent activities of many diverse groups, including organized labor unions, anarchists, nationalist groups revolting against foreign powers, and ultranationalist political organizations (White, 2006). By the 1930s, the term came to refer to practices of repression used by totalitarian states (Italy, Germany, and Russia) against their own citizens (Hoffman, 2006).

During the late 1940s and 1950s, the word *terrorism* was used to describe numerous nationalist, anticolonialist groups that emerged following the post-World War II reorganization of Europe (Hoffman, 2006). Popular views on terrorism regained their "revolutionary" connotations. Many newly independent and would-be independent states argued that any group struggling against colonial oppression and/or Western domination should not be described as terrorists but as "freedom fighters."

Post-World War II campaigns by revolutionaries in Palestine, Cyprus, and Algeria were enormously influential around the world. Terrorism, despite claims to the contrary, was successful in gaining a global audience, pleading grievances, and compelling colonial governments to address issues that would have otherwise been ignored (Hoffman, 2006). Indeed, following a successful antigovernment campaign by the Irgun group, headed by Menachem Begin, future Prime Minister of Israel, Britain's rule over Palestine formally ended and the establishment of the State of Israel was proclaimed on May 15, 1948.

In the late 1960s and early 1970s, the Palestinian Liberation Organization (PLO) fueled the "internationalization" of terrorism, first with a hijacking of an Israeli El Al flight in 1968, then with the infamous Munich Olympic Games murders of 11 Israeli athletes in 1972 by Black September, a militant splinter group. Eighteen months after the Munich tragedy, the PLO's leader, Yassir Arafat, was invited to address the United Nations General Assembly. Shortly after that, the PLO was granted special observer status in the United Nations.

The PLO provided a powerful example. Within the decade, the number of terrorist groups operating internationally or committing attacks against foreign interests had more than quadrupled (Hoffman, 2006). For the first time terrorists began to travel regularly from one country to another; publicity was greater; limitations were fewer; attacks on civilians became more routine; and death tolls went higher. These changes were facilitated in no small part by technological advances in weaponry, communications, and transportation.

From the early 1960s to the early 1980s, the term *terrorism* was also used to describe various violent left-wing groups (e.g., the Weathermen, the Symbionese Liberation Army)[1] as well as various nationalist groups (White, 2006). Left-wing terrorism coincided with the counterculture movement of the 1960s and 1970s in Europe and the United States, and, in particular, a growing dissatisfaction with the excesses of capitalism and the inequalities it bred, not only domestically but between the "developed" and "undeveloped" world (Hoffman, 2006).

Interestingly, the PLO began training other terrorist groups during this period, partly for ideological purposes but also to make money. The PLO helped train various left-wing terrorists, including the Red Army Faction from Germany. By the early 1980s, at least 40 different terrorist groups had been trained by the PLO at various camps in the Middle East (Hoffman, 2006). Perhaps as a precursor to modern groups like al Qaeda, the PLO was one of the first terrorist groups to actively pursue the accumulation of capital as an organizational priority.

In more recent years, the term *terrorism* has begun to refer to broader, less distinct phenomena, including covert warfare whereby weaker states or groups confront larger, more powerful rivals (Hoffman, 2006). Indeed, terrorists often perceive themselves as reluctant warriors driven to violence against a repressive state, a rival ethnic or nationalist group, or an unresponsive international order by desperation and a lack of viable alternatives.

Terrorists fundamentally believe that they are serving a good cause designed to achieve a greater good for a wider constituency—whether real or imagined—that the terrorists and their organizations claim to represent (Hoffman, 2006). At a post-1972 Munich conference of United Nations states, a minority of states, including many Arab and various African and Asian countries, argued that "people who struggle to liberate themselves from foreign oppression and exploitation have the right to use all methods at their disposal, including force" (Hoffman, 2006, p. 45).

Terrorism has been around for centuries, and other countries can claim far more experience (and casualties) than the United States. Since 1992, terrorist violence in Algeria has claimed the lives of more than 75,000 persons (Hoffman, 2006). More than 3,000 people lost their lives in a mix of terror attacks, riots, and retribution during the height of conflicts in Northern Ireland (Gassman, 2006). Israel's Ministry of Foreign Affairs (2006) estimated that 1,122 people were killed and 6,845 injured as a result of Palestinian violence and terrorism between September 29, 2000, and May 1, 2006. The Palestine Red Crescent Society (2006) estimated that there were 4,202 Palestinian deaths and 30,698 injuries in the West Bank and Gaza as a result of Israeli incursions between Sept. 30, 2000, and Aug. 18, 2006.[2]

STATE-SPONSORED TERRORISM

The emergence of *state-sponsored terrorism* is one of the most important developments of recent years. Some governments have embraced terrorism as a deliberate instrument of foreign policy, a cost-effective means of waging war covertly through the use of terrorists as surrogate warriors or mercenaries (Hoffman, 2006).

In the United States, the designation of a country as a "state sponsor of terrorism" is made by the U.S. Department of State (2014) based on a determination that the government of a specific country has repeatedly provided support for acts of international terrorism. Once a country is so designated, it retains this distinction until it is rescinded in accordance with statutory criteria. A wide range of sanctions can be imposed as a result of this designation, including a ban on arms-related exports and sales, prohibitions on economic assistance, and financial and other restrictions. More information on "state sponsor of terrorism" designations may be found online (www.state.gov/j/ct/c14151.htm).

Following the Iran hostage crisis of 1979, during which 52 American hostages were held by fictional "militant Iranian students" for 444 days, "acts of violence, perpetrated by terrorists secretly working for governments, were shown to be a relatively inexpensive and, if executed properly, potentially risk-free means of anonymously attacking stronger enemies and thereby avoiding the threat of international punishment or reprisal" (Hoffman, 2006, p. 299). For the terrorists, the benefits of state sponsorship are even greater: Such relationships enhance the capabilities and operational capacity of otherwise limited terrorist groups.

Another major concern is with the acquisition and potential use of weapons of mass destruction (Hoffman, 2006; Milhollin, 2004; START, 2014). Such concerns are greatly magnified through state-sponsored terrorism and are nowhere today greater than in Iran (Karimi, 2006). Iran's refusal to halt its uranium enrichment program coincided with its determination to strengthen Islamic fundamentalism in the country. Echoing the rhetoric of the 1979 Islamic revolution, Iranian president Mahmoud Ahmadinejad urged students to push for a purge of liberal and secular university teachers.

TERRORIST TACTICS

Traditionally, terrorists have used diverse tactics, including bombing, hijacking, arson, assault, kidnapping, and taking hostages. In recent years, emerging tactics have included threats of chemical and biological weapons as well as weapons of mass destruction, including nuclear weapons (Milhollin, 2004). The disruption of services through electronic hacking (cyberterrorism) is an emerging threat (White, 2006). Terrorists can use the "instrumental tools" of technology and the media to create fear and gain publicity for their cause, but such tools can also provide avenues for attacks, given the dependency of many countries on computerized technology for major structural (energy and security) and financial (banking, stock markets) systems (White, 2006). The Internet may also serve as a valuable tool for terrorists attempting to radicalize others in support of their cause (Von Behr et al., 2013).

TYPES OF TERRORISTS

Osama bin Laden (1957–2011) was often described as the "CEO" of terrorists, applying modern business administration and management techniques to run his transnational terrorist organization (Hoffman, 2004a). As businesses in the 1990s moved toward flatter, more linear, networked structures, bin Laden did the same. He used both "top-down" and "bottom-up" strategies. In the former case, especially in high-visibility attacks, he functioned like a typical CEO, defining goals and aims, issuing orders, and ensuring implementation. Using the bottom-up approach, however, he also acted like a venture capitalist, soliciting ideas from below, encouraging creative approaches, and providing funding for promising proposals.

In al Qaeda, there was no one operational style and thus no one type of terrorist. Instead, bin Laden used at least four different types of personnel: (1) the professional cadre, (2) trained amateurs, (3) local walk-ins, and (4) like-minded insurgents, guerillas, and terrorists (Hoffman, 2004a). Each may be delegated different responsibilities and tasks, and each may be driven by different motivations and justifications (see the Explanations section).

The "professional" cadre refers to the most dedicated, committed, and professional soldiers of al Qaeda, entrusted with the most important and high-value attacks. The 9/11 attackers provide the exemplar (Hoffman, 2004a). Generally, such terrorist teams are carefully selected, provided with specific targeting instructions, and generously funded.

At the next level down, "trained amateurs" receive some training and funding, but they are distinctly less professional, less dedicated, less well supported, and more expendable than the professional cadre. An example is Ahmed Ressam, who was arrested in December 1999 at Port Angeles, Washington, after trying to enter the United States from Canada

(Hoffman, 2004a). Al Qaeda had provided him with basic terrorist training in Afghanistan and gave him open-ended instructions to attack some commercial aviation target in the United States. Ressam had targeted Los Angeles International Airport because he had passed through there once. He was given only $12,000 in "seed money" and was instructed to raise the rest of his operational funds from theft (e.g., stealing cell phones and laptops). He was also instructed to recruit members for his own terrorist cell. Richard Reid, who attempted to blow up an American Airlines passenger plane en route from Paris to Miami with an explosive device concealed in his shoe, was another trained amateur.

"Local walk-ins" refer to Islamic radicals who come up with an idea for a terrorist attack on their own and then pursue funding from al Qaeda. One example is the group of Islamic radicals who, with funding from al Qaeda, planned to attack tourists at the Radisson Hotel in Amman, Jordan, on the eve of the millennium (Hoffman, 2004a).

"Like-minded insurgents, guerrillas, and terrorists" include existing groups who benefited from bin Laden's support in myriad ways, including training, material (arms), or tactical support. Bin Laden provided such aid to radical Islamic groups to further his cause of global jihad (Hoffman, 2004a). Recipients of this revolutionary philanthropy included insurgent forces in Uzbekistan, Indonesia, Chechnya, the Philippines, Bosnia, and Kashmir. In return, al Qaeda occasionally called on the logistical services and manpower provided by such groups.

Hewitt (2004) makes another useful distinction, classifying terrorist organizations according to their social and political goals: (1) *nationalist-separatist groups*, (2) *revolutionary-leftist groups*, and (3) *reactionary-rightist groups*. These groups tend to be distinct in terms of the characteristics of terrorists, their campaigns, and their targets. National-separatists primarily seek changes in territories or boundaries related to desired independence and/or new political identities. They tend to see their land as occupied by foreigners who must be driven out. Hewitt's examples include EOKA in Cyprus, the Irish Republican Army (IRA) in Northern Ireland, and the ETA group in the Basque area of Spain. Revolutionary-leftists primarily wish to alter fundamental political and social relationships and governance within an existing state. These groups wish to overthrow the existing government and replace it with a structure sympathetic to the oppressed masses. Examples include the Tupamaros of Uruguay and the Red Brigade in Italy. Reactionary-rightist groups generally seek to defend existing power relationships and inequalities or return to a previous status quo. This category includes groups such as the Ku Klux Klan in the United States, loyalist groups in Northern Ireland, and neo-Nazi groups in Germany. Such groups seek to preserve existing power relationships to the benefit of a dominant group.

To the three types of terrorist groups identified by Hewitt we add a fourth: religious terrorists (Hoffman, 2004a, 2006). Extreme religious beliefs have strongly shaped the context of terrorism in recent years. In groups like the PLO and the IRA, religious affiliation is evident, but it is their political and ethnonationalist goals that are prominent. For many others, in increasing numbers, the religious motive and character are the primary features (Hoffman, 2006). *Religious terrorism* refers to terrorism motivated either in whole or in part by a religious imperative, where violence is regarded by its practitioners as a divine duty or sacramental act. Religious terrorism includes different means of legitimation and justification than secular terrorism (Hoffman, 2006).

Religious terrorists often have different motivations (violence as a divine duty, fundamentalist principles), targets (anyone outside one's own group, not just particular enemies), rewards (martyrdom), justifications (corruption of Islamic culture and principles), and restraints (less restraint against violence because the ends justify the means: wipe out the enemy). Religious motives for terrorism have become more popular as old ideologies such as communism lie discredited, whereas the promise of benefits from the liberal-democratic, capitalist state have failed to materialize in many countries throughout the world.

The Islamic revolution in Iran in 1979 changed the landscape considerably. The Iranian revolution has been held up as an example to Muslims around the world, exhorting them to reassert the fundamental teachings of the Koran and to resist the intrusion of Western influence (especially that of the United States) into the Middle East. The goal of the hard-core fundamentalists is the creation of a "true" Islamic state. "The world today is as others have shaped it," wrote Ayatollah Baquer al-Sadr, "We have two choices: either to accept it with submission, which means letting Islam die, or to destroy it, so that we can construct the world as Islam requires" (Hoffman, 2006, p. 131). Extremist religious beliefs can provide direct motivations and justifications for violence:

> For the religious terrorist, violence is first and foremost a sacramental act or divine duty executed in direct response to some theological demand or imperative. Terrorism thus assumes a transcendental dimension, and its perpetrators therefore often disregard the political, moral, or practical constraints that may affect other terrorists. Whereas secular terrorists, even if they have the capacity to do so, rarely attempt indiscriminate killing on a truly massive scale because such tactics are not consonant with their political aims and therefore are regarded as counter-productive, if not immoral, religious terrorists often seek the elimination of broadly defined categories of enemies and accordingly regard such large-scale violence not only as morally justified but as necessary expedients to attain their goals. (Hoffman, 2006, p. 129)

TERRORIST INCIDENTS

Although all violent crime statistics are social constructions (see Chapter 1), terrorist incidents are particularly difficult to count. Definitions of terrorism and counts inevitably reflect the political and social worldviews of the particular governments, agencies, and officials collecting them (Hoffman, 2006; Jenkins, 2003; START, 2014; Turk, 2004). Matters are further complicated by the difficulties associated with all comparative crime statistics, including the level of development or underdevelopment of data reporting systems in different countries, disagreements over definitions, and the degree of willingness or unwillingness of governments to share records (see Chapter 3). We focus on two major sources of data on international terrorism here, highlighting some of the difficulties involved with reliability.

First of all, U.S. law requires the Secretary of State to provide Congress, by April 30 of each year, a full and complete report on terrorism with regard to those countries and groups meeting criteria set forth in the legislation (U.S. Department of State, 2014). This annual report is entitled *Country Reports on Terrorism*. Beginning with 2004, *Country Reports on Terrorism* replaced the previously published *Patterns of Global Terrorism*. Section 2656f(b) of Title 22 of the U.S. Code authorizes the State Department to include in its annual reports on terrorism "to the extent practicable, complete statistical information on the number of individuals, including United States citizens and dual nationals, killed, injured, or kidnapped by each terrorist group during the preceding calendar year" (U.S. Department of State, 2014). This is satisfied through the inclusion of a statistical annex to the report that sets out statistical information provided by START, a Department of Homeland Security Science and Technology Center of Excellence based at the University of Maryland. From 2004 to 2011, the data for the Annex of Statistical Information were collected by the National Counterterrorism Center, part of the Office of the Director of National Intelligence, through the Worldwide Incidents Tracking System.

The challenges in collecting valid data on terrorism through official records encouraged researchers to seek alternative sources of data, particularly unclassified, open-source (e.g., media reports) research on terrorism (LaFree & Dugan, 2007, 2009). Beginning in June 2012, START contracted with the U.S. Department of State to collect a Statistical Annex dataset and provide a report to include in the State Department's annual *Country Reports on Terrorism*. Since 2001, START has maintained the Global Terrorism Database (GTD), an unclassified event database compiled from information in open-source reports of terrorist attacks. The first version of the GTD was released in 2006 and included information on worldwide terrorism from 1970 to 1997. START routinely updates and improves the accuracy of the data. The full GTD (1970–2012) and accompanying documentation are available to the public (www.start.umd.edu/gtd).

To count incidents of terrorism, START applies the definition of terrorism in 22 U.S.C. § 2656f (d)(2): "premeditated, politically motivated violence perpetrated against noncombatant targets by subnational groups or clandestine agents." The ability to track the specific groups responsible for each incident involving killings, kidnappings, and injuries is significantly limited by the availability of reliable open-source information, particularly for events involving small numbers of casualties (START, 2014). The quality, accuracy, and volume of incident reporting vary significantly from country to country. Further, determination of what constitutes an incident of terrorism is sometimes based on incomplete information and may be open to interpretation. Neither the perpetrator's identity nor his or her specific motivation, political or otherwise, is always clear. Moreover, additional information that surfaces over time may alter the initial classification of an incident as terrorist or not. Despite these limitations, tracking incidents of terrorism can help us understand some important patterns, including the geographic distribution of incidents and characteristics of perpetrators and their victims (U.S. Department of State, 2014).

The GTD staff compiled the Statistical Annex dataset to include violent acts carried out by nonstate actors that meet all of the GTD inclusion criteria: (a) The violent act was aimed at attaining a political, economic, religious, or social goal; (b) The violent act included evidence of an intention to coerce, intimidate, or convey some other message to a larger audience (or audiences) other than the immediate victims; and (c) The violent act was outside the precepts of International Humanitarian Law insofar as it targeted noncombatants (LaFree & Dugan, 2009). The term *combatant* refers to military, paramilitary, militia, and police under military command and control, in specific areas or regions where war zones or warlike settings exist. Further distinctions are drawn depending on the particular country involved and the role played by the military and police. Diplomatic assets, including personnel, embassies, consulates, and other facilities, are also considered noncombatant targets. Although only acts of violence against noncombatant targets are counted as terrorism incidents, if those incidents also resulted in the death of combatant victims, all victims (combatant and noncombatant) are tallied.

The statutory definition of terrorism also requires the attack to be *politically motivated*. Toward this end, the GTD uses two lists prepared by the U.S. State Department: (1) foreign terrorist organizations and (2) other organizations of concern. An act attributable to a group appearing on either list is deemed politically motivated. In addition, any serious attack by any organization or individual against a government/diplomatic official or a government/diplomatic building is deemed politically motivated and is thus considered terrorism.

Finally, as the wary reader may suspect, it is particularly difficult to gather reliable or comprehensive information about terrorist incidents in countries experiencing war or postwar insurgencies, and it is difficult to distinguish terrorism from other forms of violence, including criminal, tribal, and sectarian violence. The distinction between terrorism and insurgency in Iraq is especially challenging, as some Iraqis may participate in terrorist networks as well as in tribal and sectarian violence.[3]

Given these limitations, we turn now to major patterns of terrorism reported by START. In 2013, a total of 9,707 terrorist attacks occurred worldwide, resulting in 17,891 deaths and 32,577 injuries (START, 2014). In addition, 2,990 people were kidnapped or taken hostage. Among the 10 countries that experienced the most terrorist attacks in 2013 were Iraq, Pakistan, Afghanistan, India, and the Philippines (Table 14.1). Although terrorist attacks occurred in 93 different countries in 2013, they were heavily concentrated

Table 14.1 Ten Countries with the Most Terrorist Attacks, 2013

Country	Total Attacks	Total Killed	Total Wounded	Average Number Killed per Attack	Average Number Wounded per Attack
Iraq	2495	6378	14956	2.56	5.99
Pakistan	1920	2315	4989	1.21	2.60
Afghanistan	1144	3111	3717	2.72	3.25
India	622	405	717	0.65	1.15
Philippines	450	279	413	0.62	0.92
Thailand	332	131	398	0.39	1.20
Nigeria	300	1817	457	6.06	1.52
Yemen	295	291	583	0.99	1.98
Syria	212	1074	1773	5.07	8.36
Somalia	197	408	485	2.07	2.46

Source: National Consortium for the Study of Terrorism and Responses to Terrorism (START). (2014, April). *Annex of Statistical Information: Country Reports on Terrorism 2013* (Table 2, p. 4). Retrieved from http://www.state.gov/documents/organization/210288.pdf.

geographically. More than half of all attacks (57%), fatalities (66%), and injuries (73%) occurred in three countries: Iraq, Pakistan, and Afghanistan.

A second major source of data on terrorism is the Global Terrorism Index (GTI) produced by the Institute for Economics and Peace (IEP) (www.visionofhumanity.org). The GTI systematically ranks and compares 158 countries over a 10-year period to examine the impact of terrorism. The GTI, based on GTD data, includes information on more than over 104,000 terrorist attacks from 2002 to 2012. The GTI ranks countries based on four indicators weighted over five years: (a) total number of terrorist incidents; (b) total number of fatalities from terrorism; (c) total number of injuries from terrorism; and (d) estimated property damage from terrorism. Each of the factors is weighted between zero and three, with fatalities having the highest weighting, and a five-year weighted average is applied to reflect the lasting effect of terrorist acts over time (IEP, 2013).

The global impact of terrorism peaked in 2007 and has since leveled off (IEP, 2013). The biggest increase occurred from 2005 to 2007, largely driven by events in Iraq. Only 31 out of 158 nations experienced no terrorist incidents between 2002 and 2011. While as we noted terrorism is heavily concentrated in places like Iraq, Afghanistan, Pakistan, and India (Table 14.2), it is nonetheless distributed around the world.

From 2002 to 2011, the most frequent targets of terrorist attacks were private citizens and property (29%), government (17%), and police (14%) (IEP, 2013). Military installations and personnel were targeted in only 4% of incidents. According to IEP (2013), terrorism tends to be associated with low political stability, low intergroup cohesion, human rights violations, and high levels of group grievances.

In the decade since 9/11, fatalities from terrorist attacks increased by 195%, incidents by 460%, and injuries by 224% (IEP, 2013). Interestingly, the seven countries that have suffered the most fatalities due to terrorism since 9/11 account for nearly three quarters of deaths in this period, with Iraqis suffering the most (Fig. 14.1). However, terrorism fatalities have fallen by 25% since 2007, coinciding with the winding down of the Iraq war. During the past decade, the Middle East and North Africa have seen the highest number of fatalities due to terrorism, closely followed by the Asia-Pacific region.

Table 14.2 Ten Countries Most Affected by Terrorism, 2011

Rank	Country	GTI Score	Rank	Country	GTI Score
1	Iraq	9.56	6	Somalia	7.24
2	Pakistan	9.05	7	Nigeria	7.24
3	Afghanistan	8.67	8	Thailand	7.09
4	India	8.15	9	Russia	7.07
5	Yemen	7.30	10	Philippines	6.80

GTI = Global Terrorism Index.

Source: Institute for Economics & Peace. (2013). *2012 Global Terrorism Index: Capturing the impact of terrorism for the last decade* (Table 6, p. 12). Retrieved from http://www.visionofhumanity.org/sites/default/files/2012_Global_Terrorism_Index_Report.pdf.

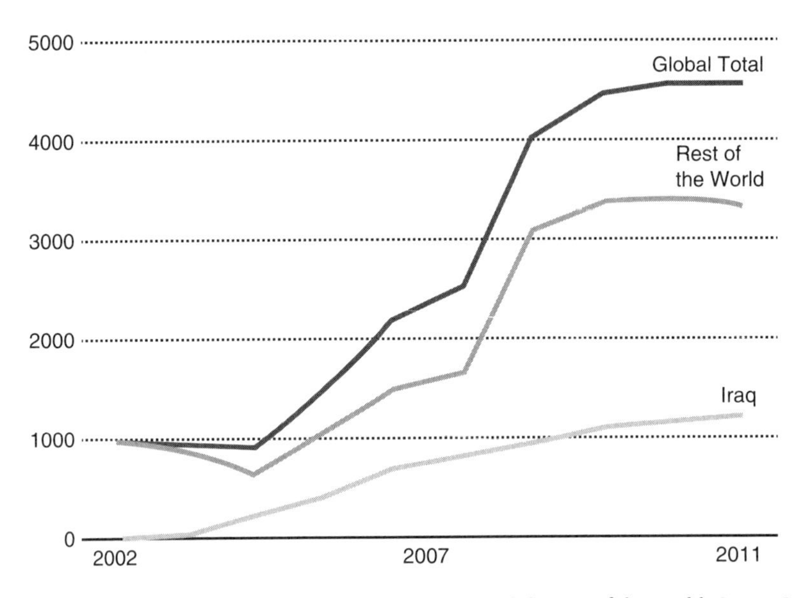

FIGURE 14.1 Number of terrorist incidents 2002–2011, Iraq and the rest of the world. *Source:* Institute for Economics & Peace. (2013). Global Terrorism Index: Capturing the impact of terrorism for the last decade (Chart 7, p. 23). Retrieved from http://www.visionofhumanity.org/sites/default/files/2012_Global_Terrorism_Index_Report.pdf..

EXPLANATIONS

STRAIN THEORY

Structural strain, or anomie, refers to societal processes that influence how individuals perceive their needs. In Merton's classical version of anomie, social structures may be inadequate to the degree that they generate discrepancies between widely held cultural goals such as success and the legitimate means to obtain those goals, such as hard work and a good education. Inadequate social structures generate strain, which is disproportionately (but not exclusively) experienced by those at the lower rungs of the social hierarchy. The gap between means and goals creates pressure toward nonconformity (deviant behavior), with the greatest pressure on those facing the greatest disjuncture.

Individual strain refers to the frictions and pains experienced by individuals as they attempt to satisfy their needs. Individual adaptations to strain include both deviance and conformity. A range of emotional and behavioral responses to strain are possible depending on an individual's social background and experience; his or her perceptions of goals, means, and opportunities; and his or her personality, social supports, and coping abilities (Agnew, 2005, 2006).

Adherence to extremist beliefs can be conceptualized as a particular adaptation to anomie or normlessness. In the "rebellion" adaptation, cultural goals and means are rejected, but new ones are substituted. Rebels attempt to alter society and create a new world where a new set of goals and means is adopted.

According to general strain theory, strains are *most* likely to result in crime when they (1) are seen as *unjust*; (2) are seen as *high in magnitude*; (3) are associated with *low social control*; and (4) create *some pressure or incentive to engage in criminal coping* (Agnew, 2001, 2005, 2006). First, sources of strain perceived as unjust are more likely to provoke anger, which increases the likelihood of violent coping (Agnew, 2001). An event is most likely to be seen as unjust when it involves the voluntary, intentional violation of a relevant justice norm. Second, strains of high magnitude reduce one's ability to cope in a nonviolent manner, reduce the perceived costs of violent coping, reduce dispositions to engage in nonviolent coping, and generate more anger. Third, strains associated with low social control include work in the secondary labor market, which is often accompanied by low pay, hard work, long hours, disrespectful or dangerous working conditions, and lengthy periods of unemployment. Such conditions facilitate low commitment to conventional norms. Fourth, strains may create pressure or incentive to engage in criminal coping when associated with exposure to others who model criminal coping and present beliefs favorable to criminal coping with that type of strain. Arguably, conditions in some regions of the Middle East meet many of these criteria, and the United States, rightly or wrongly, is often perceived by Arabs as a contributor to such strains (United Nations Development Programme [UNDP], 2005).

The first type of strain, unjust conditions, is particularly relevant. In particular, violent victimization is likely to generate perceptions of injustice. Inhabitants of most Arab countries have few rights and freedoms (UNDP, 2005, p. 9):

> Even disregarding foreign intervention, freedoms in Arab countries are threatened by two kinds of power: that of undemocratic regimes, and that of tradition and tribalism, sometimes under the cover of religion. These twin forces have combined to curtail freedoms and fundamental rights and have weakened the good citizen's strength and ability to advance.

Victims of oppressive political regimes in many Arab countries often cannot rely on the police or others to intervene on their behalf (UNDP, 2005). Democracy is often little more than illusion: "With a few exceptions, free presidential elections involving more than one candidate do not occur in Arab countries" (UNDP, 2005, p. 9).

Other conditions perceived as unjust include the presence of U.S. military forces and defense systems on Arab soil even before the U.S. invasions of Afghanistan and Iraq. The U.S. presence in the Middle East is strongly perceived as tied to exploitative economic interests in the area, particularly oil (UNDP, 2005). Many militant Muslims believe that the United States is guilty of war crimes for its support of Israel in its conflict with Palestine, and that legitimate Palestinian demands for land and an independent state have long been squelched by U.S. interests and actions in the Middle East (UNDP, 2005).

Strains of high magnitude are particularly likely to result in anger and violent coping. Three major strains have generated anger in recent years: the continued occupation of Palestinian territories by Israel, the U.S.-led occupation of Iraq, and the escalation of terrorism and civilian suffering (UNDP, 2005). The UNDP report reflects a good deal of anger about the Israeli–Palestinian conflict. During a series of strikes by Israel in the West Bank and Gaza in 2003 and 2004 (efforts that the Israeli government labels counterterrorism), 768 Palestinians were killed and 4,064 injured; 22.7% of those killed were under 18. The

Iraq war, according to UNDP (2005, p. 7), has increased suffering in a country already beset by misery: "As a result of the invasion of their country, the Iraqi people have emerged from the grip of a despotic regime that violated their rights and freedoms, only to fall under a foreign occupation that increased human suffering." As many as 100,000 Iraqis have died as a result of events associated with the war. A good deal of anger is directed toward the United States.

As the occupying powers proved unable to meet their obligations under the Geneva Conventions to protect citizens, Iraq witnessed an unprecedented loss of internal security, with killings and acts of terrorism in most parts of the country, including attacks against Iraqi and foreign civilians, international organizations, and humanitarian organizations (UNDP, 2005). The report further claims that thousands of innocent civilians were imprisoned and tortured at Abu Ghraib and other prisons.

Nor are Arab rulers immune from criticism. Post-9/11 antiterrorism strategies adopted by some Arab governments have resulted in further restriction of freedoms (e.g., censorship, prohibitions against protests) and human rights violations (e.g., abductions, torture, and imprisonment without trial) (UNDP, 2005). Many abductions or killings of citizens are never recorded; people just disappear: "The names of the victims are not mentioned, and no public investigation is conducted" (UNDP, 2005, p. 9). With the global war on terror, the report argues, the situation has worsened.

In many Arab countries, *low social control* contributes to strain. Governmental control over extremist groups is weak (UNDP, 2005). Even in Saudi Arabia, where Saudi leaders have close economic ties to the United States, leaders are hesitant to challenge hardline clerics and fundamentalist groups who preach anti-U.S. hatred because they are afraid of repercussions from large sections of their populace who have more than a grain of sympathy for the militants. Civilian casualties often outnumber those of combatants in armed confrontations between security forces and extremist groups (UNDP, 2005). Corruption, poverty, a lack of civic institutions and social services, and the perception that legal systems are biased and brutal provide conditions that terrorists exploit to create safe havens for terrorism, win sympathy, and gain new recruits (U.S. Department of State, 2014).

According to al Qaeda propaganda, the United States is a hegemonic, status quo power, opposing change and propping up corrupt and reprobate regimes that would not exist without U.S. backing (Hoffman, 2004a). Islamic militants also perceive a cultural onslaught against Islam, whereby the Western media (through television, movies, music, fashion, and the Internet) transmit immoral values contrary to the teachings of Islam. Contrary to arguments that bin Laden had no clear goals or sought only destruction of non Muslims (e.g., Bremer, 2004), bin Laden repeatedly (and prior to 9/11) stated three clear goals: (1) the removal of the U.S. military and other U.S. interests from Saudi Arabia and other countries in the Middle East, (2) the end of U.S. pressure on and sanctions against Iraq, and (3) the destruction of the U.S.–Israeli alliance and the strengthening of the Palestinians' battle against Israel (Nacos, 2004).

Many fundamentalist Islamic schools (*madrassahs*) provide for people's basic needs, including housing, food, financial support, and family support. They also provide a focus for people's rage (i.e., the United States) and *pressure or incentive to engage in violent coping.*

According to experts, many seminaries socialize the young to have strong anti-Western and anti-American sentiments, teaching them that the West is out to destroy Islam. As in many regions in the East, Pakistan's madrassahs have long offered free education and shelter to the poor (Worldwide Religious News, 2005). For many poor families living in areas where state schools do not exist or charge huge fees, madrassahs offer boys the best chance of an education, typically providing free board and religious schooling. Pakistan's estimated 10,000 Islamic seminaries came under increased scrutiny for fanning Islamic extremism following the discovery that at least one of the London bombers attended a madrassah.

Although researchers have not fully applied general strain theory to terrorism, Agnew (2004) has offered some valuable insights. He distinguishes between the "Arab street" and the "Arab basement." The "Arab street" refers to the broad mass of public opinion, which is largely pacifist (Friedman, 2002). In contrast, the "Arab basement" refers to small groups of hard-core ideologues, including Osama bin Laden and al Qaeda, who have retreated from the mainstream into subterranean campaigns of anti-Western hatred and violence. Arab leaders, according to Friedman, have become adept at coping with the Arab street. They know how to buy off or seal off its anger and how to deflect its attention onto Israel. The Arab basement, however, is more dangerous and uncontrollable. As Friedman (2002) states:

> These are small groups of super-empowered, angry men who have slipped away from the street into underground cells, but with global reach and ambitions. While issues like Israeli and U.S. policy clearly motivate them, what most fuels their anger are domestic indignities—the sense that their repressive societies are deeply failing, or being left behind by the world, and that with a big bang they can wake them up and win the respect of the world.

Although diplomacy may have some effect on the Arab street, the Arab basement is immune to such efforts: "It doesn't want a smaller Israel, it wants no Israel; it doesn't want a reformed Saudi monarchy, it wants no Saudi monarchy."

The appropriate choice of strategies to respond to terrorism, therefore, must include addressing the legitimate grievances of the Arab street: "The only sensible response is to defeat those in the Arab basement, who are beyond politics and diplomacy, while at the same time working to alleviate the grievances, unemployment and sense of humiliation that is felt on the Arab street, so that fewer young people will leave the street for the basement, or sympathize with those down there—as millions of Arabs do today." If America made clear that it was going into Iraq to empower Iraq's people to implement the recommendations of the Arab Human Development Report (UNDP, 2005), "The Arab basement still wouldn't be with us, but the Arab street just might." Arab states also have a large role to play; states must address the reasons for Arabs' lack of economic, political, and social development, including deficits of freedom, lack of women's empowerment, and the failures of modern education (UNDP, 2005).

If these arguments are valid, then it takes many years of political, social, economic, and human degradation to create the conditions ripe for terrorist groups to flourish. The so-called war on terror may thus require the "rehumanizing" of degraded societies by addressing the many acts of repression, obstruction, denial, marginalization, and autocracy that contributed to present conditions (Friedman, 2002).

Agnew (2004) suggests that further research on the factors that condition the effects of strain on terrorism might help us understand why so many strained individuals in the "Arab street" are drawn into the "Arab basement." Agnew acknowledges that such research will need to go beyond the variables normally considered by general strain theory to examine the responses of political regimes to the strains and social protests of their citizens.

The "poverty thesis" is a variant of strain theory, more closely related to Merton's original theory than recent formulations such as general strain theory (Agnew, 2005, 2006). Simply put, the poverty thesis suggests that poverty directly contributes to severe strain, and indirectly facilitates the harsh conditions that contribute to the growth of terrorism (e.g., the Arab basement). Competing arguments and evidence for and against the poverty thesis are briefly summarized below.

Jessica Stern of Harvard's Kennedy School is one proponent of the poverty thesis, although not the simplistic version that some critics incorrectly attribute to her. In testimony to the U.S. Congress shortly after 9/11, Stern (2001) argued that a war on terrorism must be fought on many fronts, including diplomacy, intelligence, and military strikes. Force, however, is not enough: "Failed and failing states are important sanctuaries as well as sources of recruits for extremist movements" (Stern, 2001, p. 127). Stern (2001, p. 130) argued that we can no longer afford to allow states to fail and conflicts to fester: "Extremists thrive when the state is no longer able to provide basic services, such as healthcare, education, and law and order. They also thrive on lingering conflicts, such as those in the Middle East, Afghanistan, Indonesia, and Kashmir." In short, *in addition to* diplomacy, intelligence, and military force, "We have a stake in the welfare of other peoples and need to devote a much higher priority to health, education, and economic development, or new Osamas will continue to arise" (Stern, 2001, p. 130).

Many Muslim scholars and politicians agree. One Hamas leader states: "It is enough to see the poverty-stricken outskirts of Algiers or the refugee camps in Gaza to understand the factors that nurture the strength of the Islamic Resistance Movement" (Pipes, 2004). In many countries where terrorism flourishes, militant Islamic organizations offer a wide range of welfare benefits (food, housing, protection, financial support) to potential recruits where governments fail to do so. Further, in a climate of destruction, war, unemployment, and depression, according to many Islamic scholars, "people seek solace, and they're going to Allah" (Pipes, 2004, p. 112). Former German Foreign Minister Klaus Kinkel stated that militant Islam reflects the economic, political, and cultural disappointment of Muslims. Israeli Foreign Minister Shimon Peres similarly argued that fundamentalism offers a way of protesting against poverty, corruption, ignorance, and discrimination (Pipes, 2004).

Poverty is not always the *primary* cause of Islamic violence, however (Pipes, 2004). For example, billions of dollars of economic assistance to the PLO have failed to stem militant Islam in that region. Further, Pipes argues, aggregate measures of wealth fail to predict where militant Islam is strong and where it is not. Many of the poorest Muslim states (e.g., Bangladesh, Niger) are not hotbeds of extremism. In contrast, many countries with flourishing economies (Saudi Arabia, Kuwait) are. A relatively small number of elites account for the vast majority of wealth and consumption in oil-rich countries, however (UNDP,

2005). Data on income inequality in Arab countries are sparse and incomplete, but even in Saudi Arabia, 21% of the population lives below the national poverty line (UNDP, 2005).

Further, many members of militant Islamic groups are fairly well off, not poor (Pipes, 2004). Pipes cites two studies by Egyptian social scientist Saad Eddin Ibrahim. One study of militant Islamists in Egyptian jails found that the typical member was in his early 20s, of rural or small-town background, from the middle or lower middle class, with high achievement and motivation, often with a science or engineering degree, and from a cohesive family. A second study found that 21 of the 34 members of a violent Islamist group had fathers with good jobs in the middle ranks of the civil service. Similarly, an examination of leadership of the militant Islamic group al-Jihad found that nearly all were university educated with middle-class backgrounds. These examples suggest that there is more activism among the well-educated middle classes than among the very poor.

Like previous generations of radicals in England, Italy, and Russia, militant Islam tends to attract competent, ambitious, motivated individuals who have become disaffected with Western lifestyles (Pipes, 2004). Certainly, the 9/11 hijackers failed to support the poverty thesis: Most came from wealthy families and had successful university careers. Many individuals who provide financial support for militant Islamic groups have substantial amounts of wealth at their disposal. Even suicide bombers come from mixed backgrounds, although few could be described as well off. Despite apparent wealth and success, though, many who join militant Islamic groups are on the fringes of elite society. They may have been excluded *socially and politically* rather than *economically*, and thus harbor a grievance.

Issues of identity and power rather than poverty may be paramount (Pipes, 2004). Driven by their own beliefs and values, Westerners too easily attribute the Arab world's problems to material issues like land and wealth, rather than religious and spiritual beliefs and adherence to principles. If anything, militant Islam recoils against the consumerism of the West, rather than turns toward it. Pipes argues that it is culture, religion, power, and identity that matter most. Islamists care more about where they stand in the world than about material wealth. Economic assets represent not the good life but strength to do battle against the West.

Silverman (2004) further discusses the importance of identity but is less dismissive of strain arguments. Many interpretations of the Qur'an are possible, he argues, but it is a distinctive subculture that provides terrorists with their identities and their ideational and physical resources. The 9/11 hijackers, for instance, perceived their actions as *jihad* (struggle) and *shahadat* (martyrdom) on behalf of Islam and its enemies. The militant Islamist subculture also provides a slanted understanding of the disputes and grievances that need to be resolved. Indeed, reactionary Islamic schools often provide the only education and the only version of Islam that youth receive. Major "identity-based" grievances include the existence of Israel and the lack of a society acceptable to Muslims. In response, militant Islam provides the justification for a "just war."

Militant Islam, however, thrives in authoritarian regimes with the least developed and open politics and the worst economic conditions for the average citizen (Silverman, 2004; UNDP, 2005). Examples include Saudi Arabia, Iran, and Egypt. Islamic revivalism in Iran arose as a response to the former shah's despotic rule. Iranian anger at the United States resulted from unwavering U.S. support of a monarch widely viewed by Iranians as an oppressive tyrant. In other places such as Lebanon, Afghanistan, Algeria, the West Bank, and the Gaza Strip, civil society has largely failed or never existed (UNDP, 2005). In such areas, militant Islam gives inhabitants an identity and a sense of what is expected and allowed in regard to behavior, and it focuses anger and frustration at a clear enemy (Silverman, 2004).

Similarly, Krueger and Maleckova (2003) argue that terrorism is less a direct response to poverty than a response to feelings of indignity and frustration developed in repressive environments. Of course, such a conclusion is perfectly compatible with general strain theory, even if the more narrow poverty thesis is questioned. A National Research Council panel (Smelser & Mitchell, 2002) argued that the regions most likely to display terrorist threats have a history of colonization, exploitation, and/or cultural penetration by Western interests. Such histories provide a credible focus for resentment and outrage (i.e., strain) in the mobilization of terrorist support.

Krauthammer (2004) argues that anti-U.S. sentiment is widespread, not just in the world of militant Islam. Much of this antipathy stems from the fact that the United States is the only remaining, unchallenged world superpower, and its economic and cultural dominance is often resented. The powerful nation-state, Krauthammer suggests, is seen by many as an archaic residue of an anarchic past and an affront to a domesticated international arena. The perception by many is that American dominance and power must be handcuffed. Such sentiments can be productively manipulated by terrorist groups like al Qaeda.

Although existing evidence for or against the poverty thesis is hardly conclusive, scholars so far have paid inadequate attention to the *different roles* that distinguish members of terrorist organizations (Hoffman, 2004a) and the *different types of terrorist groups* (Hewitt, 2004). We briefly return to two typologies discussed earlier.

Recall that Hoffman (2004a) distinguished among four different operational roles of terrorists: (1) the professional cadre, (2) trained amateurs, (3) local walk-ins, and (4) like-minded insurgents, guerillas, and terrorists. Some scholars point to the fact that most of the 9/11 hijackers came from middle- or upper-class families as firm evidence against the poverty thesis. In addition to being "bad science" (i.e., generalizing from a single incident involving only 19 individuals), such a conclusion fails to account for differences among the many individuals and groups involved in more than 11,000 terrorist incidents in 2005 alone. It is true that the 9/11 hijackers were mostly from middle- or upper-class backgrounds, but the same cannot be said of the hundreds of suicide bombers, the thousands of insurgents pouring into Afghanistan and Iraq, or the millions of citizens who sympathize with Islamic militants or vote them into political office, as with the election of Hamas in Palestine (Wilson, 2006). When one looks beyond the 9/11 hijackers (i.e., the "professional" cadre), one finds considerable evidence of strain, poverty, anger, injustice, and oppression (UNDP, 2005).

Similarly, Hewitt (2004) finds evidence that different types of groups draw membership (and sympathizers) from different class backgrounds. Although he looks at a limited number of terrorist groups, and includes none representative of the Middle East or militant Islam, his analysis is instructive. For example, the ranks of revolutionary-leftist terrorists are drawn heavily from the educated middle class (Hewitt, 2004). Of the Marxist Tupamaros in Uruguay, about one third were students and one third were professionals. Of 37 members of the

Italian Red Brigade "killed in action," 11 were students, seven were factory workers, six were unemployed, and the rest were professionals such as teachers or clerks.

Nationalist terrorists present a different profile (Hewitt, 2004). In Cyprus, for example, EOKA leaders tended to come from comfortable middle-class backgrounds, but their foot soldiers (guerillas) were overwhelmingly working-class or unemployed peasants. Of 68 EOKA members killed in action, only two were university graduates and only 24 had graduated from high school. Similarly, IRA members killed in action in Northern Ireland were of distinctly lower socioeconomic backgrounds. The most commonly documented occupation was unskilled laborer, and 89% came from wards listed as "areas of special need." Hewitt does not examine the membership of reactionary-rightist groups, but evidence suggests that many members of such groups (at least in the United States) tend to come from lower socioeconomic backgrounds (Hamm, 2002).

In short, available evidence so far is inconclusive, but simplistic arguments that terrorists in general and religious terrorists in particular come from upper-class backgrounds are untenable. Researchers so far have failed to account for critical differences among individuals and groups in their exploration of the poverty thesis more narrowly or strain theory more broadly. This remains a ripe area for further research.

SOCIAL LEARNING THEORY

As Akers and Silverman (2004) note, social learning theory is compatible with structural theories of anomie, conflict, or collective behavior. Social learning theory focuses on how attitudes and behaviors are learned though interaction with others, but such learning at the individual and group levels always occurs within a particular social and cultural context (see Akers, 1998, for further discussion).

Social learning theory proposes that criminal behavior, including terrorist acts, is acquired, reinforced, and maintained through interactions with significant others, especially one's primary group (family, peers, friends, and neighbors), but also through secondary agents of socialization (e.g., social, religious, and political organizations). Through such interactions, one may learn definitions favorable or unfavorable to deviant acts, including terrorism. These include attitudes and beliefs, rationalizations, justifications, and definitions of situations (e.g., suicide bombings) as right or wrong, moral or immoral, justified or unjustified, and ethical or unethical.

Religious terrorists, in particular, are heavily schooled in definitions conducive to anti-U.S. hatred and terrorism through the numerous Islamic schools and madrassahs discussed earlier (see also Stern, 2003). Some militant beliefs are so strongly held and promoted by groups that they compel one to act on them: "In the case of extremist and terrorist groups they are in the form of pushing negative in-group norms and attitudes toward out-groups to virulent extremes while discarding, neutralizing or counteracting whatever norms of constraint on means may be present" (Akers & Silverman, 2004, p. 21).

Differential reinforcement refers to the balance of rewards and punishments associated with the actual or perceived consequences of behavior. Rewards and punishments include not only the direct reactions of others but also the whole range of actual and expected, tangible and intangible, and symbolic rewards and punishments valued within specific subgroups. Rewards can result when one believes that violence fulfills important ideological, religious, or political goals, even anticipated transcendental rewards in heaven or hell. The greater the magnitude and salience of the reward, and the greater the frequency with which it is reinforced (through behavior, imitation, or teaching), the more likely is the behavior to be enacted. It matters little whether the supporting beliefs and definitions are true or untrue, but only that they acquire positive discriminative value and reinforcing properties for individuals. Thus, if militant Islamic groups teach that the United States is the great Satan waging war against all of Islam, and that attacks on U.S. interests and citizens are, in fact, acts that defend Islam, the veracity of this belief is irrelevant to its motivational impact on the members of militant groups.

Learning typically occurs through the indirect influence of the primary group, but it also occurs through direct training or tutelage (including the use of weapons and explosives, suicide bombing, and other terrorist techniques), indoctrination, and early childhood socialization. Extremist religious beliefs have a strongly reinforcing and mobilizing effect on adherents, and they are resistant to change (Hoffman, 2006).

Although rewards in many cases are ideological, material rewards are also possible. Suicide bombers are promised not only spiritual and transcendental rewards (paradise in the afterlife), but their families may receive cash bonuses of several thousand dollars donated by groups and governments sympathetic to their cause (Brooks, 2004). Islamist schools provide not only education but also free room and board. Stern (2001) provided this account in her post-9/11 testimony to Congress:

> The Taliban were actually born out of extremist madrassahs in Pakistan. These schools function as orphanages. Families that cannot afford to feed their children send them to these schools where they are not only educated but also clothed and fed. In the most extreme of these schools, which Pakistani officials estimate to comprise 10–15 percent of its religious schools, children are taught a distorted version of jihad. A child should be taught that jihad means doing your homework, helping the poor, and purifying the self. At these schools, children are taught about hate. . . . In a school that purportedly offered a broad curriculum, a teacher I questioned could not multiply seven times eight. Children that graduate from these schools are trained to be mullahs, but many of them can't find jobs. They are thus susceptible to their teachers' message that the best way to fulfill their religious duty is to fight on behalf of the Taliban or to join so-called *jihadi* groups. The children are also taught that Osama bin Laden is a hero. (p. 129)

Akers and Silverman (2004) further suggest that terrorism is moralistic violence that seeks to redress grievances and enforce the norms of the groups with which the terrorists identify and perceive others to have violated. In this sense, terrorist identities may be very strongly shaped by both religious and political ideologies that glorify their roles as freedom fighters and martyrs. Terrorism attempts to assert the worldview and subcultural norms of terrorists onto the larger culture or subculture, but also to bring about dramatic sociopolitical change. In this sense, terrorism is both identity-based, as others have argued, and instrumental. It is not the case that there are *no* goals, but rather that the goals are *ideological, religious, social, and political* rather than monetary or material in nature.

Social learning theory, therefore, proposes that terrorists adopt an identity promoted through extremist groups that includes attitudes, beliefs, and values that justify killing and injuring as a means to a noble end. Violence for political ends is accepted and rewarded (Stern, 2003). Extremist subcultures can provide both ideological and physical resources and a more or less coherent perspective on the grievances and struggles that are of central importance to the individual.

Although empirical support for social learning theory is widespread and cuts across many different cultures and settings, there is still little research that directly tests these principles as explanations of terrorism (Akers & Silverman, 2004). While there is much room for further research, Akers and Silverman argue that social learning theory does indeed account for at least some of the empirical patterns of terrorism already established, particularly the ideologies and attitudes favorable to violence and patterns of subgroup associations.

CONFLICT THEORY

Conflicts among dominant and subordinate groups may be resolved not only by consensual methods, but also by deception and force (Turk, 1982, 1990, 2004). Violence is a resource that may be used frequently or infrequently, effectively or ineffectively. In this view, terrorism and terror are associated with the breakdown of traditional authority structures and with efforts to create new ones. Although "critical" theories often presume that political and economic inequalities are the root causes of collective violence, "structural" conflict theories acknowledge that violence may be a product of strategic and tactical decisions in an ongoing conflict (Turk, 2004).

Awareness and resentment of political coercion and social inequality do not usually lead to terrorism, although lower-class socialization is more likely to reflect experiences of material and cultural deprivation and defeat, and higher-class socialization reflects experiences of privilege and success (Turk, 1982, 1990). Lower-class individuals are more likely to be resentful without actively resisting, however. Most subordinate persons do not readily move from resentment to resistance or violence. Within lower-class ranks, however, the imagery of terrorism is most likely to attract the young and the politically inexperienced, who have not internalized the accommodations of dominance and deference that characterize well-established authority structures.

An adequate theory of terrorism, according to Turk (2002), must develop an explanation of its causation, the dynamics of its escalation and deescalation in relation to other forms of political violence, and its impact on the stability and change of social orders. In Turk's scheme, it is necessary to analyze the social dynamics involved in the escalation from coercive to injurious to destructive violence. Terrorism is seen as the culmination of a conflict process that has escalated to an extreme form. This conflict, Turk argues, must end either in the annihilation of one party or mutual exhaustion. If participants must live in proximity and interdependence, survivors must search for a viable relationship.

This analysis seems appropriate to conflicts such as the Israel–Palestine conflict and the Northern Ireland conflict, among others. It is not clear, however, how the conflict between the United States and Islamic extremist groups such as al Qaeda might end according to this theory. Where disputants have only vague geographic ties, hold irreconcilable views, or fail to identify each other's grievances, the potential for long-lasting conflict is high. The only limits would seem to be the resources and human lives necessary to conduct terrorism and counterterrorism.

INTERVENTIONS

There is little doubt that extraordinary threats have been mirrored by extraordinary countermeasures (Turk, 2004). Post-9/11 responses to terrorism included the largest reorganization of government in the post-World War II era, a new Department of Homeland Security, new legislation (the USA Patriot Act), international cooperation to disrupt terrorist organizations and cells, and wars in Afghanistan and Iraq. Many counterterrorism measures are controversial (e.g., military actions and broadened government powers such as unauthorized wiretaps). According to critics, political pressures have resulted in the erosion of legal protections against intrusive and secret surveillance, arbitrary detention, hurtful interrogation methods, military action, assassination, and extralegal executions (Haque, 2002; Turk, 2004). Despite the enormous resources devoted to countering terrorism, surprisingly little empirical information is available on which strategies are most effective. In this section, we summarize major responses to date, including the 9/11 Report, the Patriot Act, military action, and diplomacy and international cooperation.

THE 9/11 REPORT

As the 9/11 Report (National Commission, 2004, p. 16) pointed out, the enemy is not just terrorism: "It is the threat posed specifically by Islamist terrorism, by bin Laden and others who draw on a long tradition of extreme intolerance within a minority strain of Islam that does not distinguish politics from religion, and distorts both." The commission advocated dismantling al Qaeda and prevailing over the ideology that contributes to Islamic terrorism.

The *9/11Report* concluded that the first phase of the U.S. response correctly included military action to topple the Taliban and pursue al Qaeda (National Commission, 2004, p. 17). A successful response in the long term, however, requires a multidimensional effort: "But long-term success demands the use of all elements of national power: diplomacy, intelligence, covert action, law enforcement, economic policy, foreign aid, public diplomacy, and homeland defense. If we favor one tool while neglecting others, we leave ourselves vulnerable and weaken our national effort." The commission thus proposed a three-pronged strategy: (1) attack terrorists and their organizations, (2) prevent the continued growth of Islamist terrorism, and (3) protect against and prepare for terrorist attacks.

Toward the first objective, the commission recommended that the U.S. government *identify and prioritize terrorist sanctuaries*, using national power and reaching out to other countries for assistance. For example, the commission stated bluntly that the United States should confront problems with Saudi Arabia in the open and build a relationship beyond oil that addresses human rights violations, exploitation, and repression in that country (UNDP, 2005).

To prevent the continued growth of Islamist terrorism, the United States and its allies must define their message and stand as an example of moral leadership in the world (National Commission, 2004). Such an effort requires cooperation from Muslim governments, which must offer opportunity, respect the rule of law, and tolerate differences (UNDP, 2005).

The virulent hatred expressed by many Muslims against the United States must be addressed. Toward this end, the commission argued that the United States must engage in much stronger public diplomacy to reach more people, including students and leaders outside of government. Part of this effort should include an agenda of opportunity that includes support for public education and economic openness. Such recommendations address some of the strains most conducive to violent coping (discussed earlier).

Further, the commission recommended that the United States develop a comprehensive coalition against Islamist terrorism, fashioning a common coalition approach on issues like the treatment of captured terrorists. Many critics have argued that the unilateral approach demonstrated by the United States following 9/11 was inadequate (Krauthammer, 2004). Reflecting the fear that followed 9/11, the commission recommended that the United States devote maximum effort to countering the proliferation of weapons of mass destruction. Many critics have since argued that concerns over these weapons were greatly exaggerated, especially in Iraq (Milhollin, 2004). Other recommendations included strategies to address terrorist financing, to more closely target terrorist travel through surveillance and other intelligence, and to develop stronger standards for the issuance of birth certificates and other sources of identification, such as driver's licenses.

The commission presciently suggested that the United States should determine, with leadership from the president, guidelines for gathering and sharing information in the new security systems that would be needed. Such guidelines, they cautioned, should integrate safeguards for privacy and other essential liberties. The commission warned that as government power necessarily expands in certain ways, the burden of retaining such powers remains on the executive to demonstrate the value of such powers and ensure adequate supervision of how they are used.

To achieve these goals, the commission recommended a broad reorganization of government. For example, the commission recommended unifying strategic intelligence and operational planning within a National Counterterrorism Center and strengthening the FBI and homeland defenders. Responsibility for America's national defense is now shared by the Department of Defense and by the Department of Homeland Security. The Department of Homeland Security and its oversight committees assess the types of threats the country faces to determine the adequacy of the government's plans and the readiness of the government to respond to those threats.

THE PATRIOT ACT

One of the most controversial responses to 9/11 was the USA Patriot Act of 2001 (its full name is "Uniting and Strengthening America by Providing Appropriate Tools Required to Intercept and Obstruct Terrorism"). This act was far-reaching, consisting of more than 150 sections. Changes were made to national security authorities, the substantive criminal law, immigration law, money laundering statutes, victim assistance statutes, and other areas (FBI, 2002).

On the national security front, modifications under the Patriot Act aimed at improving the process by which federal law enforcement officials obtain legal authority for conducting surveillance, searching for agents of a foreign power, strengthening the sharing and coordination of information at the national level, and issuing subpoenas for records related to national security investigations.

The act made important changes to the Foreign Intelligence Surveillance Act (FISA) of 1978. FISA provides a formal procedure, approved by Congress, for the government to obtain court orders authorizing the use of electronic surveillance and physical searches within the United States to obtain "foreign intelligence information" (FBI, 2002). This statute had previously been interpreted to mean that the gathering of foreign intelligence information, rather than criminal prosecution, had to be the primary purpose for requesting surveillance or search authority under FISA. Under changes specified by Section 218 of the Patriot Act, the gathering of foreign intelligence now must be a "significant" purpose for requesting an order from the FISA Court. As a result, personnel involved in FISA surveillance or searches are now allowed to consult with law enforcement officials to coordinate efforts to investigate or protect against attacks, terrorism, sabotage, or clandestine intelligence activities.

Other modifications to FISA include expanding the number of judges who review applications for FISA orders from seven to 11; extending the duration of electronic surveillance and search orders for certain categories of individuals determined to be agents of a foreign power; granting "roving" authority that allows the FBI to serve orders on communications carriers, including telephone carriers, cellphones, or Internet accounts; and modifying the type of business records that can be subpoenaed.

The definition of a federal crime of terrorism was modified to include offenses likely to be committed by terrorists, including a number of aircraft crimes and computer crimes. New federal offenses included attacking mass transportation systems, vehicles, facilities, or passengers; harboring or concealing persons who have committed or are about to commit a variety of terrorist offenses; expanding the prohibition on providing material support or resources to terrorists to include expert advice and assistance; and possessing a biological agent or toxin of a type or in a quantity that is not reasonably justified. The International Money Laundering Abatement and Financial Anti-Terrorism Act of 2001 was also incorporated into the Patriot Act to increase America's ability to combat the financing of terrorism (FBI, 2002).

The Patriot Act made it easier for the FBI to conduct secret searches, monitor telephone calls and emails, and obtain bank records and other personal documents in connection with terrorism investigations. Critics contended, however, that some of the counterterrorism policies eroded the same freedoms ostensibly being defended in the war against terrorism: "Regard for legalities has been subordinated to concerns with assessing levels of threat and with the demonstrated shortcomings of intelligence agencies in making and responding to such assessments" (Turk, 2004, p. 282). The provisions that were most heavily criticized included the increased monitoring of electronic communications, financial transactions, and educational records; the secret taping of attorney–client exchanges; the creation of military tribunals with the authority to try and sentence both foreign nationals and American citizens defined as enemy combatants; and the relaxing of the prohibition of assassination to permit the extralegal killing of suspected terrorists, whether foreigners or citizens. The latter provision was used to partly justify the killing of Osama bin Laden in 2011 (Silverleib, 2011).

Initial efforts to renew the act in 2005 collapsed in the Senate when four Republicans joined Democrats to block action following a *New York Times* report that President Bush had signed a secret order in 2002 authorizing the National Security Agency to eavesdrop on U.S. citizens and foreign nationals in the United States (Babington, 2005). Many felt that this executive order far exceeded the limits of the president's legal and constitutional authority. President Bush responded that he did not need explicit permission from Congress or the courts to establish a secret domestic surveillance program to eavesdrop on suspected terrorists. Bush vowed to continue the program and expressed outrage that it had become public, calling its disclosure to the media a shameful act. Jonathan Turley, a George Washington University law professor and a specialist in surveillance law, disagreed: "The President's dead wrong. It's not a close question. Federal law is clear" (Hutcheson, 2005, p. A01). The sharpest disagreements centered on broad provisions allowing the FBI to obtain records on terrorism suspects. Suspects, regardless of evidence of terrorist ties, would have very limited options for challenging searches.

In what many regard as the largest security breach in U.S. history, and what others regard as a courageous blow struck for freedom, the U.S. government faced intensive scrutiny and outrage in 2013 following unauthorized disclosures about the full extent of its national surveillance program by former National Security Agency contractor Edward Snowden (Wilson & Goldfarb, 2013). President Obama later announced plans to work on ways to tighten the provision of the Patriot Act, known as Section 215, that permitted the government to obtain the phone records of millions of Americans (Wilson & Goldfarb, 2013). He announced the creation of a panel of outsiders—former intelligence officials, civil liberties and privacy advocates, and others—to assess the programs and suggest changes by the end of the year. The National Security Agency, among the most secretive institutions in government, also released a summary of the programs it operates under provisions of FISA and the Patriot Act. Intelligence agencies also said they would set up a website with the goal of better explaining their legal authorities and actions.

MILITARY ACTION

Although Article 51 of the United Nations Charter grants nations the right of self-defense, scholars continue to debate whether the United States was legally justified under international law to undertake military action in Afghanistan and Iraq (Bremer, 2004; Ulfstein, 2004). The Bush administration offered three main reasons for the decision to invade Iraq (Jenkins, 2003): (1) Saddam Hussein was thought to be manufacturing and hiding weapons of mass destruction; (2) world support for the war against Iraq was widespread; and (3) the Iraqi regime was thought to be closely tied to al Qaeda and other terrorist groups. All three arguments have been sharply disputed.

First, no evidence of weapons of mass destruction was found either before or after the war (Kull et al., 2003–2004). Second, the unilateral decision to invade Iraq without approval from the United Nations Security Council was a huge departure from generally accepted international norms (Turk, 2004). Third, a 2006 Senate Intelligence Committee report stated that "Iraq has no past, current, or anticipated future contact with Osama bin Laden and al Qaeda" (Pincus, 2006). In fact, according to the report, Saddam Hussein considered bin Laden an enemy of the Baghdad regime. Although many agree that an effective counterterrorism strategy must include a broad range of national and international initiatives, there is much disagreement over the appropriate balance of diplomacy versus force (Bremer, 2004; Hoffman, 2004b; Turk, 2004). Postinvasion violence and insurgencies in Afghanistan and Iraq have led to acrimonious debates over military responses (Turk, 2004).

Overreliance on military solutions may actually backfire and worsen the problem. The National Intelligence Estimate, a bipartisan assessment by 16 U.S. government intelligence agencies, found that the overall terrorist threat actually grew following the U.S. invasions in Iraq and Afghanistan (Mazzetti, 2006). Approved by the Director of National Intelligence, National Intelligence Estimates are the most authoritative documents produced on national security issues. The report confirmed predictions of a National Intelligence Council report completed in January 2003, two months before the Iraq invasion. That report stated that the approaching war had the potential to increase support for militant Islam and terrorism worldwide.

The National Intelligence Estimate indicated that the Iraq war actually fueled Islamic radicalism. The radical Islamic movement expanded from a core of al Qaeda operatives and affiliated groups to include a new class of "self-generating" cells inspired by al Qaeda's leadership but without any direct connection to Osama bin Laden or his top lieutenants. This group closely resembles the "like-minded insurgents and guerillas" described by Hoffman (2004a). The National Intelligence Council had previously released a study concluding that Iraq had become the primary training ground for the next generation of terrorists, and that veterans of the Iraq war might ultimately overtake al Qaeda in the global jihad leadership. Other actions that stoked the jihad movement included the indefinite detention of prisoners at Guantánamo Bay and the Abu Ghraib prisoner abuse scandal. The judgments of the Intelligence Estimate were consistent with assessments of global terrorist threats by U.S. allies and independent terrorism experts (Mazzetti, 2006).

DIPLOMACY AND INTERNATIONAL COOPERATION

Although many disagree about military action, most agree that the U.S. counterterrorism strategy must also focus on "rebuilding the international consensus against terrorism that flourished briefly during the 1980s, but then fell into neglect" (Bremer, 2004, p. 248). Through regional and international partnerships, the United States is attempting to build networks that undermine, marginalize, and isolate terrorists; discredit terrorist ideology; and empower legitimate alternatives to extremism (U.S. Department of State, 2014). Four major types of counterterrorism initiatives are summarized by the U.S. Department of State (2014): (a) countering violent extremism (CVE), (b) capacity-building programs, (c) regional strategic initiative, and (d) international conventions and protocols. We provide a brief overview of each.

Countering Violent Extremism

CVE is part of a strategic approach that aims to deny terrorist groups new recruits. In 2009, the State Department created a CVE team in the Counterterrorism Bureau. CVE programming has three main goals: (1) build resilience among communities most at risk of recruitment and radicalization to violence, (2) counter terrorist narratives and messaging, and (3) build the capacity of partner nations and civil society to counter violent extremism. A major emphasis is the support of local efforts and building local capacity. Efforts include a broad range of international partners, including other governments, multilateral organizations, and nongovernmental actors.

One major initiative is the Center for Strategic Counterterrorism Communications, established in 2011 to lead an interagency effort to coordinate, orient, and inform government-wide foreign communications activities targeted against terrorism and violent extremism. This group attempts to counter terrorist propaganda in the social media environment, contesting space where terrorist groups are active. In 2013, the center produced over 10,000 Internet postings and 138 videos. It also engages in a variety of projects directly supporting U.S. government communicators working with overseas audiences, as well as supporting local initiatives in critical parts of the Middle East and Africa. Key areas of programming include community engagement and community-oriented policing, and media and CVE messaging.

The U.S. Department of State implements community development projects that link marginalized groups with responsible leaders in their communities to build their resilience to violent extremism and improve their capacity to counter it. Activities include providing skills training to youth, their families, and their communities; leadership development; and promoting problem-solving and conflict resolution skills. Projects also include mentoring and training law enforcement personnel in community engagement, facilitation and conflict mitigation, and communication techniques (U.S. Department of State, 2014).

The U.S. Department of State also supports media projects that reach large audiences who are facing a looming violent extremist threat. In West Africa, for example, projects include weekly radio dramas that are produced locally and are designed to empower locally credible voices that reject violent extremism. They include call-in shows with representatives from educational institutions and government officials in discussions about CVE, peace, and stability (U.S. Department of State, 2014).

A number of multilateral bodies are key partners for the U.S. Department of State in these CVE efforts. For example, the Global Counterterrorism Forum (GCTF) provides a platform for counterterrorism policymakers and experts to identify urgent needs, devise solutions, and mobilize resources for addressing key counterterrorism challenges. The

GCTF's CVE Working Group, one of five expert-driven groups, focuses on (a) using institutions to counter violent extremism, (b) measuring the impact of CVE programs, and (c) countering extremist narratives.

The United Nations is a close partner of and participant in the GCTF and its activities. The GCTF serves as a mechanism for implementing the universally agreed-upon United Nations Global Counter-Terrorism Strategy, and the GCTF complements and reinforces existing multilateral counterterrorism efforts, starting with those of the United Nation. The GCTF also partners with a wide range of regional multilateral organizations, including the Council of Europe, the Organization for Security and Cooperation in Europe (OSCE), the African Union (AU), and the Inter-Governmental Authority on Development. Other GCTF accomplishments since its launch in 2011 include the adoption of six sets of good practices intended both to provide practical guidance for countries seeking to enhance their counterterrorism capacity and to bring greater strategic coherence to global counterterrorism capacity-building efforts (U.S. Department of State, 2014).

With support from GCTF members and international partners, the United Arab Emirates launched the first international CVE Center of Excellence, Hedayah, in December 2012. Hedayah's mandate covers CVE research, dialog, and training. The U.S. Department of State supports Hedayah with funding to develop pilot training courses for governmental and nongovernmental CVE practitioners in the areas of community-oriented policing, education, youth development, and media. More information on the GCTF and Hedayah can be found at http://www.thegctf.org/.

The Global Community Engagement and Resilience Fund, launched in 2013, is the first ever public–private global effort to support grassroots CVE projects. This fund will leverage public and private sector support for community-based projects aimed at addressing local drivers of radicalization by focusing on education, vocational training, civic engagement, and women's advocacy.

Capacity-Building Programs

The success of counterterrorism efforts depends in large part on the effectiveness and ability of successful international partnerships (U.S. Department of State, 2014). High-priority efforts include improvements to partners' law enforcement and border security capabilities to tackle terrorist threats. Capacity-building programs currently include the Antiterrorism Assistance Program, Counterterrorist Finance, Counterterrorism Engagement, the Terrorist Interdiction Program/Personal Identification Secure Comparison and Evaluation System, and transnational activities under the Regional Strategic Initiatives. For further information on these programs, see the Annual Report on Assistance Related to International Terrorism (www.state.gov/j/ct/rls/other/rpt/221544.htm).

Regional Strategic Initiative

Because terrorist groups often take advantage of porous borders and ungoverned areas between countries, the Bureau of Counterterrorism created the Regional Strategic Initiative to encourage the development of regional approaches to counterterrorism. These initiative groups operate in key areas to assess threats; pool resources; and devise collaborative strategies, action plans, and policy recommendations. In 2013, groups were in place for Central Asia, East Africa, Eastern Mediterranean, Iraq and its neighbors, South Asia, Southeast Asia, the Trans-Sahara (the Maghreb and the Sahel), and the Western Hemisphere (U.S. Department of State, 2014). The Regional Strategic Initiative also funds resident legal advisors in Malaysia, Mauritania, Niger, and Turkey, and supports regional workshops focusing on border security and larger counterterrorism issues. These forums provide a venue for participants to discuss current counterterrorism issues, as well as joint efforts to fight terrorism.

International Conventions and Protocols

International law and legal guidelines have developed considerably over the past 20 years, although gaining international approval, ratification, and implementation of these principles is difficult (e.g., the 1980 Convention on the Physical Protection of Nuclear Material). A matrix of the ratification status of 16 of the international conventions and protocols related to terrorism can be found here: https://www.unodc.org/tldb/universal_instruments_NEW.html.

CONCLUSIONS

A comprehensive counterterrorism strategy must be multifaceted and balanced in its approach, and such a strategy will require considerable national and international cooperation and resources. There is little doubt that force alone will be insufficient to combat terrorism at home or abroad.

The most common response by the state to outbreaks of violence has been to suppress or control them. The greater the perceived threat to the nation's political and economic institutions, the greater the response. The prolonged use of force by any group as a means of social control, however, may impede and even prevent reform, because it will elicit strong, defensive counter-violence. Long-term solutions must address the underlying causes that give rise to grievances, and optimal strategies must include a mix of control and remedial strategies (Gurr, 1979).

An effective counterterrorism strategy must attempt to understand the inner logic that motivates terrorists (whether we agree with it or not), develop countermeasures to reduce fear, develop realistic expectations and responses, and address hostility toward the United States through a comprehensive program of international, multilateral diplomacy (Hoffman, 2004b). Terrorism is unlikely to be defeated any time soon, and counter-efforts must continually evolve and adapt (Hoffman, 2004a).

Even in a highly politicized arena, progress can be made if pundits agree on a few simple guiding principles. Toward this end, we emphasize once again that the development of effective and just interventions should be guided by a sound appraisal of patterns and causes. Otherwise we run the risks of ineffectiveness, outrageous expense, questionable morality, and perhaps making things worse.

DISCUSSION QUESTIONS

1. Define (a) *domestic terrorism*, (b) *international terrorism*, (c) *terrorist incident*.
2. Discuss the different types of terrorists and terrorist groups identified by Hewitt and others. Why are these distinctions important?
3. Is terrorism *increasing or decreasing*? How can you tell? Give specific evidence.
4. Discuss how (a) strain theory, (b) social learning theory, and (c) conflict theory help explain terrorism. Use specific evidence and examples from course materials.
5. What is the "poverty thesis"? Discuss arguments for and against this thesis.
6. (a) Describe major efforts to combat international terrorism. (b) Which, if any, of these strategies is likely to be successful, in your opinion? Why (or why not)? Use specific evidence and examples from course materials to illustrate your answer.

SUGGESTED READINGS

Hamm, M. S. (2002). *In bad company: America's terrorist underground*. Boston: Northeastern University Press.

Hoffman, B. (2006). *Inside terrorism*. New York: Columbia University Press.

LaFree, G., & Dugan, L. (2009). Research on terrorism and countering terrorism. In M. Tonry (Ed.), *Crime and justice: A review of research, Vol. 38* (pp. 413–477). Chicago: University of Chicago Press.

U.S. Department of State. (2014, April). *Country Reports on Terrorism, 2013: Executive Summary*. U.S. Department of State, Bureau of Counterterrorism. Retrieved from www.state.gov/j/ct/rls/crt/index.htm.

NOTES

1. On February 4, 1974, the Symbionese Liberation Army kidnapped 19-year-old Berkeley history major and newspaper heiress Patricia Hearst. The group's leader, Donald DeFreeze, wanted to start a revolution of the underprivileged, and he intended to do that by declaring war on those with status and money. Similarly, working in tightly constructed cells dispersed around the country, the Weathermen employed strategically targeted violence during the 1970s in an effort to overthrow the U.S. government.
2. The Palestine Red Crescent Society is a national humanitarian society that provides a wide range of health, social, and other humanitarian services for the Palestinian people throughout the Middle East. The society is a member of the International Federation of the Red Cross and Red Crescent Societies.
3. For example, many Iraqis participated in the al Qaeda-sponsored terror network headed by Abu Musab al-Zarqawi as well as sectarian violence between Shiite and Sunni Muslims. Zarqawi took responsibility for directing numerous acts of terrorism in Iraq and Jordan, including suicide bombings and the killing of soldiers, police officers, and civilians. Zarqawi was killed on June 7, 2006, near the city of Baquba, Iraq, by a U.S. air strike.

REFERENCES

Agnew, R. (2001). Building on the foundation of general strain theory: Specifying the types of strain most likely to lead to crime and delinquency. *Journal of Research in Crime and Delinquency, 38*, 319–361.

Agnew, R. (2004). A general strain theory approach to violence. In M. A. Zahn, H. H. Brownstein, & S. L. Jackson (Eds.), *Violence:From theory to research* (pp. 37–50). Cincinnati, OH: Lexis-Nexis/Anderson.

Agnew, R. (2005). *Why do criminals offend? A general theory of crime and delinquency.* Los Angeles: Roxbury.

Agnew, R. (2006). *Pressured into crime: An overview of general strain theory.* Los Angeles: Roxbury.

Akers, R. L. (1998). *Social learning and social structure: A general theory of crime and deviance.* Boston: Northeastern University Press.

Akers, R. L., & Silverman, A. L. (2004). Toward a social learning model of violence and terrorism. In M. A. Zahn, H. H. Brownstein, & S. L. Jackson (Eds.), *Violence: From theory to research* (pp. 19–35). Cincinnati, OH: LexisNexis/Anderson.

Babington, C. (2005, Dec. 18). Closed-door meetings follow roadblock of Patriot Act. *Washington Post.* Retrieved from http://msl1.mit.edu/furdlog/docs/washpost/2006-03-08_washpost_patriot_renewal.pdf.

Bremer, L. P. (2004). A new strategy for the new face of terrorism. In G. Martin (Ed.), *The new era of terrorism: Selected readings* (pp. 243–248). Thousand Oaks, CA: Sage.

Brooks, D. (2004). The culture of martyrdom: How suicide bombing became not just a means but an end. In G. Martin (Ed.), *The new era of terrorism: Selected readings* (pp. 143–147). Thousand Oaks, CA: Sage.

Combs, C. C. (1997). *Terrorism in the twenty-first century.* Upper Saddle River, NJ: Prentice-Hall.

Eggen, D. (2005, June 29). Nine more held in second London subway attacks. *Washington Post.* Retrieved June 30, 2014 from http://www.washingtonpost.com.

Federal Bureau of Investigation. (2002). *Terrorism 2000/2001.* Retrieved from http://www.fbi.gov/stats-services/publications/terror/terrorism-2000-2001.

Federal Bureau of Investigation. (2014). *Definitions of terrorism in the U.S. Code.* Retrieved from http://www.fbi.gov/about-us/investigate/terrorism/terrorism-definition.

Friedman, T. L. (2002, Oct. 23). Under the Arab street. *New York Times.* Retrieved from http://www.nytimes.com/2002/10/23/opinion/under-the-arab-street.html.

Gassman, M. (2006). *Northern Ireland still troubled.* Retrieved September 11, 2006, from http://www.peacecouncilorg/gassmanarticte.html.

Gurr, T. R. (1979). Alternatives to violence in a democratic society. In H. D. Graham, & T. R. Gurr (Eds.), *Violence in America: Historical and comparative perspectives* (pp. 491–506). Newbury Park, CA: Sage.

Gurr, T. R. (1989). Political terrorism: Historical antecedents and contemporary trends. In T. R. Gurr (Ed.), *Violence in America: Vol. 2. Protest, rebellion, reform* (pp. 201–230). Newbury Park, CA: Sage.

Hamm, M. S. (1997). *Apocalypse in Oklahoma: Waco and Ruby Ridge revenged.* Boston: Northeastern University Press.

Hamm, M. S. (2002). *In bad company: Americas terrorist underground.* Boston: Northeastern University Press.

Haque, M. S. (2002). Government responses to terrorism: Critical views of their impacts on people and public administration. *Public Administration Review, 62,* 170–180.

Hewitt, C. (2004). Terrorist violence. In M. A. Zahn, H. H. Brownstein, & S. L. Jackson (Eds.), *Violence: From theory to research* (pp. 237–250). Cincinnati, OH: LexisNexis/Anderson.

Hoffman, B. (2004a). Rethinking terrorism and counterterrorism since 9/11. In G. Martin (Ed.), *The new era of terrorism: Selected readings* (pp. 2–12). Thousand Oaks, CA: Sage.

Hoffman, B. (2004b). A nasty business. In G. Martin (Ed.), *The new era of terrorism: Selected readings* (pp. 226–231). Thousand Oaks, CA: Sage.

Hoffman, B. (2006). *Inside terrorism*. New York: Columbia University Press.

Hutcheson, R. (2005, Dec. 20). Bush stands firm on spying. *Philadelphia Inquirer.* Retrieved from http://phillynews.com.

Institute for Economics & Peace. (2013). *2012 Global Terrorism Index: Capturing the impact of terrorism for the last decade.* Retrieved from http://www.visionofhumanity.org/sites/default/files/2012_Global_Terrorism_Index_Report.pdf.

Israel Ministry of Foreign Affairs. (2006). *Palestinian violence and terrorism since September 2000.* Retrieved September 11, 2006, from http://www.mfa.gov.il/MFA.

Jenkins, P. (2003). *Images of terror: What we can and can't know about terrorism*. New York: Aldine de Gruyter (Transaction).

Karimi, N. (2006, Sept. 6). Iran's leader urges school purge. *Philadelphia Inquirer.* Retrieved from http://www.philly.com/.

Krauthammer, C. (2004). The unipolar moment revisited. In G. Martin (Ed.), *The new era of terrorism: Selected readings* (pp. 13–23). Thousand Oaks, CA: Sage.

Krueger, A. B., & Maleckova, J. (2003). Seeking the roots of terrorism. *The Chronicle of Higher Education, 49,* B10. Retrieved September 21, 2006, from http://chronicle.com/free/v49/i39/39b01001.htm.

Kull, S., Ramsay, C., & Lewis, E. (2003–2004). Misperceptions, the media, and the Iraq war. *Political Science Quarterly, 118,* 569–598.

Kushner, H. W. (1998). *Future of terrorism: Violence in the new millennium*. Thousand Oaks, CA: Sage

LaFree, G., & Dugan, L. (2007). Introducing the global terrorism database. *Terrorism and Political Violence, 19,* 181–204.

LaFree, G., & Dugan, L. (2009). Research on terrorism and countering terrorism. In M. Tonry (Ed.), *Crime and justice: A review of research* (*Vol. 38, pp.* 413–477). Chicago: University of Chicago Press.

Laqueur, W. (2003). *No end to war: Terrorism in the twenty-first century.* New York: Continuum International Publishing Group.

Mazzetti, M. (2006, Sept. 24). Spy agencies say Iraq war worsens terrorism threat. *New York Times.* Retrieved from http://www.nytimes.com/2006/09/24/world/middleeast/24terror.html?pagewanted=all&_r=0.

Milhollin, G. (2004). Can terrorists get the bomb? In G. Martin (Ed.), *The new era of terrorism: Selected readings* (pp. 188–193). Thousand Oaks, CA: Sage.

Nacos, B. (2004). The terrorist calculus behind 9–11: A model for future terrorism? In G. Martin (Ed.), *The new era of terrorism: Selected readings* (pp. 176–188). Thousand Oaks, CA: Sage.

National Commission on Terrorist Attacks upon the United States. (2004). *The 9/11 Commission Report.* Final report of the National Commission on Terrorist Attacks on the United States (Official Government Edition). Washington, DC: U.S. Government Printing Office.

National Consortium for the Study of Terrorism and Responses to Terrorism (START). (2014, April). *Annex of Statistical Information: Country Reports on Terrorism 2013.* Retrieved from http://www.state.gov/documents/organization/210288.pdf.

Palestine Red Crescent Society. (2006). Total daily numbers of deaths & injuries—West Bank & Gaza. Figures inclusive during the period September 30, 2000–August 18, 2006, Midnight. Retrieved September 11, 2006, from http://palestinercs.org/crisistables/table_of_figures.htm.

Pincus, W. (2006, Sept. 15). CIA learned in '02 that Bin Laden had no Iraq ties, report says. *Washington Post.* Retrieved from http://www.washingtonpost.com/wp-dyn/content/article/2006/09/14/AR2006091401545.html.

Pipes, D. (2004). God and Mammon: Does poverty cause militant Islam? In G. Martin (Ed.), *The new era of terrorism: Selected readings* (pp. 111–117). Thousand Oaks, CA: Sage.

Schmid, A. (1983). *Political terrorism: A research guide to concepts, theories, data bases and literature.* New Brunswick, NJ: Transaction Books.

Silverleib, A. (2011, May 6). The killing of bin Laden: Was it legal? *CNN World*. Retrieved from http://www.cnn.com/2011/WORLD/asiapcf/05/04/bin.laden.legal/.

Silverman, A. (2004). Just war, jihad, and terrorism: A comparison of Western and Islamic norms for the use of political violence. In G. Martin (Ed.), *The new era of terrorism: Selected readings* (pp. 149–160). Thousand Oaks, CA: Sage.

Smelser, N. J., & Mitchell, F. (Eds.). (2002). *Terrorism: Perspectives from the behavioral and social sciences*. Washington, DC: The National Academies Press.

Stern, J. (2001). *Preparing for a war on terrorism*. Testimony before the Committee on Government Reform, U.S. House of Representatives. Boston: Kennedy School of Government, Harvard University. Retrieved January 8, 2015, from http://www.gpo.gov/fdsys/pkg/CHRG-107hhrg77229/pdf/CHRG-107hhrg77229.pdf.

Stern, J. (2003). *Terror in the name of god: Why religious militants kill*. New York: HarperCollins.

Turk, A. T. (1982). *Political criminality: The defiance and defense of authority*. Beverley Hills, CA: Sage.

Turk, A. T. (1990). Social dynamics of terrorism. In N. A. Weiner, M. A. Zahn, & R. J. Sagi (Eds.), *Violence: Patterns, causes, public policy* (pp. 212–218). Orlando, FL: Harcourt Brace Jovanovich.

Turk, A. T. (2002). Political violence: Patterns and trends. In R. A. Silverman, T. P. Thornberry, & B. Krisberg (Eds.), *Crime and justice at the millennium: Essays by and in honor of Marvin E. Wolfgang* (pp. 31–44). Norwell, MA: Kluwer.

Turk, A. T. (2004). Sociology of terrorism. *Annual Review of Sociology, 30,* 271–286.

Ulfstein, G. (2004). Terrorism and the use of force. In G. Martin (Ed.), *The new era of terrorism: Selected readings* (pp. 233–242). Thousand Oaks, CA: Sage.

United Nations Development Programme. (2005). *The Arab human development report, 2004: Towards freedom in the Arab world*. New York: Author. Retrieved September 15, 2006, from http://www.undp.org/publications/.

U.S. Department of State. (2014, April). *Country Reports on Terrorism, 2013: Executive Summary*. U.S. Department of State, Bureau of Counterterrorism. Retrieved from www.state.gov/j/ct/rls/crt/index.htm.

Von Behr, I., Reding, A., Edwards, C., & Gribbon, L. (2013). *Radicalization in the digital era: The use of the Internet in 15 cases of terrorism and extremism*. Rand Europe. Retrieved from http://www.rand.org/content/dam/rand/pubs/research_reports/RR400/RR453/RAND_RR453.pdf.

White, J. R. (2006). *Terrorism and homeland security: An introduction* (5th ed.). Belmont, CA: Wadsworth/Thompson.

Wilson, S. (2006, January 28). Abbas calls for Hamas cabinet. *Washington Post*. Retrieved from http://www.washingtonpost.com/wp-dyn/content/article/2006/01/27/AR2006012701563_2.html.

Wilson, S., & Goldfarb, Z. A. (2013, Aug. 9). Obama announces proposals to reform NSA surveillance. *Washington Post*. Retrieved from http://www.washingtonpost.com/politics/obama-to-announce-proposals-to-reform-nsa-surveillance/2013/08/09/ee3d6762-011a-11e3-9711-3708310f6f4d_story.html.

Worldwide Religious News. (2005, July 20). *Islamic prayer schools under spotlight as breeding grounds for hatred*. Retrieved September 15, 2006, from http://www.wwrn.org/article.php?idd=17941&sec=34&con=26.

SECTION V

CONCLUSION

CHAPTER 15

PREVENTION AND PUNISHMENT: A DELICATE BALANCE

In previous chapters, we explored different types of violence (e.g., homicide, rape, robbery, hate crimes) using the *tripartite approach* (i.e., patterns, explanations, and interventions). We have already had much to say about how to reduce each type of violence. Why, then, a separate chapter on prevention and punishment? This concluding chapter summarizes several important but more *general approaches* to prevention and intervention that do not fit neatly into any one specific subtopic.

We draw on both criminal justice and public health perspectives (see Chapter 1) to argue for a more balanced approach to prevention and punishment. More and more, we are witnessing the development of creative, multimodal approaches to violence prevention and intervention. The main challenges are threefold: (1) we need to more carefully consider the appropriate balance of punishment and prevention required to reduce different types of criminal violence; (2) we need to develop better programs and policies based on valid information and knowledge; and (3) we need to better evaluate which strategies are effective and which are not.

CRIMINAL JUSTICE APPROACHES

Criminal justice approaches aimed at reducing violence typically emphasize deterrence, rehabilitation, incapacitation, or restoration goals, although distinctions between programs and policies based on these goals are less pronounced than they once were. Here, we summarize some of the major evidence for the effectiveness of each. We then discuss two controversial examples of punishment (three-strikes laws and the death penalty) and examine the limits of punishment.

CRIMINAL JUSTICE GOALS

Deterrence

Theories of deterrence predict that reduced crime will result as the certainty, swiftness, and severity of sanctions are increased. Indeed, some studies have found a reduction in crime rates (some more than others) related to the increased likelihood of apprehension, conviction, or imprisonment (Greenwood, 1982). A National Academy of Sciences panel that conducted the most thorough review of deterrence research to date found that, overall, the evidence did not strongly support the existence of deterrent effects (Blumstein et al., 1978). Where effects were found, they were stronger when the probability of arrest and incarceration was increased (i.e., *certainty*). The effect of increasing length of sentences (on crime rates) was minimal. Evidence suggested that certainty is much more important than severity.

A number of studies have examined whether an increased police presence in certain areas reduces violent crime. For example, a study of crime in the New York City subways between 1965 and 1971 showed that robberies dropped significantly after the number of uniformed officers patrolling the subway system was increased (Chaiken et al., 1974)—however, crimes were displaced to nearby locations. In the well-known Kansas City Preventive Patrol Experiment (Kelling et al., 1974), researchers varied the amount of preventive patrol (i.e., officers in patrol cars cruising neighborhoods) in different districts. Areas were matched for similarity in crime rates, population demographics, income, and calls for service. In some areas (proactive patrol), patrols were doubled or quadrupled. In other areas (the control group), nothing was changed. In another area (reactive policing), preventive patrol was eliminated entirely. After one year, there were no significant differences in crime rates or citizens' perceptions of safety. Studies have failed to consistently demonstrate any clear-cut reduction in crime due to increased police presence alone.

Although the evidence is mixed, testing deterrence theory is in reality difficult and complex (Nagin, 1998). First of all, much of the research has been based on aggregate, official statistics (e.g., Uniform Crime Reports) that contain known limitations (see Chapter 2). Second, interpreting crime rates is an extremely complex task. Many studies cannot eliminate other factors that could account for observed deterrent effects (e.g., biases in measures, regional variations in criminal statutes and procedures, differences in data collection and reporting, and other influencing factors). Third, it is difficult to determine how many *potential* offenders are deterred by any specific strategy. Doing so would require large samples of survey or interview respondents, including honest citizens as well as offenders. Some researchers attempt to assess offenders' calculation of benefits versus costs associated with specific offenses, although only occasionally in response to any specific intervention strategy (Clarke & Cornish, 1985), and only occasionally with positive benefits (Clarke, 1992).

In an interesting reconceptualization, Stafford and Warr (1993) argued that it is unnecessary to formulate separate theories of general and specific deterrence. Rather, they suggest, a single theory should focus on *indirect experience* and *direct experience* with legal punishment and punishment avoidance. This proposal makes tests of deterrence theory even more complex. Studies based on survey data, for example, would need to include measures of persons' perceptions of their own certainty and severity of legal punishment for crimes; persons' perceptions of the certainty and severity of legal punishment for others; self-reported criminal behavior, including self-reports of *direct experience* with punishment and punishment avoidance; and estimates of peers' criminal behavior, including their experiences with punishment and punishment avoidance.

Much new research is now applying these ideas to help reshape deterrence theory (Paternoster & Piquero, 1995; Piquero & Pogarsky, 2002; Pogarsky & Piquero, 2003). For now, we conclude that deterrent effects of sanctions on crime rates are not impossible to achieve, but the weight of the evidence to date has been somewhat mixed, and stronger research methods are needed (Nagin, 1998).

Rehabilitation

Numerous and diverse attempts at reforming offenders have been attempted over the years, including psychotherapy, behavior modification, vocational training, alcohol and drug treatment, and violent offender and sex offender programs. According to a National Academy of Sciences panel (Sechrest et al., 1979), at least four situations limited conclusions about the effectiveness of rehabilitation: (1) Evaluation methodologies have often been inadequate; (2) An insufficient number of programs are available to prisoners (e.g., many want and need drug treatment but cannot get it); (3) Many inmates refuse to participate; and (4) Sometimes inmates are not allowed to participate for security reasons.

More recently, researchers have argued that the "nothing works" rhetoric about rehabilitation is highly misleading (Andrews et al., 1990; Gendreau, 1996). The best studies show that some types of treatment do indeed work for some types of offenders, at least some of the time. For example, stronger treatment effects are observed when (1) behavioral or cognitive-behavioral theories guide the development of interventions, (2) high-risk offenders are targeted, and (3) interventions address the specific risks and needs of individuals (Andrews & Bonta, 2006). We still need to know much more, however, about how different factors influence treatment outcomes for different offenders.

Incapacitation

Incapacitation refers to the argument that offenders cannot commit further crimes while in prison. Generally, what is recommended is increasing sentence length to keep convicted offenders in prison longer, particularly "career criminals." Serious problems are associated with this type of *selective incapacitation, however* (Blumstein et al., 1986). Most important, we cannot predict with any accuracy whatsoever *who* is likely to become a career criminal until *after* he or she has already amassed a lengthy criminal career. It would be highly unethical and illegal to simply lock somebody up forever because we think he or she *might* become a serious criminal. There is, in other words, a huge false-positive problem: A large percentage of those who are predicted to reoffend (based on various models) indeed do not. *General incapacitation*, in contrast, argues that if we simply locked up all offenders for longer periods of time, we would significantly reduce crime. Such indiscriminate increases in punishment, however, would strain overcrowded jails and prisons even further than they are already, and projected expenses would far exceed available resources unless gigantic tax increases were imposed (Welsh & Harris, 2013).

Restoration

Restoration attempts to restore the victim and or the community to his or her prior state before the crime occurred. It is similar to retribution in the sense that crime is viewed as a disruption of the peace. Restoration, however, seeks to repair the harm that resulted from the offense, whereas retribution seeks only to apply blame and punishment.

Two broad types of programs have emerged: restorative justice and community justice (Kurki, 1999). Restorative justice strategies involve victims as well as offenders in the process of deciding on an appropriate sanction. Community justice strategies engage members of the community in the business of solving community crime problems. Both are based on the assumption that communities will be strengthened if local citizens participate in responding to crime, and both envision responses tailored to the preferences and needs of victims, communities, and offenders. Most advocates of restorative justice agree on five basic principles (Kurki, 1999):

1. Crime consists of more than violation of the criminal law and defiance of government authority.
2. Crime involves disruptions in a three-dimensional relationship of victim, community, and offender.
3. Because crime harms the victim and the community, the primary goals should be to repair the harm and heal the victim and the community.
4. The victim, the community, and the offender should all participate in determining the response to crime.
5. Case disposition should be based primarily on the victim's and the community's needs, not solely on the offender's needs or culpability, the dangers he or she presents, or his or her criminal history.

Many diverse programs based on these principles have emerged (Braithwaite, 1999; Kurki, 1999; Strang, 2004). Programs offer options such as financial restitution to victims, as well as requiring offenders to perform community service work. Still others involve the offender, the victim, and family members and friends of both parties in face-to-face encounters during which reparation steps are negotiated and empathy is encouraged. Restorative justice conferencing provides an opportunity for victim and offender to meet voluntarily, face to face, to discuss a crime and its impact and make a plan for reparations (Strang, 2004).

Evaluation evidence so far is promising (Porter, 2006; Sherman & Strang, 2004; Strang, 2004). In one of the most rigorous examinations of restorative justice outcomes to date, Sherman and Strang (2004) reported five conclusions based on randomized controlled experiments examining the effects of face-to-face restorative conferences between victims and offenders versus court prosecution or other forms of diversion. First, statistically significant benefits for crime victims (as measured by interviews), including reduced anger and anxiety and increased satisfaction with the justice process, were found. Second, consistent reductions in victims' stated desire for revenge against offenders were found. Third, statistically significant and substantial *reductions* in repeat offending (as measured by police arrest or charge data) were found in *some* tests, in *some* settings, and with *some* demographic groups. Fourth, statistically significant *increases* in repeat offending were found in *some* tests, in *some* settings, and with *some* demographic groups. Fifth, in several comparisons, restorative justice made no statistically significant difference in repeat offending.

In short, strong, consistent results were found for victim satisfaction, but not for repeat offending. More research, however, is needed to explore the different factors that might influence differential rates of program success, including differences in program implementation across sites, different social settings, the social distance between victim and offender, local police and community relations with different groups, community characteristics, and different offense and offender types (Sherman & Strang, 2004; Strang, 2004). For further information, visit the International Institute for Restorative Practices at http://www.realjustice.org.

THE DEATH PENALTY

Capital punishment was used widely in the United States until 1968, at which time it was suspended by the U.S. Supreme Court. In *Furman vs. Georgia* (1972), the Court ruled that the death penalty, at least as administered, constituted cruel and unusual punishment because it was administered in an arbitrary and discriminatory manner. The death penalties of 39 states and the District of Columbia were rendered invalid.

The death penalty was banned in the United States until a follow-up decision by the Supreme Court was issued in *Gregg vs. Georgia* (1976). Revising its earlier decision, the Court ruled against mandatory death penalty laws but allowed "aggravating and mitigating circumstances" for which the death penalty could be permitted (e.g., a murder committed in the course of a felony). Because of the seriousness and finality of the punishment, capital cases must be conducted according to higher standards of due process and more careful procedures than other cases.

Instead of deciding the defendant's guilt and imposing the death sentence in the same court proceeding, most states created "bifurcated" (two-step) proceedings with a separate trial and punishment phase. In the punishment phase, the court must consider specific aggravating factors set forth in state law (e.g., excessive cruelty, murder of a police officer, commission of a murder during a felony) as well as specific mitigating factors (e.g., offender's youthfulness, diminished intent, lack of a previous criminal record). These factors must be weighed together before a judge or jury imposes the death penalty in any case. Executions resumed in 1977, as most states revised their legislation to meet the requirements set forth by *Gregg vs. Georgia*.

The *Gregg* decision stood until 1987, when Georgia's death penalty was challenged once again on constitutional grounds, this time on the basis of racial discrimination. In *McCleskey vs. Kemp* (1987), the defendant's attorneys claimed that Georgia's law discriminated on the basis of race. Research by David Baldus and his colleagues (1994) examined more than 2,000 Georgia murder cases and found that defendants charged with killing whites received the death penalty 11 times more often than those charged with killing blacks. Even after controlling for 230 factors, such as viciousness of the crime and the quality of the evidence in each case, the death sentence was still four times more likely to be imposed when the victim was white. Even though a majority (60%) of homicide victims in Georgia was black, six out of seven offenders put to death from 1977 to 1987 were black men convicted of killing white men (Baldus et al., 1994). The Supreme Court rejected McCleskey's claim by a 5-4 vote. To show that the death penalty in Georgia was being administered in an unconstitutional manner, the Court ruled, McCleskey would have had to prove that decision makers discriminated in his own individual case, not just in a "generalized statistical study." McCleskey was executed in 1991.

Recent patterns and trends on the death sentence in the United States are shown in Table 15.1. For example, executions are rare. At year-end 2012, more than 3,000 inmates were held under sentence of death, but only 39 were executed in 2013 (Snell, 2014). The major reason is the lengthy and expensive appeals process required since the Supreme Court ruling in *Gregg vs. Georgia* (1976). Death sentences must be reviewed by both state and federal courts until the appeals process has been exhausted.

Diverse arguments are commonly made for and against the death penalty (for further reading, see Baldus et al., 1994; Bohm, 1989, 2003; Zimring & Hawkins, 1986). At least four major arguments are commonly made in favor of the death penalty: (1) public support, (2) deterrence, (3) retribution, and (4) cost-effectiveness.

First, public opinion strongly favors the death penalty, and thus democratic values should prevail, some argue. Since 1953, the Gallup Poll has asked: "Are you in favor of the death penalty for a person convicted of murder?" Support has been as low as 42% in 1966 and as high as 80% in 1994. In 2013, 60% favored the death penalty for persons convicted of murder (Gallup, 2014).

A second major argument addresses deterrence: Does the death penalty deter criminals from committing violent acts? Research conducted by Ehrlich (1975) is often cited as support for deterrent effects due to the death penalty. That study, however, has been severely criticized for its weak methodology, and most experts have questioned its conclusions (Blumstein et al., 1978; Conrad & van den Haag, 1983; Vandaele, 1978). The research evidence in favor of deterrent effects due to the death penalty is not convincing (Blumstein et al., 1978). The great

Table 15.1 Facts About Capital Punishment

- As of December 31, 2012, 36 states and the federal government authorized the death penalty.
- At year-end 2012, 35 states and the Federal Bureau of Prisons held 3,033 inmates under sentence of death.
- Four states (California, Florida, Texas, and Pennsylvania) held more than half of all inmates on death row on December 31, 2012.
- Of prisoners under sentence of death at year-end 2012, 56% were white and 42% were black. The 384 Hispanic inmates under sentence of death accounted for 14% of inmates with a known ethnicity.
- In 2013, nine states executed 39 inmates, four fewer executions than in 2012.
- Of the 39 executions in 2013, 38 were by lethal injection; one was by electrocution.
- In 2012, 20 states and the Federal Bureau of Prisons removed 111 inmates from under sentence of death: 43 (39%) were executed, 17 (15%) died by means other than execution, and 51 (46%) were removed as a result of commutations or courts overturning sentences or convictions.

Source: Snell, T. L. (2014). *Capital Punishment, 2012—Statistical Tables* (NCJ 245789). Washington, DC: U.S. Department of Justice, Bureau of Justice Statistics (BJS). Retrieved July 7, 2014, from: http://www.bjs.gov/content/pub/pdf/cp12st.pdf.

majority of murderers, for example, commit their crimes impulsively and irrationally, without much reasoning or anticipation of consequences.

Some advocates (e.g., Conrad & van den Haag, 1983) argue that the death penalty achieves justice by paying back killers for the seriousness of their crimes. Retribution becomes a moral justification for the death penalty. According to this position, the death penalty helps define the most serious of all crimes (and punishments), showing society's disapproval. The death penalty alone, advocates argue, provides sufficient retribution and reparation for surviving family members of homicide victims. Advocates also point to incapacitation as a justification; the death penalty prevents offenders from doing further harm. The portion of released homicide offenders who recommit murder is quite low, however (Zahn, 1990). Moral justifications really cannot be answered by any empirical evidence, but rather by faith: Retribution is punishment for its own sake.

Advocates also argue that the death penalty is more cost-effective than holding prisoners for the rest of their lives. This position is weak (Bohm, 1989, 2003; Conrad & van den Haag, 1983). In many cases, the mandatory appeals process ends up being more expensive than the cost of incarcerating a prisoner for life, and there is no justifiable reason in a democratic society to place a priority on cost-effectiveness where human lives are concerned. Besides, evidence suggests that it is actually more expensive to carry out a death sentence under current laws than it is to keep someone in prison for life (Bohm, 2003; Zimring & Hawkins, 1986).

Opponents of the death penalty often invoke at least three arguments: (1) improper use of state power, (2) racial discrimination, and (3) the possibility of errors. First, opponents argue, it is wrong for the government to intentionally kill citizens. How can the state advocate murder while at the same time prohibiting murder? Further, in countries (e.g., apartheid-era South Africa) and regions of the United States (e.g., Southern states) where the death penalty has been most widely used, its use has departed most conspicuously from standards of equity and humanity (Bohm, 2003; Bowers, 1974). It is hard to ignore historical lessons where the death penalty has been justified and applied under the auspices of religion (e.g., the Christian Crusades) and the coercive use of power by the state (e.g., Stalinist Russia) to enforce compliance (Bowers, 1974; Foucault, 1977).

Second, there is substantial evidence that the death penalty discriminates against minorities (Bohm, 2003; Bowers, 1974). Minorities are more likely to be arrested, charged, and convicted of capital crimes, even holding constant legal variables, such as previous criminal record; and they are at least four times more likely to be executed (Baldus et al., 1994). Statistics show clearly that blacks receive death penalty sentences far more frequently than would be expected on the basis of their criminal history alone (Bonczar & Snell, 2005).

Third, opponents argue, the death penalty is irreversible. A surprising number of people convicted of capital crimes were later found to be innocent (Bohm, 2003). Of 7,529 prisoners sentenced to death from 1973 to 2004, fully 2,598 (34%) had their sentences reduced or overturned on appeal; an additional 337 (4%) had their sentence commuted (Maguire & Pastore, 2006a).

Regardless of one's views, one cannot ignore the constitutional requirements outlined by the Supreme Court, nor can one ignore the moral arguments that fuel public support for the death penalty. On the other hand, both sides could benefit from careful examination of existing research and further valid research on critical arguments associated with the death penalty (Bohm, 2003).

THREE-STRIKES LAWS

Three-strikes laws became extremely popular in the 1990s as a means of putting away repeat offenders (Welsh & Harris, 2013). Such laws, however, were beset with a number of weaknesses, including poorly defined target populations, discrimination against minorities, lack of acceptance by prosecutors, and lack of prison space (Shichor & Sechrest, 1996). Although these laws attempted to focus on career criminals, few offenders "specialize," and prediction of who will become a high-rate offender is extremely difficult, as mentioned earlier in this chapter.

Democratic values, such as equity, may be compromised by these laws. A California study found that blacks were sent to prison under the three-strikes law 13 times more often than whites (Greenwood et al., 1994). Forty-three percent of the third-strikes inmates in California were African American, although they made up only 7% of the state's population and 20% of its felony arrests. In analyses of the federal sentencing guidelines, researchers found that African Americans received longer sentences than whites not because of differential treatment by judges, but because they constituted the large majority of those convicted of trafficking in crack cocaine, a crime Congress had singled out for especially harsh mandatory penalties (McDonald & Carlson, 1993).

Target populations for three-strikes laws were often poorly defined. During the first few years of the law's implementation in California, about 1,300 offenders were imprisoned on third-strike felonies and more than 14,000 were imprisoned for second-strike felonies. California's law called for a doubling of the prison sentence for a second felony and for a sentence of 25 years to life for a third conviction. The California law was written to cover 500 felonies, including many nonviolent offenses. Some of the felonies include petty theft, attempted assault, and burglary. Thus, about 85% of all those sentenced under the three-strikes laws were involved in nonviolent crimes. For instance, 192 marijuana possessors were sentenced for second and third strikes, compared with 40 murderers, 25 rapists, and 24 kidnappers (Greenwood et al., 1994).

Laws vary widely across states in terms of the definition of a "strike," the conditions under which the law is triggered, and the severity of the sanctions. Some state laws call for third-time offenders to receive life without parole. In others, prisoners are eligible for parole after 30 or 40 years (Greenwood et al., 1998). State prosecutors frequently avoid the three strikes laws because they see little need for them with existing sentencing laws (Welsh & Harris, 2013). Some laws were also narrowly written, making them difficult to apply. Plea bargaining and charge bargaining became common methods for circumventing three-strikes laws. Some states have not used them at all; others have applied the laws infrequently and inconsistently (Greenwood et al., 1998).

Three-strikes laws were intended to reduce serious crime by incapacitating repeat offenders and by deterring others from becoming repeat offenders. Existing evidence of effectiveness is mixed. An evaluation by the Rand Corporation found that states with three-strikes laws did not experience greater declines in crime than states without such laws (Greenwood et al., 1998). Three-strikes states did not experience greater increases in overall incarceration rates, although the likelihood of incarceration per conviction increased substantially. No consistent effects in terms of court workload or backlog were found. In California, counties varied dramatically in how the law was implemented. Strikes were dismissed in one fourth to one half of all strike-eligible cases in some counties. Rand researchers cautioned that the full effects of three-strikes laws may remain unknown until offenders imprisoned under three-strikes laws have been incarcerated longer than they would have been under previous laws. It is also difficult to control for the many other social, political, and economic factors (besides three-strikes laws) that may affect crime rates and incarceration rates (see also Auerhahn, 2003; Stolzenberg & D'Alessio, 1997; Zimring et al., 1999).

The California three-strikes law, one of the nation's toughest, had overwhelming voter support when it was approved in 1994 amid concern over violent crime. Following protracted prison overcrowding and state budget crises over the next two decades, however, California voted in November 2012 to soften the law (Leonard & Dolan, 2012). The law had targeted offenders previously convicted of at least two violent or serious crimes, such as rape or residential burglary. Proposition 36, supported by about 69% of voters, changed the law so that offenders whose third strikes were relatively minor, such as shoplifting or drug possession, could no longer be sentenced to 25 years to life in prison. Offenders convicted of third strikes for serious or violent crimes under the law can still receive the lengthy prison terms, however. About a third of incarcerated third-strikers (about 3,000 prisoners) convicted of minor third strikes could seek reduced sentences under the new law. Inmates with prior convictions for rape, murder, and child molestation cannot be released under the measure, and courts can reject a request to reduce a sentence if they determine that an individual is a danger to public safety.

Get-tough policies such as three-strikes laws provided a dramatic response to a perceived problem, but it is unlikely that such intervention is sufficient by itself to produce a substantial decrease in violent crime. Given the complexity of human behavior and the interaction of multiple causes of violence (e.g., biological, psychological, and sociological), the criminal justice system is limited in its ability to prevent violent crime.

THE LIMITS OF PUNISHMENT

The criminal justice system is intended, at least in part, to prevent crime. But how much impact do responses by police, courts, and corrections have on violent crime? It would be folly to suggest that laws determine human behavior completely or even to a great extent (Packer, 1968). What about all the other diverse causes of human (and violent) behavior? Why should individual free will (or pathology) predominate among all the diverse causes of violence suggested by social science research (Zahn, 1990)?

Many researchers have concluded after careful reviews of the evidence that the criminal justice system is, at best, quite limited in its ability to reduce violent behavior (Blumstein et al., 1978; Greenwood, 1982; Packer, 1968; Reiss & Roth, 1993). Punishment is a necessary but not sufficient condition to prevent violent crime:

> The criminal sanction is indispensable; we could not, now or in the foreseeable future, get along without it. Yet we resort to it in far too indiscriminate a way, thereby weakening some of the important bases upon which its efficacy rests and threatening social values that far transcend the prevention of crime. (Packer, 1968, p. 364)

What are some of these limits, then, and what values are threatened? First of all, criminal justice system processing is imperfect and inefficient. If the criminal justice system is to have any success in preventing violence, it must first be able to identify and apprehend violent offenders.

However, clearance rates (the percentage of reported crimes in which police make an arrest) are not very high. In 2008, 45.1% of violent crimes and 17.4% of property crimes nationwide were cleared by arrest or exceptional means (Federal Bureau of Investigation [FBI], 2009). Examples of exceptional clearances include the death of the offender, the victim's refusal to cooperate with the prosecution after the offender has been identified, or the denial of extradition because the offender committed a crime in another jurisdiction and is being prosecuted for that offense. Murder had the highest percentage of offenses cleared for violent crimes (63.6%). Clearance rates were lower for aggravated assault (54.9%), rape (40.4%), and robbery (26.8%). Most cases, if solved at all, are solved either by an on-scene arrest or a witness identifying the offender. If these factors do not occur, arrest is unlikely.

Second, even if an arrest is made, cases are filtered out at each stage of court processing, primarily because of the quality of evidence (Cole & Smith, 2004). For example, considerable portions of those who are arrested are not prosecuted. Even if prosecutions are initiated, many cases will be dismissed after closer review. Even if charges are not dismissed, offenders are not always convicted, and many plead guilty to lesser charges. Indeed, only about half of all arrests for violent crime result in a conviction. Of those, fewer than half are sentenced to state prison. Given such serious limitations, under what circumstances can we reasonably expect the criminal justice system to prevent crime, and what else is needed?

Violent offenders should not escape punishment. The vast majority, however, will be released from prison at some point, better or worse equipped to become productive members of society. To what degree can prison reduce the likelihood of recidivism? Do *some* prison programs (e.g., drug treatment, education, vocational training) work, at least for *some* offenders under at least *some* circumstances? And even more important, are there any effective strategies to prevent acts of criminal violence in the first place, before violators come to the attention of the criminal justice system? As Packer argues, the use of punishment must be qualified to some degree by other social purposes, including the enhancement of freedom and the doing of justice.

Does the Criminal Justice System Discriminate Against Minorities?

Overrepresentation of minorities in the criminal justice system, from arrest to disposition to incarceration, remains one of the most troubling problems in the adult and juvenile justice systems of the United States (Hawkins, 2003; Hsia et al., 2004; Welsh et al., 1996).

Minorities come into contact with the criminal justice system at much higher rates than whites (Hagan & Peterson, 1995). Although incarceration rates vary across counties and states, African American, Latino, Asian American, and Native American youths make up nearly two thirds of all juveniles incarcerated nationwide (Hsia et al., 2004).

At least two major explanations have been offered: (1) minorities commit more crimes and (2) the criminal justice system is racist. There is likely some truth to both, although it is extremely difficult to measure either with precision or to determine their exact balance. First, official statistics are themselves flawed (see Chapter 2). Second, racial disparities in conviction and incarceration rates are reduced (but not eliminated) when certain variables, such as the offender's current and prior offense severity, are taken into consideration (Walker et al., 1996). Ample evidence points to discrimination, although its exact prevalence is unclear. Much evidence suggests that high rates of minority youth incarceration are attributable at least partly to case-processing disparities, not merely to higher crime rates by minority youth (Feyerherm, 1995; Pope & Feyerherm, 1992). Despite increasing public and scholarly concern about relationships among race, crime, and punishment, "program initiatives/policy designed to reduce minority overrepresentation and ensure fairness in juvenile justice processing either do not exist or at least not in any significant numbers" (Pope & Feyerherm, 1992, p. 46). As Carl Pope (1995, pp. 215–216) suggested:

> Policy initiatives must not only address problems in the case processing of juvenile offenders, as noted earlier, but also pre-existing social conditions. Only by such a two-pronged attack can we have any chance of reducing crime among our youths and the disproportionate overrepresentation of minorities within the juvenile justice system.

PUBLIC HEALTH APPROACHES TO PUNISHMENT AND PREVENTION

The public health risk-based approach to prevention has gained considerable attention from criminal justice researchers and policymakers (Loeber & Farrington, 1998; Moore, 1995). Five broad approaches to prevention are discussed in this section: (1) the National Research Council's *Multilevel Risk Approach* (Reiss & Roth, 1993); (2) the *evidence-based practices and programs* (EBPP) approach; (3) the Office of Juvenile Justice and Delinquency Prevention's (OJJDP) *Comprehensive Strategy for Serious, Violent, and Chronic Juvenile Offenders* (Howell, 2009); (4) *community-based approaches;* and (5) the *Blueprints for Healthy Youth Development initiative.*

THE MULTILEVEL RISK APPROACH

Despite abundant social science evidence over the years that violent crime is related to time, place, culture, and social structure, criminological researchers and policymakers have heavily emphasized individual offenders' motivations (Harris et al., 2000). Calls for multilevel, interdisciplinary approaches (e.g., examining the relative explanatory power of individual, institutional, social structural, and cultural factors associated with violence) have become more frequent in recent years, partially as a result of the greater sophistication of information and computing systems, and partially as a result of the influence of the public health perspective.

The National Academy of Sciences Panel on the Understanding and Control of Violent Behavior, comprising an international panel of experts from a variety of disciplines, was established in 1989 to review existing knowledge and make recommendations to control violence (Reiss & Roth, 1993). One of its main conclusions was that we have many promising directions for intervention and prevention to pursue from research findings, but better measures and more controlled research (especially evaluations of promising efforts) are needed to identify causes and opportunities for prevention. Using the risk approach to classify different predictors, they proposed a matrix consisting of two main dimensions: (1) *temporal proximity* (closeness in time) of a predictor to the violent event and (2) the *level of analysis* at which that predictor is observed.

Levels of analysis refer to different units of observation and analysis, including macrosocial, microsocial, psychosocial, and biological (e.g., neurobehavioral). Macrosocial factors are characteristics of large social units, such as communities, cities, states, and countries. Macrosocial risk factors for violence include both social structural (e.g., poverty, unemployment) and cultural (e.g., group and subgroup values about the acceptability of violence in specific circumstances, exposure to media violence) variables. Microsocial factors are characteristics of encounters among people (e.g., family and group dynamics, situational factors such as availability of weapons, organizational and institutional processes). Psychosocial factors include individual characteristics (e.g., personality, learned rewards) or temporary states (e.g., influence of alcohol, stress) that influence interactions with others. Biological or neurobehavioral factors, primarily in the brain, include chemical, electrical, and hormonal influences on behavior.

The multilevel approach carries important implications for the study and prevention of violence. Consistent with the risk-based approach of the public health perspective, the panel suggested that the effective prevention and intervention of violence will depend on breaking one or more specific links in the chain of events preceding a violent incident. Multiple options for intervening and increased interagency collaboration are called for:

> Violence problem-solving will require long-term collaboration and new organizational arrangements among local law enforcement, criminal justice, schools and public health, emergency medicine, and social service agencies, all working with program evaluators and other researchers. (Reiss & Roth, 1993, p. 10)

EVIDENCE-BASED PRACTICES AND PROGRAMS

Implementation research suggests that identifying EBPPs that yield positive client outcomes is an essential step in improving services for adolescents who come into in contact with the juvenile justice system. For example, many "evidence-based" interventions are often slow to be disseminated (Kilbourne et al., 2007), poorly implemented (Bourgon & Armstrong, 2005), and difficult to sustain (Brown & Flynn, 2002, Miller et al., 2006). There are particular challenges in introducing EBPPs into juvenile justice agencies, which are slow to be exposed to EBPPs and often isolated from practice and research (Lipsey et al., 2010). Typical barriers to implementation of EBPP include cyclic funding, vacillating support for juvenile offender programs, and an emphasis on punishment rather than treatment.

It is thus important to understand the effective components of the program or practice being implemented. Approaches to implementing EBPP have included guidelines (American Psychological Association, 2006; National Institute on Drug Abuse, 1999, 2006), dissemination of EBPP information, and regulatory policies (e.g., state EBPP requirements for obtaining funding). Although a key feature of health systems (Institute of Medicine, 2002), the EBPP movement has so far had limited penetration into the juvenile justice system. Examples include assessment and placement practices, reintegration and aftercare services for juvenile offenders, juvenile drug courts, and school- and community-based interventions (Lipsey et al., 2010).

The *Standardized Program Evaluation Protocol* translates guidelines for effective juvenile justice programs into practical form (Lipsey et al., 2010). This empirically grounded framework is intended to help juvenile justice systems systematically assess their existing services along a continuum of care ranging from primary to tertiary prevention and then target relevant services for change. Assessment of service delivery includes the fundamental elements of valid risk and needs assessments, the matching of the level of risk and need to the appropriate service, and ensuring that the services provided are effective at improving outcomes.

A database for the meta-analysis of the effects of delinquency interventions consisted of 548 studies that spanned the period 1958 to 2002 (Lipsey et al., 2010). These studies represented all the intervention research that could be located through an extensive search for published and unpublished reports of research that met four criteria: (a) The research was conducted in an English-speaking country and reported in English; (b) The juveniles studied were between 12 and 21 years of age; (c) The program's effect was measured on at least one delinquency outcome variable (e.g., rearrest, reconviction, return to court supervision); and (d) The outcomes of the target intervention program were directly compared to those of a control group of similar juveniles who did not receive the intervention.

The effectiveness of these programs was accounted for by a small number of factors. Close attention to these factors can thus provide reasonable assurance that those programs will be effective for reducing recidivism. Evidence-based programs should address four major principles shown to be characteristic of the most effective programs: (a) *Target high-risk cases*. In particular, provide the most effective programs possible to the highest-risk cases. Because effective programs applied to low-risk cases will have small effects, it is not cost-effective to provide more than minimal, low-cost services to such cases; (b) *Use programs that take a therapeutic approach* to changing behavior by focusing on constructive personal development. Minimize programs based on a control or deterrence philosophy; (c) Favor those program types that have shown the largest effects in research studies when *matching programs to the needs and problem areas of the juveniles served*; and (d) *Implement* the selected programs well. Monitor each program to ensure that it is delivered as intended and that all the juveniles assigned to it receive at least an amount of service that corresponds to the average reported in the research on that type of program.

Juvenile justice agencies can thus compare their current services to best practices shown in the research to improve outcomes for juvenile justice–involved youth. This is done via an automated and ongoing process of quality improvement across virtually all services provided by juvenile justice agencies. The Standardized Program Evaluation Protocol approach allows for the retention of local programs and provides a quality assurance mechanism across the continuum of care (Lipsey et al., 2010).

Each of the factors found in the meta-analytical results to be related to program effectiveness is represented in the Standardized Program Evaluation Protocol and is associated with a specific number of points. The maximum overall score is 100 points. The number of points associated with each factor is derived from the statistical models used in the meta-analyses to predict program effects on recidivism. Those factors with stronger predictive relationships were assigned proportionately more points. The Standardized Program Evaluation Protocol assesses five domains: (1) *Primary Service* (program type)—classified as high, moderate, or low average effect size based on meta-analytic research (35 points); (2) *Supplemental Service*—additional services if distinct from primary approach (5 points); (3) *Treatment Amount* (duration: 10 points; contact hours, 15 points); (4) *Treatment Quality*—extent to which the program was implemented as intended for each juvenile recipient (15 points); and (5) *Youth Risk Level* (20 points). Projects in North Carolina and Arizona have demonstrated that the Standardized Program Evaluation Protocol can be implemented statewide or countywide, and scores were closely related to client outcomes (Lipsey et al., 2010).

OFFICE OF JUVENILE JUSTICE AND DELINQUENCY PREVENTION'S COMPREHENSIVE STRATEGY FOR SERIOUS, VIOLENT, AND CHRONIC JUVENILE OFFENDERS

The Standardized Program Evaluation Protocol corresponds well to the OJJDP's Comprehensive Strategy (CS) for Serious, Violent, and Chronic Juvenile Offenders, a continuum-of-care framework for guiding state and local system reforms to address juvenile delinquency in a cost-effective manner (Howell, 1995, 2003, 2009). The CS encourages helping youths throughout their development, while responding to juvenile crime in a way that ensures public safety.

The CS is a two-tiered system for responding proactively to juvenile delinquency (Fig. 15.1). In the first tier, prevention, youth development, and early intervention programs are used to reduce the likelihood that at-risk youth will come into contact with the juvenile justice system. If those efforts fail, then the juvenile justice system, the second tier, proactively addresses the risk factors and associated treatment needs of offenders. At the same time, supervision proportionate to the risk to public safety posed by the respective offenders must be applied. In the CS framework, the supervision and control components in response to assessed risks and needs are referred to as *graduated sanctions*. The CS is structured around levels of care moving from least restrictive (e.g., programs for all youth) to most restrictive (e.g., training schools).

The CS was based on an influential risk-based approach known as the *Social Development Strategy* (Catalano & Hawkins, 1996; Hawkins & Catalano, 1992; Howell, 1995). According to this strategy, known risk factors for delinquency and substance abuse can be

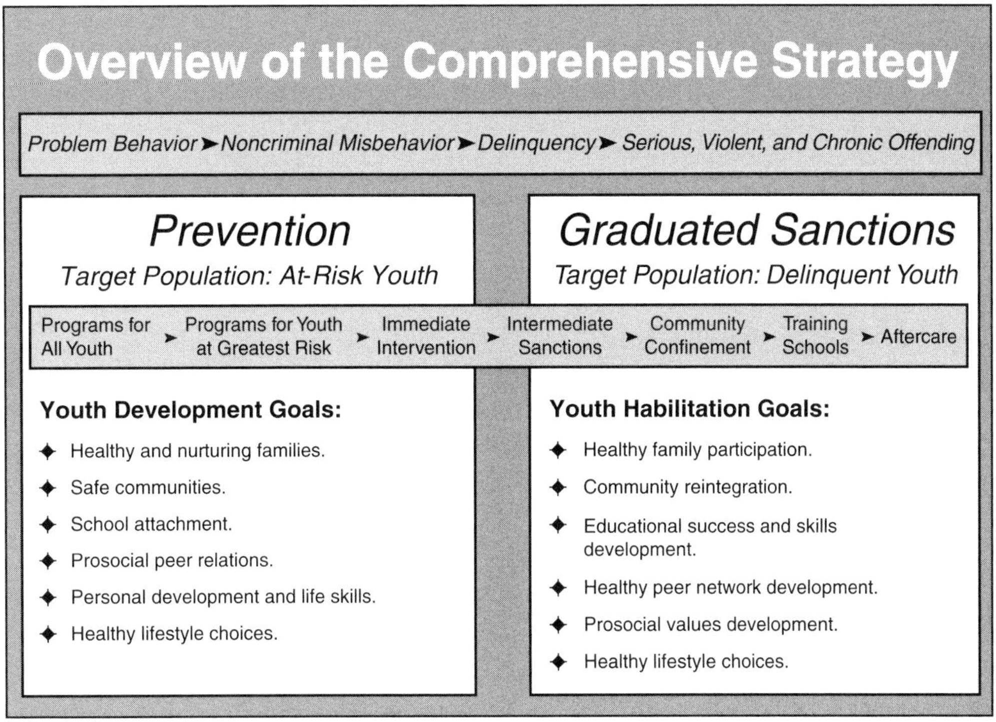

Overview of the Comprehensive Strategy

Problem Behavior ➤ Noncriminal Misbehavior ➤ Delinquency ➤ Serious, Violent, and Chronic Offending

Prevention	*Graduated Sanctions*
Target Population: At-Risk Youth	*Target Population: Delinquent Youth*

Programs for All Youth ➤ Programs for Youth at Greatest Risk ➤ Immediate Intervention ➤ Intermediate Sanctions ➤ Community Confinement ➤ Training Schools ➤ Aftercare

Youth Development Goals:

- Healthy and nurturing families.
- Safe communities.
- School attachment.
- Prosocial peer relations.
- Personal development and life skills.
- Healthy lifestyle choices.

Youth Habilitation Goals:

- Healthy family participation.
- Community reintegration.
- Educational success and skills development.
- Healthy peer network development.
- Prosocial values development.
- Healthy lifestyle choices.

FIGURE 15.1 The Comprehensive Strategy. *Source:* Coolbaugh, K., & Hansel, C. J. (2000). The comprehensive strategy: Lessons learned from the pilot sites (Bulletin, NCJ 178258). Washington, DC: Office of Juvenile Justice and Delinquency Prevention.

reduced by enhancing known "protective" factors. Healthy beliefs and clear standards for behavior in the family, school, and community (i.e., protective factors) directly promote healthy behavior in children. By encouraging bonding with people and institutions (e.g., families, peer groups, schools, and communities) that promote healthy beliefs and clear standards, the model suggests, youths will be encouraged to adopt similar beliefs and standards. Individual characteristics (e.g., prosocial orientation, intelligence, resilient temperament), however, are important because they affect a child's ability to perceive opportunities, develop skills, and obtain recognition.

The CS was based on decades of research and evaluations in the fields of criminal and juvenile justice, public health, and youth development (Bilchik, 1998; Howell, 2009). Research has consistently documented certain risk factors for violent juvenile offending (Greenwood, 1992; Hawkins et al., 1995; Howell, 1995; Loeber & Farrington, 1998; Reiss & Roth, 1993; Roth, 1994). At the individual level, risk factors include pregnancy and delivery complications, hyperactivity, concentration problems, restlessness, risk-taking behavior, early aggressiveness, early involvement in other forms of antisocial behavior, and beliefs and attitudes favorable to deviant or antisocial behavior. Family factors that increase risk include delinquent siblings, criminal behavior of parents, harsh discipline, physical abuse or neglect, poor family management practices, low levels of parent–child involvement, high levels of family conflict, parental attitudes favorable to violence, and separation of the child from family. School factors associated with higher risk include academic failure, low commitment to education, truancy, early dropout, frequent changes of schools, association with delinquent peers, and gang membership. Community or neighborhood factors include high population density, high residential mobility, high poverty rate, availability of weapons and drugs, and a high rate of adult involvement in crime.

In a 1992 reauthorization of the Juvenile Justice and Delinquency Prevention Act of 1974, Congress established the Title V Incentive Grants for Local Delinquency Prevention Programs (Pub. L. 93–415; 42 U.S.C. 5601 *et seq.*), known as the Community Prevention Grants Program. Title V grants supported the implementation of many local, collaborative, and community-based delinquency prevention plans focused on implementing the CS (Caliber Associates, 2006). We summarize here five key objectives of the CS and review corresponding prevention and intervention strategies.

The first objective of the strategy was to provide immediate intervention and appropriate sanctions and treatment for delinquents. One broad strategy involved graduated sanctions. Sanctions refer to a system of responses to delinquency that combine individual accountability with intensive treatment and rehabilitation services. These sanctions are graduated to the degree that they fit the offense and the juvenile's previous history of delinquency. This requires consideration and balancing of various criteria, such as the seriousness of the delinquent act, the potential risk for reoffending, the risk to public safety, and the offender's rehabilitation needs. The most intensive treatments are reserved for juveniles who most need them (e.g., intensive, residential drug and alcohol treatment), while the most intensive punishments (e.g., secure detention, rather than camps, ranches, or farms) are reserved for those who earn them. Comprehensive, valid, risk and needs assessments are required to determine the appropriate punishment or treatment response for any juvenile.

Safe Futures was one programmatic response to the first objective. Under the Safe Futures Project, OJJDP provided approximately $1,400,000 a year for five years to each of six communities: Boston, Seattle, St. Louis, Contra Costa County and Imperial County (both in California), and the Fort Belknap Indian Community in Montana (Morley et al., 2000). Safe Futures assisted communities in developing collaborative efforts to reduce youth violence and to improve the service delivery system by creating a continuum of care for youths and their families. Both primary and secondary prevention strategies were used. Collaborative efforts included the participation of local human service and juvenile justice systems, health and mental health services, child welfare and education, and police, probation, courts, and corrections agencies. In Boston, for example, a coalition of community and government agencies established a total support network to address the multiple needs of juvenile offenders and their families. Extensive participation included neighborhood residents and youths, community-based service providers, schools, churches, housing authorities, probation, police, and corrections. A key aspect of this program was its emphasis on increasing local administrative control and decision making through neighborhood governance boards established in each of the three target areas (Kracke & Special Emphasis Division Staff, 1996).

The second objective of the plan was to prosecute serious, violent, and chronic juvenile offenders in criminal court. The primary focus was on offenders who have committed serious crimes, have a lengthy history of delinquency, have failed to respond to treatment, or all of these. In public health parlance, tertiary prevention is emphasized by this objective. In particular, almost every state has adopted or strengthened waiver and transfer mechanisms that allow juveniles, under specific conditions, to be tried as adults in criminal court. Such legislation varies dramatically from one state to another, however, and reliable information on the impact of such strategies is still lacking. Related policies include changing state laws to make juvenile records more accessible to school, human services, and justice personnel. In many states, a juvenile's record no longer stays sealed when he or she reaches adulthood; previous juvenile offenses can now be used in criminal proceedings. Confidentiality of juvenile records, once a cornerstone of the *parens patriae* philosophy, has also been weakened, ostensibly to improve sharing of information among human services personnel and to improve coordination of different treatment services delivered by different agencies (Harris et al., 2000).

The third objective of the plan was to reduce youth involvement with guns, drugs, and gangs. Partnerships to Reduce Juvenile Gun Violence was an OJJDP initiative that attempted to enhance and coordinate prevention, intervention, and suppression activities by strengthening linkages among community groups, schools, law enforcement, and the juvenile justice system. For example, if law enforcement agents became more acquainted with community residents, it was hoped that they would learn more about problems in neighborhoods and be more successful in enlisting support for community crime prevention efforts. Three critical factors were addressed: (1) juvenile access to guns, (2) the reasons young people carry guns, and (3) the reasons they choose to use guns to resolve conflicts. In the Boston Violence Prevention Project (Braga et al., 2001; Kennedy, 1997), city, state, and federal representatives helped establish and support a large network of community-based job, recreation, and prevention programs for juveniles (see also Chapter 12). Such efforts, illustrative of secondary and tertiary prevention techniques, coincided with police and probation crackdowns on high-risk offenders.

Other strategies focused specifically on reducing gang violence. Research supported through OJJDP's National Youth Gang Suppression and Intervention Program, based on the work of Irving Spergel in Chicago, suggested that effective strategies to reduce gang violence must focus on individuals, institutions, and communities (Burch & Chemers, 1997). Coordinated strategies associated with the sustained reduction of gang problems include community mobilization (e.g., citizens, youth, community groups, and agencies), social and economic opportunities, such as special school, training, and job programs, social intervention (especially youth outreach and work with street gangs), gang suppression (i.e., formal and informal social control procedures administered by justice agencies and community groups), and organizational change and development (i.e., appropriate organization and integration of strategies and potential reallocation of resources among involved agencies).

Based upon these findings, OJJDP implemented and tested its Comprehensive Response to America's Youth Gang Initiative in a number of jurisdictions across the United States (OJJDP, 2009). The model's key feature is a strategic planning process designed to empower communities to assess their own gang problems and develop antigang strategies and program activities. A strategic planning tool developed by OJJDP is available at no cost. OJJDP's Socioeconomic Mapping and Resource Topography (SMART) system is available online (www.smartgis.info).

The fourth objective was to provide opportunities for children and youths. When they are well planned and well implemented, prevention and intervention activities focused on enhancing prosocial skills and increasing opportunities for youth have been effective in reducing serious delinquency (e.g., Howell, 1995; Lipsey & Wilson, 1998; Lipsey et al., 2000). Such programs include counseling, building interpersonal skills, mentoring, after-school activities, conflict resolution training, remedial education, and vocational education. In a multisite study, participation in five community-based after-school programs run by nonprofit groups reduced rearrest rates for juveniles in one community but not another (Welsh et al., 1999). Program implementation and organizational stability were major factors influencing impacts.

Mentoring programs, such as the Juvenile Mentoring Programs (JUMP) funded by OJJDP, have also demonstrated some success in reducing delinquency. Advocates of mentoring argue that such programs address at-risk children's critical needs for positive adult contact, support, monitoring, and child advocacy. Such needs are particularly high in impoverished communities where delinquency rates are highest. Mentors and youths make a significant commitment of time and energy to develop relationships devoted to personal, academic, or career development, and social, athletic, or artistic growth. In the Big Brothers/Big Sisters program, the youth and the volunteer mentor meet for about four hours, two to four times per month, for at least one year. Developmentally appropriate activities may include taking walks; attending a play, movie, school activity, or sporting event; playing catch; visiting the library; grocery shopping; watching television; and sharing thoughts and ideas about life. Professional staff and national operating standards provide uniformity in recruitment, screening, matching, and supervision of volunteers and youths. Opportunities and support are provided for volunteers, as well as youths and their parents. A national evaluation of the Big Brothers/Big Sisters program found that youths involved in the program were 46% less likely to start using drugs, 33% less likely to exhibit aggressive behavior, and 27% less likely to start using alcohol than their peers (Grossman & Garry, 1997; Ingersoll, 1997). Schools, as sites where juveniles spend a majority of their weekday time, also offer primary opportunities for prevention and intervention efforts, but not in isolation from concerned citizens, communities, and other agencies (see Chapter 10).

The fifth objective dealt with breaking the cycle of violence by addressing youth victimization, abuse, and neglect. Considerable evidence has shown that childhood victimization experiences are related to subsequent delinquency and adult criminality. For example, Thornberry (1994) found that children who had been victims of violence were 24% more likely to report engaging in violent behavior as adolescents than those who had not been maltreated earlier. Widom (1992) reported that child abuse increased the risk of future delinquency and adult criminality by almost 40%. Many have begun to ask how such "cycles of violence" can be broken.

The Safe Kids/Safe Streets initiative by OJJDP was designed to help youth at risk for abuse and neglect; to encourage communities to strengthen the response of their criminal and juvenile justice systems to child abuse and neglect; and to enhance system coordination with child and family service agencies (Ingersoll, 1997). In Burlington, Vermont, a community-wide stakeholder collaborative was organized to address specific needs identified by a community survey. Activities included providing additional resources to new and existing prevention efforts targeting at-risk families and child and adolescent victims of abuse; strengthening interagency protocols and collaboration; training the police, courts, and juvenile providers in effective means of supporting families affected by child abuse, neglect, or both; and involving stakeholders in a community governance structure (Westat, 2005). In a national evaluation of Safe Kids/Safe Streets (Gragg et al., 2005), evaluators did not observe any changes in reported child maltreatment during the term of the study, although they described accomplishments expected to reduce maltreatment, delinquency, and other problem behaviors in the long run. Across sites, the most frequently reported effects were improvements in communication and cooperation among those who deal with child abuse and neglect, improvements in multiagency responses to children affected by domestic violence, improved community education on child abuse and neglect, expanded prevention programs, and improved information sharing and case tracking across agencies.

Although the CS was based on known risk factors derived from empirical research, and its objectives were based on established findings and principles from empirical research, few evaluations of its overall effects have been conducted. Part of the difficulty is due to the complexity of the multiple approaches implemented in many different jurisdictions across different states and attendant difficulties associated with research design. Although the CS was implemented in more than 50 localities in 20 states across the country, few sites have completed comprehensive evaluations (Howell, 2003). Of those that have, results were encouraging (Howell, 2003).

The Orange County, California, 8% Early Intervention Program included the first known implementation of the CS graduated sanctions component (Schumacher & Kurz, 2000). Initial research found that a small number (8%) of first-time offenders were arrested repeatedly over a three-year period, accounting for 55% of repeat cases. Common risk factors for this group included involvement in crime at an early age, significant family problems (abuse, neglect, criminal family members, and/or a lack of parental supervision and control), problems at school (truancy, failing more than one course, or a recent suspension or expulsion), drug and alcohol abuse, and behaviors such as gang involvement, running away, and stealing. The 8% "wraparound" approach was developed to target first-time offenders under 16 who exhibited at least three of the major risk factors. The program attempted to increase structure, supervision, and support for families; make potential "8%-ers" accountable; ensure that youths and families understood the importance of school; and promote prosocial values, behavior, and relationships. Large-scale interagency cooperation ("wraparound" services) was a cornerstone of the program. This intervention was identified as a Model program by the American Youth Policy Forum and as a Promising program by OJJDP. Later renamed the Repeat Offender Prevention Project, California conducted a statewide randomized, experimental evaluation of the program. Overall, youths who participated had significantly better health, education, and justice system outcomes than their counterparts in the control group (California Board of Corrections, 2002; Orange County Probation Department, 2001).

Several other sites combining the CS early intervention, prevention, and graduated sanctions components have produced positive results. These include Breaking Cycles in San Diego (Burke & Pennell, 2001) and Operation Eiger in Baton Rouge (Lizotte & Sheppard, 2001). Further evaluation of implementation and long-term effectiveness is still needed, however (Howell, 2003).

COMMUNITY-BASED APPROACHES

Effective community-based strategies focus on enhancing opportunities and reducing risk factors in specific neighborhoods and usually involve a variety of diverse community, non-profit, and faith-based groups in addition to justice and/or social service agencies (Curtis, 1985). Community-based interventions often target individuals, families, schools, and structural conditions (e.g., unemployment) in specific areas (Welsh et al., 1996, 1999). Below, we briefly discuss several notable examples.

Several large-scale efforts in the 1970s were aimed at strengthening families in the poorest communities, including federally funded Child and Family Resource Centers located in different communities across the country. These centers provided a wide range of services to families (e.g., day care, tutoring, parenting skills, family counseling). A review by the U.S. General Accounting Office stated that these centers enhanced family functioning at very low cost, and they may have reduced delinquency indirectly by improving parent–child relations and school performance (Curtis, 1985). Other programs targeted minority youth unemployment in high-crime communities. Many of the better federal job-training programs of the 1960s and 1970s were successful at reducing crime, improving earnings, and reducing long-term costs. Training for adequate jobs, however, must be provided. If job training only leads to dead-end jobs, illegal opportunities may become even more attractive. Youths' decisions to remain in legitimate jobs depend not only on money, but on intrinsic job satisfaction and gaining respect from their peers. Despite evidence of their success, most of these programs were eliminated or severely curtailed due to federal budget cuts in the 1980s (Curtis, 1985).

Other partnerships in specific communities have attempted to facilitate the cooperation of justice and human service agencies. For example, the Yale/New Haven Child Development-Community Policing Program engages community policing officials and mental health professionals in addressing child victimization and family violence (Marans & Berkman, 1997). Through federal support, nearly 300 communities developed Children's Advocacy Centers, which act as information clearinghouses, provide training and technical assistance, and coordinate the response of judicial and social service systems to child abuse (Ingersoll, 1997).

Long-term economic and social development must also be addressed as part of an effective community-based strategy (Clear, 2007). Capable community organizations have become increasingly involved in crime prevention through programs aimed at strengthening community involvement, employment and economic development, family supports and services, and a host of other activities (e.g., block watches, home security). Economic development is a necessary goal to improve the quality of residents' lives in many areas, including to crime. Creating financial self-sufficiency is at least as important as reducing illegal opportunities or addressing other causes of crime (Clear & Karp, 2000).

Innovative and promising community-based violence prevention strategies attempt to address risk factors at multiple levels. Chicago's Operation CeaseFire attempts to reduce violence by changing community norms about violence, changing perceptions of the risks and costs associated with violence, and widening decision alternatives for individuals involved in conflicts (Skogan et al., 2009). These strategies require a variety of components working together in the community simultaneously, including street intervention, client outreach, clergy involvement, community mobilization, educational campaigns, and policing and prosecution strategies focused on high-risk offenders. Read the case study below and discuss how each one of the three components of the tripartite strategy (patterns, explanations, and interventions) works together in CeaseFire.

CEASEFIRE: A PUBLIC HEALTH APPROACH TO REDUCE SHOOTINGS AND KILLINGS

Source: Ritter, N. (2009). CeaseFire: A public health approach to reduce shootings and killings (NCJ 228386). *NIJ Journal, 264*, 20–25.

The bloodshed in some of the Windy City's toughest neighborhoods declined substantially with the advent of the CeaseFire violence reduction program. A rigorous evaluation of the program, sponsored by the National Institute of Justice, confirmed anecdotal evidence that had already led officials in other cities to adopt Chicago's CeaseFire model. Researchers found that CeaseFire had a significant positive impact on many of the neighborhoods in which the program was implemented, including a decline of 16% to 28% in the number of shootings in four of the seven sites studied.

"Overall, the program areas grew noticeably safer in six of the seven sites, and we concluded that there was evidence that decreases in the size and intensity of shooting hot spots were linked to the introduction of CeaseFire in four of those areas. In two other areas shooting hot spots waned, but evidence that this decline could be linked to CeaseFire was inconclusive," the researchers reported.

Led by Wesley Skogan, a political science professor at Northwestern University, the evaluation team meticulously measured CeaseFire's impact on shootings and killings in Chicago. [1] The researchers spent three years evaluating the program. The findings are encouraging.

What Is CeaseFire?

CeaseFire uses prevention, intervention and community-mobilization strategies to reduce shootings and killings. The program was launched in Chicago in 1999 by the Chicago Project for Violence Prevention at the University of Illinois at Chicago School of Public Health. By 2004, 25 CeaseFire sites existed in Chicago and a few other Illinois cities. Some of the program's strategies were adapted from the public health field, which has had notable success in changing dangerous behaviors. For example, public health campaigns have helped to decrease smoking and increase childhood immunizations. In fact, the program's executive director, Gary Slutkin, is an epidemiologist who views shootings as a public health issue.

As the researchers note in their report, a significant amount of street violence is "surprisingly casual in character." Men shoot one another in disputes over women, or because they feel they have been "dissed." Simply driving through rival gang territory can be fatal. In the gang world, one shooting can lead to another, starting a cycle of violence that can send neighborhoods careening.

CeaseFire uses various tools to target this violence:

- Community mobilization
- A major public education campaign
- Services, such as GED programs, anger-management counseling, drug or alcohol treatment, and help finding child care or looking for a job, that can improve the lives of at-risk youth, including gang members.

In their evaluation, the researchers detail the program's approaches to building collaborations in the CeaseFire sites. The successes and pitfalls were many, as could be expected in a complex program that required law enforcement agencies, businesses, service providers, schools, community groups, political leaders, and one of CeaseFire's most important partners, churches, to work together.

(continued)

(continued)

Of all of the program's facets, the most notable involves hiring "violence interrupters." CeaseFire's violence interrupters establish a rapport with gang leaders and other at-risk youth, just as outreach workers in a public health campaign contact a target community. Working alone or in pairs, the violence interrupters cruise the streets at night, mediating conflicts between gangs. After a shooting, they immediately offer nonviolent alternatives to gang leaders and a shooting victim's friends and relatives to try to interrupt the cycle of retaliatory violence. Violence interrupters differ from community organizers or social workers. Many are former gang members who have served time in prison, which gives them greater credibility among current gang members.

CeaseFire's message travels from violence interrupters to gang members, from clergy to parishioners, and from community leaders to the neighborhood through conversations, sermons, marches, and prayer vigils. The message appears on banners at post-shooting rallies, which are a major part of the program. The message is simple: "The killing must stop!"

Measuring Results

The evaluation included two parts: process and outcomes.

In the process evaluation, the researchers looked at how the program worked in the field. They interviewed CeaseFire staff, police, social service workers, and business, religious and community leaders at 17 sites. The researchers also interviewed 297 gang members and street youth to get their assessment of the program.

The evaluation of outcomes was challenging because the researchers had to find comparable areas without the program to make valid comparisons to CeaseFire neighborhoods. They found seven such sites within the city of Chicago.

Statistical analysis: Analysis based on 17 years of data showed that, as a direct result of CeaseFire, shootings decreased 16% to 28% in four of the seven sites studied. The researchers called this decrease in gun violence "immediate and permanent" in three of the sites and "gradual and permanent" in the fourth site.

Hot spots analysis: Using crime mapping techniques, the researchers compared shooting patterns before and after CeaseFire started to those in areas that had no CeaseFire program. Six of the sites grew noticeably safer overall, but the researchers could credit this to CeaseFire in only four of those areas. In two sites, shooting hot spots waned, but there was not enough evidence to link this to CeaseFire.

Gang social network analysis: Gang killings declined in two CeaseFire sites. The researchers also looked at the proportion of gang homicides that were sparked by an earlier shooting. This violence was a special focus of the violence interrupters. In four sites, retaliatory killings decreased more than in the comparison areas.

Impact on Young People

The researchers also looked at CeaseFire's impact on gang members and other at-risk street youth ("clients") that the program targeted. More than 80% of CeaseFire's clients had past arrests, 56% had spent more than a day in jail, 20% had been to prison, and about 40% had been on probation or parole. Most CeaseFire clients had been involved in a gang. Nearly 60% had only a grade school education.

Many clients said in interviews that they had received significant help from CeaseFire. More than three fourths of the clients said they needed a job; 87% of that group received significant help. Of the 37% who said they wanted to get back into school or a GED program, 85% said they had received help through the program. Nearly every one of the 34% who told the researchers that they wanted help in leaving a gang reported that they had received such guidance. However, although two thirds of the clients became active in CeaseFire after they had formed a relationship with a violence interrupter—and indeed, half of them took part in marches and vigils after a shooting occurred in their neighborhood—70% of the clients were still in a gang when they were interviewed.

That said, the researchers found that CeaseFire had a positive influence on these at-risk youth. "A striking finding was how important CeaseFire loomed in their lives," the researchers stated in the report. "Clients noted the importance of being able to reach their outreach worker at critical moments—when they were tempted to resume taking drugs, were involved in illegal activities, or when they felt that violence was imminent."

CeaseFire also had a positive influence on the violence interrupters themselves. The program employed 150, many of whom had been in a gang and served time in prison. CeaseFire gave them a job in an environment where ex-offenders have limited opportunities and, the researchers note, "Working for CeaseFire also offered them an opportunity for personal redemption and a positive role to play in the communities where many had once been active in gangs."

Challenges and Cautions

Evaluating Chicago CeaseFire was not a neat laboratory experiment. Because the program runs in the real world, boundaries were not always clear between CeaseFire neighborhoods and other neighborhoods. For example, the violence interrupters had to go where gang members and other potential perpetrators of gun crime (and their potential victims) lived or hung out. "Spillover" between targeted areas and other areas was inevitable, although the researchers pointed out that this could have resulted in underestimating the program's impact.

Other programs, such as Project Safe Neighborhoods, were running in and around some of the CeaseFire sites during part of the time the researchers evaluated the program. Despite their best efforts to avoid such areas when selecting comparison sites, it was not always possible to do so. When this occurred, the researchers stated they were unable to determine empirically that CeaseFire alone was responsible for the decrease in violence.

Other issues made it difficult to discover the exact effect of CeaseFire in as straightforward and precise a way as policymakers and citizens might like. For example, in looking at the statistical data about violence, the researchers had to pick a month as the pre- and post-CeaseFire demarcation. However, pinpointing a precise date for the start of a program as large and multifaceted as CeaseFire is not easy. Community-mobilization and public education efforts got under way at different times in different areas, and the hiring of violence interrupters came a few years after the program started.

Another issue to consider when looking at the findings is that the researchers were able to examine only events that were reported to and recorded by police.

Finally, one overarching caveat to keep in mind is that Chicago experienced a huge drop in violence beginning in 1992. [2] As the researchers state in their report, "The reasons for this decline are, as elsewhere in the nation, ill-understood, and we could not account for possible remaining differences between the target and comparison areas in terms of those obviously important factors."

Still, It Worked

Despite these caveats, the evaluation showed that the program made neighborhoods safer. CeaseFire decreased shootings and killings (including retaliatory murders in some of the sites), making shooting hot spots cooler and helping the highest-risk youth.

The full report contains an extensive discussion of many topics, including:

- How sites were selected and organized, and how the central CeaseFire management worked
- Challenges in areas with notably weak community bases
- The crucial role of local police in providing immediate information about a shooting. This cooperation was not automatic, and readers may want to learn more about how this evolved.

Like other criminal justice programs, CeaseFire was vulnerable to the vagaries of funding fluctuations. Policymakers in particular will want to read sections of the evaluation to understand how the program was funded and the role that fluctuations played throughout the years. Also, CeaseFire was a small-scale program. Although it varied among the sites, the typical CeaseFire site's annual budget during the period covered in the evaluation was about $240,000. In the summer of 2007, the program was dramatically downsized because of budget cuts. The researchers found that they did not have enough data to do a rigorous statistical analysis of this cutback's impact. They did state, however, that "[a] detailed examination of the existing data did not reveal any dramatic shifts in crime following the closures [of CeaseFire sites], when compared to trends in the comparison areas."

CeaseFire is still running in 16 Chicago communities and six other Illinois cities. The CeaseFire model is going national. Recently, CeaseFire has collaborated with the Baltimore City Health Department to set up the model in four sites. Parts of the model are being implemented in Kansas City, MO, and officials are considering implementing it in Columbus, OH; Detroit; Jacksonville, FL; and New Orleans. Other programs modeled on CeaseFire are being launched in eight New York cities, including Albany, Buffalo, New York City, Rochester, and Syracuse.

The NIJ evaluation was supported by the Bureau of Justice Assistance and the Office of Juvenile Justice and Delinquency Prevention.

For More Information

- An executive summary and the full report are available at http://www.skogan.org/files/Evaluation_of_CeaseFire-Chicago_Main_Report.03-2009.pdf
- CeaseFire website: http://ceasefirechicago.org/

Notes

1. Skogan was the lead investigator on the NIJ-funded evaluation. Other researchers who participated in the evaluation include So Yung Kim (Korea Advanced Institute of Science and Technology); Richard Block (Loyola University Chicago); Andrew Papachristos (University of Massachusetts Amherst); and Susan Hartnett and Jill DuBois (Northwestern University).
2. Crime and violence decreased throughout Chicago in both the target and the comparison sites during the time that the researchers considered data, so they used fairly complex analyses to examine whether crime dropped significantly, hot spots visibly moved or cooled, and gang homicide weakened more in the CeaseFire sites than in the comparison areas.

BLUEPRINTS FOR HEALTHY YOUTH DEVELOPMENT

The Blueprints for Healthy Youth Development initiative (formerly "Blueprints for Violence Prevention") is a comprehensive effort to provide communities with a set of programs whose effectiveness has been scientifically demonstrated (www.blueprintsprograms.com). With support from the Annie E. Casey Foundation, the Center for the Study and

Prevention of Violence at the University of Colorado at Boulder identifies and replicates effective youth violence prevention programs across the United States. Outcomes have been expanded to include not only problem behavior but also education, emotional well-being, physical health, and positive relationships.

Program effectiveness is judged based on an initial review by the center and a final review by an advisory board comprising six experts in the field of violence prevention. The standard for proven effectiveness includes four criteria: (1) an experimental or quasi-experimental design with random assignment or matched control group; (2) evidence of a statistically significant deterrent effect on delinquency, drug use, and/or violence; (3) replication in at least one additional site with demonstrated effects; and (4) evidence that the deterrent effect was sustained for at least one year following treatment. To date, more than 1,250 programs have been reviewed. Eleven programs have met strict scientific standards of program effectiveness. We briefly describe these 11 here (for further information, see: www.blueprintsprograms.com).

1. *Nurse Family Partnership* is a program that sends nurses into the homes of at-risk pregnant women bearing their first child to ensure the health of the mother and child (Nurse Family Partnership, 2010). Home visits promote the physical, cognitive, and emotional development of the children and provide general support and parenting instruction to the parents from the prenatal period to two years after the birth of the child. Six- to 12-year follow-up studies of children showed significant reductions in aggressive and criminal behavior and improvements in intellectual functioning, mental health, and quality of relationship with mothers.
2. *Promoting Alternative Thinking Strategies* (PATHS) is a multiyear, school-based prevention model for elementary school youths designed to promote emotional and social competence, including the expression, understanding, and regulation of emotions. Evaluations demonstrated significant improvements in social problem solving, emotional understanding, and self-control, and higher scores on peer sociability.
3. *Multisystemic Therapy* targets specific factors in a youth's ecology (family, peers, school, neighborhood, and support network) that contribute to antisocial behavior. This is a short-term, intensive program by credentialed therapists that has been proven effective for decreasing antisocial behavior of violent and chronic juvenile offenders.
4. *Multisystemic Therapy for Sexual Offenders* focuses on aspects of a youth's ecology that are functionally related to the problem sexual behavior and includes reduction of parent and youth denial about the sexual offenses and their consequences; promotion of the development of friendships and age-appropriate sexual experiences; and modification of the individual's social perspective-taking skills, belief system, or attitudes that contributed to sexual offending. Families are provided family therapy, youth are provided individual therapy, and services are delivered over a period of five to seven months. Therapists have three to five families on their caseloads, and rotating members of the team are available to respond to crises 24 hours a day, seven days a week. Studies have demonstrated significant reductions in arrests for both sexual and nonsexual offenses and significant improvements in peer and family relationships.

5. *Functional Family Therapy* is a family treatment model designed to engage and motivate youths and families to change their communication, interactions, and problem-solving patterns. It has been applied successfully to a variety of problem youths (with problems ranging from conduct disorder to serious criminal offenses, such as theft or aggravated assault). Studies have demonstrated consistent reductions in substance abuse, rearrest, and recidivism, and significant improvements in family functioning.
6. *Life Skills Training* is a three-year primary prevention program that targets the use of cigarettes, alcohol, and marijuana (the initial year includes 15 lessons; booster sessions are provided in years two and three). The program provides general life skills and social resistance skills training to junior high and middle school students to increase knowledge and improve attitudes about drug use. Numerous studies have demonstrated the effectiveness of this program in reducing tobacco use, alcohol and illicit drug use, delinquency, and violence.
7. *Multidimensional Treatment Foster Care* is an effective alternative to residential treatment for adolescents who have problems with chronic delinquency and antisocial behavior. Youths are placed in well-supervised foster families for six to nine months and undergo weekly individualized therapy. Foster families receive weekly group supervision and daily telephone monitoring. Biological parents learn behavior management techniques to ensure that gains made in the foster setting are maintained after the youth return home. Studies show significant reductions in arrest, incarceration, and violent offending due to the program.
8. *Project Towards No Drug Abuse* is a drug abuse prevention program that targets heterogeneous samples of youth ages 14 to 19. A set of 12 in-class interactive sessions builds motivational and decision-making skills targeting the use of cigarettes, alcohol, drugs, and violence-related behavior. It has been tested at traditional and alternative high schools using true experimental designs. Reductions in cigarette smoking, alcohol use, marijuana use, hard drug use, and victimization have been found at one- and two-year follow-up periods.
9. *Brief Alcohol Screening and Intervention of College Students* (BASICS) is a preventive intervention for college students 18 to 24 years old. It targets students who drink heavily and are at risk for alcohol-related problems such as poor class attendance, missed assignments, accidents, sexual assault, and violence. BASICS is designed to help students make better alcohol-use decisions based on a clear understanding of the risks associated with problem drinking, enhanced motivation to change, and the development of skills to moderate drinking. The program involves two brief interviews that prompt students to change their drinking patterns. Significant reduction in binge drinking and problem drinking were reported.
10. *The New Beginnings program* is a group-based intervention for divorced mothers and their children. It consists of 10 two-hour group sessions held either for mothers or concurrently for mothers and their children. Groups are led by two master's-level clinicians. The intervention focuses on changing aspects of the child's environment that directly involve the child, including increasing effective discipline strategies, increasing mother–child relationship quality, and decreasing exposure to conflict between

parents. There are two individual phone sessions that are structured but also allow for tailoring the program to specific needs. Program skills are taught through presentations, role-playing, and videotapes. Significant effects include reductions in childhood behavioral problems and aggression, improved mother–child relationship quality, and better maternal use of effective discipline strategies.

11. *Positive Action* is a school-based program that includes school-wide climate change and a detailed curriculum with lessons two to four times a week—approximately 140 15-minute lessons for grades K to 6 and 82 15- to 20-minute lessons for grades 7 and 8. Lessons for each grade level are scripted and age-appropriate. The first unit, which includes the Thoughts-Actions-Feelings about Self Circle, provides an introduction to the nature and relevancy of positive and negative actions and behaviors. Units 2 through 6 teach the positive actions for the physical, intellectual, social, and emotional areas. There are two school-wide climate development kits (elementary and secondary) and a counselor's kit. The kits reinforce the classroom curriculum in the practice and reinforcement of positive actions. After three program years, there were school-wide reductions in grade retention, suspensions, and absenteeism and school-wide improvements in reading and math proficiency and teacher- and student-reported school supportiveness.

WHEN VIOLENT CRIME GOES DOWN, DO WE KNOW WHY?

How can we explain the decreases in violent crime since 1993, the largest in more than 30 years? Significant decreases in homicides have been recorded since 1991, when a peak rate of 10.5 per 100,000 was recorded. The murder and nonnegligent manslaughter rate of 5.5 per 100,000 recorded in 2000 and 2004 was the lowest recorded since 1965 (Maguire & Pastore, 2006b). Substantial drops in other violent crimes (e.g., robbery, rape, aggravated assault) were observed during the same period. How much is this downward trend related to criminal justice policies, prevention strategies, economic or social conditions, or other factors (e.g., changes in age distributions, drug markets, and weapon availability)?

Experts generally agree that changes in the use of weapons are important in understanding peaks and valleys in homicides, particularly juvenile homicides (Blumstein & Rosenfeld, 1998; Blumstein & Wallman, 2000). The growth in homicides by young people from 1985 to 1993 was entirely due to homicides committed with handguns. Decreases since 1994 are similarly due to decreases in handgun-related homicides. These trends were most pronounced for large cities and appear to be related to the rise and fall of crack markets and violent drug markets in large cities.

Observed decreases in violent crime from 1993 to 2000 may also have been partially due to economic upturn (e.g., reduced unemployment rates), police crackdowns on illegal markets, increased incarceration rates, and increased youth involvement in legitimate labor markets. It is extremely difficult, however, to parcel out specific causes for decreased violence: probably all played some role in interaction with one another (Blumstein & Rosenfeld, 1998; Blumstein & Wallman, 2000).

Social institutions (i.e., mutually shared and reinforced patterns of norms, rules, and laws) provide another potential explanation for decreases in violence (LaFree, 1998). In the peaceful post-World War II years, social institutions (e.g., political, economic, and family) were strong. In the 1970s, public trust in political institutions plummeted; economic inequality, inflation, and decline of labor unions all reduced confidence. The traditional family of the 1950s was severely weakened in the 1970s (e.g., both parents working, more single parents, higher divorce rates). Violent crime rates increased dramatically from 1963 to 1974. American society fought back against institutional decline by investing heavily in other institutions, especially criminal justice, education, and welfare. All three put downward pressure on crime rates, LaFree (1998) argues.

Curtis (1998) suggests that many people had written off inner cities at the peak of the crack problem in the late 1980s and early 1990s. But how do we explain the sudden decline in violent crime in these neighborhoods, especially in New York City? Curtis cites ethnographic research in two New York City neighborhoods to suggest that many youths began to withdraw from public life as violence around them increased. He further suggests that community activism against violence played a role, even though economic vitality can hardly be said to have increased markedly. At the same time, aggressive policing against drug gangs and long prison sentences helped reduce the influence of large drug gangs because many downsized and many disbanded. Remaining distributors became more discreet and moved indoors, and turf battles were eliminated.

Fagan, Zimring, and Kim (1998) argue that those who gave credit to police strategies for declines in crime in New York City had little evidence for their claims. Why was there a steady decline in nongun homicides long before former Mayor Rudolph Giuliani and former Police Commissioner William Bratton took office and began their multifaceted war on crime? As Fagan and colleagues (1998, p. 13) noted:

> The trend in nongun homicide for more than a decade remains a pleasant mystery that shrouds the whole explanation of variations in New York City homicide in fog. Even the best statistical data on incidence will not yield easy answers on causation.

CONCLUSIONS

We have reviewed diverse prevention and intervention efforts throughout this book. These examples serve to illustrate the broad, interdisciplinary nature of prevention and intervention required to reduce rates of violence in our society. Violence prevention must strive for an appropriate balance between punishment and prevention, between reactive and proactive approaches, between legal and educational interventions, and between social development and social control.

Much further research on risk factors and causes of violence is desirable, and more rigorous, valid evaluations of program effects are needed. Valid analyses of risk factors and causes are prerequisites for designing effective violence reduction strategies (Welsh & Harris, 2013). In the absence of such information, untested assumptions and hunches will continue to drive critical policy decisions, and unacceptably high rates of injuries and deaths will persist.

Despite perceptions by many that violence in the United States is out of control and beyond control, careful examination indicates that violence is more prevalent among some groups than others, occurs more in some places than others, and involves certain types of situations and participants more often than others. There is reason for optimism as researchers and practitioners work together to explore and evaluate rational approaches to reducing violence.

Significant challenges remain, however. Successful interventions cost money and a significant investment of human resources. It is not yet clear that local, state, or federal government officials are prepared to sustain a commitment to approaches based on valid research and knowledge, rather than policies calculated to win votes at election time. Nor is it clear that government officials will fund evaluation studies at the level necessary to determine what works. A dearth of valid evaluations has hindered progress in our knowledge about what works. Everyone seems to agree that better coordination and cooperation among government, private, and nonprofit agencies is needed, but little attention is devoted to exploring how to make such relationships work given the diverse backgrounds and agendas of participants (Welsh & Harris, 2013).

Perhaps the best that can be said for now is that violence prevention in the United States has a promising but unpredictable future. To the degree that interventions can reasonably balance punishment and prevention, and take a rational approach based on existing and emerging knowledge, that promise may yet be realized.

DISCUSSION QUESTIONS

1. Define and discuss (a) deterrence, (b) rehabilitation, (c) incapacitation, and (d) restoration. For each, discuss available evidence and limitations.
2. Discuss major *arguments* and *evidence* in favor of and against (a) the death penalty and (b) three-strikes laws.
3. Describe *major risk factors* for violent juvenile offending: (a) individual, (b) family, (c) school, and (d) community.
4. What are Evidence-Based Practices and Programs (EBPPs)? What does this term mean, and what are the criteria for designating something as an EBPP?
5. Describe OJJDP's Comprehensive Strategy for Serious, Violent and Chronic Juvenile Offenders. Discuss the five objectives and give one example of each.
6. Describe how Operation CeaseFire works and discuss evidence for its effectiveness.
7. Describe *Blueprints for Healthy Youth Development*. Give one specific example.
8. Why did violent crime go down after 1993? Make an argument, and give specific evidence from course materials to support your answer.
9. According to Riedel and Welsh, "Violence prevention must strive for an appropriate balance between punishment and prevention, between reactive and proactive approaches, between legal and educational interventions, between social development and social control." (a) What do they mean? (b) Do you agree or disagree with this statement? Why? Give specific examples from course materials to support your argument.

SUGGESTED READINGS

Farrington, D. P., & Welsh, B. C. (2008). *Saving children from a life of crime: Early risk factors and effective interventions*. New York: Oxford University Press.

Greenwood, P. W. (2007). *Changing lives: Delinquency prevention as crime-control policy*. Chicago: University of Chicago Press.

Lipsey, M. W., Howell, J. C., Kelly, M. R., Chapman, G., & Carver, D. (2010). *Improving the effectiveness of juvenile justice programs.* Washington, DC: Center for Juvenile Justice Reform, Georgetown Public Policy Institute.

Skogan, W. G., Hartnett, S. M., Bump, N., & Dubois, J. (2009). *Evaluation of CeaseFire-Chicago* (NCJ 227181). Washington, DC: U.S. Department of Justice. Retrieved from https://www.ncjrs.gov/pdffiles1/nij/grants/227181.pdf.

REFERENCES

American Psychological Association. (2006). Presidential task force on evidence-based practice. Evidence-based practice in psychology. *American Psychologist, 61*(4), 271–285.

Andrews, D. A., & Bonta, J. (2006). *Psychology of criminal conduct* (4th ed.). Cincinnati, OH: LexisNexis/Anderson.

Andrews, D. A., Zinger, I., Hoge, R., Bonta, J., Gendreau, P., & Cullen, R. (1990). Does correctional treatment work? A clinically relevant and psychologically informed meta-analysis. *Criminology, 28,* 369–404.

Auerhahn, K. (2003). *Selective incapacitation and public policy: Evaluating California's imprisonment crisis.* Albany: State University of New York Press.

Baldus, D. C., Woodworth, G., & Pulaski, C. A., Jr. (1994). *Equal justice and the death penalty: A legal and empirical analysis.* Boston: Northeastern University Press.

Bilchik, S. (1998). *A juvenile justice system for the 21st century* (NCJ 169276). Washington, DC: Department of Justice, Office of Juvenile Justice and Delinquency Prevention.

Blumstein, A., Cohen, J., & Nagin, D. (Eds.). (1978). *Deterrence and incapacitation: Estimating the effects of criminal sanctions on crime rates.* Washington, DC: National Academy of Sciences.

Blumstein, A., Cohen, J., Roth, J. A., & Visher, C. (Eds.). (1986). *Criminal careers and career criminals* (2 vols.). Washington, DC: National Academy of Sciences.

Blumstein, A., & Rosenfeld, R. (1998). Assessing the recent ups and downs in U.S. homicide rates. *National Institute of Justice Journal, 237,* 9–11.

Blumstein, A., & Wallman, J. (Eds.). (2000). *The crime drop in America.* New York: Cambridge University Press.

Bohm, R. M. (1989). Humanism and the death penalty, with special emphasis on the post-Furman experience. *Justice Quarterly, 6,* 173–195.

Bohm, R. M. (2003). *Deathquest II: An introduction to the theory and practice of capital punishment in the United States* (2nd ed.). Cincinnati, OH: Anderson.

Bonczar, T. P., & Snell, T. L. (2005). *Capital Punishment, 2004.* Bureau of Justice Statistics Bulletin (NCJ 211349). Washington, DC: U.S. Department of Justice, Office of Justice Programs.

Bourgon, G., & Armstrong, B. (2005). Transferring the principles of effective treatment into a "real world" prison setting. *Criminal Justice and Behavior, 32,* 3–25.

Bowers, W. J. (1974). *Executions in America.* Lexington, MA: Lexington Books, D.C. Heath.

Braga, A. A., Kennedy, D. M., Waring, E. J., & Piehl, A. M. (2001). Problem-oriented policing, deterrence, and youth violence: An evaluation of Boston's Operation Ceasefire. *Journal of Research in Crime and Delinquency, 38,* 195–225.

Braithwaite, J. (1999). Restorative justice: Assessing optimistic and pessimistic accounts. In M. Tonry (Ed.), *Crime and justice: A review of research* (Vol. 25, pp. 1–127). Chicago: University of Chicago Press.

Brown, B. S., & Flynn, P. M. (2002). The federal role in drug abuse technology transfer: A history and perspective. *Journal of Substance Abuse Treatment, 22,* 245–257.

Burch, J. H., III, & Chemers, B. M. (1997). *A comprehensive response to America's youth gang problem* (Fact Sheet #40). Washington, DC: Department of Justice, Office of Justice Programs, Office of Juvenile Justice and Delinquency Prevention.

Burke, C., & Pennell, S. (2001). *What works: San Diego County's breaking cycles program* (NCJ 205580). San Diego, CA: San Diego Association of Governments (SANDAG). Retrieved September 28, 2006, from http://www.sandag.org/uploads/publicationid/publicationid_573_951.pdf.

Caliber Associates. (2006). *National evaluation of the Title V Community Prevention Grants Program* (NCJ 212214). Washington, DC: U.S. Department of Justice, Office of Justice Programs, Office of Juvenile Justice and Delinquency Prevention.

California Board of Corrections. (2002). *Repeat Offender Prevention Program: Final Report to the Legislature*. Sacramento, CA: CA Board of Corrections. Retrieved from http://www.cdcr.ca.gov/Divisions_Boards/CSA/CPP/Docs/Final%20Evaluation.pdf

Catalano, R. F., & Hawkins, J. D. (1996). The social development model: A theory of antisocial behavior. In J. D. Hawkins (Ed.), *Delinquencyand crime: Current theories* (pp. 149–197). New York: Cambridge University Press.

Chaiken, J. M., Lawless, M., & Stevenson, K. A. (1974). *The impact of police activity on crime: Robberies on the New York City subway system* (R-1424-NYC). Santa Monica, CA: Rand Corporation.

Clarke, R. V. (1992). *Situational crime prevention: Successful case studies*. New York: Harrow & Heston.

Clarke, R. V., & Cornish, D. B. (1985). Modeling offenders' decisions: A framework for policy and research. In M. Tonry & N. Morris (Eds.), *Crime and justice: An annual review of research* (Vol. 6, pp. 147–185). Chicago: University of Chicago Press.

Clear, T. R. (2007). *Imprisoning communities: How mass incarceration makes disadvantaged neighborhoods worse*. New York: Oxford University Press.

Clear, T. R., & Karp, D. R. (2000). *The community justice ideal: Preventing crime and achieving justice*. Boulder, CO: Westview.

Cole, G. F., & Smith, C. E. (2004). *The American system of criminal justice* (10th ed.). Belmont, CA: Wadsworth/Thompson.

Conrad, J. P., & van den Haag, E. (1983). *The death penalty: A debate*. New York: Plenum.

Coolbaugh, K., & Hansel, C. J. (2000). *The comprehensive strategy: Lessons learned from the pilot sites* (NCJ 178258). Washington, DC: Office of Juvenile Justice and Delinquency Prevention.

Curtis, L. A. (Ed.). (1985). *American violence and public policy: An update of the national commission on the causes and prevention of violence*. New Haven, CT: Yale University Press.

Curtis, R. (1998). The improbable transformation of inner-city neighborhoods: Crime, violence, drugs, and youths in the 1990s. *National Institute of Justice Journal, 237*, 16–17.

Ehrlich, I. (1975). The deterrent effect of capital punishment: A question of life or death. *American Economic Review, 65*, 397–417.

Fagan, J., Zimring, F., & Kim, J. (1998). Declining homicide in New York City: A tale of two trends. *National Institute of Justice Journal, 237*, 12–13.

Federal Bureau of Investigation. (2009). *Crime in the United States 2008*. Retrieved December 21, 2009, from http://www.fbi.gov/ucr/cius2008/index.html

Feyerherm, W. H. (1995). The DMC initiative: The convergence of policy and research themes. In K. K. Leonard, C. E. Pope, & W. H. Feyerherm (Eds.), *Minorities in juvenile justice* (pp. 1–15). Thousand Oaks, CA: Sage.

Foucault, M. (1977). *Discipline and punish*. New York: Pantheon.

Furman vs. Georgia, 408 U.S. 238 (1972).

Gallup. (2014). Death penalty. Retrieved July 8, 2014, from: http://www.gallup.com/poll/1606/death-penalty.aspx.

Gendreau, P. (1996). The principles of effective intervention with offenders. In A. T. Harland (Ed.), *Choosing correctional options that work: Defining the demand and evaluating the supply* (pp. 117–130). Thousand Oaks, CA: Sage.

Gragg, E., Cronin, R., Schultz, D., & Eisen, K. (2005). *National evaluation of the Safe Kids/Safe Streets program: Final report executive summary* (NCJ 210269). Washington, DC: U.S. Department of Justice, Office of Justice Programs, Office of Juvenile Justice and Delinquency Prevention.

Greenwood, P. W. (1982). The violent offender in the criminal justice system. In M. E. Wolfgang & N. A. Weiner (Eds.), *Criminal violence* (pp. 320–346). Beverly Hills, CA: Sage.

Greenwood, P. W. (1992). Substance abuse problems among high-risk youth and potential interventions. *Crime and Delinquency, 38*, 444–458.

Greenwood, P. W., Everingham, S. S., Chen, E., Abrahamse, A. F., Merritt, N., & Chiesa, J. (1998). *Three strikes revisited: An early assessment of implementation and effects* (NCJ 194106). Washington, DC: U.S. Department of Justice, Office of Justice Programs, National Institute of Justice.

Greenwood, P. W., Rydell, C. P., Abrahamse, A. F., Caulkins, J. P., Chiesa, J., Model, K. E., & Klein, S. P. (1994). *Three strikes and you're out—Estimated benefits and costs of California's new mandatory-sentencing law.* Santa Monica, CA: RAND Corporation. Retrieved September 29, 2006, from http://www.rand.org/publications/MR/MR509/.

Gregg vs. Georgia, 428 U.S. 153 (1976).

Grossman, J. B., & Garry, E. M. (1997). *Mentoring—A proven delinquency prevention strategy* (NCJ 164834). Washington, DC: U.S. Department of Justice, Office of Justice Programs, Office of Juvenile Justice and Delinquency Prevention.

Hagan, J., & Peterson, R. D. (1995). Criminal inequality in America: Patterns and consequences. In J. Hagan & R. D. Peterson (Eds.), *Crime and inequality* (pp. 14–36). Stanford, CA: Stanford University Press.

Harris, P. W., Welsh, W. N., & Butler, F. (2000). A century of juvenile justice. In G. LaFree, R. Taylor, R. Bursik, & J. Short (Eds.), *Criminal justice 2000.* Vol. 1. *The changing nature of crime* (359–425). Washington, D C: U.S. Department of Justice, National Institute of Justice.

Hawkins, D. (Ed.). (2003). *Violent crime: Assessing race and ethnic differences.* New York: Cambridge University Press.

Hawkins, J. D., Arthur, M. W., & Catalano, R. F. (1995). Preventing substance abuse. In M. Tonry (Ed.), *Crime and justice: A review of research* (Vol. 19, pp. 343–427). Chicago: University of Chicago Press.

Hawkins, J. D., & Catalano, R. F. (1992). *Communities that care: Action for drug abuse prevention.* San Francisco: Jossey-Bass.

Howell, J. C. (Ed.). (1995). *Guide for implementing the comprehensive strategy for serious, violent, and chronic juvenile offenders* (NCJ 153681). Washington, DC: U.S. Department of Justice, Office of Justice Programs, Office of Juvenile Justice and Delinquency Prevention.

Howell, J. C. (2003). Diffusing research into practice using the comprehensive strategy for serious, violent, and chronic juvenile offenders. *Youth Violence and Juvenile Justice, 3*, 219–245.

Howell, J. C. (2009). *Preventing and reducing juvenile delinquency: A comprehensive framework* (2nd ed.). Thousand Oaks, CA: Sage Publications.

Hsia, H. M., Bridges, G. S., & McHale, R. (2004). *Disproportionate minority confinement: 2002 update* (NCJ 201240). Washington, DC: Office of Juvenile Justice Delinquency and Prevention.

Ingersoll, S. (1997). The national juvenile justice action plan: A comprehensive response to a critical challenge. *Juvenile Justice, Journal of the Office of Juvenile Justice and Delinquency Prevention, 3*(2), 11–20.

Institute of Medicine. (2002). *The future of public health in the 21st century.* Washington, DC: Institute of Medicine.

Kelling, G. L., Pate, T., Dieckman, D., & Brown, C. E. (1974). *The Kansas City preventive patrol experiment: A summary report*. Washington, DC: Police Foundation.

Kennedy, D. M. (1997). *Juvenile gun violence and gun markets in Boston. Research preview.* Washington, DC: Department of Justice, Office of Justice Programs, National Institute of Justice.

Kilbourne, A. M., Neumann, M. S., Pincus, H. A., Bauer, M. S., & Stall, R. (2007). Implementing evidence-based interventions in health care: Application of the replicating effective programs framework. *Implementation Science, 2*, 42.

Kracke, K., & Special Emphasis Division Staff. (1996). *Safe futures: Partnerships to reduce youth violence and delinquency.* Fact Sheet #38. Washington, DC: Department of Justice, Office of Justice Programs, Office of Juvenile Justice and Delinquency Prevention.

Kurki, L. (1999). *Incorporating restorative and community justice into American sentencing and corrections. Sentencing & Corrections: Issues for the 21st Century.* Papers from the Executive Sessions on Sentencing and Corrections, No. 3 (NCJ 175723). Washington, DC: U.S. Department of Justice, Office of Justice Programs, National Institute of Justice. Retrieved September 28, 2006, from http://www.ncjrs.org/pdffiles1/nij/175723.pdf.

LaFree, G. (1998). *Losing legitimacy: Street crime and the decline of social institutions in America*. Boulder, CO: Westview Press.

Leonard, J., & Dolan, M. (2012, Nov. 8). Softer 3-strikes law has defense lawyers preparing case reviews. *Los Angeles Times*. Retrieved from http://articles.latimes.com/print/2012/nov/08/local/la-me-three-strikes-20121108

Lipsey, M. W., Howell, J. C., Kelly, M. R., Chapman, G., & Carver, D. (2010). *Improving the effectiveness of juvenile justice programs*. Washington, DC: Center for Juvenile Justice Reform, Georgetown Public Policy Institute.

Lipsey, M. W., & Wilson, D. B. (1998). Effective interventions with serious juvenile offenders: A synthesis of research. In R. Loeber & D. P. Farrington (Eds.), *Serious and violent juvenile offenders: Risk factors and successful interventions* (pp. 313–345). Thousand Oaks, CA: Sage.

Lipsey, M. W., Wilson, D. B., & Cothern, L. (2000). *Effective intervention for serious juvenile offenders* (NCJ 181201). Washington, DC: U.S. Department of Justice, Office of Juvenile Justice and Delinquency Prevention.

Lizotte, A., & Sheppard, D. (2001). *Gun use by male juveniles: Research and prevention* (NCJ 188992). Washington, DC: U.S. Department of Justice, Office of Juvenile Justice and Delinquency Prevention. Retrieved from http://www.ncjrs.gov/pdffiles1/ojjdp/188992.pdf.

Loeber, R., & Farrington, D. P. (Eds.). (1998). *Serious and violent juvenile offenders: Risk factors and successful interventions*. Thousand Oaks, CA: Sage.

Maguire, K., & Pastore, A. L. (Eds.). (2006a). *Sourcebook of criminal justice statistics*, Table 6 .0002.2004. Retrieved September 29, 2006, from http://www.albany.edu/sourcebook/pdf/t60002204.pdf.

Maguire, K., & Pastore, A. L. (Ed.). (2006b). *Sourcebook of criminal justice statistics*, Table 3.106.2004. Retrieved September 29, 2006, from http://www.albany.edu/sourcebook/pdf/t3J062004.pdf.

Marans, S., & Berkman, M. (1997). *Child development community policing: Partnership in a climate of violence*. Bulletin. Washington, DC: U.S. Department of Justice, Office of Justice Programs, Office of Juvenile Justice and Delinquency Prevention.

McCleskey vs. Kemp, 478 U.S. 1019 (1987).

McDonald, D. C., & Carlson, K. E. (1993). *Sentencing in the courts: Does race matter? The transition to sentencing guidelines, 1986–1990*. Washington, DC: Department of Justice, Bureau of Justice Statistics.

Miller, W. R., Sorensen, J. L., Selzer, J. A., & Brigham, G. S. (2006). Disseminating evidence-based practices in substance abuse treatment: A review with suggestions. *Journal of Substance Abuse Treatment, 31*, 25–39.

Moore, M. H. (1995). Public health and criminal justice approaches to prevention. In M. Tonry (Ed.), *Crime and justice: A review of research* (Vol. 19, pp. 237–262). Chicago: University of Chicago Press.

Morley, E., Rossman, S. B., Kopczynski, M., Buck, J., & Gouvis, C. (2000). *Comprehensive responses to youth at risk: Interim findings from the Safe Futures initiative* (NCJ 183841). Washington, DC: U.S. Department of Justice, Office of Justice Programs, Office of Juvenile Justice and Delinquency Prevention.

Nagin, D. (1998). Criminal deterrence research at the outset of the twenty-first century. In M. Tonry (Ed.), *Crime and justice: An annual review of research* (Vol. 23, pp. 1–42). Chicago: University of Chicago Press.

National Institute on Drug Abuse. (1999). *Principles of drug addiction treatment: A research-based guide* (NIH-99-4180). Washington, DC: National Institute of Health, National Institute on Drug Abuse.

National Institute on Drug Abuse. (2006). *Principles of drug abuse treatment for criminal justice populations: A research-based guide.* Rockville, MD: Author.

Nurse Family Partnership. (2010). *Nurse Family Partnership: Helping First Time Parents Succeed.* Retrieved January 23, 2010, from http://www.nursefamilypartnership.org.

Office of Juvenile Justice and Delinquency Prevention. (2009). *Best practices to address community gang problems: OJJDP's comprehensive gang model.* Washington, DC: U.S. Department of Justice, Office of Juvenile Justice and Delinquency Prevention. Retrieved January 23, 2010, from http://www.ncjrs.gov/pdffiles1/ojjdp/222799.pdf.

Orange County Probation Department. (2001). *Intervention program evaluation: Evaluating the success of the 8% Early Intervention Program.* Retrieved September 28, 2006, from http://www.oc.ca.gov/Probation/solution/contentipe.asp?h=ipe.

Packer, H. L. (1968). *The limits of the criminal sanction.* Stanford, CA: Stanford University Press.

Paternoster, R., & Piquero, A. R. (1995). Reconceptualizing deterrence: An empirical test of personal and vicarious experiences. *Journal of Research in Crime and Delinquency, 32*, 251–286.

Piquero, A. R., & Pogarsky, G. (2002). Beyond Stafford and Warr's reconceptualization of deterrence: Personal and vicarious experiences, impulsivity, and offending behavior. *Journal of Research in Crime and Delinquency, 39*, 153–186.

Pogarsky, G., & Piquero, A. R. (2003). Can punishment encourage offending? Investigating the "resetting" effect. *Journal of Research in Crime and Delinquency, 40*, 95–120.

Pope, C. E. (1995). Equity within the juvenile justice system: Directions for the future. In L. K. Kempf, C. E. Pope, & W. H. Feyerherm (Eds.), *Minorities in juvenile justice* (pp. 201–216). Thousand Oaks, CA: Sage.

Pope, C. E., & Feyerherm, W. H. (1992). *Minorities and the juvenile justice system: Final report.* Washington, DC: Office of Juvenile Justice and Delinquency Prevention.

Porter, A. (2006). *The Jerry Lee program research on restorative justice: Promising results.* Restorative Practices E-Forum, April 13, 2006. Retrieved September 28, 2006, from http://www.realjustice.org/library/jerryleeresearch.html.

Reiss, A. J., Jr., & Roth, J. A. (Eds.). (1993). *Understanding and preventing violence (Vol. 1).* Washington, DC: National Academy Press.

Ritter, N. (2009). CeaseFire: A public health approach to reduce shootings and killings (NCJ 228386). *NIJ Journal, 264*, 20–25.

Roth, J. (1994). *Understanding and preventing violence.* NIJ Research in Brief (NCJ-145645). Washington, DC: U.S. Department of Justice, National Institute of Justice.

Schumacher, M., & Kurz, G. (2000). *The 8% solution: Preventing serious, repeat juvenile crime.* Thousand Oaks, CA: Sage.

Sechrest, L., White, S. O., & Brown, E. D. (1979). *The rehabilitation of criminal offenders: Problems and prospects.* Washington, DC: National Academy of Sciences.

Sherman, L. W., & Strang, H. (2004). *Restorative justice: What we know and how we know it.* Working paper, Jerry Lee Program on Randomized Controlled Trials in Restorative Justice. Retrieved September 28, 2006, from http://www.sas.upenn.edu/jerrylee/research/rj.htm.

Shichor, D., & Sechrest, D. K. (Eds.). (1996). *Three strikes and you're out: Vengeance as public policy.* Thousand Oaks, CA: Sage.

Skogan, W. G., Hartnett, S. M., Bump, N., & Dubois, J. (2009). *Evaluation of CeaseFire-Chicago* (NCJ 227181). Washington, DC: U.S. Department of Justice. Retrieved from: https://www.ncjrs.gov/pdffiles1/nij/grants/227181.pdf

Snell, T. L. (2014). *Capital Punishment, 2012—Statistical Tables* (NCJ 245789). Washington, DC: U.S. Department of Justice, Bureau of Justice Statistics. Retrieved July 7, 2014, from: http://www.bjs.gov/content/pub/pdf/cp12st.pdf

Stafford, M. C., & Warr, M. (1993). Reconceptualization of general and specific deterrence. *Journal of Research in Crime and Delinquency, 30*, 123–135.

Stolzenberg, L., & D'Alessio, S. J. (1997). "Three strikes and you're out": The impact of California's new mandatory sentencing law on serious crime rates. *Crime and Delinquency, 43*, 457–469.

Strang, H. (2004). *Repair or revenge: Victims and restorative justice.* New York: Oxford University Press.

Thornberry, T. (1994). *Violent families and youth violence.* Fact Sheet. Washington, DC: U.S. Department of Justice, Office of Justice Programs, Office of Juvenile Justice and Delinquency Prevention.

Vandaele, W. (1978). Participation in illegitimate activities: Ehrlich revisited. In A. Blumstein, J. Cohen, & D. Nagin (Eds.), *Deterrence and incapacitation: Estimating the effects of criminal sanctions on crime rates* (pp. 319–335). Washington, DC: National Academy of Sciences.

Walker, S., Spohn, C., & DeLeone, M. (1996). *The color of justice.* Belmont, CA: Wadsworth.

Welsh, W., & Harris, P. (2013). *Criminal justice policy and planning* (4th ed.). Waltham, MA: Anderson/Elsevier.

Welsh, W., Harris, P., & Jenkins, P. (1996). Reducing overrepresentation of minorities in juvenile justice: Development of community-based programs in Pennsylvania. *Crime and Delinquency, 42*, 76–98.

Welsh, W., Jenkins, P., & Harris, P. (1999). Reducing minority over-representation in juvenile justice: Results of community-based delinquency prevention in Harrisburg. *Journal of Research in Crime and Delinquency, 36*, 87–110.

Westat. (2005). *Findings from the Safe Kids/Safe Streets national evaluation: Kid Safe, Burlington, Vermont.* Washington, DC: U.S. Department of Justice, Office of Justice Programs, Office of Juvenile Justice and Delinquency Prevention. Retrieved September 29, 2006, from http://www.ncjrs.gov/pdffiles1/nij/grants/210280.pdf.

Widom, C. S. (1992). *The cycle of violence.* Research in Brief. Washington, DC: Department of Justice, Office of Justice Programs, National Institute of Justice.

Zahn, M. A. (1990). Intervention strategies to reduce homicide. In N. A. Weiner, M. A. Zahn, & R. J. Sagi (Eds.), *Violence: Patterns, causes, public policy* (pp. 379–390). New York: Harcourt, Brace, Jovanovich.

Zimring, F. E., & Hawkins, G. (1986). *Capital punishment and the American agenda.* Cambridge, MA: Cambridge University Press.

Zimring, F. E., Kamin, S., & Hawkins, G. (1999). *Crime & punishment in California: The effect of three strikes and you're out.* Berkeley, CA: Institute of Governmental Studies Press.

AUTHOR INDEX

Abelson, R. P., 250
Addington, L. A., 32
Adler, F., 5, 7
Agnew, R., 96, 211, 298–99, 301, 302
Akers, R. L., 98, 207, 305, 306, 307
Akiyama, Y., 30, 32
Alaniz, M. A., 273
Allport, G., 144
American Psychological Association, 335
Amir, Y., 148
Anderson, C. A., 249, 251
Anderson, C. S., 208
Anderson, D. C., 208
Anderson, E., 210
Anderson, K. R., 181, 182*t*, 183
Andrews, D. A., 325
Anti-Defamation League (ADL), 145
Aos, S., 122
Archer, D., 55–56
Armstrong, B., 334
Arsenault, S., 179
Arthur, M. W., 280, 337
Associated Press, 138
Ateyo, D., 3
Athens L. H., 80
Auerhahn, K., 270, 271, 272, 273, 331

Babington, C., 311
Bahr, S. J., 163, 164, 164*t*
Bailey, W. C., 175
Baldus, D. C., 327, 328, 329
Ball, J. C., 267
Bandura, A., 250
Barnes, R., 260
Barr, R., 250
Bart, P. B., 122
Basile, K. C., 156
Bauer, R. A., 23
BBC News, 269, 270
Beaton, S., 209
Beattie, R., 30
Beck, A., 245, 246, 248
Bedau, H. A., 175
Beech, T., 119
Begley, S., 201
Beha, J. A., III, 103
Benedict, J. R., 4
Berendes, H. W., 172
Berger, P. L., 5
Bergesen, A., 142
Berk, R. A., 173
Berkman, M., 342
Berkowitz, A., 125
Berkowitz, L., 250
Bernard, T. J., 207
Best, J., 6, 13, 77
Beuscher, P. A., 56
Bianchi, K., 83
Biderman, A. D., 31
Bienen, L., 119
Bilchik, S., 337
Binbaum, H. J., 115
Bjerregard, B., 226
Black, D., 81–82
Black, M. C., 156, 157
Blackshaw, L., 126
Blankenship, J., 281
Block, C. R., 12, 26–27
Block, R., 94
Blumer, H., 142
Blumstein, A., 12, 83, 244, 277, 324, 325, 328, 331, 348
Bohm, R. M., 328, 329, 330
Bonczar, T. P., 329
Bonta, J., 325
Borg, M. J., 81
Borges, S., 118
Botvin, G. J., 280
Boudreaux, M. C., 164

Bourget, D., 163
Bourgois, P., 274
Bourgon, C., 334
Bowden, E., 135, 147
Bowden, M., 136
Bowers, W. J., 103, 256, 329
Bowie, V., 179
Braga, A. A., 234, 235, 236, 237, 255, 257, 257*f*, 339
Braithwaite, J., 326
Brantingham, P. J., 87
Brantingham, P. L., 87
Bremer, L. P., 300, 311, 312
Brenner, R. A., 172
Brezina, T., 211
Bridges, G. S., 332, 333
Brooks, D., 306
Brown, B. S., 334
Brown, E. D., 325
Brown, R. M., 43, 44, 50, 54
Browne, A, 169–70
Brownmiller, S., 116–17
Brownstein, H. H., 4, 5, 6
Buerger, M., 101, 236, 237, 247–48, 273
Bull, J. L., 104
Bune, K. L., 145
Burch, J. H., 339
Burdon, W. M., 127
Bureau of Justice Statistics, 34, 35, 67, 67*t*, 93*t*, 94–95, 110, 112, 112*f*, 113*t*, 114, 140*t*, 268
Bureau of Labor Statistics, 186
Burgess, A. W., 115
Burke, C., 342
Burns, K. S., 172
Burt, M., 118
Bushman, B. J., 249, 250, 251
Butler, F., 333, 339
Butzin, C. A., 281

Caldwell, A., 248, 273
Caliber Associates, 338
California Board of Corrections, 342
Callahan, P. T., 104
Cal/OSHA, 181, 196
Campbell, J. C., 157
Canter, D., 87
Cantor, D., 34, 35
Cao, Y., 281
Caplan, N., 119
Cardarelli, A. P., 70
Caringella-MacDonald, S., 120
Carlson, K. F., 330
Carlson, M., 250
Carmody, M., 125, 126
Cartmill, R. S., 271, 273
Catalano, R. F., 168*t*, 336
Cauffman, E., 207
Cavanagh, D., 70
Center for Substance Abuse Research, 271
Centers for Disease Control, 39
Cernkovich, S. A., 207, 211
Chaiken, J. M., 98, 103, 324
Chaiken, M. R., 98, 267
Chappell, D., 179
Chemers, B. M., 339
Chermak, S., 237
Chesney-Lind, M., 207
Chester, C., 73
Chew, K. S. Y., 162
Child Trends Data Bank, 165
Clarke, R. V., 324
Clear, T. R., 342, 343
Clifton, W., Jr., 104
Clinard, M. B., 228
Cloward, R., 96, 230
Cohen, 189–90
Cohen, A. K., 229
Cohen, J., 102
Cohen, L., 93, 247
Cohen, L. E., 189
Cole, G. F., 332
Combs, C. C., 288
Comstock, G. A., 249
Conklin, J. E., 94
Conly, C., 94, 101, 102
Conrad, J. P., 328, 329
Cook, D. E., 250
Cook, P. J., 94, 242, 244, 245, 246, 249, 257, 257*f*, 259, 260, 261
Coolbaugh, K., 337*f*
Cooper, J., 142
Cornish, D. B., 324
Coser, L. A., 142
Cothern, L., 340
Craig, K. M., 141, 143
Craig, S. E., 162
Crittendon, P. M., 162
Cronin, J., 71, 72
Crosset, T. W., 4
Crow, W. J., 104
Crume, T. L., 162
Cullen, F. T., 191
Cumming, G. F., 127, 128
Curry, G. D., 232, 233, 235
Curtis, L. A., 342
Curtis, R., 349

Daiger, D., 208, 209
D'Alessio, S. J., 331
Daly, K., 94
Dansereau, D., 281
Davis, H., 179–80
Dawsey, D., 136, 143
Day, D. M., 128
Deane, C., 102
Decker, S. H., 71, 72, 99, 102, 103, 192, 234, 248, 273
Dees, M., 135, 147
Delany-Shabazz, R. V., 216
DeLeone, M., 333
Denno, D. W., 270, 271, 272, 274, 276, 277, 282
DiCristina, B., 56
Di Martino, V., 179
Disha, I., 138

Dolan, M., 331
Douglas, J. E., 115
Drake, E. K., 122
Dryfoos, J. G., 280
Duffala, D., 104
Dugan, L., 171, 295
Duhart, D. T., 186
Dunworth, T., 277, 278, 279
Durlak, J. A., 280
Durose, M. R., 121
Dutra, R. L., 164
Dutton, D. G., 170, 174
Duwe, G., 73

Earls, F., 209
Eck, J. E., 72, 84
Edgerton, R. B., 274
Edwards, T. J., 30, 31*t*, 32
Eggen, D., 287
Egger, S. A., 77, 83, 87, 88
Egley, A., Jr., 238
Ehrlich, I., 328
Elias, M. J., 212
Elliott, D., 206
Ellis, L., 118
Esbensen, F.-A., 224, 226
Ewigman, B., 162
Ewing, C. P., 162, 167

Fagan, J., 173, 174, 274, 275, 275*f*, 349
Falkin, G. P., 280, 281
Farrington, D. P., 206, 207, 333, 337
Fazio, F. H., 142
Federal Bureau of Investigation, 6, 15, 24, 25, 27, 28, 29, 30, 31, 37, 65, 66*t*, 69, 73, 76, 94, 98, 110, 113*f*, 114, 136, 137, 139, 139*t*, 140*t*, 141, 157, 161, 161*t*, 259, 288, 289, 309–10, 332
Federal Bureau of Prisons, 281
Felson, 93, 247
Felson, M., 189–90, 192–93
Felson, R. B., 80, 192
Ferracuti, F., 81, 231
Feyerherm, W. H., 333
Field, G., 281
Finkelhor, D., 32, 117, 162, 164
Fisher, B., 191
Fisher, J. C., 76, 77
Flynn, P. M., 334
Foley, L. A., 148
Fornango, R., 96, 97, 253, 254
Foucault, M., 329
Fowler, 157, 158, 158*t*
Fox, J. A., 72, 73–74, 74*t*, 75, 77, 80, 87
Fox, R. S., 208
Friedman, T. L., 301
Frosech, D., 75
Furby, L., 126

Gallagher, C. A., 127
Gallup Poll, 328
Gammage, J., 201
Gannon, T. A., 119
García-Moreno, C., 159, 160, 161
Garry, E. M., 340
Gartin, P., 101, 247–48, 273
Gartner, R., 55–56
Gassman, M., 291
Gates, D. F., 276, 277
Gauffman, 207
Geerken, M., 38
Geist, A., 119
Gelles, R. J., 14, 155
Gendreau, P., 325
Gerber, J., 277
Gerould, A. L., 207
Giannini, A. J., 272
Gidycz, C., 114, 118
Gillespie, C. K., 170–71
Gilmartin, P., 118
Giordano, P. C., 13, 207, 211
Glaser, D., 37
Godwin, J., 87
Goldfarb, Z. A., 311
Goldsmith, D. S., 280
Goldstein, P. J., 268, 269
Goode, E., 52, 275
Gottfredson, D. C., 206, 207, 208, 211, 213, 214*t*, 215, 217
Gottfredson, D. M., 8, 14
Gottfredson, G. D., 208, 209, 210, 213, 214*t*, 215, 217
Gottfredson, M. R., 14, 81, 207
Gove, W. R., 30, 38
Gragg, E., 341
Grattet, R., 136
Green, D. P., 142–43
Greenbaum, S., 244
Greenberg, J., 192, 211–12
Greenberg, M., 192, 211–12
Greene, J. R., 208, 210
Greenfeld, L. A., 115, 123
Greenwood, P. W., 11, 72, 98, 267, 324, 330–31, 337
Gregg, C., 253
Griswold, J., 104
Grossman, J. B., 340
Groth, A. N., 115
Gurr, T. R., 289, 315

Hagan, F. E., 37, 38
Hagan, J., 207, 333
Hagedorn, J., 224, 226
Haggerty, K. D., 75
Hahn, R., 211–12
Hall, E. A., 281
Hamm, M. S., 288, 305
Handy, W., 12
Hanna, J. L., 210
Hansel, C. J., 337*f*
Hansen, W. B., 280
Hanson, R. K., 126
Haque, M. S., 308
Harlow, C. W., 139
Harrell, E., 184, 184*t*, 185*t*, 186, 187*t*, 227, 330
Harries, K. D., 12, 14, 66

Harris, P. W., 15, 16, 103, 201, 259, 325, 330, 333, 339, 349, 350
Harvey, M. H., 118
Hass, M. E., 179
Hate Crime Statistics Act (HCSA), 136
Hawkins, D., 332
Hawkins, G., 328, 329, 331
Hawkins, J. D., 280, 336, 337
Hazelwood, R. R., 115
Heath, D. B., 277
Heide, K. M., 165, 166–67, 166*t*
Heinle, K., 269, 270
Hellman, D. A., 209
Hellriegel, D., 208
Hendricks, S. A., 181, 182*t*, 183
Henson, B., 179
Herman, M., 142
Herman-Giddens, M. E., 162
Hewitt, C., 293, 304–5
Hickey, E. W., 77–78, 79
Hickman, L. J., 126, 127
Hiller, M. L., 281
Hills, S. L., 5
Hindelang, M. J., 81, 206, 207
Hirschi, T., 97, 206, 207, 209, 231
Hoag, C., 277
Hoffman, B. ., 288, 289, 290–94, 300, 304, 306, 312, 315
Hollabaugh, L. C., 118
Holmes, R. M., 77
Holmes, S. T., 77
Hopkins, M., 191, 192
Horiuchi, G. T., 6, 13
Howard, J., 194, 195, 196, 197, 198*t*
Howell, J. C., 216–17, 333, 336, 337, 340, 341, 342
Hsia, H. M., 332, 333
Hudson, S. M., 118
Huesmann, J. R., 249, 250
Hughes, M., 38
Huizinga, D., 206, 226
Humphrey, S. E., 114
Hunter, R. D., 104
Hutcheson, R., 311
Hybyl, L. G., 206

Inciardi, J. A., 267, 281
Ingersoll, R., 206
Ingersoll, S., 340, 341, 342
Institute for Economics & Peace (IEP), 297, 297*t*, 298*t*
Institute of Medicine, 335

Jackson, A., 114
Jacobs, B., 98, 99, 100*f*
Jacobs, J. B., 136, 137, 145–46, 149
Jankowski, M. S., 13
Jarvis, J. P., 32, 69, 70, 71, 72
Jeffery, C. R., 104
Jenkins, E. L., 181, 182*t*, 183
Jenkins, P., 6, 76, 77, 78, 206, 207, 208, 288, 294, 311
Jenness, V., 136
Jensen, E. L., 277
Jimenez, S., 135
Johnson, B., 267, 268
Johnson, B. D., 95
Johnson, K., 75
Jones, E. D., III, 260
Jones, E. E., 142

Kahn, A. S., 114
Kamin, S., 331
Karberg, J. C., 268
Karch, D. L., 39
Karimi, N., 292
Karp, D. R., 343
Katz, J., 98, 99
Kazdin, A. E., 207
Keel, T. G., 72
Keim, J., 122
Kelleher, M. D., 172, 174, 175
Kelley, E., 193–94
Kelling, G. L., 103, 324
Kemp, J., 205*t*
Kennedy, D. M., 234, 235, 236, 254–55, 257*f*, 339
Kilbourne, A. M., 334
Kim, J., 349
Kinderman, C., 34, 35
Kirk, D. S., 211
Kitsuse, J. I., 5, 16
Kiviahan, C., 162
Kivivuori, J., 58
Klebold, S., 207
Kleck, G., 244, 246, 260
Klein, M. W., 223–24, 226, 230, 233, 235, 237, 238
Klinger, D. A., 81
Knight, K., 281
Koper, C. S., 260
Kosa, R., 85, 86
Koss, M. P., 114, 118
Kracke & Special Emphasis Division Staff, 338–39
Kramer, R. C., 4
Krauthammer, C., 304, 309
Krebs, C. P., 114
Krohn, M., 207
KRON-TV, 110
Krueger, A. B., 304
Kruttschnitt, C., 121
Kubrin, C. E., 102
Kull, S., 312
Kunz, J., 163, 164, 164*t*
Kurki, L., 326
Kurz, G., 341
Kushner, H. W., 288

Lab, S. P., 84
LaFree, G., 56, 120, 295, 348–49
Lam, J. A., 217
Land, G., 162
Lane, R., 43–44, 46–49, 54, 55, 73
Langan, P. A., 121
Langton, L., 66
Laqueur, W., 288
Latessa, E. J., 191
Laufer, W. S., 5, 7
Lauritsen, J. L., 209
Lavin, M., 98, 267

Lawler, E., 208
Lawless, M., 103, 324
Lawrence, R. A., 207
Lawton, B. A., 279, 280
LeBoeuf, D., 216
Lee, M. R., 71, 274
Leonard, J., 331
LePage, A., 250
Levin, J., 72, 73–74, 74*t*, 75, 77, 80, 87, 144, 145, 146–47
Lewis, E., 312
Linville, P. W., 142
Lipsey, M. W., 211, 212–13, 334–36, 340
Lipton, D. S., 267, 280, 281
Liska, A., 207
Litwin, K. J., 81–82
Lizotte, A., 342
Lockwood, D., 202
Loeber, R., 333, 337
Loftin, C., 38, 260
Lord, W. C., 164
Lösel, F., 126, 127
Lott, J. R., Jr., 260
Lowe, L., 281
Luckenbill, D. F., 81, 94, 246, 266
Luckmann, T., 5
Ludwig, J., 256, 257, 259, 260
Luongo, A. J., 279, 280
Lynch, J. P., 31, 34, 35, 190–91
Lyons, C. J., 70, 71

MacAndrew, C., 274
MacCrae, D. J., 23
MacDonald, J. M., 102
MacKenzie, D. L., 126, 127
Maguire, K., 329, 348
Mahoney, J., 148
Makepeace, J. M., 170
Malamuth, N., 117, 118
Maleckova, J., 304
Malesky, A., 122
Maltz, M. D., 23
Marans, S., 342
Marder, D., 92, 96, 97
Marolla, J., 117, 118
Marques, J. K., 127, 128–29
Marsh, J. C., 119
Marshall, L. E., 129
Marshall, W. L., 129
Martin, G. R., 127, 128
Martin, S., 144, 281
Marvell, T., 256
Massey, J., 207
Massing, M., 277
Matza, D., 97, 118, 143
Maxfield, M. G., 31, 32
Maxson, C. L., 223–24, 226, 237, 238
Mazerolle, P., 211
Mazzetti, M., 312
McClain, P. W., 162
McCrae, D. J., 23
McDevitt, J., 144, 145, 146–47, 236, 237
McDonald, D. C., 330
McDonald, M. A., 4
McDonald, S., 216
McDowall, D., 38, 256
McGarrell, E., 237
McGeever, K., 102
McGuire, E., 84
McHale, R., 332, 333
McKay, H. D., 106n1, 209
Melnick, G., 281
Mercy, J. A., 9, 10
Merton, R. K., 142, 228–31, 229*t*
Messner, S. F., 58, 102, 209, 211
Michael, R. T., 114
Microsoft, 46, 47
Miczek, K., 270, 271, 272, 274
Miederanders, M., 128
Mikula, G., 193
Milhollin, G., 291, 292, 309
Miller, J., 99, 100, 238
Miller, S. L., 170
Miller, W. B., 225, 230–31
Miller, W. R., 334
Mills, G., 277, 279
Mitchell, F., 304
Moody, C., 256
Moore, J., 226
Moore, M., 8, 9, 10, 11
Moore, M. H., 257*f*, 333
Morales, E., 280
Moriarty, A. R., 216
Morley, E., 338
Morrison, S., 125
Muehlenhard, C. L., 118
Mueller, G. O. W., 5, 7
Muirhead, Y. E., 72
Mullen, J., 193–94
Mulligan, E., 46
Mulvey, E. P., 207
Mumola, C. J., 268, 280

Nacos, B., 300
Nagin, D., 171, 324, 325
Nash, J. R., 5, 49, 50
National Center on Addiction and Substance Abuse, 188–89, 267
National Clearinghouse on Child Abuse and Neglect, 169
National Commission on Addiction and Drug Abuse, 189
National Commission on Terrorist Attacks upon the United States, 288, 308, 309
National Consortium for the Study of Terrorism and Responses to Terrorism (START), 288, 291, 294, 295, 296, 296*t*
National Crime Victimization Survey, 140*t*
National Gang Center, 224, 224*t*, 226*t*
National Institute for Occupational Safety and Health (NIOSH), 181, 194–95
National Institute for the Prevention of Workplace Violence, 193, 196
National Institute of Justice, 267
National Institute on Drug Abuse, 281, 335
National Intimate Partner and Sexual Violence Survey (NISVS), 155, 157, 157*t*

National Research Center (NRC), 242, 244, 245, 246, 248, 249, 251, 253, 255, 256, 258, 259, 260–61
National School Safety Center, 201
Nelson, C., 127, 128–29
Newman, G., 3, 56
NIJ, 267
Niolon, 157, 158, 158*t*
Nolan, J., 32
Nurco, D. N., 267
Nussbaum, P., 121

O'Brien, R. M., 33, 122
O'Carroll, P. W., 9, 10
Office of Juvenile Justice and Delinquency Prevention (OJJDP), 340
Office of National Drug Control Policy, 267
Ohlin, L., 96, 230
Oldham, G., 208
O'Neil, J. A., 267
Ontario Ministry of Children and Youth Services, 232
Orange County Probation Department, 342
Ormrod, R., 32
Ousey, G. C., 71, 274
Ovenden, C., 125
Overpeck, M. D., 172
Owens, R. G., 208, 211

Packer, H. L., 331, 332
Paik, H., 249
Parker, K. F., 81
Parker, R. N., 270, 271, 272, 273
Pastore, A. L., 329, 348
Paternoster, R., 325
Paulson, S. K., 241
Payne, A. A., 210
Pearson, F. S., 209
Peipert, T., 241
Pennell, S., 248, 273, 342
Perone, S., 179, 180–81
Petee, T. A., 73, 165, 166*t*
Peters, J., 281
Petersilia, J., 72, 98, 267
Peterson, R. D., 175, 333
Petri, B., 193
Philadelphia Inquirer, 109, 110, 124
Philbrick, J. H., 179
Piehl, A. M., 235, 255, 339
Pierce, G. L., 103, 256
Pincus, W., 312
Pipes, D., 302, 303
Piquero, A. R., 211, 325
Pithers, W. D., 127, 128
Pittman, D., 12
Planty, M., 66, 242, 243*f*, 244, 245
Poe-Yamagata, E., 244
Pogarsky, G., 325
Poggio, E. C., 24, 30
Pokorny, A. D., 12
Polizzi, D. M., 126, 127
Polk, K., 120
Pope, C. E., 333
Porter, A., 326
Potter, K. A., 136, 137, 145–46, 149
Prendergast, M. L., 281
Prothrow-Stith, D., 9, 96
Ptacek, J., 4
Pulaski, C. A., Jr., 327, 328, 329
Purtell, R., 254

Ramsay, C., 312
Rand, M. R., 12, 34, 35, 36, 67*t*, 69
Rantala, R., 30, 31*t*, 32
Raudenbush, S. W., 209
Reed, M., 207
Regoeczi, W. C., 69, 71, 72
Reiss, A. J., Jr., 3, 7, 82, 104, 209, 244, 245, 249, 253, 255, 258, 260, 261, 266, 269, 273, 281, 331, 333, 334, 337
Rennison, C. M., 12, 36
Resnick, P. J., 163
Rhodes, W. M., 94, 101, 102
Riedel, M., 13, 24, 26, 29, 34, 55, 68, 70, 71, 72, 159
Ritter, N., 343
Robers, S., 202–4, 204–5*t*, 206
Roberts, A., 70, 71
Robison, S. M., 30
Rogan, D. P., 12, 248
Rosenfeld, R., 12, 83, 84, 96, 97, 171, 209, 211, 253, 254, 348
Rosenthal, H. M., 30
Rossi, P. H., 94, 99, 245
Rossman, D., 103
Rossmo, D. K., 87
Roth, J., 3, 7, 104, 209, 244, 245, 249, 253, 255, 258, 260, 261, 266, 269, 273, 281, 331, 333, 334, 337
Rubel, R. J., 208
Rudovsky, D., 253
Russell, D. E., 118
Ryan, P., 6

Sagi, P. C., 69
Saltz, R. F., 273
Saltzman, L. E., 156
Sampson, R. J., 102, 209, 274
Sanday, P. R., 114, 117
Sanders, W. B., 224
Sarche, J., 109
Savolainen, J., 58, 59
Schank, R. C., 250
Scheckner, S., 206
Schmid, A., 288
Schmitt, E. L., 121
Schmucker, M., 126, 127
Schumacher, M., 341
Scully, D., 117, 118
Sechrest, D. K., 330
Sechrest, L., 325
Sedensky, S. J., 73
Sellers, C. S., 98, 207
Sellin, T., 30
Shaffer, J. W., 267
Shaw, C. R., 106n1, 209
Shaw, J. W., 12
Shelden, R. G., 207

Sheley, J. F., 84, 175, 234
Sheley, J. K., 244, 248
Sheppard, D., 342
Sherif, C. W., 141
Sherif, M., 141
Sherman, L. W., 12, 101, 104, 173, 247–48, 251, 273, 326, 327
Shichor, D., 330
Shively, M., 138, 141, 145, 149
Sibbitt, R., 144
Sickmund, M., 204, 244
Silberman, C. E., 54
Silverleib, A., 311
Silverman, A. L., 303–4, 305, 306, 307
Simpson, D., 280, 281
Simpson, J., 207
Skogan, W. G., 15, 343
Sloane, J., 248
Slocum, J., Jr., 208
Smelser, N. J., 304
Smith, 226
Smith, C. E., 332
Smith, D. C., 254
Smith, S. C., 157, 158, 158*t*
Snell, T. L., 328, 328*t*, 329
Snipes, J. B., 207
Snyder, H. N., 204, 244
Southern Poverty Law Center (SPLC), 135, 148
Sparks, M. R., 179
Spector, M., 5, 16
Spelman, W., 84
Spergel, I. A., 232, 233, 235
Spivak, H., 96
Spohn, C., 333
Stafford, M. C., 324
State of California, 14
Steffensmeier, D., 207
Stern, J., 302, 305, 306, 307
Stevenson, K. A., 103, 324
Stiffman, M. N., 165
Stokes, R., 210
Stolzenberg, L., 331
Strang, H., 326, 327
Straus, M. A., 14, 155
Strolovitch, D. Z., 142, 143
Stucky, T. D., 102
Subra, B., 249
Sullivan, J., 201
Sutherland, E. H., 143
Swartz, J., 4
Sykes, G., 97, 118, 143

Tajfel, H., 142
Tanzer, N., 193
Taylor, B. M., 34, 35
Taylor, R. B., 103, 279, 280
Thornberry, T., 207, 227, 232, 340
Time magazine, 188
Tobler, N. S., 280
Toby, J., 208, 209
Tolson, E. R., 216
Toscano, G. A., 179
Trento, A. J., 273
Trifiletti, L. B., 172
Truman, J. L., 66, 67*t*, 69, 78, 93, 111, 242, 243*f*, 244, 245
Trumble, A. C., 172
Turk, A. T., 294, 307, 308, 310, 312
Turner, R., 85, 86

Ulfstein, G., 311
United Nations (UN), 56
United Nations Development Report (UNDP), 299–300, 301, 302–4, 308, 309
United Nations Office on Drugs and Crime, 25, 57, 58*f*
University of Iowa Injury Prevention Center, 182
Urban Archives, 123, 124
Urbina, I., 4
U.S. Census Bureau, 142
U.S. Department of Justice, 37, 122
U.S. Department of State, 291, 294, 295, 300, 312–14, 315
U.S. Government Accountability Office, 122
U.S. Secret Service, 207
U.S. Senate, 77

Vandaele, W., 328
van den Haag, E., 328, 329
van Ommeren, A., 128
Van Winkle, B., 234
Vigil, J. D., 231–32
Von Behr, I., 292

Waegel, W. B., 72
Walker, L. E., 169
Walker, S., 16, 333
Wallman, J., 348
Ward, T., 118, 119
Waring, E. J., 235, 255, 339
Warr, M., 324
Weber, W., 179
Weinrott, M., 126
Weis, J. G., 206
Weis, K., 118
Welch, D., 142
Welch, W. M., 142
Wellford, C., 71, 72, 170
Welsh, W. N., 9, 15, 16, 103, 201, 202, 206, 207, 208, 209–10, 211, 215, 217, 259, 281, 325, 330, 332, 333, 339, 340, 342, 349, 350
West, S. G., 163
Westat, 341
Wexler, H. K., 280, 281
White, J. R., 289, 290, 292
White, S. O., 325
White House, 276, 277
Whitlock, M. L., 226
Widom, C. S., 340
Wiersema, B., 38
Williams, K. R., 170
Wilson, D. B., 213, 340
Wilson, J. J., 216
Wilson, M. M., 136, 138, 141
Wilson, S., 304, 311
Wilson, S. J., 211, 212–13
Wilson, W. J., 274

Wilson-Brewer, R., 217
Winfree, L., 226
Wintermute, G., 84
Wish, E. D., 95, 267
Wisiniewski, N., 114, 118
Wolfgang, M. E., 30, 81, 231
Wong, J. S., 142, 143
Woodworth, G., 327, 328, 329
Wooldredge, J. D., 191
Workplace Shootings, 193
World Almanac and Book of Facts, 67, 76
World Health Organization (WHO), 56, 159, 160
Worldwide Religious News, 301
Wright, J. C., 250
Wright, J. D., 84, 94, 99, 102, 103, 175, 234, 244, 245, 248
Wright, R. T., 98, 99, 100*f*, 192

Yun, S. C., 231–32

Zahn, M. A., 69, 329, 331
Zajac, G., 281
Zimring, F., 258, 328, 329, 331, 349

SUBJECT INDEX

Note: Page numbers followed by '*f*' and '*t*' refers to figures and tables.

Abu Ghraib prisoner abuse scandal, 300, 312
ADAM. *See* Arrestee Drug Abuse Monitoring program
Adams, John, 44
Adam Walsh Child Protection and Safety Act (2006), 122
ADL. *See* Anti-Defamation League
Afghanistan War, 299, 308, 311–12
African Americans
  death penalty and, 329
  gang violence and, 226
  hate crimes and, 138, 141
  homicide data, 9, 26, 82, 83, 165
  indentured servitude of, 46–47
  lynchings of, 48–49
  Nat Turner Rebellion, 47–48
  physical assault, rape, stalking data, 157
  school violence and, 210
  serial killers, 78
  slavery of, 47–48
  teenage hopelessness, 96
  three-strikes laws and, 330
Age
  aggravated assault victimization by, 67–68, 67*t*
  arrest clearances and, 70
  of child homicide victims, 163–64, 164*t*
  family violence data, 163–64, 164*t*
  firearm victims and, 242, 243*f*, 244
  gang data, 225, 226*t*
  homicide patterns, 64–68, 73–74, 74*t*
  of rape and sexual assault data, 111–12, 112*f*
  robbery data, 94
  school violence data, 202–4, 204–5*t*
  in SHR, 29
  in UCR data, 28–29
  in WHO classification data, 56
  workplace violence data, 184*t*, 185, 187*t*
Aggravated assault, 12, 14, 227
  by gender, age, race in 2009, 67–68, 67*t*
  NCVS data on, 65, 66, 69
  total rate in 2009, 69
  victim-offender relationship, 69
  in workplace, 179
Aggression in workplace, 192–93
Ahmadinejad, Mahmoud, 292
Ahmed, Ramzi, 288
Air Force Office of Special Investigations, 85
Alaska Natives
  intimate partner violence data, 157
  physical assault data, 157
  rape data, 157
Alcohol and drugs, violence role of, 266–86
  examples, 266
  homicide rates association, 271
  intimate partner violence association, 167, 170
  patterns, 267–69
  during Prohibition era, 51–54
  rape and sexual assault association, 110, 114, 115, 120
  school violence association, 213, 215, 217
  workplace violence association, 189
Alcohol and drugs violence explanations
  biological and psychological effects, 270–73
  cultural hypothesis, 273–74
  differential association theory, 98
  routine activities theory, 101, 273
  situational, 275–76
  structural, 274–75
Alcohol and drugs violence interventions
  criminal justice approaches, 276–80
  illegal markets disruption, 279–80
  primary prevention programs, 280
  public health approaches, 280–81
  rehabilitation programs, 280–81
  War on Drugs, 276–77
  Weed and Seed, 251–52, 277–79
Algier, Horatio, 228
Allen family feud, 44
American Indians. *See* Native Americans
American Revolution, 43, 44, 45
American Youth Policy Forum (AYPF), 341
America's Youth Gang Initiative, 340
Amman, Jordan tourist attack, 293
Amphetamine abuse, 272
Anderson, "Bloody Bill," 50

Annie E. Casey Foundation, 345
Annual Report on Assistance Related to International Terrorism, 314
Anselmi, Albert, 53
Anti-Defamation League (ADL), 138, 145
Anti-Muslim and Middle Eastern hate crimes, 138
Antiterrorism Assistance Program (ATA), 314
Arab Human Development Report, UNDP, 301
Armed robbery, 94, 99, 174
Arrest clearances, 80, 84–88
  characteristics associated with, 70, 81–82
  Chicago data (1989-1991), 82
  decline of, 81
  defined, importance of, 69–70
  drug-related homicide, 71
  gender, race/ethnicity, age, 70
  NIBRS measures of, 69–70
  organizational and investigational variables, 72
  for rape and sexual assault, 114
  trends, 79
  UCR data, 69, 79*f*
  victim-offender relationship, 71–72
  weapons and felonies, 71
Arrestee Drug Abuse Monitoring (ADAM) program, 267, 282n1, 282n2
Aryan Nations incident, 135, 147–48
Asian and Pacific Islander
  physical assault data, 157
  rape data, 157
Assassinations, political, 43, 288, 289, 311
Assaults. *See also* Rape and sexual assaults
  aggravated, 12, 14, 65–69, 67*t*, 179, 227
  physical assault data, 157
ATA. *See* Antiterrorism Assistance Program
ATF. *See* Bureau of Alcohol, Tobacco, Firearms and Explosives
Attucks, Crispus, 44
Aurora, Colorado movie theatre mass murder, 75, 241
AYPF. *See* American Youth Policy Forum

Barbour, Richard L., 92
Bartley-Fox gun law, in Massachusetts, 103, 255–56
BASICS. *See* Brief Alcohol Screening and Intervention of College Students
Battered wives or intimate partners, 80, 169–73
Behavioral Sciences Unit (BSU), of FBI, 77
Behavior of Law (Black), 81
Benton, Thomas Hart, 44
Berry, Shawn, 135
Bianchi, Kenneth "Hillside Strangler," 83
Bias Incident Investigating Unit (BIIU), New York City, 144
Bias-motivated hate crimes, 138, 140*t*, 145
Big Brothers/Big Sisters program, 340
BIIU. *See* Bias Incident Investigating Unit
Billy the Kid, 49
bin Laden, Osama, 292–93, 300, 306, 311, 312
Biological factors
  in alcohol and drugs violence, 270–73
  in serial homicides, 82–83
Blueprint for the Future of the Uniform Crime Reporting Program, 24
Blueprints for Healthy Youth Development initiative, 345–48
Bootlegging, 52–53
Boston gang violence interventions, 233–37
Boston Gun Project, 238, 254–55
Boston Violence Prevention Project, 339
Brady Act, for gun purchases, 84, 258–59
Branch Davidian compound assault, 289
Breaking Cycles early intervention program, in San Diego, 342
Brewer, Lawrence Russell, 135
Brief Alcohol Screening and Intervention of College Students (BASICS), 347
Brinkman, Christopher, 136
Bryant, Kobe, 109, 121
BSU. *See* Behavioral Sciences Unit
Bullying, 204, 206
Bureau of Alcohol, Tobacco, Firearms and Explosives (ATF), 234, 242, 248–49
Bureau of Counterterrorism, Regional Strategic Initiative, 314–15
Bureau of Economic Analysis, of U.S. Department of Commerce, 96
Bureau of Justice Assistance, Weed and Seed program, 251–52, 277–79
Bureau of Justice Statistics, 24, 140*t*, 202
Bureau of Labor Statistics, on workplace homicides, 182
Burr, Aaron, 44
Bush, George W., 311, 312–13
Butler, Richard, 147–48
Byrd, Billy Ray, 196
Byrd, Carrie, 196
Byrd, James, Jr., 135

California Division of Occupational Safety and Health (Cal/OSHA), 181–84, 182*t*
Cannabis (marijuana, hashish), 270, 272
Capital punishment. *See* Death penalty
Capone, Al "Scarface," 53–54
Case reviews, 85–87
CDC. *See* Centers for Disease Prevention and Control
Census Bureau, U. S., 24, 35, 142
Center for the Study and Prevention of Violence (CSPV), 345–46
Centers for Disease Prevention and Control (CDC), 57, 202
Cherokee nation, 45–46
Chicago crime, during Prohibition era, 53
Chicago Project for Violence Prevention, 343
Child abductions, 77, 164
Child abuse, 169, 172, 175
  homicide of children, 163–64, 164*t*
  intimate partner violence affected by, 170
  legislation about, 174
  maltreatment, 165
  National Clearinghouse data, 169
  NIBRS data on, 32
  serial homicide and, 83
  Shaken Baby Syndrome, 162
  SIDS, 162
  underreporting of, 14, 162
Child Development-Community Policing Program, of Yale/New Haven, 342
Children killing parents, 165–67, 166*t*
Children's Advocacy Centers, 342
Civil lawsuits, for hate crimes, 147–48

Civil legal sanctions, for intimate partner violence, 173
Civil War, 48–51, 54, 289
Cocaine, 6, 272
Code R (sexual assault victim), 109
Cold-case squads, 84–87
Collective gang, 227
Colosimo, "Big Jim," 53
Columbine High School incident, 201, 207, 241–42
Combatant terrorists, 295–96
Committee on Juvenile Delinquency and Youth Crime, of John F. Kennedy, 230
Communities, 208–11, 236
  causes of violence, 16
  prejudice, 144
  about rape and sexual assault, 121–22
  safety, personal liberty conflict with, 8
  U.S. Department of State development projects, 313
Community-based approaches, 342–43
Community Oriented Police Service Anti-Gang Initiative, 225
Community Prevention Grants Program, of Juvenile Justice and Delinquency Prevention Act, 338
Community Relations Division (CRD), Baltimore County, 145–46
Community Service Officers (CSOs), 145
Comparative Crime Data File (1900-1970), 56
Comprehensive/multimodal school-based violence prevention programs, 211, 213
Comprehensive Response to America's Gang Problem, of OJJDP, 225
Comprehensive Strategy (CS) for Serious, Violent, and Chronic Juvenile Offenders, of OJJDP, 336–42, 337*f*
Compressed gang, 227
Conflict model, of law creation, 5
Conflict resolution, as school violence prevention strategy, 215–16
Conflict subculture, 230
Conflict theory, for terrorism, 307–8
Confluence Model of Sexual Aggression, 118–19
Consensus model, of law creation, 5
Content analysis, in violence research, 13
Continuum of care model, for offenders, 281
Control theory, of robbery, 97
Convenience Store Security Act (1990), 105
Corollary homicide victims, in intimate partner violence, 157–58, 158*t*
Corporate violence, of Deepwater Horizon, 4
Countering violent extremism (CVE), 313–14
Counterterrorism Engagement, 314
Counterterrorism initiatives, 312
  capacity-building programs, 314
  CVE, 313–14
  international conventions and protocols, 315
  Regional Strategic Initiative, 314–15
Country Reports on Terrorism, 294–95, 296*t*
CPTED. *See Crime Prevention through Environmental Design*
CRD. *See* Community Relations Division
Crime Classification Manual, of FBI, 115
Crime in the United States, 65, 161, 161*t*, 163
Crime Prevention through Environmental Design (CPTED), 104
Crime rates, 24
  amount compared with, 25
  criticism of, 26–27
  formula defined, 25–26
  U.S., in 2012, 25
Criminal coping pressure or incentive, in strain theory for terrorism, 300–301
Criminal intent, in workplace violence, 181–82
Criminal justice approaches
  for alcohol and drugs violence, 276–80
  death penalty, 174, 327–30, 328*t*
  punishment limits, 331–33
  for robbery, 102–3
  three-strikes laws, 330–31
Criminal justice goals
  deterrence, 323–25
  incapacitation, 325
  rehabilitation, 325
  restoration, 325–27
Criminal justice perspective, of criminal violence, 8–9
Criminal justice system
  criminal courts, 8
  law enforcement, 8
  minorities discrimination, 332–33
Criminal legal sanctions, for intimate partner violence, 173
Criminal subculture, 230
Criminal violence, 3–19. *See also specific types*
  causes, 16, 17
  challenges of research, 13–15
  contemporary trends in, 54–59
  corporate, 4
  in early U.S., 43–45
  incarceration impact on decline of, 84
  international data on, 56–59
  measures of, 23–39
  media impact on, 249–51
  perspectives, 7–11
  psychological, 5
  research methods, 12–13
  socially approved activities, 3–4
  sports, 3–4
  theoretical perspectives, 11–15
  violence transformation to, 5–7
Criminological perspective, of criminal violence, 7–8
Criminology, defined, 7
CS. *See* Comprehensive Strategy for Serious, Violent, and Chronic Juvenile Offenders
CSOs. *See* Community Service Officers
CSPV. *See* Center for the Study and Prevention of Violence
Cultural deviance, 230–31
Cultural hypothesis or theories
  for alcohol and drugs abuse, 273–74
  of arrest clearances, 81, 82
  firearm availability and, 248–49
  on violence cause, 17
Cultural risk factors, 10
Custer, George Armstrong, 46
Customer-client workplace violence, 182
CVE. *See* Countering violent extremism
Cyber-bullying, 204, 206
Cyberterrorism, 292
Cycle of violence, 169–70

Dangerous jobs, in workplace violence, 187–88
Daniels et al. vs. City of New York et al., 253
Date rape, 110, 114
DEA. *See* Drug Enforcement Administration
Death penalty, 174, 327–30, 328*t*
Dees, Morris, 147
Delinquent Boys (Cohen), 229–30
Department of Commerce, U.S., 96
Department of Defense, 309
Department of Education, U. S., 202
Department of Health and Human Services, U. S., 57
  Youth Gang Drug Prevention Program, 225
Department of Homeland Security, 295, 308, 309
Department of Justice, U. S., 17, 136
Department of State, U. S., 313
Department of Youth Services (DYS), 234
Detached street-based worker programs, 233
Deterrence, 9, 323–25, 324
Differential association theory, 98, 143
Differential opportunity theory, 96
Differential reinforcement, 305–6
Dillinger, John, 54
Diplomacy and international cooperation, 289, 312
  capacity-building programs, 314
  CVE, 313–14
  international conventions and protocols, 315
  Regional Strategic Initiative, 314–15
Distributive justice, 193
District of Columbia Firearms Control Regulations Act (1975), 260
DNA analysis, 86
Domestic homicides, 71
Domestic terrorism, 288
Drexler, Melissa, 172
Drug-crazed killers, 6
Drug Enforcement Administration (DEA), 234
DRUGFIRE spent shell casing analysis, 86
Drug-related homicides, 71, 269
Drug-related violence, 23, 268–70. *See also* Alcohol and drugs
Drug Use Forecasting Program, 248, 282n1
Dueling, 44
DYS. *See* Department of Youth Services

East Side White Pride skinhead group, 135
EBPP. *See* Evidence-based practices and programs
8% Early Intervention Program, 341–42
Eighteenth Amendment, of U.S. Constitution, 51, 52
Eighth Amendment, of U.S. Constitution, 174
Emancipation Proclamation (1863), 48
Employee assistance programs, as workplace violence prevention policy, 196
Enrollment Act (1863), 48
Environmental designs, as workplace violence prevention policy, 194–95
EOKA Greek Cypriot paramilitary organization, 293, 305
Evidence-based practices and programs (EBPP), 334–36

False positives, 83
Family violence, 14, 55, 70, 164*t*
  juvenile offenders and, 167, 174–75
  stake-in-conformity hypothesis, 173, 174
  strategies for reducing, 174–75
  trends, 167–69
Family violence, of other family members
  towards children, 169
  children killing parents, 165–67, 166*t*
  parental homicides, 163–65
Family violence explanations
  intimate partner violence, 169–72
  violence towards children, 172
FBI. *See* Federal Bureau of Investigation
Fear and avoidance, as school violence pattern, 202
Federal Bureau of Investigation (FBI), 65, 73, 76, 115, 202, 227, 288. *See also Uniform Crime Reports*
  BSU of, 77
  on hate crimes, 137, 138, 139*t*
  National Center for the Analysis of Violent Crime, 85
  USA Patriot Act and, 308, 310–11
Federal Civil Rights Act, 146, 147
Federal firearms licensees (FFLs), 256, 258
Federal Gun Control Act (1968), 258
Federal legislation, civil rights and, 146–47
Felicia "Snoop" Pearson (character), 100–101
Females, 118
  arrest clearances, 70
  attitude toward violence, 160
  firearms and, 242
  gang violence and, 226
  hate crimes, 141
  murder patterns, 73–74, 74*t*
  as robbery victims, 95
  serial homicides by, 77–78
  uncleared homicides for, 82
Feminist theories, 99–101, 116–17
Feuds, 44
FFLs. *See* Federal firearms licensees
FFT. *See* Functional Family Therapy
Filicide, 163
Finland, homicide rates in 1995-2011, 58–59, 58*f*
Firearms, violence role, 241–65. *See also* Gun-control legislation; Handguns
  fatality data, 242, 243*f*, 244
  flow of, 257–58, 257*f*
  gang violence, 227, 234, 248
  school violence and, 241–42, 244
  self-defense motivation, 246
  straw purchases, 241–42, 257
  in workplace violence, 181, 189
Firearms, violence role explanations, 251
  cultural theories and availability, 248–49
  media violence, 249–50
  routine activities and illegal markets, 247–48
  symbolic interaction theory, 246–47
Firearms, violence role interventions
  Boston Gun Project, 238, 254–55
  gun control legislation, 84, 103, 241–42, 255–60
  illegal gun markets disruption, 238, 247–48, 251–55, 343–45
  injury prevention programs, 261
  Operation Ceasefire, in Boston, 234–37, 254–55
  Operation CeaseFire, in Chicago, 343–45
  right-to-carry laws, 260–61
Firearms, violence role patterns and trends
  acquisition, ownership, use of, 245–46
  crimes involving, 242

offender characteristics, 244–45
victims of, 242, 243, 243*f*, 244
FISA. *See* Foreign Intelligence Surveillance Act
Five Points gang, 53
Floyd, "Pretty Boy," 54
Forcible fondling, 110, 111
Forcible rape, 27, 29, 37, 110, 113*f*, 114, 161
Forcible sodomy, 161
Ford, Robert, 51
Foreign Intelligence Surveillance Act (FISA), 310, 311
Forrest, Nathan Bedford, 48
Fourteenth Amendment, 174
Freedom fighters, 55, 190
French Revolution, 289
Functional Family Therapy (FFT), 346
Furman vs. Georgia, 327

G8. *See* Group of Eight summit
Gangs and gang violence, 164, 223–40, 255
characteristics of, 223
demographics of, 225–26, 226*t*
FBI assistance for dealing with, 227
firearms use, 227, 234, 248
gang membership designation, 224*t*
homicides, 70, 227, 228, 237
NYGS data, 223, 225
OGC and, 52–54, 270
Operation CeaseFire in Chicago and, 344
organization and types of, 226–27
prevalence and extent of, 225
social banditry and, 49–51
study (1991), 13
types of, 226–27
Gangs and gang violence explanations
cultural deviance, 230–31
interactional theory, 232–33
social control, 231–32
strain theories, 228–30
Gangs and gang violence interventions, 233
Boston programs, 233–37
detached street-based worker programs, 233
organizational change and development, 233
suppression, 233, 235–36
Gangs and gang violence patterns and trends, 223–28
definitions, 223–24
growth and changes, 225–28
Gay, lesbian, bisexual, and transgender (GLBT) community, 145
Gay and Lesbian Anti-Violence Project, 138
GCTF. *See* Global Counterterrorism Forum
Gender
aggravated assault victimization by, 67–68, 67*t*
arrest clearances, 70
of child homicide victims, 164, 164*t*
homicide patterns, 64–68, 73–74, 74*t*
intimate partner violence data, 158*t*
robbery data, 95
serial homicides by, 77–78
stalking data, 156, 157*t*
uncleared homicides for, 82
workplace homicides by, 187*t*
General Accounting Office, U. S., 342
General Strain Theory (GST), 96
Geneva Conventions, 300
Giffords, Gabrielle, 241
Giunta, Joseph, 53
GLBT. *See* Gay, lesbian, bisexual, and transgender
Global Counterterrorism Forum (GCTF), 313–14
Global Terrorism Database (GTD), of START, 295
Global Terrorism Index (GTI), of IEP, 297, 297*t*, 298*f*
Going postal, 72, 188–89
Graham-Tewksbury feud, 44
Grays Ferry, in Philadelphia, 135–36, 143
Gregg vs. Georgia, 327, 328
Group conflict theories, of hate crimes, 141–42
Group of Eight (G8) summit, 287
GST. *See* General Strain Theory
GTD. *See* Global Terrorism Database
GTI. *See* Global Terrorism Index
Gun-control legislation, 241–42
altering gun uses and storage, 255–56
banning assault weapons, 259–60
Bartley-Fox laws, 103, 255–56
Brady Act, 84, 258–59
District of Columbia handgun ban, 260
gun dealers regulation, 258
gun lethality reduction, 256
limiting gun sales, 258–59
market-based interventions, 256–60
screening buyers, 258–59
Gun markets, disruption of illegal, 247–48
Boston Gun Project, 238, 254–55
Kansas City Gun Experiment, 251–53
Operation CeaseFire, Chicago, 343–45
Operation Ceasefire, in Boston, 254–55
SQF tactic, 253–54
Guzik, Jake "Greasy Thumb," 53

Habitual Offenders Survey, 98
Halloween sadism, 6, 13
Hallucinogens, 272
Hamilton, Alexander, 44
Handguns. *See also* Firearms, violence role
Brady Act influence on, 84, 258–59
decreases in homicide with, 83, 348
District of Columbia ban of, 260
gang members turning in of, 255
homicides use of, 59, 68, 71, 242
lack of forensic evidence left by, 71
Latinos and Whites homicides decline, 83
right-to-carry laws on, 260
Hargis-Cockrell feud, 44
Harris, Eric, 201, 249
Harvard Negotiation Project, 216
Hate Crime Data Collection Guidelines, of FBI, 137
Hate crimes, 135–52
bias-motivated, 138, 140*t*, 145
definitions, 136–37
examples, 135–36
FBI on, 137, 138, 139*t*
incidence and motivations, 140*t*
juvenile offenders and, 144
patterns and trends, 137–41
prejudice in, 136–37
types of, 139, 140*t*

Hate crimes explanations
  defended neighborhood perspective, 142
  group conflict theories, 141–42
  social learning theory, 143–44
  strain theory, 142–43
Hate crimes interventions
  civil lawsuits, 147–48
  educational strategies, 148–49
  law enforcement responses, 144–45
  legislation, 145–47
  police bias investigation units, 144–45
  Teaching Tolerance program, of SPLC, 147, 148
Hate crimes laws
  reporting statutes, 146
  sentence enhancements, 146
  substantive laws, 145–46
Hate Crimes Resource Manual for Law Enforcement and Victim Assistance Professionals, 149
Hate Crime Statistics Act (HCSA) (1990), 136, 146
Hatfield-McCoy feud, 44
HCSA. *See* Hate Crime Statistics Act
Heroin, 271–72
Hickok, Wild Bill, 49
Hierarchical Linear Modeling techniques, 208
Hierarchy Rule, 31, 32
Holmes, James, 75, 249
Homicides, 37, 65–88, 66*t*, 165, 271. *See also* Serial homicides; Workplace homicides
  age, gender, race patterns, 64–68
  arrest clearances, 69–72, 81–82
  assault compared to, 12, 14
  clearance rates increase, 84–88
  cross-national, 57
  firearms and, 242, 243*f*, 244
  gang, 70, 227, 228, 237
  handguns used in, 59, 68, 71, 348
  impersonalization of, 55
  interventions, 83–84
  intimate partner, 68, 69, 156–58, 158*t*, 167, 168*f*, 169, 170–72
  multiple murders, 72–78
  records, 38–39
  subcultural theories for, 81
  symbolic interaction explanation, 80–81
  transnational comparisons, 57–59
  UCR types of, 65
  uncleared, 71, 82, 88
  U.S. rates of, 12, 25, 57, 58–59, 58*f*, 65, 78, 78*f*
  victim-offender relationship, 71–72
  victims, by sex and race 1999-2012, 74*t*
  WHO definition of, 56
Homicide victimization rates
  African-Americans and whites, in Los Angeles, 26
  by age, gender and race, 64–68
  Baltimore and Austin, in 2012, 25
  New York and Chicago, in 2012, 24–25
  recording by UCR compared to NCVS, 35, 36
Hotel Rule, of NIBRS, 31
Hussein, Saddam, 312

Ibrahim, Saad Eddin, 303
ICS. *See* Index of Consumer Sentiment
IEP. *See* Institute for Economics and Peace
Illegal markets disruption
  for alcohol and drugs violence, 279–80
  for firearms violence, 247–48, 251–55
Incapacitation, 9, 325
Incarceration and recidivism, 84, 121–22, 127–29
Incest, 110, 111
Indentured servitude, 46–47
Index of Consumer Expectations, 96
Index of Consumer Sentiment (ICS), 96–97
Indian Removal Act (1830), 45
Infanticides, 54, 163
Institute for Economics and Peace (IEP), GTI of, 297, 297*t*, 298*f*
Instrumental aggression theory, 193
Interactional theory, on gang violence, 232–33
International Money Laundering Abatement and Financial Anti-Terrorism Act (2001), 310
International rape and sexual assaults, 159–60
International terrorism, 289, 312–15
Interventions
  for alcohol and drugs violence, 251–52, 276–81
  for firearms violence, 84, 103, 234–38, 241–42, 247–48, 251–61, 343–45
  for gangs and gang violence, 233–37
  for hate crimes, 144–49
  for homicides, 83–84
  for intimate partner violence, 173–74
  public health, 9
  for rape and sexual assaults, 119–29
  for robbery, 102–5
  for school violence, 211–15
  terrorist, 308–15
  for workplace violence, 193–94
Interviews
  ADAM on adult male arrestees, 267
  with armed robbers, 99
  with incarcerated felons, 245
  of inmates on firearm acquisition, 245
  with jurors, in rape cases, 120
  of rape and sexual assault victims, 110, 123
  with rapists, 117
  as research method, 13
  with robbery victims, 97, 104
  with victims, 33–38
  of victims with protection orders, 173
Intimate partner violence, 155–78
  alcohol and drugs association, 167, 170
  corollary homicide victims, 157–58, 158*t*
  cycle of violence, 169–70
  decline in, 167, 168*f*, 169
  homicides, 68, 69, 156–58, 158*t*, 167, 168*f*, 169, 170–72
  legislation in, 84
  NISVS study on, 156–59
  perpetrator victims in, 158–59
  threatening and denigrating behavior, 5, 156
  WHO on, 159
Intimate partner violence interventions
  batterer treatment, 173
  civil legal sanctions, 173
  criminal legal sanctions, 173
  research on, 174

Intimate partner violence patterns and risks
frequency and severity of, 159–61
in other countries, 159
race and ethnicity, 157–59
risk factors for, 160–61
sexual violence, 160
women's attitude toward violence, 160
Intimate partner violence types
physical violence, 156, 157*t*
psychological aggression, 156
rape, 156, 157*t*
stalking victimization, 156, 157*t*
Iran hostage crisis of 1979, 291
Iraq War, 299–300, 308, 311–12
Ireland (Northern Ireland) terrorism, 291, 293, 305, 307
Islamic *jihad* (struggle), 303
Islamic Resistance Movement, 302
Islamic revolution, in Iran, 294
Islamic *shahadat* (martyrdom), 303
Islamist terrorism, 308–9
Israeli El Al flight hijacking, 290

Jackson, Andrew, 44, 45
James, Frank, 50, 51
James, Jesse Woodson, 49, 50, 51
James-Younger gang, 49–51
Johnson, Andre, 92, 97
Johnson, Lyndon, 8, 96
JUMP. *See* Juvenile Mentoring Programs
Justice, workplace violence and, 193
Justice Research and Statistics Association, 33
Juvenile Justice and Delinquency Prevention Act (1974), 338
Juvenile Mentoring Programs (JUMP), 340
Juvenile offenders. *See also* School violence
alcohol and drug abuse prevention strategies, 277
Columbine High School incident, 201, 207, 241–42
conflict resolution training, 215–16
differential association theory and, 98
family violence and, 167, 174–75
firearm use, 244–45
hate crimes and, 144
homicides, 174–75
OJJDP strategy for, 336–42, 337*f*
UN survey data, 56
victimization by gangs, juveniles, 164

Kaczynski, Theodore "Unabomber," 55
Kansas City Gun Experiment, 251–53
Keenan, Victoria (hate crime victim), 135
King, John William, 135
Kinkel, Klaus, 302
Klebold, Dylan, 201, 249
Klein, Ed, 201
Ku Klux Klan, 144–45, 293

Lanza, Adam, 249
Larceny rates, UCR compared to NIBRS, 32
Latinos
arrest clearances, 70, 80, 82
handgun homicides decline, 83
homicide victims, 70, 82, 83, 88
infant homicides, 165
intimate violence data, 157
physical assault data, 157
serious assault rates, 68
stalking data, 157
Law enforcement, 8, 12, 144–45
Legislation. *See also specific legislation*
child abuse, 174
federal, civil rights and, 146–47
for gangs and gang violence, 233
gun control, 84, 103, 241–42, 255–60
hate crimes, 145–47
in intimate partner violence, 84
Trail of Tears case, 45–46
Life Skills Training prevention program, 347
Lincoln, Abraham, 48
Little Big Horn battle, 46
London subway terrorist attacks, 287
Lying and buying firearms, 257
Lynchings, 48–49

Madrid terrorist train attack, 287
Males, 118
drinking patterns, 273
firearms and, 242, 244
gangs, 226
hate crime and, 141
murder patterns, 73–74, 74*t*
as robbery victims, 95
as workplace violence victims, 184
Malvo, Lee Harvey, 76
Market-based interventions, gun-control legislation and, 256–60
Martin-Tolliver feud, 44
Martyrdom. *See* Islamic *shahadat*
Mass murders, 73–75, 74*t*, 241
Matthew Shepard and James Byrd, Jr. Hate Crime Prevention Act (2009), 136
McCaffrey, Paddy, 48
McCleskey vs. Kemp, 327–28
McVeigh, Timothy, 289
Measures of violence, 23–39, 69–70. *See also* National Crime Victimization Survey; National Incident-Based Reporting System; *Uniform Crime Reports*
Media, 86
family violence focus, 166
male-female portrayals, 118
mass murders and, 75
rape stereotypes, 114
serial killers representation, 6, 77
unusual violence focus, 7
U.S. Department of State projects of, 313
violence, impact of, 249–51
Western, Islam and, 300
Megan's Law (1996), 122
Mérida Initiative., 270
Methamphetamine, 272
Metzger, John, 147
Metzger, Tom, 147
Mexican drug cartels, 269–70
Middle East, 138, 299
terrorism, 297
Military action, against terrorism, 311–12
Minorities discrimination, 332–33

Model Hate Crime Law, of ADL, 145
Moran, George "Bugs," 53
Morphology or horizontal distribution of individual hypothesis, for arrest clearances, 82
Motor-vehicle theft, 32
MST. *See* Multisystemic therapy
Muhammad, John Allen, 76
Multifactor theories, for rape and sexual assaults, 118–19
Multiple murders, 72–78
Multiplier effects, for workplace violence, 180–81
Multisystemic therapy (MST), for sexual offenders, 346
Munich Olympic Games terrorist act, 290
Murder. *See* Homicides

National Academy of Sciences
  deterrence research, 324
  Panel on the Understanding and Control of Violent Behavior, 3, 104, 325, 334
National Archive of Criminal Justice Data, 24
National Center for Health Statistics (NCHS), 37, 57, 80
National Center for the Analysis of Violent Crime, of FBI, 85, 115
National Center on Addiction and Substance Abuse, 189, 267
National Clearinghouse on Child Abuse and Neglect, 169, 174, 186
National Counterterrorism Center (NCTC), 309
National Crime Victimization Survey (NCVS), 12–13
  on aggravated assaults, 65, 66, 69
  on firearms, 242
  gang violence and, 227
  on hate crimes, 137–39, 140*t*
  incidents collected methods, 35
  information collected types and methods, 34–35
  limitations of, 37–39
  modern usage of, 35–39
  on offender drug or alcohol use, 268
  rape and sexual assault definition, 110
  redesign of, 33–35
  on robbery, 35, 36, 37, 92–93
  strengths of, 36–37
  on teacher victimization, 206
  Victim Risk Supplement study, 190–91
  violence statistics, policy, practice, 38–39
  on workplace violence, 184, 186, 190
National Criminal Justice Reference Service, 17
National Drug Control Strategy, 276
National Incident-Based Reporting System (NIBRS), 24
  advantages and disadvantages, 32–33
  arrest clearance data, 69–70
  criticism of, 32
  Hotel Rule of, 31
  rape and sexual assault definition, 110–11
  on robbery, 30, 32
  UCR compared to, 30–33, 31*t*
  on victim-offender relationship for victims under age 18, 161, 161*t*
National Instant Criminal Background Check System (NICS), 259
National Institute for Occupational Safety and Health (NIOSH), 194, 195
National Institute of Justice, 17, 225
National Intelligence Council, 312
National Intelligence Estimate, 312
National Intimate Partner and Sexual Violence Survey (NISVS), 156–59
National Research Council (NRC), 242, 333–34
National-separatist groups, 293
National Study of Delinquency Prevention in Schools, 210, 213, 214–15, 214*t*
National Violent Death Reporting System (NVDRS), 39
National Youth Gang Survey (NYGS), 223, 225
Native Americans, 54. *See also* Cherokee nation; Little Big Horn battle; Trail of Tears
  intimate partner violence data, 157
  rape data, 157
  white warfare with, 45–46
Nat Turner Rebellion (1831), 47–48
Naval Criminal Investigative Service (NCIS), 85
NCHS. *See* National Center for Health Statistics
NCIS. *See* Naval Criminal Investigative Service
NCTC. *See* National Counterterrorism Center
NCVS. *See* National Crime Victimization Survey
Neo-Nazi groups, 135, 293
Neotraditional gang, 227
Neutralization techniques, for robbery, 97
New Beginnings program, 347–48
New York City Draft Riots (1863), 48
NFP. *See* Nurse Family Partnership
NIBRS. *See* National Incident-Based Reporting System
Nichols, Terry, 289
NICS. *See* National Instant Criminal Background Check System
9/11 Report, 308–9
NIOSH. *See* National Institute for Occupational Safety and Health
NISVS. *See* National Intimate Partner and Sexual Violence Survey
Noncombatant terrorist, 295–96
Noncriminal violence, 43
Nonfatal violence
  gunshot injuries and, 242, 243*f*, 244
  school violence, 204
  in workplace, 72, 184–89
Nonnegligent manslaughter
  FBI statistics, 65, 76
  2012 data, 14
  UCR data, 65
Northern Ireland terrorism, 291, 293, 305, 307
North Side gang, in Chicago, 53
NRC. *See* National Research Council
Nurse Family Partnership (NFP) program, 346
NVDRS. *See* National Violent Death Reporting System
NYGS. *See* National Youth Gang Survey

Obama, Barack, 126, 241, 311
O'Bannion, Dion, 53
Occupationally related deaths, 4
Offenders. *See also* Rapists and sexual offenders
  by age, gender, race in 2012, 66*t*
  dangerous, 10
Office of Juvenile Justice and Delinquency Prevention (OJJDP), 225, 336–42, 337*f*
Office of Sex Offender Sentencing, Monitoring, Apprehending, Registering, and Tracking (SMART), 121–22

OGC. *See* Organized crime or gang
OJJDP. *See* Office of Juvenile Justice and Delinquency Prevention
Oklahoma City Federal Building bombing, 288, 289
Omnibus Crime Control and Safe Streets Act (1968), 23
Operation CeaseFire, Chicago, 343–45
Operation Ceasefire intervention, Boston, 234–37, 254–55
Opiates, 271–72
Opportunistic behavior, of rape offender, 116
Opportunity reduction strategies, 103–5
Organizational causes of violence, 16
Organization or collective action hypothesis, of arrest clearance, 82
Organized crime or gang (OGC) activity, 52–54, 270

Palestine Red Crescent Society, 291, 316n2
Palestinian Liberation Organization (PLO), 290
Panel on the Understanding and Control of Violent Behavior, of National Academy of Sciences, 3, 104, 325, 334
Parental homicide, 163–65
Participant observation, in violence research, 13
Partnerships to Reduce Juvenile Gun Violence, 339
PATHE. *See* Positive Action Through Holistic Education
PATHS. *See* Promoting Alternative Thinking Strategies
Patricides, 165–66, 166*t*
Patriot Act. *See* USA Patriot Act
PCP drug, 272
Peer mediation, in schools, 216–17
Perpetrator victims, in intimate partner violence, 158–59
Personal liberty, community safety conflict with, 8
PLO. *See* Palestinian Liberation Organization
Policies and procedures, as workplace violence prevention policy, 195–96
Political assassinations, 43, 288, 289, 311
Positive Action Through Holistic Education (PATHE) Project, 217, 348
Power assertive behavior, of rape offender, 116
Power reassurance behavior, of rape offender, 116
Predatory stranger offenses, 101
Predicate offenses, 136, 150n1
Prejudice, 136–37, 144
President's Commission on Law Enforcement and Administration of Justice, in mid-1960s, 33, 225
Preston, Thomas, 43–44
Prevention and punishment, 323–56
  criminal justice approaches, 323–33
  public health approaches, 333–48
  violent crime decrease, 348–49
Primary prevention, 10, 280
Prison-based drug treatment, 280–81
Procedural justice, 193
Program for Young Negotiators, 216
Prohibition era, 51–54
Project Towards No Drug Abuse (Project TND), 347
Promoting Alternative Thinking Strategies (PATHS), 346
Psychological aggression and violence, 5, 156
Public health approaches, 11
  on alcohol and drugs violence, 280–81
  Blueprints for Healthy Youth Development initiative, 345–48
  community-based approaches, 342–43
  EBPP, 334–36
  Multilevel Risk Approach, of NRC, 333–34
  OJJDP CS, 336–42, 337*f*
  Operation CeaseFire in Chicago, 343–45
Public health perspectives, of criminal violence, 8–11

al Qaeda, 287, 290, 292–93, 300, 304, 307–8, 312, 316n3
Quantrill, William Clarke, 50

Race
  aggravated assault victimization by, 67–68, 67*t*
  arrest clearances and, 70
  of child homicide victims, 164
  criminal justice system and, 332–33
  gangs and, 226
  hate crimes data, 141
  homicide patterns, 64–68, 73–74, 74*t*
  intimate partner violence, 157–58
  minorities discrimination, 332–33
  serial homicides and, 78
  U.S. Census on changing mix, 142
  workplace and non-workplace violence data, 184*t*, 185
  workplace violence by, 187*t*
Racial conflict, 43
RAF. *See* Red Army Faction
Rand Inmate Surveys, 267
Rape and sexual assaults, 4, 102, 109–34
  alcohol and drugs association, 110, 114, 115, 120
  arrest clearances for, 114
  characteristics, 111–14
  definitions, 110–11
  examples, 109–10
  international, 159–60
  interviews with victims of, 110, 123
  as intimate partner violence type, 156, 157*t*
  mythology of, 118
  patterns and trends, 111–14
  screening questions, 34–35
  underreporting of, 14, 112, 113*t*
  victim at rape crisis center, 109
  victim-offender relationships, 114
Rape and sexual assaults explanations
  feminist theories, 116–17
  multifactor theories, 118–19
  psychiatric perspectives, 115–16
  social cognitive theories, 117–18
Rape and sexual assaults interventions
  incarceration and recidivism, 121–22, 127–29
  rape reform law, 119–21
  sex offender notification and registration laws, 121–22, 130n2
  sex offender treatment programs, 126–29
  sexual violence education, 124–26
  victim resistance, 122–23
  victim services, 123–24
Rape and sexual assaults types
  date rape, 110, 114
  forcible fondling, 110, 111
  forcible rape, 27, 29, 37, 110, 113*f*, 114, 161
  incest, 110, 111
  sexual assault with object, 111
  sodomy, 110, 161
  statutory rape, 110
Rape shield laws, 120–21

Rapists and sexual offenders, 117, 121–22, 126–29, 130n2, 346
Rational choice, in workplace, 192–93
Reactionary-rightist groups, 293
Reactive policing, 324
Reagan, Ronald, 276
Recidivism, 121–22, 127–29
Red Army Faction (RAF), German terrorist group, 290
Rehabilitation, 9, 280–81, 325
Reid, Richard, 293
Religious terrorism, 293–94, 305
Reporting statutes, as hate crimes law, 146
Repression in totalitarian states, 289, 301, 308
Research, 12–13, 12–15, 77, 174
Resistance by victims of crime, 94, 122–23
Ressam, Ahmed, 292–93
Restorative justice strategies, 325–27
Retreatist subculture, 230
Revolutionary-leftist groups, 293
Right-to-carry laws, 260–61
Risk factors, 9–10
Robber's Cave experiments, 141
Robbery, 12, 92–108, 324
  armed robbery, 94, 99, 174
  death compared to injuries from, 94
  defined, 92
  drug use and, 267
  firearms and, 242, 244
  gang violence and, 227
  Hotel Rule, 31
  incidents or examples, 92
  interviews with victims of, 97, 104
  location, 94, 101–2
  NCVS data on, 35, 36, 37, 92–93
  NIBRS data on, 30, 32
  patterns and trends, 92–95
  rape and, 95, 117
  risk and rewards considerations, 98
  UCR data on, 27, 92, 94
  UN survey data, 56
  victims, 94–95, 97, 104
  weapon use, 94
  workplace violence and, 186, 192
Robbery explanations, 95, 100*f*
  control theory, 97
  differential association theory, 98
  differential opportunity theory, 96
  feminist theory, 99–101
  Habitual Offenders Survey theory, 98
  neutralization techniques, 97
  routine activities theory, 101–2
  social bonding theory, 97
  strain theory, 96–97
  symbolic interaction theory, 98–99
Robbery interventions, 102–5
  criminal justice approaches, 102–3
  opportunity reduction strategies, 103–5
Roper v. Simmons, 174
Routine activities theory, 101–2, 189–92, 247–48, 273

al-Sadr, Baquer (Ayatollah), 294
Safe Kids/Safe Streets initiative, 341
Saint Valentine's Day Massacre, 53
Same-sex relationships
  intimate partner violence, 156
  power and control issues, 171
  serial killers and, 6
Sandy Hook Elementary School shootings, 241, 249
Scalise, John, 53
School violence, 9, 141, 201–22
  alcohol and drugs association, 213, 215, 217
  Columbine High School incident, 201, 207, 241–42
  community characteristics for, 209–10
  examples of, 201
  firearms use, 241–42, 244
  National Study of Delinquency Prevention, 210, 213–15, 214*t*
  Sandy Hook Elementary School shootings, 241, 249
  school disorder explanations, 206–11
  Virginia Polytechnic Institute incident, 201, 241
School violence interventions, 214–15
  comprehensive/multimodal programs, 211, 213
  selected/indicated, 211, 212
  special schools or classes, 211, 212–13
  universal, 211–12
School violence pattern and trends
  fear and avoidance, 202
  incidents and disciplinary actions, 203–4
  school security responses, 203
  self-reported violence, 206
  student victimization, 204, 204–5*t*, 206
  teacher victimization, 206
School violence prevention strategies, 214*t*
  conflict resolution, 215–16
  organization and climate changes, 217
  peer mediation, 216–17
Secondary prevention, 10–11
September 11 attacks, 138, 287–88
Seraw, Mulugeta (hate crime victim), 135, 147
Serial homicides
  biological factors in, 82–83
  explanation for, 82–83
  FBI definition of, 73
  mass murders compared to, 72–73
  media representation of, 6, 77
  racial profile, 78
  research-based tracking techniques, 77
  terrorism compared with, 55, 76
  trends, 79–80
  U.S. yearly estimates, 76
Serial killers, 6, 77, 87–88
Seung-Hui Cho, 201
Seung Ki Leung, 92
Sex offender
  notification and registration laws, 121–22, 130n2
  treatment programs, 126–29
Sex Offender Registration and Notification Act (SORNA), 122, 130n2
Sex Offender Treatment and Evaluation Project (SOTEP), California, 128–29
Sexual assault. *See* Rape and sexual assaults
Shaken Baby Syndrome, 162
Shepard, Matthew (hate crime victim), 135
Sherrill, Patrick, 72, 188, 195
SHR. *See* Supplementary Homicide Reports
SIDS. *See* Sudden Infant Death Syndrome

Situated transaction theory, 275–76, 275*f*
Slavery, 47–48
SMART. *See* Office of Sex Offender Sentencing, Monitoring, Apprehending, Registering, and Tracking; Socioeconomic Mapping and Resource Topography
Snowden, Edward, 311
Social banditry, 49–51
Social bonding theory, 97, 206–7
Social categorization process, 142
Social cognitive theories, 117–18, 249
Social control hypothesis, 299–300
  for arrest clearances, 82
  on gang violence, 231–32
  for school violence, 211
  of serial homicides, 82
Social Development Strategy, 336–37
Social disorganization theory, 106n1, 209
Social learning theory, 143–44, 305–7
Socially constructed perspective, of criminal violence, 4–6
Socioeconomic Mapping and Resource Topography (SMART), of OJJDP, 340
Socioeconomic status, 12, 82
Sodomy, 110, 161
Sorenson, Paul Stanley, 85
SORNA. *See* Sex Offender Registration and Notification Act
SOTEP. *See* Sex Offender Treatment and Evaluation Project
Southern Poverty Law Center (SPLC), 138, 142, 147, 148
Specialty gang, 227
SPLC. *See* Southern Poverty Law Center
Sports violence, 3–4
SQF. *See* Stop, question, and frisk
Stake-in-conformity hypothesis, 173, 174
Stalking, 156, 157*t*
START. *See* Study of Terrorism and Responses to Terrorism
State-sponsored terrorism, 291–92
Statutory rape, 110
Stop, question, and frisk (SQF) crime prevention tactic, 253–54
Strain theory
  of gang violence, 228–30
  of hate crimes, 142–43
  of robbery, 96–97
  of terrorism, 298–305
Stratification hypothesis, for arrest clearance, 81
Straw purchases, of firearms, 241–42, 257
Struggle. *See* Islamic *jihad*
Student Civil Rights Project, 148
Student victimization, 204, 204–5*t*, 206
Study of Terrorism and Responses to Terrorism (START), National Consortium for, 288, 295–96
Subcultural theories, 81, 230, 231
Substance abuse. *See* Alcohol and drugs
Substantive laws, against hate crimes, 145–46
Sudden Infant Death Syndrome (SIDS), 162
Supplementary Homicide Reports (SHR), of UCR, 29–30, 32, 38, 162
Survey of Prison Inmates, 246–47
Symbionese Liberation Army, 316n1
Symbolic interaction theory, 80–81, 98–99, 246–47
Systemic drug-related violence, 268–70

Taliban (Sunni Islamist political movement), 306, 308
Teacher victimization, 206
Teaching Tolerance program, of SPLC, 147, 148
The Teen Files: The Truth about Hate TV special, 149
Terrorism and terrorists, 208, 287–319. *See also* al Qaeda
  definition, types of, 288–89, 292–94, 296, 304, 305
  examples, 287–88
  incidents, 294–97, 296*t*, 297*t*
  as moralistic violence, 306
  Northern Ireland, 291, 293, 305, 307
  repressive environments response, 304
  serial homicides compared with, 55, 76
Terrorism explanations
  conflict theory, 307–8
  social learning theory, 305–7
  strain theory, 298–305
Terrorism interventions
  diplomacy and international cooperation, 312–15
  military action, 311–12
  9/11 Report global strategy, 308–9
  USA Patriot Act, 308, 310–11
Terrorism patterns and trends
  historical background, 289–91
  incidents, 294–97
  state-sponsored terrorism, 291–92
  terrorist tactics, 292
Terry vs. Ohio, 253
Tertiary prevention, 11
Theoretical perspectives, of criminal violence, 11–15
Three-strikes laws, 330–31
Torres, Arturo Reyes, 193
Torrio, Johnny, 53
Torrio-Capone gang, in Chicago, 53
Traditional gang, 227
Trail of Tears, 45–46
Train attacks in London and Spain, 287
Training Guide for Hate Crime Data Collection, of FBI, 137
Tripartite approach to violence, 15–17, 269, 323
Twin Towers terrorist attack, 287

UCR. *See Uniform Crime Reports*
UN. *See* United Nations
Uncleared homicides, 71, 82, 88
UNDP. *See* United Nations Development Programme
Uniform Crime Reports (UCR), of FBI, 13, 24, 65
  advantages and disadvantages, 32
  Age, Sex, Race, Ethnic Origin of Persons Arrested forms of, 29, 32
  arrest clearance data, 69, 79*t*
  described, 27
  on familial homicide, 163
  on firearms, 242
  hate crime data, 138, 139–40
  Hate Crime Statistics Program, 137, 138
  homicide types or divisions, 85
  NIBRS compared with, 30–33, 31*t*
  program, 28*f*
  rape and sexual assault definition, 110
  Return A forms of, 29, 32
  on robbery, 27, 92, 94
  SHR of, 29–30, 32, 38, 162
  violent crime data collection, 27–29
United Arab Emirates, CVE Center of Excellence, 314

United Nations (UN)
  crime surveys, 56
  Global Counter-Terrorism Strategy, 314
  Security Council, 312
United Nations Development Programme (UNDP), 299–301
United States (U.S.). *See also specific departments*
  assaults and homicides in, 65–66
  crime rates, in 2012, 25
  homicide rates in, 12, 25, 57, 58–59, 58*f*, 65, 78, 78*f*
  marijuana legalization, 270
  Middle East presence, 299
  serial homicides, 76
  violence in early, 43–45
USA Patriot Act (2001) (Uniting and Strengthening America by Providing Appropriate Tools Required to Intercept and Obstruct Terrorism), 308, 310–11

Victim-offender relationships, 71–72
  in aggravated assault, 69
  in homicides of intimates, 168*t*
  mass murders, 74–75
  for victims under age 18, 161, 161*t*
  for workplace violence victims, 185*t*
Victim Risk Supplement study, of NCVS, 190–91
Victims of crimes
  of aggravated assault, 67–68, 67*t*
  child homicide, 163–64, 164*t*
  Code R, 109
  corollary homicide, 157–58, 158*t*
  firearm, 242, 243*f*, 244
  homicide, 24–25, 26, 35, 36, 64–68, 74*t*
  interviews with, 33–38, 97, 104, 110, 123, 173
  Latinos homicide, 70, 82, 83, 88
  of mass murders, by sex and race in 1999-2012, 74*t*
  perpetrator, 158–59
  rape and sexual assault, 110, 123–24
  resistance by, 94, 122–23
  robbery, 94–95, 97, 104
  varying responses of, 14
  workplace violence, 184
Violence. *See* Criminal violence
Violence Prevention Curriculum for Adolescents, 216
Violent Crime Control and Law Enforcement Act (1994), 259–60, 281
Virginia Polytechnic Institute incident, 201, 241

Waco domestic terrorism bombing, 288
Wahl, Ruth, 92
Warfield, Jesse, 135
War on Drugs, 276–77
Weapons. *See also* Firearms; Handguns
  arrest clearances, felonies and, 71
  banning assault, 259–60
  effect, 250–51
  in mass murders, 75
  robbery use, 94
Weapons of mass destruction (WMD), 291–92, 311–12
Weathermen left-wing terrorist group, 290, 316n1
Weed and Seed program, 251–52, 277–79
Whites
  handgun homicide decline, 83
  Native Americans warfare with, 45–46
  patricide, 165–67, 166*t*
  stalking data, 157
  teenage hopelessness, 96
WHO. *See* World Health Organization
Wild Bill Hickok, 49
Williams, Raheem (hate crime victim), 135–36
Williams, Warren (hate crime victim), 135–36
Williams, Wayne, 78
Williams, Yerodeen, 92
WMD. *See* Weapons of mass destruction
Women Organized against Rape (WOAR), in Philadelphia, 123
Worker on worker workplace violence, 182–83
Workplace homicides, 179–80
  dangerous jobs, 187–88
  demographic characteristics of victims of, 186
  offender types, 187*t*
Workplace violence, 179–200
  aggravated assault, 179
  Cal/OSHA classification of, 181–84, 182*t*
  demographics and occupational characteristics, 184–88
  empirical evidence, 197–98
  employers cost from, 179
  firearms in, 181, 189
  harassment, 195
  interventions, 193–94
  multiplier effects, 180–81
  policy elements, 198*t*
  specific policies, 197–98
  victim-offender relationship, 185*t*
Workplace violence, nonfatal
  dangerous jobs, 186
  demographic and occupational characteristics, 184–86
  going postal, 72, 188–89
Workplace violence explanations
  rational choice and aggression, 192–93
  routine activities, 189–92
Workplace violence prevention policies and strategies
  administrative controls, 195
  employee assistance programs, 196
  environmental designs, 194–95
  outplacement services, 196
  policies and procedures, 195–96
  screening and selection, 195
  supervisor and employee training, 196
World Health Organization (WHO), 56–57, 159
World Trade Center terrorist attack, 287–00
World War I, 44
World War II, 290

Yates, Andreas, 163
Younger, Cole, 49–51
Younger, James, 50, 51
Younger, John, 50
Younger, Robert, 50
Yousef, Ramzi Ahmed, 288